Liability Claim Concepts and Practices

Liability Claim Concepts and Practices

ROBERT J. PRAHL, CPCU
Assistant Vice President - Claims
State Auto Insurance

STEPHEN M. UTRATA, CPCU
Branch Claims Manager
State Auto Insurance

Coordinating Editor
FREDERICK R. HODOSH, Ph.D., J.D., CPCU
Vice President and General Counsel
Insurance Institute of America

First Edition • 1985

INSURANCE INSTITUTE OF AMERICA
720 Providence Road, Malvern, Pennsylvania 19355

First Printing • October 1985

Library of Congress Catalog Number 85-80059
International Standard Book Number 0-89462-022-3

Printed in the United States of America

Foreword

Over the years, the American Institute for Property and Liability Underwriters and the Insurance Institute of America have responded to the educational needs of the property-liability insurance industry by developing new programs.

The American Institute maintains and administers the program leading to the Chartered Property Casualty Underwriter (CPCU) professional designation.

The Insurance Institute of America offers programs leading to the Certificate in General Insurance, the Associate in Claims (AIC) designation, the Associate in Management (AIM) designation, the Associate in Risk Management (ARM) designation, the Associate in Underwriting (AU) designation, the Associate in Loss Control Management (ALCM) designation, the Associate in Premium Auditing (APA) designation, the Accredited Adviser in Insurance (AAI) designation, and the Associate in Insurance Accounting and Finance (AIAF) designation as well as the Introduction to Property and Liability Insurance (INTRO) Course.

This is the first text to be developed by the Institute for use in the AIC program. Throughout the development of this series of texts it has been—and will continue to be—necessary to draw on the knowledge and skills of Institute staff members. These individuals will receive no royalties on texts sold, and their writing responsibilities are seen as an integral part of their professional duties. We have proceeded in this way to avoid any possibility of conflicts of interests.

We invite and welcome any and all criticisms of our publications. It is only with such comments that we can hope to provide high quality texts, materials, and programs. Comments should be directed to the curriculum department of the Institutes.

Edwin S. Overman, Ph.D., CPCU
President

Preface

In recent years, as the number of educational programs offered by the American and Insurance Institutes has been increasing, more and more of the textbooks used in these courses have been published by the Institutes, replacing texts of other publishers. The major impetus for this development came from the Chartered Property Casualty Underwriter (CPCU) program which, ever since its restructuring into ten parts in the late seventies, has utilized texts that have been specifically written to meet its educational objectives. Similarly, the programs in Underwriting, Production, Premium Auditing, Research and Planning, Insurance Accounting and Finance, and the Introduction to Property and Liability Insurance course have, from the start, been based on Institute-published textbooks.

Liability Claim Concepts and Practices represents the first step in this process for the Associate in Claims (AIC) Program. It is one of the texts used in the initial course in liability claims adjusting and follows in the footsteps of books authored by claims practitioners long involved in sharing their wealth of experience with claims people at the threshold of their careers. The new work represents the educational philosophy of the Program: a balanced educational effort combining practice-oriented materials with an overview of basic principles of claims, insurance, legal, and other related fields involved in everyday claim work.

After a general description of the major claim department functions and a discussion of the role of the adjuster, two chapters deal with the importance and meaning of coverage, an indispensable area of knowledge that must be mastered before the first claim can be handled. Chapters 4 and 5 delve into the meaning of legal liability, the understanding of which is crucial for anyone dealing with liability claims. Chapters 6 and 7 introduce the reader to the process of claim investigations with separate treatment for the most frequently encountered types of claims. Chapters 8 and 9 analyze the "payoff" stage of the claim process: evaluation and settlement, with Chapter 9 concentrating on the recognition and elimination of the causes of failure in the disposition of a claim. The text concludes with a discussion of the basic concepts of reserving and an overview of the interaction of the claim function with other operating departments of insurance companies.

The authors are indebted to many knowledgeable insurance and law professionals for their assistance. Space does not permit a complete listing, but special recognition is due to Eugene D. Garan, Claim Examiner; Brent Mackey, Special Representative; John Melvin, Claims Counsel; Booth Muller, CPCU, Unit Claim Manager; and Robert G. Whitney, Resident Vice President, all of State Automobile Mutual Insurance Company; Edward G. Kagels, Esquire, of Cleveland, Ohio; and Thomas A. Savignac, Assistant Vice President, Northwestern National Insurance Group, for their valuable advice.

The burden of reviewing and evaluating every chapter promptly and thoroughly fell on three long-time claims practitioners and teachers, John Majka, CPCU, CLU, Senior Vice President, Germantown Insurance Company; Samuel M. Meeks, CPCU, AIC, Resident Vice President, Western Employers Insurance Company; and John J. Roberts, CPCU, Division Manager, State Farm Mutual Automobile Insurance Company. Their always thorough and prompt work has given the authors a measure of assurance that the book might achieve its objective, namely fulfilling the educational needs of the new claims person.

Robert J. Prahl
Stephen M. Utrata
Frederick R. Hodosh

Table of Contents

Chapter 1—Functions of the Claim Department and the Adjuster 1

Technical Functions~*Providing Procedures for Reporting Claims; Assigning Claims to Adjusters; Assisting in Determining Coverage; Reviewing Files to Ensure Proper Disposition; Counseling Adjusters in the Resolution of Legal Liability Questions; Defending Lawsuits; Pursuing Subrogation Claims; Establishing Proper Reserves; Claim Evaluations*

Personnel Functions~*Hiring Adjusters; Training Adjusters; Planning for Future Needs*

Types of Adjusters~*Staff Adjusters; Independent Adjusters; Agents; Public Adjusters*

The Self-Insured Firm's Need for the Claim Function

The Role of the Adjuster~*Investigation; Evaluation; Negotiation; Settlement; Paying the Fair Amount; Controlling Costs; The Value of Intangible Damages*

The Adjuster's Fields of Knowledge~*Auto Construction and Repairs; Medical Knowledge; Accounting; Building Construction; Product Manufacturing; The Law*

Attributes of a Successful Adjuster~*Inquiring Mind; Self-Discipline and Work Organization; Human Relations Abilities; Integrity and Honesty; Loyalty; Statement of Principles*

The Role of the Attorney in Insurance Claims~*The Claimant's (Plaintiff's) Attorney; The Defense Attorney; Conflicts of Interest*

Types of Claims~*Auto Liability Claims; Personal and General Liability Claims; Products Liability Claims; Completed Operations Liability Claims; Liability versus Property Claims*

Sources of Knowledge and Information

The Claim Field as a Career

Chapter 2—The Importance and Meaning of Coverage 35

The Elements of a Contract~*Agreement; Competent Parties; Genuine Assent; Consideration; Legal Purpose; Form Required By Law*

Distinctive Features of Insurance Contracts~*Intangible and Aleatory; Contract of Adhesion; Rule of Strict Construction and Ambiguity; Personal Contract of the Utmost Good Faith; Reasonable Expectations; Examples of Ambiguous Policy Language*

Personal Auto Policy—Liability Analysis~*Insuring Agreement; Supplementary Payments*

Chapter 3—The Importance and Meaning of Coverage, Continued 61

Personal Auto Policy~*Exclusions; Additional Limitations; Coverage versus Liability; Limit of Liability; Out of State Coverage; Other Insurance*

Why Knowledge of Coverage Is Important~*Hionis Decision; Standard Venetian Blind Decision; Ady Decision*

Coverage Problems~*Waiver and Estoppel; Reservation of Rights Letter; Nonwaiver Agreement; Declaratory Judgment Action*

Excess Liability~*Punitive Damage Suits*

Chapter 4—The Meaning of Legal Liability 95

Introduction

Common and Statutory Law

Criminal and Civil Law

Torts ~ *Types of Torts*

Legal Liability Based on Negligence ~ *Elements of Negligence; Determining Negligence in Premises Liability Claims; Other Factors Considered in Determining Negligence*

Legal Liability Based on Contract and Statute

Main Principles of Law Affecting Liability Claim Handling ~ *Joint Tortfeasor Liability; Vicarious Liability; Contributory Negligence; Comparative Negligence; Automobile Guest Statutes; Immunity; Bailments*

Chapter 5—The Meaning of Legal Liability, Continued 147

Imperfections of the Tort Liability System

Remedies ~ *Financial Responsibility Laws; Compulsory Auto Insurance; Uninsured Motorists Insurance; Underinsured Motorists Insurance; No-Fault Automobile Insurance*

Bad Faith and Excess Liability ~ *Sources of Bad Faith; Discovery Process May Involve Claim Personnel; Conclusion*

The Evolutionary Process of Law

Defenses ~ *Contributory Negligence; Assumption of Risk; Avoidable Consequences; Unavoidable Accident; Act of God; Emergency Defense; Last Clear Chance; Seat Belt Defense*

The Role of Damages ~ *First-Party Damages; Third-Party Damages; Disability; Verification of Damages; Verification of Medical Charges; Independent Medical Examinations; Collateral Source Rule; Emotional Distress Claims; Prenatal Injury Claims; Damages in the Form of Interest; Pre-Judgment Interest*

Chapter 6—The Investigative Process 195

Introduction ~ *Categories of Liability; Telephone Adjusting*

Planning the Investigation ~ *Recognizing Coverage Questions; Recognizing Liability Questions; Recognizing Questions Related to Damages; Planning the Work Schedule*

Planning the Interview ~ *Contacting the Claimant or Insured; Contacting Witnesses*

Sources of Information ~ *Police Report; Diagrams; Photographs; Weather Reports; The Use of Experts*

Investigating the Injury Aspect of the Claim ~ *Hospital Records; Interview with Treating Physician; Other Official Reports*

Reporting ~ *Kinds of Reports; Potential Problems with Discovery; Claim Reports to Underwriting*

Statement Taking ~ *Written Statements; Recorded Statements; Special Problems Associated with Statement Taking; Conclusion*

Appendix to Chapter 6

Chapter 7—Types of Claims Investigation 291

Auto Claims ~ *Introduction; Uninsured Motorists Claims; Statute of Limitations; Underinsured Motorists Claims; Auto Damage Claims; Actual Cash Value and Replacement Cost; Auto Theft Claims; Auto Arson Claims; Automobile Flood Claims; No-Fault Auto Insurance Claims*

Public Liability Claims ~ *Status of Claimant; Causes of Falls*

Products Liability Claims ~ *Exclusions; Privity; Legal Basis of Products Liability Claims; Res Ipsa Loquitur; Duty to Warn; Proximate Cause and Intervening Acts; Investigation Procedures; Duty of Safe Design; Statute of Limitations*

Professional Liability Claims

Workers' Compensation Claims ~ *Benefits; Sources of Coverage; Subrogation of Workers' Compensation Claims; Occupational Illness or Disease*

Chapter 8—The Evaluation and Settlement of Injury Claims 341

Introduction

Factors Affecting Claim Evaluation ~ *Importance of Medical Report and the Doctor Interview; Medical Terminology; Other Considerations or Issues*

Methods of Evaluating Claims ~ *X Times Special Damages; Total/Partial Disability Approach; Unit of Time; Judgment/Experience Method; Round Table*

Examples of Claim Evaluation ~ *Case One Evaluation—Clear or Probable Liability; Case Two Evaluation—Questionable Liability*

Settlement Negotiations ~ *Determining Case Readiness for Negotiations; Planning the Approach to Negotiations; Characteristics of a Good Negotiator; Initiating the Negotiations Process; Handling the Attorney Threat*

The Offer ~ *The First Offer; Negotiating with Attorneys*

Closing the Claim—The Release ~ *Types of Releases and Settlement Agreements; Setting Aside of Releases; Alternative Approaches to Settlement; Reducing Claim Costs*

Appendix to Chapter 8

Chapter 9—When the Negotiation Process Breaks Down 431

First-Party Disputes ~ *Coverage Disputes; Damage Disputes*

Third-Party Disputes ~ *Damage Disputes with the Claimant; Liability Disputes; Contributory Negligence and Comparative Negligence; Need for a Thorough Investigation; Inter-Company Arbitration*

Forces Influencing the Decision to Settle the Claim ~ *Local Statutes and Ordinances; Regulatory Requirements; Consumer Protection Agencies*

The Legal Process ~ *Protecting the Insured; Discovery Procedures; Pretrial Conferences; the Trial; the Appeal; the Negotiation Process after Suit has been Filed; Authority to Settle; Balancing the Interests*

Summary

Chapter 10—Reserving 457

Introduction ~ *What Is a Claim Reserve? Why Are Claim Reserves Necessary? How Are Claim Reserves Established? Types of Reserves; Establishing Individual Case Reserves; Projecting Claimant's Total Special and General Damages—the Projection Sheet*

Chapter 11—The Role of the Claim Department in the Company 477

Introduction ~ *Underwriting Department; Agency (Sales); Accounting Department; Data Processing Department; Marketing Department*

Corporate Structures ~ *Types of Insurance Companies; Risk Management/Investment of the Insurer; Economics of the Insurance Company*

Bibliography 489

Index 491

CHAPTER 1

Functions of the Claim Department and the Adjuster

TECHNICAL FUNCTIONS

The major purpose of a claims department of an insurance company is to properly and fairly dispose of all claims made against the company and its insured. In order to accomplish this, several functions must be carried out by the members of the department, the most important ones being:

- providing the procedure for claims reporting,
- assigning claims to adjusters,
- assisting adjusters in determining coverage,
- reviewing files to ensure proper disposition,
- counseling adjusters in the resolution of legal liability questions,
- arranging for the defense of lawsuits,
- pursuing subrogation,
- establishing and maintaining proper reserves, and
- assisting adjusters and defense counsel in evaluating claims.

Investigation and claims settlement are the main reasons for all the support work described in the foregoing list of functions. The only way that the company can determine its liability position is by obtaining the necessary statements and other investigation. Only then can it be decided whether payment will be made, or the claim denied or compromised. The support work occurs between the time that the claim is reported and closed.

Providing Procedures for Reporting Claims

It is necessary for the company to establish a system of reporting the claims to the company. Such reporting comes either directly from the insured or from agents or brokers. A number of methods can be used to report a claim, ranging from the telephone call from the insured to the company to the sophisticated system of reporting to a company person who immediately enters the information into the computer. Whatever the system, it must be efficient enough to process the claims in a timely manner to allow immediate service by the adjuster.

Assigning Claims to Adjusters

Assuming that an insurance company employs a staff of adjusters, the distribution of work among the staff involves many considerations. First, the staff must be sufficiently trained to process the variety of claims received. The size of the staff must be large enough so that each member can maintain a tolerable workload. Further, proper balance in number and load of assignments is required to ensure fairness to the entire staff.

Often, adjusters are assigned to exclusive territories or work areas in which they service claims. Since the adjuster receives all claims that occur in that territory, the department workload balance can be disturbed, depending on the timing and the volume of claims received. Companies must maintain a close watch on their claim assignments to be sure that they obtain quality as well as quantity of work from their adjusters.

Assisting in Determining Coverage

Before a claim can be paid, coverage must be confirmed; thus coverage verification is the first order of business after a notice of claim is received. There are two elements of coverage: (1) policy verification and (2) contract construction. For the most part, verification of coverage poses no problem. Policies or endorsements are obtained and checked and the facts of the loss as originally reported are matched to the coverage. Many companies now confirm coverage through the use of computer terminals instead of viewing the actual policies or endorsements. This practice will become more common as more companies become computerized. If the facts match the coverage, the adjuster goes on to the next order of business.

If a contract construction or "coverage" problem exists, it must be recognized and resolved as soon as possible. If any question occurs, it is necessary to have the company and the insured sign a non-waiver agreement, or to send a reservation of rights letter to the insured before attempting an investigation of the facts.

The agreement or the letter is used to reserve the rights and/or defenses under the terms of the insurance policy. To proceed without one in a case of questionable coverage can be greatly detrimental to the company since the omission can later foreclose or reduce the company's ability to enforce its rights. (The non-waiver agreement and the reservation of rights letter are discussed further in Chapter 2.)

The company must establish its position regarding coverage as early as possible and must then make it immediately known to its insured. This should be done by letter to the insured, explaining the applicability of coverage, or its absence, and giving specific reasons.

Property and casualty insurance claims are presented by both first and third parties. The terms "first party" and "third party" arise from the fact that the insurance policy is a legally enforceable contract. The insured is designated the "first party" and the insurance company the "second party." A third party is neither an insured nor an insurer, in a pure sense, but someone else who has a right to recover under the policy. First-party losses are those where the insured sustains financial loss for which he or she is entitled to recovery under the insurance contract. As a result of the contractual relationship, the insurer owes the insured a duty to act in good faith and to investigate and pay all first-party losses in a timely and fair manner.

By virtue of the liability coverage in the policy, the company promises to pay on behalf of the insured all sums for which the insured becomes legally liable, and to defend the insured against all claims covered under the policy, whether valid or not.

It is necessary for the claimant to prove that the insured's actions were the proximate cause of the claimant's damage or injury. Such actions would apply to negligence as well as to strict liability when dealing in products liability claims. The differences between negligence and strict liability will be discussed in later chapters. Only after the claimant has proven the insured's liability can he or she be successful in perfecting such a claim. If there is the least bit of difficulty in the processing of the claimant's loss, the relationship may become adversary to the point of losing control of the claim. By loss of control is meant that the claimant has retained an attorney to represent that person's interests, and all negotiations thereafter must be conducted with the attorney.

Reviewing Files to Ensure Proper Disposition

Claim adjusters often need supervisory assistance or direction to keep them on the right path. Additionally, on occasion, adjusters receive unusual claims where the supervisor's expertise provides an added dimension to the adjuster's claim handling ability.

As a supervisor reviews the file, many items are checked. Have the contacts with the insured and claimant been made in a timely manner? Has the necessary investigation been completed promptly? Have all developments been properly documented? Is the adjuster observing diary dates and marking the file accordingly? As the supervisor reviews the file, it must speak for itself. If the file does not answer a question or contain needed information, the work has not been done, in the supervisor's mind.

It should be noted that it is often easy for an adjuster to do work on a file and not report that work to the file. This occurs because the adjuster is busy on other pursuits or fails to organize the work. The adjuster should be careful to avoid such pitfalls.

Counseling Adjusters in the Resolution of Legal Liability Questions

As the adjuster develops the facts in a claim file, it is not always easy to determine the respective legal liability of the parties involved. In some cases, such as in rear-end type accidents, legal liability is obvious. If the liability rests with the insured, the only question that remains concerns damages. In other situations, it is not that simple. As an example, if the accident occurs in an intersection where the insured and the claimant both allege that each had the green light, the adjuster must fully investigate the facts by seeking witnesses who can clarify the circumstances. It may be necessary to canvass the scene for unknown witnesses, such as store employees or customers, gas station employees, or residents in nearby houses. Photos of the damaged vehicles and of the accident scene should be obtained. A diagram should also be constructed, displaying the physical layout. If the investigation does not clearly reveal liability, then legal precedents must be reviewed to determine the strength of the defenses available. If they are not clearly favorable, then payment should be seriously considered, either for the entire damage or for a compromise amount.

The important thing to consider here is that a complete investigation is the only way to determine liability. If the essential fact questions involving liability are not addressed and answered, no one can pinpoint the liability. It is best to obtain the necessary investigation of the facts before the question of liability is discussed with the supervisor.

Defending Lawsuits

It is inevitable that an adjuster will work on a claim file that develops into a lawsuit. This subject matter will be described in detail in Chapter 9. Lawsuits are mentioned at this time because the handling of litigation is an important function of the claim department. High priority should be placed on lawsuits due to their nature. Lawsuits must be answered within a certain time and they must be assigned to legal counsel for immediate attention. If this does not occur, the rights of both insured and insurer may be waived and substantial financial loss occur.

The critical action for an adjuster upon receipt of a new lawsuit is to report it to the supervisor or claim manager so that it may receive the proper consideration and action.

Pursuing Subrogation Claims

Although most claim department activity involves paying claims, one area involves the collection of money—subrogation. Subrogation is defined as "the substitution of one person in place of another with reference to a lawful claim, demand, or right."[1]

A typical subrogation claim occurs where an insured's automobile is struck in the rear while stopped for a traffic light. If collision coverage is available, the company must pay (on demand) the collision damage, subject to the amount of the deductible. The company is then subrogated against the wrongdoer, or his or her insurance company, for the amount of damage paid. When this money is collected by the claim department, it becomes a credit in the accounting process.

Subrogation provides an excellent source of income for the company. Needless to say, success in this area can be very beneficial.

Establishing Proper Reserves

A loss reserve is an accounting liability entry indicating that certain amounts have been set aside to cover the expected costs. There are various methods of establishing loss reserves, which are described in Chapter 10.

Undoubtedly, establishing loss reserves is one of the most important functions of the claim department, since reserving directly affects the company's financial standing. Consequently, understating the reserves drastically affects the solvency of the company, while overstating the reserves would also distort its financial status.

Claim Evaluations

Upon establishing that its insured is legally liable for the damages resulting from an accident, it then becomes necessary for the claim department to evaluate the damages that must be paid. If the damages are limited to physical property, it is relatively simple to establish the value. This is done by estimating the cost of repairs or by the cost of replacement if the item is damaged beyond repair.

Evaluation becomes more difficult when dealing with bodily injuries. How does one establish the value of soft-tissue injury, a fractured leg or arm, or a facial scar? There is no secret formula or computer approach used to arrive at such values. Dollar values are based on adjuster experience and knowledge of costs of previous settlements as well as recent jury awards in the prevailing jurisdiction. It takes time to acquire this knowledge and experience. Companies establish settlement "authority" ranges, from zero to policy limits, based upon adjuster ability and experience.

In more serious injuries, the adjuster will undoubtedly confer with the supervisor or claim manager to take advantage of their greater experience and knowledge to arrive at proper values.

PERSONNEL FUNCTIONS

The above described functions could not be fulfilled without a knowledgeable and motivated staff. Procuring and maintaining such a staff is a task of claim management equal in importance to the disposition of the claims itself.

Hiring Adjusters

Assuming that the claim department maintains its own staff, the claim manager must interview and hire adjusters when the need arises. This process requires that the manager be familiar with the company's hiring practices, job requirements, salary ranges, and benefit structure. Adequate time must be devoted to the actual interview as well as additional time in comparing information, and finally, selecting the right person. As can be seen, the entire hiring process becomes very involved, almost making it necessary for the claim manager to be a specialist in the personnel area as well as in claims.

Special consideration must be given by the manager to the calibre of person who will be hired. The applicant must be able to perform the job, and equally important, the newly hired person must be willing to make the insurance claim profession a career. While difficult to ascertain at the time of employment, such devotion to duty is indispensable due to the cost and amount of training that is involved in developing a good adjuster.

Training Adjusters

The level of training of a newly hired adjuster depends on his or her prior experience. If an experienced adjuster has been selected, the training will probably be limited to specific company procedures. This training takes a comparatively short time and the new, but experienced, adjuster can be ready to work with very little assistance. On the other hand, if the new employee has no experience, the training will consume a great deal of time. In addition to on-the-job training, the new adjuster may also be required to participate in organized training schools, seminars, and correspondence or self-study courses.

Training time can be very extended, depending on the company's requirements, particularly if the adjuster will handle "multiple-line" claims. These are claims involving both property and liability coverages. Such claims require knowledge of specific contract language as well as considerable technical information for investigation and settlement.

In spite of the length of time that it takes to develop and train an adjuster, such time should be regarded as an investment that will pay handsome dividends in the future, not only for the adjuster, but also for the employer. This price must be paid for competent, proficient claims activity.

Proper salary administration begins in the planning and budgetary stages, particularly in the area of salary ranges and individual salary adjustments. Most companies use some form of merit approach to salary administration, where desirable and proficient employees are compensated in keeping with their perceived contributions. If companies did not use some program such as this, every employee would simply obtain an "across the board" increase. Obviously, this approach to salary administration requires no management attention and actually discriminates against the employees who are doing a superior job. Personnel retention would quickly become a problem in such a situation.

When individual performance is recognized and rewarded, the manager must evaluate all employees on a consistent basis, on predetermined and recognized standards. Companies employ various forms or methods of evaluation. While the motivation theorists tell us that salary is not really a motivator, it clearly acts as a great dissatisfier if paid in an unfair or inadequate manner.

Planning for Future Needs

Proper claims administration does not just "happen." It begins with detailed planning by the claim manager, and with support and input from the supervisors. The manager must consider present and anticipated future premium volume, since premium volume translates into claims, claims into workload, and workload into personnel needs. The predicted fluctuations in premium generate changing departmental budgets, which must be monitored along with other departmental performance statistics.

Planning may profitably begin with a "situation analysis," which describes both internal and external conditions affecting the department's ability to perform its assigned function. The manager then makes projections based upon what he knows and what he expects to occur.

From this analysis process flows specific departmental objectives, along with a plan for achieving them. The plan, which includes training, litigation prevention and management approaches, and a variety of other activities, provides a general framework for the department's work, a standard against which performance can be measured on a broader scale than case-by-case evaluation. Without this structure and direction departments may become mired in day-to-day detail that contributes little to overall success.

TYPES OF ADJUSTERS

Heretofore, "claim representatives" have been mentioned in a generalized manner, as though there were only one kind. Claim persons are categorized into several separate classes. Among these are the staff adjuster, the independent adjuster, and the agent. In addition, there are public adjusters who work in insurance claims. All but public adjusters work on behalf of the insurer; conversely, the public adjuster works on behalf of (and is paid by) the insured.

Throughout this work the terms "adjuster," "claim representative," and "claims person" are used interchangeably to designate the person involved in the direct investigation and disposition of insurance claims. The terms "claim supervisor," "claim examiner," and "claim manager" refer to supervisory personnel overseeing the work of the first group.

Staff Adjusters

A *staff adjuster* is an employee of the insurer and processes all of that insurer's claims, usually for a salary. Some adjusters specialize in particular coverage lines or types of claims; others accept all assignments, regardless of line. This could include auto liability, general liability, property, plate glass, inland marine and ocean marine losses, among others. The staff adjuster may work as a field claim representative or as an office claim representative.

Field Claim Representatives The field claim representative's duties include meeting personally with insureds, claimants, witnesses, and service-related people. Also, the field adjuster inspects damage, takes photos, and makes diagrams of the scenes of various accidents. The field adjuster may also serve as a support person for the office adjuster, performing any duties necessary to facilitate field adjuster duties.

Since the field adjuster is mobile, little time is generally spent in the claim office. On the other hand, the field adjuster prepares reports for the claim file and confers with the supervisor regarding coverage and liability questions while in the office, so time spent inside is necessary and vital to the claim operation.

Office Claim Representatives Office claim representatives (OCRs), or telephone adjusters as they are sometimes called, spend virtually all of their time investigating and settling claims from within the claim office. The telephone unit may work in connection with a drive-in claim office for damaged autos, or it may operate as a separate entity. All contacts are made either by telephone or correspondence. They may obtain telephone statements, as well. As stated previously, if the OCR needs field assistance with a portion of the investigation, the field adjuster provides the necessary support. If a drive-in claim office is included in the company's operation, the insured or claimant drives the damaged auto to the drive-in location. While the appraiser prepares a repair estimate, the OCR obtains a recorded statement from the driver. If sufficient information is received and payment is warranted, it is possible for the OCR to issue a payment to the insured or claimant at that time.

Maintaining staff adjusters is a significant expense. The claims operation must justify that expense as a wise use of funds. While the handling of the claim provides the major benefit to the insured from the policy, staffing must be arranged on a cost-effective basis and in keeping with premium volume.

Field and Office Adjusters Compared In comparing the field adjuster with the office adjuster, it is possible to find advantages and disadvantages in both approaches to adjusting claims. With the field adjuster's mobility, it is possible to inspect large and small losses to determine their accurate value. Also, since the field claim representative meets personally with the public, an assessment may be made of the impression an individual witness would make to a jury. Most importantly, mobility permits face-to-face settlement negotiations with insureds and claimants. The disadvantage in using field adjusters relates to the cost per case. It is expensive to transport the adjuster from place to place. The expense factor also increases as a function of travel time. A consequence of this method of processing claims is that only a limited number of calls can be completed in the course of the normal work day. Other expenses involve the cost of making telephone calls from phone booths or other locations, plus other incidental expenses, such as parking fees, toll fees, and the like.

Since the office claim representative is not mobile, the expenses for this method of processing claims are limited to his or her salary and office expenses. There are no transportation or incidental expenses. The telephone is provided by the employer, undoubtedly at a less expensive rate than individual calls. In addition, the OCR can investigate and process more claims in the same period of time, because there is no need to travel. Since more claims can be processed in the same amount of time, the number of adjusters needed will decrease accordingly.

However, it is not possible for the OCR to inspect the damage, and as a result, it is possible that an inflated amount will be paid toward the settlement of the claim. Another disadvantage is that telephone contact does not permit observing the other party to the same extent as by face-to-face meeting.

Some insurers combine the use of field claim representatives with OCRs to gain a very effective and efficient staff of adjusters.

Independent Adjusters

Independent adjusters do not work for the insurer, but work for bureau organizations or are independent adjusters. When independent adjusters become involved in a claim, it is because that claim has been assigned to them by the insurer.

The independent adjuster may operate at one or more locations. Insurers may assign the total investigation and settlement, or only a portion of the total claim, depending on need. The independent adjuster is an independent contractor and charges the insurer for services rendered on each individual assignment, or on a contract or retainer basis.

These adjusters provide a valuable service merely by being available when needed on a temporary, fill-in-basis. For example, during times of a catastrophe, independent adjusters from distant places as well as near locations assist by providing their services to quickly resolve the insuring public's devastating problems. Also, they are available during staff vacation and illness periods.

Some insurance companies do not maintain staff adjusters but rely solely on independent adjusters to process all of their claims. In such situations, the insurer may contract with certain independent adjusters at various locations and may even provide the adjuster with drafts and draft authority to facilitate the settlement of claims. The insurers claim volume in these areas will dictate the manner in which the claims will be assigned to the independent adjuster.

Agents

The agent is included in our discussion as an adjuster because agents do, in fact, settle many claims. For the most part, they work with first-party losses when the insured's property is damaged by an insured peril, or on comparatively minor automobile losses, such as towing, glass, and collision claims, up to a certain value. Some agents also settle claimants' auto property damage claims; however, this claim work is most often performed by an adjuster, as it requires specific knowledge of negligence laws. In most cases, when agents settle claims, they also have a designated amount of draft authority in order to make a loss payment and quickly close the claim.

Public Adjusters

The public adjuster is employed by the insured to protect that interest, usually with respect to property damaged by fire, wind, or some other peril. This adjuster prepares the insured's claim and negotiates the settlement with the staff or independent adjuster. The public adjuster's services are paid for by the insured, usually in accordance with a contract for service.

THE SELF-INSURED FIRM'S NEED FOR THE CLAIM FUNCTION

Some businesses, usually larger firms, by-pass the insurance method and absorb predictable losses. Although we refer to these firms as self-insured, the term self-insurance is really a contradiction. Insurance involves the transfer of the risk of loss; self-insured firms retain this risk of loss. In order to determine its risk of loss with some degree of credibility, the self-insurer must be able to predict its usual or routine losses by having a large number of exposures. Further, the self-insurer must have sufficient resources available for the payment of these fortuitous losses when they occur.[2]

These plans are common in today's business world and can be an effective method for dealing with losses. Distinction must be made, however, between a funded plan and passive lack of insurance. The latter is an example of poor risk management and can be dangerous for a business or company, as a large loss can close the doors of the business.

When a loss involving a self-insurer occurs, the self-insurer must have the means of investigating the loss, to determine liability. These losses can be assigned to independent adjusters. They can also be handled by the excess insurer, or by the self-insurer's own staff. Excess insurance is a necessary part of a responsible self-insurance program. While these policies may be written in different ways, the overall effect is to limit the insured's exposure in the event of catastrophic loss.

Self-insureds often have an insurance department, risk management department, or an individual who is familiar with losses to determine that investigations are sufficient and to guide the claim to a conclusion.

As the claim representative becomes involved in self-insured claims, it becomes evident that the question of coverage has vanished—and the only questions to answer are those of liability and value.

THE ROLE OF THE ADJUSTER

Through claim adjusters, insurance companies fulfill their promises to promptly compensate insureds or others for losses sustained. Thus, the responsibility of the adjuster is great indeed. Up until the time of loss, the insured has received only promises; now, with a loss presented, the insurer must make good on that promise. To accomplish this, the adjuster will have to perform a number of tasks, grouped under the headings of investigation, evaluation, negotiation, and settlement.

Investigation

After determining that coverage is in order, the adjuster next contacts the parties involved in the claim. These initial contacts acknowledge the fact that the insurer is aware of the loss and is prepared to do what is required to arrive at a proper conclusion. Timing and content both enter into the effectiveness of the initial contact effort.

Invariably, this contact determines the future course of the claim. If it is made promptly, the adjuster has taken the first positive step toward developing a favorable relationship with the insured or claimant. Occasionally, it may be impossible for the claim representative to meet with the individual immediately, but a simple telephone call will often suffice for the person who is looking and waiting for help. Most individuals are not unreasonable in their demands and, therefore, are usually appreciative and relieved by that early, first telephone call.

There is another important reason for making that early first call, either in person or by telephone. That consists of the opportunity for the claim representative to obtain a recorded statement from the insured, the claimant, or witnesses. The recording device must always be in readiness to allow response to such opportunities. In some cases, this may be the only time this person will be willing to give a statement. Thus, the opportunity must not be missed. Further, the facts of the accident are still fresh in mind, so this first contact provides the most favorable time to preserve them for the claim file.

In addition to statements, investigations involve other activities. In many cases, the police report forms an important element of the file. At the onset, this report may be the adjuster's only guide to what happened. It may also contain other important information, such as names of all parties connected with the accident, the type and extent of injuries, names of witnesses, names of insurance companies, who was arrested or cited, cause of citation, where the autos were towed, and so on. As a precaution, it should be noted that the police report serves only as a guide; it does not replace the careful and complete investigation by the adjuster.

Photos and a diagram of the scene are often important. They permit a better understanding of the accident facts and may even identify a previously unsuspected witness in some situations. Other investigation often includes the inspecting and photographing of property damage, as well as detailed estimates of repair costs.

Dealing with injured persons constitutes the major portion of many investigations. When making the first contact with an injured party, the adjuster obtains medical authorization forms so that medical information can be released. Without signed authorization, the medical file remains privileged information, thereby increasing the difficulty of a thorough evaluation of the injuries. Also, authorization forms are necessary to obtain wage loss information from employers or other custodians of records.

As the investigation progresses, the claim representative must report on developments as they occur. As previously stated, if the information does not appear in the file, one assumes that the investigation was not conducted. Incomplete and untimely reporting destroys the value of an otherwise proficient investigation.

Persistence has particular significance in the investigation of claims. It means that the adjuster must persist until all available pertinent information is collected. By acting in this manner, the adjuster keeps the facts fresh in mind and has a perceptible rhythm working to his or her benefit. On the other hand, if the facts are gathered in a dilatory, piecemeal fashion, with portions obtained perhaps days apart, it is difficult to get the "feel" of the claim, and as a result, the investigation suffers in quality, or even worse, goes uncompleted.

Evaluation

After completion of the investigation, the claim representative must make use of the information. First the adjuster must determine if the insured is liable, and if so, the extent of that liability. If liability exists, then the injury must be valued on the basis of the information received from the treating physician and/or hospital. Earlier in this chapter, it was suggested that the claim supervisor should assist in determining the extent of liability as well as the value of the injury where needed. But the competent adjuster forms his or her own independent analysis and evaluation, expressed in the form of a recommendation for discussion.

Negotiation

In order to be a successful negotiator, the claim representative must also be a successful salesperson. Taken a step further, the negotiation or selling process can be even more effective when the negotiator knows the person on the other side of the negotiating table. The first time around in any process is usually the hardest. The same is true in negotiating a claim settlement. If the time has been taken to get to know the claimant or the claimant's attorney, one can be sure that, in most cases, negotiations will proceed more successfully. The same rapport must be established with attorneys as with insureds and claimants. The subject of settlement negotiations will be explored in detail in Chapter 9.

Settlement

When a settlement of a claim has been reached, the adjuster must be certain that all the elements of the settlement are understood and accepted by all concerned. This includes obtaining the necessary signatures on the release, identifying various interests involved, and the amounts agreed. Nothing seems as exasperating or embarrassing as a revived claim thought to be closed.

Paying the Fair Amount

By many state laws and as a general practice, insurers pay a fair amount for loss or damage sustained as the result of a covered loss. If this concept is not followed, the insurer not only suffers financial problems, but may subject itself to expensive punitive litigation. Of course, these constraints apply to company practice, not what occurs in an occasional instance.

For instance, if a company consistently overpays claims, it will not take long for knowledge of this practice to spread. The company will pay out more for claims than the income received from normal premium receipts. Such an insurer develops financial difficulty and will perhaps become insolvent.

Conversely, a company that constantly underpays claims encounters different problems. Its reputation also spreads, and eventually this company loses a great deal of business due to voluntary cancellations or nonrenewals by the insureds. Cash flow becomes a problem, and this may include a lack of funds to pay losses already on the books. In addition, this company may generate more than its share of complaints from its insureds and claimants. When this happens, the state Insurance Department will intervene, creating more problems for the company.

It is obvious, then, that the only way to adjust claims is to pay a fair amount for the loss. And this can only be done after proper investigations have been made by adjusters.

Controlling Costs

The duties related to the adjuster's job consist of adjusting the values of property to injury if the values are overstated or understated. These adjustments may involve various aspects of value determination, such as:

1. the value of intangible damages,
2. replacement value,
3. depreciation, and
4. betterment.

The Value of Intangible Damages

When personal property is damaged, it can be described and classified with ease. For example, the automobile involved in an accident was a 1981 Gas Saver, 4-door sedan. Or the fishing rod that was damaged was a Lucky Rod, Model A601. With such exact description and classification, the value of the property can be established with relative ease. This can be done by checking catalogues, checking advertisements, visiting retail stores, or calling sources by telephone.

On the other hand, the value of an injury claim is more difficult to establish. There are no price lists or catalogues that can be used as reference. As noted previously in this chapter, establishing injury values requires experience and medical reports from the treating physician and/or hospital. Consideration must be given to the objective and subjective findings and to other factors, such as degrees of permanent injury and/or scars.

Replacement Value One method of concluding a property damage loss is through replacement of the item with one of like kind and quality. This solution eliminates consideration of prior use or wear and tear; therefore, this method is generally used in casualty claims only when the damaged property is new or has little wear and tear.

Actual Cash Value When personal property is damaged, it frequently has been used or worn for some period of time. Such use causes wear and tear on the object, and consequently, when damage occurs, the value of that use must be considered. This, in turn, is based on the long standing insurance principle of indemnity, which says that a payee should not be allowed a profit from insurance recoveries. The basis of a property damage evaluation is called Actual Cash Value (ACV). The most common method in arriving at ACV is by use of the simple formula:

Replacement cost new less depreciation = ACV

Depreciation can be determined by mutual agreement between owner and adjuster or from depreciation tables. Perhaps the easiest method is to allow the owner to suggest the depreciation factor since the owner has the best knowledge of the age and condition of the object. Usually, the owner will be fair in establishing depreciation values. Of course, there exists the converse argument, wherein the owner feels since the damaged object was perfectly useful and since the owner had no intention of buying a new one the adjuster should waive the depreciation. The adjuster should be able to persuade the owner that some value of the damaged item has already been derived, and that fairness prompts payment only for the remaining value. At this point, it may be well for the adjuster to compare other examples of depreciation, such as when a defective tire is being replaced by the manufacturer. In such a case, it is common to measure the wear on the tire and for the manufacturer to pay for only the portion which has not been used. If the claimant is not willing to accept depreciation, the adjuster must either make an instant decision on the matter, or refer the situation to the claim supervisor or claim manager to determine what action should be taken.

There is still another factor that can be associated with the actual cash value of property and that is when obsolescence is present. Obsolescence is common in items such as old stereo tapes, old sheet music, some clothing and other similar examples. Webster's Dictionary defines obsolescence as "being out of date" or "going out of use."[3] Generally, it is not difficult to recognize such property; the problem lies in arriving at an agreed value.

"Betterment" is comparable to depreciation, and at times "betterment" is used in lieu of "depreciation." Webster defines betterment as "improvement," compared to the definition of depreciation as being a "reduction in value."[4] When the adjuster thinks or talks about betterment, it is merely another way of describing the need for depreciation to be applied.

THE ADJUSTER'S FIELDS OF KNOWLEDGE

The adjuster must become expert in the interpretation of insurance coverages, a skill developed through training and repeated analysis of the various policies. In fact, the claim person must become familiar with the law of contracts in general, as many of the phases of investigation are based on contract law.

Since insurance policies are legal contracts, they may serve as the first exposure to contractual construction. Other examples are mortgages and liens which hold insureds, insurers, and claimants in contractual privity. The adjuster must be aware of various duties associated with these contracts as these may well become the adjuster's own duties, in the handling of losses to property referred to in these contracts.

As the adjuster continues to investigate claims, he or she may encounter other contracts such as leases, construction contracts, and hold-harmless agreements. The subject of contractual duties and liabilities is not one that can be properly explained in a few paragraphs. The purpose here is to illustrate that contracts are a portion of the adjuster's overall responsibility requiring training and knowledge.

While the adjuster is primarily an insurance person, let us consider some other fields that may be encountered depending on the case assigned.

Auto Construction and Repairs

When an auto is damaged, the adjuster must be in a position, at the very least, to ascertain if the repair estimate is in line with the damage. Such knowledge requires familiarity with the names of the parts of the car and being able to identify them. The adjuster also has to know how to read an auto repair manual to determine costs. Many adjusters are expected to prepare their own estimates of damage and to obtain an agreed repair price with the body shop.

As we all know, America's love affair with the automobile has generated annual model changes that affect body parts changes as well as changes in cost. These annual changes require an ongoing educational program, particularly for those who specialize in auto physical damage claims. In addition, with the energy crisis came the need for smaller, lighter autos. This propelled us all the way from automobiles with traditional frames to autos with a unitized body and no frames at all. Also, manufacturers now assemble their products with new high strength steel, which weighs less. As a result of these changes, many old methods of repair have become outdated, making it necessary for the repairers and adjusters to re-educate themselves in new repair processes that are essential with new auto bodies.

Medical Knowledge

As a person who must evaluate, negotiate, and settle bodily injury claims, the adjuster must gain more than a passing knowledge of injuries that result from trauma. This requires sufficient familiarity with human anatomy, so that the adjuster recognizes the portion of the body involved. This includes knowing not only the skeletal system, but also other anatomical systems as well.

After the adjuster obtains the medical reports, these must be scrutinized to determine the location, type, and extent of injury, and the diagnosis and prognosis must be sufficiently understood before a value can be placed on the injury. In this process, the adjuster should be able to recognize natural illnesses and conditions, and separate them from traumatic injury. Within this realm must be considered pre-existing conditions, such as arthritis being aggravated by trauma.

During the analysis of the medical reports, the adjuster should not hesitate to refer to a medical dictionary when needed. In this manner, the adjuster's medical knowledge is constantly expanded.

As the claim representative learns these various medical terms, he or she should remember that his or her knowledge is not on the professional level of a physician, and as a result, the claim person must never attempt to diagnose an injury, or counsel an injured person. These actions must be left to the physicians.

Accounting

In the area of inventory and stock losses, the need for accounting knowledge becomes apparent. These losses may come about as the result of an insured's negligence, causing the necessity for a manufacturer or retailer to close the business on a temporary basis. When this occurs, the adjuster's accounting talents are needed to sort out the real loss, which is accident related. The adjuster's accounting knowledge limits payments to those properly covered under the policy.

It is possible that the claim may be large or complicated enough to warrant the services of a professional accounting firm to counsel and act on behalf of the insurer. In these cases, the claim representative must have sufficent knowledge of accounting principles to be able to understand the information and reports submitted by the accounting expert.

Building Construction

An insured's negligence can cause substantial damage to dwellings, as well as to commercial or industrial buildings. The adjuster must be knowledgeable in comparing estimates of damage to the damaged property itself. Along these lines, the adjuster must also be aware of local building codes.

Product Manufacturing

The expertise needed for the investigation and processing of products liability claims can be as broad as the number of products being manufactured. This is true as the nature of the product may require mastering an entirely new field.

In this age of remarkable progress, one sees the almost daily appearance of new products on the market. Each of these products may be capable of producing injury or some type of loss to the consumer. As a result, investigations of losses in this field present a diverse challenge to the claim person.

The Law

Very little detail on the law will be given in this section, although this subject weighs heavily in the performance of the adjuster's duties and knowledge. Since this text deals primarily with liability claims, the investigation of facts in order to determine liability in the context of the applicable law is of the greatest importance.

Although some of the insured's negligence may also include a criminal act, such as a violation of a traffic law, the essence of the claim person's thrust will center around the civil law. Such considerations pertain to what the ordinarily prudent person would do in a situation and, generally, what actions, contrary to the prudent person's activities, would constitute negligence and result in liability.

The adjuster's familiarity with the law will also include various legal doctrines applicable to negligence, common law, statutes, defenses, and other procedures relative to the proper processing of claims.

ATTRIBUTES OF A SUCCESSFUL ADJUSTER

Inquiring Mind

An inquiring mind is an important characteristic of the claim representative. To illustrate this point, consider the adjuster who receives a new assignment which in itself does not fully describe the facts or full results of the accident. Not only must coverage be confirmed, but also other claim possibilities for which coverage may be claimed must be anticipated. Inquisitiveness can also be essential for the entire investigation process. For example, during the process of obtaining a statement a witness may suggest information that may open an entirely new area for inquiry. By following up and asking more questions, the adjuster may obtain information that changes the entire approach to the defense of the claim. Certainly, such "finds" may be rare; however, the ability to perceive them separates a good claim representative from less accomplished adjusters.

Adjusters may develop many good characteristics but fail to keep progressing in knowledge and ability. This can change former success into a rut. This occurs when one begins to treat regular adjusting duties with such a lack of attention and concern that necessary details are no longer completed. Claim representatives should take refresher courses to re-learn the basics and maintain the techniques of proper adjusting practices.

Claim supervisors often complain that adjusters do not research and resolve their own coverage questions. Consider this example. Suppose the insured's car was being driven by someone other than a named insured when it was involved in an accident. In this instance, the coverage item must be investigated with much the same detail as the factual situation. The adjusters should obtain statements to determine everything pertinent about the use of the automobile, then compare those facts to the policy verbiage, then make a decision as to whether coverage applies. Claim representatives should normally submit recommendations on coverage, along with their investigative report, for supervisor approval. The supervisor may agree or disagree with the adjuster's recommendation. Often it seems much easier for the adjuster to request the supervisor's decision without any research on the part of the adjuster. Such a manuever not only saves time, but it also saves the adjuster the need to make a decision. When such a practice occurs, negative results become evident in many areas of the claims operation. First, the adjuster is prevented from actively participating in the educational process of learning coverage. Second, a response from the supervisor may not be forthcoming for some time, particularly if the question of coverage is routed through the mail. Third, the adjuster is prevented from making a total commitment to the duties related to the position and, as a result, will never be considered a good claim representative. Fourth, it becomes necessary for the claim supervisor to take the time to research the question and provide the answer to the adjuster as quickly as possible, delaying the supervisor's review of other files.

Adequate innovation in procedure may be needed to complete a particular claim. At times, innovative ideas meet resistance from supervisors, since not all new ideas will be beneficial. The claim representative may have to convince the supervisor the idea is plausible. As an example, the use of structured settlements has become popular and can be a superior method of settling some cases. Someone took risks initially in developing the technique or we would not have that avenue for settling claims today.

Self-Discipline and Work Organization

Self-discipline is critical to the good claim representative. Without it, the most talented person would find it difficult to succeed in the adjusting profession. The principal reason for this is that the claim representative works alone in disposing of the claims which have been assigned to him. He or she alone can determine when to make appointments, when to report on claims, and when to perform any other phase of the job. Each claim is a separate entity, with individuals who are all unique. For this reason, it is impossible to "standardize" the adjuster's duties. Thus the adjuster must learn to organize work so that important activities are performed first, and that nothing of consequence is overlooked.

One critical aspect of self-discipline is the ability to start work in the morning at the correct time. Since field adjusters usually do not report to the claim office every morning, special diligence must be observed to get started on time. Otherwise, it would be impossible to conclude all of the assigned work.

Although the office claim representative (OCR) follows a more regimented schedule, it is also necessary for that adjuster to be prepared to start work as soon as is required in the morning. Unless a rest period or break is permitted, the OCR should not waste time idly drinking coffee and carrying on nonbusiness discussions.

Self-discipline also carries into the realm of proper organization for both the field adjuster as well as the OCR. Included is the use of an appointment calendar, the scheduling of a daily itinerary (for the field), and keeping current with the department's diary system.

The use of the appointment calendar is important for several reasons, all of which assist the adjuster to complete the required work in a timely manner. The calendar is used to mark and keep track of all appointments. By using the appointment book or calendar, the claim representative controls his own work day and can maximize the effect of the available working hours. Equally important, the use of the appointment book commits the adjuster to handling his claims in an organized manner, compared with making field calls without appointments, often a waste of the adjuster's time, as the persons visited may be out shopping, working, or may have other plans.

The use of the appointment book serves to remind the adjuster to stay current in the diary of claim files. The suggestion is made here for the adjuster to mark new diary dates on the corresponding dates in the calendar. Each morning, the files that appear on diary can be pulled, worked on, and reported on. In this manner, keeping current should pose no problem. This same method is equally beneficial for the OCR in maintaining a file diary.

The daily itinerary is ideally prepared to take the claim representative on field calls in a circular manner, winding up near the starting point if possible. This method prevents backtracking, or zig-zagging back and forth, wasting precious time and energy. Scheduling field calls is not always an easy function, particularly in a catastrophe which covers a large area. In such cases, it is better to subdivide the area, simplifying scheduling and working in each section on a different day.

When emergency claim assignments are received they must take precedence over more routine matters. When these occur, the adjuster must react immediately and reorganize his work plan. If the action requires postponing an appointment, the adjuster must contact the person to be seen, and set the meeting for another date and time. Failure to do so is not only discourteous but may result in the alienation of an otherwise cooperative party.

Although OCRs usually do not make field calls, the same organizational principles apply to their daily routines. They must be as well-organized as the field claim representative. For example, the use of the appointment book is especially important to the OCR if the office contains a drive-in facility. The appointment system for scheduling estimates and taking statements works exceptionally well in a drive-in as it eliminates the need for the customers to wait, on a first come-first serve basis.

In addition, the diary system for maintaining current status on files also applies to the OCR and must be kept current to assure prompt activity. Failure by either the field claim representative or the office claim representative to apply these principles will permit the "job to control the adjuster," instead of the adjuster being in command of the duties to be performed.

Human Relations Abilities

The ability to relate to other people in a favorable manner is a very important ingredient of the successful claim representative. Adjusters deal with insureds, claimants, witnesses, and various individuals who provide services. Since this is the case, it follows that the adjuster should learn all that is possible about people skills. Later, the claim person will study how to develop these skills and to establish a common ground, empathy, and rapport.[5]

Integrity and Honesty

Integrity is defined as "adherence to a code of moral, artistic or other values."[6] Values, in the case of claims, depend largely on the provisions of the insurance policy applicable at the time of loss. As the representative of the insurance company, the adjuster acknowledges and accepts a variety of responsibilities and, in the process, becomes a fiduciary agent of the insurer. To be a fiduciary agent means "relating to or involving a confidence or trust."[7] In the case of the adjuster, the insurer places a great deal of trust in the claims person in areas of determining and committing the company to coverage, or determining the absence of coverage, which may later result in costly litigation. Also, the claims person frequently has blank field drafts which can be converted to cash. Draft authority, granted by the company, allows the adjuster to write drafts for relatively large amounts of money. As a fiduciary agency, the claim person must maintain the highest degree of honesty and trustworthiness.

In dealing with the issue of honesty, employers concern themselves with those aspects of their business which are the most vulnerable to employee dishonesty. In the case of a large retailer, employee dishonesty concerns center around stock shortages and/or employees who have access to cash, such as cashiers. The employer, therefore, can concentrate on securing those known limited areas of risk and be fairly sure that these problems will be kept at a minimum. On the other hand, an insurer is vulnerable in several other ways. First, the only stock involved would be the usual furniture, fixtures, and office supplies necessary to run an insurance company. Obviously, the employer will take the proper action to secure these items and prevent loss or damage. The greater danger to an insurer centers on the fact that adjusters have direct access to financial information and systems.

The claim person can avoid trouble and suggestions of dishonesty in a number of ways. For example, when reporting on a file, only accurate facts should be related. This applies to all information received, as well as reporting on the adjuster's personal activities.

Since the adjuster pays for the repair of damaged property, it is possible to become involved improperly with service-related persons who will go to extremes to secure business for their company. Some firms offer pay-offs to an adjuster in return for steering the work to that service company. This dishonest practice is grounds for immediate termination of the guilty adjuster. The great majority of adjusters avoid this conduct, but such situations have occurred in the past, and when encountered, the end result is embarrassing and disastrous to the adjuster, as that person's reputation and means of livelihood can be destroyed.

The disposition of salvage and property affords yet another area where integrity problems are encountered. Most insurers have a company rule stating that employees are not permitted to purchase directly or indirectly, or in any way obtain possession of, any salvage that becomes available as a result of one of that company's claims. The violation of this rule can result in instant termination. Needless to say, it is important for the claim representative to be familiar with company rules and abide by them totally. If there are any questions relating to these matters, or if the adjuster is offered some personal financial incentive to engage in any of these activities, the claim manager should be notified immediately.

Loyalty

When adjusters are employed by an insurer, they are expected to display a proper degree of loyalty. Loyalty should rule out negative discussions about the company, particularly unfounded, or selfish or malicious matters. Additionally, the claim person should produce a full day's work for the salary received. It is not unreasonable to expect such loyalty from any employee. In truth, many employers extend themselves and provide extra benefits to employees that often are taken for granted. In return, the employer requires reasonable loyalty and production from the employee.

Statement of Principles

The insurance policy is the basis for many distinct activities of the claim representative. Since the policy is a legal contract and the adjusters deal intimately with its terms, it is possible for the adjuster's duties to approach the practice of law. In an effort to properly distinguish the differences, a code of conduct has been adopted by the National Conference of Lawyers, Insurance Companies, and Adjusters. The original agreement appeared in 1939. Since then, revisions have occurred, whereby the code was shortened, without changing the original intent. The code appears in its entirety in Appendix A.

Briefly, some of the primary concerns dealt with by the code include (1) division of claims into first-party and third-party claims; (2) that companies or representatives cannot deal directly with a claimant known to be represented by an attorney, without the attorney's knowledge; (3) that legal advice should not be dispensed to claimants; (4) that any conflict of interest should be made known to the policyholder; (5) that a copy of a statement or transcript should be furnished to the subject, at request and at no charge to the subject; and (6) that a claimant should not be advised to refrain from obtaining legal advice.

This code was most recently revised in 1982. All adjusters are expected to be familiar with it and follow it accordingly.[8]

THE ROLE OF THE ATTORNEY IN INSURANCE CLAIMS

The Claimant's (Plaintiff's) Attorney

A new claim representative soon encounters a claimant or plaintiff's attorney as he or she handles third-party claims. Ordinarily, the first notice of the involvement of the attorney comes from a letter or representation, a lien letter, or verbal notice from the claimant that he or she is legally represented. If the notice is verbal, the adjuster should insist on formal notice in writing to properly document that attorney's involvement in the claim.

Certain courtesies are owed to the claimant's legal representative and must be observed for a number of reasons. The most obvious reason is that adjusters should be courteous to all persons with whom they interact in their daily work. Also, if the proper courtesies are not extended to the claimant's attorney, the adjuster cannot reasonably expect cooperation in return. Further, the Statement of Principles referred to earlier provides guidelines that reinforce the need for such courtesies.

In defining these courtesies, we start with acknowledging the receipt of a retainer letter. A simple telephone call can accomplish this minor task. During that telephone conversation, the adjuster should also advise the attorney of the adjuster's name, address, phone number, and claim file number, if such a number is needed to identify the adjuster's file. Also, depending on the amount of discussion the claim representative had with the claimant previously, it may be necessary to obtain other information from the attorney at that time.

For the new adjuster, dealing with an attorney for the first time can be a frightening experience, but only because the claim person approaches it that way. In most cases, claimants' attorneys are understanding and the adjuster builds up groundless fears. Fortunately, this feeling soon disappears, and the adjuster soon learns that the attorney is just another person who must be contacted and dealt with in the process of negotiating and settling a claim.

In this section, reference is made to "claimant's attorney" instead of "plaintiff's attorney." A plaintiff is a party initiating a lawsuit. As long as a lawsuit has not been filed, the former reference is proper. After a suit is filed, then the claimant may properly be called the plaintiff.

When the claimant's attorney takes the responsibility for representing a claimant, he or she must do all that is legally proper to obtain the best results for that client. This fact should be kept in mind when it appears that the attorney is being unreasonable.

As with all personal associations, it is necessary to establish a rapport with the claimant's attorney before proceeding with the business of settling claims. Although this can be done by telephone as well as in person, it is recommended that a personal visit be made, at least for the first claim that involves that attorney. In this manner, both parties establish a relationship which can be beneficial in resolving the current claim as well as for future claim needs. It is common knowledge that people who deal regularly with each other by telephone seldom really know anything about the other person. Perhaps the earlier a meeting is accomplished, the earlier success can be obtained in settling claims. Since an office claim representative normally does not leave the office, a personal visit may not be practical. In those instances, a pleasant telephone voice will go a long way toward establishing the necessary rapport. In some geographic areas, some attorneys visit the adjuster for the purpose of discussing and negotiating a claim. Such opportunities for personal meetings should not be forfeited.

Claimant and attorney relationships are usually based on a contractual agreement which includes payment to the attorney on a contingent fee basis. In these fee structures, the claimant pays the attorney an agreed-upon percentage of the settlement amount or court award. If the case is tried and the trial results in a defendant's verdict, then the claimant's (now plaintiff's) attorney receives no fee. In the meantime, however, the plaintiff may pay all expenses and court costs that have been incurred or these may be advanced by the attorney. The expenses often represent a large amount of money, consequently all parties to the lawsuit must give serious consideration to early disposal of the claim.

The Defense Attorney

After the plaintiff's attorney files a lawsuit, the insurer must provide a defense lawyer to protect the insured's rights. After the lawsuit is filed, the claimant becomes the plaintiff and the insured, or party against whom the claim is made, becomes the defendant. They are both litigants and the process involving the disposition of the lawsuit is known as litigation.

The defense counsel's involvement in the claim comes about in a unique manner. Since the liability policy provides a defense for the insured for all covered matters, a defense lawyer must be provided when the insured is served with the summons and complaint—the "suit papers." The assignment of the defense lawyer is made by the insurer, in most cases, and all legal fees are likewise paid by the insurer. This arrangement is unique because the defense lawyer actually represents only the insured.

The insured is not only expected, but required, to cooperate with the defense counsel, in the defense of the lawsuit. The defense attorney reports periodically to the claims person who supervises the lawsuit, and close contact is maintained during development on the suit.

Conflicts of Interest

Under normal circumstances the control of the insured's attorney by the insurance company poses no problem. But under certain circumstances, called conflicts of interest, the relationships take on troublesome ramifications. Conflicts of interest emerge most often in connection with coverage problems. To illustrate, assume that XYZ Contracting Co. has purchased a liability insurance policy from ABC Insurance Company. Assume further that when suit papers alleging liability on the part of XYZ are received, it becomes apparent that a possible coverage question exists. The liability policy states that ABC Insurance Company will provide a defense, but it must be related to a covered claim. The insurance company assigns the defense of the lawsuit to an attorney to represent the insured or the defendant. The insurer pays all legal expenses.

Since a coverage question exists, the insurer also retains another defense lawyer to represent its own interests. That is necessary since the attorney representing the insured cannot "wear two hats" by also representing the insurer. At this point, ABC Insurance Company is paying two legal firms in the same file. As a procedural matter, the claim person must also advise the insured by letter that the defense is being provided as a courtesy until the coverage question has been resolved. The insurer must act in good faith in the resolution of all case issues.

The situation with two attorneys continues until the company decides to provide the coverage, or until the court rules on the question. In the overall approach, the claim person must recognize the conflict and act prudently. Most certainly, a competent defense lawyer will bring this to the attention of the claim representative so that proper action can be taken.

As we proceed further in the ever-changing arena of insurance claims, the plaintiff attorneys have developed another troublesome problem. This involves the theory of file separation within the claim department. This theory appears when an insured is attempting to perfect a bad faith claim against the insurer. The theory holds that a conflict of interest can apply to the claim representative as well as to the attorney. For example, in the foregoing situation, it is argued that it is impossible for the claim examiner and the adjuster to "wear two hats," i.e., consider both the merits of the claim against the insured and the potential policy violation by the insured without prejudicing the rights of the insured. As a result, some persons recommend that the file be separated and examined by different supervisors representing the individual interests of insurer and insured. Each party should refrain from discussing the file contents with the other party. In this manner, the insurer can realistically testify that all actions were conducted in the spirit of ultimate good faith.

TYPES OF CLAIMS

The property and casualty insurance industry provides many types of coverages as has already been described. These coverages can be categorized into two areas in the liability insurance field—personal lines and commercial lines. Personal lines includes the individual's private auto(s) covered under the automobile policy, or personal liability covered in a homeowners policy. The second area deals with commercial liability policies which can involve commercial automobiles coverage, general liability, products liability, and completed operations. Other types of casualty coverages are available, but those mentioned cause the greatest concern and activity for the adjuster. Very often, the insurer determines the claim representative's exposure to this variety of coverages. Most companies specialize in the type of business they write, such as predominantly personal lines or commercial lines coverage. As a result, a claim representative may be assigned all general liability claims and no automobile or personal liability claims. The opposite may also occur, again, depending on the employer's specialty.

Auto Liability Claims

In the personal lines area, the auto liability claims can take on a certain routine in the context of investigation. This routine includes confirmation of coverage, statements from the insured, claimants, and witnesses, photos of the autos and of the scene, diagram of the scene, police report, medical reports, and lost wages information. Then the claim is evaluated, negotiated, and settled. This routine may vary as to quantity of statements or other reports that are needed, but by and large, the handling of auto liability claims is done within these described parameters.

Personal and General Liability Claims

On the other hand, personal liability claims and general liability claims may involve any conceivable kind of activity which results in injury or damage to a claimant. These activities can relate to the ownership of property, usually in the area of slip or fall type claims in dwellings or commercial buildings or outside the premises.

Products Liability Claims

Products liability claims have proven to be very active and expensive in recent years. These claims are incurred as the result of faulty products which were manufactured, processed, distributed, or sold by an insured. The handling of these claims can be as diverse as the types of products involved.

Where the auto liability claims involve the alternate legal principles of tort or "no-fault" liability, products claims may involve either tort, contractual, or strict liability. The claim representative must be able to recognize roadmarks, as in a map, to determine the direction of needed investigation. The principles of tort, no-fault, and strict liability will be discussed in detail in later chapters. At that time, the differences in these legal principles will clarify the reason for the need for a well-trained, knowledgeable adjuster to work on these claims.

Completed Operations Liability Claims

Akin to the products claims is the field of completed operations liability. The difference between the two is that in products liability, the proximate cause of the injury or damage relates to the product, whereas in completed operations liability, the proximate cause is related to the work or service performed by the insured.

As an example of a completed operations claim, think of a roofing contractor who has been hired to replace the roof on a dwelling. After the job has been completed, a heavy storm causes extensive interior damage to the dwelling, necessitating the repair of plaster and the redecorating of all four rooms on the second floor of the house. Investigation reveals that the roofer incorrectly installed the metal flashing, thereby allowing rain water to enter the house. With the application of completed operations coverage, the roofer's insurer would pay for the damage resulting from the roofer's negligence, but would not pay for the repair of the defective work on the metal flashing itself. These losses arise only after the insured completes the work.

In this illustration, it is readily evident that the adjuster must have proficiency in confirming and understanding the coverage, conducting an investigation to determine the presence or absence of negligence, and have sufficient technical knowledge to understand the construction principles involved.

Liability versus Property Claims

From a casualty standpoint, a claim representative is often involved in damage claims involving a third-party claimant's property.

Damage to personal property may consist of a smashed vehicle or to destruction or mutilation of other personal property. Examples of damage to personal property include golf clubs stored in the trunk of a car damaged in a collision, a bicycle struck by a car, damaged clothing resulting from a fall, or an expensive lamp, owned by a neighbor, and broken by an insured.

With respect to damage to real property, on many occasions autos or trucks go out of control and strike dwellings or other buildings, causing substantial damage. While it is true that the owner's property insurer may step in to cover the loss under a first-party contract of insurance, the loss inevitably will be directed to the insurer of the negligent driver. In such situations, the casualty adjuster must be knowledgeable to the extent that the repair estimate can be reviewed and adjusted, if necessary, to make sure that the claim will not be overpaid. In addition to damage caused by auto, it can also arise from other causes, such as the roofer who was responsible for the interior damage to the dwelling.

Losses may become more complicated when they involve furniture and fixtures in commercial buildings or damage to inventory of retailers or manufacturers. These cases may necessitate the need for accountants, engineers, or other experts, depending on the type of inventory and type of loss. Inventory in the process of being manufactured may have to be separated from finished products, or from raw material. Such claims are often very technical and complicated to adjust.

SOURCES OF KNOWLEDGE AND INFORMATION

There are a number of sources of information, training, and knowledge available to anyone who seeks them. Most insurers conduct their own in-house seminars which concentrate on the prevailing topic of the day for the insurer. In addition, trade and professional groups within the industry conduct panel discussions, seminars, and workshops, the subject of which is usually directed toward the specialty of the individual groups. These presentations are well advertised and registration forms are readily available.

Usually, such self-training programs are sponsored by larger companies that need large numbers of staff adjusters and appraisers for positions throughout the country. In some cases, training facilities include not only classrooms and related equipment, but also small auto repair shops and mock-up models of portions of dwellings and buildings. Overall, the equipment is usually the latest sophisticated material, tools, and facilities. Naturally, such programs are very expensive to maintain, explaining why only the larger national insurers can afford them in their budgets.

Additional commercial sources of technical information provide valuable information. For example, Fire, Casualty and Surety Bulletins (FC&S), published by the National Underwriter Company,[9] provide answers to questions presented by subscribers as well as other data. These bulletins can often be used as a ready reference for obtaining the current interpretation of coverage relative to intent and to any existing case law.

When it comes to the formal training in the classroom, the insurer has several sources. There are commercial training schools that feature various specialties in their educational programs, including auto damage estimating and dwelling and building construction estimating techniques. These classroom training programs may last from a few days to several weeks.

An important source of training and education is the Insurance Institute of America (IIA) and the American Institute for Property and Liability Underwriters (AIPLU). The IIA presents organized material for a number of specialty courses, including the Associate in Claims (AIC) course for adjusters. The completer of the AIC course, in addition to receiving the AIC designation, automatically earns credit for two of the ten CPCU (Chartered Property Casualty Underwriter) courses offered by The American Institute. Experience shows that both the AIC and the CPCU designations are highly coveted within the industry, as they represent a great deal of study and successful completion of difficult national examinations.

Various textbooks are available to the adjuster or the examiner for ready reference in the handling of claims and losses. Supervisors and home office staff may be available to train or simply to answer questions. Finally, in specific matters dealing with an individual file and involving the law or questions of liability, the claim person can rely on defense counsel for specific assistance.

THE CLAIM FIELD AS A CAREER

The discussion in this chapter has dwelt in some detail on the various aspects of the duties of the claim representative. It is hoped that it adequately relays the message that these duties involve a career and not just a job.

From the day a person starts adjusting claims, a great amount of time is spent on and attention given to, learning the technical aspects of claim assignments. As previously related, those aspects involve many subjects and require considerable time and expense in training. Certainly, these educational processes serve their purpose. The claim representative enjoys an incomparable opportunity to gain an education which is varied in scope and contributes to the good of society.

A natural question refers to the opportunities for advancement. These opportunities may lead in either of two directions. One may be the supervision of claim representatives and administration of claim departments. This, traditionally, was the only route of advancement available to a successful adjuster. The theory was if the individual was a good adjuster, he or she would also make a good supervisor. This idea persisted in spite of the fact that the two areas of activity are substantially different from each other. We already know something of the type of work the adjuster does in the course of handling daily claim assignments. In this process, the adjuster develops skill and, perhaps, after a few years, will become qualified for consideration for the job of supervisor or examiner. In these positions, the individual directs other employees and may be required to discipline another employee. There are many occasions when these supervisory duties are totally repugnant to some. In a short period of time, these persons learn that they would rather be involved in the technical aspect of claims than in supervision. In the past, and in many cases presently, that decision would preclude any form of advancement: individuals involved in the technical aspects of claims would remain within the classification of adjuster with that classification's limitations of salary range.

Within recent years, several insurers have entered into an era of personnel administration called "career pathing." In the claims field, career pathing permits the adjuster to advance either in the technical area or in the administrative sector.

In either case, an adjuster can progress up through participating in predetermined educational programs while working within the desired field. Claim persons still start out as adjusters and continue in that category until a sufficient amount of experience and education have been achieved. Then, assuming that their performance is satisfactory, they move into the selected career area and begin their movement through the designated growth levels.

Chapter Notes

1. John Gage Allee, ed. *Webster's Encyclopedia of Dictionaries* Cedar Knolls, NJ: Wehman Brothers, 1975, p. 1011.
2. Robert I. Mehr and Emerson Cammack, *Principles of Insurance,* 7th Ed. (Homewood IL: Richard D. Irwin, Inc., 1980), p. 555.
3. Allee, pp. 939 and 946.
4. Allee, p. 258.
5. Willis P. Rokes, *Human Relations in Handling Insurance Claims,* 2nd Ed. (Homewood, IL: Richard D. Irwin, Inc., 1981), p. 164.
6. *Webster's New Collegiate Dictionary* (Springfield, MA: G. & C. Merriam Co., 1965).
7. Webster's.
8. Corydon T. Johns, *An Introduction to Liability Claims Adjusting,* 3rd Ed. (Cincinnati, OH: The National Underwriter Co., 1982), pp. 13, 14, 621, 622.
9. FC&S Bulletins, The National Underwriter Co., Cincinnati, OH.

CHAPTER 2

The Importance and Meaning of Coverage

The work of the claim adjuster involves essentially three areas of claim handling: *coverage, liability,* and *damages.* This chapter is devoted to what can be called the first step in the adjusting process—that of coverage confirmation or, in the more involved cases, coverage analysis. Before the issues of liability and damages can be resolved, the coverage aspect of the loss or claim must first be decided. (Liability and damages are treated in Chapters 4 and 5.)

THE ELEMENTS OF A CONTRACT

Agreement

Insurance contracts are subject to the same general laws that govern ordinary contracts. In all contracts, for example, certain elements must exist for the contract to be binding and enforceable. Those elements are agreement (offer and acceptance), competent parties, genuine assent, consideration, legal purpose, and form required by law.

For an agreement to be completed, there must be both an offer and an acceptance. With regard to insurance contracts, ordinarily the prospect or applicant for insurance makes an offer when he or she requests insurance or completes an application. The insurance company indicates its acceptance when it issues the policy.

In situations involving large commercial accounts where the applicant can negotiate to some degree with the insurer, the policy issued by the company may simply be a response to the applicant's inquiry and, therefore, may be regarded as merely an offer. The applicant may reject or accept the offer of that particular policy. In such a case, when the policy is issued by the insurer and accepted by the applicant with payment of the premium, then an offer and an acceptance will have been completed.

Whether or not an agreement will have been achieved will depend on the particular circumstances of the transaction. Once again, the general rule is that the applicant's request for insurance or completion of an application serves as the offer while the company's issuance of the policy represents the acceptance.

Most insurance transactions are conducted through agents. Some companies utilize their own salaried employees to sell insurance, others use independent agents who may represent several companies, while still others use what can be referred to as "exclusive agents" who sell only for that particular company. Whatever the method used, these agents possess varying degrees of authority, or "binding" authority, with regard to accepting or rejecting risks.

As a practical matter, most agents have authority to orally bind coverage on the spot. The rush and complexities of modern business life require that insurance often be immediately obtainable. The most common way to obtain insurance is to request it from an agent, either by telephone or in person. Here the applicant has made an offer and the agent with binding authority can accept it immediately even without receiving a premium payment. The typical response from an agent after such a request might be: "You are covered." At this point the agreement has been consummated.

Realistically speaking, this is the manner in which most insurance transactions are completed. A written binder, providing information about the coverage and terms of the agreement, may be issued as temporary evidence of insurance until the actual policy is issued. However, an oral agreement can be effective without the issuance of a written binder.

The law of agency holds that an agent working within the scope of his or her authority with an insurer can create a contractual obligation for that insurer. Even when the agent is acting *outside* the insurer's grant of authority, he or she may create such liability for the insurer. This can occur if it appears to the applicant that the agent has authority to act in such a manner and the applicant is unaware of any such restrictions imposed upon the agent. This is known as *apparent authority* and it is a concept with which claim people must be familiar to properly perform the task of coverage determination. An agent's actions regarding insurance transactions can be a crucial factor in the ultimate decision concerning coverage. Though technically there may be no coverage, certain words or actions on the part of an agent may have created coverage or the inference of coverage.

In those situations where an agent has acted outside the scope of his or her authority and bound coverage, and thereafter the application sustains a loss, the insurer will be required to pay for the loss. The insurer, however, will have a right of action against the agent based on the fact that the agent violated the agency contract.

Competent Parties

That parties to a contract must be competent refers to the fact that they must be legally capable of entering into a contract. Individuals who may not be legally capable of making a valid contract include minors (under age eighteen or twenty-one depending upon the state), insane persons, and people under the influence of alcohol or drugs. Insurance companies too must have legal capacity, which means they must be properly chartered and properly licensed by the states in which they conduct business.

Generally speaking, the law protects those who are often unable to protect themselves from being taken advantage of in making contracts. A minor, for example, ordinarily can regect or disaffirm a contract entered into while incompetent. The contract is said to be voidable at the minor's election. There are exceptions to this rule for contracts involving necessities which generally include things relating to the health, education, and comfort of the minor.

Genuine Assent

Genuine assent or agreement of the parties to a contract must exist if the contract is to be enforceable. If one of the parties did not consent to the contract, he or she may avoid it. Genuine assent may be lacking because a mistake was made by either or both of the parties or assent of one of the parties was obtained through fraud, undue influence, or duress.

Consideration

Ordinarily, a promise is binding on someone only when he or she has received consideration. Consideration is what the person making the promise demands and receives as the price for his or her promise.

In an insurance contract, the consideration given by the insured is the payment of the premium or the promise to pay the premium. The consideration given by the company is its promise to pay the insured (or pay on behalf of the insured in liability insurance) upon the happening of an event insured against. In property and liability insurance, immediate payment of the premium is not required in order for the contract to be valid. An implied promise to pay the premium is sufficient. Otherwise, an agent could not orally bind coverage and, as noted earlier, this is the common practice utilized to conduct insurance transactions.

Legal Purpose

A contract must have a lawful purpose and be consistent with public policy and interest. This is true for insurance contracts as well. Insurance obtained on stolen goods, for example, would not be valid. Fire insurance obtained by an insured with the intent of subsequently burning the property and profiting from the loss will not be recoverable, provided the insurer can establish the necessary circumstantial evidence to show the insured committed arson.

A distinction must be made here between evidence necessary in a criminal action and that necessary in a civil action. Before an insured will be prosecuted for the crime of arson, the state must be able to establish its case beyond a reasonable doubt. In a civil case, where the insurer and insured (rather than the state and the insured) are the parties to litigation, the insurer need only show a "preponderance of evidence" or the *weight* of the evidence, to implicate the insured in arson. Strong circumstantial evidence that the insured committed arson may be sufficient for the insurer to successfully resist paying the claim. The insurer will atempt to show that the fire was intentionally set, that the insured had the *opportunity* to set the fire, and that the insured had a financial *motive* (overinsurnace, for example).

One final note on legal purpose—the concept of insurable interest has relevance here. In order for an individual to have an insurable interest, he or she must stand to lose financially in the event of a loss. If insurable interest is lacking, the policy is considered illegal and void. An individual cannot purchase a homeowners policy on a neighbor's property in the hope that it will burn and provide the purchaser of the policy with a profit. The individual who purchased the policy has nothing to lose, but much to gain. Aside from the obvious moral hazard here, the contract is invalid because it involves gambling, not insurance.

Form Required By Law

Despite what many people may think, most contracts are oral. However, there are situations where the law requires that a contract be written in order to be enforceable. These requirements, created by statute, are referred to as *Statutes of Fraud.* Their purpose is to provide a degree of certainty regarding contracts and to reduce the possibility of fraud.

In most states, the contract must be in writing in order to be enforceable in the following six situations:

1. contracts involving the sale of land,
2. agreements that cannot be performed within one year,
3. promises to answer for the debt of another,
4. promises made in consideration of marriage,
5. promises made by executors of decedents' estates to pay debts of estates from executors' own funds, and
6. contracts involving sale of personal property in which the sales price is $500 or more.

As mentioned earlier, oral contracts in insurance are valid. Statute of fraud provisions have been held not to be applicable to insurance agreements. Aside from the fact that some states have specific statutory requirements that certain insurance contracts be in writing in a "standard" form, it would be very difficult indeed to conduct the selling and claim handling aspects of the insurance business without a written policy setting out what is and what is not covered. For these reasons and because of the highly technical nature of insurance, it is customary practice to issue written policies to insureds.

Although an insured carries out his or her part of an insurnace contract by paying the premium, the contract remains executory on the part of the insurer. Executory means that some act prescribed in the contract remains to be performed by one of the parties, namely the insurer. Naturally, the insurer will not execute its part of the agreement until a specified event occurs.

DISTINCTIVE FEATURES OF INSURANCE CONTRACTS

Insurance contracts are subject to the same rules which apply to contracts in general. However, the uniqueness of the insurance product itself, as compared to other economic goods, creates several distinctive features which are associated with insurance contracts.

Intangible and Aleatory

Because an insured pays a premium but doesn't receive anything material or physical in return unless a loss is sustained, insurance has been characterized as being an "intangible" product. Though insurance brings many immediate benefits to individual insureds in the form of peace of mind, loss prevention services, etc. and to society in general by providing a basis for credit and creating investment capital, the characterization of insurance as an intangible is to some degree true. The payment of a claim really consummates the insurance contract—and not all insureds have losses or make claims. But then this is the nature of insurance. A small, fixed premium (small in relation to the risk the insured transfers to the insurer) is paid in return for the assurance that a potentially large loss will be covered.

Since in an insurance contract money is paid for protection against a future, uncertain event, the contract is said to be *aleatory.* This means that performance depends on a contingent event and that the values exchanged (premium payment versus potential loss payment) are not equal.

Contract of Adhesion

Since an insurance policy is drafted or written by the insurer and accepted by the insured without any discussion or negotiation, insurance contracts are said to be *contracts of adhesion.* The insured ordinarily has no voice in establishing the terms of the policy and simply *adheres* to the policy terms as drawn by the insurer. (It should be noted that many large commercial insureds are in a position to negotiate or bargain with the insurer regarding coverage and the policy eventually agreed upon may very well not be considered a contract of adhesion.)

When policy language is clear and unambiguous, the parties to the contract are usually bound by its terms. In other words, no forced or strained interpretation of the policy which would defy reason would be permissible. Clear and unambiguous words and phrases should be interpreted in their plain, ordinary sense.

It is a generally accepted rule of contract law that a party to a contract is responsible for having knowledge of the contract provisions. In written contracts in general, an individual will be bound by the terms whether they were read and understood or not. While an insured can be held to a knowledge of the terms of the insurance contract even though he or she may not have read it,[1] the courts have generally shown some reluctance to hold insureds responsible for having read or having understood their policies. (Recall the courts' thinking in the Ady and Hionis decisions discussed earlier.)

Courts are quick to recognize the highly technical nature of insurance and the fact that insurance policy language is often complicated and not easily understood by the average insured. Based on this view, there is often a tendency on the part of the courts to attempt to balance the unequal bargaining positions of insureds and insurers by giving the insured the benefit of the doubt whenever this appears reasonable.

Rule of Strict Construction and Ambiguity

The fact that an insurance policy is a contract of adhesion means that any doubt or ambiguity in a policy provision will be resolved against the party who drafted it. Since the insurer drafted the policy, any question concerning its meaning will be decided against the insurer and in favor of the insured. The rationale behind this principle is that since the insurer chose the policy language, it can be assumed that the insurer has sought to limit its scope. Fairness dictates that any doubt as to the meaning of the language used should be resolved in favor of the insured. To do otherwise, and employ a narrow and technical construction, would result in an injustice.[2]

Despite the fact that some policies actually are not written by the insurer but are "standardized," meaning that they contain statutorily required language, the rule of strict construction against the insurer still prevails.

Personal Contract of the Utmost Good Faith

It is well established that an insurance policy is a personal contract requiring the highest degree of good faith on the part of both parties. Failure to disclose vital information, or dishonesty or fraud on the part of either party, will result in the contract being voidable at the option of the innocent party.

Reasonable Expectations

The principle of *reasonable expectations,* an extension of the doctrine that an insurance contract is a contract of adhesion, has been applied in a growing number of court cases in the last two decades or so. (It was a significant factor in the Hionis case.) The principle holds that an insurance policy should be interpreted as affording the coverage that a reasonable person would expect to have purchased. Put another way, an insured is entitled to coverage for losses which he or she reasonably expects will be covered under the particular insurance policy purchased even if a close reading of all policy provisions indicates a contrary intent by the drafter of the policy.

Policy language is to be interpreted in light of the reasonable understanding of a layperson, not a lawyer. Even though policy language may exclude a loss or claim in unambiguous terms, if the exclusion is inconsistent with the reasonable expectations of an insured, it may be invalid.

Another approach to interpreting insurance coverage is to consider the *purpose* of the provision or, in particular, the exclusion. What is really intended to be excluded by the exclusionary language?

This appears to some extent to revert to the more conservative approach to contract interpretation in which the intent of the parties is a prime consideration. Although the *rule of purpose,* as it is sometimes called, may appeal to insurers, many courts are reluctant to apply it since its application would seem frequently to favor the insurer. While the *intent* of the policy is important, if the language of the policy does not clearly express that intent, courts will be reluctant to consider "intent" as the overriding factor in contract interpretation. Modern day realities suggest rather strongly that it is not so much the intent of the policy which is controlling, but rather what the policy *says* and how it is interpreted by the average insured.

What does all this mean for the claim person? It means that claim people must not only be able to read and interpret insurance policies; they must also know whether the current attitude and thinking of the courts will affect those interpretations. This assumes that in order to do an effective claim handling job, adjusters need to develop familiarity with court decisions and legal trends affecting the area in which they handle claims. This can be acquired through good training and supervision as well as by close contact with local defense counsel and with active claim associations. Information about coverage issues and impending claim problems can be found in periodic insurance publications such as *The Fire, Casualty & Surety Bulletins,* the *Policy Forms & Manual Analyses,* and *For The Defense* to name a few. The Question & Answer section of *The Fire, Casualty & Surety Bulletins* is particularly informative with regard to topical coverage issues.

It also is recommended that claim people train themselves to be alert to ambiguous policy language in insurance policies. It happens frequently that several adjusters will "roundtable" or discuss a coverage question and arrive at a variety of conflicting conclusions. When a group of adjusters cannot agree on a coverage interpretation, it may indicate that the particular word, phrase, or provision is ambiguous and unclear. If a genuine ambiguity does exist, the interpretation most favorable to the insured ordinarily is applied. In claims involving a substantial coverage question, most company procedures call for the issue to be submitted to claim management or supervisory personnel for final resolution. Adjusters, however, should attempt to develop their skills by analyzing the issue and making a specific coverage recommendation first, provided this does not conflict with company claim procedures.

Examples of Ambiguous Policy Language

There is no clear evidence at the present time that the move to readable policies has brought about a reduction in ambiguous policy language. Coverage disputes continue and the courts, which traditionally have tended to find ambiguity with relative ease, show no signs of changing their attitudes.

It is not possible to list all of the policy terms and phrases which might be susceptible to a claim of ambiguity, but some words and phrases appear more often than others to be the subject of argument, and sometimes litigation. The following is a partial list of words and phrases that have been called "ambiguous:"

"Business Pursuits" The *business pursuits* exclusion in homeowners policies is ambiguous. The policy defines business in the following manner: *Business* includes trade, profession, or occupation. The policy indicates what "business" *includes,* but not what it is. Many insureds are involved in activities which, though they might remotely be called a business, are not the trade, profession, or occupation of the insured. It is a fact that many people who work a full-time job also are involved in after-hour activities which may or may not supplement the income earned in their primary job. Some of these may more closely resemble a hobby than a business and some may be engaged in regularly or irregularly. People involved in these activities seemingly can claim with some justification that their full-time job, not their secondary endeavor, is their "business" and provides their means of livelihood.

Ordinarily, if the supplemental activity is conducted on a *regular* or *continuous* basis for the purpose of making a *profit,* it can be considered a business pursuit. Claims involving bodily injury or property damage arising out of business pursuits of the insured are not covered by the homeowners policy, which is designed to cover *personal* liability, not *business* liability. (An endorsement to the homeowners policy which provides coverage for business pursuits of an insured is available but it is subject to limitations for certain professions.) Claims involving what appears to be a business activity of the insured must be investigated thoroughly and the claim person's ultimate decision must take into consideration any court cases in the jurisdiction which might be relevant. An exception to the exclusion (which means coverage would apply) if the activity causing the injury or damage is *ordinarily incidental to nonbusiness pursuits* complicates the matter further. Each case, having its own unique set of facts, must be decided on its individual merits.

"Aircraft" Another controversial term from a coverage standpoint is "aircraft." The word appears in three separate parts of the homeowners policy. Initially, it appears as an exlusion in the Property Not Covered provisions under Coverage C Personal Property; secondly, as an insured peril under the perils section; and finally, as an exclusion under the liability section. The homeowners policy covers neither damage to aircraft owned or operated by an insured nor bodily injury or property damage arising out of an insured's ownership or use of an aircraft. These exposures are more appropriately covered by specific aircraft or aviation insurance. However, the homeowners policy does cover damage to the insured's property caused by aircraft because this is an exposure, which although remote, is nevertheless faced by modern homeowners.

The controversy of the meaning of the term arises when losses involve such instruments as parasails, hang gliders, model airplanes and the like. The adjuster faced with such a claim will find that the term *aircraft* is not defined in the policy.[3] Keeping in mind the well established principle that ambiguities are resolved in favor of the insured, the term "aircraft" can be interpreted differently in each part of the policy in which it appears so that the insured will benefit from each ambiguity.

"Operated or Used by the Insured" The meaning of the phrase *operated or used by the insured* in automobile liability insurance is sometimes the subject of dispute. A recent court decision held that the term "operated by" was ambiguous and therefore included the insured's operation of vehicles indirectly through the use of carriers or bailees for hire.[4]

"Care, Custody or Control" The *care, custody or control* exclusion in automobile and general liability policies is a frequent source of controversy. Note the conjunction in the exclusion is "or," not "and"; therefore, the presence of any *one* of these elements will render the exclusion applicable.

The controversy arises in attempting to estabish when property is in the insured's care, custody *or* control. For example, is a customer's car which is being washed in a car wash in the care, custody or control of the car wash establishment? The adjuster needs to determine whether the customer was in or out of the car when it was damaged and whether the car was locked into and "controlled" by any kind of mechanical tracking device. If the customer was out of the car and it was locked into a tracking device, the "control" element would appear to be present and the exclusion in the car wash operator's liability policy would apply.

"Insured" The word *insured* itself is often said to be ambiguous. Particularly in commercial liability policies where the term *insured* appears in an exclusion, the question whether "the" insured applies equally to "an" insured or "any" insured can be troublesome. In addition, whether the term includes "employees" of the insured is another area of occasional dispute when the definition of "insured" is silent on this question.

"Furnished for Regular Use" Automobile liability policies normally exclude the insured's use of nonowned vehicles which are available or furnished for the regular use of an insured. What is meant by *regular use?* Can the insured's continuous use of a nonowned car for only one day constitute regular use? The question arises typically in car rental situations. There is really no uniform rule regarding what constitutes regular use. Some companies, but certainly not all, feel comfortable with the position that anything beyond three weeks would constitute regular use.

"Intentional Act" According to the *intentional act* exclusion, bodily injury or property damage caused intentionally by an insured is not covered. However, even though the *act* by the insured might have been intentional, if the resulting injury or damage is not, the exclusion will not apply; that is, coverage will be provided.

These are just some examples of insurance terminology that has proved troublesome for claim people in the past. It is difficult, if not impossible, to make general rules about handling these policy questions. Each claim must be considered in light of its particular circumstances and decided accordingly.

In concluding the discussion of the unique characteristics of insurance contracts, it needs to be emphasized that adjusters must recognize that these features call for special handling of coverage disputes. Claim people must view insurance policy language not merely in light of the average insurance or business person's understanding of coverage, but also in light of the average *layperson's* reasonable understanding of the protection afforded. This means continually keeping abreast of the latest court decisions, insurance department regulations, and legal trends in a particular state as well as not losing sight of the fact that insurance is essentially a customer service contract that vitally affects the insured's well-being.

The image of the insurance industry suffers when insurers initially deny claims and then, under the threat or pressure of a lawsuit, do an about-face and pay these claims. Adjusters should be reluctant to deny a claim unless they can confidently and rationally support their denial. On the other hand, if a questionable claim is denied and a shaky defense is entered on behalf of the insurer, insurers need not be so inflexible that they cannot compromise such a case to prevent a precarious defense from being litigated.

Cases which have been denied and resisted with little support or an inadequate defense strategy have often proved disastrous for insurers. Much of the adverse or bad law on the books today from the standpoint of insurers has stemmed from claims that probably never should have been denied or defended in the first place.

In the final analysis, it can be said with relative certainty that the aim of the courts is to achieve fairness and equity in coverage disputes. Since insurance is a highly technical subject, yet essential to the economic health of society, the courts tend to balance what they often perceive as the unequal bargaining positions of the insured and insurer by giving the benefit of any doubt to the insured. In the interests of justice as well as practicality, adjusters must keep this in mind as they handle insurance claims.

PERSONAL AUTO POLICY—LIABILITY ANALYSIS

The personal auto policy (PAP), an ISO form, has been selected for analysis here because of its wide application across the country. Since the subject of this text is liability claim handling, and because page limitations must prevail concerning how much space can be devoted to a study of coverage, the analysis is necessarily confined to the liability section of the policy.

The personal auto policy (PAP) is considered a *readable* policy; it is printed in large type and uses simplified language designed to make the policy easier to read and understand than traditional insurance contracts. While simplifying the policy language has not eliminated the number of coverage questions (and may actually have increased such questions due to the newness of the forms), most insurance practitioners agree that the move to simplified, everyday language is a step towards opening communications between insurers and insureds.

Like all insurance policies, the PAP contains the traditional four parts of an insurance contract that set out the coverages, limitations, and qualifications of the agreement. These four parts are the *declarations, insuring agreement, exclusions,* and *conditions.* The PAP uses slightly different terminology—the "conditions" are referred to as *general provisions.* In addition, the policy contains sections titled *definitions* and *duties after an accident or loss.*

With regard to the kinds of insurance protection provided, the policy includes coverage for (1) *liability* (2) *medical payments* (3) *uninsured motorists,* and (4) *damage to the insured's auto.* Each coverage part has its own insuring agreement and exclusions. Terms appearing in bold print in the body of the policy are defined on page 1, *Definitions.*

Although some policy provisions will be reprinted in the text as the analysis proceeds, in order to derive optimal benefit from the analysis, adjusters are advised to keep a policy nearby since proper coverage analysis requires moving back and forth between the various provisions.

An insurance policy is not designed to be *memorized* but to be *read*—and read over again each time a coverage question arises. The claim person with real expertise in contract analysis is not embarrassed by the fact that he or she needs to read the policy in order to answer coverage questions. Quite the contrary; attempting to answer such questions "off the top of one's head" may be not only careless but dangerous as well. Frequently, too much is at stake to be guessing at answers. Adjusters should make every effort to be sure of their answers by reading the actual policy language involved.

The Declarations section "individualizes" the policy. It contains information such as the insured's name, policy number, policy period, description, and identity of automobile(s), rate classification, coverages, premium charges, and endorsements.

The insuring agreement describes the insurer's promise to the insured. It tells how the insurer will respond to a covered claim. Certain terms appear in bold print and are defined in the *Definitions* section of the policy. Insuring agreements ordinarily are quite broad in scope but are modified and limited by exclusions.

Exclusions limit the scope of the insuring agreement to take into account the fact that some hazards are not insurable. Exclusions are incorporated in insurance policies for various reasons: to minimize or eliminate moral hazard, to eliminate risk which are more appropriately covered by other insurance, or to eliminate risks with catastrophic potential. The conditions or general provisions sets out the obligations of the insured and insurer. Common conditions include subrogation, cancellation and assignment provisions. The personal auto policy also includes a *Duties After an Accident or Loss* section, which defines the insured's duties in the event of a covered claim or loss.

Frequently, upon receipt of notice of an accident, all the adjuster needs to do to confirm coverage is check the Declarations page to see that the accident took place within the policy period, that a "covered auto" was involved, and that the driver was insured under the policy. Many companies today utilize computers for this purpose, thereby eliminating the need to pull the "paper" policy or daily.

In cases where an essential question of coverage exists, however, adjusters will often find it necessary to read the policy for answers to their questions. The insuring agreement is the logical starting point.

Insuring Agreement

PART A—LIABILITY COVERAGE

> We will pay damages for bodily injury or property damage for which any **covered person** becomes legally responsible because of an auto accident. We will settle or defend, as we consider appropriate, any claim or suit asking for these damages. In addition to our limit of liability, we will pay all defense costs we incur. Our duty to settle or defend ends when our limit of liability for this coverage has been exhausted.
>
> **"Covered person"** as used in this Part means:
> 1. You or any **family member** for the ownership, maintenance or use of any auto or **trailer.**
> 2. Any person using **your covered auto.**
> 3. For **your covered auto,** any person or organzation but only with respect to legal responsibility for acts or omissions of a person for whom coverage is afforded under this Part.
> 4. For any auto or **trailer,** other than **your covered auto,** any person or organization but only with respect to legal responsibility for acts or omissions of you or any **family member** for whom coverage is afforded under this Part. This provision applies only if the person or organization does not own or hire the auto **trailer.**

Note that certain words and phrases are not defined in the policy. For example, "damages," "bodily injury," "property damage," "legally responsible," and "accident" are not defined. *Covered person* is defined and the broad meaning of this phrase will be discussed shortly. First, however, a comment about the undefined terms is in order.

Undefined Terms

Damages. The common or plain meaning of a term must be used in the absence of a specific definition in the contract. The term "damages" refers to *compensatory* damages such as expenses for medical bills and lost wages as well as damages for loss due to pain and suffering, disfigurement, and so on. It may also include *punitive* damages if the laws of the state permit such damages to be insurable. Some courts have held that the term "damages," since its meaning in the policy is not restricted to compensatory damages, can include those of a punitive nature as well.

Another issue with regard to punitive damages is the idea that the whole purpose of the assessment of such damages—to *punish* the wrongdoer—seemingly is defeated if the payment is made by a party other than the wrongdoer. Despite this line of reasoning, laws in some states hold such damages to be covered under liability insuring agreements.

Bodily Injury. Bodily injury refers to physical injury, sickness, disease, death, or pain and suffering.[5] Note that the policy says "bodily" injury, not "personal" and the distinction is important. The phrase "personal injury" is actually broader than "bodily injury" Bodily injury is one type of personal injury, but not all personal injuries are bodily injuries. An injury to a person can involve the ***body*** or the ***personality*** of an individual. When the term "personal injury" is used in an insurance policy, it refers to situations involving humiliation, libel, slander, defamation of character, and the like. It might help make the distinction clearer if adjusters think of bodily injury as injury to one's body, and personal injury as injury to one's personality or character. The PAP covers claims against an insured for bodily injury but not the *broader term* for personal injury.

Property Damage. This includes physical damage or destruction of property, including loss of use of the property. Examples are damage to an automobile as a result of an accident, reasonable car rental charges incurred by the claimant while his or her car is being repaired, or damage to property other than automobiles caused by an insured as a result of an auto accident.

A situation that can be confusing when confronted for the first time involves injury to animals. Animals, while living creatures, are not humans and actually are considered chattel or property under the law. As a result, the subjective elements of *damages* such as pain and suffering, inconvenience, disfigurement, and so on are not considered in evaluating such claims. Injury to animals is treated as property damage, not bodily injury.

Legally Responsible. This phrase has a broad meaning and is not confined merely to negligence. An insured can be legally responsible by *contract* and by *statute* as well as by *negligence.* Since the PAP does not contain a contractual liability exclusion (some companies may use ISO endorsement PP 00 03, which contains a contractual *limitation* rather than an exclusion), coverage applies to damage an insured causes to a rental car he or she is using when the rental contract makes the insured legally responsible. This is true even when the vehicle is damaged through no negligence on the part of the insured.

Accident. The PAP is written on an "accident" basis rather than an "occurrence" basis, the latter being the basis upon which general liability insurance is written. "Accident" means an event which is *sudden, unexpected,* and usually *definite* in time and place. *Occurrence* is a broader term and in general liability policies is defined as "an accident, including continuous or repeated exposure to conditions, which results in bodily injury or property damage neither expected nor intended from the standpoint of the insured.[6]

A liability policy written on an occurrence basis would cover injury or damage resulting from gradual or continual exposure to certain conditions. For example, suppose employees of a concrete and gravel company make repeated trips in their dump trucks to and from a sand and gravel pit in the course of their work at various job sites. In order to get to the pit, the trucks are driven back and forth over a residential street adjacent to the site. Over the course of time, dust and other road substances such as dirt and grease generated by the trucks discolor the exterior of houses along the street as well as laundry hung out to dry. Claims by the residents are made against the insured concrete company for the damages. These damages are caused by an occurrence, not an accident.

Another example of an occurrence would be a situation in which a person sustains a partial hearing loss and develops a nervous disorder over the course of time as a result of the noise created by an insured's repeated use of a jackhammer in nearby construction activity.

It is virtually impossible to pinpoint when the "accident" actually took place in these cases. The injury or damage did not result suddenly nor can it be traced to a definite time and place. Obviously, it would not be practical from an insured's standpoint to carry general liability insurance on an accident basis and, in the interest of adequate protection, these policies are offered on an occurrence or "claims made" basis.[7] The PAP, however, which covers the automobile liability exposure, is on an accident basis because the exposure is adequately covered on this basis.

Who Is a "Covered Person"? The meaning of "covered person" is explained in a four-part definition immediately after the insuring agreement. **Covered person** as used in this Part means:

1. You or any **family member** for the ownership, maintenance or use of any auto or **trailer.**

Reading and understanding this seemingly simple sentence requires referring back to page 1, Definitions, for the meaning of several of the terms used in the sentence:

> You (the named insured and, if a resident of the same household, the spouse of the named insured) or any *family member* (a person related to *you* by blood, marriage or adoption who is a resident of your household, including a ward or foster child) is a covered person for the ownership, maintenance or use of any auto or *trailer* (a vehicle designed to be pulled by a private passenger auto or pickup, panel truck or van. Trailer also means a farm wagon or farm implement while towed by a private passenger auto or pickup, panel truck or van).

This particular part of the definition of *covered person,* in its simplest form, means that an insured is covered for the ownership, maintenance, or use of any auto or trailer. This is a broad statement of coverage. The insured's occasional use of a borrowed truck, even a large truck such as dump truck, for example, to move heavy furniture over a weekend, can be covered under the PAP. The only thing that could preclude coverage is the possible application of one of the policy exclusions. If the use of the nonowned truck is an isolated instance and is not connected with any business of the insured, liability coverage would be available to the insured. Liability coverage for damage to the truck itself, however, would be excluded under exclusion A. 3, discussed later.

2. Any person using your **covered auto.**

Now the focus is on people other than the named insured or family members who use a *covered auto.* Here again the adjuster is referred to page 1, Definitions, for the lengthy definition of *your covered auto.*

Your covered auto means:

1. any vehicle identified in the Declarations.
2. a newly acquired private passenger auto or pickup, panel truck or van.

An insured has automatic coverage for thirty days when any such vehicle is acquired during the policy period. (Broad coverage is available on *replacement* vehicles, as noted later.) In order to continue coverage beyond the thirty-day period, the vehicle must be reported to the company.

As originally written, the PAP did not cover *business* use of a pickup, panel truck, or van. Later, however, endorsement PP 00 03 was introduced in most states in which the PAP had been approved. This endorsement provides thirty-day automatic coverage on a pickup, panel truck, or van acquired as a replacement or additional vehicle and used in business.

If an acquired vehicle *replaces* a vehicle already insured in the policy (as opposed to being an *additionally* acquired vehicle), it will have the same coverage as the vehicle it replaced. Liability insurance on a replacement *private passenger* auto, or a replacement pickup, panel truck, or van *not* used in business is automatically inluded for the duration of the policy period. If a pickup, panel truck, or van is used in any business, other than farming or ranching, liability coverage applies automatically for *only* thirty days and the vehicle must be reported to the company within that time in order for coverage to be extended beyond thirty days. Furthermore, if the insured wishes to add or continue *physical damage* insurance on any replacement vehicle, he or she must report the vehicle to the company and request the coverage within 30 days after acquisition.

A question may arise whether an insured is covered for a collision or comprehensive loss during the initial thirty-day period if physical damage insurance had not been carried on the previous vehicle. In other words, if the insured carried no collision insurance on the previous vehicle, acquired a replacement vehicle, and then twenty days later, collided with a tree and damaged the replacement vehicle, could the option to purchase collision insurance retroactive to the date the car was acquired be exercised, thereby enabling the insured to have coverage for the collision loss?

It would seem that a fair case for coverage can be made because the policy provides thirty-day "grace period" of sorts during which the insured can decide whether or not to purchase physical damage insurance. The insured has thirty days in which to *add* physical damage insurance and the policy is silent on precisely when the coverage will take effect. Based on the reasoning applied in the rule of strict construction, this lack of clarity, as demonstrated by the contract's silence on this question, could very well be decided in the insured's favor. This reasoning would give the insured the option to add collision coverage to be effective prior to the date of loss. The vagueness of this part of the provision leaves the question open and adjusters are advised, if the question arises, to check with their companies to see if a position has been taken.

If the vehicle is not a replacement vehicle, but an *additional* vehicle, the insured will have the broadest coverage currently provided on any existing vehicle insured in the policy.

In summary, *liability* insurance on a *replacement* private passenger auto, or *replacement* pickup, panel truck, or van *not* used in business is automatically included for the duration of the policy with no requirement that the vehicle be reported to the company. (A replacement pickup, panel truck, or van used in farming or ranching is afforded the same broad coverage.)

Coverage on any additionally acquired vehicle—private passenger, pickup, panel truck, or van—as well as coverage on a replacement pickup, panel truck, or van used in business is automatic for only thirty days. Finally, a question exists regarding when physical damage insurance can be added to a replacement vehicle when no such coverage was carried on the vehicle it replaced. Adjusters are advised to check with their companies, should a question arise, to determine if the company has taken a position on this question.

The remaining two parts of the definition of "your covered auto" are:

3. any trailer owned by the named insured. (Note that the trailer need not be identified in the Declarations and liability coverage will still apply. Physical damage insurance, however, is not provided unless the trailer is shown in the Declarations or, if a newly acquired trailer, it is reported within thirty days after acquisition.)
4. any nonowned auto or trailer which is used as a "temporary substitute vehicle."

A temporary substitute vehicle is described as a nonowned vehicle that is used temporarily as a substitute for a "covered auto" because the latter is out of normal use because of its breakdown, repair, servicing, and so on. In such a case, the temporary substitute vehicle becomes a covered auto. Liability coverage under the insured's policy for a temporary substitute vehicle is *excess* over any collectible liability insurance which may be carried on the temporary substitute vehicle. (See the Other Insurance clause.)

Once again, claim people will see how they must move back and forth among policy provisions to read and understand the policy. This pattern of movement becomes quite routine with experience and practice.

With the discussion of the meaning of "your covered auto" completed, this brings us to paragraph 3. of the definition of "covered person."

3. With regard to *your covered auto,* any person or organization is a covered person but only with respect to legal responsibility stemming from acts or omissions of another person covered under the policy.

This is a particularly broad coverage provision, the extent of which newer claim employees may not fully appreciate early in their careers.

Suppose that the insured, Gary Smith, is very active in his church (or club or other organized endeavor) and is asked by the church to chaperone and drive a group of children to a church sponsored picnic. On the way to the picnic, he rear-ends another vehicle and the driver of that vehicle sustains injuries. The injured person's attorney, upon learning that Smith was using his vehicle on church (or club) business, sues both Smith and the church. Smith's PAP will defend both parties, the church qualifying as a covered person under paragraph 3. of the definition of *covered person.*

Other examples of persons or organizations that can be *covered persons* under this provision are the insured's employer when the insured uses his or her own auto on company business as well as a neighbor's employer in the event the insured loans his car to the neighbor for the neighbor's business use.

The applicability of the fourth and final part of the definition of *covered person* appears to be somewhat remote as far as actual claim situations are concerned.

4. With respect to any auto or trailer, other than a covered auto, any person or organization is a covered person but only with respect to legal responsibility stemming from acts or omissions of the named insured, a resident spouse or any *family member* who is covered under the policy. There is no coverage under this part, however, if the person or organization owns or hires the auto.

For example, suppose the insured runs a work-related errand for his or her employer in a car borrowed from a friend and is involved in an accident because of his or her negligence. The insured's employer would be a covered person as far as the insured's negligent acts are concerned. The friend, however, as *owner* of the car, would not be a covered person as it would be expected that the friend would have his or her own insurance.

An interesting related question is whether the insured's employer would also be a covered person under the neighbor's policy and, if so, which policy would be primary? Looking at the neighbor's PAP policy, paragraph 3., regarding a covered auto, any person or organization is a covered person but only with respect to legal responsibility for acts of a person for whom coverage is afforded. Since coverage is afforded for the insured under the neighbor's policy, the insured's employer would also be a covered person under the neighbor's policy.

The question of which policy is primary is answered by the *Other Insurance* clause on page 4 of the PAP. The liability coverage available on a nonowned car is excess. In other words, primary coverage follows the car. Therefore, the neighbor's policy (since the car involved is owned by the neighbor) is primary. The insured's policy also is available, if needed, but on an excess basis.

The idea that coverage is extended to include far more individuals than the person specifically named in the policy is known as the "omnibus clause." Early auto insurance policies covered only the named insured but eventually coverage was extended to anyone driving the vehicle with the named insured's permission. Hence, a permissive user is sometimes referred to as an "omnibus insured." Though the term is used infrequently today, its dictionary meaning—"covering numerous objects or items...," is unquestionably manifested by the broad meaning of "covered person." See Exhibit 2-1 for a summary of the meaning and applicability of "covered person."

When one considers that the insurer will pay damages for bodily injury or property damage for which any *covered person* becomes legally responsible because of an auto accident, it becomes clear that the grant of coverage in the liability insuring agreement is quite broad indeed. It is limited only by the exclusions which will be discussed

Exhibit 2-1
Covered Person

Definition/Meaning	Applicability
1. You or any *family member* for the ownership, maintenance or use of any auto or *trailer.*	Named insured, resident spouse and all *family members* are covered for use of *any* auto, including trucks, provided no exclusion applies to preclude coverage.
2. Any person using *your covered auto.*	Any person using the insured's covered auto with a reasonable belief that he or she is entitled to do so is covered. Again, exclusions must be checked for possible application.
3. For *your covered auto*, any person or organization but only with respect to legal responsibility stemming from acts or omissions of a person covered under the liability section of the policy.	Any person or organization (to which any insured belongs or for whom any insured is employed) for legal responsibility stemming from acts or omissions of any person insured under the policy. Examples include the insured's church or club while insured is engaged in church or club sponsored trip or the insured's employer while insured is using personal auto on company business.
4. For any auto or trailer, other than a covered auto, any person or organization but only with respect to legal responsiblity stemming from acts or omission of the named insured, a resident spouse or any *family member* covered under the policy. No coverage if the person or organization owns or hires the auto.	Example: Insured runs a work related errand for his or her employer in a friend's car and has an auto accident. Insured's employer would be covered as far as the insured's actions are concerned. The friend, however, as owner of the car, would not be covered.

shortly. But first it is necessary to explain the other promise of the insurer which is included in the agreement—the promise to *defend.*

Duty to Defend The insurer actually makes two separate promises in the liability insuring agreement. The first is to *pay* for damages; the second, to *defend,* the insured.

Though there is a stated limit in the policy concerning the amount the insurer will pay for damages, there is no such limit as far as the cost of defense is concerned. Expenses incurred in defending an insured are *in addition to* the limit of liability and actually are unlimited in terms of money expended. Note that the policy says: "In addition to our limit of liability, we will pay all defense costs we incur." However, the duty to defend ceases when the policy limits have been exhausted by the payment of claims. (The ramifications of this provision will be discussed subsequently in these pages.)

It is customary to view the promise or duty to defend as being greater than the duty to pay damages. This view is accurate because frequently no liability, or a question of liability, will exist, and an insurer might not have to pay a claim. Regardless of the liability situation, however, an insurer may have to defend its insured once a lawsuit against the insured is commenced. The insurer must defend (if it chooses not to settle) any suit against an insured for bodily injury or property damage arising out of an auto accident in which the facts alleged come within the coverage of the policy.

A problem exists when a summons and complaint are served upon an insured and the fact situation of the accident creates questions about whether coverage actually applies. In cases where an accident seems to involve a policy exlusion, for example, the insurer must look to the plaintiff's allegations as expressed in the complaint to determine if it must provide a defense for the insured. If the complaint alleges anything which conceivably could come within the scope of the liability coverage, even if untrue, the insurer must defend its insured. The *complaint* then will determine whether or not an insurer owes its insured a defense.[8]

One example of this kind of situation is a case in which the insured is alleged to have been at a certain place at a certain time and to have negligently caused an auto accident. Perhaps the plaintiff claims to have gotten the insured's license plate number or other identifying element which prompted the lawsuit, but the insured denies involvement and can substantiate that he was nowhere near the accident scene at the time in question. Based on the allegations in the complaint, the claim is covered and the insurer must defend its insured even though the claim, in fact, may be groundless.

Another situation where a question of defense may exist is a case in which the insured may have intentionally caused injury or damage. (Note that the first exclusion in the PAP refers to intentionally caused injury or damage.) In the complaint, the plaintiff will likely allege a *negligent* act as well as an intentional act. Negligence, of course, is covered by the PAP; and based on this one aspect of the complaint alone, the insurer is obligated to defend its insured. Ordinarily, it will do so under a *reservation of rights* or *nonwaiver agreement.* This approach is taken so that if the outcome of the litigation confirms that a legitimate coverage defense existed, the insurer will have protected its right under the policy to deny coverage and will not be compelled to pay *damages* assessed against an insured for a claim which was not covered in the first place. To do otherwise, that is, to answer a complaint and defend its insured where a policy defense may exist, without first reserving it rights, an insurer will have waived or lost its right to later assert that policy defense when the case is decided at trial.

Another aspect of the defense provision that needs to be emphasized is that when a lawsuit is turned over to defense counsel to defend an insured, the defense attorney's prime obligation is to the insured, not the insurance company. When a coverage question is involved or develops as the case proceeds, defense counsel may be confronted with a serious conflict of interest. Counsel cannot properly defend an insured and at the same time adequately protect the insurer's possible coverage defense. When confronted with such a conflict, the defense attorney may withdraw from the defense of the insured and recommend that the insured be permitted to retain its own counsel at the insurer's expense. The original attorney then would represent the interests of the insurer, and the insured would have separate counsel representing its interests. Recent court cases have held that separate counsel must be retained when such conflicts of interest develop.

Another occasional problem with the defense provision involves the question of when the duty to defend ceases. The policy states quite clearly that the duty to defend ends when the the limit of liability has been exhausted. Thus, when a claim is settled or a judgment is rendered for the policy limit, the duty to defend ceases at that point. If a judgment is rendered against the insured for the policy limit, the insurer will pay that amount as damages as well as pay all legal expenses it incurred in the course of litigation. At this point, the duty to defend has ceased for the insurer.

If after the policy limit has been exhausted, a claimant who was thought not to be injured in the accident sues the insured, the insurer would be under no obligation to defend the insured. This is true provided it can be shown that the insurer conducted a thorough investigation and had no reason to believe the claimant had a potential injury claim. If the insurer's investigation was inadequate or negligent, a problem involving possible bad faith might confront the insurer and this is a matter for discussion later in the text.

Though the policy language is clear on when the duty to defend ceases, experience demonstrates that in actual practice, the provision is occasionally the subject of controversy.

Questions arise most frequently when there are multiple claimants and all claims cannot be settled within the policy limit(s). For example, suppose that there are three bodily injury claimants in a case in which the insured carried a $50,000 single limit policy and is clearly at fault for the accident. The adjuster settles two claims for $15,000 each and offers the remaining $20,000 to the third claimant who is represented by an attorney. The attorney rejects the offer, indicating that the case is worth $40,000 at the very least.

In all likelihood, the insurer in such a case would very much like to pay $20,000, exhaust its limit of liability, and have the case over with. However, if the attorney starts a lawsuit, the insurer must defend its insured because it has not exhausted its limit of liability.

The insurer cannot pay the plaintiff (once suit is instituted the "claimant" is then referred to as the "plaintiff") $20,000 and abandon its duty to defend its insured.

Where an insured is clearly liable to multiple claimants and the value of these claims exceeds the insured's liablity limits, an insurer may file an *interpleader* action. In an interpleader action, the insurer submits the entire matter to the court and asks it to allocate the available limits of liability among the claimants. By such an action, an insurer is able to avoid allegations of bad faith.

Supplementary Payments

Coverage for Supplementary Payments may be viewed as an extra benefit associated with the promise to settle or defend claims. Like the costs incurred in defending the insured, supplementary payments are payable *in addition to* the limit of liability of the policy.

Bail Bonds The insurer agrees to pay up to $250 for the cost of a bail bond. A bail bond guarantees that the accused will appear in court. In order for payment for the bond to be made, an auto accident must cause bodily injury or property damage which is covered under the policy. A bail bond required because of a traffic violation *alone* — e.g., speeding or driving while intoxicated—without an accident is *not* covered.

Appeal Bonds These are required when the insurer, on behalf of the insured, decides to appeal a decision to a higher court. An appeal bond guarantees that the insured will pay the judgment, plus interest and costs, if the appeals court should uphold the decision against the insured.

Release of Attachment Bond If an insured's property is attached as the result of a lawsuit, he or she may have the property released, provided a release of attachment bond is purchased and given to the court. The bond guarantees that the insured (defendent) will pay any damages or court costs, should the case be decided in the plaintiff's favor.

Note that an insurer is not obligated to actually furnish these bonds but simply to pay the premium or cost of the bonds.

Interest When a judgment is appealed, for example, the insurer must pay interest on the judgment even if it exceeds the insured's limit of liability. Once the insurer offers to pay any judgment up to its policy limit, along with the accrued interest, its obligation ends.

Loss of Earnings The insurer agrees to pay up to $50 a day to an insured for loss of earnings as a result of attending a hearing or trial.

Other Expenses The reasonable cost of a hotel as well as reasonable travel expenses incurred by an insured in coming to the trial or to the office of the insurer's attorney for a deposition are examples of expenses covered here.

Chapter Notes

1. *Blue Ridge Textile Co. vs. Travelers Indem. Co.* 181 A 2d 354 (Pa.) and *Universal Underwriters Co. vs. Semig* 182 NW 2d 354 (Mich.)
2. *Couch on Insurance* 2d 15:77, pp. 809–811.
3. The 1984 edition of the homeowners policy developed by the Insurance Services Office incorporates qualifying language in the liability exclusion which indicates that "aircraft" does not include model aircraft of the hobby variety not used or designed for the transportation of people or cargo. This makes it clear that the liability section of the policy does *not* exclude (and therefore covers) injury or damage caused by such model aircraft.
4. *Motor Coils Manufacturing Co. vs. American Ins. Co.* 454 A 2d 1044 (Pa. Superior Court).
5. Claims for mental anguish or emotional distress are generally allowed as long as the emotional distress arises from a bodily injury. Some states allow claims for emotional distress even when actual bodily injury from the impact is not sustained. The so-called "fright" injury where emotional shock results from being involved in a close call, or the emotional distress caused by the sight of dead insects or rodents in food are examples of such situations. A number of courts have considered such emotional injury to be bodily injury.
6. ISO's new Commercial General Liability policy, 11/85 edition, defines *occurrence* as meaning "an accident, including continuous or repeated exposure to substantially the same general harmful conditions." The "expected nor intended..." language of the earlier policy appears as a specific exclusion in the 11/85 edition.
7. A "claims made" policy applies to injuries which occur before the policy's inception date as well as those which occur during the policy period provided the claim is reported during the policy period. A "tail" provision is added which extends, without time limitation, the period in which claims for injury that occurred before a policy's termination will be covered.
8. In some jurisdictions, there is an obligation to look "behind" the complaint. If the complaint alleges an excluded act, for instance, but the insurer knows that the true, unpleaded, factual basis for the claim brings it within the coverage of the policy, it must defend its insured. *Albuquerque Gravel Products Co. vs. American Emp. Ins. Co.* 282 F. 2d 218, 220 (CA 10, 1960).

CHAPTER 3

The Importance and Meaning of Coverage, Continued

PERSONAL AUTO POLICY

Exclusions

As indicated earlier, the broad statement of coverage in the liability insuring agreement is limited only by the exclusions. The resolution of coverage questions must begin with the insuring agreement, but resolution cannot be complete until the exclusions are reviewed for possible applicability.

The insurance company's promise to pay damages for injury or damage is conditioned upon the fact that no exclusions are applicable.

Exclusions Applying to Persons The exclusions are separated into sections A and B. The exclusions in section A refer to activities or situations involving the *person* seeking insurance which are not covered. The emphasis of the exclusions in section B is on *vehicles,* the ownership, maintenance or use of which is not covered.

A.1. Intentional Injury or Damage. The company will not pay damages for bodily injury or property damage intentionally caused by any covered person. This exclusion is a necessary part of the policy because deliberate or intentionally caused injury or damage is not an accident. Frequently, however, while the act of an insured may have been intentional, a question may exist whether the resulting injury or damage was intended by the insured. The exclusion does not rule out coverage for intentional acts, just intentional injury or damage.

When such questions arise, the insurer must promptly advise its insured that it will conduct a detailed investigation of the question and that it reserves its rights under the policy pending completion of the investigation. The insurer may send the insured a reservation of rights letter or have a nonwaiver agreement signed by the insured. Upon completion of its investigation, the insurer must promptly decide whether it will provide coverage for the claim and advise the insured accordingly.

A.2. Damage to Property Owned or Transported. Direct damage insurance, not liability insurance, is the appropriate method for insuring owned or transported property. A related reason for the exclusion is that individuals cannot be held liable for damage they cause to their own property.

A.3. Rented to, Used by, or in the Care of. This is perhaps the most complex liability exclusion partly because of the rather lengthy *exception* to the exclusion. An "exception" to an exclusion allows coverage to apply for the excepted situation.

All liability insurance policies contain such a "care, custody or control" type of exclusion. It is based on the belief that providing liability insurance for damage to property over which an insured exercises complete control encourages indifference or even carelessness concerning the protection of that property. Therefore, damage to such property is not covered in the event a liability claim by the owner of the damaged property is made against the insured.

If an insured rents or borrows a cultivator, for example, leaves it in the driveway and accidentally backs the car over it, no coverage is provided by the PAP for the claim made against the insured by the owner of the cultivator. (Section I coverage of homeowner forms 2 and 3 should respond to this loss under the *Vehicles* perils.)

Two important exceptions apply to this exclusion. The first refers to damage to a residence or private garage which is rented to, used by, or in the care of an insured. If the insured, while driving into his or her rented garage, misjudges the distance and collides with the side of the garage, coverage is available to pay for the damage. Keep in mind, however, that the exception refers to a residence or private garage which is rented to or in the care of an insured, not to such property which is *owned* by the insured. Damage to owned property is excluded by Exclusion 2.

The other exception, which undoubtedly is one of the most significant provisions in the policy, refers to a private passenger auto, trailer, or pickup, panel truck, or van which is *not* owned by or furnished or available for the regular use of the named insured or any *family member. (Family member* is defined on Page 1.) This means that damage to any of the aforementioned type of vehicles which the insured borrows or rents is covered provided that the insured is legally responsible for the damage. This is particularly important in light of the fact that coverage for nonowned vehicles is not provided under the physical damage insurance of Part D of the policy. Physical damage insurance is limited to "covered autos" and a specific exclusion applies for damage to temporary substitute vehicles. Thus, the only coverage available for damage to nonowned vehicles in the PAP is under the liability section of the policy as an exception to this exclusion.

In order for coverage to apply under the exception, certain criteria must be met:

1. The nonowned vehicle must *not* have been furnished or available for the regular use of the named insured or any *family member.*
2. The insured must be legally responsible for damage to the nonowned vehicle.

If an insured drives her resident son's car, which is not insured, to the supermarket and damages the car en route, no coverage is available under the insured's policy for damage to the son's car. Since the son's car is owned by a *family member,* the exception to the exclusion—for a private passenger auto *not* owned by. . .any *family member*—does not apply. Thus, the exclusion remains in effect.

If, however, the insured had borrowed a neighbor's car instead, and damaged that car in the same manner, coverage for damage to the car is provided. The neighbor's car was not owned by the insured or family member; nor was it furnished or available for their regular use. (This exclusion in no way affects the liability coverage available for damage to *other* property; that is, to property which is *not* rented to, used by, or in the care of an insured.)

The Car Rental Situation. As mentioned earlier, an insured may become legally responsible by negligence, by contract, or by statute. Most car rental firms provide liability and physical damage insurance on their rental vehicles but the latter coverage ordinarily is subject to a deductible of anywhere from $250 to $1,000. Typical rental contracts hold the renter responsible for damage to the rental car up to the deductible amount, unless the renter exercises, for an additional premium, the "buy back" option to eliminate the deductible. In the event the deductible is not eliminated, the contract frequently holds the renter responsible regardless of how the damage was caused, even if through no fault of the renter.

For example, a renter properly parked a car in front of his or her home and during the night a hit-and-run motorist demolished it. The typical rental contract makes the renter responsible for the damage in the amount of the deductible. Is the renter covered for damage to the rental car under his or her PAP?

The answer is yes. The renter has contractually assumed liability for damage to the vehicle which makes him or her legally responsible. Since the PAP does not contain a contractual liability exclusion, the renter can look to his or her PAP for coverage as an exception to Exclusion 3.

What Constitutes Regular Use? A final question regarding the exclusion is what constitutes "regular use"? Most insurers will agree that a two- or three-day car rental is not regular use. Some insurers go as far as saying that a two-week rental would not be considered regular use. Anything over two or three weeks, however, approaches the "danger zone" beyond which coverage may be in jeopardy. Adjusters should be certain they know their company's position on the question of what constitutes regular use.

One last point needs to be made about the subject of *regular use.* Although the *extended nonowned coverage* endorsement (PP 03 06) is typically used to provide liability coverage for the insured's use of a nonowned vehicle that is furnished for his or her regular use, the endorsement will not cover damage to the vehicle itself. For example, suppose an insured with extended nonowned coverage who drives a nonowned vehicle furnished for regular use strikes another vehicle, causing damage to both vehicles and injury to the other driver. The extended nonowned coverage endorsement, which deletes several liability and medical payments exclusions of the PAP, provides liability coverage for damage to the other vehicle and for injury to the other driver. However, since the endorsement does not eliminate Exclusion A. 3., this exclusion still prevails to preclude coverage for damage to the vehicle driven by the insured—because that vehicle *is* furnished for the insured's regular use.

Adjusters need to be sure to obtain a copy of the car rental contract and read it thoroughly. While these contracts are generally similar, provisions sometimes vary regarding the situations in which the renter will be held responsible for damage. For example, some contracts excuse the renter for damage caused by acts of nature such as hurricanes or tornadoes or by riot, vandalism, and so on. Other contracts simply require the insured to return the car in the same condition it was in when rented. A decision whether an insured is legally responsible cannot reasonably be made without first reviewing the specific rental contract in question.

A.4. Workers' Compensation. No coverage applies if an employee of any insured is injured in an auto accident while in the course of employment. For example, if the insured and his or her employee are making a delivery in the course of their employment and the insured rear-ends another vehicle causing injury to the employee, the employee's claim against the insured is not covered. This exposure is appropriately covered by workers' compensation insurance.

However, *domestic* employees—housekeepers, gardeners, and so on—are not always subject to workers' compensation laws and, in such cases, coverage is provided if a domestic is injured in an auto accident involving an insured driver.

Note the policy states that the exclusion does not apply to injury to a domestic employee *unless* workers' compensation benefits are "required or available" for the domestic. This means that even though workers' compensation insurance covering the domestic may not be carried, if state law *requires* that it be carried, the exclusion will apply. Adjusters, therefore, must know the circumstances under which their state's workers' compensation law applies to domestics in order to determine the applicability of the exclusion.

A.5. Carrying Persons or Property for a Fee. This exclusion is designed to avoid the public or private livery exposure where a vehicle is held out for hire. The exposure can be covered by commercial auto insurance. Little has been written about the specific language of this exclusion. Carrying people or property for a fee may involve an isolated instance or a continuous activity designed to make a profit. The latter case is clearly not covered, but adjusters should make a thorough investigation when only an isolated instance is involved as well so that if the claim is denied, the denial can be substantiated by the facts.

Note the exception to the exclusion for a share-the-expense car pool. If passengers pay a modest amount to help defray the insured's expenses of automobile operation, coverage will not be excluded in the event of an accident. When the insured earns a regular *profit* from the car pool operation, however, the exclusion applies.

A.6. Auto Business Exclusion. The selling, repairing, servicing, parking, and so on of automobiles is a commercial auto or garage exposure, not a personal one. A garage policy, with both garage liability and garagekeepers insurance, is the appropriate insurance form for this exposure.

As is the case with so many exclusions, an important exception applies to this exclusion. The exclusion does not apply to the ownership, maintenance, or use of a covered auto by the named insured, any *family member* or any partner, agent, or employee of the named insured or *family member.* If any of these individuals drive a covered auto while employed or engaged in an automobile or garage business, coverage applies. For example, a PAP insured who is a mechanic in a car dealership is covered if involved in an accident while driving his or her own car en route to a customer's home to charge a dead battery.

The insured takes her car in for repairs to a local service station. While the service station's mechanic is test-driving the car after repairs are made, he is involved in an accident. Is there any liability coverage provided for the mechanic under the insured's PAP?

Liability coverage for any person employed or engaged in the auto business, including road testing or delivery, is excluded, unless the exception applies. The mechanic's use of the vehicle would not activate the exception in this instance.

A.7. General Business Exclusion. This exclusion is designed to preclude coverage for business use exposures other than the auto business exposure which is already eliminated in the preceding exclusion. Here again, an exception to the exclusion is applicable, and the exception is quite extensive. The general business exclusion does not apply to use of a private passenger auto, to a pickup, panel truck, or van *owned* by the named insured or resident spouse, or to a *trailer* pulled by any of these vehicles. The exclusion was revised by ISO endorsement PP 00 03 to *except* farming and ranching from the exclusion which means, of course, that use of a vehicle in farming or ranching is covered. A PAP policy endorsed with PP 00 03, therefore, would afford the insured coverage for use of even a nonowned pickup, panel truck, or van used in farming or ranching.

In summary, an insured is covered while using in any business (except the auto business) a covered auto (private passenger, pickup, panel truck, or van) or a nonowned private passenger auto or a *trailer* pulled by either a covered auto or *nonowned* private passenger auto. However, an insured is not covered for business use of a nonowned pickup, panel truck, or van (except if used in farming or ranching) or the business use of any larger vehicle such as a dump truck, bus, and so on.

A.8. Unauthorized Use of Vehicle. Previous auto policies contained a requirement that in order for coverage to apply, the use of the vehicle must have been with the permission of the owner. Problems were often encountered, however, in establishing whether a driver actually had the owner's permission and consequently, the permission requirement was eliminated in the PAP.

The emphasis now is on whether the person using a vehicle had a "reasonable belief" that he or she was entitled to its use. It is believed that this language is less restrictive than the previous language which required permission of the owner. The policy does not provide liability coverage for any person using a vehicle without a reasonable belief that the person is entitled to do so. While the obvious purpose of the exclusion is to eliminate coverage for the car thief, it also gives an insurer support for resisting claims where other unauthorized use of the vehicle has been established.

The reference in the exclusion to "any person" seemingly can be interpreted literally. If the insured's teenage son takes the car without his parents' permission and has an accident, and investigation confirms that the son drove the vehicle with clear knowledge that his use was unauthorized, can the exclusion be invoked to deny coverage? In other words, does the reference to "any person" include an insured's son who is a resident of the parents' home?

While the answer to this question is subject to company interpretation, it is quite possible that if statements of both parents and the son are obtained and confirm the absence of reasonable belief, liability coverage for the son can be declined. Taking this step further, if the parents are sued as owners of the vehicle, the insurer will be required to defend them. However, the insurer would not be required to pay a claim for damages unless the parents were held legally responsible. If it can be demonstrated that the son's use of the auto was unauthorized and that he knew it, legal responsibility on the parents' part seemingly will be difficult to establish. A number of claim people, however, feel that unless legal action is taken by the parents against the son for his unauthorized use of the vehicle, a denial of coverage under these circumstances will not be sustained in a court of law.

A.9. Nuclear Energy Exclusion. The PAP will not apply if an insured is covered under a nuclear energy liability policy. Federal legislation requires firms which own or operate nuclear facilities to be insured through nuclear energy liability insurance. Nuclear energy policies contain what can be referred to as an *omnibus clause* which covers, without restriction, anyone (including the PAP insured) responsible for a nuclear accident covered by the policy, except the U.S. government. Though chances are remote that a PAP insured would ever be involved in an accident covered by a nuclear energy liability policy, if such an incident did occur, the insured would be covered under that policy and would not need his or her PAP.

An example used by ISO will help demonstrate the applicability of the exclusion. Suppose an insured collides with a truck carrying nuclear material covered by the nuclear energy liability policy of the nuclear facility. If the collision causes a nuclear incident and a claim or suit against the insured results, the nuclear liability policy will provide coverage. If no nuclear incident results, but the driver of the truck is injured and makes a claim against the insured, the PAP will apply, not the nuclear liability policy.

The exclusion is activated only when an insured is covered by a nuclear liability policy. If no such policy exists, the PAP will apply.

Exclusions Applying to Vehicles

B.1. Vehicles Having Less than Four Wheels. The exclusion is designed to preclude coverage for the use of a motorcycle, moped, and the like. Such vehicles can be specifically insured under their own policies or, if company procesing is available, the Miscellaneous Type Vehicle endorsement (PP 03 23) may be attached to the PAP.

B.2. Vehicles Owned by or Furnished for the "Named Insured's" Regular Use. The use of any vehicle, other than a covered auto, which is owned by the named insured or furnished or available for his or her regular use, is excluded. The purpose of this exclusion is to eliminate the situation where an insured might own several vehicles, and by simply insuring one of those vehicles the insured gets coverage for all the vehicles.

Similar rationale is involved with the second part of the exclusion for a vehicle furnished or available for the insured's regular use. The exposure created by a vehicle furnished for the insured's regular use is comparable to that of an owned auto. As noted earlier in the text, for an additional premium charge, the insured can obtain *extended nonowned coverage* (PP 03 06) which eliminates this exclusion (among others) and provides liability coverage for the use of a vehicle furnished or available for the insured's regular use.

An example of a claim which would not be covered because of this exclusion is the use of a company car furnished the insured by the employer. Since the company car is not a "covered auto" and is furnished for the insured's regular use, the exclusion would apply to preclude coverage under the PAP.

The term "available" for regular use could refer to an arrangement whereby the insured's employer makes a group of cars available to its employees through a pool. Even though an employee may use a different car each day, it probably can be said that the employee's *access* to the pool makes the car *available* for his or her regular use.

It is difficult to make general statements about this exclusion because each case will have its own unique set of circumstances. Adjusters handling claims involving vehicles which may be furnished or available for an insured's regular use will need to conduct a sound investigation. The investigation should cover such items as permission, previous history regarding use of the vehicle, accessibility to car keys, garaging, and intent of the parties involved.

B.3. Owned by or Furnished for Any "Family Member's" Regular Use. This exclusion, read in conjunction with the preceding exclusion, has caused its share of confusion in the past. The purpose of the exclusion is simply to eliminate coverage for a vehicle owned by or furnished or available for the regular use of a *family member.* In other words, if the insured's teenage son owns a car which he decides he cannot afford to insure, his use of the car will not be covered under his parents' PAP. (If he insured the vehicle under a separate policy, the exclusion would still apply because the son's vehicle would not be a "covered auto" under the parents' PAP.)

The exclusion is necessary in view of the broad grant of coverage expressed in the insuring agreement. The insurer agrees to pay damages for injury or damage for which any *covered person* becomes legally obligated because of an auto accident. A "covered person" includes any *family member* for the use of *any* auto. Without this exclusion, coverage would be available if the son caused an auto accident while driving his own vehicle even though that vehicle might be uninsured or insured in another policy.

Note the important exception to the exclusion for use of the son's vehicle by the named insured or resident spouse. While the son is not covered under his parent's PAP for his use of the vehicle, his parents, as named insureds, are covered for their use of the vehicle.

Now if it can be said that the son's car is furnished or available for the regular use of the parents as well, then even the parents' use of the vehicle would be excluded. The parents' use of the car is excluded not by this exclusion but by the *preceding* exclusion which eliminates coverage for the use of any vehicle furnished or available for the named insured's regular use.

Herein lies the distinction between these two exclusions. Exclusion 2 rules out coverage for the *named insured* and *resident spouse* for their use of any vehicle owned by them or furnished or available for their regular use which is not insured under the policy. Exclusion 3 rules out coverage for any *family member* for the use of any vehicle owned by or furnished or available for the regular use of the *family member* which is not insured under the policy. However, exclusion 3 affords coverage (by way of an exception) for the named insureds' use of a vehicle owned by or furnished or available for the regular use of a *family member*—provided the vehicle is not furnished or available for the named insureds' regular use.

The insureds' working daughter lives at home and owns her own car which she had insured under a separate policy but the policy lapsed. Assume the car is *not* available for the parents' regular use. If the daughter has an accident in her uninsured vehicle, she cannot look to her parents' PAP for coverage. Though she is a *family member* under her parents' PAP, the vehicle is not a *covered auto* under that policy and it is furnished for her regular use. Thus, exclusion 3 will be invoked to preclude coverage for the daughter.

On the other hand, if one of the parents borrowed the daughter's car (with her permission) in an emergency and had an accident, the parent would be covered under his or her PAP, as the exception to exclusion 3 would be activated.

Additional Limitations

Two significant limitations which are not actually a part of the PAP but apply as mandatory endorsements are the *contractual liability limitation* of $1,000 (PP 00 03) and the *liability coverage exclusion* (PP 03 26). These endorsements are mandatory with the PAP in those states where the endorsements have been approved and where insurers have adopted them. Not every state has approved the endorsements; nor has every insurer in states where they have been approved, adopted them.

Contractual Liability Limitation The endorsement containing this limitation (PP 00 03) has already been introduced in the text with reference to the amended definition of *your covered auto*. The part of that endorsement which is of interest now concerns the imposition of a $1,000 limitation on vehicle property damage for liability assumed by any insured under a contract. The purpose of the limitation is to restrict coverage in situations where an insured rents a car and it is damaged through no negligence on the insured's part. As noted earlier, car rental contracts frequently hold the renter responsible for any damage to the vehicle, regardless of fault.

In the event a vehicle rented to (or used by or in the care of) an insured is damaged through no negligence on his or her part—say, the vehicle is vandalized or struck by a hit and run motorist—payment under the PAP is limited to $1,000. (This, of course, assumes that the endorsement is attached to the PAP.) Keep in mind that if the insured *negligently* causes damage to a rental car, the $1,000 limitation does not apply and full coverage is available if needed.

It needs to be emphasized that not all car rental firms provide liability and physical damage insurance on their rental cars. In the past several years, many "cut-rate" or "discount" car rental firms have emerged which offer a lower rate but either do not provide insurance or offer it as an option for an additional charge. These firms do quite a lot of business with insurance companies which refer insureds and claimants whose cars have been disabled to them because of their less expensive rates. The rental vehicle is considered a "temporary substitute auto" under these circumstances and is insured as a "covered auto" under the renter's PAP.

With an unrestricted PAP, that is, absent the $1,000 limitation, no coverage problem is anticipated because the temporary substitute auto is a "covered auto" by definition. Even if it takes a month or two for the damaged car to be repaired, the insured will have coverage for use of the rental car. The "furnished or available for regular use" exclusion does not apply to a "covered auto."

A potential problem does exist, however, with regard to the risk of damage to the rental car itself when the $1,000 limitation applies.

Suppose that in an auto theft, rental reimbursement, or liability claim, an insurer directs the individual to a car rental agency or firm that does *not* provide any insurance on the rental car. As mentioned previously, the rental car is a "covered auto" under these circumstances and covered under the renter's PAP. Assume further that the rental car is seriously damaged by a hit and run motorist or that it is stolen while legally parked and locked in front of the renter's house. The renter is entitled to $1,000 from his or her PAP but the remainder of the loss apparently will be borne by the renter personally. Not a particularly happy event for the PAP insured who suddenly learns of such a dilemma. (The problem does not exist when the car rental firm provides auto physical damage insurance on the rental vehicle. Ordinarily, the deductible is less than $1,000 and, if desired, the renter can eliminate the deductible in its entirety for an additional charge.)

Faced with having to come up with this money from personal funds, the renter may very well turn to his or her PAP insurer and claim that it created the dilemma by sending the insured to a car rental firm which failed to provide necessary insurance. The renter may have a valid point if an insurer actually directed him or her to such a rental firm without explaining the limitation.

To avoid this potential problem, at least one insurer recommends that its claim people do not send insureds or claimants to car rental firms that do not provide auto physical damage insurance. It also instructs its adjusters to inform insureds or claimants of the contractual property damage limitation so that they can confirm with car rental firms that auto physical damage insurance is provided for customers and that the deductible is not in excess of $1,000.

Liability Coverage Exclusion "We do not provide Liability Coverage for any person for bodily injury to you or any *family member.*" (PP 03 26)

This seemingly simple exclusion has been the subject of considerable discussion among insurance people. Like the contractual liability limitation just discussed, the liability coverage exclusion has been adopted as a mandatory endorsement with the PAP by insurers in a large number of states where the endorsement has been approved. The intent of the exclusion actually is to prevent any insured from making a bodily injury recovery from his or her auto liability insurance policy.

The exclusion has created some controversy because in many states the doctrine of intrafamily immunity, which bars claims among members of the same family, has long been eliminated. Thus, liability insurance has been available in these states to cover claims or suits among family members. Some insurance people have suggested that it seems somewhat regressive to insert an exclusion precluding coverage for claims which previously have been covered without offering insureds an option to "buy back" the coverage.

The exclusion was also introduced in states which still bar suits by one family member against another and this is not a particular problem. In fact, it might be asked why an exclusion barring intrafamily claims is even necessary when such claims are already prohibited by the laws of the state. The rationale for including such an exclusion is the belief of insurers that the presence of the exclusion will demonstrate to any court hearing a suit between family members, the insurer's clear intent to exclude such claims. It is significant that courts that have tried the issue of intrafamily immunity for the first time in a particular state (that is, where the immunity doctrine was being challenged), have said that if an exclusion barring such claims had been included in the policy, it would have been honored. Such judicial commentary served as the impetus for introducing the exclusion even in states which have not abrogated intrafamily immunity.

Some insurers have filed, and use, similar endorsements independently. Court decisions regarding this type of exclusion endorsement (sometimes referred to as the "household" exclusion) vary among the states. Adjusters should know their state's position regarding the validity of this type of exclusion.

Though the main thrust of the exclusion concerns claims among members of the same family, the scope of the exclusion goes far beyond the intrafamily situation. The insurer states that it does not provide liability coverage for "any person" for bodily injury to you or any *family member.* The reference to "any person" demonstrates the fact that it is not merely confined to members of the same family.

The following example illustrates the broad scope of this exclusion: Gary Smith is driving Al Scott's car while Scott is a passenger in the vehicle. Smith falls asleep at the wheel and drives into a tree. Scott is seriously injured and sues his friend Smith. The liability coverage exclusion in Scott's PAP rules out coverage for Smith as a permissive user insofar as injury to Scott is concerned. (In the absence of the exclusion, Smith would be covered under Scott's policy and Scott's insurer would pay Scott's bodily injury claim.)

With no liability coverage available under Scott's policy, Scott can look to Smith's policy if one is in effect. If Smith is uninsured, Scott will have no liability insurance available to pay his claim for bodily injury.

A remote but possible solution is for Scott to make an uninsured motorists claim under his PAP, provided he carries this coverage. While it is true that the PAP states that an "uninsured motor vehicle" does *not* include any vehicle owned by or furnished or available for the regular use of an insured (see page 6 of the PAP), the fact that uninsured motorists protection is statutorily mandated might void this particular policy language in some states. Courts in a number of states have already said that policy language which is in conflict with the uninsured motorist statute is invalid. (See previous discussion of the *Ady* case in this text which held, in effect, that uninsured motorists insurance follows the person, not the auto.)

Coverage versus Liability

Coverage and liability are distinct concepts, the former referring to the insurer's contractual obligation to pay for damages and defend claims, and the latter focusing on the insured's legal responsibility.

When both coverage and liability exist simultaneously, a claim will be paid by the insurer. When there is coverage, but no liability, or questionable liability, ordinarily the claim will be resisted or defended or, when circumstances warrant, compromised. Where there is liability on the insured's part but no coverage, the insured must be informed that coverage is not available and given an explanation of why it does not apply. Claim people must be able to distinguish between coverage and liability so that they will know how to respond to a particular claim.

Claims involving coverage with no liability are quite common. A claimant makes a sudden left turn in front of the insured who is driving within the speed limit and has the clear right of way. A claimant runs a stop sign controlling traffic on a side street and collides with the insured who is driving on the main thoroughfare.

In cases where there is liability on the insured's part but no coverage, a policy exclusion is usually involved. For example, investigation reveals that the insured deliberately drove into the car dealership show room window because the dealership sold the insured a "lemon" and would not assume responsibility for it. (Exclusion A.1.) The insured accidentally drove through the rear wall of the garage when his foot slipped off the brake. (Exclusion A.2.)

In the following situation, neither liability nor coverage is present. While in a hurry, the insured backs out of the driveway and accidentally collides with his second car which is parked across the street. There is no collision coverage on the second car. Since a person cannot be held liable for damage he or she causes to his or her own property, there is no legal responsibility in this case. Coverage is also lacking in view of exclusion A.2.

Limit of Liability

The limit of liability shown in the Declaration for liability insurance is the most the insurer will pay for damages resulting from any one accident. This is the case regardless of the number of covered persons, claims made, vehicles or premiums shown in the Declarations, or vehicles involved in the accident. This provision is necessary to prevent the stacking of limits in cases where two or more cars or individuals are covered under one policy with a separate liability premium charge shown for each car. If an insured is involved with a claim in which the amount demanded exceeds the limit of liability, he or she could argue for stacking the limits for each car insured. The limit of liability provision technically prevents this from occurring. (There also is a provision in Part F of the policy—Two or More Auto Policies—that is designed to accomplish the same purpose when more than one policy with the same insurer is in effect.) Before enforcing these "anti-stacking" provisions, adjusters must make sure that they have not been invalidated by statute or court decisions in their state.

Out of State Coverage

This provision protects an insured while driving in a state which may require higher insurance limits than those required by the insured's home state. It also provides an insured with any coverage required of a nonresident driving in a state, including no-fault auto insurance benefits. For example, suppose that an insured who meets his or her state's financial responsibility limits of $12,500/25,000 bodily injury liability insurance drives through a state which requires minimum limits of $20,000/40,000 bodily injury coverage, including basic no-fault benefits, and the requirement extends to nonresidents driving in the state. While the insured is in that state, his or her PAP is automatically converted to provide the limits and coverages required by that state.

This broadened coverage feature, an acknowledgment that America is a mobile and motoring society, is built into the policy at no additional premium charge. Furthermore, there is no requirement that the insured pay an additional premium even if a claim payment exceeds the stated policy limits.

Other Insurance

There are two distinct parts of the Other Insurance provision. Probably the one most commonly encountered by adjusters involves the *primary/excess* situation where an insured is driving a nonowned vehicle. If the insured borrows a neighbor's car and has an accident, the insured is a *covered person* under both the neighbor's policy and his or her own policy. Assume the insured is sued for $100,000 and a judgment is rendered in that amount. If the neighbor's liability limit is $25,000 and the insured's is $100,000, how is the judgment divided between the two policies?

The answer is found in the Other Insurance provision. The insured's policy says that any insurance the company provides for liability arising out of the use of a nonowned vehicle is *excess* over any other collectible insurance. Therefore, the insured's PAP is excess and the neighbor's policy—since the car is an *owned* auto from the neighbor's standpoint—is *primary.* This is what is meant by the phrase "primary coverage follows the car." In this case, the neighbor's policy will pay $25,000 and the insured's policy will pay the remainder of the judgment, or $75,000. In the event the neighbor's car was uninsured, the insured's policy would become primary. (Keep in mind that while a "temporary substitute auto" is a *covered auto* by definition, the liability coverage available for the auto is on an excess basis because a temporary substitute auto is still a nonowned vehicle.)

The other part, or first part of this provision, involves a situation in which two or more insurance policies apply to the claim on the same basis; in other words, where all the policies appear to apply on a primary basis.

For example, an insured is eager to change insurance companies to save money on her auto insurance premium. In her haste to make the change, there is a mix-up and the new policy is made effective three weeks before the existing policy expires. During that three-week period when two polices are in effect, the insured has an accident for which she is responsible and a claim is made for $30,000. The limit of liability in the existing policy, with Company A, is $50,000, while the new limit of liability, with Company B, is $100,000. Each insurer will pay only the proportion of the claim that its limit of liability bears to the total limits available. With a claim for $30,000, Company A will pay $10,000 and Company B will pay $20,000.

$$\text{Company A} \frac{\$50{,}000 \quad \text{(Company A's limit)}}{\$150{,}000 \quad \text{(Total limits)}} \times \$30{,}000 \text{ loss} = \$10{,}000$$

$$\text{Company B} \frac{\$100{,}000 \quad \text{(Company B's limit)}}{\$150{,}000 \quad \text{(Total limits)}} \times \$30{,}000 \text{ loss} = \$20{,}000$$

Total settlement from both companies $30,000

One final point needs to be made about the Other Insurance provisions. When the PAP was first introduced, some adjusters took the position that the reference in the last sentence to "any other collectible insurance" included not only liability insurance but collision or comprehensive insurance as well. Thus, in the case where an insured borrowed a neighbor's car and negligently damaged it, and the neighbor carried collision insurance, the collision insurance was regarded as other collectible insurance and the insured's liability insurance (also available to pay for the vehicle damage) was considered excess. What usually happened was that the owner's collision insurance would pay for the bulk of the loss and the driver's liability coverage simply picked up the deductible.

According to ISO, which drafted the PAP, this position was incorrect. The vehicle owner's physical damage insurance is *not* to be considered other collectible insurance. ISO reasons that since the first sentence of the Other Insurance provision specifies "liability insurance," that is the controlling aspect, and the reference in the last sentence to other collectible insurance should be read: "other collectible *liability* insurance."

The correct interpretation of this provision impacts claim adjustment in the following manner. If the owner of the vehicle (in the case described above) wishes to make a collision claim with his or her insurer, the insurer must pay the claim and will *not* be able to subrogate against the driver of the vehicle. This is because the provision entitled "Our Right To Recover Payment" on page 10 of the PAP states that the collision insurer's right to recover (or right to subrogate) does not apply under Part D (physical damage insurance) to a permissive user.

The deductible portion of the claim aside, the driver's PAP (liability section) will not apply unless the owner forgoes a collision claim and presses the driver to make claim under his or her PAP. Should this happen, the PAP insurer will be required to pay for the entire damage since it cannot say with any reasonable basis that the PAP is excess to the owner's collision coverage.

WHY KNOWLEDGE OF COVERAGE IS IMPORTANT

Although all insurance people—agents, underwriters, and claim people alike—share in the responsibility of understanding and explaining the policy, in most companies the ultimate decision regarding coverage rests with the claim department. For this reason as well as others which will be mentioned shortly, the responsibility for coverage interpretation placed on claim people is significant.

If it is to deny coverage, a company must be prepared to defend its position with clear and concise policy language. Courts across the country are unanimous in holding that questionable or ambiguous policy language will be resolved in favor of the policyholder, and against the company which wrote the policy and had the opportunity to make it clear and understandable.[1]

Many companies, realizing the risks associated with claims of bad faith for wrongfully denying coverage, require that coverage denials of claims of any consequence be reviewed and approved by management or even home office claim personnel before a denial is made to an insured. (The subject of bad faith and excess liability claims is discussed in Chapter 5.)

In addition, many unfair claim practice laws require that denials of coverage be made in writing and include reference to the specific policy provision and language upon which the denial is based.

These factors combined with the influx of new "readable" policy forms that began in the mid-1970s and continues today, challenge insurance people to develop and maintain a working knowledge of coverage. Related to this, many companies, in an effort to hold on to what they perceive as their competitive edge in the marketplace, continually add new coverages and develop new endorsements. The combination of these factors increases the number of policy forms with which adjusters must be familiar and places a heavy burden on them to keep up with their changing products.

Compounding the problem of understanding coverage is the fact that updating insurance policies into the "vernacular," or everyday, readable format, is a monumental task and one which is not necessarily flawless. Mistakes are made, provisions are inadvertently omitted, and paragraphs are unclear, necessitating still further changes in policy forms which the adjuster is responsible for learning. It is probably true that there has been as much, if not more, change in the language and format of insurance policies in the last ten years than in the previous fifty years—and there are strong indications that the trend will continue well into the future.

All of these developments present a major challenge to the adjuster whose responsibility it is to interpret policy language. And rare indeed is the claim person who can be said to possess a "commanding" knowledge of the policy contracts in his or her portfolio of forms. It would seem that in this area of coverage analysis, a great opportunity exists for ambitious claim people to develop their knowledge and be recognized as skillful policy analysts.

A look at a few court decisions involving coverage disputes will lend further support to the view that insurance people need to be knowledgeable about insurance policies with which they work. These cases are particularly relevant to claim people because they demonstrate how the courts analyze questions of coverage.

Hionis Decision

A significant decision, despite the fact that it was subsequently overturned, was *Hionis vs. Northern Mutual Ins. Co., 327 A.2d 363* (1974). This case is especially interesting from a coverage analysis standpoint because of the dilemma it created for insurers as well as for the valuable insights it provided regarding the manner in which courts interpret coverage questions.

Hionis went far beyond the principle that ambiguities in policy language should be resolved in the insured's favor.[2] The Pennsylvania Superior Court case held that even where a particular exclusion is clear and unambiguous, it may not be relied upon unless the insurance company can prove that the exclusion was explained to the insured and that the insured understood it. One attorney, observing the harshness of this doctrine, has said that Hionis is to insurance law what the Miranda warning is to criminal law.[3]

The decision as predicated on the court's perception that most insureds have little understanding of insurance contracts and since the insurer selects the policy and the language to be used, it has a duty to be sure the insured gets what he or she needs and, if not, to explain the limitations so that additional coverage may be obtained, if available. Establishing that policy exclusions were read and understood by the insured is a difficult and impractical, if not impossible, task.

The reasoning of the case applied primarily to unsophisticated insurance buyers—the average homeowner and perhaps small business firms—who ordinarily rely on the knowledge and expertise of an agent or broker to select needed coverages for them. A larger business firm with a risk manager or attorney, for example, did not need the benefit of the Hionis doctrine. Nor would it have been applied to an individual with independent knowledge of the insurance field. Furthermore, where it would have been unreasonable for an insured to expect to be covered for a particular risk or loss, an insurer would not have been required to show that an exclusion was explained and understood by the insured.

Standard Venetian Blind Decision

In 1983, almost ten years after it was decided, the impact of Hionis was substantially restricted by the Pennsylvania Supreme Court in *Standard Venetian Blind Co. vs. American Empire Insurance Co.* 469 A.2d 563.

This case involved exclusions (n) and (o) of the comprehensive general liability policy, the exclusions for property damage to the named insured's products and to work performed by or on behalf of the named insured.

In the case, a portico constructed by Standard Venetian Blind Co. collapsed and damaged some materials stored underneath it. The insurance company agreed to pay for the damage to the materials but refused to pay for the collapsed portico based on the exclusions referred to above for damage to the insured's products and to work performed by the insured.

While both the trial court and, on appeal, the Superior court, found that the exclusions were presented in a clear and unambiguous manner, they nevertheless held for coverage. Relying on the Hionis rule, these courts affirmed coverage because the insured had neither been informed of the exclusions nor had them explained to it.

On appeal to the highest court in the state, the Pennsylvania Supreme Court, however, the Hionis rule was rejected. The supreme court said that an exclusion is enforceable as long as it is expressed in clear and unambiguous language. The court went on to say that the burden imposed by Hionis forces the courts to give less significance to the written contract which historically has been the true test of the parties' intent. Application of the Hionis rule would permit an insured to avoid clear and unambiguous exclusionary provisions, the court added. In concluding, it observed that where the exclusion is clearly worded and conspicuously displayed, the insured may not avoid the consequences of the exclusion by presenting evidence that he or she failed to read it or understand it.

Although the highest court in Pennsylvania has essentially rejected the Hionis doctrine, it has also acknowledged the unequal bargaining positions of insurance companies and purchasers of insurance. This acknowledgment leaves the door open to some extent for courts to reject even clear and unambiguous policy language when the effect of an exclusion would be unconscionable. In other words, if the result of applying the clear intent of an exclusion would be so harsh as to defy the reasonable understanding of the parties to an insurance contract, the exclusion will not be upheld.

While the threat of the Hinonis rule has been significantly diminished in Pennsylvania, it is possible that attempts will be made to limit *Standard Venetian Blind* to disputes involving commercial insureds, since the case dealt with such an insured. Only time will tell whether Hionis will still be a factor in coverage disputes involving the average or less sophisticated insureds.

In any event, courts in other states have followed the Hionis view. An Ohio case, in particular, seems to bear the closest resemblance to it.[4]

Ady Decision

In *Ady vs. Western American Ins. Co. 433 NE2d 547 (1981),* the Ohio Supreme Court held invalid an uninsured motorists exclusion which precluded coverage when an insured was occupying an owned vehicle which was not insured under the policy. In the case, Terry Ady was operating a motorcycle when he was injured by an uninsured motorist. Ady had uninsured motorists coverage in a policy covering the motorcycle but since his claim exceeded those limits, he sought additional uninsured motorists insurance under his father's policy with Western American. The claim was denied based on the exclusion noted earlier.

The actual exclusion read as follows:

> This insurance does not apply: (b) to bodily injury to an insured while occupying a highway vehicle (other than an insured highway vehicle) owned by the named insured, any designated insured or any relative resident in the same household as the named or designated insured.

Ady was an insured under his father's policy but was operating a vehicle (motorcycle) which though *owned* by an "insured," was not *insured* under the father's policy. Therefore, the exclusion was invoked by the insurer.

In concluding that the exclusion was invalid, the court observed that the public policy behind the uninsured motorists statute was to protect persons injured in automobile accidents from losses which, because of the negligent motorist's lack of liability coverage, would otherwise go uncompensated. The court went on to say that the public policy requires broad coverage and does not limit it merely to those who have purchased separate insurance on all vehicles. The court was emphatic in expressing the view that the statute is designed to protect *persons,* not automobiles. Insurance companies use preprinted, multiple page forms with which most insureds are unfamiliar and which are accepted by them without question or negotiation. Because of the unequal bargaining positions of the insurer and insured, companies must bear the burden of showing that the insured was aware of any restriction and that the insured understood it and agreed to it. Exclusions should be conspicuous and exclusionary language clear and easily understood by a layperson and there should be evidence that the insured agreed to the exclusion.

The court concluded that the exclusion was invalid because it was in conflict with the uninsured motorists statute and because it was not clear and conspicuous.

What is particularly perplexing about this case is that the Ohio Supreme Court overruled its earlier decision in *Orris vs. Claudio 406 NE2d 1381,* a case decided less than two years before Ady. In Orris, the court *upheld* an identical uninsured motorists exclusion. (In the past few years, this particular exclusion has been the subject of litigation in a number of states with decisions going both ways; some upholding the exclusion and others declaring it void.)

The inconsistency displayed by the Ohio Supreme Court in the Orris and Ady decisions has seemingly dealt a blow to the long standing doctrine of *stare decisis.*[5] This doctrine holds that where the court has once established a principle of law as applicable to a certain set of facts, it will follow that principle and apply it to all future cases where the facts are essentially the same. The doctrine allows accepted and established legal principles to be followed on a consistent basis and maintains a degree of security and certainty in the law.

This case demonstrates that claim adjusters should be especially sensitive to issues involving uninsured motorists insurance because the coverage is mandated by state law. For this reason, courts tend to look rather negatively at any policy provision which may conflict with the purpose of the particular uninsured motorists statute.

The Ady decision (as well as the Hionis decision before it was overturned) demonstrates that insurance people can be held responsible for explaining policy limitations or exclusions to their policyholders. Though this responsibility may seem to refer mainly to individuals responsible for form writing and selection of coverage, including agents in their role as insurance advisors, it impacts upon claim people as well. Since claim people ordinarily make the final call regarding coverage, they must be aware of any court decisions which address the area of insurance coverage, even those which may more specifically involve an agent's responsibility than that of an adjuster. The law of agency holds that a company (principal) is responsible for the acts or omissions of its agent and this often makes the agent's role a crucial factor in coverage resolution.

The reasoning expressed by these courts and the terms employed in their analysis have particular significance to the principles of insurance contract law. Before proceeding to an analysis of the personal auto policy and the related case discussion exercise, it will be helpful first to describe the general characteristics of a contract and, in particular, the unique features of insurance contracts.

COVERAGE PROBLEMS

Up to now, this text has concentrated on demonstrating to claim people the need to develop and maintain a working knowledge of coverage. This chapter deals with the proper insurer response necessary when a coverage question is recognized. The chances of recognizing coverage questions in a timely manner are significantly increased if claim people possess a sound knowledge of the insurance contracts with which they work.

Waiver and Estoppel

It is important, however, for claim people not only to be able to recognize coverage questions promptly, but also to be able to act immediately upon such recognition to advise an insured that a problem which may preclude insurance protection exists. An insurer's prolonged silence in the face of a potential coverage question can constitute a waiver of its rights under the policy resulting in its being estopped (prevented) from later asserting a valid coverage defense.

Waiver means the voluntary relinquishment of a known right by the insurer. *Estoppel* is the result of a waiver, which prevents an insurer from asserting a right because that right has been waived. In the context of insurance claims, waiver occurs most often as a result of actions taken by an insurer which imply that coverage has been accepted when in reality a question of coverage exists. For example, the failure of an insurer to advise an insured of a coverage question until three months after the claim is reported in a case where investigation indicates injury is intentionally caused constitutes a waiver of the insurer's right to later assert the intentional injury exclusion.

The question is not so much when the coverage problem was recognized, but when it *could* have been recognized in the course of a proper investigation. Thus, in all probability, an insurer will not be able to reserve its right to deny coverage when a policy violation or applicable exclusion is recognized for the first time months after an accident if, through reasonable investigation, it could have been recognized in the early stages of the claim. Obviously it is imperative that insurers conduct a prompt and complete investigation when coverage disputes are involved.

The threat of waiver and estoppel encourages insurers to act promptly to advise an insured of any coverage dispute and to decide as quickly as reasonably possible whether to provide or decline coverage.

Coverage disputes can develop for a variety of reasons. The following situations are examples of coverage disputes that require prompt action on the insurer's part:

1. late notice of an accident,
2. an accident involving a vehicle which is owned by an insured but not designated in the policy,
3. date of accident does not fall within the policy period,
4. a question whether an "insured" driver had a reasonable belief he or she was entitled to the use of the vehicle,
5. applicability of an exclusion,
6. failure to cooperate, and
7. fraud on the insured's part.

As a practical matter, gathering the necessary facts to intelligently decide such questions often entails a lengthy investigation. Yet courts have held that a lapse of time or a delay in advising an insured of a coverage dispute constitutes waiver and estoppel.

How then may an insurer conduct the necessary investigation without waiving its right to later deny coverage should investigation confirm that no coverage exists? Insurers have essentially three devices which they may utilize to handle coverage disputes. These devices are (1) *a reservation of rights letter,* (2) *a nonwaiver agreement,* and (3) *a declaratory judgment action.*

Reservation of Rights Letter

When a company sends a reservation of rights letter to its insured, it is, in effect, accepting the claim with qualifications. The insurer has pointed out the nature of a coverage dispute and states that while it will investigate the claim, it reserves its rights under the policy to deny coverage to anyone claiming protection under the policy in the event investigation reveals that coverage does not apply.

The purpose of a reservation of rights letter is twofold: (1) to protect the insurer so that it may avoid waiver and estoppel and (2) to inform the insured(s) that a coverage problem may exist and provide an opportunity for the insured to retain his or her own counsel, at his or her expense, if desired. It is only fair that the insured be promptly made aware of any situation which might jeopardize his or her coverage. First of all, an insurer should deal honestly and candidly with its insured so that there is no uncertainty regarding the actions which will be taken. The reservation of rights letter advises the insured of a potential problem and prevents him from being lured into a false sense of security regarding coverage. Secondly, a reservation of rights could very well mean that the insured will be without coverage and defense and will need to consider making other arrangements for his or her protection immediately.

The answers to the following questions about reservation of rights letters will help to highlight the important aspects of such letters.[6]

1. When should a reservation of rights letter be sent?

A reservation of rights letter should be sent as soon as the claim person recognizes a potential coverage problem such as late notice, an applicable exclusion, failure to cooperate, and so on.

The question occasionally arises whether the adjuster can conduct an initial investigation of the coverage question before actually sending the letter. While a specific answer to this question will depend on a particular company's procedures for handling coverage disputes, as a general rule any delay in sending the reservation of rights letter is risky. If it is clear or probable that a definite coverage question is involved, the safe course is to promptly notify the insured(s) via a reservation of rights letter. (Many insurers believe that the letter should be preceded by either a telephone call to the insured or a face to face mention of the potential question so that the letter does not shock or panic the insured and create an immediate adversary situation. Common sense and courtesy should serve as the adjuster's guide with respect to the extent of communication he or she will have with the insured.) On the other hand, if there is only a remote possibility that coverage may not apply, it would seem that the adjuster is entitled to make a prompt inquiry into the question to determine if a real problem or dispute exists before sending a reservation of rights letter. The main idea to keep in mind if notification of the insured is to be held up is that unreasonable delay will result in waiver or estoppel.

2. To whom should a reservation of rights letter be sent?

To any insured who is likely to claim coverage under the policy, including the attorney of that person, should one be involved. Likewise, the insured's agent or broker should be advised of the coverage problem, personally or by copy of the reservation letters.

3. What information should be contained in a reservation of rights letter?

The name of the insured, date of accident, policy/claim number, and the specific policy provision involved, whether it is an exclusion, condition, definition, and so on should be identified. It is important that the adjuster actually quote the relevant policy language. The coverage question must be clearly defined and the insured must be informed of his or her right to retain personal counsel in view of the possible conflict over coverage.

It is optional to include an additional "catch-all" reservation to handle any unforeseen coverage problems that might arise during the course of the claim. The additional reservation or "savings clause," as it is sometimes called, might read: "There may be other reasons why coverage does not apply. We do not waive our rights to deny coverage for any other valid reason which may arise."

Even where the additional reservation or savings clause is included, if another issue (other than the one upon which the original reservation is based) arises, the adjuster should send another reservation of rights letter covering the additional issue. If this is not done, the insurer will be subject to waiver and estoppel on the additional question.

Companies usually furnish their claim employees with samples or guides of reservation of rights letters and nonwaiver agreements while other companies may rely exclusively on counsel to send such letters or draw up such agreements. A sample reservation of rights letter is shown in Exhibit 3-1. It is a mistake to view the sample, or any sample letter for that matter, as a form letter. The term "form letter" tends to give the false impression that one basic letter will fit all occasions. On the contrary, the sample letter should be viewed merely as a guide, as each letter needs to be specifically tailored to the particular claim situation.

Nonwaiver Agreement

A *nonwaiver agreement* is similar to a reservation of rights letter except that it is *signed* by the insured and a company claim representative. For this reason, it ordinarily is considered to carry more weight than a reservation of rights letter. (A sample nonwaiver agreement is shown in Exhibit 3-2.)

Some insurers favor a nonwaiver agreement if a claim is in suit and a decision on coverage cannot be made until trial. Other insurers regard a reservation of rights letter to be sufficient. No attempt will be made in this text to encourage the use of one method over the other as this is essentially a company decision which ordinarily is made with the advice of counsel.

As a general rule, three elements are necessary in order for a reservation of rights or non-waiver agreement to be effective.[7]

Exhibit 3-1
Notice of Reservation of Rights

_______________, 19_____

TO

RE: Insured:
Claimant:
Date of Loss:
Policy Number:

We have received notice of an occurrence which took place at ______ on ____(date)____. As a result of this occurrence coverage has been requested under policy number ____________ which was issued to ____(NA)____ by ____(Company Name)____ ____________. There is a question whether coverage under the policy applies to this occurrence.

The nature of the coverage question is as follows: ____________

____

____

____(Company Name)____ will continue to handle this claim even though a coverage question exists. However, no act of any company representative while investigating, negotiating settlement of the claim or defending a lawsuit shall be construed as waiving any Company rights. The Company reserves the right, under the policy, to deny coverage to you or anyone claiming coverage under the policy.

There may be other reasons why coverage does not apply. We do not waive our right to deny coverage for any other valid reason which may arise.

You may wish to discuss this matter with your own personal attorney. In any event, we would be pleased to answer any questions you might have concerning our position as outlined in this letter.

Very truly yours,

____
Insurance Company

BY ____________________
For the Company

Exhibit 3-2
Nonwaiver Agreement

Policy of insurance number ________________ was issued to ____NI____ by ____Co.____ to cover the period from ________ to ________. Coverage under this policy of insurance has been requested for occurrence which took place on _Date_ at ____Place____. A dispute has arisen about whether or not there is insurance coverage under the policy to protect ____NI &/or other____ for any liability which is a result of the reported occurrence. The reason for the question of coverage is ________________________

____

____

Nevertheless, ____(NI &/or other)____ ____(request or requests)____ that the ____Name____ Company investigate, negotiate, settle, deny or defend any claim or suit arising out of such accident or occurrence as it deems necessary. ____Name____ Company agrees to proceed with such handling of this case but only on condition that such action taken will not waive any right the Insurance Company may have to deny any obligation under the policy contract, nor be considered an admission of any liability on the part of the company. It is further agreed that such action will not waive any rights of the insured.

There may be other reasons why coverage does not apply. We do not waive our right to deny coverage for any other valid reason which may arise.

Nothing in this agreement precludes ____NI &/or other____ from retaining personal counsel for his or her own protection.

Either party to this agreement may at any time terminate the agreement upon notice in writing and proceed under his/her own unrestricted rights.

Signed this ______ day of ____________, 19____.

________________ Witness	________________ Insured
	________________ Additional Insured
________________ Witness	________________ Insurance Company
	BY: ________________ For the Company

1. It must be communicated to the insured. Since proof of receipt of the document by the insured is important, the letter should be sent by certified mail, return receipt requested.
2. It must be timely. As mentioned earlier, a real possibility exists that the insured may be without coverage and defense and will need time to consider retaining other counsel or finding other means of protection. Generally, an insurer is required to notify its insured of a potential coverage question as soon as it is recognized, or *could* have been recognized, in the course of a proper investigation.
3. It must adequately and fairly inform the insured of the insurer's position. This refers to the need to clearly inform the insured of the specific nature of the coverage dispute. As noted earlier, if a policy provision is involved, it should be stated in detail. It must be clear to the average insured from a reading of the letter or agreement what the coverage question is all about. In addition, the document should always refer to the insured's right to retain his or her own counsel.

Once the reservation of rights letter has been sent or the nonwaiver agreement signed and secured in the file, the adjuster's task is only partially completed. The next step entails making a final decision whether coverage will be accepted or declined or, if in suit, whether the case will proceed to trial under a reservation of rights or nonwaiver agreement.

The fact that a reservation of rights or nonwaiver agreement has been consummated does not mean that the adjuster can sit back indefinitely and let the claim proceed undirected. The insurer must take a definitive position regarding the coverage dispute with due diligence, if reasonably possible. An insurer which does not act in a timely manner to inform an insured of its final position is subject to waiver or estoppel even though it has sent a reservation of rights letter or secured a nonwaiver agreement. Put candidly, coverage disputes are pressure situations and only a prompt and complete investigation of the issues and a final coverage decision can relieve the pressure.

Upon completion of the investigation of the coverage issue, the adjuster should promptly and completely report his or her findings to the supervisor, or to a higher authority, if that is what company procedures call for, and make specific recommendations for handling. Although companies have their own procedures for handling coverage disputes which must be controlling, there is considerable merit to encouraging adjusters to make their own decisions and recommendations. By requiring the adjuster to make recommendations, he or she is compelled to analyze the problem and make a decision. Since the recommendations will be reviewed by supervisory or management personnel, there is little or no danger that a wrong decision will be acted upon. Yet the entire exercise can be an invaluable growth experience for the adjuster, whether the decision is put into action or not.

Declaratory Judgment Action

The third method of handling a coverage dispute is for the insurer to bring an action for *declaratory judgment.* In a declaratory judgment action, the insurer (or insured) presents the coverage question to the court and asks the court to declare or determine the rights of the parties under the policy. It may be used as a substitute for a reservation of rights letter or non-waiver agreement or in addition to these two methods.

A declaratory judgment action is particularly useful when an insurer faces a substantial third-party claim in conjunction with a significant coverage question. If commenced promptly, it has the advantage of providing a decision on the coverage question before the serious third party claim is litigated. If the judgment declares coverage is in effect, the insurer knows that its policy applies and can concentrate on choosing its best course of action with regard to the disposition of the claim. If the judgment declares that an exclusion applies or that the policy is not in force, the claim is closed as far as the insurer is concerned.

A declaratory judgment action may be the only means of avoiding waiver and estoppel should an insured refuse to sign a nonwaiver agreement or reject in writing a reservation of rights letter.

Declaratory actions play an important role in handling coverage disputes and may even avoid claims for punitive damages. Claim people need to be conscious of situations in which declaratory actions could be effective in deciding coverage disputes. When such situations are recognized, the appropriateness of such actions should be discussed with claim management and defense counsel.

EXCESS LIABILITY

The general subject of excess liability as it relates to extra-contractual liability and bad faith is discussed in Chapter 5. Extra-contractual liability refers to liability which is in addition to that which is covered by the actual insurance policy. It includes such things as claims for punitive damages or verdicts in excess of the policy limits in which an insurer's improper claim handling is alleged to be the cause of the additional damages. This is a subject of growing concern and will be covered rather extensively in the next chapter.

For now, the discussion focuses on suits in excess of policy limits and suggests the steps necessary to protect both the insured and the company. When an insured is sued and the *ad damnum* (prayer for damages) is in excess of the policy limits, the insurer must notify the insured of this fact and inform him of the right to retain personal counsel. The customary method used to so notify the insured is an *excess letter.* The content of the letter varies somewhat from company to company. Samples of typical excess letters are shown in Exhibit 3-3 and 3-4

An excess letter should include the following information:

1. Policy number and name, address, and telephone number of defense counsel assigned to defend the insured.
2. The amount sued for as well as the policy limit(s). It is important that the insured be shown the amount of the suit as it relates to the amount of coverage so that the excess or uncovered amount of the claim is clearly discernible to the insured.
3. The letter should explain explain that the company will defend the insured and pay the cost of defense but that in the event of a verdict in excess of the policy limit(s), the policy will not cover the excess amount. For this reason, the insured should be advised of his or her right to retain another attorney at his or her own expense to handle the uncovered portion of the suit. In conjunction with the notification of the right to retain personal counsel, the insured should be offered the opportunity to have his or her counsel, if retained, work with defense counsel which will be providing the insured's defense.
4. Many insurers believe it is a good idea to specifically request that the insured refrain from giving any information to anyone other than a company representative or defense counsel. In addition, the insured is asked to keep the company and counsel advised of his or her current address and telephone number in the event the insured is needed for a deposition, to complete interrogatories, or to testify at the actual trial.

It also is important that the claim person keep the insured apprised of the status of the lawsuit, including notification of any offers or demands which might be made. The insured may wish to personally participate in the settlement as far as the excess amount of the suit is concerned, if he or she is financially able.

Exhibit 3-3
Excess Letter 1

DATE

INSURED OR DRIVER'S NAME AND ADDRESS

RE: CLAIM

DEAR (INSURED, DRIVER):

We have forwarded a copy of your claim file to [NAME OF ATTORNEY/NAME OF FIRM, ADDRESS, AREA CODE AND TELEPHONE NUMBER]. We have asked this firm to proceed with your defense in the lawsuit brought against you by ______________________. You do not have to appear in court on the date stated in the legal papers, as the law firm will appear for you. They will notify you if you are required to make an appearance in court at a later date. Under the terms of your policy, this firm is entitled to your complete cooperation throughout the handling of this litigation. Members of this law firm may desire to discuss the lawsuit with you. They will notify you when they desire you to call at their office. Please comply with all requests the law firm may make.

Because the amount claimed against you in this suit is in excess of the protection afforded by this policy, there may be a personal liability for damages on your part. In view of your possible personal liability you may wish to retain an attorney of your own choosing, at your own expense, to represent you personally and to appear in this matter, in addition to the law firm we have selected and will compensate.

It may be necessary to contact you on short notice. We request that you immediately notify this office, as well as the attorneys designated above, as to any change in your present address or telephone number, even though it may be a temporary change.

Defense counsel will do its best to keep you advised of all developments in your case. We appreciate your cooperation and look forward to working with you.

Should you have any questions, please feel free to contact either myself or the defense counsel selected to defend this lawsuit.

____

(Claim Representative)
(Telephone Number)

bcc: Attorney

Exhibit 3-4
Excess Letter 2

DATE

INSURED OR DRIVER'S NAME AND ADDRESS

RE: CLAIM

DEAR (INSURED, DRIVER):

You have been named as a defendant in a lawsuit which was filed in ___(COURT)___. Our policy, ___(NUMBER)___, provides for your defense in this action. We have requested that ___(ATTORNEY'S NAME, ADDRESS AND PHONE)___ take charge of your defense. This law firm is well qualified in negligence law, so your interests will be thoroughly protected within the limits of the policy. Our company will pay for the cost of your defense.

The amount asked for by the person suing you is ___$ (AMOUNT)___. Your insurance policy limit is ___$ (AMOUNT)___. This means your policy limit is not high enough to cover the amount for which the other party is asking.

If a judgment against you should be made for an amount in excess of your policy limit, you would be personally responsible for the excess amount. You may want to retain another attorney at your own expense to handle the uncovered portion of this lawsuit. If you wish, you may associate your own personal attorney with the law firm named above which will be providing your defense. You have a right to do this and our company and the law firm in charge of your defense will extend full cooperation to you.

In addition, the suit is seeking punitive damages which are not covered under your insurance policy. As a result, you may wish to have your own personal attorney handle this portion of the lawsuit for you.

Please do not give anyone a statement or discuss this lawsuit with anyone other than a representative of our company or counsel for your defense. We request that you extend your cooperation to the attorney selected for your defense who will be contacting you shortly.

It will be very important for us to be able to locate you when the need arises. Please keep myself and defense counsel advised of your current address and phone number.

Defense counsel will do its best to keep you advised of all developments in your case. We appreciate your cooperation and look forward to working with you.

Should you have any questions, please feel free to contact either myself or the defense counsel selected to defend this lawsuit.

____
(Claim Representative)
(Telephone Number)

bcc: Attorney

Punitive Damage Suits

In a growing number of lawsuits, the complaint includes a count for punitive damages as well as compensatory damages. Whether coverage is available under liability insurance to pay for punitive damage claims depends on the laws or court decisions of the state in question.

The fact that the term "damages" is not defined in standard liability insurance policies has led some courts to hold that "punitive damages" are as much a part of damages as compensatory damages and, therefore, are insurable. Other courts have reasoned that to make punitive damages insurable defeats their purpose of punishing the wrongdoer by allowing the wrongdoer to transfer responsibility to an insurer. For this reason, these courts have held that it is against public policy to allow the assessment of such damages to be insurable. In still other states, no position has been taken on the insurability of punitive damages.

In states where statutes or court decisions hold that punitive damages are *not* insurable, the insurer must advise the insured who is a defendant in a lawsuit seeking punitive damages, that the policy does not cover such damages. Ordinarily, the suit will contain a count for general damages, which is covered, and a count for punitive damages. The insurer has a duty to defend its insured with respect to the count for general damages, but not the count seeking punitive damages. The insured must be advised that the insurer is under no obligation to pay for punitive damages or defend the punitive damage count. The insured must also be advised that he or she has a right to retain personal counsel for protection against the claim for punitive damages. (Sample Excess Letter 2, shown in Exhibit 3-4 paragraph 4, in particular, demonstrates how this can be handled.)

This concludes the discussion of the importance and meaning of coverage. The next chapter concentrates on the second step in the adjusting process, that of determining legal liability.

Chapter Notes

1. Ronald A. Anderson, *Couch on Insurance* 2d 15:73 (Rochester, N.Y. The Lawyers Co-operative Publishing Company 1959), pp. 776–782.
2. Gerard P. Harney, "A Little Known—But Crucial—Decision," *The National Underwriter,* Property and Casualty Insurance Edition, 26 March 1982, p. 19.
3. Harney, p. 19.
4. Dorothy H. Dey, "Recent Insurance Cases," *For The Defense,* November 1982, p. 10.
5. *The Ohio Underwriter* carried an interesting editorial on this subject in which two judges debated the application of *stare decisis.* The editorial quoted one Ohio Supreme Court justice who expressed frustration at the threat to the stability of the law brought about by changes in the composition of the high court created by the election process. (Ohio elects, rather than appoints, its Supreme Court justices.) Suggesting that if *stare decisis* is only valid under the condition of a non-changing pattern of the membership of the court, that is..."hardly a satisfactory condition of stability of the law upon which lower courts and practitioners in Ohio may reasonably rely." "Important Supreme Court Election," *The Ohio Underwriter,* June 1982, p. 60.
6. Much of the material on reservation of rights letters was culled from a talk by our associate, John B. Melvin, State Auto Claims Counsel, before company claim managers in September, 1983.
7. An excellent article on reservation of rights and nonwaiver agreements appeared in *UPDATE,* Summer 1983, a publication of Underwriters Adjusting Company, 180 Maiden Lane, New York, N.Y. 10038. The article, "Waiver and Estoppel: Creation and Prevention," was written by John H. Mauney, Claims Counsel and Administrative Assistant, Home Office Claims, of Underwriter Adjusting Company.

CHAPTER 4

The Meaning of Legal Liability

INTRODUCTION

Once coverage has been verified with respect to a particular claim, the equally serious task of determining legal liability must begin. This chapter addresses the concepts and issues that must be understood and resolved before a proper determination of legal liability can be made.

Although an extensive knowledge of law is not necessary in order for adjusters to make liability decisions, some basic knowledge of the law, particularly tort law, is essential. Adjusters should work toward developing and expanding their knowledge of the law as it relates to their jobs as claim adjusters. This entails keeping abreast of the latest court decisions and legislation in their particular jurisdictions which may have an impact on their insureds' legal liabilities.

An individual can become legally responsible or legally liable by *negligence*, by *contract* or by *statute*. In order to get a clearer perspective on how one becomes legally liable, it is necessary to understand the meaning and relationships of concepts such as *common law* and *statutory law*, *civil* and *criminal* law, and *torts* and *negligence*.

COMMON AND STATUTORY LAW

Every person possesses certain legal rights granted by common law and statutory law. These include very basic rights such as the right to liberty, reputation, and personal and property protection as well as the right of privacy and the right to vote.

Common law originated in England as unwritten law and was

brought to America during the colonization period. It was developed and expanded during the course of American history. Essentially, common law consists of a body of principles based on customs and usages that have been adopted by society. It also includes court decisions that have recognized and followed these customs and usages over the years. Common law also is referred to as *case* law or *precedent* law.

By contrast, statutory law is *codified* law enacted by state legislatures or by Congress. It expresses the will of the people through their elected officials. Statutory law may amend the principles of common law. Workers' compensation laws, no-fault auto insurance laws, and some comparative negligence laws are examples of statutory laws that have revised common law.

CRIMINAL AND CIVIL LAW

The fact that every individual possesses legal rights based on common and statutory law imposes certain duties on every person to avoid harm to others. When these legal rights are violated, the injured party is entitled to restitution. The act violating an individual's legal rights may be criminal or civil in nature. *Criminal law* is designed to protect the well-being of society at large; because of the harm to the public welfare which results from criminal activity, government takes responsibility for prosecuting and punishing the wrongdoer. A person convicted of a crime—murder, arson, or reckless driving for example,—may be imprisoned or fined, or may incur both of these penalties. In a criminal case, the victim receives no financial compensation.

In *civil law,* the focus is on the violation of an individual's *private* rights due to the breach of certain duties owed that individual by another. Unlike criminal law, remedies in a civil action are provided for the injured party in the form of *money damages.* Insurance claim people are concerned primarily with civil law, not criminal law, but occasionally the two interact in claim situations. Because of this interaction, claim people need to be able to distinguish between civil and criminal law to the extent that the differences may affect coverage or legal liability. For example, a criminal act that results in bodily injury or property damage ordinarily activates the intentional injury or damage exclusion in liability insurance policies. In addition, a violation of a statute may be so improper that it is automatically considered negligence without regard to whether due care was exercised. This idea will be expanded subsequently when *negligence per se* is discussed.

TORTS

Acts or omissions, not including contracts, which violate the private rights or standards of human conduct established by common and certain statutory laws to protect individual rights are called *torts.* A tort is a *civil* wrong that results in injury or damage to another for which recovery in money damages is the remedy. The wrongdoer, or person who violates these legal rights or standards, is called a "tortfeasor." (Civil wrongs can arise from a *contract* as well as a tort. Unlike tort liability, which is a liability imposed by law, contractual liability is voluntarily assumed by a person. Both of these civil wrongs can make an individual legally liable and insurance coverage can be provided by liability insurance. Practically speaking, adjusters will deal primarily with civil wrongs arising from torts rather than contracts.)

An act that violates another's legal rights may be both a crime and a tort. If one person assaults another, the act of assault is a crime for which the person may be prosecuted by a governmental authority. It also is a civil wrong or tort for which money damages may be recovered by the injured party. Similarly, the theft of an auto is both a crime (larceny) and a tort (conversion). In addition, vehicular homicide or manslaughter can result in the motorist's being prosecuted for a crime as well as being sued for tortious or negligent conduct in a civil action for damages by the estate of the deceased.

It needs to be emphasized that criminal and civil actions are separate and distinct matters; that is, they are handled by separate legal actions at separate trials. In addition, the degree of proof necessary to establish a case differs in a criminal and civil action. In a criminal action, the government must establish its case against the wrongdoer *beyond a reasonable doubt* while in a civil action, the injured party need only establish his or her case by the *preponderance of the evidence.*

Although it has been stated that an act that violates a legal right can be both a crime and a tort, certainly not all torts are crimes. In fact, ordinary negligence or carelessness, the most common type of tort that claim people will encounter, is not criminal.

Types of Torts

There are three kinds or classes of torts: *intentional, strict liability* (liability without fault), and *negligence.*

Intentional Tort The person committing an intentional tort actually intends to cause injury or damage. It is a deliberate act.

Examples of intentional torts include *assault* (placing a person in fear of bodily harm); *battery* (actual infliction of bodily harm); *defamation* (wrongful injuring of another's reputation without justification), including libel (defamation conveyed by sight, i.e., written word, newspapers, photos, etc.) and *slander* (defamation conveyed by speech, i.e., made orally); *malicious prosecution* (where prosecution is started without probable cause); and *conversion* (wrongful taking of another's property).

Insurance protection for intentional torts is not provided in standard liability insurance policies. However, coverage for some intentional torts can be obtained by the purchase of a *personal injury coverage* endorsement. These endorsements are not necessarily uniform by insurer and the scope of coverage may vary depending upon the applicable exclusions and should be scrutinized carefully by adjusters.

Strict Liability (Liability without Fault) In this case, liability exists regardless of fault or negligence. The law generally takes the view that where an activity is extremely dangerous to the public, liability for injury or damage arising out of such activity will be imposed even though there may be no negligence on the part of the person conducting the dangerous activity. Strict liability generally applies to ultrahazardous activities such as blasting operations, storage of explosives, or the keeping of wild animals. It also is applicable to products liability claims under some circumstances. In many states, the owner of a dog that bites someone is subject to strict liability. Claims based on strict liability are insurable.

Negligence This is the most significant area of tort law from the standpoint of liability claim handling. While it is true that adjusters will handle claims where an insured has become legally responsible by contract and by statute, the great majority of liability claims involve tort liability. Furthermore, of the three classes of torts, negligence is by far the most common one which adjusters will encounter.

It must be kept in mind that the terms "tort" and "negligence" are not synonymous. *Tort* is a broader term encompassing negligence as merely one of three kinds of torts. In addition, adjusters need to make a distinction between "intentional tort" and "negligence." Intentional injury or damage is not negligence. Negligence is equivalent to carelessness or the lack of proper care. It is carelessness *without* the intent to injure.

LEGAL LIABILITY BASED ON NEGLIGENCE

Negligence is the failure to exercise the degree of care required of a reasonably prudent person in any given situation. Legal liability arises when negligence results in injury or damage to another. Stated in another way, negligence is an act (or failure to act) which violates a right recognized by common or statutory law. A cause of action for negligence arises when carelessness or neglect on the part of one person causes injury or damage to another.

The test or standard against which the acts or omissions of an individual are measured is the "reasonably prudent person" standard. This standard will, of course, vary according to the circumstances of an accident, but it has proved quite workable in actual practice. If, in a given case, it can be said that a person failed to act in a manner in which a reasonably prudent person would have acted under the same circumstances—or acted in a manner in which a reasonably prudent person would *not* have acted under the same circumstances—the person is said to be negligent. The claim adjuster is continually comparing the actions of the parties to an accident against this reasonably prudent person standard in determining liability in a particular claim.

Elements of Negligence

In describing the various factors that need to be considered in determining negligence or legal liability, it is appropriate to begin in a general manner with the elements of negligence. In order to establish liability for negligence, the general rule is that the claimant, or the person making the claim, must demonstrate that the following four elements were present:

1. a legal duty was owed,
2. a careless breach of that duty occurred,
3. a causal relationship or connection between the negligent act and the resulting injury or damage, and
4. damages (bodily injury or property damage) occurred as a result of the breach of duty.

Legal Duty The duty owed arises from the standards of human conduct established by law to protect legal rights. Put simply, the duty referred to here is the duty to use care in one's activities so as to avoid harm to others.

Breach of Duty In order to determine whether a legal duty was breached, the claim person must measure the actions or omissions of the parties to an accident against the "reasonably prudent person" standard described earlier. As will be explained later in these pages, the degree of care required will vary according to the circumstances of the particular accident.

Causal Relationship—Proximate Cause The fact that a duty was owed and subsequently breached by the wrongdoer does not necessarily mean that the wrongdoer was negligent. There must be a direct causal relationship or connection between the breach of duty and the resulting injury or damage. Once causal relationship is established, the negligent act or omission can be said to be the *proximate cause* of the injury or damage. Proximate cause is a particularly important concept in negligence. An injured party cannot recover unless the negligent act is the proximate cause of the resulting injury or damage.

A cause is proximate when it sets in motion the chain of events that result in the loss without the intervention of any unforeseeable, new, or independent force. The proximate cause is that which immediately causes the injury and without which the injury would not have occurred. It is the efficient or dominant cause—the one that necessarily sets the other causes in motion. There must be a natural and unbroken chain of causation from the negligent act to the infliction of injury or damage in order for the insured's negligence to be considered the proximate cause of that injury or damage. In short, a cause is considered to be the proximate cause if it is shown to have led to the loss and no intervening act occurs which is more directly responsible for the loss.[1]

A common test for determining proximate cause is the "but for" rule. If no damage would have occurred *but for* the insured's negligence, then the insured's negligence is the proximate cause of the damage. The question that can be asked is: If the insured's negligent act is eliminated, would injury or damage have been sustained? If injury or damage would have resulted even in the absence of the insured's act, then the insured's negligent act was *not* the proximate cause.

If the insured, while backing his car into the garage, bumped the next door neighbor, causing him to trip over the lawnmower he was pushing and break his arm, the insured's negligence would be the proximate cause of the neighbor's injury. But if the insured were backing up and stopped to let the neighbor pass, and the neighbor simply tripped over the lawnmower due to his own carelessness, the insured's backing of the vehicle, which may have momentarily distracted the neighbor did not cause him to fall. The proximate cause of the injury is the neighbor's carelessness.

The but for test, while helpful in most cases, has limited value when multiple parties and contributory acts of negligence are involved.[2] Where two motorists collide in an intersection and one vehicle is forced by the impact into a parked car, the but for rule can lead to a position that the negligence of neither driver individually caused the accident. If the negligent act of the first motorist is eliminated, then the accident would not have occurred but for the negligence of the second motorist. The first motorist can argue, therefore, that his or her negligence was *not* the proximate cause of the damage to the parked car. On the other hand, the second motorist can make the same argument to his favor. The result is that the owner of the damaged parked car cannot recover from either motorist.

To avoid this unreasonable result, the *substantial factor* test was adopted by the courts. In the above example, application of the substantial factor test would hold that neither driver could escape liability by arguing that his or her act alone did not cause the accident because the accident would have resulted anyway by the negligence of the other driver. On the contrary, each driver is liable for the damage he or she causes even though the other driver is reponsible for part of the damage. In short, both drivers are answerable for damage caused by their combined conduct.

Illustrations of Proximate Cause. In a case where the insured, while driving a covered auto, strikes the rear of the claimant vehicle causing damage to it and injury to the claimant, there is little question that the insured's negligent act is the proximate cause of the loss. The questions that should come to the adjuster's mind are:

> What is the duty owed?
> Was there a careless breach of that duty?
> Was the careless breach of the duty the proximate cause of the accident?
> Did the damages result from the breach of the duty?

These questions are relatively easy to answer in this case. The insured owes other people using the highway the duty to operate his or her vehicle in a safe manner so as to avoid harm to others. The means in which the insured struck the claimant makes it pretty clear, in the absence of any extenuating circumstances such as a sudden stop or backing up by the claimant, that the insured breached a duty owed the claimant. Likewise, proximate cause and damages are easy to establish in this case. The adjuster merely needs to confirm the damage and injury, either by visual inspection or by securing a repair estimate or appraisal and a medical report or bill. In short, the insured was negligent in causing this accident and the claimant will be paid for his or her damages.

As a practical matter, most claims are more complex and establishing negligence is not simple. Suppose that the adjuster receives an accident report indicating that a claim is being made against the insured for negligence in causing the claimant to lose control of her vehicle and collide with a parked car. The report shows that the claimant's vehicle sustained property damage and that the claimant sustained a head injury. The insured indicates that there was no contact between the insured and claimant vehicles. Preliminary investigation reveals that the insured ran a stop sign while the claimant had no traffic controls. The insured states that he ran the stop sign but did not realize an accident had occurred until he "heard" the collision of the claimant's vehicle with the parked car. At this point, the adjuster may begin to form a picture in his mind of probable liability on the insured's part.

Suppose, however, that subsequent investigation by the adjuster leads to the discovery of an independent eyewitness who states that she was standing at the intersection waiting to cross the street when the accident occurred. Thus, she had a good view of the entire accident. Specifically, the witness states that she saw the insured and claimant approaching the intersection at a right angle and that the insured, having failed to stop at the sign, entered the intersection about two seconds before the claimant. But the witness adds that prior to entering the intersection, she saw the claimant driver drop a lit cigarette and, in attempting to find and extinguish the cigarette, the claimant took her eyes off the road and collided with a parked car immediately after she crossed the intersection.

Although the claimant alleged that the insured's running the stop sign put her into an emergency situation causing her to lose control of the vehicle and strike the parked car, the eyewitness testimony from a disinterested witness seemingly proves otherwise. Clearly, this presents the question: was the proximate cause of the accident the insured's running the stop sign or the claimant's dropping the lit cigarette and losing control of her car?

The questions of causal relationship and proximate cause are equally important in "fall down" cases. For example, a homeowner owes a duty to a social guest to refrain from affirmative acts of negligence and to warn of any known hidden dangers of which the guest may be unaware. If a guest falls on the kitchen floor and breaks her arm, the immediate question that must be answered is: What caused the guest to fall?

Assume that the kitchen floor was covered by linoleum and that the investigation reveals that a small part of the linoleum was loose and turned up and that this was partially hidden from view because of overhanging cabinets.

If the guest attributes her fall to the condition of the linoleum, known to the insured, but of which she was unaware, it is apparent that the homeowner's negligence is responsible for the injury to the guest.

Stated precisely, the homeowner breached the duty to warn that was owed the guest and the breach of the duty led to the guest's injury.

On the other hand, if the guest attributes her fall to reasons other than the defect in the floor, such as tripping over her own feet, there no longer is a connection between the breach of the duty to warn and the resulting injury. In other words, the breach of the duty was not the proximate cause of the guest's injury.

Unless the four elements of negligence are present in a claim, legal liability does not exist. This is why it is so important for adjusters to conduct a good investigation on claims they are assigned. The extent of the investigation will depend upon the nature of the damages and injury as well as the complexity of the accident itself.

The question of causal relationship also can be a factor with respect to the *injury* being claimed as a result of an accident. The claimant with a chronic back problem or other pre-existing injury may claim that the first sign of the injury came when the insured struck him or her in the rear. While the insured will be responsible for aggravating the claimant's injury if, in fact, the impact rekindled an old injury, the insured will not be responsible for the injury if it can be confirmed that no aggravation and no further injury resulted from the impact. Practically speaking, claims involving alleged back injuries or other injuries which may have preexisted, must be thoroughly and imaginatively investigated in an effort to determine whether causal relationship exists. This entails such steps as obtaining a medical history on the claimant, checking employment records and background, conducting an extensive activity check, obtaining a comprehensive medical exam, and so on.

Another situation concerning causal relationship that creates occasional confusion, especially for new claim people, is that involving illegally parked cars. Suppose the insured parks his or her car in a no-parking zone near an intersection. Later, two speeding cars approaching the intersection collide when they simultaneously reach the intersection, and one of the cars is pushed into the insured's parked car. The insured will not be held responsible for the accident for parking his car in an illegal manner. The proximate cause of the accident was not the illegal parking of the car but the excessive speed and carelessness of the two motorists who collided in the intersection.

On the other hand, where the insured parks too close to an intersection in violation of a parking ordinance, thereby blocking the oncoming motorist's view of a stop sign, the insured may be responsible for an accident that can be attributed to the insured's improper parking of the car. If it can be said that the proximate cause of the accident was the improperly parked car which blocked the motorist's view of the stop sign, the insured will be held legally liable for damages sustained by the claimant in the accident.

Intervening Cause. In order to understand the concept of proximate cause, the claim person must be able to distinguish it from that of *intervening cause.* An example should help to clarify this distinction.

Suppose the insured runs a red light and collides with an oil truck and shortly thereafter, the oil, which begins leaking from the truck as a result of the impact, ignites spontaneously and causes serious damage to nearby buildings. The insured's negligence is considered the proximate cause of the damage to the buildings as well as the damage to the oil truck.

However, suppose that in another case, the same impact took place but that thirty minutes later, cleanup is almost completed and the danger of a flash fire no longer exists. A bystander lights a match and carelessly throws it into the remaining oil which had accumulated from the impact and the oil ignites and the ensuing fire damages a nearby building. In this case, the insured's negligence was the proximate cause of the damage to the oil truck, but it was not the proximate cause of the fire damage to the building. *An intervening cause,* the bystander's throwing the lit match, actually caused the building damage. If it can be said that *without* this foreseeable intervening act, the fire damage to the building would *not* have occurred, then the intervening act becomes a new, independent cause and the proximate cause of the building damage.

Another example of intervening cause might involve a post-accident situation where a claimant who was not injured in the accident is out of his or her vehicle after the impact and is struck by a passing motorist. The claimant cannot attribute the injury caused by the passing motorist as being proximately caused by the driver who caused the first accident. The striking of the claimant by the passing motorist was a new and independent act or intervening cause which then becomes the proximate cause of the claimant's injury.

In summary, just because the insured may be negligent and the claimant has sustained damages, it cannot automatically be assumed that the insured's negligence was the proximate cause of the claimant's damages. A good investigation is essential in order to connect proximate cause and damages and, when appropriate, to rule out possible preexisting injuries or discover any relevant intervening cause.

Damages Even though the first three elements of negligence are present, without damages there can be no claim. An insured may have struck the claimant's vehicle in the rear, but if the impact was light and no damage or injury resulted, the claimant cannot recover from the insured.

In claims involving foreign substances in food products, sometimes the claimant will make a claim but will have neither consumed the product nor gotten sick. If this is confirmed in a statement, the adjuster can decline the claim on the grounds that no injury was sustained by the claimant. This can be a sensitive situation and the adjuster must employ empathy and tact in declining the claim. It is a fairly common practice in such situations for the insured food manufacturer to offer additional food products to the claimant at no charge anticipating that this will rectify the situation. (The subject of damages is covered in Chapter 5)

In summary, the four elements of negligence—legal duty owed, careless breach of that duty, causal relationship/proximate cause, and damages—must be present before an individual will be considered legally liable based on negligence. Adjusters should condition themselves to look for these four elements in every liability claim they encounter.

Determining Negligence in Premises Liability Claims

The premises "fall-down" case involves some additional factors that must be considered in determining whether the premises owner is legally liable for injuries sustained by others while on the premises.

Status of Claimant The owner of property—a private dwelling as well as a commercial property—is responsible for exercising a certain degree of care in maintaining the premises so that people who enter the premises are not exposed to unreasonable risks of injury. Essentially, in the majority of jurisdictions, the degree of care owed by a property owner is based on the *status* of the person on the premises. People on the property of others are classified under one of three categories: (1) business invitee, (2) licensee (social guest), and (3) trespasser.

Business Invitee. A *business invitee* is one who is on the premises or in the building by either express or implied invitation. The person usually is there for a business purpose in which some financial benefit might be received by the owner. The possibility, not the actuality, of financial benefit to the owner is sufficient to make the person a business invitee.

With regard to commercial buildings or retail stores, examples of business invitees include customers (or potential customers), carpenters, or installers who are called to the premises by the owner to perform the work of their trade. Salespeople who are invited on the premises or who are there either by appointment or otherwise also are considered invitees.

With regard to a private home, individuals who enter the premises to render a service are considered invitees. This would include mail carriers, delivery people, meter readers, and so on.

The premises owner owes a business invitee the duty of ordinary and reasonable care to keep the premises in a reasonably safe condition. This means that the owner must make reasonable inspections of the premises. In addition, the owner is under a duty to warn the invitee of any latent (hidden) defect known by the owner of which the invitee may be unaware. Finally, the owner must refrain from any affirmative acts of negligence which might cause injury.

A *licensee* is on the property for his or her own convenience and is not forbidden to be there. With respect to private residences, the social guest is probably the most common example of a licensee. With respect to a retail store, a person coming in merely to use the restroom or to pass through the store to get to the rear parking lot (if these facts are established through investigation) is a licensee.

The duty owed a licensee is less than that owed to a business invitee. The premises owner owes a licensee or social guest a duty to warn of any latent defects and to refrain from affirmative acts of negligence. A licensee takes the premises as he or she finds them and the owner is under no duty to prepare for the licensee's arrival by inspecting the premises.

While a premises owner owes a duty to both invitees and licensees to warn of any defect on the premises, the duty does not apply to the licensee, unless the owner has notice of the defect. "Notice" is a particularly significant factor in investigating premises liability claims involving licensees. Without notice of a defect, there can be no duty to warn of the defect; there is no duty to inspect as is the case of a business invitee.

Trespasser. A *trespasser* is a person who is on one's premises without permission or legal right to be there. A person who cuts through another's fenced yard will be considered a trespasser, as long as this has not been done repeatedly for a long time and become accepted by the owner. A hunter on "posted" grounds is another example. In general, the owner of land is not liable for harm to trespassers caused by failure to put the land in a reasonably safe condition or to carry on his or her activities so as not to endanger them.

The landowner has no responsibility for defective conditions he or she did not know about, even though their existence could have been discovered by ordinary inspection. No duty of inspection is owed to a trespasser. In addition, there is no duty to alter a dangerous natural condition for the benefit of trespassers even though their presence on the land can be anticipated or is known. If, for example, a landowner sees a trespasser about to walk into an excavation, he or she is under no obligation to warn the trespasser or to aid the trespasser if he or she falls into the excavation. However, certain exceptions to this rule have developed:

1. If the presence of a trespasser is discovered, the landowner commonly is required to exercise reasonable care as to any active operations the owner may carry on, and possibly as to any known highly dangerous artificial condition on the land.
2. If the landowner knows that trespassers frequent a particular place or area, he or she is required to exercise reasonable care as to activities and highly dangerous artificial conditions.
3. The landowner usually has the duty to exercise reasonable care in regard to trespassing children under the following conditions:
    - the premises involves an unreasonable risk of harm,
    - the child does not understand or appreciate the danger, and
    - the utility of maintaining a condition is slight as compared to the risk.

This last exception is based in part on the *doctrine of attractive nuisance,* which provides that a landowner owes reasonable care to trespassing children in regard to something on the land that meets the following conditions:

- it is attractive to children,
- it is artificial and uncommon, and
- children could be protected against danger by exercise of reasonable care by the landowner.

A swimming pool is the usual example of an attractive nuisance.

This situation was recognized in many states through the doctrine of *attractive nuisance.* Courts of these states take the position that a property owner on whose land such potentially dangerous conditions exist, owes a duty to children, even though they may actually be trespassers, to take precautions to protect them from injury arising out of such conditions. In other words, where the property owner knows or should know, through the exercise of reasonable care, that children are likely to trespass on his premises, he will be responsible for the failure to take the necessary precautions to avoid unreasonable harm to these children. Generally, the duty does not apply to natural conditions which exist on the land.

It is important that adjusters be aware that a person's status can change while on a particular premises. For example, an individual may come into a store to browse, and at that point, is an invitee. (As noted earlier, the mere *possibility* that a purchase might be made is sufficient to classify the individual as a business invitee.) Suppose that moments later, the same individual gets curious and follows an employee carrying a mannequin through the store. The employee, who is followed by the shopper, goes through doors marked "Employees Only," and the shopper follows. What is the shopper's status now? If you said *trespasser,* you would be correct. He or she is considered a trespasser who has no business and no right being in the stockroom having ignored a clearly visible sign posted to keep customers out. It is not always easy to determine a claimant's status and detailed questioning of the parties involved in the accident by the adjuster will frequently be necessary.

Change in Significance of Claimant's "Status" Although determining the claimant's status is important in deciding the ultimate question of legal liability, the courts in several states have mitigated the significance of the status distinctions of invitee, licensee, and trespasser. In rejecting the claimant's *status* as the primary basis for determining the degree of care owed, and ultimately legal liability, the courts have focused on "foreseeability" and reasonable care as more proper criteria.

In other words, if it is reasonably foreseeable that a person may enter the premises, the owner must exercise reasonable care for that person's safety. In some cases, courts have indicated that status will still be a consideration in determining negligence, but status will not be the sole consideration.

The imposition of a duty of reasonable care does not appear to create an unfair or unreasonable burden on the property owner—especially when the person's status will still apparently have some relevance in determining negligence.

Maintenance and Control of Premises Another important consideration in handling premises liability fall down cases, especially commercial cases, is determining who is responsible for maintenance and control of the premises. The owner may lease the premises to another party who may have this responsibility. In an owner-tenant relationship, the adjuster must obtain a copy of the lease, if one exists, in order to determine who has responsibility for maintenance and control and for repairs to the premises.

In summary, determining the claimant's status (less significant in some jurisdictions than in others) and responsibility for maintenance and control of the premises are two essential elements of any commercial premises liability investigation. Investigation of such claims is discussed in more detail in Chapter 7.

Other Factors Considered in Determining Negligence

Other factors to be considered in determining whether an individual is negligent are the *degree of care* required, *foreseeability, burden of proof,* and *negligence per se.*

Degrees of Care As noted earlier, legal liability for negligence is based on the failure to exercise the care a reasonably prudent person would exercise under similar circumstances. The general standard or test then is ordinarily that of "reasonable care." What is "reasonable" is a variable standard that depends upon the circumstances of the accident. The *degree of care* required will vary specifically according to the particular conditions existing at the time of the accident. It also could be affected by any special characteristics of the person whose conduct is being measured.

For example, suppose a motorist is driving his or her car at a speed of forty-five m.p.h. in a forty-five m.p.h. zone and is involved in an accident with a second motorist. From this limited information, it is impossible to tell which motorist is negligent. The fact that the first motorist was driving within the speed limit is not enough to conclude that he or she is free of negligence. The circumstances of the accident must be investigated to arrive at the cause.

Changing the situation somewhat, suppose the road was covered with ice and a group of young school children was playing unsupervised at the corner as the motorist approached. Would a reasonably prudent person drive at a speed of 45 m.p.h. under these circumstances? Here again, the adjuster must compare the actions of the parties to an accident against the reasonably prudent person standard. The degree of care required will vary according to the circumstances surrrounding the accident. Driving at forty-five m.p.h. in a forty-five m.p.h. zone may be quite reasonable in some circumstances while it may constitute negligence in others.

Generally, the reasonably prudent person standard applies to all people regardless of the level of intelligence or education. A person with physical limitations, say a lack of depth perception or slower reaction time than normal, ordinarily is not permitted a lesser standard of care than the reasonable person standard. As a result of these physical limitations, such a person simply must exercise greater care to meet the standard of reasonable care.

However, children represent a special case. Ordinarily, they are held to a duty to exercise that degree of care which could be reasonably expected of people with their age, intelligence, and experience. Courts in some states have held that children under the age of seven are incapable of being negligent. Children between the ages of seven and fourteen may be charged with negligence if it can be established that they possess the intelligence to exercise reasonable care. In other words, the child's actions will be compared to other children between the ages of seven and fourteen to determine the standard of reasonable care. Children over the age of fourteen are judged in the same manner as adults.

A person with special skills or knowledge will be measured against the reasonable person possessing similar special skills. A medical doctor, therefore, must act in the manner in which a reasonable person with the knowledge and training of a medical doctor would act under the circumstances. If the doctor's actions were those of a reasonable person not having this special medical skill or knowledge, the doctor's actions would be considered improper and negligent.

The law also can be classified in terms of degrees of care or negligence. These classifications consist of *slight negligence, ordinary negligence,* and *gross negligence.*

Slight negligence refers to a situation in which a person has a duty to exercise a *high* degree of care and has failed to do so, which results in an accident. A situation in which a person is engaged in a potentially dangerous activity that exposes others to greater harm than they would be exposed to under normal, less dangerous conditions is an example.

Ordinary negligence refers to the failure to exercise reasonable care, or the care a reasonably prudent person would exercise under similar circumstances. It refers to the care required under normal circumstances as opposed to the care required when a person is engaged in dangerous activities.

Gross negligence refers to the failure to exercise even slight care. It implies a greater degree of carelessness than ordinary negligence as well as a total lack of concern for the consequences of one's actions. Gross negligence is a factor in cases involving automobile guest statutes, discussed later in this chapter.

Foreseeability Another factor that affects the determination of negligence is *foreseeability.* Generally, an individual is considered negligent when injury or damage which is reasonably foreseeable or reasonably anticipated occurs. On the other hand, where injury or damage cannot be reasonably anticipated, the individual ordinarily will not be charged with negligence. An individual's responsibility is limited to those situations the reasonably prudent person can foresee under similar circumstances.

For example, a person driving a new car who is involved in an accident when the brakes suddenly fail will not be considered negligent. The sudden brake failure could not have been reasonably anticipated under the circumstances. However, suppose that the car in question was an older car and the last time it was serviced, the owner was told by the mechanic that the brake line was substantially worn and in need of replacement. Despite this warning, the owner continued to drive the car for several weeks. One day, while driving within the speed limit on a main thoroughfare, the brakes suddenly failed and caused the driver to lose control of the car and hit a pedestrian. Obviously, in this case, it cannot be said that the brake failure could not have been anticipated.

A homeowner also is under a duty to reasonably anticipate or foresee that persons entering the premises may by exposed to certain risks. If the carpet inside the front door, for example, is loose and bunches up every time the door is opened, creating a risk that a guest might trip or fall, the homeowner must warn the guest of the risk. It is reasonably foreseeable that a guest could be injured as a result of this condition.

The concept of foreseeability actually places a limit on the scope of the reasonably prudent person standard. Suppose, for example, that two motorists collide in front of a retail store with the result that the gasoline tank of one of the cars explodes and several people, both in the cars and on the street, are injured. Due to the explosion damage to the retail store and the fact that debris from the impact blocks entrance to the store, a three-week shutdown with a substantial loss of earnings results.

When the owner learns of the extent of the damage and loss, he has a heart attack while a relative who invested in the business develops a bleeding ulcer he attributes to the loss of earnings caused by the accident. In addition, the owner's sister must cancel her scheduled Mexican vacation to be by her brother's side while he recuperates from the heart attack. She makes a claim for the sizable deposit she loses when her vacation is canceled. For which of these claims will the two motorists who caused the accident be responsible? Or put another way, how far does the "foreseeable zone of danger" extend?

It is reasonable to expect that both occupants of the vehicles as well as bystanders could be injured as a result of this accident in which a gasoline fire ensued from the impact. It also is reasonable to anticipate that a nearby business establishment might be damaged as a result. Modern day realities might even suggest the possibility, in at least some jurisdictions, that the "fright" injury or heart attack sustained by the business owner could be construed to be reasonably foreseeable under the circumstances. But beyond this point, we have transgressed the so-called "foreseeable zone of danger" within which the cause of an accident and resulting injury or damage can be reasonably connected. There must be a limit beyond which the courts will not connect cause and effect.

If the act is one which an individual should, in the exercise of ordinary care, have anticipated was likely to result in injury or damage to others, then the individual is liable for any injury or damage proximately resulting from it. This is true even though the individual could not have anticipated the particular nature of the injury which resulted. A person will be liable for the proximate results of his or her own acts, but not for remote damages or injury.

Burden of Proof Another important aspect of the determination of legal liability based on negligence involves the question of whose responsibility it is to prove negligence. Ordinarily, the person making the claim must prove his or her case. This means that the *burden of proof* is placed upon the claimant or, when the case is in suit, the plaintiff. The plaintiff must prove that the insured or defendant was negligent, the negligence was the proximate cause of the accident, and the injury or damage resulted from the accident. The plaintiff also must be able to demonstrate that he or she was not guilty of any contributory negligence which, depending upon the state, either bars or limits recovery by the plaintiff.

Under common law, contributory negligence on the part of the plaintiff is a bar to recovery. In states which have modified common law by installing *comparative negligence* laws, usually only substantial contributory negligence (50 percent or more) on the plaintiff's part will bar recovery. It must be emphasized, however, that there are different kinds of comparative negligence laws and the percentage of contributory negligence which will bar recovery varies by the kind of law in effect as well as by the particular state involved. (The subjects of contributory and comparative negligence are examined more closely later in the chapter.)

Unlike criminal actions where the prosecution must prove its case beyond a reasonable doubt, the plaintiff in a civil action needs only to prove his or her case by a *preponderance of the evidence.* This means that the weight of the evidence must be in favor of the plaintiff. Keep in mind that the four elements of negligence—duty owed, duty breached, proximate cause, and damages—must exist before legal liability based on negligence can be established. All of these elements must be present in convincing fashion before the plaintiff can prevail in the case. Not only must injury or damage be proved, but it must be shown to have been proximately caused by the defendant's negligence.

There are circumstantial evidence situations, however, where the burden of proof placed on the plaintiff, though not eliminated entirely, is minimized to a substantial degree. Specifically, cases in which the doctrine of *res ipsa loquitur* can be applied, lighten the plaintiff's burden of proof significantly. Translated, *res ipsa loquitur* means "the thing speaks for itself." Generally, it can be applied when an inference of negligence can be drawn from the circumstances of an accident and where the cause of the accident is not apparent. When *res ipsa loquitur* is applicable, the plaintiff need not prove specific acts of negligence against the defendent. Negligence may be inferred from the happening of the accident but the plaintiff must show that the following elements were present:

1. the accident was caused by an agency or instrumentality within the exclusive control of the defendant,
2. there was no contributory negligence on the part of the plaintiff,
3. the accident was a kind which ordinarily does not occur in the absence of negligence, and
4. there is no direct evidence as to the cause.

Suppose, for example, that a person is walking on the sidewalk in a moderately busy metropolitan community when suddenly a flower pot falls from a windowsill above her. The flower pot strikes the person on the head, causing serious injuries. Subsequently, the injured party determines the identity of the tenant in the building from whose window the flower pot fell and, through her attorney, institutes a lawsuit against this individual. If the plaintiff can show that (1) the flower pot was within the exclusive control of the defendant, (2) there was no contributory negligence on the plaintiff's part, (3) the accident would not have occurred in the absence of negligence, and (4) there is no direct evidence as to the cause, *res ipsa loquitur* will apply. Seemingly, the aforementioned elements can be established in this case which would make the doctrine applicable.

When *res ipsa loquitur* applies, there is a presumption that the defendant was negligent. However, the presumption may be rebutted by the defendant. If the defendant can show that either someone else was negligent, that the plaintiff was contributorily negligent, that the defendant did not have exclusive control of the instrument, or that the accident could have occurred without anyone's negligence, *res ipsa loquitur* will not be applied.

Essentially, the doctrine makes it somewhat easier for the plaintiff to establish his or her case. The doctrine has been held to apply in some jurisdictions to exploding bottle cases, collapsing buildings, falling elevators, and boiler explosions. Each case is different, however, and must be determined on its individual merits. *Res ipsa loquitur* is not necessarily an easy doctrine to apply and insurance defense counsel will usually fight its application strenuously.

Another area in which the plaintiff's burden of proof is minimized is in cases where dangerous or hazardous activities are conducted and legal liability is based on *strict liability.* In these cases, the plaintiff need not prove that the defendant was negligent, but merely has to show that injury or damage resulted from the dangerous activity.

Negligence Per Se Up to now, it has been emphasized that negligence must be proved by the plaintiff before the defendant can be held legally liable. Although this is the general rule, there are cases where negligence is automatically presumed *without* the necessity of proof. These cases usually involve either the violation of a statute, particularly traffic violations, or conduct which is so obviously imprudent in itself that there can be no question in the minds of reasonable persons that the act was negligent. Such a violation or imprudent conduct is said to constitute *negligence per se;* that is, negligence in and of itself, or as a matter of law, without the need for argument or proof. The principle of negligence per se applies when a violation of law causes an accident which the law was designed to prevent.

Though violations of law such as speeding, reckless driving, or running a stop sign may constitute negligence per se in some jurisdictions, it is wrong to assume that any violation of a statute or traffic code automatically creates negligence per se. As noted above, the violation of the law must have caused or contributed to an accident the law was designed to prevent. Specifically, when the injured party is within the class of people the statute is designed to protect, and sustains the type of injury contemplated by the statute, the violation generally constitutes negligence per se.[3] In such case, the wrongdoer is automatically considered negligent unless evidence can be found which would justify or excuse his or her actions.

However, simply because a person parks his or her car in a no parking zone and it is struck after two cars collide in a nearby intersection, does not mean that negligence per se applies. Such a situation will not constitute negligence per se unless it can be established that the illegally parked car was in some way the proximate cause of the intersection accident. (Recall the previous discussion about the car that was parked too close to the corner in violation of a statute, thereby blocking an oncoming motorist's view of the stop sign with the result that an accident occurred. If the no parking statute was designed to prevent such an accident, then the principle of negligence per se could very well apply.)

The same is true in cases where a car involved in an accident is not properly registered or a driver is unlicensed. Negligence cannot automatically be presumed in such cases. These laws usually are intended to raise revenue for the state and not necessarily to protect persons from harm on the highways. The fact that a vehicle was not registered or that a driver was not licensed *usually* has nothing to do with the cause of an accident.

The extent to which the principle of negligence per se will be applied depends upon the state in question. Most states follow the view that a violation of a statute that causes an accident the statute was designed to prevent constitutes negligence per se. Other states will not go quite this far but hold that the violation of a statute at least creates a presumption of negligence which can be rebutted with proof to the contrary. Still other states regard the violation of the statute merely as evidence of negligence; in other words, one factor to be considered in determining whether or not there was negligence.

One final comment about the violation of statutes is in order. Generally, the judgment or decision of a traffic court is not admissible in a related civil case where money damages are sought. Thus, a conviction in traffic court is not admissible in a civil case. There is, however, one significant exception to the general rule. In many jurisdictions, when an individual pleads guilty to a traffic offense in a traffic court proceeding, the *guilty plea* is admissible in the related civil case. It is particularly important, in light of this exception, that claim people refrain from ever advising an insured to plead guilty to a traffic offense. Aside from the obvious problem it can create for an insured who is a defendant in a related civil suit, advising an insured in this manner is equivalent to giving legal advice or practicing law, which adjusters are prohibited from doing. Adjusters should seek the advice of legal counsel when confronted with such questions.

LEGAL LIABILITY BASED ON CONTRACT AND STATUTE

Legal liability based on negligence has been examined in considerable detail in the foregoing pages. Legal liability based on contract was alluded to in Chapter 3 with respect to the discussion of coverage for damage to a rental car under the personal auto policy. As noted previously, liability based on negligence is a liability imposed by law while liability based on contract is voluntarily assumed by a person.

While the personal auto policy does not contain a contractual liability exclusion, standard general liability forms do contain such an exclusion. Since contractual assumption of liability by commercial insureds represents a substantial exposure, insurers are reluctant to provide the coverage without receiving a suitable additional premium to cover the increased exposure. Contractual liability insurance, therefore, is available by endorsement for an additional premium.

An example of legal liability based on statute can be found in state statutes that provide that parents are liable for willful or malicious damage to property of others committed by their children. Most states have enacted such statutes, which are subject to a limited amount of recovery. The provisions of the statutes vary from state to state and adjusters should be familiar with the specific statute in effect in their state. (Some of these statutes include bodily injury that is willfully caused by a child.)

That such claims are covered under homeowners policies, in spite of the intentional damage exclusion, requires some clarification. It is true that the child who intentionally damages the property of another is not covered. However, although the child intentionally caused the damage, the parents did not. Legal liability is imposed upon the parents by statute, and since they did not intentionally cause the damage, the exclusion would not apply to them. Thus, the homeowners policy, which covers the legal liability of the insured (in this case, the parents), will respond to such claims. As noted earlier, however, liability under these statutes is subject to a monetary limit and the insurer is liable only to the extent of that monetary limit.

Another example of liability imposed by statute can be found in what is called the "family purpose doctrine." This doctrine, which has been adopted by statute as well as by judicial decision in some states, holds essentially that the head of a family who owns a car used by a family member may be held responsible for the negligence of that family member. The doctrine was designed to assure that a financially responsible individual would be available to pay for damages. With the advent of uninsured motorists insurance and complusory auto insurance laws, this doctrine seemingly is not as necessary as it was in the past. In many states, the doctrine does not exist.

MAIN PRINCIPLES OF LAW AFFECTING LIABILITY CLAIM HANDLING

The preceding discussion concerning how one becomes legally responsible is intended to build the foundation upon which these basic concepts can be expanded. Starting with an examination of the various kinds of law, the elements of negligence, and the concepts of foreseeability, burden of proof, and negligence per se, the discussion now moves on to an explanation of the various doctrines and principles which modify and affect the application of the law of torts. In particular, the following principles or concepts will be examined: joint tortfeasor liability, vicarious liability, contributory negligence, comparative negligence, guest statutes, interspousal and intrafamily immunity, governmental immunity, and bailments.

Once these principles and their effect on claim handling are considered, the defenses which can be raised by an insured will be discussed. At that point, the imperfections of the tort liability system as well as the actual remedies which have been implemented to minimize the deficiencies in that system will be explored.

Joint Tortfeasor Liability

Injury or damage arising from negligence may be caused by two or more wrongdoers. When two or more individuals cause an accident that results in injury or damage to another, they are said to be "joint tortfeasors." Historically, a distinction was made between "joint" and "concurrent" liability. "Joint" liability technically refers only to situations where individuals act in concert and with common intent to cause an injury. "Concurrent" liability or negligence refers to situations where the independent or separate acts of two or more individuals concurrently (at the same time) produce a single accident which causes injury. Over time, the meaning of "joint tortfeasors" has taken on this latter, broader view involving concurrent negligence.

Generally, joint tortfeasors are jointly and severally liable for damages caused by their negligence. Thus, if driver 1 and driver 2 negligently collide at an intersection and the impact forces driver 1 to strike a house on the corner, the homeowner may recover his or her damages from either driver 1 or driver 2, or from both drivers together. If the homeowner decides to sue only driver 1 and makes a full recovery, the recovery extinguishes his or her cause of action. In effect, a full recovery from driver 1 also eliminates the homeowner's claim against driver 2. Once total damages are recovered, the claimant's cause of action ceases because recovery in excess of total damages is not permitted.

In short, joint and several liability means that the damaged party can recover his or her entire damages from either tortfeasor individually or from all tortfeasors together, but recovery can never be for more than the total damages. As a practical matter, plaintiff's attorneys usually will include all tortfeasors who could possibly be responsible for the accident in the lawsuit.

There is another type of situation in which two or more tortfeasors cause injury or damage which is referred to as "successive" rather than "concurrent" neligence. Put simply, successive tortfeasors are those whose independent acts injure the claimant *successively* or in quick succession. An example would be a case where a car is struck in relatively quick succession by two other cars. The damage to the first car was caused by successive independent tortfeasors and generally each tortfeasor will be jointly and severally liable for the total damages, unless the precise damage caused by each tortfeasor can be established.

With joint and several liability being the general rule, it is possible that one of several wrongdoers could end up paying for the entire claim. When a joint tortfeasor pays more than his or her proportionate share of a claim, that tortfeasor may be entitled to *contribution* from the other tortfeasors to the extent of the excess payment. This will depend upon the law in effect in the particular state in question.

Common law does not recognize a right of contribution among joint tortfeasors. This means that if a cause of action is brought against one of several joint tortfeasors and a judgment is recovered, the tortfeasor responding to the damages would have no cause of action against, or any right of contribution from, the other tortfeasors. However, many states have modified the common law through enactment of the *Uniform Contribution Among Tortfeasors Act* or some variation of this act. This statute creates a right among joint tortfeasors in favor of the joint tortfeasor making the payment. Such statutes vary somewhat from state to state and, understandably, claim people should be familiar with the statute in their state, if one exists.

Some states determine the amount of contribution on a comparative or percentage-of-fault basis while others use a mathematical or pro rata method of dividing the liability by the number of defendants. It usually matters little to the plaintiff how liability is apportioned when multiple tortfeasors are jointly and severally liable. The plaintiff may recover from either defendant or from all defendants, and is not particularly interested in which defendant pays what amount. Insurers, however, will look at percentages of fault in cases involving multiple defendants whom they insure either because the applicable contribution statute apportions liability on the basis of comparative fault or simply as a matter of convenience in resolving disputes.

In the previous example in which two cars collided in the intersection and the impact forced one car into a house, the two percentages of fault attributable to both drivers so that the homeowner's claim for damages can be resolved. The same process of attributing fault is exercised by insurance adjusters in multiple-car accidents involving injured passengers so that the passenger claim may be amicably settled.

Where one individual is compelled to pay damages caused by another solely on the basis of a relationship which existed between the two parties, the individual paying the damages is entitled to *indemnity* from the individual whose active negligence caused the damages. *Indemnity* must be distinguished from *contribution.* Indemnity involves a transfer of the *whole* loss from the passive tortfeasor to the tortfeasor actually responsible for the damages. The actively negligent party actually reimburses the nonnegligent party who has already paid the claim. On the other hand, *contribution* is a sharing of the loss between the joint tortfeasors based on the fact that they share responsibility for the accident.

Indemnity applies typically to situations in which one tortfeasor is *vicariously* liable for the negligence of another. Vicarious liability refers to a situation where the liability of one person is imputed to another who is not guilty of active negligence. In an employer-employee relationship, for example, the employer who has paid damages caused by an employee's negligence is entitled to indemnity from the employee. (The doctrine of vicarious liability is examined in detail in the following pages.)

Frequently, one joint tortfeasor will be in a better position than the others to pay the claim. An employer-employee situation is a good example. An employer frequently will be insured and on this basis is considered more collectible than an employee, who may or may not be covered under the employer's policy. If the plaintiff directs the claim against the employer and makes a full recovery, technically the employer can seek indemnity from the employee. If the employee is covered under the employer's insurance policy, however, the insurer who pays the claim on behalf of the employer cannot exercise its subrogation right against the employee. The result would be that the employee could come to the insurer and demand a defense based on the fact that the employee is insured under its policy. A subrogation claim under these circumstances obviously would serve no purpose. Even when an employee is *not* an insured under the policy, an insurer often will forgo its subrogation right to make claim against the employee either as a matter of company policy or for public relations reasons. So while the employer has a right to seek indemnity from an employee, this right is not always exercised for the aforementioned reasons.

Essentially, indemnity will apply to situations where a nonnegligent or passive tortfeasor (who was not personally guilty of any negligence but who has the "right to control") is compelled to pay damages based on his or her relationship with the other joint tortfeasor whose active negligence caused the accident.

Vicarious Liability

Until now, the discussion of negligence has concentrated entirely on the direct liability or negligence of the wrongdoer. There are, however, situations in which another person may also be liable for injury or damage caused by the negligence of the wrongdoer. When the liability of one individual is based upon the tort of another, that individual is said to be *vicariously* liable. *Vicarious* liability is liability that is *imputed* to another essentially because of a relationship which exists between the parties. The most common relationship in which vicarious liability is involved is known as "agency."

Agency is a relationship based upon an express or implied agreement whereby one person, the agent, is authorized to act under the control of and for the principal.[4] A principal is liable for the acts of an agent committed within the scope of the agency relationship that cause injury or damage to a third party. The basis of this liability is the doctrine of *respondeat superior* (let the master respond).

In order for a relationship to constitute a genuine agency relationship in which the doctrine of respondeat superior applies, two elements must be present. The agent must have *authority* to act for the principal and must be under the *control* of the principal. It must be kept in mind that the doctrine does not relieve the agent of liability but it does create additional liability on the part of the principal for injury or damage to a third person. While the agent is *directly* liable for the injury or damage, the principal is *vicariously* liable. Within the insurance claim business, the terms "vicarious liability," "imputed liability," and *"respondeat superior"* are often used synonymously.

The rationale behind the principle of vicarious liability is based on the attitude that since the principal stands to benefit by the agent's activities conducted on behalf of the agency, the principal should be responsible for any harm done by the agent. In addition, the principal usually is in the best position to pay for the damages. The fact that the principal is responsible is considered a cost of doing business and can be passed on to customers in the form of higher prices. Protection for claims against the principal can be secured by the purchase of liability insurance.

With respect to liability claim handling, the most common situations or agency relationships in which vicarious liability will be a factor are employer-employee relationships, partnerships, joint ventures, independent contractors and parental-family relationships.

Employer-Employee This is probably the most common type of principal-agent relationship involving the doctrine of *respondeat superior* that adjusters will encounter. An employer is vicariously liable for the negligent act of an employee committed within the scope or course of employment. If the employee deviates or acts outside the scope of employment, his or her negligence is not imputed to the employer. Determining whether a specific act is *within* or *outside* the scope of employment often requires a detailed investigation. There are no simple rules to follow which will generate an instant answer to this question.

When confronted with such questions, adjusters must determine what the employee's job entails and what he or she is commonly expected to do with regard to the performance of the job. Only then will the adjuster be able to begin to analyze whether the employee's activity which caused an accident was a departure from the general category of work which the employee was hired to perform. Adjusters should look at the time and location of the accident to see if they were within the normal perimeters of the employment agreement. They should also consider whether the employee's act was intended to benefit the employer or the employee himself. Usually, if the negligent act is committed to benefit the employer's business or interests, the employer will be held vicariously liable, even though the act may have been contrary to the employer's instructions. While personal acts of the employee which are done to advance his or her own interests will not make the employer liable, personal acts that are merely incidental to the job but still within the scope of employment will impose vicarious liability on the employer.

A typical illustration of a departure from the scope of employment would be an employee's deviation from a scheduled delivery or business trip. Suppose a delivery of merchandise is being made from one city to a city in another state. While making the trip, the employee decides to spend an afternoon in a favorite pool hall some twenty miles off the main route to the city of destination. Once the employer leaves the main route, he or she has probably stepped outside the normal scope of employment. Should the employee negligently cause an accident while driving to or from the pool hall, the employer will have a good argument to resist the imposition of vicarious liability. Whether the deviation was major or minor will have a significant bearing on whether or not the employee was within the scope of employment when the accident occurred.

It needs to be emphasized that an *office* employee is not in the course of employment until he or she actually gets to work; yet such an employee ordinarily is outside the course of employment as soon as he or she leaves the office. Thus, while driving to and from work, the office employee is outside the scope of employment. On the other hand, an *outside* employee, such as a field sales representative or field claim adjuster, has much greater latitude as far as the scope of employment is concerned.

Another troublesome area involves intentional torts committed by an employee. Generally, if the employee's assault or other intentional act is within the scope of employment, the employer is vicariously liable for any injury that results. Even though there may be a question whether the act was within the scope of employment, if the employee's act, regardless of how poor the judgment, is committed to benefit the employer, the employer is vicariously liable.[5] A purely personal assault with no thought on the employee's part of benefitting the employer will not make the employer vicariously liable.

While up to this point the emphasis has been on *vicarious* liability imposed on an employer, keep in mind that under some circumstances, the employer may also be *directly* liable for acts committed by an employee. For example, when an employee is directed by the employer to act in such a way that injury or damage to another results, the employer is directly responsible for the resulting injury or damage. In addition, an employer is directly liable for injury caused by an employee who possesses a vicious propensity to harm others when, through a reasonable background check, the employer could have discovered the employee's propensity toward violence at the time he or she was hired.

Although an employee may possess immunity from suit for his or her negligence, the employer may not share such immunity. For example, where the employee, while in the course of employment, injures his wife or child, he is immune from suit in jurisdictions which prohibit interspousal or intrafamily suits. However, in many jurisdictions, the family immunity rule does not extend to the employer. The employee's wife or child can still sue the employer who will be vicariously liable for the injuries.

Finally, it must be remembered that the employer's *vicarious* liability is dependent upon the employee's *direct* liability. If the employee is found to be free of negligence, the doctrine of respondeat superior cannot make the employer vicariously liable.

Partnerships Each partner is an agent of the partnership. When a partner commits a tort while acting within the scope of the partnership business, each partner is vicariously liable for injury or damage caused by that tort. Partners are jointly and severally liable, which means that the injured party can sue any one of the partners or all of them. Limited partners, however, do not have the "right to control"; therefore, they are insulated from the imputation of legal liability.

Joint Ventures A joint venture is an enterprise organized by two or more people, usually to achieve a specific purpose. To qualify as a joint venture, the participants must be involved in a common endeavor with each maintaining a right of control as to how it will be accomplished.

When a joint venture is established to conduct a business, it is essentially a limited partnership (or partnership with a limited purpose) and the liability of one member is imputed to each other member as in a partnership. In many jurisdictions, the operation of an automobile for a common purpose, e.g., a specific trip or vacation, may be a joint venture. If two or more people rent or use a car for a common purpose and all maintain an equal right of control, the temporary enterprise is considered a joint venture. If during the course of such a joint enterprise, the driver negligently strikes a pedestrian, all joint participants are liable for the pedestrian's injury. As is the case in a partnership, the pedestrian may sue any one of the joint venturers, or all of them.

Independent Contractors Technically, an independent contractor is neither an agent nor an employee of the employer or person with whom the contract for work is made. Generally then, the employer or person who contracts with an independent contractor is not liable for injury or damage to a third party caused by the negligence of the independent contractor. In the typical independent contractor situation, the employer has no control over the means or methods by which the contractor performs the job. Generally, if the employer does not retain control over the independent contractor or supervise the work in any way, the liability of the contractor is not imputed to the employer.

In some cases, the question of who actually controls the work is not clear and adjusters will need to conduct a detailed investigation to resolve this question. This may include closely scrutinizing the actual contract between the parties as well as obtaining detailed information as to the manner in which the work was performed. If investigation reveals that the employer did exercise some control or supervision over the independent contractor, an employer-employee relationship may exist, and a negligent act of the contractor could be imputed to the employer.

Questions that need to be answered in deciding whether an employer-employee relationship exists include the following:

- Is there any provision in the contract for control or supervision of the independent contractor?
- Are the hours fixed by the employer?
- Are tools or equipment supplied by the employer?
- Is the independent contractor paid by units of time? (Generally, an independent contractor is responsible to the employer as to the result of the work performed, but not as to the particular methods used to complete the work.)
- Does the employer deduct income taxes or provide any benefits such as workers' compensation insurance?

Affirmative answers to these questions indicate that an employer-employee relationship exists.

As is often the case with principles of legal liability, there are some exceptions to the general rule. Although generally, an employer is not liable for the negligence of an independent contractor, certain duties cannot be delegated to another. Thus, the employer will remain legally liable with respect to these "nondelegable" duties.

Situations involving nondelegable duties include the following:

Dangerous Activity. With respect to ultrahazardous activities, such as blasting or wrecking, the employer is generally held liable for any resulting injury or damage, regardless of whether an employee or an independent contractor conducted the operation. Both the employer and the contractor are liable for ensuing damages on the basis of strict liability (or liability without fault) in view of the ultrahazardous nature of the activity.

Work Involving Public Thoroughfare. If construction is being conducted in close proximity to a public sidewalk or street, the employer or person for whom the work is being done has a duty to the general public to prevent any obstructions which would endanger the general public. Safety devices such as barricades, warning signs, etc. must be maintained. The employer cannot abandon his or her responsibility here by delegating it to an independent contractor.

License Requirements. When a license is required to conduct certain activities and the person licensed delegates the performance of the activity to another, the person licensed remains liable for the negligence of the other person. A public utility, for example, may not discharge its responsibility by contracting a job to an independent contractor.

Negligent Selection of an Independent Contractor. When an independent contractor selected by an employer is found to be incompetent, and this fact would have been discovered by the employer with the exercise of reasonable care, the employer is liable to third persons for injury or damage caused by the incompetent contractor. With respect to insurance agents and independent adjusters, whether a genuine independent relationship exists between principal and agent will depend essentially upon the right of the insurer to control the conduct of the individual in the performance of his or her duties. Since both insurance agents and independent adjusters usually represent multiple companies and generally control their own activities, establishing vicarious liability on the insurer for their negligent acts seemingly would be unlikely.

However, if after applying the previously discussed considerations for establishing whether an employer-employee relationship exists, the claim person finds that the agent or adjuster is basically in the employ of one company and closely supervised by that company, the individual might be considered an employee by some courts.

Keep in mind that while the employer is not vicariously liable for the negligent acts of an independent contractor, the employer remains liable for any *direct* negligence on his or her part.

Parental-Family Liability Generally, a husband is not liable for the torts of a wife and vice versa; nor is a parent liable for the torts of a child. A family relationship is not automatically construed to be an agency or employer-employee relationship. On the other hand, where a clear agency relationship can be established, such as where the parent actually authorizes or instructs a child to act in a certain way and an injury results, the parent will be liable for the child's negligence.

Other exceptions to the general rule that a parent is not liable for the negligent acts of a child include liability statutorily imposed upon the parents, liability based on the negligent entrustment of a dangerous instrumentality, or liability that stems from other direct negligence on the part of the parents.

As explained earlier most states have statutes that impose liability of a vicarious nature upon parents whose minor children willfully or maliciously cause damage to the property of others. An example is the family purpose doctrine, which makes the head of a family responsible for injuries caused by a family member's use of the family car. Statutes in some states go as far as imposing vicarious liability upon a vehicle owner for injury or damage which is caused by *any* permissive user.

In addition, a parent is liable for his or her direct negligence in giving a child a dangerous instrument, such as a loaded gun. A parent has a duty to exercise reasonable care in supervising his or her child so as to avoid harm to others. Is it not reasonably foreseeable that giving a loaded gun to a young child who does not appreciate the dangers associated with the instrument, can cause serious harm to others? If a parent fails to exercise reasonable care and permits the child to get possession of a gun and injury results, the parent is guilty of negligence.

The same is true when a parent fails to warn a third party of a child's vicious propensities of which the parent is aware and which result in injury to a third party. This is particularly true with reference to a babysitter who is watching the child for the first time and is unaware of the child's vicious tendencies. Of course, the extent of the danger to others will determine the degree of care required of the parents.

Finally, if a parent furnishes a car to a minor child who is unfamiliar with its use and, while driving the car, the child causes injury to another, the parent may be liable on the basis of negligent entrustment. A car in the hands of such an inexperienced, untrained driver becomes a dangerous instrumentality.

Contributory Negligence

The importance of the concept of contributory negligence cannot be overstated. Not only is it a consideration as a defense in most liability claims, but it serves as the basis for the settlement of claims involving the law of *comparative negligence* as well.

Under common law, a claimant cannot recover for injuries caused by another's negligence if his or her own negligence has contributed to the injury. The negligent act of the claimant is viewed, along with the negligent act of the defendant, as a concurrent and contributing cause of the accident.

The claimant's conduct, like that of the defendant, is measured against the reasonably prudent person standard. If the claimant's actions fail to measure up to that standard, the claimant will be considered contributorily negligent and no recovery will be made. Technically, this is true even if the claimant's negligence is slight in comparison to that of the insured or defendant. In actual practice, however, this rule is not followed quite so strictly. Insurance adjusters realize that there is considerable risk in denying a claim based on slight contributory negligence when the claimant's injuries or damages are significant. When confronted with such situations, the claim person often will adjust or compromise these claims. To let such a case go to trial where a a jury will decide the outcome exposes the company to serious risk. Whether that risk will be assumed by the insurer depends upon the particular case in question.

Not too long ago, the principle of contributory negligence was in effect in the majority of states, but this is not the case today. As a result of what many people perceived as the harshness of the doctrine of contributory negligence, this common law rule has been modified in most states by installation of *comparative negligence* laws. In states applying comparative negligence, the claimant's contributory negligence ordinarily will not bar his or her recovery unless it is substantial. Recovery will be limited, however, by the percentage of the claimant's contributory negligence. (If, for example, the claimant's damages are $1,000 and he or she is 30 percent contributorily negligent, the claimant's recovery would be $700.)

It is evident, therefore, that contributory negligence has not been eliminated as a factor in claim settlements under comparative negligence. On the contrary, contributory negligence, or the percentage of contributory negligence attributed to each party to the accident, is the key determinant of *whether* a claimant will recover, or of *how much* a claimant will recover under comparative negligence.

At this point, the intent is simply to introduce the concept of contributory negligence as a necessary preliminary step for an examination of the more widely applicable principle of comparative negligence. Subsequently in this chapter, the concept of contributory negligence will be revisited when it is examined as one of the key defenses available to an insured.

Comparative Negligence

The principle of comparative negligence has its origins in maritime law and has long been applicable to a number of federal statutes as well. In 1910, Mississippi became the first state to enact a comparative negligence law. The movement among the states to adopt comparative negligence was slow and uneventful during the first half of the century. In the mid 1960s, however, the pace began to accelerate so that today comparative negligence laws apply in more than forty states. (A current state by state status of comparative negligence as of May 1, 1984 is shown in Exhibit 4-1). Such laws have been adopted either by statute or by court decision. (Most states have adopted comparative negligence by statute.)

Comparative negligence laws are intended essentially to mitigate the harshness of the doctrine of contributory negligence. As mentioned earlier, if the law of contributory negligence is strictly followed, a person cannot recover for damages sustained in an accident if he or she contributed to it. This is true even though the claimant's degree of negligence may be slight in comparison to that of the other person(s) involved in the accident.

In comparative negligence jurisdictions, the complete bar to recovery created by the doctrine of contributory negligence (when the claimant is contributorily negligent) is eliminated. Comparative negligence laws enable claimants to recover a portion of their damages even when they are substantially at fault. However, the claimant's recovery is reduced by his or her percentage of contributory negligence. As previously illustrated, a claimant who is 30 percent at fault recovers only 70 percent of his or her damages from the other individual involved in the accident. Generally, the claimant will recover only if his or her negligence is *not as great as* or *no greater than* that of the defendant. Under a *pure* comparative negligence law, however, a claimant may recover even when his or her negligence is greater than the defendant's.

Kinds of Comparative Negligence Laws Basically, there are three kinds or types of comparative negligence laws. They are categorized as follows: (1) pure, (2) modified "not as great as," or 49 percent rule, or (3) modified "no greater than," or 50 percent rule. (Some states have laws which are classified as "slight versus gross," in

Exhibit 4-1
Status of Comparative Negligence (As of May 1, 1984)*

Jurisdiction	Status	Authority	Year Adopted	Type
Alabama	No	—	—	—
Alaska	Yes	Kaatz v. State, 540 P.2d 1037 (Alaska 1975)	1975	Pure
Arizona	No	—	—	—
Arkansas	Yes	Ark. Stat. Ann. 27-1763 to 1765 (1979)	1955	49%
California	Yes	Li v. Yellow Cab Co., 13 Cal. 3d 804,532 P.2d 1226, 119 Cal. Rptr. 858 (1975)	1975	Pure
Colorado	Yes	Colo. Rev. Stat. Ann. 13-21-111 (1973 and Supp. 1982)	1971	49%
Connecticut	Yes	Conn. Gen. Stat. Ann. 52-572h (West Supp. 1982)	1973	50%
Delaware	Yes	Del. Sen. Bill #381	1984	50%
District of Columbia	No	—	—	—
Florida	Yes	Hoffman v. Jones, 280 So. 2d 431 (Fla. 1973)	1973	Pure
Georgia	Yes	Ga. Code Ann. 105-603 (1968)	†	49%
Hawaii	Yes	Haw. Rev. Stat. 663-31 (1976)	1969	50%
Idaho	Yes	Idaho Code 6-801 (1979)	1971	49%
Illinois	Yes	Alvis v. Ribar, 85 111.2d 1, 421 N. E. 2d 886 (1981)	1981	Pure
Indiana	Yes	Indiana code 34-4-33-2 (Senate Bill 419)	1985	50%
Iowa	Yes	Goetzman v. Wichern, 327 N. W. 2d 742 (Iowa 1982)	1982	Pure
Kansas	Yes	Kan. Stat. Ann. 60-258a (1982)	1974	49%
Kentucky	Yes	Hilen v. Hays, 82 Court of Appeals 2566 (1984)	1984	Pure
Louisiana	Yes	La. Civ. Code Ann. art. 2323 (West Supp. 1983)	1979	Pure
Maine	Yes	Me. Rev. Stat. Ann. tit. 14, 156 (1980)	1965	49%

Maryland	No	—	—	—
Massachusetts	Yes	Mass. Gen. Laws Ann. ch. 231, 85 (West Supp. 1982)	1971	50%
Michigan	Yes	Placek c. City of Sterling Heights, 405 Mich. 638, 275 N. W. 2d 511 (1979)	1979	Pure
Minnesota	Yes	Minn. Stat. Ann. 604.01, subd. 1 (West Supp. 1983)	1969	50%
Mississippi	Yes	Miss. Code. Ann. 11-7-15 (1972)	1910	Pure
Missouri	Yes	Gustafson vs. Benda 611 S. W. 2d 11 (1983) Mo. Supreme Court Case #63857	1984	Pure
Montana	Yes	Mont. Code Ann. 27-1-702 (1981)	1975	50%
Nebraska	Yes	Neb. Rev. Stat. 25-1151 (1979)	1913	Slight/ Gross
Nevada	Yes	Nev. Rev. Stat. 41.141 (1981)	1973	50%
New Hampshire	Yes	N.H. Rev. Stat. Ann. 507:7-a (Supp. 1979)	1969	50%
New Jersey	Yes	N.J. Stat. Ann. 2A:15-5.1 (West Supp. 1982)	1973	50%
New Mexico	Yes	Scott v. Rizzo, 96 N.M. 682, 634 P.2d 1234 (1981)	1981	Pure
New York	Yes	N.Y. Civ. Prac. Law 1411 (McKinney 1976)	1975	Pure
North Carolina	No	—	—	—
North Dakota	Yes	N. D. Cent. Code 9-10-07 (1975)	1973	49%
Ohio	Yes	Ohio Rev. Code Ann. 2315.19 (Page 1981)	1980	50%
Oklahoma	Yes	Okla. Stat. Ann. tit. 23,13 (West Supp. 1982)	1973	50%
Oregon	Yes	Or. Rev. Stat. 18.470 (1979)	1971	50%
Pennsylvania	Yes	Pa. Stat. Ann. tit. 42, 7102(a) (Purdon 1982)	1976	50%
Rhode Island	Yes	R.I. Gen. Laws 9-20-4 (Supp. 1982)	1971	Pure

South Carolina	Yes	S. C. Code Ann. 15-1-300 (Law. Co-op 1977) (Applies only to motor vehicle accidents)	1962	50%
South Dakota	Yes	S.D. Codified Laws Ann. 20-9-2 (1979)	1941	Slight/ Gross
Tennessee	No	Although it is not considered comparative negligence, Tennessee law does apportion the plaintiff's recovery for "remote" contributory negligence and bars recovery for "proximate" contributory negligence.		
Texas	Yes	Tex. Rev. Civ. Stat. Ann. art. 2212a (Vernon Supp. 1982)	1973	50%
Utah	Yes	Utah Code Ann. 78-27-37 (1977)	1973	49%
Vermont	Yes	Vt. Stat. Ann. tit. 12, 1036 (Supp. 1982)	1970	50%
Virginia	No	—	—	—
Washington	Yes	Wash. Rev. Code Ann. 4.22.010 (Supp. 1982)	1973	Pure
West Virginia	Yes	Bradley v. Appalachian Power Co., 256 S. E. 2d 879 (W. Va. 1979)	1979	49%
Wisconsin	Yes	Wis. Stat. Ann. 895.045 (West Supp. 1982)	1931	50%
Wyoming	Yes	Wyo. Stat. 1-1-109 (1977)	1973	49%

†Georgia statute traces to the 19th century.

*Source: *Non-Use of Motor Vehicle Safety Belts As An Issue in Civil Litigation*, David Westenberg, Sommerville, MA. 02143. Prepared For National Highway Traffic Safety Administration, Washington, D.C. Reproduced by National Technical Information Service, U.S. Department of Commerce, Springfield, Va. 22161.

which the claimant can recover when his or her negligence is slight and the defendant's is gross by comparison.)

A *pure* comparative negligence law, as previously mentioned, is one which permits the claimant to recover a portion of his or her damages even when his or her negligence is greater than the defendant's. As noted earlier, the recovery is reduced by the percentage of the claimant's negligence. Thus, an injured claimant can be as much as 90 percent at fault and still recover 10 percent of his or her damages under a pure comparative negligence law. In fact, the only time a claimant will be barred from recovery is when the defendant is totally blameless.

A dramatic illustration of this kind of law is found in a relatively recent New York case. In the case, a claimant who tried to commit suicide by throwing himself in front of a subway train recovered $650,000 from the New York City Transit Authority. The person's injuries were severe and it was decided that the operator of the subway train was negligent in not stopping the train sooner. Slight negligence on the part of the operator, therefore, enabled the injured person, who clearly bore the major responsibility for the accident, to recover a substantial sum under a pure comparative negligence law.

Under a *modified* "not as great as" law, the claimant can recover as long as his or her negligence is *not as great as* (or less than) the defendant's. This is also known as the "49 percent rule." If the claimant is as much as 49 percent at fault, he or she can recover the remaining percentage of his or her damages. For example, a claimant who is 40 percent at fault can recover 60 percent of his or her damages. However, if the claimant is 50 percent at fault, no recovery can be made.

The other variation of a modified law is referred to as the "no greater than" or "50 percent rule." The "no greater than" version is broader than the "not as great as" version because the former approach provides for recovery as long as the claimant's negligence is *no greater than* the defendant's. The case where two motorists are each deemed to be 50 percent at fault illustrates the difference between these two variations. In a state which applies the "not as great as" variation, the claimant who is 50 percent at fault is prohibited from making any recovery. In a "no greater than" state, the claimant will recover 50 percent of the damages because even though the claimant is 50 percent at fault, his or her negligence is *no greater than* the defendant's. If the claimant's negligence is 51 percent or more, there is no recovery.

How Comparative Negligence Works Ohio's modified "no greater than" law (50 percent rule) is used to illustrate how such a comparative negligence law affects claim settlements. The Ohio law makes each negligent party liable for a portion of the claimant's total damages. This is calculated by multiplying the claimant's total damages by a fraction in which the numerator is the tortfeasor's percentage of fault and the denominator is the total percentage of fault attributable to all tortfeasors. The claimant's percentage of fault (contributory negligence) is not included in the denominator. See Exhibit 4-2.

In Illustration 3, A recovers from C even though his or her negligence is four times as great as that of C. C, of course, can recover

Exhibit 4-2
Comparative Negligence Illustrations

Illustration 1

A sues B and C
A is not negligent
B is 30% negligent
C is 70% negligent
A's damages are $20,000
A recovers $20,000

B pays $\frac{30\%}{100(\%)} \times \$20{,}000 = \$6{,}000$

C pays $\frac{70\%}{100(\%)} \times \$20{,}000 = 14{,}000$

Total recovery $20,000

Illustration 2 — A is partially at fault; otherwise same situation as in Illustration 1.

A is 10% negligent
B is 30% negligent
C is 60% negligent
A recovers $18,000 ($20,000 – $2,000 (A's contributory negligence)

B pays $\frac{30}{90}$ (total % of all defendants' negligence excluding claimant's contributory negligence) x $18,000 = $6,000.

C pays $\frac{60}{90} \times \$18{,}000 = \$12{,}000$

Total Recovery $18,000

Illustration 3

A sues B and C
A is 40% negligent
B is 50% negligent
C is 10% negligent
A's damages are $20,000
A recovers $12,000 ($20,000 – $8,000 (A's contributory negligence)

B pays $\frac{50}{60}$ (total % of all defendants' negligence) x $12,000 = $10,000 less A's negligence).

C pays $\frac{10}{60} \times \$12{,}000 = \$2{,}000$

Total Recovery $12,000

his or her damages from A and B, and even B can recover from A and C. However, B would only recover half of his or her damages.

Claim people need to keep in mind that the particulars of comparative negligence laws may vary from state to state. While in Illustration 3, A will recover from C in Ohio, this is not true in all other states which have a similar type of comparative negligence law. Some states prohibit one party from recovering from another whose negligence is less than the party making claim.

Multi-car accidents present additional problems because of the mathematics involved and of the variations in the laws from state to state. The rule in some jurisdictions is that when the injured person's negligence is equal to or greater than that of each defendant individually, there is no recovery. This is true even if the injured person's negligence does not equal that of all the other defendants combined. Thus, there would be no recovery in a three-car accident in which each driver is assessed with 33⅓ percent negligence. In Ohio, however, each party would recover two-thirds of his or her damages in such a situation.

Another area which causes occasional confusion concerns contribution among joint tortfeasors. Under some comparative negligence laws, each tortfeasor will pay a pro-rata share of the claimant's damages despite the fact that they may be negligent in differing degrees. In other states, the amount recoverable is apportioned according to the percentage of comparative fault of each tortfeasor.

In some states, the injured party collects nothing from a joint tortfeasor whose negligence is less than his own, but will collect the entire amount of recoverable damages from the tortfeasor whose negligence is greater. For example, in a case where the injured party is 40 percent negligent, the second driver 10 percent negligent, and the third driver 50 percent negligent, the injured person collects nothing from the second driver and 60 percent from the third driver. The person whose fault contributes most to the accident is liable for the entire amount of the injured person's recovery which in this case is 60 percent (100 percent less injured person's negligence).

Need for Investigation The task of assessing fault against the parties to an accident is the responsibility of the claim adjuster and, in those cases that go to trial, the jury. Detailed accident investigations frequently need to be conducted before an accurate assessment of liability can be made. In this sense, there is no difference between the way a claim will be investigated under comparative negligence and that under contributory negligence. As a matter of fact, there is support for the position of many claim practitioners that claims under comparative negligence need to be more thoroughly investigated to substantiate the apportionment of fault between the parties.

In order to make an accurate assessment of liability, statements will have to be taken from the parties involved in the accident and from witnesses. Diagrams and photos of the accident scene will need to be secured along with police reports, weather reports (when necessary), and any other items that will help piece together a reasonably accurate picture of how the accident occurred.

The state motor vehicle or traffic code may be of help to adjusters who must reduce a claimant's recovery because the claimant has violated a particular traffic law and is partially responsible for an accident. Adjusters may refer to the particular traffic code that was violated as an aid in explaining why they are diminishing the claimant's settlement.

Relationship of Comparative Negligence to Other Actions Comparative negligence laws generally apply to all negligence actions—auto accidents, fall-downs, and so on. Products liability claims may or may not be subject to a state's comparative negligence law. Products claims may be based on negligence, warranty, or strict liability. Actions for breach of warranty or strict liability may not be subject to comparative negligence depending upon the state. Some states specifically eliminate the law's applicability to an action based on strict liability. Ordinarily, comparative negligence will not apply to intentional acts. If a statute bars the defense of contributory negligence, comparative negligence usually will not apply. Comparative negligence, for example, ordinarily will not apply to a dog-bite statute.[6]

Some states have merged the defenses of contributory negligence and assumption of risk by statute, whereas others have refused to do so where the statute is silent on this question. In addition, most comparative negligence states have abolished the doctrine of last clear chance. (This doctrine is explained in Chapter 5.)

The question of joint and several liability can be a significant issue with regard to comparative negligence laws. Some states in which comparative negligence laws were adopted have, in the process, abolished the principle of joint and several liability. The following example illustrates how this will affect a plaintiff's recovery:

A sues B and C
A is not negligent.
B is 60 percent negligent.
C is 40 percent negligent.
A's damages are $20,000.
B is uninsured and insolvent.

If joint and several liability applies, A will recover his entire damages of $20,000. Even though B is uncollectible, A can recover fully from C, who is jointly and severally liable with B for all damages caused by their joint negligence. If joint and several liability does *not* apply, A will recover only $8,000 from C (40 percent of $20,000). In the absence of joint and several liability, the tortfeasors are *separately* liable for A's damages. Since B is uncollectible, A can only recover the portion or percentage of his damages which are attributable to C's negligence.

Still another area of concern involves absent tortfeasors, or those who, for some reason, are not a party to the lawsuit. The question is: Can the jury consider the negligence of a tortfeasor who is not a party to the suit? Some comparative negligence laws address this question specifically and indicate that the negligence of a "nonparty" can be considered by the jury in arriving at the apportionment of damages among the codefendants. The laws of other states may be silent on this issue or specifically prohibit consideration of the negligence of a nonparty. Nonparties may include individuals who are immune from suit such as a spouse, family member or employer, so-called "phantom" vehicles or individuals who have already been released from the claim through a limited release form or a "covenant not to sue."

Actually, many of the foregoing issues are not settled within the actual comparative negligence law but are resolved subsequently through litigation.

Conclusion Comparative negligence, in one form or another, is now the law in more than forty states. It is expected that the trend toward adoption of such laws will continue through the eighties. Seemingly, a growing number of legislators across the country view comparative negligence as a realistic and reasonable concept which is more acceptable to the general public and more in tune with today's socio-economic tempo than the common-law doctrine of contributory negligence.

From a claims standpoint, it has always been difficult to convince the average claimant that his or her 10 percent or 20 percent contributory negligence means that recovery for damages cannot be made. By contrast, a claimant can better understand, and usually accept, the logic that because he or she contributed to the accident, an amount representing this contribution will be deducted from the recovery.

Automobile Guest Statutes

A minority of states have passed *automobile guest statutes* which affect a passenger's recovery. These statutes exempt the driver from liability for injury to a guest unless the driver is guilty of something more than ordinary negligence.

Generally, a *guest* is one who is in the car for a social purpose, as opposed to a business purpose. If the driver-owner is paid by the passenger, or if any discernible, substantial benefit other than payment by the passenger is received, the passenger is *not* considered a guest and may recover for injuries caused by the *ordinary* negligence of the driver. A passenger in a share-the-expense car pool arranged purely for business reasons, without any social purpose, is *not* considered a guest. Yet, an informal arrangement involving the sharing of expenses among friends will not necessarily eliminate a passenger's guest status.[7] In the latter situation then, the passenger will likely remain a guest and will need to prove something more than ordinary negligence against the driver in order to recover for injuries sustained while a passenger in the car.

The rationale behind guest statutes is based on the belief that the ordinary guest or passenger who rides free, so to speak, is not entitled to hold the driver responsible unless the latter is guilty of gross negligence or willful, wanton, or reckless conduct. Guest statutes vary from state to state with regard to the specific nature or degree of fault which will make a driver liable for injuries sustained by guests. The intent of these statutes is also aimed at discouraging collusion between the guest and the driver.

If a "gratuitous" passenger (one who rides free) is seriously injured when the driver of the car in which he or she is riding rear-ends another car, the passenger cannot recover unless gross negligence or wanton or reckless driving on the operator's part can be established. On the other hand, if the passenger has paid for the ride, or benefits in some other way and is not considered a guest, he or she need only prove ordinary negligence against the driver in order to recover.

Guest statutes, like the doctrine of contributory negligence, are considered by many to be out of touch with today's realities. Why, it is asked, should a seriously injured guest passenger be prevented from recovering from the negligent driver simply because their relationship was of a social rather than a business nature? In the last decade, a number of states have repealed their guest statutes and modern day realities suggest this trend will continue.

Immunity

Immunity exists when an individual who negligently causes injury is exempt from liability. The two kinds of immunity addressed in the following pages are *intrafamily* immunity and *governmental* immunity.

Intrafamily Immunity Under common law, lawsuits among family members—husband and wife or parent and child—are not permitted. Therefore, a husband cannot be legally liable for injury to his wife which is caused by his negligence, and vice versa. Likewise, parents cannot be liable for injury to a child; nor can a child be liable for injury to a parent caused by his or her respective negligence.

The rationale behind the common law position was that such suits create an adversary relationship between family members and disrupt family harmony. In addition, it was felt that there would be incentives for fraud and collusion among family members if such lawsuits were permitted and liability insurance was available to pay for such claims.

Intrafamily immunity actually is separated into two distinct subject areas: *interspousal immunity* (between husband and wife) and *parent-child immunity* (child versus parent and vice versa).

Interspousal immunity developed originally from the idea that in the eyes of the law, husband and wife were one. Though the modern day emphasis on equal rights has significantly altered this attitude, the immunity has nevertheless persevered and still exists in a number of states. Once again, the reluctance to abolish this immunity was based on the concern that family harmony would be disrupted and that fraud and collusion would ensue when insurance was available, if suits between spouses were permitted.

In more recent times, this reasoning has fallen into various stages of disrepute because it is believed to be unfounded. In many states, the interspousal immunity doctrine has been completely abolished. In other states, it has been partially abolished such as in a case where one spouse dies as a result of an accident caused by the surviving spouse. In such cases, a lawsuit against the surviving spouse by the estate of the deceased is permitted. The reasoning is based on the idea that the death of either spouse ends the family relationship and family harmony is no longer an issue. Consequently, the estate of the deceased spouse may sue the surviving spouse or, when the deceased party was responsible for the accident, the injured surviving spouse may sue the estate of the deceased.

Parent-child immunity, like interspousal immunity, was based on concerns of disruption of family tranquility and possible fraud and collusion. This immunity applies whenever there is a claim between an *unemancipated* minor child and a parent. An "unemanicapted" child is one who is under legal age, which in most jurisdictions is either age eighteen or twenty-one. An *emancipated* child is one who becomes legally free from parental authority either by reaching legal age, by getting married, or by otherwise getting released from parental authority with the parents' consent. Thus, a minor (under legal age) who is married or otherwise released from parental authority can be construed to be emancipated and, therefore, can sue a parent or be sued by a parent. In short, where parent-child immunity exists, an *unemanicipated* child *cannot* sue a parent or be sued by a parent.

The immunity applies to any family situation: natural father and mother, stepfather or stepmother, or any other person who stands in place of a parent (*in loco parentis*) to the child.[8]

Generally, the date of the accident will control and not the time of suit. For example, if an accident occurs when a minor is under legal age, the minor will not be permitted to institute suit when he or she reaches legal age. At the time of the accident, the minor could not maintain the action, and the fact of attaining legal age will not create a cause of action where none existed before.

Although it is true that the doctrine of intrafamily immunity (both interspousal and parent-child immunity) exists today in a number of states, there appears to be a trend toward the abolition of this doctrine. The existence of liability insurance no doubt has more than a little to do with the trend. A recovery by one family member against another who is covered by insurance will enable the injured party to pay for medical expenses and lost income. It will also provide monetary consideration for pain and suffering and other intangible elements of the injury.

One final comment about intrafamily immunity is in order before moving on to the subject of governmental immunity. As discussed in Chapter 3, many states have approved the *liability coverage exclusion* (PP 03 26) for use with the personal auto policy as a means of precluding coverage for claims or suits between family members. The exclusion applies in states where intrafamily immunity still exists as well as in states where the immunity has been abolished. Some insurers have for years used their own similar exclusion (often referred to as the "household" exclusion) to achieve the same purpose. In addition, the 7-82 and 4-84 editions of the homeowners policy developed by the Insurance Services Office contain an intrafamily exclusion in the liability section of those forms. (For a review of some of the problems associated with the *liability coverage exclusion*, see the discussion of this subject in Chapter 3.)

Governmental Immunity The doctrine of sovereign or governmental immunity was derived from English common law which held that "the king can do no wrong." The king, being an absolute monarch, was accountable to no one, even when he made errors or mistakes. American law adopted the same principle except that the immunity applied to governmental bodies such as the states and the federal government. Aside from the role historical inheritance played in our adoption of the immunity doctrine, it was also felt that public funds and public activities should not be subject to tort liability claims.

States can, however, usually by specific statute, consent to be sued if certain established procedures are followed by the plaintiff. For the most part, the states may prescribe their own requirements concerning the limitations and conditions upon which suit may be brought. Such suits usually are handled by "court of claims acts." The federal government has also consented to be sued under the Federal Tort Claims Act. These acts represent a limited waiver of governmental immunity but not a complete abolition of the doctrine.

It is important that claim people understand that in states where governmental immunity still exists, the immunity is applicable only to activity which is of a "governmental" nature. When a particular function is governmental, the governmental unit is not subject to tort liability. However, where a governmental body engages in an activity which can be characterized as a "business" activity, the activity is viewed as being private and *proprietary* and the governmental body is subject to tort liability. Where a governmental body has no direct obligation to perform certain duties or tasks, for example, but does so for the comfort and convenience of the public, the activity is considered proprietary.

It is sometimes difficult to distinguish between "governmental" and "proprietary" functions of government. If the activity could just as well have been performed by a private firm or individual, it is in all likelihood a proprietary function and the governmental unit performing the task can be sued in tort liability should injury or damage result from the negligent acts of its agents or employees. Generally, activities which involve such things as planning, regulation, making and enforcing ordinances, crime and fire prevention, preservation of the public health, and education of the young are considered governmental functions and immunity applies.

Examples of activities which can be construed to be proprietary in nature include the following: operation and/or maintenance of a sports stadium or public hall, a public golf course or swimming pool, a municipal bus or rail system, an airport, a public parking garage, a hospital, a zoo, a state fair, a municipal water works or electric utility. In these cases, the governmental body is viewed as a private entity and is *not* immune from suit.

When Insurance Applies In some states, the courts have taken the position that the purchase of liability insurance constitutes a waiver of governmental immunity to the extent of the limits of the insurance policy. Other states have rejected this view. On the one hand, it seems illogical for a governmental body to purchase insurance and then when a claim is made, be able to deny recovery based on the immunity. Seemingly, such situations might appear to be designed merely to enrich insurance companies. On the other hand, it might possibly be reasoned that insurance will protect the governmental body against claims arising out of its proprietary functions, but would not waive the defense of governmental immunity for governmental activities.

Like many of our common law doctrines, the doctrine of governmental immunity seems to be somewhat out of fashion with today's socio-economic tempo. Many states have rejected the doctrine as being out of touch with modern thinking and one state supreme court which recently abrogated the doctrine in part, referred to it as a "legal anachronism."

Bailments

A *bailment* is the transfer of possession of *personal* property by its owner to another for some specific purpose with the understanding that when the purpose is fulfilled, the property will be returned to the owner. (Real estate or real property can never be the subject of a bailment.)

It needs to be emphasized that a bailment involves only a transfer of *possession* of property. For this reason, a bailment is to be distinguished from a "sale" in which title and ownership are transferred as well. In a bailment situation, the owner of the property or goods is called the *bailor* and the person (or business) who receives the property is the *bailee.* A bailment can be either an express contract (usually written) where the terms are specified, or an implied contract, the latter being implied from the facts of the situation.

In order for the transfer of property to constitute a bailment, the following characteristics must be present:

1. ownership of the property is retained by the bailor,
2. temporary possession and control is exercised by the bailee, and
3. possession is ultimately returned to the bailor unless the bailee is instructed to further transfer the property to a third party.

Keep in mind that a bailment does not exist unless the owner actually transfers the property to another person and that person accepts care or custody of the property. Thus, parking one's car in a theater parking lot before seeing a movie or docking one's boat in an open space at a marina is not considered a bailment because the property has neither been transferred by the owners of the property nor accepted by the owners of the premises. It is merely a lease of an area.

Claim people encounter bailment situations with relative frequency in their claim handling. When a person leaves his or her car at a garage for servicing, or clothes at a dry cleaner for cleaning, a bailment exists. Aside from these so-called "business" bailments, "gratuitous" bailments, which are of a social nature and do not involve the exchange of money, are equally common. Ordinarily, any time an individual leaves personal property with another or uses or cares for the property of another, a bailment relationship exists.

If you loan your lawn mower to a neighbor so that he can cut his or her lawn, a gratuitous bailment is present. The bailee has temporary possession of your lawn mower and must return it in the same condition as when received. The bailee is under a duty to exercise a certain degree of care in the use of your mower. The degree of care required will depend upon the nature of the bailment. Expressed another way, the degree of care required depends upon who benefits from the bailment. With this in mind, bailments are classified in the following manner:

1. for the mutual benefit of the bailor and bailee,
2. for the sole benefit of the bailor, or
3. for the sole benefit of the bailee.

Once the particular bailment relationship is classified, the adjuster can determine the degree of care required of the bailee. For example, in a mutual benefit bailment, the bailee must exercise ordinary and reasonable care (recall the reasonable person standard discussed previously) with respect to his or her use of the bailed property. A mutual benefit bailment is one in which both parties benefit. The previously mentioned business bailments are examples of mutual benefit bailments. When an individual takes his or her car to a garage for servicing, both parties benefit. The car owner (bailor) gets the car serviced and the garage (bailee) gets paid for its service work.

The other two kinds of bailments usually are considered gratuitous in that ordinarily no money is exchanged between the parties.

A bailment for the sole benefit of the bailor is illustrated by the situation in which a vehicle owner asks a neighbor to take the car and run an errand for him. Where benefit is being derived solely by the bailor (owner), the bailee only owes a duty of *slight* care in the use of the vehicle.

If this situation were reversed so that the car was loaned to the neighbor solely because of the neighbor's need to run an errand or do something that required the use of a car, a bailment for the sole benefit of the bailee would exist. Since the bailee is the only person benefiting from use of the car, a *high* degree of care is imposed upon the bailee.

When confronted with a claim involving a bailment, adjusters must first classify the type of bailment involved before they can determine the degree of care required and decide whether the bailee's actions constitute negligence.

It needs to be emphasized that mere loss or damage to the bailed property does not make the bailee automatically responsible to the bailor, in the absence of a specific agreement to that effect. Thus, if an individual borrows the property of a friend—a car, a bicycle, or a television set—and while in the borrower's care, the property is stolen, the borrower is not liable unless his or her actions constitute negligence. If the car was properly parked and locked, or if the television set was safely secured in the individual's home, and the items were stolen by someone, the borrower (bailee) is not liable.

This must be distinguished from the rental car situation discussed in Chapter 3. In the rental car situation, the renter (bailee) signs a contract which specifically makes him responsible, regardless of fault, if the car is damaged or stolen. Here there is a *contractual* assumption of liability which includes explicit terms concerning the bailee's responsibilities. In the gratuitous bailment situation, specific terms or agreements of this nature are ordinarily absent and legal liability will be based solely on whether the property was damaged as a result of the bailee's *negligence.*

A bailment can arise whenever the owner of property loans, conveys, transfers, or delivers the property to another for a certain purpose with the understanding that the property will eventually be returned to the owner.

Agency versus Bailment An important aspect of bailment concerns the rights of an absent owner of a car which, while driven by a bailee, is damaged in an accident. The issue is whether the absent owner can recover for damage to his or her car when the bailee himself shares responsibility for the accident with another motorist. As it was explained in the discussion of vicarious liability, if an employer-employee relationship with the "right to control" exists between owner and driver, the driver's negligence is imputed to the owner. In such case, both the owner and driver are barred from recovery from third parties for their respective damage or injury. In a bailment situation, however, the negligence of the driver is not imputed to the absent owner in the absence of an actual agency relationship or a specific statute to that effect. (Recall that some states have statutes which make a vehicle owner liable for the negligent act of any permissive user.)

In a number of states, the absent owner can recover from the other motorist even when that motorist's negligence is slight in comparison to that of the bailee. In other words, the bailee may bear the major responsibility for the accident but if the other driver is even slightly responsible, the absent owner can recover from the latter. This is known as the "bailment rule." Of course, the bailor has a right of action against the bailee, too, and if he does not sue both parties, the other driver may join the bailee as an additional defendant.

Joint and Several Liability and Insurance Two additional factors need to be considered when discussing an absent owner's recovery possibilities under bailment situations. The first is the question of whether joint and several liability applies, and the second is the question of insurance itself.

If the principle of joint and several liability applies to a bailment, the absent owner may recover his or her damages in full from the adverse driver (the other driver, not the bailee) as long as the adverse driver was to some degree at fault. This is true even when the bailee is primarily at fault for the accident. Recall that where joint and several liability applies, the damaged party may recover his or her total damages from both wrongdoers together or from either wrongdoer separately.

On the other hand, where joint and several liability is not a factor, as under some comparative negligence statutes where the principle has been abolished, the absent owner cannot recover *total* damages from either wrongdoer. In such cases, each wrongdoer is liable for a portion of the damages attributed to his or her negligence.

When insurance is not a factor, this may not be a problem. The absent owner technically can make claim against the bailee (permissive user) and/or the adverse driver and recover accordingly. Where insurance is involved, however, this is not necessarily the case. If the bailee has a personal auto policy and the owner can persuade the bailee to make claim for the damage to the car under the liability portion of the bailee's PAP, the owner will likely be able to recover in full. The owner can recover from both drivers according to their comparative fault provided they are both insured or solvent. (Remember that the PAP provides coverage for damage to nonowned cars used by the insured, which is caused by his or her negligence under the liability section of the policy.)

On the other hand, if the owner encounters a delay or other problems with the bailee's insurer and decides to make a collision claim with his own insurer, a problem arises. When the absent owner makes a collision claim and the claim is paid by the insurer, the insurer ordinarily cannot subrogate against the permissive user. As a matter of fact (as explained in Chapter 2), Part F—General Provisions of the PAP contains a provision referred to as *Our Right To Recover Payment* which states: "Our rights do not apply under Part D against any person using your covered auto with a reasonable belief that that person is entitled to do so." This provision specifically prevents an insurer from making a subrogation claim against a permissive user. Thus, a collision insurer's subrogation claim can only be directed against the adverse driver(s).

In jurisdictions which follow the bailment rule and where the principle of joint and several liability applies, if the adverse driver is even slightly at fault, the insurer can recover in full from the adverse driver. Where joint and several liability does not apply, however, a full recovery cannot be made against one driver when both drivers share fault for the accident. As explained earlier, where joint and several liability does not apply, each driver is liable for a portion of the damages attributed to his or her negligence. Therefore, since the collision insurer will not be able to make claim against the bailee (permissive user), its only recourse is against the adverse driver and recovery will be based on the portion of the damages attributable to the adverse driver's negligence.

One additional comment about the rights of a vehicle owner is in order before moving on to a discussion of the defenses available to insureds. (As noted earlier, in the absence of an actual agency relationship or specific statute, a bailee's negligence is not imputed to the absent owner of the vehicle. However, when the owner is a passenger in his or her car while it is being driven by a bailee, some states hold that the bailee's negligence (including his or her contributory negligence) is imputed to the owner and bars the owner's recovery for damage to the vehicle. This position is based on the belief that the owner's presence in the car constitutes that necessary element of control over the bailee which allows the latter's negligence to be imputed to the owner. Keep in mind, however, that not all states follow this view.

In the more general area of rights and liabilities of vehicle owners, it generally can be said that a vehicle owner is not responsible for damages caused by the negligence of a permissive user (in the absence of agency or a specific statute which holds otherwise).

There are, however, some exceptions to the general rule. Where there is a defect in the car of which the owner is aware, such as faulty brakes, defective steering, or bald tires and the driver is not so informed, the owner will be responsible for any injury or damage caused by the defect. Recall that the negligent entrustment of a car to an incompetent may make the owner responsible as well.

The applicability of the aforementioned concepts and principles concerning bailment and vehicle ownership, in general, varies somewhat from state to state. As a consequence, adjusters should be certain they are up to date regarding the position their state has taken on these matters.

Chapter Notes

1. Mark S. Rhodes, *Couch on Insurance,* 2d (Rev ed) 74:712 (Rochester, NY: The Lawyers Co-operative Publishing Co., 1983), p. 1022.
2. James H. Donaldson, *Casualty Claim Practice,* 3d ed. (Homewood, IL: Irwin-Dorsey Limited, 1976), pp. 38, 39.
3. Ronald A. Anderson, *The Insurer's Tort Law,* 2d ed. (Ephrata, PA: Science Press, 1971), p. 108.
4. Ronald A. Anderson and Walter A. Kumpf, *Business Law,* 9th ed. (Cincinnati, OH: South-Western Publishing Co., 1972), p. 253.
5. Donaldson, p. 220.
6. James L. Graham, attorney, Graham, Dutre & Nemeth, Columbus, Ohio, *Ohio's New Comparative Negligence Statute,* p. 6.
7. Pat Magarick, *Successful Handling of Casualty Claims* (Brooklyn, NY: Central Book Company, Inc., 1974), pp. 77, 78.
8. Donaldson, p. 100.

CHAPTER 5

The Meaning of Legal Liability, Continued

IMPERFECTIONS OF THE TORT LIABILITY SYSTEM

The tort liability system, which focuses on *fault* as the basis for determining whether injured accident victims will recover for their injuries, is imperfect. Although the foregoing discussion has demonstrated that tort law has changed significantly in that it has been expanded to keep pace with society's changing values, today's tort liability system still contains inequities and inadequacies concerning the manner in which accident victims are compensated. While much of the following commentary applies to the overall tort system, it concentrates on the auto liability problem, which is perhaps the most evident as far as the public is concerned. Some background on the problems inherent in tort liability is necessary before proceeding to a discussion of the remedies used to minimize these problems.

The effectiveness of tort liability as a means of compensating accident victims has been questioned for a long time. As far back as the 1930s,[1] studies on the tort liability system criticized it for providing inadequate compensation or no compensation at all to injured accident victims. In general terms, there was too much uncertainty over whether injured victims would receive adequate compensation or be compensated at all for their injuries. Recovery under an adversary system depended on fault, and this had to be determined through investigation. However, not all accidents lent themselves to a ready determination of fault, and a large and growing number of these were going into litigation for final resolution. The increasing volume of cases clogged court calendars and delayed final outcomes, thus prolonging uncertainty about recovery. In the meantime, seriously injured accident victims went uncompensated until the courts were ready to hear their cases.

Even when the victims did win, the expenses of investigation and legal proceedings combined with attorney fees paid out of the recovery often left the injured party with little more than out-of-pocket expenses, if that. While many seriously injured persons were inadequately compensated, minor injury claims were often overpaid out of practical considerations; that is, it was more economical to pay off these claims than to keep the claim file open indefinitely.

Another problem with the fault system, whose ultimate arbiter is the trial court, is the role that appearance, chance, emotion, and attorney skills play in the final outcome. These factors, which ordinarily are unrelated to the merits of the case, may cause a deserving individual to go uncompensated or an undeserving party to be overpaid.

Frequently, the problem was not so much determining who was responsible for the accident, but rather *collecting* from the responsible party who may have been insolvent or uninsured.

Still another problem was that auto insurance costs were rising at an alarming rate. The supremacy of the automobile as America's primary mode of transportation had been firmly established, and an increasing accident frequency magnified the weaknesses of the system.

REMEDIES

Attempts to eliminate or minimize the problems associated with the tort liability system included the following approaches: financial responsibility laws, compulsory auto insurance laws, uninsured motorists insurance, underinsured motorists insurance, and no-fault auto insurance.

Financial Responsibility Laws

A financial responsibility law requires motorists to furnish evidence of financial responsibility. (Financial responsibility laws apply in all states.) Ordinarily, this evidence need not be shown until after an accident, although a number of states require that such evidence be demonstrated when the car is registered. In actual practice, motorists who are involved in accidents in which a stated amount of property damage (which varies by state) is incurred, or where any bodily injury is sustained, must submit proof of financial responsibility usually in the form of an insurance policy or a bond. If motorists are not insured, they are required to furnish security which will satisfy any judgment that might be made against them arising from the accident. Most states today have security-type laws, which means that motorists must provide security to cover liability arising out of the immediate accident.

Some states use a security and proof type of law that requires the motorist to submit not only security to pay for a judgment resulting from the immediate accident but proof of financial responsibility for *future* accidents as well. Failure to satisfy the financial responsibility law can result in a suspension of the motorist's license and registration.

In effect, financial responsibility laws do not mandate the purchase of liability insurance but they do provide a strong incentive to purchase insurance.

Compulsory Auto Insurance

Compulsory auto insurance laws, unlike the majority of financial responsibility laws, require that evidence of financial responsibility be shown when the car is registered. In compulsory auto states, auto liability insurance is mandatory. While such laws are stronger than financial responsibility laws, they do not guarantee that all motorists in a particular state will be insured. Statistics on the subject have indicated that as much as 15 percent of the motoring public remains uninsured even where auto insurance is compulsory.

Proponents of compulsory auto insurance laws cite the need for guaranteed protection against the risk of being injured by a negligent driver who is uninsured and financially irresponsible. Opponents dislike the idea that insurance is forced on all car owners regardless of their driving performance and record. In addition, opponents assert that the bureaucracy and red tape of administering a compulsory auto system often increases the costs of auto insurance.

Uninsured Motorists Insurance

Uninsured motorists coverage provides an insured protection when he or she is injured through the *negligence* of an uninsured or hit and run motorist. In order for the insured to recover, the other motorist must be at fault.

The personal auto policy (PAP) enumerates four situations in which a vehicle will be considered *uninsured.* They are:

1. When there is no bodily injury liability bond or policy on the negligent driver's car.
2. Where there is such a bond or policy but its limit of liability is less than the minimum limit(s) specified by the financial

responsibility law of the insured's state. (This provision applies to an accident with an out-of-state motorist whose required financial responsibility limits are less than those required by the insured's state.)

3. A hit-and-run vehicle whose operator or owner cannot be identified and which hits an insured or a vehicle an insured is occupying or the insured vehicle itself. (Note the requirement of "physical contact" which has been voided in some states by court decision).
4. Where a bond or policy applies but the bonding or insurance company has denied coverage or becomes insolvent.

Claim people need to be familiar not only with the actual policy language of the uninsured motorists provision but with their state statute as well. Since uninsured motorists insurance is statutorily mandated, adjusters must pay particular attention to the statute and be especially sensitive to claim disputes involving this coverage.

Uninsured motorists insurance can protect insureds from the risk of being injured by an uninsured or hit and run motorist. In some states, uninsured motorists laws include protection for property damage as well as bodily injury, and some insurers *voluntarily* offer uninsured motorists property damage insurance in states where it is not mandated by law. A segment of the insurance industry believes that uninsured motorists insurance covering the bodily injury and property damage exposures would preclude the need for compulsory auto insurance laws to which many insurers object for reasons previously noted.

Underinsured Motorists Insurance

While *uninsured* motorists coverage protects insureds from the risk of being injured by a motorist who is uninsured or insolvent, insureds face an equally serious risk from drivers who carry auto liability insurance with limits inadequate to fully compensate the injured insured. Since the negligent driver has some insurance, the insured's uninsured motorists coverage will not be applicable. This represented a serious void in coverage before the advent of *underinsured* motorists insurance.

State legislatures saw this deficiency and today virtually all states have enacted underinsured motorists statutes, making the coverage available to insureds who want to purchase it. Statutes vary by state but generally underinsured motorists insurance responds when the liability insurance available to the injured person from the negligent motorist's policy is less than the injured person's underinsured motorists coverage. For example, suppose that the insured has underinsured motorists insurance of $50,000 and is injured by a negligent motorist who has bodily injury liability limits of $15,000 per person. Assuming that the value of the insured's bodily injury claim exceeds the negligent driver's limit of $15,000, the insured may collect under the underinsured motorists insurance of his own policy (if he carries the coverage). Ordinarily, there is a set off for the amount of liability insurance available to the injured person; that is, recovery is reduced by all sums received from the negligent driver's policy. Thus, the insured recovers $15,000 from the negligent driver's insurer and, assuming an injury case worth in excess of $50,000, $35,000 ($50,000 less $15,000) from his underinsured motorists insurance for a total recovery of $50,000.

Underinsured motorists insurance is a relatively new coverage and questions have emerged concerning set off provisions, stacking, other insurance provisions, and protecting subrogation rights, which have not been resolved in all states. Adjusters are advised to be familiar with the underinsured motorists statute in their state since the statute may address these questions and to seek the advice of supervisory and management personnel in resolution of these questions.

No-Fault Automobile Insurance

Many of the inequities of the traditional tort liability system which precipitated the enactment of no-fault laws were previously mentioned. Formal criticism of the tort liability system was expressed as early as 1932 in the Columbia Report. The Report indicated that the system frequently resulted in inadequate compensation or no compensation at all for injured auto accident victims either because they were negligent or because the negligent party was insolvent.

It is true that the basic principles of negligence law were developed before the advent of the automobile. Present day realities combined with the growing applicability of auto liability insurance tend to negate the use of negligence as the criteria for determining recovery in the opinion of some insurance people. Fault or negligence law was designed to impose retribution and promote individual responsibility by making the negligent party pay for his or her wrong. But the existence of liability insurance prevents the wrongdoer from personally bearing the financial burden. Why then, so the reasoning goes, should the tort liability system still be used to assess fault when its fundamental purpose has been defeated by auto liability insurance?[2]

Another criticism of the tort liability system involved the fact that the expenses of investigation and trail incurred in the system diverted funds which could otherwise be paid directly to injured victims in the form of benefits. Proponents of no-fault saw this situation as wasteful and unfair. A no-fault plan, they claimed, would eliminate or at least minimize the need for investigation and trail.

In the late 1960s, considerable attention became focused on these inadequacies of tort liability, especially in light of the fact that auto insurance costs were rising at an alarming rate. Public pressure, fueled by a handicapped tort system, was mounting for auto insurance reform.

Though these inadequacies by themselves were, in the minds of reformers, sufficiently formidable to justify auto insurance reform, yet another significant factor removed any doubt on the part of no-fault advocates that no-fault offered the best solution for compensating auto accident victims. That factor was the example of workers' compensation insurance and, in particular, the apparent success of that system as a means of compensating injured workers without any regard to fault. There was a striking parallel between the impetus for workers' compensation laws at the turn of the century and the later motivation for no-fault auto insurance. Both concepts emerged in response to a failing tort liability system that placed an undue burden on the injured party to prove fault, this being the only means of recovery. Workers' compensation laws were passed to deal with the problem of compensating workers injured as a result of mounting industrial accidents while no-fault plans were aimed at more adequately compensating victims of rising auto accidents.

Prior to the enactment of workers' compensation laws, injured workers had to prove fault on the part of the employer before they could recover. The employer had at its disposal the traditional defenses of contributory negligence, assumption of risk, and the fellow servant rule. This seemingly harsh system had not worked as a reasonable mechanism for compensating injured workers. With the passage of workers' compensation laws, injured workers gave up their right to sue their employer but in return, were guaranteed compensation for their medical expenses and a portion of their lost earnings regardless of how the accident was caused. For all intents and purposes, fault was no longer a factor in work-related accidents. In addition to medical expense coverage, rehabilitation services also were available when necessary. This was considered a much more realistic and equitable approach to handling the growing problem of compensating victims of industrial accidents.

Observing these obvious similarities between workers' compensation insurance and proposed no-fault auto plans, proponents urged that a workers' compensation approach, already an established and workable system, be applied to the automobile compensation problem.

In 1965, Robert E. Keeton, professor of law at Harvard University, and Jeffrey O'Connell, professor of law at the University of Illinois, wrote *Basic Protection For The Traffic Victim,*[3] which summarized the work of the authors to that time and, significantly, included a model bill, incorporating key features seen in today's no-fault laws.

In the early 1970s, the stage was set for a more responsive automobile compensation system, and public pressure became sufficiently strong to compel legislators in several states to act.

On New Year's Day, 1971, the first no-fault auto insurance plan in the United States took effect in Massachusetts. In the five years that followed, Americans saw a flurry of legislative activity concerning no-fault, which culminated in the passage of no-fault auto insurance laws in twenty-four states. (Currently, no-fault auto insurance laws apply in twenty-three states and the District of Columbia.)

Types of No-Fault Laws The provisions of these twenty-four laws vary from state to state, but generally, no-fault laws can be classified into the following three types: modified, add-on, and voluntary plans.[4] The most common type, the *modified* plan, limits the right to sue but stops short of actually eliminating it. In exchange for this partial relinquishment of the right to sue, the injured person is entitled to a package of benefits commonly referred to as Personal Injury Protection or PIP benefits. PIP benefits ordinarily cover medical expenses, lost income, survivors' loss, and expenses for replacement services.[5] (Replacement services refer to expenses incurred for household help, child care, necessary yard work, and so on. which the injured person is unable to perform because of the injury.)

These benefits are paid promptly on a first-party basis without regard to fault. Like collision insurance, individuals go directly to their own insurer for payment of these first-party or PIP benefits, not to the third party's insurer.

Unlike modified plans, *add-on* plans do not limit the right to sue but simply expand the typical provisions of Medical Payments insurance and add lost income coverage. Benefits similar to PIP benefits are provided, but the tort liability system is not affected.

A *voluntary*[6] plan is one which offers individuals first-party coverage similar to PIP benefits strictly on a voluntary basis. In other words, these plans are not created by legislation. Insurers may offer such coverage if desired and insureds may purchase the coverage if they want, but there are no obligations on either side. Both the offer and the acceptance of coverage are optional. As with add-on plans, the tort liability system is unaffected.

An occasionally mentioned fourth type of no-fault plan or proposal is a "pure" plan. A pure no-fault auto plan, which would completely eliminate the right to sue, exists only in theory. No such law has been enacted nor is one contemplated at the present time.

Modified Plans Since modified plans are the only plans which actually change the tort liability system and are said to most closely resemble a genuine no-fault approach, our discussion concentrates on these plans. The modified plans of Massachusetts and Michigan, in particular, are used to illustrate not only the similarities of modified laws but their range of distinctions as well.

The modified plan, in exchange for the limitation on the right to sue, grants a broad range of PIP benefits to the injured person without regard to fault. Most modified laws place a ceiling on total medical benefits offered, although a couple of states provide unlimited medical and rehabilitation benefits, unlimited both in *time* and *amount.*

The Massachusetts law, for example, pays up to $2,000 per person for medical expenses or funeral expenses incurred within two years from the date of accident as well as for loss of earnings up to 75 percent of the individual's average weekly wage. Coverage for replacement or essential services also is available, and insureds may purchase additional medical expense coverage at their option.

In contrast, Michigan's law provides *unlimited* medical and rehabilitation benefits, funeral expenses up to $1,000, 85 percent of lost income subject to a fluctuating ceiling based on changes in the cost of living, replacement service benefits up to $20 a day, and survivors' loss benefits subject to the same fluctuating limit as lost income protection. Payment for lost income, replacement services, and survivors loss can continue for as long as three years if warranted by the extent and seriousness of the injury.

Under no-fault, an injured person ordinarily has access to fairly comprehensive coverage for *economic* loss such as medical expenses, lost income, and the like. Since modified no-fault laws restrict the right to sue, claims for *noneconomic* loss such as pain and suffering, inconvenience, loss of consortium, disfigurement, and so on can be made only under certain circumstances. Whether an individual can make a tort liability claim for noneconomic loss depends upon the extent of medical and hospital expenses and the seriousness of the injury. The mechanism utilized in modified plans to determine whether such a tort claim can be made is known as a *threshold.*

Tort Threshold The threshold is the unique or distinguishing feature of modified no-fault laws. Put simply, a threshold is a "border" beyond which an injured person must pass, in terms of medical and hospital expenses or of the extent of injury, before that individual can resort to tort liability. Only when the threshold is exceeded, may the injured person present a tort liability claim for noneconomic loss. (Tort liability claims for uncompensated *economic* loss, i.e., medical and hospital expenses, lost income, and so on, can be made when actual economic loss exceeds the benefits provided by the law. In other words, if actual lost wages or replacement services expense exceed the benefit limits provided by the law, the injured person can sue to recover the excess.)

Thresholds can be either *monetary* or *verbal.* (The difference between these two approaches in their application to claim situations can be significant as will be noted shortly.) Monetary thresholds are commonly called "dollar" thresholds while verbal or injury thresholds refer to the extent and seriousness of the injury. A comparison of these provisions in the Massachusetts and Michigan laws will illustrate the difference between them.

The Massachusetts law contains a dollar threshold which says that an injured person cannot make a tort liability claim for noneconomic loss such as pain and suffering, and so on, unless medical expenses exceed $500. The threshold provision goes on to list certain kinds of injuries that, if sustained, would permit a tort action. Thus, the provision actually is a combination dollar/verbal threshold. It is called a dollar threshold primarily to distinguish it from a purely verbal threshold.

Michigan's law, on the other hand, contains a verbal threshold; that is, the *amount* of medical expenses has no effect on the right to sue. Tort liability claims for pain and suffering are not permitted in Michigan unless the injury results in death, serious impairment of body function, or permanent serious disfigurement. There is no reference to any monetary figure which if exceeded would allow a tort action as there is in the Massachusetts law.

A simple example will show the distinct applications of these two approaches.

Suppose that an individual incurs $506 in medical bills as a result of a soft tissue injury sustained in a two-car accident. In Massachusetts, the individual can resort to the tort liability system—which means he or she can make a claim against the other motorist and, if necessary, sue that motorist. A third-party liability claim is permitted because the injured person has exceeded the $500 threshold. At this point, whether the injury is serious is immaterial. The injured party has already exceeded the "dollar" portion of the threshold and thus regains his or her right to a tort action.

This is not necessarily the case in Michigan. Remember, the Michigan no-fault law contains a verbal threshold; there is no reference to any dollar amount. The sole determinant of whether an injured person can sue for pain and suffering is the seriousness of the injury. The injury must involve a serious impairment of body function or a permanent serious disfigurement before a liability claim can be pressed. The amount of medical bills will not affect the possibility of a tort claim.

It does not matter whether medical bills are $200 or $1,500. The focus is on the seriousness of injury, not the amount of medical bills.

In Michigan, the injured person would need to establish that the injury was "serious" as described in the threshold provision before a liability claim for noneconomic loss could be pursued. Generally, a soft tissue injury will not qualify. Under these circumstances in Massachusetts, a tort claim for pain and suffering is allowed; but in Michigan, the injured person's recovery would probably be limited to economic loss.

Much criticism is lodged at plans with low dollar thresholds as being ineffective in limiting tort liability claims. Contrary to reducing such claims, critics contend that dollar thresholds actually *invite* claims by posing as a target, in terms of accumulating medical and hospital bills, at which claimants can take aim. Once exceeded, the injured person can make claim for the more subjective or "weightier" elements of an injury claim such as pain and suffering, mental anguish, and so on. Low dollar thresholds and consistently high inflation make it relatively easy to exceed the dollar thresholds of a number of no-fault plans.

Verbal thresholds, in contrast, remove the incentive to accumulate medical bills because the amount of medical expenses has no effect on the right to sue. Admittedly, the question of whether an injury is serious may in itself be the subject of occasional litigation; nevertheless, verbal thresholds do remove the incentive for some injured persons (who may not be seriously injured) to inflate their medical expenses or prolong their treatment.

Clearly then, the threshold feature is of major significance in a modified no-fault plan. Depending upon how strongly it is written, tort liability claims may be reduced substantially or be virtually unaffected.

The results of a study prepared by the Alliance of American Insurers in March, 1984, suggest that cost savings have generally occurred in no-fault states with strong thresholds, particularly those with verbal thresholds. In states with weak tort thresholds, however, costs are likely to be higher than under the tort system.

Other Important Provisions of No-Fault Auto Plans Any comprehensive examination of no-fault auto insurance would be deficient without a general discussion of a typical plan's approach to subjects like *interstate driving, coordination of benefits, vehicles covered, source of primary coverage,* and *subrogation.* (Since a state-by-state analysis at this point would be exhaustive, the following comments are general in nature.)

The aim of no-fault plans is to be as far-reaching as possible with regard to vehicles covered and the scope of territorial protection. For this reason, most no-fault laws apply to all motor vehicles subject to motor vehicle registration—private passenger and commercial vehicles alike. Motorcycles generally are not covered although a few states do bring motorcycles within the scope of their no-fault laws or at least make coverage optional.

The fact that America is a motoring and mobile society is reflected in no-fault legislation. Typically, insured residents of a no-fault state are covered while using the vehicle anywhere in the United States, its possessions or territories, or Canada. Conversely, most states provide no-fault benefits for nonresidents driving in the no-fault state. Ordinarily, all auto insurers licensed to write in the no-fault state must stipulate that every auto insurance policy written, regardless of where it is issued, will provide the coverage required by the no-fault state when the nonresident is in that state. Nonadmitted insurers usually are requested to make the same pledge.

With regard to duplication of benefits, many no-fault laws try to minimize situations where benefits from several insurance sources are paid to an injured person. A relatively common provision in modified no-fault laws states that benefits received from federal or state insurance programs such as social security or workers' compensation insurance are deducted from no-fault benefits payable. In other words, PIP benefits are secondary or excess to these governmental insurance plans. (Benefits payable under *Medicare*, however, are now excess to benefits recoverable under no-fault auto insurance.) Benefits available from *private* health insurance are not subject to this deduction. An injured person usually can duplicate benefits available from private health and no-fault insurance.

In an effort to contain the cost of auto insurance, some states have introduced *coordination of benefits* provisions which make either health or auto insurance primary with the requirement that the excess insurance source reduce its premium accordingly. Another way to reduce premiums is to carry a deductible on PIP benefits. Optional deductibles ordinarily are available in no-fault plans.

No-fault laws vary depending on whether primary PIP coverage follows the automobile or the individual. When coverage follows the car, injured occupants of a motor vehicle collect PIP benefits from the vehicle owner's policy. When injured as a pedestrian, an insured receives benefits from the insurer of the vehicle which struck him.

When coverage follows the individual, an injured person receives benefits from his own policy even if injured while an occupant of another vehicle. The same is true if the individual is injured as a pedestrian. When more than one source of PIP benefits are available on a primary basis, benefits normally are prorated among the various coverages so that payments in excess of the actual loss are not received.

In the event that no insurance is available from any source—perhaps an individual does not own an automobile and is injured as a pedestrain by an uninsured vehicle or as an occupant of an uninsured vehicle—*an assigned claim plan* is available in many no-fault states. Such plans make PIP benefits available to victims of such uninsured accidents.

With regard to subrogation, the majority of no-fault states permit such recovery from a negligent driver's insurer to the extent of PIP benefits paid, or at least provide for reimbursement to the PIP insurer if the PIP insured makes a liability recovery. Like the other provisions discussed here, subrogation provisions vary somewhat from state to state. Some no-fault states have eliminated subrogation altogether.

Another point to keep in mind is that the existence of no-fault insurance does not eliminate the need for auto liability insurance. Once the threshold is exceeded, or when actual economic loss exceeds the benefit limit provided by the law, an injured person can resort to tort liability. Motorists, therefore, must maintain their liability insurance if they want protection for such tort liability claims. Another reason for liability insurance is the fact that property damage claims in all but one state are still handled under tort liability.[7] Furthermore, a no-fault insured traveling in a state that has not enacted a no-fault law limiting tort liability can be sued by an injured auto accident victim without restriction.

It also is true that coverages such as uninsured motorists protection and even medical payments insurance are still necessary. Such coverages may not respond as often as they did under a tort liability system—because under no-fault, medical payments coverage ordinarily is excess over PIP benefits and thresholds often bar liability claims—but they, nevertheless, are available when they are needed. Uninsured motorists coverage is needed to protect an injured person who finds that there is no insurance covering the vehicle which caused the accident. Once the threshold is exceeded, the injured party's uninsured motorists insurance would respond. Although no-fault auto insurance impacts upon the tort liability system, it does not eliminate the need for traditional automobile liability or associated coverages.

Strengths and Deficiencies of No-Fault Insurance At this point, the reader should once again consider the previously noted inadequacies of tort liability which served as the impetus for the enactment of no-fault laws. No-fault auto insurance laws were created in response to a failing tort system which, according to reformers, placed an undue burden on injured persons to prove fault. Proponents of auto insurance reform believed that a system based on fault was incapable of adequately and fairly compensating the growing number of auto accident victims. This was a social problem, they contended, that required a social solution. In their minds, no-fault auto insurance was the only logical answer.

In several respects, no-fault auto insurance represents a marked improvement over the tort system that existed in the 1960s in the manner in which auto accident victims are compensated. Under no-fault, payment for economic loss is made promptly because there is no need to delay payment until the investigation is completed and fault is determined.

No-fault plans also minimize the classical adversary confrontation between claimant and insurance company because under no-fault, more claims are handled on a first-party basis. In addition, insureds have the advantages of dealing directly with their own insurance company, and claim representatives are in a position to generate good public relations through the claims process. In serious injury cases and those involving rehabilitation, the claim representative has a real opportunity to develop empathy and rapport with the claimant (insured) by acting in a counseling capacity and by providing prompt and efficient service.

Although there is no real evidence to suggest that no-fault auto insurance has brought about a reduction in insurance costs—inflation being the main reason—it has generally returned a larger portion of the premium dollar to the accident victim in the form of benefits. Since fewer premium dollars go for the expenses of investigation and trial preparation, more money is available to policyholders. (Exhibit 5-1 shows the relative change in injury coverage costs under no-fault. The no-fault experience in 1982 is measured against what the estimated average loss costs—pure premiums—for 1982 would have been if no-fault had not been enacted.)

Though it is true that no-fault auto insurance has some definite strengths, this is not to imply that it is without its critics. Some critics contend that no-fault auto insurance has not gone far enough in restricting use of the tort liability system. Many no-fault laws leave tort liability virtually untouched while weak thresholds in a number of modified plans render those plans ineffective in limiting tort claims.

On the other side of the coin, many attorneys claim that thresholds restricting tort claims must not be too severe because pain and suffering can and does occur with less serious injuries. Following this reasoning, severe thresholds would be harsh and unfair to a great many auto accident victims. It is unfortunate that sometimes the end result of this bargaining process is a no-fault law which neither restricts tort claims nor pays sufficient PIP benefits to seriously injured accident victims.

As noted earlier, the threshold often becomes a target of sorts, because once exceeded, the potential recovery increases to encompass

Exhibit 5-1
Relative Change in Injury Coverage Costs*

	Year No-Fault Effective	Threshold at Time of Study	Relative Change in Injury Coverage Costs[2]
Verbal Threshold			
Florida	1972	Verbal[1]	–21%
Michigan	1974	Verbal	–17
New York	1974	Verbal[1]	– 6
Threshold $1,000 or More			
Minnesota	1975	$4,000[1]	– 2%
Hawaii	1974	$1,500	+37
Kentucky	1975	$1,000	–29
North Dakota	1976	$1,000	-19
Threshold Less than $1,000			
Pennsylvania[3]	1975	$ 750	+53%
Colorado	1974	$ 500 ($2,500 effective 1-1-85)	+15
Georgia	1975	$ 500	+15
Kansas	1974	$ 500	– 9
Massachusetts	1971	$ 500	–33
Utah	1974	$ 500	–13
Connecticut	1973	$ 400	+14
New Jersey	1973	$ 200	+65
Add-On States			
Oregon	1972	None	– 8%
Delaware	1972	None	+17
Maryland	1973	None	+26

[1] The verbal threshold in Florida became effective in 1976. The verbal threshold in New York became effective in 1978. Prior to 1978, Minnesota's threshold was $2,000.

[2] The latest year of no-fault experience (1982) measured against what the estimated average loss costs (pure premiums) would have been in 1982 if no-fault had not been enacted.

[3] Pennsylvania repealed its modified no-fault law and replaced it with an add-on plan effective October 1, 1984.

Note: The District of Columbia was not included in the analysis since its no-fault law did not become effective until October 1, 1983. Nevada repealed its law effective January 1, 1980 and was not included in the analysis.

*Reprinted, with permission, from *The Cost of No-Fault*, March, 1984, Alliance of American Insurers.

the more subjective elements of a bodily injury claim such as pain and suffering, permanency, and mental anguish. Not only is a weak dollar threshold ineffective in reducing tort claims, but it also serves as an incentive to incur medical bills, and exceed the threshold, and encourages abuse and overutilization of medical services.

Another deficiency of current no-fault plans is that little effort is being made to reduce the overall cost of auto insurance. True, there are offsets or anti-duplication provisions as far as social security and workers' compensation insurance are concerned, but much more could be done in the area of coordination of benefits. It is common for injured persons to receive benefits for the same elements of loss from multiple sources; that is, many auto accident victims receive PIP benefits as well as private health insurance benefits. This duplication is costly. Making one insurance source primary and reducing the cost of the excess source of benefits accordingly, may help reduce or at least contain the cost of auto insurance. Some no-fault states have already moved in this direction as noted earlier in the discussion.

Yet another area of concern is the provision in some laws of unlimited medical and rehabilitation benefits. Unlimited medical coverage creates serious problems in setting claim reserves, and the potential payout, possibly over the injured person's lifetime, can be enormous. Some insurers might be discouraged from entering or continuing to write business in no-fault states which provide unlimited benefits.[8] Finally, there are those who feel that no-fault auto insurance is yet another example of government encroachment upon private enterprise. In their minds, no-fault auto insurance simply is not necessary and has not produced any positive impact upon the auto compensation system that would not have occurred in the absence of no-fault legislation.

For many of these reasons, Pennsylvania has done a turnaround of sorts and repealed its modified no-fault law, replacing it with a noncompulsory add-on plan effective October 1, 1984. Pennsylvania's new plan eliminates the tort threshold and requires a minimum of $10,000 in PIP medical benefits, income loss benefits with a monthly maximum of $1,000 and a total maximum of $5,000, and funeral benefits of $1,500. Insurers must also make available additional PIP medical coverage of at least $100,000 and additional income loss coverage of $50,000.

In addition, in order to provide protection for the catastrophic injury exposure, a $5.00 fee is required of owners of vehicles registered in Pennsylvania. The fee is designed to provide a fund to cover a person's medical expenses in excess of $100,000. The new law also requires that motorists carry both uninsured motorists and underinsured motorists insurance in amounts equal to their liability coverage.

The costs of Pennsylvania's modified no-fault system were high, as can be seen in Exhibit 5-1. The threshold was criticized for being significantly responsible for this increase because it served as a target which injured persons were required to meet in order to make a liability claim. Because the value of a claim is often based on the quantity of medical treatment, the liability recovery is also inflated. The Pennsylvania experiment is being watched closely by legislators, insurers, and attorneys alike.

Conclusion Looking back to the early 1970s when twenty-four states enacted some form of no-fault legislation, it becomes quite clear that the momentum for no-fault auto insurance has all but vanished today.[9] This change in attitude may be a response to a perception that the tort system has improved to the point at which radical reform is no longer necessary.

In any event, tort liability has evolved significantly over the past several decades. In this evolutionary process, many of the inequities of an earlier tort system seemingly have been removed. In particular, guest statutes and intra-family immunity doctrines, which precluded recovery for a large group of injured persons, have been eliminated in a growing number of states.

Statutes and laws installing *comparative negligence* rules have quite literally swept the country in the last decade and currently apply in more than forty states.

As mentioned previously, comparative negligence laws enable accident victims to recover a portion of their damages (including pain and suffering) even when they bear a substantial share of the blame for an accident. This approach, which allows recovery on a share-of-fault basis, represents a significant improvement in the manner in which auto accident victims are compensated under tort liability. Although a deduction is taken which represents the injured person's share of fault—and few argue with the logic of this principle—more people are able to recover under comparative negligence.

In addition to these developments, a more positive claims attitude on the part of insurers seems to be emerging. This is likely stimulated by internal factors such as company policy, consumer consciousness, etc., as well as by external factors such as the impact on insurers of adverse bad faith and punitive damage awards and unfair claim practice laws. Unfair claim practice laws require companies to deal openly and promptly with insureds and claimants or face appropriate penalties.

When all of these factors are combined, the picture portrayed is that of an expanded and relatively workable tort liability system. Though still imperfect, it certainly represents a major improvement over the situation which existed just prior to the surge of no-fault legislation in the early seventies. With many of the inadequacies of that earlier tort system removed and a negative attitude toward government involvement in business gaining strength, it is no great mystery why the no-fault movement has slowed almost to a halt. Understandably, the more tort liability is expanded, the less pressure there is for no-fault auto insurance.

Though no-fault auto insurance may no longer be as fashionable as it once was, it is a bit risky to presume that the expansion of tort liability has dealt a death blow to the no-fault movement. As tort liability continues to expand, will society find that it can no longer afford the growing generosity of this expansion, combined with the soaring injury awards and settlements and huge administration costs of the tort system? And should this attitude emerge, will the search for a more efficient system lead to a resurgence of the no-fault movement?[10] These questions are left for time to answer.

BAD FAITH AND EXCESS LIABILITY[11]

Recent years have seen the appearance and gradual spreading of court decisions in the field of insurance law resulting in new theories of liability and in the unexpected assessment of damages.

It has been customary to refer to these developments as "extra-contractual liability" because they go beyond the letter of the insurance contract and the obligations of the insurer under it. The courts that subscribe to such theories of liability will read into the insurance contract additional obligations on the part of the insurance company and its agents, employees, and representatives that are not expressed in the policy. If the court finds violation of these, the defendants can be held responsible in amounts in excess of the liability contemplated by the written policy contract.

It is a general rule that every contract implies the exercise of good faith and fair dealing between the parties to the contract. The failure of either party to fulfill this obligation is referred to as "bad faith." Since an insurance policy is a contract, the same general rule applies to insurance policies. The implied covenant of good faith does not arise out of the policy itself, but is a legally recognized principle apart from the policy.

A bad faith claim generally involves an insurance company and its insured and arises out of the handling of a claim. It can arise from the handling of a first-party claim or a third-party claim. In a bad faith case, the company's conduct is really on trial, more so than its actual decision or the particular coverage question which might have led to the bad faith claim. Thus, the insurer's claim handling, not the policy itself, is the basis for the claim or suit.

Originally, the measure of damages or amount recoverable in a breach of contract or bad faith claims was limited to (or could not exceed) the monetary value or subject of the contract itself. It was limited, therefore, to damages which could be shown to result *directly* from the breach as opposed to consequential damages which could include punitive or exemplary damages. In time, however, a bad faith breach of contract began to be viewed by the courts as being an independent tort or wrong for which a greater measure of recovery, including punitive damages, could be allowed.[12]

The insurer is faced with liability beyond that represented by the policy limit(s) and because of this, bad faith claims are said to be claims involving *extra-contractual liability.* Extra-contractual liability is liability imposed upon the insurer which is separate and distinct from the liability covered by the insurance policy. It can be said that bad faith is to insurance companies what products liability is to manufacturers and malpractice is to professionals.

Ordinarily, there must be a showing of malice, fraud, or oppression on the insurer's part before punitive damages will be awarded. Keep in mind that actual malice may be inferred from an insurer's conduct and from circumstances surrounding the claim. Furthermore, the exposure to punitive damages can exist by a mere breach, without malice, of the covenant of good faith and fair dealing.[13]

Historically, the tort of bad faith or outrageous conduct stems from third-party liability claims where damages were assessed for an insurer's failure to settle within policy limits.[14]Such liability is referred to as excess liability and involves suits against the insured in excess of policy limits. (In Chapter 3, guidelines for handling excess suits were included along with sample excess letters.)

It must be kept in mind that when an insurer handles a claim or defends a claim against an insured, it must place its insured's interest on at least an equal footing with its own. When an insurance company refers the defense of a lawsuit against its insured to defense counsel, counsel is protecting and defending the insured, not the company.

If an excess verdict results and the insured can show that it occurred because of the insurer's mishandling or negligence, the insurer will be compelled to pay the portion of the verdict which exceeds the policy limits (as well as the covered portion of the verdict). The insured may sue the insurer directly or, in some states, may assign the right to sue to the plaintiff who was awarded the recovery against the defendant insured. In order to prevail in the suit, the insured must prove that the insurer violated the covenant of good faith and fair dealing in the handling of the claim.

Whenever the insured's liability is clear or probable, the plaintiff's injuries are serious, and the value of the claim approaches or exceeds the policy limits, the possibility of an excess verdict exists. An even more difficult situation may occur when injuries are serious but liability is questionable or doubtful because there may be a stronger inclination on the insurer's part to defend such a suit, thus exposing the insured to an excess judgment. Claim people must be alert to these situations because the insured faces a potential excess verdict. The insurer owes its insured an adequate investigation of the third-party claim and must deal in good faith with its insured regarding the evaluation and negotiation of the claim. In addition, the insurer must communicate with and keep the insured regularly apprised of the status of the claim.

When a claim person evaluates a claim, it should be evaluated strictly on its own merits and without any consideration as to the limits of the policy. That is, evaluate the claim as if the policy has no limits. Once the value is determined, make a reasonable offer based on that value. Only when the value established exceeds the limits of the policy will those limits be a factor in the settlement.

Sources of Bad Faith

Investigation One of the common sources of bad faith claims is the *investigation* itself. The investigation must be complete and thorough concerning both the liability question and the damages aspect of a claim. Since the claim file is ordinarily discoverable in a bad faith suit (which means that the plaintiff attorney will eventually have access to the claim file), the file should be as complete as reasonably possible. This does not mean that every file requires an intensive, elaborate investigation, but it does mean that sufficient information must be obtained to allow the claim person to make an intelligent decision based on the facts.

In a bad faith action, the plaintiff (insured) is claiming that the insurer committed an error and was negligent in the handling of the claim, which caused the insured to sustain damages. If the claim file is incomplete, this may demonstrate proof of an inadequate investigation and a failure on the insurer's part to protect properly its insured's interests. In short, the insurer's decision concerning the handling of the claim must be supported by the claim file.

Settlement Negotiations Another possible source of bad faith is the conduct of *settlement negotiations.* Discussions with the plaintiff's attorney must be documented in the file. The adjuster must respond promptly to all demands of plaintiff's counsel and the response should be in writing. If the attorney makes a demand and the claim file is not complete, the attorney must be advised of what information is lacking and required from him. The file may be lacking current medical information or verification of medical bills, or a physical examination may be necessary before the claim can be evaluated. In addition, the insurer may need depositions of the parties involved in the accident to which it will likely be entitled in the discovery process. On the other hand, the file may be complete except that liability is questionable.

Regardless of the status of the claim, the attorney should be advised one way or the other as to what the insurer needs or what it is prepared to do or offer at this time. Experience suggests that if sufficient medical information is in the file to evaluate the claim and the company intends to settle, that a prompt and reasonable offer should be made. Generally, the claim will not get any less expensive with the passage of time. An early settlement based on a relatively complete file is usually the best settlement.

On occasion, a plaintiff's attorney will send adjusters a demand letter and place a time limit on the demand. When this occurs, the adjuster must respond to the attorney within the time designated. This is not to say that the adjuster must make an offer if there is insufficient information in the file, but he or she must respond, if only to ask for an extension of time in order to complete the file. Ignoring such a deadline could prove damaging to the insurer.

Suppose, for example, that the plaintiff's attorney gives an adjuster fifteen days in which to respond to a demand for settlement and the adjuster fails to respond or ignores the demand. If the case goes to trial and there is an excess verdict, the plaintiff's attorney can argue that the company had an opportunity to settle the claim but ignored it and forced the matter to trial. This may very well constitute bad faith on the company's part for obviously ignoring the opportunity to settle.

In order to avoid bad faith, an adjuster should respond in writing to such demands by attorneys. If the case is one for settlement but the demand is unreasonable, a counteroffer should be made in writing. If liability is doubtful and the case is one for defense, the attorney should be so advised.

Inadequate Defense *Inadequate defense* is another area where insurers may be exposed to claims of bad faith. Occasionally insurers will be uncertain regarding whether coverage applies until the outcome of the trial. If an insurer simply refuses to defend a claim involving a question of coverage, it may subject itself to a bad faith claim including an award of punitive damages. In these situations, insurers ordinarily will defend the insured under a reservation of rights or nonwaiver agreement. An insurer's failure to reserve its rights under these circumstances will prohibit the insurer from denying a claim after completion of the trial when the facts reveal that no coverage actually applied.

Unfair Claim Practices Acts Another source of such litigation concerns *unfair claim practices acts.* Unfair claim practices acts address many aspects of claim handling, including an insurer's responsibility for prompt communications with its insureds, adequate investigation, detailed explanations of coverage denials, and so on. Generally, such laws require that insurers handle claims promptly, which means prompt investigations, evaluation and, where warranted, prompt settlement. Ordinarily, if an insurer is found to have violated a provision of an unfair claim practices law with such frequency as to indicate a general business practice, penalties can be assessed against it by the state insurance department. Although the provisions of unfair claim practice acts generally do not allow a claimant to sue an insurer for the violation of the act, some states permit a claimant to bring a separate tort action for bad faith directly against an insurer. Case law in California and West Virginia provide that the plaintiff in such litigation must first win the basic or underlying suit before he or she can sue the insurer. In the California case, *Royal Globe vs. Superior Court 592 P. 2d 329 (1979),* the court held that either a first party or third party claimant could, under some circumstances, start an action directly against an insurance company for a single violation of the unfair claim practices act. In Montana, however, the court has ruled that a favorable verdict in the underlying case is *not* necessary in order to bring the secondary tort action.[15]

Claim File Reporting Another source of potential bad faith claims is *claim file reporting.* Claim adjusters can unwittingly make written remarks in a claim file which will come back to haunt them in the event the file is later subpoenaed in a bad faith suit. Claim people must refrain from making derogatory, personal, or unprofessional comments in the claim file. Such comments can be damaging and costly to the company as well as personally embarrassing to the adjuster who made them.

An example of a comment from an actual claim file which should have been avoided involved a case where the adjuster was attempting to explain why an individual was away from home frequently. The adjuster noted that the person spent a lot of time traveling to Texas, the Bahamas, and Mexico and made the following remark in the claim file: "What business he is in, I do not know, but he has us wondering and thinking the worst." As it turned out, this individual was an expert construction pipe welder who worked on oil rigs and specialized in welding joints of X-ray quality. His prolonged absences from home were, therefore, easily explained. However, the innuendo in the adjuster's comment is potentially dangerous.

Other examples of remarks which should be avoided in the claim file are:

> "I can save on the policy limits."
> "I will pay this under medical payments and forget about the uninsured motorists claim because the specials will satisfy the insured."
> "Mr. Claimant, if you retain an attorney, you'll have to wait a few years for a recovery and it will cost you one-third."

Personal comments of a derogatory nature about the claimant, insured, doctor, or lawyer must be avoided. Claim people should keep in mind the thought that someday the comment put in the file may be read back while its author is on the witness stand in a bad faith trial. Common courtesy and common sense can avoid this potentially dangerous source of bad faith litigation. It is dangerous to editorialize or emotionalize; comments should be restricted to the facts.

Additional sources of bad faith include wrongful denial of coverage (or inadequate explanation of the denial), unreasonable delay in the handling of a claim regarding decisions on coverage, liability, or damages, misrepresentation of coverage (or failure to advise of a specific coverage), and unreasonable settlement offers designed to "steal" a claim.

Discovery Process May Involve Claim Personnel

What happens when a bad faith suit is actually filed? Just what and whom is the plaintiff's attorney looking for? Soon after the complaint is filed, the attorney will begin the discovery process, usually with a request for the adjuster to answer interrogatories. The attorney will want to approach the company personnel who played any part in the handling of the claim. If the only name that the attorney has is that of the adjuster, then it can be expected that the adjuster will eventually be subpoenaed, along with the claim file, and asked a number of questions. The questions asked of the adjuster in the interrogatories as well as in depositions will involve not only the investigation of that paricular claim but also general claim procedures and the identity of other claim personnel who were involved with the claim.

It is at the time that depositions are taken when mistakes or misjudgments that the adjuster made several years earlier may resurface. It is at this time that the adjuster may wish that he or she had taken a little more time or exercised more care in completing the investigation. The fact that the adjuster was busy back when the claim occurred and could not give it sufficient attention will not be much of an excuse some years later when that pressure is long removed. All of these problems can be avoided but they must be avoided from the beginning. Once the act of bad faith is committed, it is too late; it is there forever. The emphasis should be on doing what is proper right from the start.

Claim people need to be aware that in a bad faith suit, the plaintiff's attorney will delve into the inner workings of the insurance company in an effort to learn what claim handling "standards" have been established by the company. When the standards are determined, the attorney will try to show that the adjuster handling the claim breached or failed to meet those standards.

In an effort to determine these claim handling standards, the attorney will subpoena claim manuals, training manuals, claim bulletins, and perhaps even pertinent memos of what the company requires and expects of its claim personnel. If there is a lack of written material in claim manuals, training guides, and so on, the attorney may point to the absence of such information as evidence of bad faith in itself on the company's part for not giving sufficient guidance to its claim personnel. On the other hand, if claim manuals and training manuals contain too much detail in regard to what is required of claim personnel, the company may have unintentionally created standards which, for the most part, are difficult to attain by most adjusters. In such a case, it may be rather easy for a plaintiff's attorney to show that an adjuster failed to meet the claim handling standards established by his or her company. For this reason, insurance companies should exercise care and discretion in producing their claim and training manuals.

It is also possible, when the dispute involves coverage, that the plaintiff will subpoena underwriting manuals and company advertising and promotional literature related to certain insurance policies. If more coverage is promised or implied in the policy brochure than is actually provided by the policy itself, there may be grounds for requiring the insurer to provide coverage when technically none existed.

In addition, plaintiff's attorneys are looking for inconsistencies in claim handling. For example, if an insurer pays a claim which technically is not covered, perhaps because it involves a large insured or agent, it may be subject to a bad faith claim. If an attorney representing another insured with less "leverage" can show that a similar claim was paid previously, the insurer may be compelled to pay the current claim even though technically it, too, is not covered.

Conclusion

While only a small number of claims are the subject of bad faith litigation, claim people should be conscious of the exposure insurers face in this regard in light of the threat of a judgment for punitive damages. (Exhibit 5-2 shows by state whether punitive damages may be awarded and whether they are insurable.) Specifically, adjusters should be able to identify conduct which can lead to bad faith claims. In this way, they can learn to avoid such conduct in their everyday claim handling.

Claim people must make every effort to communicate with claimants and insureds alike. Let the person making a claim know precisely what he or she must do to process the claim and bring it to a close. Adjusters should be objective and fair. They should document their files and communicate with their supervisors on a regular basis.

The claim file should be written up keeping in mind that it could be reviewed by an insurance department representative or subpoenaed by a plaintiff to be read to a judge or jury.

Above all, adjusters need to use their experience and claim sense to recognize those claims which represent potential problems and give them the necessary attention from the start. In most cases, a good claim adjuster can anticipate which claims might turn into problem claims. Early recognition of a potential problem case is the key.

Finally, adjusters should not be reluctant to ask supervisory claim personnel for help. While most companies want their adjusters to make their own decisions, this does not preclude their using supervisors or managers as a sounding board as to the propriety of those decisions. Many companies, in an effort to avoid or minimize the bad faith exposure, require that certain claims (those in which coverage is about to be denied or those involving an excess verdict exposure, for example) be submitted to management or home office claim personnel before action is taken. These companies do not discourage individual decision making but rather acknowledge the fact that occasionally another opinion regarding a claim issue is helpful. In addition, they emphasize that when the adjuster needs the benefit of the thinking of others, a support team of experienced claim practitioners is available.

THE EVOLUTIONARY PROCESS OF LAW

By now it should be evident that the law is not static; rather, it is a continually evolving process. While on the one hand the law provides society with stability, on the other it is not so rigid that it refuses to respond to society's changing views and values. One need only look at the withering away of the many common-law doctrines and principles and the corresponding expansion of the tort liability system to appreciate the meaning of this evolutionary process.

Other notable examples of the evolutionary process of law include the human rights movement of the past few decades, the expansion of the right to vote, and the changing law of the marketplace which saw the attitude of "let the buyer beware" fade into oblivion.

The law of a century or even a decade ago may seem harsh and unreasonable by today's standards. Today's law reflects changes in social and economic life as well as changes in the basic attitudes and needs of people. It is safe to say that the law changes, and will continue to change, as society's attitudes and values change.

DEFENSES

Until now, the discussion has concentrated on how an individual becomes legally liable and what rights of recovery may be available to an injured person. At this juncture, we change direction somewhat and examine the *defenses* available to an insured that can bar or mitigate a claimant's recovery.

Contributory Negligence

Contributory negligence is often referred to as the first and foremost defense available to a defendant. As stated previously, contributory negligence on the claimant's part bars recovery in those jurisdictions that have not adopted comparative negligence. It may also bar recovery in comparative negligence states if it is sufficiently substantial. Even where it does not bar recovery under comparative negligence, a claimant's contributory negligence will *limit* recovery, discounted according to the claimant's percentage of contributory negligence.

The claimant, as well as the defendant, is obligated to exercise reasonable care in his or her activities. Though a claimant may be injured through the negligence of a third person, if the claimant's actions contributed to the injury, the claimant is guilty of contributory negligence and cannot recover in states where the doctrine of contributory negligence still applies. The claimant has failed to measure up to the reasonably prudent person standard and this will bar recovery. Although contributory negligence is a valid defense in claims based on negligence, it cannot be asserted in cases involving intentional injury or damage caused by the insured or defendant.)

When investigating liability claims, adjusters must continually be alert to evidence of contributory negligence on the claimant's part. With respect to fall-down claims, the claimant has a duty to look where he or she is going. When a claimant stumbles or falls over an object or

Exhibit 5-2
State By State Punitive Damages Review—1983*

State	May Punitive Damages Be Awarded?	Are Punitive Damages Generally Insurable?
Alabama	Yes	Yes
Alaska	Yes	No precedent
Arizona	Yes	Yes
Arkansas	Yes	Yes
California	Yes	No unless insured not personally at fault.
Colorado	Yes	No
Connecticut	Yes	No
Delaware	Yes	No precedent
Florida	Yes	No unless liability vicarious
Georgia	Yes	Yes
Hawaii	Yes	No precedent
Idaho	Yes	Yes
Illinois	Yes	No unless liability vicarious
Indiana	Yes	No unless liability vicarious
Iowa	Yes	Yes
Kansas	yes	No
Kentucky	Yes	Yes
Louisiana	Generally not	Yes
Maine	Yes	No
Maryland	Yes	Yes
Massachusetts	Generally not	No precedent
Michigan	No	Probably yes
Minnesota	Yes	Yes, unless conduct intentional
Mississippi	Yes	Yes
Missouri	Yes	Yes as respects false arrest
Montana	Yes	No precedent
Nebraska	No at common law	No precedent
Nevada	Yes	No precedent
New Hampshire	Yes	Probably yes

New Jersey	Yes	No unless liability vicarious
New Mexico	Yes	No precedent but appears yes
New York	Yes	No
North Carolina	Yes	No
North Dakota	Yes	No precedent
Ohio	Yes	No precedent
Oklahoma	Yes	No unless liability vicarious
Oregon	Yes	Yes unless conduct intentional
Pennsylvania	Yes	No unless liability vicarious
Rhode Island	Yes	Probably yes
South Carolina	Yes	Yes
South Dakota	Yes	No precedent
Tennessee	Yes	Yes
Texas	Yes	Yes
Utah	Yes	No precedent
Vermont	Yes	Yes
Virginia	Yes	Probably yes
Washington, D.C.	Yes	Probably not
Washington	No unless statutory	No precedent
West Virginia	Yes	Yes
Wisconsin	Yes	Yes
Wyoming	Yes	No precedent
Total	46 Yes	
	5 No	
Insurable	7 No	
	7 No unless liability vicarious	
	37 Yes or no precedent	

*Reprinted, with permission, from *Punitive Damages Review—1983*, a publication of Wilson, Elser, Edelman and Dicker, Attorneys at Law, Graybar Building, 420 Lexington Avenue, New York, New York, 10170.

debris left in the path, it does not automatically mean that there is legal liability on the insured's part. If the object were large enough for the average person to see, the claimant may be guilty of contributory negligence. Frequently, in fall-down claims, a good investigation may reveal that a claimant was in a great hurry when the accident occurred and, if sufficiently developed, this may be solid evidence of contributory negligence.

In auto accidents, a claimant's speed, failure to yield or exercise caution at a busy intersection, or even lack of concentration may constitute contributory negligence. Any time it can be said that the cause of an accident can be attributed in part to the claimant's own failure to use the care required under the circumstances the claimant will likely be guilty of contributory negligence.

Children Whether a child can be guilty of contributory negligence is an essential issue in any investigation involving injuries to a child. Earlier in this chapter, it was indicated that, historically, a child under the age of seven is considered incapable of criminal intent. In most jurisdictions, this historical position has been extended to civil negligence law. Thus, a child under seven is ordinarily legally presumed to be incapable of negligence as well as contributory negligence. In those jurisdictions, this presumption is not rebuttable, which means that it cannot be argued that the child's actions constitute contributory negligence and should bar his or her recovery. In effect, contributory negligence has no meaning with respect to a child under the age of seven.

This does not mean, however, that adjusters should simply get out the checkbook when dealing with infant claims such as a child pedestrian knock-down. While the adjuster cannot use the defense of contributory negligence, if he or she can show through investigation that the insured was free of negligence, the claimant child ordinarily will not recover. It is of no consequence that a parent's negligence in failing to properly care for the child pedestrian may have resulted in or contributed to the child's being injured. The parent's negligence in such a situation cannot be imputed to the child to bar his or her recovery. Once again, the issue which determines if recovery will be made is whether or not the driver was negligent.

With respect to children over the age of seven, no arbitrary standard is imposed and the child's actions will be objectively compared to other children of his or her age and level of intelligence, experience, and education to determine whether the child is guilty of contributory negligence.

Vicarious Liability The negligence of a wrongdoer can be imputed to another person in certain situations. Agency with its "right to control," is probably the most common type of situation in which the contributory negligence of an agent or employee may be imputed to the principal or employer. As stated previously, if an agency relationship exists between a driver and a car owner and an accident results from the joint negligence of the driver and another motorist, the negligence (as well as the contributory negligence) of the driver is imputed to the owner. This may prohibit the owner from recovering his or her damages from the other motorist, depending on whether contributory negligence or comparative negligence is the law in that particular state. The same is true with regard to the driver's negligence being imputed to the owner in a claim made by the other motorist against the owner. In other words, the owner would be vicariously liable for the injury or damage sustained by the other motorist.

In a bailment situation, the contributory negligence of a bailee is *not* imputed to the owner because, ordinarily, the necessary element of the right to control the bailee (which is indicative of agency) is lacking.

Passengers Generally, passengers who sustain injuries while riding in a car are free of contributory negligence. As a practical matter, injured passengers will recover from the responsible driver(s). A partial exception, of course, is created by guest statutes, which require a showing of gross negligence on the part of the driver of the car in which the guest passenger was riding before the passenger can recover from that driver. The passenger's claim against the other driver, however, would not be affected by the guest statute.

Since in most situations the injured passenger will be able to make a recovery, adjusters should make prompt efforts to contact and control injured passenger claimants and to determine the seriousness of their injuries. It should be kept in mind, however, that in those cases where a joint venture or other agency relationship between the driver and passenger can be established, there may be grounds for barring recovery and these situations must be investigated thoroughly.

Assumption of Risk

When a person *voluntarily* and *knowingly* exposes himself or herself to a danger of injury, the person is said to have assumed the risk of such injury. *Assumption of risk* has been defined as a voluntary exposure to a known risk of injury. When a person assumes a risk in this manner, he or she is prevented from recovering from the negligent party. Recovery is not permitted even though the injured person may have exercised due care for his or her own safety. However, in order for the defense to be successful, the injured person must be shown to have had knowledge of the danger and to have voluntarily exposed himself or herself to the danger. If the potential danger was unknown to the claimant, the defense cannot be invoked.

The doctrine of assumption of risk is often associated with spectator injuries sustained at sporting events, such as auto racing, baseball, or hockey games. It is also a factor in pedestrian knock-down claims, such as when a claimant is struck by a car after walking between parked cars or while crossing in the middle of the intersection, or where a person voluntarily becomes a passenger in a car driven by someone who is obviously intoxicated or known to drive recklessly.

Comparative negligence statutes in a number of states have changed the status of assumption of risk as a separate defense. While some states have merged contributory negligence and assumption of risk by statute or by judicial decision, other states have retained it as a separate defense. Adjusters should be familiar with the status of the doctrine of assumptions of risk in their states.

Avoidable Consequences

The principle of *avoidable consequences* is related somewhat to that of contributory negligence but is of lesser significance. The defense of avoidable consequences applies *after* an accident has occurred and affects only *subsequent* injury or damage. It imposes a duty on the claimant to mitigate his or her damages. If the claimant fails to take proper care after an injury and complications result, the defense may be invoked to bar recovery for that portion of the claimant's injuries which can be attributed to his or her lack of care.

Unavoidable Accident

This defense may be effective where it can be established that an accident could not have been anticipated or prevented by the insured's use of reasonable care. When it can be shown that an accident was no one's fault, the accident can be characterized as an "unavoidable accident."

The question of *foreseeability* is an important factor in such cases. Sudden illness such as a heart attack or blackout by an insured while driving, which results in an accident, is an example of a case in which this defense may be invoked. For the defense to be effective, it must be demonstrated that the illness could not have been foreseen by the insured through the exercise of reasonable care. If, for example, the insured had been diagnosed by his or her doctor as having a brain tumor or serious heart ailment and was warned not to drive, an auto accident that occurs when the insured blacks out at the wheel would not be an unavoidable accident. Since the accident could have been avoided had the insured exercised reasonable care and better judgment, the defense of unavoidable accident cannot be asserted to bar the plaintiff's recovery.

Another example of an unavoidable accident may include a pedestrian knock-down involving a young child where the insured driver is free of negligence. A child under the age of seven cannot be guilty of contributory negligence even though he or she may have suddenly run between parked cars into the insured's car. The fault, if any, is the child's and since fault cannot be assessed against such a child, the accident is considered unavoidable. Another situation in which the unavoidable accident defense may be appropriate is sudden, unanticipated fog or smoke that virtually eliminates road visibility.

Act of God

An *act of God,* which is somewhat related to the defense of unavoidable accident, is regarded as a force of nature that cannot be reasonably foreseen or prevented by the exercise of reasonable care and prudence. It is both inevitable and unavoidable since human intervention can neither control nor influence it. A common situation to which the defense of act of God may be applied is a weather-related accident, such as one resulting from lightning, tornadoes, or earthquakes.

At times, an accident will be caused by a concurrence or combination of an act of God and the insured's negligence. In such cases, the insured ordinarily is responsible for his or her negligent acts and the plaintiff will recover. Where an act of God is the sole and proximate cause of an injury, however, there will be no recovery by the plaintiff.

If the insured is driving home from work in a severe thunderstorm and a tornado forms and picks up the car, forcing it into a nearby building, the insured is free of negligence based on the act of God defense. But if the town is under a tornado warning with touchdowns reported throughout the area, and residents are told to stay indoors or head for cover, the person who continues to drive after sighting a tornado under these conditions will not have much success invoking the defense if he or she has a weather-related accident.

Another situation where the defense may be successful is in the case of a sudden ice storm that makes driving, and even walking, virtually impossible. If it can be established that the road freeze was sudden, that motorists could not control their vehicles, and that the exercise of reasonable care could not have prevented the accident, the defense may be appropriate. The defense of unavoidable accident may also be pleaded in such a case.

Emergency Defense

An individual confronted with an emergency situation is not held to the same degree of care as when he or she has time to think and consider various courses of action. This is true as long as the individual's negligence did not create the emergency. If the person responds to the emergency in a way in which a reasonably prudent person would have responded, he or she will not be deemed negligent. In other words, if there is some justification for the action taken, the person is not considered negligent.

Last Clear Chance

Application of the doctrine of *last clear chance* excuses a plaintiff whose contributory negligence has put him or her in a position of peril, provided the defendant had recognized the peril in time to avoid an accident, but failed to do so. Expressed another way, where two individuals have been negligent, the individual having the last clear chance or opportunity to avoid the accident is solely responsible for the accident. This is true despite the plaintiff's contributory negligence. The negligence of the person who had the last opportunity to avoid the accident is considered the proximate cause of the accident.

Before the doctrine can be applied, it must be established that the defendant was aware of the plaintiff's vulnerability to danger or, through the exercise of reasonable care, should have been aware of it. It also must be demonstrated that the defendant actually had an opportunity to avoid the accident.

Suppose, for instance, that the plaintiff failed to see a stop sign until he or she had just entered an intersection and then jammed on the brakes and accidentally stalled the car in the middle of the intersection. If the defendant, who was driving on the cross street and was not subject to any traffic controls, saw the plaintiff stalled in the intersection in time to avoid the accident, but failed to do so, the plaintiff's contributory negligence in failing to properly stop will not bar his or her recovery. The defendant's negligence in failing to avoid the accident is the proximate cause of the accident.

The scope of this doctrine varies among the states which recognize it and it is noteworthy that most comparative negligence states have abolished the doctrine.[16]

Seat Belt Defense

Although it is not a universally accepted defense in auto accident cases, the seat belt defense does represent a potentially effective means to bar or reduce a plaintiff's recovery in a large number of states. The objective of the defense is to prove that the plaintiff's failure to use an available seat belt caused or enhanced his or her injuries and that, consequently, the plaintiff's recovery should be barred or mitigated accordingly.

For the defense to be successful, the defendant must prove that the plaintiff failed to use the safety or seat belt and then evidence must be introduced showing a causal relationship between that failure and the injuries sustained. Ordinarily, it will be necessary for the insurer, on behalf of the defendant, to have an accident reconstruction or engineering expert, as well as a medical expert, testify as to causal relationship. Then, the defendant must request that the judge charge the jury as to the possible legal consequences of the expert testimony. Finally, the jury will reach its verdict, which will include a determination of the plaintiff's damages. The plaintiff's damage may or may not be reduced for the failure to use a seat belt depending upon how much weight, if any, the jury gives to the seat belt related evidence presented by the defendant.

The potential for success of the seat belt defense is greater in cases involving head-on collisions or one-car accidents with a fixed object. In such cases, it usually can be shown that the impact would not have caused the plaintiff to strike the windshield or be ejected from the car had he or she been wearing a seat belt. In right-angle collisions, when the front of the defendent's car strikes the side of the plaintiff's car, resulting in a broken arm or leg, whether the plaintiff was wearing a seat belt may be quite irrelevant. In many such cases, the injury could have occurred with or without the seat belt being fastened. The adjuster will need to make the determination whether to assert the seat belt defense depending on the particular circumstances of each accident.

It is not an easy task for a defendant to utilize the seat belt defense successfully. The defense has been resisted strenuously by plaintiff attorneys. When preparing a seat belt defense, counsel will usually assert the defenses of contributory negligence, avoidable consequences, or assumption of risk as reasons why the plaintiff's recovery should be barred or limited. While these defenses may appear formidable, courts in a number of states have rejected their application in conjunction with the seat belt defense.

THE ROLE OF DAMAGES

First-Party Damages

Damages play an important part in the functioning of the insurance mechanism. As has already been mentioned, the liability insurance policy contractually relates the insured and insurer, with the insured referred to as the first party. The insurer is the second party to the contract, although such reference is seldom if ever used in insurance or legal terminology. The claimant becomes the "third party," even though not a party to the contract.

The automobile insurance policy grants a number of coverages to the insured. They protect the insured's property, or the insured's right to make claim for certain expenses arising out of injuries. For example, coverage is afforded for damage to an auto caused by collision and the various perils included in the comprehensive coverage of the policy. The latter relate to fire, theft, vandalism, glass breakage, and a host of other perils. It is important to know that comprehensive coverage is an "all-risks" physical loss coverage, with all damage covered except that which is excluded. The opposite is true of collision coverage, which is a "named peril" type of coverage, wherein only the named and described peril is covered, such as "collision and upset." Other ancillary coverages include tow and labor costs, transportation, and rental coverages.

Under the PAP, collision coverage is available to the insured whenever the insured's auto has been damaged by the peril of collision or upset. This coverage enables the insured to obtain immediate repairs to the auto described in the policy, subject to a deductible, whether or not the insured was negligent. As long as the policy is in force, the insurer must respond when a claim is made. Often, collision coverage is used even if the insured is not negligent, such as when there is a question of liability in the other party's mind, on a question of coverage involving the negligent party's policy.

Closely related to collision coverage is auto rental coverage, which may be involved following loss from any of the perils except total theft of the auto. This coverage is subject to stipulated maximum daily rates and a stipulated total limit.

Coverage for total auto theft is available in the comprehensive coverage section, along with all other perils that are not excluded (except collision and upset). Transportation coverage is built into the comprehensive coverage to pay the insured's transportation expenses, beginning forty-eight hours after the theft. A separate premium charge and payment is not required for this coverage. Similar to the rental coverage, this coverage also stipulates the maximum amount of coverage per day and a total limit on the amount.

The tow and labor costs coverage is available when the insured's auto breaks down and requires either labor at the scene or towing. In this situation, there is also a limit of coverage, such as $25 or $50.[17]

Third-Party Damages

In the context of third-party situations, damages are defined as being "the sum recoverable by a plaintiff who has sustained injuries or loss, because of wrongful acts of the defendant."[18]

When damages are being considered within the legal framework they are classified as to their nature and purpose. These classifications are nominal damages, compensatory damages, and punitive (or exemplary) damages.

Nominal damages are awarded in situations where no actual damage has been sustained, but the claimant's rights have been violated by the defendant. An example of such a situation would be a case of trespassing, with no harm done by the tresspasser.[19]

Of the greatest importance to the adjuster are compensatory damages, divided into two areas: "special damages" and "general damages."

Special Damages "Specials" consist of out-of-pocket expenses incurred by the plaintiff resulting from such charges as medical or hospital bills, prescriptions, therapy, x-rays, and loss of compensation for work the plaintiff has been unable to perform because of the injuries sustained.

When considering these "specials," the adjuster must be certain that the charges included are for damage or injury resulting from the accident only, and no other charges which are not accident related.

In addition, the adjuster must consider not only "specials" that have been incurred in the past, but also those that are anticipated in the future. Such future projections may prove difficult to ascertain in the area of medical treatment, depending on the injury and the general health of the claimant. Also, projections may be difficult from the standpoint of future loss of wages, as they depend on the talents of the claimant, the type of work involved, and many other factors. In serious injury cases, it is not unusual for the claimant to employ an economist to project future earning losses. As a result, the defense may also retain an economic expert to testify in favor of the defense.

General Damages Unlike special damages, which are determined by incurred expenditures or by some other definite measurable process, general damages comprise certain elements that require persons to form an opinion on value.[20] Such circumstances may include pain and suffering, disfigurement, disability, loss of consortium and the like, all as the result of an injury.

Pain and Suffering. All injuries involve some degree of pain and suffering and judging the value of this may be difficult. Is the degree of severity determined on the basis of objective or subjective findings? This is an important question, as it determines if severity is measured by the results of clinical testing (objective), or by the result of what the claimant says is wrong in the description of the injury (subjective). In an objective finding, a doctor is able to clinically test a part of the body and confirm the existence of injury on the examination. A subjective finding is based solely on the claimant's statement that she "has headaches every day and her back aches almost always."

Evidence of pain and suffering is usually a critical area of concern for the adjuster. This is true, even in the case of fatalities, when it can be established that the deceased was conscious for a period of time. Presentation of such factual information can lead a jury to return a large verdict. It is the duty of the claim representative to investigate and uncover such critical facts, as they may completely change the course of the defense of the claim.

Disfigurement. Claims involving disfigurement often result in large settlements or verdicts. Some accident illustrations of disfigurement claims include a claimant going through the windshield of an auto, resulting in facial lacerations and scars or serious burns resulting from the breakage of a faulty coffee pot, full of hot coffee. A vicious dog bite can severely scar the face of a child. Such scars take a long time to heal and may remain unsightly, requiring extensive surgical revision.

An important consideration in disfigurement claims is whether a defense medical examination should be requested, and if so, when the examination should take place. There are times when a defense medical examination only confirms what the plaintiff's doctor has already reported. The purpose for a defense examination is to demonstrate maximum improvement of the scarring and, therefore, it should be timed accordingly.

Loss of Consortium. Consortium is defined as "the right of conjugal fellowship of husband and wife."[21] For the purposes of this discussion, we refer specifically to sex, society, and services (the "three S's"). In these broad parameters, "sex" means the right for spouses to have sexual relations with each other; "society" means the entitlement to companionship; and "services" means the right of household duties from a spouse.[22] If any of these rights is violated by a negligent party, such violation is the basis for a cause of action against the liable person.

Historically, common law dictated that only the husband could make a claim for loss of consortium. The wife was not permitted to make such claims as the courts did not recognize the wife as being equal to the husband. In the recent past, however, many states have reversed this position and presently recognize the same rights for the wife as for the husband.[23]

While there is no doubt that the tort system requires the negligent party to reimburse the claimant for losses sustained, there still remains the duty of the claimant to mitigate the damage. This simply means that the claimant should try to keep the damage at a minimum. For example, if the claimant knows that an auto accident caused sufficient damage to the radiator to cause a leak, the claimant should either take the precaution of getting the radiator repaired or stop driving the car, in order to prevent further damage. In a situation where the claimant's auto is damaged and not drivable and he or she makes claim for loss of sales due to the lack of transportation, rental cars are available to the claimant to prevent such loss of use or similar claims.

Disability

While considering damages, the aspect of disability becomes an important factor in the overall value of a claim, especially when the claimant has incurred some degree of permanent disability. In the less serious claims, an injury may cause the claimant to be temporarily disabled for a short period of time and the disability, whether partial or total, ends with the injured party's resuming normal activities. In such cases, the value is not too difficult to establish by virtue of medical reports and establishing the lost wages.

The claim becomes more complicated and expensive when a permanent disability is involved, such as the loss of motion or movement of the joint of a finger by some percentage amount or possibly, a permanent total disability of the individual, preventing that person from pursuing an established livelihood. In the former example, the percentage of disability to the finger joint will assist in evaluating the injury. In all probability, an additional sum of money added to the value will assist in settling such a claim, providing that the disability does not hinder the claimant unduly in pursuing her livelihood.

In the latter example, the totally disabled person will have to rely on the settlement to sustain him or her and any dependents in the future, and as a result, the adjuster faces a claim representing a high value. Although it may be possible to rehabilitate a totally disabled person to pursue another type of livelihood, the settlement value, in all probability, will remain quite high. In addition to the projected loss of employment, values will also depend on other variables, such as medical costs, possible remodeling of the dwelling to accommodate physical needs, and pain and suffering.

Verification of Damages

The process of investigating claims not only includes the analysis of medical information, but also the actual steps involved in the acquisition of the medical reports and records. Since medical information is privileged, it is necessary to have medical authorization forms signed by the claimant, which upon presentation to the doctor or hospital personnel enables them to supply the adjuster with the requested medical reports and bills.

If the adjuster is working in a large metropolitan area, the arrangements for medical reports undoubtedly will be on an impersonal basis, involving busy physicians who have little time to discuss or explain a patient's medical condition to a claim person. In fact, it may be a major feat to obtain the information within a reasonable time.

In addition, large metropolitan hospitals produce such large amounts of paperwork that the arrangement for medical reports and records must be done by the numbers, just to maintain some semblance of order and organization.

Due to the sensitivity and privileged nature of the information, the doctors and hospitals must also be careful that they are not exposing themselves to a liability situation by permitting the information to be released without the appropriate authorization. Another possible situation in a metropolitan area may require only original authorizations to be used for acquiring the desired medical information. Consequently, the practice of making photocopies of one original authorization may not be sufficient for the need of these suppliers.

On the other hand, the claim representative may work in a small town or city where the doctors or the medical records secretary may be acquainted with the adjuster. Such relationships permit a freer and friendlier atmosphere in which to work. This is not to suggest that such situations promote unethical practices, but merely that it may be easier to arrange for the reports in a proper manner. The doctor may even have time to discuss an injury (with proper authorization, of course) with the adjuster.

The medical authorization forms must be signed and dated by the claimant (or parent if a minor is injured) and should be obtained at the first possible opportunity. At that time, assuming that the claimant is not represented by an attorney, the adjuster should take the necessary steps to establish rapport, discuss the accident, take the claimant's statement, and obtain the medical authorizations. If these items are not obtained on the first visit, they may not be available during the second visit, as the claimant may be legally represented at that later date.

If the first contact with the claimant is made by an office claim representative (OCR) by telephone, it is imperative that the matter of medical authorizations be discussed and understood by the claimant. Further, the OCR must follow through by mailing the authorization forms to the claimant for signature, and include a postage-paid envelope to facilitate the return mail at no cost to the claimant. In addition, the file should be placed on a short diary to be certain that the forms are returned quickly. Caution should be taken to use the forms as quickly as possible, as they are dated. In some instances, the supplier of medical information will not accept authorizations that are not recently dated.

The importance of the first meeting with the claimant or insured cannot be stressed too much. As noted, proper relationships must be established in order to maintain control of the claim. In this context, "control" is meant to have established a strong enough relationship with the claimant that the claimant is willing to deal directly with the adjuster. In addition, the claimant must be put on record in statement form in order to preserve the facts, and then the medical forms must be signed.

Still another important aspect of maintaining control and building the foundation of the relationship is providing the claimant with sufficient information as to what will be required of the claimant (or insured) and what he can expect from the adjuster. It is helpful to the claimant if the adjuster explains the various steps to be taken in the processing of the claim and approximately when these procedures will occur. In this manner, the all important element of communication is set into motion. The claimant knows what to expect and, in that sense, the claim representative is making a commitment to that claimant as to future transactions. Of course, each commitment must be kept by the adjuster, without fail. If this procedure is followed, there will be no complaint calls received and the adjuster will enjoy complete control of the claim, instead of the claim controlling the adjuster.

Verification of Medical Charges

Occasions may occur when it is necessary to verify the cost of medical treatment as submitted by the claimant, such as when the claimant requires hospitalization. Subsequently, the adjuster is presented with medical information indicating that the injury from the accident involves a fracture of the tibia in the left leg, lacerations, and contusions. The medical costs amount to a substantial sum, including all charges incurred in the hospital. How can the adjuster be sure that all of the medical charges are the result of the injuries sustained in the accident?

At times, it may be obvious that some of the charges are for the treatment of another illness or medical condition. On the other hand, it can be difficult for the lay person to detect such charges. In such cases, the services of a trained individual, who can check the charges and determine if there are overcharges, duplications, or charges for treatment of medical conditions not related to the accident, may be necessary. When a claimant is hospitalized for more than one type of treatment, the hospital does not maintain separate billing records for each condition being treated; therefore, there is a need for such verification.

In considering such verification procedures, the adjuster must be aware that these services are expensive. It is wise for the insurer to establish a minimum-charge threshold before the billing is to be submitted for verification. For example, the company might decide that the medical bills per claimant must amount to $5,000 or $10,000 before they can be submitted for verification.

Independent Medical Examinations

Reasons for Requesting an Independent Examination In some instances, an independent medical examination is necessary to defend against claims that appear to be unrealistic as to injury sustained, degree of permanent injury, or in some other way. If, for example, the adjuster's investigation shows a slight impact to the rear of the claimant's auto in a rear-end type of accident, and the claimant is claiming a fractured vertebra, certainly an independent medical exam should be requested and ordered. In another case, the degree of permanent damage may be seriously questioned by the adjuster and justifies a request for the opinion of another physician.

Other factors may be taken into consideration, such as discovery rules, healing factor of injuries, and early examination.

Legal Consideration of Discovery Rules. It is possible that the court rules of discovery in the jurisdiction may play an important part in the decision whether independent medical exams should be requested. Some jurisdictions may permit only one examination prior to trial; consequently, proper timing is of great importance. Other jurisdictions may allow more than one exam, which makes it easier to decide in certain situations.

Healing Factors of Injuries. It is only natural that the independent medical examination take place at a time most advantageous to the defendant. Since time is a great healer, it is wise to wait as long as possible for such exams. This is particularly true in cases of fractures, scarring, and disfigurement cases such as burns. Although these signs of injury will not disappear, the passage of time goes a long way to diminish the visual effects of such shock losses.

Possibly Fraudulent Claims. It is advisable to request an early exam if a fraudulent injury claim is suspected. Should the adjuster be confronted with this situation, the claimant will undoubtedly strongly resist such early examining. Under these circumstances, the adjuster should follow the suggestions and advice of the supervisor or manager and, above all, be extremely careful in making any accusations that cannot be proven.

Selection of a Medical Examiner or Expert The selection of a medical expert should be made only after proper consideration is given to all phases of the defense of the claim, including the timing of the examination, type of expert, and who the expert will be. The adjuster can discuss these aspects of consideration with the examiner, claim manager, or defense counsel in the area. The defense attorney's opinion in such matters is important as that is the individual who will be defending the insured if a lawsuit is filed.

As previously indicated, the timing of the examination is important, both from the standpoint of the healing of the injury, as in a scar, and also regarding the rules of the court where only one examination is permitted.

Not all medical doctors wish to become involved in providing independent medical exams, nor are they all qualified. Many physicians prefer to concentrate on the task of practicing medicine and do not wish to become involved with the legal aspects of injuries. In fact, it is possible that some doctors may not want to treat a patient on a regular basis if the medical condition is the result of an accident and is involved in a claim or a lawsuit.

Medical Examiner's Qualifications. Medical specialists who are willing to participate in medico-legal cases should be well qualified to do so. Among the particular qualifications are the following.

Professional Credentials. The physician should, of course, have graduated from a well-known medical school and have expertise in the specific area of medicine in question. "Board Certification" is an important credential, as it represents certification by the expert's peers and involves a number of criteria the expert must fulfill. The doctor must practice in the specialty field for a number of years, the amount usually determined by the Board and must submit to oral and written examinations before the certification can be obtained.

Many medical experts also devote time to teaching in medical schools, not only for the purpose of sharing their knowledge, but also to stay current in the medical progress of their specialty.

Finally, a specialist often shares his knowledge and experience through publications involving the specialty, describing latest techniques and, possibly, medical breakthroughs.

Fair and Objective. It would be foolish for the insurer to want a medical examiner to report favorably for the insurer under any circumstances. First, the doctor would jeopardize a reputation and, secondly, the insurer should want a fair and objective report of the medical findings. If they are unfavorable to the insurer, it is best to reevaluate the claim and perhaps negotiate a settlement immediately. In many jurisdictions, it is required that plaintiff's attorney be supplied with a copy of the independent medical report. As a result, the adjuster must be prepared for any eventuality in the report.

Willingness to Testify. If the doctor is willing to examine and produce a report to the insurer, he or she must also be willing to testify. This can be time-consuming for the doctor; therefore, the need for testimony should be made clear to the doctor beforehand. Of course, the medical expert is fully compensated for time and services when such need occurs.

Until recently, the doctor had to testify in the courtroom at a time and date suitable only to the court. Such arrangements were not always compatible with the doctor's schedule, necessitating further delays in the trial of the case. This problem has been eliminated in the last few years with the use of video equipment, used directly in the doctor's office. When it is determined that the medical expert's testimony is required, the necessary arrangements are made between the expert and plaintiff's and defendant's counsel. The testimony is taken and preserved until it is presented in evidence in the trial. This method has proven to be an efficient manner of presenting testimony, saving time and expenses.

The Independent Medical Examination Report When the medical examination is being arranged by the claim representative, the doctor must not only be apprised of the specific areas of particular interest, but also of the person to whom the report should be addressed and mailed. The report should not be addressed to the claim representative, as that information would be noted by the jury if the report is presented in evidence. Knowledge that an insurance company is involved in the claim may well prejudice the jury and cause a mistrial. There are several ways that the report can be addressed. The first is to simply address the report "To Whom It May Concern" and mail it directly to the adjuster. The second method is to address the report to the insurer's defense counsel in that locality and mail the report directly to the adjuster. Care should be taken by the physician not to caption the medical report with terminology such as "Your Insured" or to include a claim number in the caption.

The medical report should start out with a brief explanation as to how the injury occurred, as related by the claimant. Included in this will be various important dates, such as date of accident, and dates of treatment. Also, the examining doctor should relate any causal connection of the injury to the accident.

Following should be information dealing with previous medical history as well as the history of the current injury to date. If the previous history is significant in any manner, all pertinent information should be obtained and included in the report.

The report should continue with the description of the examination that was conducted, including the various tests that were conducted, and the results.

Next would come the diagnosis of the injury. It may include and explain the objective findings which result from the tests, and the subjective information from the claimant.

The final segment of the independent medical report typically deals with the doctor's conclusions and opinion as to the prognosis, that is, the expectation of recovery or the extent of permanency, if any.

Collateral Source Rule

The collateral source rule is applicable in tort claims in some states. Briefly, the Rule holds that even though the damaged party has other resources to pay for medical expenses and lost wages, the person causing the damage, the tortfeasor, remains responsible for these. The "collateral sources" may be health and accident insurance policies paid for by the claimant, or Blue Cross or Blue Shield. It is possible for the claimant to collect medical expenses several times in some cases. In some states, particularly where no-fault insurance is applicable, the law may rule out collateral source payments.

Emotional Distress Claims

Emotional distress claims are sometimes unaccompanied by physical injury or an impact. Initially, the nonimpact emotional distress claims were ruled in favor of the defendant, as the courts felt that it is too difficult to prove damages.

> Initially, such causes of action were not permitted: If the right of recovery in this class of cases should be once established, it would naturally result in a flood of litigation in cases where the injury complained of may be easily feigned without detection, and where the

> damages must rest upon mere conjecture or speculation. The difficulty which often exists in cases of alleged physical injury, in determining whether they exist and, if so, whether they were caused by the negligent act of the defendant, would not only be greatly increased, but a wide field would be opened for fictitious or speculative claims. To establish such a doctrine would be contrary to principles of public policy.[24]

These common-law rulings were first changed by the state of New York in Battalla v. State of New York, (10 NY 2d 237). Subsequently, various other states have followed to allow such emotional distress claims without impact.[25]

Prenatal Injury Claims

On occasion, an adjuster must be concerned with a claim involving an unborn child. As in many other situations, the law is changing in this area, making it necessary for the claim representative to be attentive to the current legal status of such claims. The unborn infant is referred to as a fetus, and common law has held that the fetus is "considered to be a part of the mother's anatomy until birth"[26] and, therefore, could not be included in a claim even though it could be shown that the injury was sustained while in the form of a fetus.

In recent years, however, various courts have held that a viable fetus can be the subject of a legal claim. A viable fetus is one that can sustain life outside the womb.[27]

Damages in the Form of Interest

Whenever the tort system is the basis of deciding the amount of damages, consideration must be given to amounts of money earned in interest. For many years, the interest was charged following a judgment in favor of the plaintiff, while it was appealed by the defendant. Such appeal procedures can take a considerable length of time, thereby delaying payment of the award to the plaintiff. Subsequently, if the defendant lost the appeal, not only the judgment awarded would be paid to the plaintiff, but also interest on this amount for the length of time of the delay of payment. This is called post-judgment interest. In Ohio, for example, the interest is now applied at a rate of 10 percent per annum. Depending on the amount of the award, the interest accrued may prove to be a substantial amount, making it necessary to give serious thought when considering an appeal.

Post-judgment interest can also be charged by the court when the defendant unreasonably delays the payment of the claim.

Pre-Judgment Interest

Some states also allow a pre-judgment interest, but as in Ohio, for example, this charge is allowed only in cases based on:

> tortious conduct and not settled by agreement of the parties, (interest) shall be computed from the date the cause of action accrued to the date on which the money is paid, if upon motion of any party to the action, the court determines at a hearing held subsequent to the verdict or decision in the action that the party required to pay the money failed to make good faith effort to settle the case and that the party to whom the money is to be paid did not fail to make a good faith effort to settle the case.[28]

Chapter Notes

1. Robert C. Witt and Jorge Urrutia, "An Overview and Assessment of No-Fault Plans," *CPCU Journal*, March 1984, p. 10. The authors refer to the Columbia University Council for Research in the Social Services Report by the *Committee to Study Compensation for Automobile Accidents* (Philadelphia: International Printing Company, 1932).
2. Witt and Urratia, p. 11.
3. Published by Little, Brown and Company, Boston, 1965.
4. As of May 11, 1984, modified no-fault auto insurance laws apply in the following states: Colorado, Connecticut, Florida, Georgia, Hawaii, Kansas, Kentucky, Massachusetts, Michigan, Minnesota, New Jersey, New York, North Dakota, Utah, and the District of Columbia. States with add-on plans include Arkansas, Delaware, Maryland, Oregon, Pennsylvania, South Carolina, South Dakota, Texas, and Virginia.
5. Since the state by state situation may change with time, the reader may wish to refer to the appropriate state law or to a generally available insurance technical publication for the most current information. Two popular sources of this information are *The Fire, Casualty & Surety Bulletins* and the *Policy Form & Manual Analyses.* Another possible source is *Analysis of Automobile No-Fault Statutes.*
6. Such plans are available in Washington and Wisconsin.
7. In Michigan, tort liability is abolished with respect to property damage except in cases where the damage is less than $400.
8. New Jersey offers reinsurance for medical expenses over $75,000.
9. It is somewhat ironic that aside from the enactment of a modified no-fault law in the District of Columbia, the only no-fault legislation in the last several years was the repeal of no-fault laws in two states. Nevada repealed its modified law effective January 1, 1980, and Pennsylvania did likewise effective October 1, 1984.
10. This interesting and unconventional view of the future of no-fault compensation schemes was expressed by P.S. Atiyah in an article entitled "No-Fault Compensation: A Question That Will Not Go Away," *The Insurance Law Journal*, November 1980.
11. The discussion of bad faith is based, in part, on a two-part article written by John Melvin, in the company claim bulletin, *The Claims-Gram* Vol. XXIV-No. 4, December, 1982 and Vol. XXV, No. 1, April, 1983.
12. *Gruenberg vs. Aetna Insurance Company,* 510 P. 2d 1032 (1973), a California case, as cited by Alan R. Miller, Attorney, Robins, Zelle, Larson & Kaplan, Wellesley, MA. 02181, in a presentation before the Property Insurance Committee of the American Bar Association in Dallas, Texas, August 1979. The presentation was entitled "Overview and Historical Development of the Problem of Bad Faith and Punitive Damages," pp. 1 and 2.

13. *Travelers Indemnity Co. vs. Armstrong* 384 N.E. 2d. 607,618 (Indiana App. 1979).
14. Miller, p. 1.
15. David M. Smith J.D., Senior Vice President, Wausau Insurance Company, Wausau, WI as reported in *CQ, Claims Section Quarterly,* Vol, 2, No. 3, Spring 1984, in article entitled "Watching Out For Bad Faith," p. 3.
16. James L. Graham, *Ohio's New Comparative Negligence Statute,* p. 6.
17. Personal Auto Policy, PP 00 02 (6-80) BF, Insurance Services Office; Reference First Party Coverages.
18. Pat Magarick, JD, LL.M., *Successful Handling of Casualty Claims,* (Brooklyn, NY: Central Book Co. Inc., 1974), p. 49.
19. Ronald A. Anderson, *The Insurer's Tort Law,* 2nd Edition, (Ocean City, NJ: The Littoral Development Co., 1971), p. 82.
20. Corydon T. Johns, *An Introduction to Liability Claims Adjusting,* 3rd Ed. (Cincinnati, OH: The National Underwriter Co., 1982), p. 530.
21. *Webster's New Collegiate Dictionary* (Springfield, MA: G. & C. Merriam Co,, 1981).
22. James H. Donaldson, *Casualty Claims Practice,* 3rd Ed. (Homewood, IL: Richard D. Irwin, Inc., 1976), p. 155.
23. Donaldson, p. 154.
24. Donaldson, p. 148.
25. Donaldson, p. 149.
26. Donaldson, p. 157.
27. Donaldson, p. 157.
28. General Assembly of the State of Ohio, Amended Substitute House Bill No. 189, Section C. (Effective 7-5-82).

CHAPTER 6

The Investigative Process

INTRODUCTION

It was stated earlier that the job of the claim adjuster involves essentially three areas of claim handling: *coverage, liability,* and *damages.* One claim executive, expanding on this concept, holds the view that adjusting actually is a nine step process: the three steps of (1) investigation, (2) evaluation, and (3) negotiation of *coverage;* the three steps of (1) investigation, (2) evaluation and (3) negotiation of *liability;* and, finally, the three steps of (1) investigation, (2) evaluation, and (3) negotiation of *damages.*[1] This viewpoint helps put the primary role of investigation into perspective. Investigation must *precede* evaluation and negotiation, and is concerned not only with liability but with coverage and damages as well.

Investigation is getting the facts about coverage, liability, and damages. The adjuster must determine how, when, where, and why the accident happened. The purpose of investigation is to secure the necessary facts so that a claim can be evaluated and settled or, in some instances, defended.

The right and duty of an insurance company to investigate claims against its insured is granted by the insurance policy itself. In many policies, the liability *Insuring Agreement* specifically states that the company may investigate and settle any claim or suit as it considers appropriate. If the right and duty to investigate is not specifically addressed in the *Insuring Agreement* (as is the case with the Personal Auto Policy), it will be granted in the *Duties* or *Conditions* section of the policy in the so-called "cooperation" clause. Part E—Duties After an Accident or Loss of the Personal Auto Policy states: "A person seeking any coverage must: 1. Cooperate with us in the investigation, settlement or defense of any claim or suit. . . ."

It is certainly understandable that before an insurer can decide whether to deny or pay a claim, it must be able to investigate the claim. The policy clearly gives the insurer this right, and the insured is under a contractual obligation to cooperate with the company as it conducts its investigation.

The investigative process involves inquiry, verification, and comparison of the information obtained. Adjusters must not only *obtain* information but they must also *verify* and *compare* that information through other available sources. The investigative approach, that is, the level of energy and imagination employed, will vary by adjuster. Some adjusters thrive on the leg work and people contact which are essential to an intensive investigation while others are less inclined to knock on doors in search of witnesses or physical evidence.

With respect to verification and comparison, the insured's statement should be checked against the police report and verfied by any witnesses to the accident. Adjusters frequently will find it necessary to observe the scene of an accident, especially in more serious or complex cases. In addition, damages such as medical or hospital expenses can be verified by a physician or hospital report or bill (with the necessary authorization from the claimant) or by a medical exam. Lost income can be verified by a wage or salary report from the employer (again, with the necessary authorization), and property damage can be verified by an appraisal or sometimes by a photograph.

As the adjuster conducts the investigation, he or she should be continually comparing new information with that already obtained so that any conflicts may be immediately recognized. When newly acquired information contradicts previously known information, the adjuster must reexamine the information and, in many cases, conduct further investigation to eliminate the conflict or determine which is the more credible version of the accident.

How much investigation should be conducted? The extent of investigation will depend on the nature and complexity of the accident or loss, and to a considerable degree, the company's claim philosophy. Cases involving coverage questions, serious injuries or questions of liability will need to be more extensively investigated than minor claims where fault is easily determined.

An intersection auto accident in a comparative negligence state involving several cars with a question of liability and serious injuries will require a prompt and thorough investigation. On the other hand, rear-end collision with minor injuries may require a minimum of investigation and may be handled rather routinely. A premises "fall-down" case in a supermarket parking lot, where responsibility for maintenance and repairs appears to be with an independent firm, and a lease between the supermarket and the landlord containing a hold-harmless agreement, might require a comprehensive investigation.

Categories of Liability

Since the discussion of the investigative process will repeatedly make reference to the various categories of liability as they relate to the insured, it is necessary that these liability categories be explained before proceeding any further.

When an insured's liability is characterized as *clear*, it means that there is no real question that the insured was entirely at fault for the accident and the claim is one for settlement (assuming that coverage is in order). An example of a clear liability auto case is one in which the insured strikes the claimant in the rear, provided there are no extenuating circumstances such as a sudden stop by the claimant.

A case of *probable* liability on the insured's part simply means that while it may not be a clear-cut case of liability, the insured was probably at fault for the accident. In other words, it is likely that based on the facts, the insured would not prevail if the case were litigated. An example of a probable liability case might be an intersection accident where the insured was facing a stop sign and did not come to a full stop, while the claimant was subject to no traffic controls. While there may be some room for argument for the imposition of some contributory negligence on the claimant in such cases, the details and circumstances of the accident point convincingly to the insured's negligence.

When an insured's liability is viewed as *doubtful*, it means that in all likelihood the insured was not negligent or legally liable for the accident. The doubtful liability classification is sometimes used to describe a case in which the insured is virtually free from liability as well.

The category which creates the greatest challenge for adjusters is that of *questionable* liability. In a case of questionable liability, it is unclear which party bears primary responsibility for the accident. It may be a case where each party is contributorily negligent for the mishap and there may be a genuine question whether a defense of the claim can be successful. An uncontrolled intersection accident and an accident involving a question of which driver had the green light are examples of questionable liability cases. Questionable liability claims may be defended, depending upon the circumstances of the case and the laws of the particular jurisdiction, but more often than not, these cases are compromised.

In a clear or probable liability case, the investigation needed to determine the liability aspect of the claim may be minimal. The coverage and damages aspect of the claim, however, may need to be extensively investigated.

When there is doubtful or no liability on the insured's part, a minimum of investigation may be necessary. But if the claim is one that is being pressed by the plaintiff, and will need to be defended, a thorough investigation will be necessary and warranted so that a successful defense can be developed and presented at trial.

A *questionable* liability claim will also require a thorough investigation of liability and damages. Whether the claim is denied or negotiated to a compromise, the adjuster will need to support his or her decision with a well documented claim file.

Telephone Adjusting

It is necessary at the outset to acknowledge the significant role of telephone adjusting in modern day claim handling. Since the majority of claims are minor in dollar amount and can be disposed of rather routinely and with a minimum of investigative effort, many companies utilize inside telephone claim units to handle the large majority of their claims. Low or fixed dollar amount, high volume claims such as collision, comprehensive, or property damage, and even medical payments and minor bodily injury claims, can be appropriately handled by telephone claim units. Most companies utilizing this claim handling approach also assign the more complex cases. They often require personal contact and a more extensive investigation by their field claim adjusters or by independent adjusters.

Although the view of insurance claim executives toward telephone adjusting has fluctuated over the years, it is safe to say that today telephone adjusting is a well-established and well accepted claim handling method. The motivation for installation of these claim units was essentially economic. The rationale is simply that the large volume of claims which require little or no investigation (and actually comprise the large majority of reported claims) can be more economically and efficiently handled by inside or office telephone adjusters. Most insurers acknowledge this view and prefer this approach to that of incurring the considerable expense of using field claim adjusters to handle these high volume, routine claims. The exclusive use of field claim adjusters with company cars to handle virtually all claims appears to be out of fashion today, except in isolated cases.

Today's competition among insurers mandates that companies reduce their overhead expenses, and telephone adjusting is one effective means of accomplishing this end. Furnishing agents with draft authority on relatively minor, routine claims represents another approach being used by many insurers to reduce expenses and to enhance claim service.

Most insurers believe that it is more economical to handle the mass of routine claims from inside the office than to personally investigate every claim, notwithstanding the fact that there is a risk that some claims will occasionally be underinvestigated and overpaid. Practically speaking, there appears to be a willingness among most company claim executives to assume this risk in light of the savings gained from the use of inside telephone adjusting units and the relative success of this approach.

Telephone claim units are volume or quantity oriented for the most part. Since claims handled by such units *generally* are small or routine and require a minimum of investigation, the telephone adjuster can handle a considerably larger volume of claims than his or her counterpart in the field.

The kinds of claims handled by telephone units depend basically on company claim philosophy. Actually, the structure or design of telephone units can be as diverse as the companies which employ these claim handling units. Some companies limit the telephone units to minor property damage claims, assigning all bodily injury claims and moderate to severe property claims to field adjusters. Other companies have their telephone units handling small to moderate bodily injury claims as well, including the negotiation and settlement of such claims. Still other companies operate almost exclusively with telephone adjusters who handle virtually all claims and actually play somewhat of a dual role. Though most of their time is spent in the office, they will occasionally do their own field or leg work on their claims or assign limited outside work to independent adjusters.

The point is that there is not necessarily and "ideal" or "generic" telephone unit. As noted earlier, the structure of these units and the type of claims they handle will vary according to company claim philosophy and, to some extent, the ability and experience of the adjusters who comprise these units.

It must be kept in mind that most, it not all, companies that have adopted this claim handling method are satisfied that considerable investigation can be accomplished from the telephone. Telephone adjusters, for example, can secure telephone recorded statements of insureds, claimants, and witnesses alike. They can obtain police and fire reports and with proper authorization can verify lost wages and medical and hospital expenses as well as obtain doctors' reports on claimants. Inspections or appraisals can be assigned to staff field adjusters or appraisers or to independent appraisers with instructions to submit the appraisal to the telephone adjuster for settlement.

Although modern day realities virtually assure the continued use of telephone claim units in conjunction with field claim adjusting, two cautions are frequently advanced with regard to the manner in which telephone adjusting is conducted. First, if the telephone units are handling anything more than routine claims, managers should be sure that adjusters are properly trained and capable of handling the more complicated claims. Secondly, adjusters need to be taught to recognize early the potentially troublesome claims which really are not suited for volume oriented claim handling but rather require the face-to-face personal contact and attention of an experienced field claim adjuster.

Typical claim situations in which personal contact is ordinarily necessary are those involving substantial property damage when the damage must be visually inspected and those requiring outside field work. The latter might include an inspection of the accident scene, where perhaps skid marks are evident or where some obstruction is a factor, or simply a case where a good witness canvass is necessary. In addition, cases which are particularly complicated or those requiring sensitive settlement negotiations are better suited for personal handling. Finally, whenever a telephone adjuster faces the risk of losing control of a bodily injury claimant, prompt outside field contact with the claimant should be considered.

PLANNING THE INVESTIGATION

Investigation begins with the accident report. (Examples of *ACORD* automobile and general liability accident reports are found in Exhibits 6-1 and 6-2. The *ACORD* accident report form is a standard form which is used by most insurance companies.)

Whether the claim is assigned to an office telephone adjuster or field claim adjuster, the accident report should be reviewed and checked carefully. This is true regardless of whether the adjuster begins the investigation in the field without any direction from his or her supervisor or receives the assignment directly from the supervisor with specific items of investigation being assigned. As the adjuster studies the accident report, he or she should make notes of any unusual circumstances or problems associated with the claim.

The way in which claim adjusters organize their work varies by company. Ordinarily, field claim adjusters will either make copies of the accident report or make entries into an assignment book for use in their field claim handling. Office telephone adjusters may work exclusively from the claim file, which is diaried according to a particular schedule. Since computers are used extensively in many company claim operations today, some office telephone adjusters may use the computer,

Exhibit 6-1
ACORD Automobile Loss Notice

ACORD AUTOMOBILE LOSS NOTICE

SET TAB STOPS AT ARROWS

DATE (MM/DD/YY): 8-10-8

PRODUCER	PRODUCER PHONE (A/C, NO., EXT.)	FOR COMPANY USE ONLY		
Engel Agency 1000 E. Broad Street Columbus, Ohio 43216	614 464-0000			
	COMPANY		POLICY NUMBER	CAT. #
	Institute Insurance Co.		PAP 1000 000	
CODE / SUB CODE	POLICY EFF. DATE (MM/DD/YY)	POLICY EXP. DATE (MM/DD/YY)	DATE (MM/DD/YY) & TIME OF LOSS	PREVIOUSLY REPORTED
	6-3-8	6-3-8	8-8-8 2 P.M.	X NO

INSURED

NAME AND ADDRESS	INSURED'S RESIDENCE PHONE (A/C, NO.)	INSURED'S BUSINESS PHONE (A/C, NO., EXT.)
Teddy Smith 100 Lane Drive Buckeye Lake, Ohio 43244	222-0000	345-0000
	PERSON TO CONTACT: Teddy Smith	WHERE TO CONTACT: Business WHEN: 9-5
	CONTACT'S RESIDENCE PHONE (A/C, NO.)	CONTACT'S BUSINESS PHONE (A/C, NO., EXT.)

LOSS

LOCATION OF ACCIDENT (INCLUDING CITY & STATE)	AUTHORITY CONTACTED & REPORT NO.	VIOLATIONS/CITATIONS
Intersection of Connell Ave. & Main St., Buckeye Lake, OH	Buckeye Lake	None

DESCRIPTION OF ACCIDENT (USE REVERSE SIDE, IF NECESSARY)

Insured driving north on Connell Avenue stopped at stop sign and after proceeding into intersection was struck in left rear quarter panel by vehicle 2. Vehicle 2 speeding in easterly direction on Main Street.

POLICY INFORMATION

BODILY INJURY	PROPERTY DAMAGE	SINGLE LIMIT	MED. PAY.	OTHER THAN COLL. DED.	OTHER COVERAGES & DEDUCTIBLES (UM, NO-FAULT, TOWING, ETC.)
25,50,000	10,000		1,000	no. ded.	UM/UIM 50,000 Rental Reimbursement T & L.
LOSS PAYEE				COLLISION DED.	
Fantasia Savings & Loan				100	

INSURED VEHICLE

VEH. NO.	YEAR, MAKE, MODEL	V.I.N. (VEHICLE IDENTIFICATION)	PLATE NO.
1	1983 Chevy Citation	1X100AB1300000000	ABC-162

OWNER'S NAME & ADDRESS	PHONE (A/C, NO., EXT.)
Insured	

DRIVER'S NAME & ADDRESS (CHECK IF SAME AS OWNER) ☐	RESIDENCE PHONE (A/C, NO.)	BUSINESS PHONE (A/C, NO., EXT.)
Insured		

RELATION TO INSURED (EMPLOYEE, FAMILY, ETC.)	DATE OF BIRTH	DRIVERS LICENSE NUMBER	PURPOSE OF USE	USED WITH PERMISSION ☐ YES ☐ NO

DESCRIBE DAMAGE	ESTIMATE AMOUNT	WHERE CAN VEHICLE BE SEEN	WHEN	OTHER INSURANCE ON VEHICLE
left quarter panel	$4,400	Tamborine Auto Body		

PROPERTY DAMAGED

DESCRIBE PROPERTY (IF AUTO, YEAR, MAKE, MODEL, PLATE NO.)	OTHER VEH. OR PROPERTY INSURED	COMPANY OR AGENCY NAME & POLICY NO.
1984 Cutlass Ciera	X YES ☐ NO	

OWNER'S NAME & ADDRESS	BUSINESS PHONE (A/C, NO., EXT.)	RESIDENCE PHONE (A/C, NO.)
Ralph Morgan	555-0000	350-0000

OTHER DRIVER'S NAME & ADDRESS (CHECK IF SAME AS OWNER) ☐	BUSINESS PHONE (A/C, NO., EXT.)	RESIDENCE PHONE (A/C, NO.)
Same		

DESCRIBE DAMAGE	ESTIMATE AMOUNT	WHERE CAN DAMAGE BE SEEN
Front End.	$Total	Morgan's Auto Body

INJURED

NAME & ADDRESS	PHONE (A/C, NO.)	PED.	INS. VEH.	OTHER VEH.	AGE	EXTENT OF INJURY
Insured			X		32	Head, Shoulder
Ralph Morgan				x	45	Head, Nose
Sandy Scott				x	36	Facial, Head

WITNESSES OR PASSENGERS

NAME & ADDRESS	PHONE (A/C, NO.)	INS. VEH.	OTHER VEH.	OTHER (SPECIFY)
Unknown, but there were bystanders at corner				
service station and at bus stop				

REMARKS (INCLUDE ADJUSTER ASSIGNED)

Passenger Scott taken to General Hospital; Insured and Morgan to Buckeye Lake Emergency Clinic.

REPORTED BY	REPORTED TO	SIGNATURE OF PRODUCER OR INSURED
Insured	Agnes Wilks	

ACORD 2 (8/82) NOTE IMPORTANT CALIFORNIA, FLORIDA, IDAHO, AND NEW YORK INFORMATION ON REVERSE SIDE

Exhibit 6-2
ACORD General Liability Loss Notice

SET TAB STOPS AT ARROWS

acord® GENERAL LIABILITY LOSS NOTICE (OTHER THAN AUTOMOBILE)

DATE (MM/DD/YY): 11-29-8

PRODUCER:
Robust Ins. Agency
10 First Place
Andover, PA

AGENCY CODE | SUB CODE

PRODUCER PHONE	COMPANY	POLICY NUMBER
215-666-0000	Institute Insurance Co.	GL-0000000

DATE (MM/DD/YY) & TIME OF LOSS	POLICY EFF. DATE (MM/DD/YY)	POLICY EXP. DATE (MM/DD/YY)	PREVIOUSLY REPORTED
11-2-8, 4 P.M. (A.M. / P.M.)	3-24-8	3-24-8	YES / NO X

FOR COMPANY USE ONLY: TEST FORM

INSURED

NAME & ADDRESS (AS IT APPEARS ON POLICY)	RESIDENCE PHONE	PERSON TO CONTACT (NAME & ADDRESS)	RESIDENCE PHONE
AJAX Supermarkets Inc. 1502 Indian Mound Road Andover, PA	215-532-0000 BUSINESS PHONE: 777-0000	Jack Brady, Manager	BUSINESS PHONE:

LOSS

LOCATION OF ACCIDENT (INCLUDE CITY & STATE): 1502 Indian Mound Road, Andover, PA

AUTHORITY CONTACTED: ?

DESCRIPTION OF ACCIDENT (USE REVERSE SIDE, IF NECESSARY):
Customer in supermarket fell on wet spot and lettuce leaf on floor. Wet spot may have been caused by a leak in the roof.

POLICY INFORMATION

COVERAGE PART OR FORM NO. (INSERT FORM NOS. & EDITION DATES): OL & T

LIMITS	LIABILITY	MED. PAY.	PRODUCTS	CONTRACTUAL	OTHER (SPECIFY)	DEDUCTIBLE
BI	25,000	500				
PD	5,000					
CSL						

UMBRELLA IN FORCE? YES | NO | CARRIER: | LIMITS:

TYPE OF LIABILITY

PREMISES: INSURED IS ☐ OWNER ☐ TENANT ☐ OTHER

TYPE OF PREMISES: Supermarket

OWNER'S NAME & ADDRESS (IF NOT INSURED): General Building Corp.

OWNERS PHONE:

PRODUCTS: INSURED IS ☐ MANUFACTURER ☐ VENDOR ☐ OTHER:

TYPE OF PRODUCT:

MANUFACTURER'S NAME & ADDRESS (IF NOT INSURED):

MANUFACTURERS PHONE:

WHERE CAN PRODUCT BE SEEN?

OTHER LIABILITY (EXPLAIN)

INJURED/PROPERTY DAMAGED

NAME & ADDRESS: Marilyn Jones

PHONE:

AGE: 54 SEX: F OCCUPATION: Unknown

EMPLOYERS NAME & ADDRESS:

PHONE:

DESCRIBE INJURY: Broken ankle, bruised knee, back

☐ FATALITY

WHERE TAKEN: ?

WHAT WAS INJURED DOING? Customer

DESCRIBE PROPERTY (TYPE, MODEL, ETC.)

ESTIMATE AMOUNT

WHERE CAN PROPERTY BE SEEN?

WHEN?

OWNER'S NAME & ADDRESS

PHONE

WITNESSES

NAME & ADDRESS	RESIDENCE PHONE	BUSINESS PHONE
Matilda Winters (Claimant's niece)		

REMARKS

REPORTED BY: Jack Brady

REPORTED TO: Andy Adjuster

SIGNATURE OF PRODUCER OR INSURED

ACORD 3 (TEST FORM)

NOTE: IMPORTANT CALIFORNIA AND FLORIDA INFORMATION ON REVERSE SIDE which automatically issues claim status request reports at periodic intervals, as a means of identifying files which need to be reviewed.

Whatever the method employed by companies to organize claim assignments, adjusters need to think about and analyze the claims assigned to them so that they may be prepared to conduct an orderly and intelligent investigation. When accident reports are reviewed, adjusters should be thinking in terms of *coverage, liability,* and *damages.* Analyze what coverage is provided, what the liability situation is, and what damages are being claimed. As an adjuster gains more experience, the important points or unusual aspects of a claim will stand out in the adjuster's mind as he or she examines the loss report.

Recognizing Coverage Questions

The first aspect of the claim that should be checked is *coverage.* The coverage review actually is a two step process. The first step, which can be described as a basic coverage verification, is to check the information typically provided in the *declaration page* of a policy against the information contained in the accident report. Here the adjuster checks the name of the insured, the date of the accident to verify that it falls within the policy period, the year, make, and VIN of the car involved in the accident (if an auto accident), the coverage limits and endorsements, any applicable deductible, the loss payee, and so on.

Once coverage is verified from this aspect, the adjuster should then check coverage from a *contractual* standpoint; that is, does the set of facts as described in the accident report come within the scope of coverage? Are there any exclusions applicable? For example, if the insured ran into the front of an auto dealership, he or she would, in all probability, be legally liable for the damages. But if the investigation revealed that the dealer had sold the insured a "lemon" and refused to help rectify the situation, and then, in an act of revenge, the insured intentionally drove into the showroom window of the auto dealership, there would be no *coverage.* As explained previously in the text, liability policies contain an intentional injury/damage exclusion that would be invoked by the insurer in this situation.

Sources of Coverage Information Although the investigation can be started without actual confirmation of coverage, the claim cannot be settled until coverage has been confirmed. It is important, therefore, that coverage be verified before the adjuster goes too far with the investigation. Furthermore, there is also the danger that if the investigation is well underway and then coverage is denied, the insured may claim that he or she had been led to believe that coverage was in order and the insurer may have waived the coverage question, or be estopped from asserting its coverage defenses. (The problem of waiver and estoppel and the proper use of reservation of rights letters and nonwaiver agreements were examined in Chapter 3).

Coverage can be verified from several sources. They are:

1. the agent's daily—(the daily is simply a copy of an insurance policy which is kept as the agent's record),
2. the company underwriting file,
3. the computer, and
4. receipt for premium payment from agent or insurance company employee, held by policy holder.

Agent's Daily. The field claim adjuster who works out of home or from the agent's office will likely verify coverage from the agent's daily. The agent's daily ordinarily consists of a policy, including the declarations and any applicable endorsements. This normally represents an accurate way for adjusters to verify coverage and to obtain current coverage information available on the insured.

Underwriting File. Ordinarily, companies keep on file a copy of the policy including the declarations and applicable endorsements so that coverage can be verified from within the company as well as from the agent's office. With the advent of the computer, efforts are being made by many companies to eliminate or minimize paper flow wherever reasonably possible. As a result, some companies have replaced, to varying degrees, paper files with the computer and are using the computer as the main source of policy information.

Computer. In recent years, many insurers have computerized their operations. The extent of this computerization varies considerably from company to company. The goal of eliminating or minimizing paper flow and substituting the computer as the modern day source of information occupies a priority position on the planning agenda of many insurance companies. Many companies have progressed considerably toward achieving this goal.

The incentive for computerizing or automating claim handling and processing is basically economic. Computerization can achieve reduced expenses as well as provide claim-related statistics and reports to help company executives to both analyze claim performance and recognize developing problems. Adjuster workload, salvage and subrogation recoveries, average claim costs, expense control, and case reserve development represent some of the information that can be provided efficiently by computers.

Many companies have computerized their claim operations to the extent that claim personnel can enter claims, verify coverage, set reserves and close claims via computer. The computer can be programmed to automatically issue claim status request reports at periodic intervals so that the claim handler or supervisor can conduct the necessary file reviews. Some companies are issuing claim drafts or checks via computer. It is inevitable that in the very near future, computers will play an even greater role in claim processing as more and more companies computerize their operations.

Some problems associated with computerization include employee resistance to what often is a substantial change in methods and procedures, initial unanticipated problems with the system, and computer downtime. Seemingly, these problems are resolved in time and actually are minor in comparison to the improved processing and efficiency brought about by a tested and proven computer system. *Downtime* simply means that the computer stops operating for any number of reasons. This can be an occasional and irritating problem but experience indicates that it is not a pervasive one.

Direct Bill Receipts. In an effort to reduce expenses and increase efficiency, many independent agency companies have installed what is referred to as "direct bill" procedures for billing and receiving premium payments. This means simply that the premium bill is sent by the company directly to the policyholder. In other words, the agent does not get involved with collecting premium payments from the insured when a direct bill procedure has been installed for a certain line of insurance. The agent usually gets a copy of the bill that is sent to the insured and, if the insured delays paying the premium, the agent receives a copy of the late notice which is sent to the insured.

A problem may arise when an insured does not pay or is late in paying. Though the agent usually receives copies of any reminder letter or termination notice the company sends the insured, because of general time lag, the agent may not know for certain at any specific point during the renewal period of a policy whether the insured has paid the premium. This means that the agent's records will not always be totally current or accurate. In such cases, field claim adjusters who ordinarily rely on the agent's daily for coverage confirmation will need to check further with the company to confirm that the premium was paid. In a computerized claim operation, this payment information is usually available on a computer terminal payment screen which the claim person can check to determine whether the premium payment has been received by the company.

Coverage Question Procedures Once the adjuster recognizes a coverage question, whether it be an applicable exclusion, a problem with an accident date not falling within the policy period, or the car involved in the accident not being a covered auto, he or she should immediately alert the supervisor or examiner to the problem and seek advise accordingly.

It is important that adjusters have access to actual policy forms and endorsements so that they can eliminate guesswork when interpreting coverage. Remember to develop the sound habit of *reading* the policy, rather than assuming the needless risk of trying to memorize the policy.

It may be that upon recognition of a coverage question or problem, additional investigation is needed in order to determine whether coverage applies. As noted in Chapter 2, it is important for claim people not only to be able to *recognize* coverage questions promptly but also to be able to *act* immediately upon such recognition to advise an insured that a problem exists which may preclude insurance protection. An insurer's silence in the face of a potential coverage question may constitute *waiver* and/or *estoppel.* Put simply, an adjuster cannot act in a manner which would imply that coverage has been accepted when in reality a question of coverage exists.

The question is not so much *when* a coverage question is recognized, but when it *could* have been recognized in the course of a proper investigation. Clearly, it is important that insurers reserve their rights under the policy when a coverage question exists. This can be done either by sending a reservation of rights letter to the insured or by obtaining a signed nonwaiver agreement. It is equally important that the adjuster conduct a prompt and thorough investigation of the coverage issue.

It is worth repeating the typical situations in which coverage disputes require prompt action on the insurer's part:

1. late notice of accident,
2. an accident involving a car which is owned by an insured but not listed in the policy,
3. the date of accident does not fall within the policy period,
4. a question whether an "insured" driver had a reasonable belief that he or she was entitled to the use of the car,
5. applicability of an exclusion,
6. failure to cooperate, or
7. fraud on the insured's part.

Whenever any of these situations has a bearing on a claim, the adjuster will need to conduct a detailed investigation of the particular issue. The adjuster should make notes of what needs to be accomplished in the investigation. It is essential that the adjuster have a plan rather than conduct the investigation in a random manner.

If statements will be obtained, which is usually the case, the adjuster should also make notes regarding the important or unique points that will need to be covered in the various statements.

The important thing is that the adjuster give sufficient thought to *what* is to be accomplished and to *how* it is to be accomplished. A well thought-out and planned investigation will normally result in a more informed and proper decision being made concerning the resolution of the coverage question.

Recognizing Liability Questions

The objective of the liability investigation is to determine who is legally liable or, put simply, who is at fault. Occasionally, this is readily apparent from the accident report itself but ordinarily an investigation of the liability question will need to be conducted.

Once again, as adjusters review the accident report they should analyze the accident and decide what specific information will be necessary to determine liability. The adjuster should make notes and outline what the proposed investigation will cover so that the investigation can proceed in an orderly fashion. At times, it may help for the adjuster to draw a rough sketch or diagram of the accident, to be completed or polished at a later date when the parties to the accident have been contacted and the investigation is well underway.

Adjusters will need to gather both phsysical and oral evidence in an effort to determine liability. *Physical* evidence refers to such things as diagrams, photographs, debris from the accident, while *oral* evidence refers to oral testimony which is best exemplified by statements of the parties or witnesses to an accident.

Recognizing Questions Related to Damages

Continuing with the review of the accident report, the adjuster should carefully observe the nature and extent of property damage and of any bodily injures that are reported. Frequently, the accident report will give the adjuster some idea of the seriousness of the accident. However, this is not always true and that is why a prompt investigation is necessary.

Inspections of the damaged property should be made promptly if there is any chance that the insurer will be making payment on the claim. Furthermore, injured claimants should be immediately contacted to demonstrate to the claimant that the company is interested in the claim and that it intends, through the adjuster, to assist the claimant in a reasonable manner with the processing of the claim. In this way, the adjuster can develop a rapport with the claimant and establish what is known in claim language as claimant *control.*

"Control" simply means that the adjuster has acted and represented himself in an open and straightforward manner which gains the claimant's confidence and trust. The claimant is made to feel that in

Exhibit 6-3
Medical Authorization Form

To the Hospital or Doctor Concerned:

Please furnish the bearer with copies of your records and complete any medical reports desired together with any additional information known to you, relative to diagnosis, treatment and prognosis of my injuries and my condition; also the amount of your bills to date, as well as probable final bill for services rendered to and for me, such as bearer may desire.

Signature ____________________

Address ____________________

Date ____________________

working directly with the adjuster, the claim can be settled promptly, in a fair and reasonable manner.

It is at this time that the adjuster should obtain signed medical authorizations from the claimant. A medical authorization permits the adjuster not only to secure hospital reports and medical reports from the treating physician but also to ask any questions of the doctor which the adjuster feels are necessary in order to properly evaluate the injury claim. (A typical medical authorization and medical report form are shown in Exhibit 6-3 and 6-4 respectively.)

As the investigation proceeds, the adjuster will need to confirm the nature and extent of the injuries. Ordinarily, this can be accomplished by obtaining a medical or hospital report, X-rays (if any were taken), and medical bills. It may be necessary to arrange a physical examination of the claimant by a physician selected by the company. If there is a question of *causal relationship,* that is, whether the claimant's injury was actually caused by the accident an exam may be desirable. The use and appropriateness of medical examinations were discussed in detail in Chapter 5.

If the claimant is represented by an attorney, the adjuster, of course, must deal exclusively with the attorney and may not contact the claimant directly unless permission is granted by the attorney. For this reason, injury information initially may be quite sketchy and the adjuster is to some extent at the mercy of the claimant's attorney regarding specific injury information.

Exhibit 6-4
Attending Physician's Report

DATE OF REPORT ______________________

NAME OF PATIENT ______________________ AGE ________ MARITAL STATUS ______________________

ADDRESS ______________________ OCCUPATION ______________________

CITY AND STATE ______________________ TELEPHONE ______________________

DATE OF FIRST EXAMINATION ______________________ WHO WAS PRESENT ______________________

PLACE OF FIRST EXAMINATION ______________________

EVIDENCE OF OLD INJURIES ______________________

OF DISEASE ______________________

OF INTOXICATION ______________________

PATIENT RECEIVED FIRST AID OR OTHER PRIOR TREATMENT FOR THIS INJURY FROM ______________________

PREVIOUS MEDICAL HISTORY ______________________

____

PATIENT'S ACCOUNT OF INJURY

DATE AND HOUR OF INJURY ______________________

PLACE AND MANNER OF OCCURRENCE ______________________

____

DESCRIPTION OF INJURY

____

____

TREATMENT

DATE OF TREATMENTS ______ WHERE GIVEN? ______

NATURE OF TREATMENT ______

WERE X-RAYS TAKEN ______ BY WHOM ______ DATE ______

FINDINGS ______

NUMBER OF STITCHES TAKEN ______ LOCATION OF STITCHES ______

DISPOSITION OF CASE

TAKEN HOME OR TO HOSPITAL ______ NAME OF HOSPITAL ______

DATE OF DISCHARGE ______

DIAGNOSIS ______

______

PROGNOSIS AND PERMANENCY OF INJURY

______

______

______

PERIOD OF DISABILITY:
TOTAL DISABILITY FROM ______ ,19 ______ TO ______ ,19 ______ PARTIAL DISABILITY FROM ______
______ ,19 ______ TO ______ ,19 ______

NATURE AND EXTENT OF ANY PERMANENT DISABILITY ______

AMOUNT OF BILL TO DATE $ ______ PHYSICIAN'S SIGNATURE ______

EST. AMOUNT OF FINAL BILL $ ______ CITY ______ STATE ______

Obtaining Information from the Claimant's Attorney Experience indicates that too many adjusters fail to press the claimant's attorney for medical information. They ask the attorney to indicate the nature of the injury and the amount of the special damages but when the attorney replies that he or she does not have any information yet, adjusters too often drop the matter right there. Claim supervisors see far too many claim files where the adjuster reports that "the attorney does not have any specials yet" and that represents the extent of the adjuster's efforts to obtain information about the injury.

It must be kept in mind that the fact that the attorney accepted the case in the first place usually means that he or she spoke directly with the claimant and has some knowledge of the nature and extent of the injuries. When the attorney replies that he or she does not have any injury information, the adjuster might reply in the following manner; "I realize that you may not have any details as yet, but you can give me at least a general idea of the injury for my file, can't you? I mean, did your client break a bone or are we talking about soft tissue injuries here? Was there any hospitalization? Did Mr. Claimant lose any time from work? What kind of work does he do? What part of the body was injured? Can you tell me whom the claimant is being treated by?"

This kind of approach has worked well for some claim people. In most instances, the attorney has at least some information about the injury. When talking to attorneys for the first time, adjusters should develop a more persistent approach to obtaining this information. If the inquiry is approached in a courteous manner, adjusters should be successful in obtaining information about the claimant's injuries which is often necessary for reserve purposes as well as for properly directing the remaining investigation. Injury information regarding disability, prognosis, and permanency is also essential in order to know when to set up a medical examination of the claimant.

Activity Check If this approach fails, however, there is always the traditional *activity* or *neighborhood* check, a door-to-door canvass of the claimant's neighborhood in an effort to determine the current medical condition and level of physical activity of the claimant.

Activity checks must be conducted carefully so as not to invade the privacy of the claimant. Since the objective of the activity check is to obtain information about the claimant's injuries and current activities, the questions asked by the adjuster must be confined to that subject. Activity checks can be useful in obtaining such information when it is unavailable from any other source. It is sometimes necessary to conduct this type of investigation for reserve purposes, that is, to get sufficient information about the claimant's injury so that a realistic reserve can be set.

On occasion, however, activity checks can create problems. It is not uncommon for a "friendly" neighbor to alert the claimant that someone from the insurance company is asking questions and this might compel the claimant to call his or her attorney or even the police. Adjusters sometimes return to the office after conducting an activity check to find an urgent message from the claimant's attorney requesting the adjuster to call immediately. When the adjuster calls, the attorney may reprimand the adjuster for upsetting the claimant in this manner. It is advisable for the adjuster to respectfully apologize for upsetting the claimant but to add that the company is entitled to medical and injury information about the claimant, and the neighborhood canvass was the only way that the information could be obtained. If the adjuster can make this point without alienating the attorney, the subsequent flow of information between the adjuster and the attorney actually may be enhanced.

As a caution, adjusters should be aware of their company's position on conducting neighborhood checks and should make certain that there is no applicable law in the state which might restrict or prohibit such investigative activity.

Planning the Work Schedule

It is important that adjusters conduct their investigation in a logical and orderly manner. The investigation should be planned and scheduled so that information or evidence which may be available for only a short time is obtained first. Damaged property, for example, must be inspected and perhaps photographed before repairs are made. Diagrams and photographs of the accident scene should be obtained promptly because frequently time is of the essence. This is especially true if weather conditions such as snow or ice were a factor in the claim. Usually, there is little value in taking photos in May or June of a premises fall-down case involving snow and ice that occurred in February. Although the photos will provide a general picture of the scene of the accident, they cannot possibly depict the scene as it was at the time of the accident. That will be impossible to preserve unless the accident is reported in a timely manner and the adjuster acts promptly to get to the scene and photograph it.

The proposed investigation for an auto accident with property damage to both vehicles and injuries to occupants of both vehicles might include the following notes written by the adjuster:

1. R/S Insured (R/S means recorded statement),
2. R/S claimant driver, secure M/A (M/A means medical authorization),

3. R/S claimant passenger, secure M/A,
4. R/S witness,
5. P.R. (P.R. means police report),
6. Inspect Insured's and Claimant's car,
7. Diagram, and
8. Photos of scene.

This reflects the adjuster's opinion of what is needed in the way of investigation. The adjuster will attempt to obtain these items within a reasonable time frame, handling the items on what he or she considers a priority basis.

If these particular notes were those of an office claim adjuster, obviously the completion of some of the items would need to be assigned to the field. For instance, the vehicle inspections, diagram, and photos of the scene would need to be secured by an outside adjuster or appraiser. If the recorded statement of the claimant or witness could not be obtained by the telephone adjuster, the field adjuster would be called upon to complete these items as well.

The point is that the adjuster needs to make an outline or a plan of the investigation so that it may be conducted in an organized manner.

PLANNING THE INTERVIEW

Before contacting the parties to an accident, the adjuster should be properly prepared. Preparation requires a close review of the accident report so that the adjuster may be generally familiar with how the accident happened. Whether a police report was made and whether any witnesses have been identified should be noted. If the accident occurred on a busy street, the adjuster should make a note to ask (if the claim is being handled from the office) or to find out (if handled by a field adjuster) if there were any bystanders or buildings in the vicinity of the accident, which might be a possible source of witnesses. In addition, the extent of the damage to the vehicles as well as the points of impact along with the nature and extent of injuries should be noted.

The adjuster will want to make a note of any nonroutine questions, perhaps those concerning points that may be unique to this particular accident, that he or she may wish to ask the insured, claimant, or witness in the statements. While it is true that standard statement guides are available to adjusters for various kinds of accidents or losses, each accident has its own unique set of circumstances to which the actual statement must be tailored by the adjuster. For example, if a brake failure is alleged by either the insured or claimant, this allegation will need to be covered completely in the statement.

Ordinarily, the statement will be much more effective if the adjuster plans in advance the portion of the interview concerning the brake failure, so that all relevant questions will be asked and answered in the interview. In addition, a claimant who alleges that a minor impact accident caused of serious back injury will need to be questioned extensively on prior medical history and causal relationship in the statement.

Although the insured is under a contractual obligation to cooperate with the adjuster in the investigation of the claim, a claimant or witness is under no such obligation. Usually, the adjuster has only one opportunity to obtain a statement from a claimant or witness. The importance of obtaining an informative and comprehensive statement during that initial contact cannot be overemphasized. Adjusters are well advised to conduct the initial investigation as comprehensively as possible, almost as if the case were going to trial.

It is important that a claimant be contacted immediately so that the adjuster may develop a rapport with the claimant and establish *control.* Immediate contact on the part of the adjuster demonstrates concern and interest in the claimant's situation and often creates an atmosphere of cooperation. Most companies have adopted an *immediate contact* rule that requires that adjusters contact claimants within a specified time, usually within twenty-four hours from the date the claim is assigned to the adjuster.

The purpose of immediate contact is to establish claimant control so that the claim may be amicably resolved directly with the claimant.

In making appointments, field adjusters should try to schedule a driving pattern or route in which they can make the maximum number of calls with a minimum amount of driving. Many adjusters plan calls in a somewhat "circular" pattern so that they can complete the last call of the day in the general vicinity of where they started. This seems particularly important today in view of the fact that many companies are operating with more telephone adjusters and fewer field adjusters, the latter being expected to handle a larger territory in many instances. With this approach, there also is a minimum of driving time and mileage between calls. If such a schedule can be developed on a weekly basis, the adjuster will likely have a productive week.

As mentioned earlier, during the initial contact, the adjuster should attempt to develop a rapport with the claimant and establish claimant control. It is also important at this time that the adjuster attempt to obtain a statement from the claimant and to secure a medical authorization.

In scheduling their work, adjusters should be aware of the many demographic changes in society in recent decades. Of particular note is the fact that in 40% of all families, both the husband and wife now work compared with 12% in 1959, and the ratio continues to increase.[2] The

probability that claimants, particularly female clai
at home during the day might have been great ten
Today, however, adjusters frequently will need
work or in the office. The alternative is a lot of
work for the adjuster and, understandably, m
avoid this. (Some companies have experimented
week for office telephone adjusters in which they work
This has proved relatively successful in that adjusters have been able to contact parties to an accident in the early evening hours when they are returning home from work.)

Realistically speaking, many people can take the time to be contacted by telephone or even to be met personally at work or in the office. It is advisable, however, that the adjuster first telephone the person to make an appointment. If the adjuster cannot persuade the claimant to see the adjuster at work, other arrangements, perhaps not as convenient for the adjuster, will need to be made.

Another demographic change which affects the claim business is immigration. Immigration, mostly from Asian and Latin American countries, will account for most of the population growth in the next ten years.[3] Some adjusters in southern Florida are learning to speak Spanish so that they can deal more effectively with the growing Spanish-speaking population in that area.

Contacting the Claimant or Insured

The question of whether the claimant or the insured should be contacted first is occasionally the subject of debate among claim people. Quite frankly, there is no definitive answer to this question; the answer will depend on the circumstances of the claim. When establishing claimant control is the overriding factor in a claim, such as where liability is clear and the claimant's injuries are serious, the claimant should be contacted first. Related to this, the claimant probably should be contacted first when there is no real question of liability (where liability is clear or probable) and the insured has pretty much established fault in the accident report. When the insured's accident report creates some question about liability, occasionally a quick telephone call to the insured can clarify the question, and then the claimant can be contacted. After the initial claimant contact is made, the adjuster can follow up with the insured for his or her detailed version.

The *insured* probably should be contacted first when the liability situation is complicated or unclear. In such cases, the insured's detailed version of the accident is necessary before a reasonably clear picture of how the accident occurred can be formed. In addition, when a coverage

…n exists, the adjuster ordinarily will want to contact the insured …re the claimant.

No Contact Considerations Actually, there will be cases in which the adjuster decides not to contact the claimant. The accident report may indicate that the claimant was not injured or that the injury was minor and it appears that no claim will be pressed. In addition, liability may be questionable or doubtful and the best course of action may be to refrain from contacting the claimant because contact would only encourage a claim. This is a delicate matter and adjusters should confer with their supervisors regarding the pros and cons of claimant contact under these circumstances.

The wisest course of action may be to conduct the investigation from the insured's side only; that is, to secure statements from the insured and any witnesses, to obtain the police report, photos, and so on, but to refrain from contacting the claimant. If a claim eventually is made, at least the major portion of the investigation will have been completed. Once again, the adjuster should be guided by company policy and the supervisor's judgment.

Obtaining the Claimant's Cooperation When it is considered necessary (as it is in most cases) that the claimant be contacted, such contact should be made promptly in an effort to gain the claimant's confidence and trust and thereby establish control of the claim. It is important that after an accident the claimant receive some immediate assurance of the company's interest in and consideration of the claim. In addition, the sooner the adjuster contacts the claimant, the better the chance that the adjuster will get an accurate and true account of the accident.

The settlement of a claim is in a very real sense a psychological process in which the adjuster plays a multifaceted role; that of provider of information, counselor and sales person. On occasion, the claimant's response to the adjuster's initial contact may be guarded and uncooperative. Perhaps the claimant is angry with the insured and transfers his or her anger to the adjuster, or maybe the claimant simply perceives the adjuster to be an adversary and this acts as a barrier to cooperation. Whatever the reason, the adjuster should be courteous and considerate of the claimant's position and feelings.

It needs to be remembered that the claimant is under no legal obligation to cooperate with the adjuster or to give a statement and the adjuster cannot compel the claimant to cooperate. However, before paying a claim, the adjuster needs information which frequently only the claimant can provide. The adjuster should indicate to the claimant that before a decision can be made with respect to payment of the claim, the adjuster needs to obtain the claimant's version of the accident as well as specific information about the injuries sustained and the medical expenses incurred. In other words, if the claim is paid, the payment must be justified. The adjuster must be able to demonstrate both the reason for settling the claim and the reason for paying the particular amount.

Although the adjuster cannot insist on a statement, efforts should be made to secure a statement from the claimant. Sometimes all that can be obtained is a completed claimant's form or an unsigned statement. Depending on the extent of the liability question, these alternatives to a signed or recorded statement may or may not be sufficient. In a clear or probable liability case, there may be no need to pursue a statement from a claimant who resists all such attempts by the adjuster.

With respect to injury and medical bills, ordinarily the adjuster will need a physician's report and copies of all medical bills being claimed. Where liability is clear or probable and medical expenses minor, the bills may be sufficient for settlement purposes.

Ordinarily, once it is explained to the claimant that the claim cannot be processed until the claimant cooperates and provides the necessary information, the claimant realizes that it is in his or her best interests to cooperate.

First Call Settlements Frequently, a claim can be settled during the initial meeting with the claimant. However, unless adjusters consciously look for such opportunities, they may not be recognized. The ideal case for a first call settlement is a clear or probable liability case where the claimant has sustained minor or less serious injuries. But even questionable liability cases are sometimes appropriate for first call settlements.

The field adjuster is in a particularly good position to make first call settlements because he or she can personally observe the claimant, see the effects of the injuries, and sense whether the claimant will be receptive to settlement on a first call basis. This is not to say that first call settlements cannot be made by telephone adjusters in their initial telephone conversations with the claimant. The field adjuster, however, can be especially persuasive in view of the fact that he or she can often give the claimant a draft or check immediately and secure the necessary release.

First call settlements may be one of the most underutilized claim tools possessed by a claim department. The savings in time and expense can be substantial. A claim reserve need not be set up nor will the claim file need to be maintained or reviewed periodically by a supervisor. In addition, the adjuster need not conduct additional investigation because the file is closed almost immediately. This also results in savings in postage and telephone time in corresponding or communicating with the parties to an accident or in requesting police reports.

Despite the fact that detailed medical information may not be available at that moment, if the case otherwise warrants a first call settlement, adjusters should take advantage of the opportunity. Sometimes a telephone call to the doctor while the adjuster is in the claimant's presence will get the necessary information with respect to the medical bills and diagnosis of the injury upon which the adjuster can base the settlement offer.

Experience suggests rather strongly that claim settlements do not get any less expensive with time. Frequently, the best settlement is an early settlement. It must be kept in mind, however, that not all cases lend themselves to settlement on a first call basis. In some instances, pressing for an early settlement might be tactless and insensitive. The adjuster must gain the experience and develop the judgment to be able to recognize those situations in which a first call settlement is warranted and the claimant is receptive to a settlement on that basis.

Contacting Witnesses

With respect to claim investigations, a *witness* is someone who has personal knowledge of the accident through direct observation. Usually, a witness is one who has seen or heard the accident and can furnish evidence regarding the cause of the accident and the damages sustained by the parties involved. A witness can also be called upon to give evidence or testify in court regarding the accident.

It needs to be noted at the outset that this discussion of witness contacts concerns "ordinary" witnesses rather than *expert* witnesses. Expert witnesses are those who possess a special skill, experience, or educational degree that qualifies them to testify on matters relating to their particular area of expertise. Medical doctors, engineers, and scientists are examples of expert witnesses. Doctors may testify about causal relationship and engineers or scientists about the cause of a building collapse or structural defect.

Generally, *ordinary* witnesses are limited to furnishing evidence about the facts of an accident as observed by them. They usually are not permitted to testify as to their opinions or conclusions. There are some exceptions, however. An ordinary witness may be allowed to express an opinion about such things as the speed of cars, the emotional state of another, the drunk or sober condition of another, the identity of a person by his appearance or voice (e.g., telephone conversations) or the value of objects or services with which he or she is familiar.[4]

The evidence furnished by a witness must be *relevant, material,* and *competent* in order to be admissible at trial. All three elements must be present. If there were not some reasonable limits placed on the evidence which could be entered in a case, the outcome of a trial might be prolonged indefinitely by the introduction of meaningless evidence.

Relevant evidence is evidence which has a definite bearing on the case.

Material evidence refers to essential information about the accident. It is evidence that goes to the heart of the matter and that must serve to establish a case one way or the other. The fact that a person speaks in a foreign tongue may be relevant for identification purposes, but it is not necessarily material. If the issue is simply whether the person was negligent in the manner in which he drove his car, the fact that he or she speaks only French or Italian would probably not be material. If, on the other hand, it could be demonstrated that the person could not read or understand the meaning of a yield sign or stop sign, then such evidence is material.

Competent evidence refers to the qualifications of the source of the evidence. It means that the witness must be fit or capable of testifying. A witness who was intoxicated at the time of the accident, for example, would not meet the test of competency.

Witnesses are often the key to clarifying the liability situation in an accident. Although occasionally the police report will contain the names of witnesses, or the insured will be able to furnish this information, frequently, witnesses are unidentified. Even when they are identified, there still may be *other* witnesses who can furnish valuable information about an accident if they are located. When a claim warrants the activity, a neighborhood canvass of the accident scene should be conducted. This ordinarily entails a personal building-to-building or house-to-house search of the accident scene for people who may have witnessed it or arrived on the scene immediately after it occurred. It is here where an adjuster's imagination and interviewing skills can be demonstrated.

In many cases, there is someone who may have seen or heard something (or who may know someone in this category) whose testimony could have a significant bearing on the claim. It is important that when people are questioned under these circumstances they be asked about the existence and whereabouts of other possible witnesses. It must be kept in mind also that not every witness need be an "eyewitness." Information about injuries or comments made by the parties to an accident frequently can be very valuable in addition to evidence furnished by eyewitnesses.

Promptness in contacting witnesses is essential to a good investigation. The adjuster needs to make contact with the witness when the recollection of the accident is still fresh in his or her mind. If contact is delayed, there is always the risk that the witness may forget important aspects of the accident or may become indifferent or develop resistance for fear of getting involved.

Adjusters should properly identify themselves when contacting witnesses and inform the witness that they represent the insured. An atmosphere of integrity and professional courtesy should be fostered and maintained by the adjuster so that the witness's cooperation will continue up to trial, if that is necessary.

Classification of Witnesses Witnesses are classified according to their *attitude* and *liability position* regarding the accident as *friendly, unfriendly, supporting, adverse,* or *hostile.*

A *friendly* witness is one who demonstrates a favorable attitude and cooperates with the adjuster in the investigation. The witness may simply feel an obligation to come forth and tell the truth as his or her civic responsibility or he or she may be a friend of the insured or claimant who simply wants the truth to be told.

Although the witness may cooperate fully with the adjuster, his or her position on liability may not support the insured. Such a witness may be classified as *friendly* as to attitude but *adverse* as to position or viewpoint on liability. If the witness's position is favorable to the insured's interests, he or she would be considered a *supporting* witness.

An *unfriendly* witness is one who does not cooperate in the investigation of the claim. The attitude of resistance may stem from a desire to avoid getting involved, from a dislike of insurance companies, or even from basic antisocial behavior. In the event that this witness's version of the accident, if one could be obtained, was favorable to the insured, the witness would be an *unfriendly* but *supporting* witness. Usually, such a witness will be of little help to the insured's case unless some cooperation can be obtained.

It is important that adjusters understand that a witness is under no legal obligation to cooperate or give a statement to the adjuster. While it is true that once a lawsuit is started, a witness can be compelled to testify at trial by subpoena, such an action runs the risk of alienating the witness with the result that his or her testimony may be useless or, worse yet, detrimental to the insured's case.

A *hostile* witness is one whose response to the insured is more than unfriendly and adverse. A hostile witness actually displays an attitute of bias or prejudice against the insured. For some reason, the witness may hold a personal dislike for the insured. This attitude may be influenced by the insured's race or nationality, by his or her occupation or position in society, or perhaps because the witness dislikes the insured's physical features or personality. Whatever the reason for the prejudicial behavior, such witnesses usually are of little or no help to the insured's cause.

Sources of Witnesses As noted earlier, the police report occasionally will contain the names and addresses of witnesses, or the insured will be able to identify witnesses to the accident. In many cases, however, this information will not be readily available to the adjuster. The task of identifying and locating witnesses in such circumstances is the adjuster's responsibility.

In addition to the insured and the police report, people who were with the insured or claimant frequently are good sources of information with respect to the cause of the accident and the nature and extent of the injuries sustained. In auto accidents, *passengers* may be able to furnish important information about the accident. In premises fall-down cases, any person who might have accompanied the claimant at the time of the accident may be a valuable source of information.

Statements should be secured from these people promptly. If they indicate that they did not actually see the accident and cannot comment specifically as to the cause, a statement to that effect should be taken. Such a statement is referred to as a *negative statement.* Negative statements can be very important in the defense of a claim where an individual suddenly decides, long after the accident, that he or she did witness the accident and agrees to furnish evidence which blames the insured. If the adjuster had earlier obtained a negative statement from this "witness," the statement could be used either to discourage such later testimony from the witness or to refute it, if need be.

Other sources available to identify witnesses include:

1. The motor vehicle report filed by the adverse driver. (Some states make this information confidential.)
2. Service people who may have been in the vicinity of the accident such as mail carriers, bus drivers, police officers, newspaper carriers, and so on. (This obviously requires some leg work. An adjuster can go to the scene of the accident at the approximate time it happened, and may find such service people available. Many such people are in the vicinity of the accident scene every working day at about the same time, since their jobs entail making deliveries or pickups on a regularly scheduled basis.)
3. Tow truck operators who may have removed the cars from the scene. (The police report will usually contain such information.)
4. Photographers with access to police radios who regularly take photos of serious accident scenes to make them available for a charge to attorneys and insurance companies. (Experienced adjusters usually know where to locate these photographers.)

5. Newspaper accounts of the accident. Sometimes a reporter will include the names of witnesses in his or her newspaper report of the accident. (Newspaper photographers should also be checked for information about witnesses.)
6. Newspaper advertising for witnesses. If the case warrants, advertising in the newspaper for witnesses can sometimes be effective in locating witnesses. "Witnesses" who come forth in response to such ads, however, must be closely scrutinized for motivation and integrity.
7. Neighborhood canvass. Most of these sources can be contacted by inside telephone adjusters as well as by field adjusters. Even the neighborhood canvass, if telephone adjusters have access to a telephone street directory, could conceivably be handled from the office. Practically speaking, however, the search for witnesses seemingly can be handled more expeditiously by the field adjuster. Patience, time, and a lot of energy are the basic ingredients necessary for locating witnesses when no witnesses are identified by the insured or by the police. The search can be a slow process with no guarantee of success. Ordinarily then, the claim will need to be sufficiently serious before such an expenditure of the adjuster's time is warranted. How frequently an extensive neighborhood canvass will be undertaken varies by company, and adjusters are advised to be fully aware of their company's position on this aspect of investigation. The neighborhood canvass has occasionally proved to be very valuable, but the chances of success are greater if the canvass is made promptly after the accident.

It is important that adjusters ask the witness to identify someone who will always know where the witness can be located. In addition, the adjuster should obtain the witness's social security number, name and address of the employer, and the identity of relatives or close friends who live nearby. If it appears that a case is heading for trial and a problem arises with regard to locating a witness, this kind of information will aid the adjuster in locating the witness at the time of trial.

If questioning the witness's neighbors, relatives, or employer is unsuccessful in locating the witness, the adjuster may check with the local post office for a forwarding address or send the witness a certified or registered letter, return receipt requested.

When interviewing an important witness, the adjuster should get the names, ages and the identity of the school their children are attending. Should the witness move, school records must be transferred, and the transferring school will know where they are transferred. The adjuster may then go to the transferee school and get the witness's new address.

SOURCES OF INFORMATION

Police Report

While it is true that a police report is an important document with respect to the investigation of a claim, adjusters need to understand that in most cases, a police report represents second-hand information or hearsay. Ordinarily, it contains basically what other people have told the police officer, unless the officer actually witnessed the accident. In those cases where an investigating officer is dispatched to the scene almost immediately after the accident occurs, his or her report regarding the position and condition of the cars in the street, location of debris, and conditions of the drivers and occupants may be particularly helpful. It must be kept in mind, however, that since the police report often incorporates what is known as "hearsay evidence," it cannot necessarily be viewed as an infallible document.

On the positive side, the police report ordinarily contains the names and addresses of those involved in the accident as well as the names and addresses of any witnesses. It also includes information about claimed injuries, points of impacts and vehicle damage, contributing factors to the accident, and any traffic violations or arrests. In most cases, there is a sketch or diagram of the accident made by the investigating officer from information furnished by the drivers and witnesses, if any.

If the case warrants, and this will depend to a large extent on company claim philosophy, police officers should be contacted and interviewed. Though it may be difficult, if not impossible, to obtain a statement from a police officer, sometimes casual conversation about the accident will generate important information about the liability situation as well as the injuries sustained. Information about complaints alleged, attention given to injured persons and accusations or comments made by the drivers themselves, may shed important light on the case. The willingness of police officers to discuss an accident varies by jurisdiction, but the adjuster will never know what might be gained from a police interview unless such an interview is attempted.

Diagrams

Frequently, a diagram of the accident scene is helpful in forming a picture of how the accident happened. In the more serious cases, adjusters will want to personally inspect the accident scene as soon after the accident as possible.

A diagram can be an important part of a file. It should carefully document all permanent physical landmarks, traffic controls, signs, and so on to portray the scene as it appeared at the time of the accident. Accident investigation templates with sufficient symbols to draw a fairly detailed diagram usually are available from a variety of sources. Many companies supply their adjusters with such templates or symbols for diagramming accidents.

Ideally, a diagram should be drawn to scale so that it will portray, as accurately as possible, the accident scene. It should also contain a legend or table showing the date, time, and location of the diagram, the date of the accident, the name of the adjuster who made the diagram (optional), and any other identifying marks which might be particularly important such as landmarks, obstructions, and so on.

The diagram also should indicate directions. For example, *north* is always at the top of the diagram. The names of the streets, the location of traffic controls, location of lights, the presence of any obstructions such as trees, shrubs, or other impediments, the presence of any hills or slopes, with some indication of the distances between these items, should also be included in the diagram. The point of impact of the cars involved or, if a fall-down case, the specific location of the fall, should be shown as well.

When statements are being taken in person, it is a good idea to request that the party being interviewed, whether an insured, claimant or witness, make a diagram (usually prior to the statement) which can serve as a basis for discussion. The individual should be asked to sign or initial the diagram and it should be made a part of the claim file along with the statement. (A diagram of the Teddy Smith accident—see Automobile Loss Notice, Exhibit 6-1—appears in Exhibit 6-5.)

Photographs

When evidence that is material to a case must be preserved, such as skid marks on snow and ice cases, it is essential that photographs be taken promptly. It is advisable, where warranted, to have professional photographs. Skid marks, for example, usually do not last for more than a few days, so time is of the essence. Of course, if professional photographs cannot be arranged or taken promptly, the adjuster should take his or her own photos of the scene. Skid marks or other road factors such as broken pavement or potholes, should be measured and described on a tab or tape and attached to the photographs. The location and nature of debris from an auto accident may also be of considerable value and should be photographed.

Exhibit 6-5
Diagram of Auto Accident

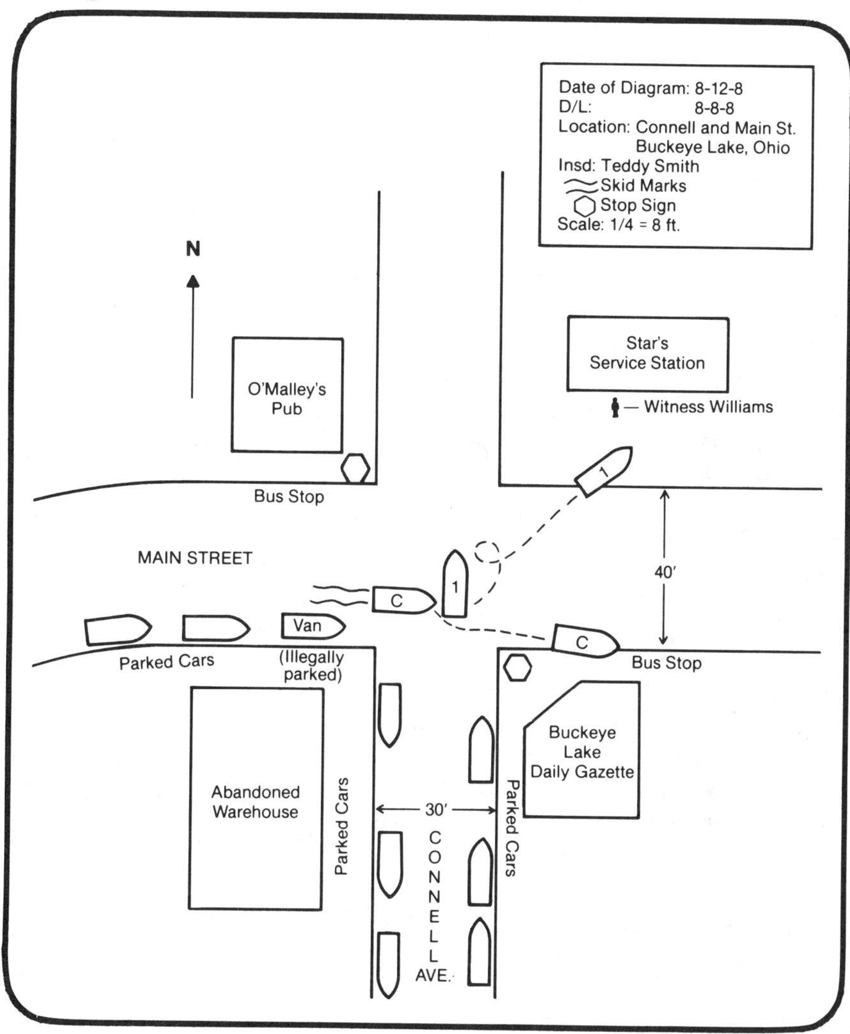

In serious cases, photos of the scene of the accident, regardless of whether there are any remaining visible objects from the accident, can be valuable when the adjuster or supervisor is trying to formulate a picture of how the accident occurred. Of equal importance with respect to photos is the position of the cars at the accident scene. When taking photographs of the points of impact and damages to the vehicle, pictures should be taken from several angles.

Photos should be identified as to date of accident, date, time and place of the photograph, and direction of the view. This information should be included in the tab which is attached to the photo.

As mentioned earlier, some photographers are linked to local police departments with two-way police radios and make it a practice of photographing the scenes of serious accidents for the purpose of selling the photos to interested parties such as insurance companies and attorneys. Because of the potential value of such photographs, adjusters should learn the identity and location of such photographers. It is also important to keep in mind that a newspaper photographer or even a television camera person may have photographs or videotape that recorded the aftermath of a serious accident and the media may be available for review by the adjuster.

Finally, when selecting a professional photographer, it is important to choose a photographer with some care. The criteria should be quality of the photography as well as the reliability and witness quality of the photographer. Will he or she make a good and credible witness?

Weather Reports

Weather can be a factor in automobile as well as premises fall-down claims. In such cases, weather reports should be obtained. They are particularly helpful in claims that are reported too late for the adjuster to be able to personally inspect the scene and preserve it with photographs. Some claims are reported months or even years after the accident occurred. A premises fall-down case in which it is alleged that the accumulation of snow and ice caused the claimant to fall is a good example of a claim where weather reports can be useful. The adjuster can secure weather reports for the several days or weeks preceding an accident (even when the request for these reports is made long after the accident occurred) which will indicate the extent and kind of precipitation which occurred in the area. Weather reports are available from any branch of the National Weather Service, from local airport authorities or from independent meteorological organizations. Monthly summary reports of weather by location may be obtained from the National Climatic Center, Asheville, North Carolina 28801.

The Use of Experts

Experts render a valuable service to the defense of a claim if their conclusions are of a favorable nature. Conversely, their service would not be desirable if the liability is known to be against the insured or if the injury in question is well etablished. To use an expert in these instances would only serve to strengthen the plaintiff's position.

Examples of experts that may be used in the process of disposing of a claim are medical specialists, accident reconstruction experts, engineers, climatological experts, accountants and others, depending on the nature of the claim.

Medical Specialists As discussed previously, the need for the medical specialist may occur frequently. As a general rule, it is wisest to delay the defense medical examination to permit the progress of the healing process, many times resulting in a favorable prognosis. It is recommended that defense counsel choose the expert as that attorney is well versed in the capabilities of most experts who are best qualified and available.

Accident Reconstruction Expert The use of the accident reconstruction expert is needed in cases where injuries are serious and liability cannot be conclusively determined by information otherwise available. By using physical facts such as the point of impact, type of road surface, weather, skid marks and the coming-to-rest point of the vehicles, the expert may be able to arrive scientifically and mathematically at an accurate conclusion regarding the type and direction of motion of all vehicles involved in the crash. In addition, the speed of all vehicles is also accurately determined, thus demonstrating the full negligence or comparative negligence of one or more of the parties to the crash. At times, this expert may be employed to determine the identity of the driver of a vehicle if there is a dispute on this point.

Chemical Engineer Products liability claims, particularly those that relate to ingested products are often the subject for an engineer, who can determine the chemical content of the product and establish whether it was the cause of the injury. The insect or vermin in a soft drink may be the best example of such a claim. Most often, it is found that the foreign matter has not produced a toxic substance and that the claim is based only on the presence of the matter in the liquid. Such information greatly reduces the value of this type of claim.

Construction Engineer Any number of claims may require the services of the construction engineer, both from the aspect of collision with an object as well as for damage resulting from the liability of a contractor. If a gasoline tanker trailer collides with a bridge abutment, there are two potential causes of damage. The first would be the damage done to the abutment and the integrity of the entire bridge because of the impact. The second cause would be the explosion of the gasoline. The construction engineer can inspect the bridge, test it and determine the extent of damage. In this process, it may be necessary to enlist the aid of other professionals such as chemists, stress analysts and physicists to arrive at a conclusion.

On occasion a structure collapses while in the process of construction or after it has been completed. The construction engineer can analyze the damage and determine the liability, perhaps pointing to a subcontractor or possibly defective building materials.

Automotive Engineers In a society where millions of cars are being used daily, there are many claims involving alleged defective automobiles, causing injuries or fatalities. The use of automotive engineers becomes an important element both in the pursuit and the defense of these claims. The defects may involve anything from tires, to gear shifts, to improper design. Extremely large verdicts have been awarded in some of these claims with a great deal of accompanying publicity. By the same token, defense verdicts have also been rendered but usually not with the same amount of media attention.

Climatological Experts The climatologist has proven to be a valuable source of expertise in establishing the weather conditions when they are alleged to be involved in an accident.

The National Oceanic and Atmospheric Administration (NOAA)[5] provides detailed weather information for each hour of every day of the year at many locations. A subscription for this data can be purchased for a nominal fee. The information is released on a monthly basis and is valuable in determining the weather conditions at the time of the accident. The data is gathered in one location of the geographical area in question, usually at the main airport. Unfortunately, the weather can be substantially different at a location five or ten miles away, thus necessitating the need for the climatologist.

Experts in this field acquire weather data from numerous sources located throughout the local area, including amounts of rainfall, snowfall and other climatological conditions. This information, added to modern electronic equipment enables the expert to pinpoint conditions in any given area of concern, thus answering any question presented in the course of the claim.

Accountants In most cases, the services of an accountant are required to assist in evaluating property losses resulting from fire, theft, or burglary of inventory or stock and in cases where business interruption claims are made. On occasion the need for this type of expert is present in liability claims as well. A car or truck may crash into a building, housing a retail store or a factory, causing loss of merchandise or stock, and closing the business until repairs are made to the building. Such claims require an immediate investigation to determine liability, and if it is present, to employ an accountant to accurately establish the value of the loss. Unless such expert is retained, there may be a danger that the liability insurer will have to pay for shortages, obsolescence, or other improper charges.

Overall, the use of an expert can prove to be of great advantage.

Caution must be exercised to use the expert under the proper circumstances as the cost involved is substantial. It must also be realized that the plaintiff undoubtedly will use the same type of expert; thus, it behooves the defense to choose the best one it can find.

INVESTIGATING THE INJURY ASPECT OF THE CLAIM

The principle that investigation begins with the accident report applies equally to the investigation of coverage, liability, and injury or damages. The injuries reported should be carefully examined with a view toward determining precisely how they were caused. Once the investigation gets underway, the adjuster will attempt to determine the nature and extent of the injuries and confirm that causal relationship exists between the accident and the injuries. Whenever it is discovered that an injury similar to the current injury was sustained previously by the claimant, the adjuster should secure a medical history from the claimant. This entails gathering specific information about prior injuries, treatment, lost time from work, and disability.

In addition, current medical information needs to be obtained. The adjuster must determine the names and addresses of physicians who are treating the claimant, the identity of the hospital, if hospitalization was necessary, and whether any X-rays were taken or other special methods of treatment were rendered. Hospital records, depending upon the length of the stay in the hospital, can be quite voluminous. The records will include notes which were taken on admittance, a medical history, the results of any lab tests or X-rays, nurses' notes concerning the claimant's condition and activity while in the hospital, diagnosis and condition of the claimant when discharged, drugs and medication received, and surgery reports.

It is also important that the adjuster obtain some approximation of the claimant's projected or actual disability as a result of the accident. If employed, how long will the claimant be unable to work at his or her normal occupation? If not employed, how long will the claimant be unable to function as he or she did prior to the accident? In order to properly evaluate a bodily injury claim, adjusters need to determine the length of disability. This includes defining the length of the claimant's *total* disability (where the claimant is virtually unable to function such as when he or she is bedridden, in a wheelchair or dependent upon crutches) and the length of the claimant's *partial* disability (where some activity or limited work is performed, but the claimant has not recovered sufficiently to function in a normal manner).

Defining disability varies from claimant to claimant. It depends upon such things as the claimant's physical activity, the nature of his or her work and, at times, the claimant's desire to get back to normal activity or work. The construction worker who breaks a leg, for example, ordinarily will be out of work longer than an office claim adjuster or accountant who can get around and perform his or her tasks on crutches or with a cane. In short, the individual claimant's manner and style of living and working must be considered in determining the claimant's disability.

Other factors which need to be considered in evaluating an injury claim are the claimant's *prognosis* and, related to this, whether the claimant has sustained any *permanency* as a result of the accident.

A *prognosis* is a forecast of the course or future of an injury. In other words, what is the degree of recovery expected? The other factor concerns the question of *permanency.* For example, will the claimant have any restriction of motion as a result of a knee, hip or back injury, or any loss of strength as a result of a broken bone? In the case of scarring, the location of the scar and its long-term cosmetic effect are important factors in evaluating the claim. The adjuster will need to consider how the permanency aspect of the claim will affect the life style of the particular claimant.

Much of the injury information considered here can be obtained from the claimant and ideally, should be secured in a signed or recorded statement. Statements are discussed subsequently in this chapter.

Other sources of claimant injury information include the insured, the police report, witnesses, the claimant's employer, individuals questioned in an activity or neighborhood check, and the *central index bureau.* The latter organization collects records of bodily injury claims made against subscriber companies. When a subscriber company receives a bodily injury claim, information about the claimant, such as name and address, reported injuries, age, social security number, occupation, date and place of accident, treating doctor, and so on, is reported to the bureau. Any information about the claimant's previous claim activity which the bureau has on file is reported to the subscriber company. As a result, the subscriber company gains information about the person's claim history including previous injuries sustained. In addition, one of the chief purposes of the index bureau is to alert companies to the "professional" claimant or individual who attempts to make a living by presenting inflated, groundless or fraudulent claims.

Not all insurance companies subscribe to the index bureau. Thus, the service is not as comprehensive as many industry people would like it to be. A growing area of concern with respect to the index bureau is the effect such an organization might have on a claimant's right of privacy. Some people have questioned whether collecting or sharing such information about members of the public who make insurance claims is an invasion of their privacy. To date, the authors are unaware of any specific action being taken to restrain the activity of the index bureau. The bureau continues to operate in a manner which assists the insurance industry in recognizing questions of relationship and identifying claim conscious individuals, and attempts to minimize and discourage fraudulent claims.

Hospital Records

The importance of carefully examining hospital records cannot be overemphasized. It is not uncommon to see a seasoned claim person using a magnifying glass when reviewing hospital records on a serious injury claim. (In fact, the use of a magnifying glass is recommended.) Any claim person who has had to struggle with reading admittance notes or nurses' or surgeons' notes understands the seriousness of this recommendation. These notes are essential in getting a complete picture of the claimant's injuries.

Admittance notes sometimes reveal that an accident did not happen in the manner alleged by the claimant but suggest rather that the insurance claim might have been an afterthought or even a fabrication. Admittance notes may reveal additional information or leads for additional investigation or they may make reference to previous injuries. They need to be carefully reviewed by adjusters handling serious injury claims.

It also is essential that the adjuster learn as much about the claimant's medical history as possible and the hospital records ordinarily include such information. Furthermore, nurses' notes can provide valuable information about the claimant's condition in the hospital, any medication taken, and the results of lab tests or X-rays, all of which convey vital information about the claimant.

Interview with Treating Physician

Aside from obtaining medical and hospital records, there are times when a personal interview of the treating physician, either face to face or by telephone, will be beneficial. A signed medical authorization from the claimant, of course, is necessary before this can be accomplished. Practically speaking, it is not easy to arrange an interview with a doctor today, but occasionally it is necessary and the adjuster should make the effort.

At one time, this practice was rather standard as far as the bodily injury claim adjuster's duties were concerned. Activity checks, too, were fairly common when the adjuster could not obtain medical or injury information in any other way.

The authors acknowledge the fact that the claim practices are changing and that these investigative techniques are conducted with less frequency today, if at all. However, there is no intent to infer that these elements of investigation have become passé. On the contrary, there are cases where an interview with the claimant's doctor is both warranted and necessary in order to determine causal relationship or to assess the real value of the claim.

With respect to activity checks, when a claimant is represented by an attorney who simply refuses to furnish any medical information, an activity check of the claimant is often the only way to obtain medical information for reserve purposes.

Ordinarily, there is no substitute for face-to-face communications, but if a doctor cannot, or will not, see the adjuster in person, the telephone is a practical and satisfactory alternative. Unlike a medical report, in an interview, the doctor can answer the adjuster's questions about disability, prognosis, permanency, or causal relationship. Some adjusters will even request and obtain a recorded statement or additional written report from a doctor, but if that fails, the adjuster should at least make notes of the conversation.

In some cases, as discussed previously, the insurance company will want to select its own doctor to examine the claimant. The examining doctor should be informed about the claimant's injury in as much detail as reasonably possible and should be furnished any medical reports, X-rays, and so on which may be available, before the claimant is examined.

Other Official Reports

Autopsy Report and Death Certificate In cases where death results from an accident or from a cause which is not readily apparent, an *autopsy* is usually perfomed on the deceased. An *autopsy* is a scientifically detailed examination of the body of the deceased in an effort to determine the cause of death. These reports ordinarily can be obtained upon payment of the required fee from the local medical examiner's office. Autopsy reports are particularly important in cases where there is a possibility that the claimant's death may have been caused by a factor other than the accident, such as a heart attack or blackout, which preceded the accident.

A *death certificate* identifies the cause of death and any contributing factors and is valuable to claim people when knowledge or confirmation of the precise cause of death is necessary.

Toxicology reports may also be requested when the adjuster suspects the claimant might have been drinking prior to or at the time of the accident. Such reports will indicate whether alcohol or any other drugs or toxins were in the deceased's bloodstream at the time of death.

School Records The information obtained from a claimant's school records can be significant in developing a profile of the claimant's physical and mental activities before and after the accident. Information about attendance, grades, athletic ability, time lost from school due to the accident, and so on can help determine the seriousness of the claimant's injuries.

Motor Vehicle Reports Most states require that motorists involved in an auto accident where there is property damage over a specified amount or any bodily injury, complete an accident report to be filed with the state motor vehicle department. The accessibility of these reports by insurance companies varies from state to state. In some states, the reports are confidential and cannot be obtained by insurers, while in other states they can be obtained and are admissible as evidence against the particular motorist, should the motorist admit fault.

Information about an individual's driving record and accident history is also available in some states. Underwriters, for example, frequently request this kind of information regarding an applicant for auto insurance.

It is important that adjusters know what motor vehicle information is available about motorists in their state.

Traffic or Criminal Court Hearings Although the evidence presented at traffic court hearings generally is not admissible in a subsequent civil trial, much valuable information can be gathered from the hearing. Ordinarily, there is considerable consistency between the evidence furnished in a traffic hearing and that furnished in a subsequent civil case.

At times, it is advisable for adjusters to attend the traffic court hearing and to take notes and document the claim file as to what evidence was presented at the hearing. It is important to remember, however, that claim people should refrain from advising or representing the insured in a criminal matter. Advising or counseling an insured in this manner constitutes the practice of law. The insured should be advised to refer any inquiries concerning the criminal case to his or her personal attorney for the aforementioned reason.

Other reports or records which are sometimes helpful or necessary for adjusters to obtain include the following:

- *Income tax returns*—for purpose of verifying lost earnings.

- *Military records*—for background information on the claimant; if discharge records are available, they also may be quite helpful.
- *Laboratory or test results*—to determine the cause or reason for a product failure or parts failure.
- *Divorce Proceedings*—when a factor in a claim, the record of the divorce proceeding is necessary in an effort to determine dependency information.

REPORTING

The need for reporting should be quite evident. Adjusters cannot afford to rely on memory. The information they obtain in an investigation must reach the claim file within a reasonable time. Other people also need to know what is happening in a case. Supervisors, managers, and sometimes defense attorneys find themselves in positions where they are compelled to make a decision in the adjuster's absence. As noted earlier, the file must speak for itself and provide these individuals with sufficient information to make a proper decision when called for. Furthermore, the adjuster may not always be around to answer questions about a claim. Adjusters resign, they get transferred, and they take vacations, or become ill. The information upon which proper decisions need to be based must be in the claim file.

In addition, in order to properly reserve a claim, sufficient information is necessary. This information should be reported in the claim file. Many companies establish case reserves shortly after the loss is reported. Furthermore, coverage questions must be recognized promptly so that proper claim handling can be effected. Not only are reports necessary, but they should be made promptly so that proper action may be taken in a timely manner.

An adjuster may be a great investigator and claim analyst but if he or she cannot, or does not, communicate the information gathered in an investigation, these superlative investigative or analysis skills often will not be recognized. The information gained from a claim investigation must be communicated to the supervisor and, when relevant, to defense counsel.

In addition, in the interests of order and common sense, an adjuster's decisions and actions on a claim must be justified in the claim file. An adjuster communicates through the claim file in the form of an investigative report. That report can be a hand written memo, a handwritten field report *form,* or a dictated report with various captions. The particulars of reporting requirements and format vary from company to company. The bottom line is that the file must speak for itself. Reporting helps adjusters organize their thoughts and enables them to see what has been accomplished on a claim and what still needs to be accomplished.

It is true that adjusters are in large part judged by the manner in which they *report* their activity on a claim. The question is occasionally raised whether insurance claim people put too much emphasis on reporting to the detriment of actual performance. In other words, if actual claim handling and results are outstanding, is there really a need for a detailed and time-consuming report? While it is true that there may be cases in which a good perfomer is not a good reporter (and this may sometimes act to his or her detriment), it is essential that the outcome of the claim be supported in the file. There must be justification for the action taken (whether the claim is settled or denied) and that justification must be evident in the claim file.

While a detailed report may not be necessary, some indication of why the specific aciton was taken should be noted. Some companies feel that hand written memos or preprinted *form* reports are quite sufficient in the large majority of claims. Other companies prefer dictated reports with specific captions. In addition, reports may also be necessary for regulatory review should a complaint be filed later.

Kinds of Reports

Generally, there are three kinds of claim reports: (1) the initial or first field report, (2) the interim or status report, and (3) the full formal report.

Initial Reports Ordinarily, *initial* reports are submitted by the adjuster within thirty days after report of the claim. The format of these reports varies by company. Some are hand written while others are written or typed on *preprinted* forms with several captions. Still other companies require that their adjusters dictate initial reports, using several captions.

The captions usually included in initial reports are:

1. date, time and place of accident,
2. coverage information and coverage question,
3. accident description,
4. insured data,
5. claimant data,
6. assessment of liability,
7. injury and damages,
8. subrogation possibilities, and
9. recommendations for future handling.

In addition, many companies require adjusters to furnish information about case reserves as well as underwriting or risk information concerning the insured.

An example of an initial report appears in Exhibit 6-6. Both the initial report and the status report (Exhibit 6-7) are based on the *Teddy Smith* case. (See ACORD 2 accident report form in Exhibit 6-1.)

This report contains a space for reserve information and also includes captions for date the *claim is received,* date the *insured is contacted,* and date the *claimant is contacted.* These captions are included to emphasize the importance of timely contacts with parties to the claim. Unfair claim practice acts usually require that such parties be contacted within a specified time. The report also provides space at the bottom for the claim examiner to add comments and to recommend future handling. This particular report comes in triplicate. One copy is retained by the claim adjuster, and the original and remaining copy are sent to the supervisor or examiner, the original of which he or she may return to the adjuster for recommended future handling.

With the widespread utilization of telephone claim units, there may be less emphasis on reporting since many of these claims are closed on initial contact with the insured or claimant, or shortly thereafter. Experience suggests that much of the reporting by telephone claim units is in the form of hand written memos. This is compatible with the general purpose of telephone claim units, which is to facilitate the claim handling process by processing and disposing of the high volume type of claims quickly.

Some companies waive a detailed initial report when a claim has been settled on a first call basis. The file still needs to be documented but some companies accept a hand written memo explaining the basis of the settlement as sufficient. Of course, the extent of reporting on an initial report will vary according to the nature and extent of the claim.

Interim or Status Report *Interim* or *status* reports are very important with respect to claims which are still active beyond the initial thirty days. It is necessary that adjusters periodically update claim files on the status of investigation or settlement negotiations. Once again, the file must speak for itself and file content must be current so that the progress and status of the claim file will be evident to anyone reviewing the file. The nature and format of interim or status reports also vary by company. These reports may be hand written or dictated.

An example of an interim or status report is shown in Exhibit 6-7. Some of the captions contained in this report from are identical to those found in the initial report. The status report contains specific checklist columns for *automobile, property, general liability* or *workers' compensation,* and *bodily injury.* (These reports are typed for

Exhibit 6-6
Initial Claim Set Up Report

Return to Claim Rep. ______

Date 8-20, 19 8

CLAIM NUMBER

BR.	POLICY NO.	MOD./SEQ.
01	1 000 000	

Date of Loss 8-8-8 Coverage Question No If yes, explain below.

Insured Teddy Smith Age 32 Married yes

Check if Principal Operator ☒ If not, indicate principal operator ______

Driver this accident ______ Age ___ Relationship to insured ______ Resides with insured ☐ yes ☐ no

ACCIDENT DESCRIPTION: (must be completed for all losses) Insured N/B on Connell Ave. came to full stop at SS, then proceeded into intersection and was struck in left rear ¼ panel by Vehicle 2.

If **TOTAL LOSS** indicate whether: PD ☒ Coll ☐ Comp ☐

Vehicle Identification(year, make, ser. no., license no.) 1983 Chev. Citation

Speedometer Reading ______ Use— Pleasure ☐ Business ☐ Farm ☐ Drives to work actual miles ☐ one way

Was anyone arrested? ______ Convicted? ______ License Suspended? ______ If yes, who ______

IF PROPERTY OR INLAND MARINE LOSS, STATE-ACV of Property ______, Building Replacement Cost ______,

Approximate Building Age ______, Condition of Premises ______

Subrogation Possibilities - If yes, complete the following:

Adverse Party: Owner ______ Driver ______

______ Address ______ Address ______

Insurer ______ Insurer Contacted? ______ Has state accident report been filed? ______

For Control Office Use Only:
AIA Code
Chargeable: yes ☐ no ☐
Acc. state

If risk questionable or undesirable, explain ______

______ Should Risk be Reviewed by Underwriter? ______

CLAIM IDENTIFICATION SECTION

CL	ID	TR	CU	Name	Coverage	Reserve	Payment	Draft No.	Date Closed
				Insured	Coll.	4,400			
				Insured	MP	500			

				Ralph Morgan	PD	9,000			
				Ralph Morgan	BI	1,500			
				Sandy Scott	BI	10,000			

FIRST FIELD REPORT

Date Claim Received 8-11-8 Date Insured Contacted 8-11-8 Date Claimant Contacted 8-11-8

Liability: ☐ Clear ☐ Probable ☒ Questionable ☐ Doubtful

Liability Opinion and Recommendations (Comment here on any coverage question and subrogation status)

Insured controlled by stop sign. but extenuating circumstances here. Clt. Morgan apparently speeding and Joe Jones cited for improper parking (See Police Report) which might have hindered both drivers' visibility. Jones is a reporter for Buckeye Gazette and was rushing to meet 2 p.m. deadline for evening edition. He parked his car anywhere he could to bring his story to editor. Unfortunately, Jones is uninsured and doesn't appear to be collectible. Injuries to Scott look fairly serious. Apparently will be some facial scarring from hitting the windshield in addition to a deviated septum. Too soon to tell if surgery will be needed. Collision and PD inspections arranged. I have control of Scott. Following up with Morgan's insurer for contribution on Scott's claim.

Claim Representative Andy Adjuster #

Andy: Note PR says Scott not wearing a seat belt! Have you canvassed scene for witnesses? By next report, lets pin down liability and get detailed information on Morgan and Scott's BI claims.

Claim Examiner Susan Supervisor #

Exhibit 6-7
Field Claim Status Report

TO: Susan Supervisor (EXAMINER/CLAIM REP.) DATE: 9-25-8

NAMED INSURED: Teddy Smith CLAIM NUMBER: 01 1000 000

CLAIM REP. Andy Adjuster DATE OF LOSS: 8-8-8

NEXT REPORT DUE 11-30-8

Indicate Activity Done: (✓)

AUTO

(✓) 1. Loss Report
(✓) 2. Driver's statement
( ) 3. Permissive use statement
( ) 4. Passenger statement
( ) 5. Claimant statement
(✓) 6. Witness statement
(✓) 7. Diagram
(✓) 8. Photos
(✓) 9. Police report
(✓) 10. Itemized repair estimate/bill
( ) 11. Title verified
( ) 12. Sales tax pd
( ) 13. Mortgagee verification
( ) 14. Proof of loss
( ) 15. Subrogation
( ) 16. Releases
( ) 17. UM or UIM clm
( ) 18. NATB report
( ) 19. Total Loss Report
( ) 20. ______

PROPERTY

( ) 1. Loss Report
( ) 2. Insured's statement
( ) 3. Witness statement
( ) 4. Diagram/Rm. dimensions
( ) 5. Photos
( ) 6. Police/Fire Report
( ) 7. Damage inspected
( ) 8. Itemized estimate-checked
( ) 9. Mortgagee verification
( ) 10. Proof of Loss
( ) 11. Subrogation
( ) 12. PILR
( ) 13. Reserve
( ) 14. Receipts or Proof of Purchase
( ) 15. Inflation Protection considered
( ) 16. Title verified
( ) 17. Anti-abandonment ordinance considered
( ) 18. Cause/origin determined
( ) 19. ______

GENERAL LIABILITY/ WORKERS' COMPENSATION

( ) 1. Loss Report
( ) 2. Insured's statement
( ) 3. Claimant's statement
( ) 4. Witness statement
( ) 5. Diagram
( ) 6. Photos
( ) 7. Police report
( ) 8. Copy of lease
( ) 9. Other relevant contracts
( ) 10. Claimant status (Invitee, licensee, etc.)
( ) 11. Product description, manuals etc.
( ) 12. Product defect
( ) 13. Potential co-defendants (discuss below)
( ) 14. WC first report
( ) 15. W.C. interim report
( ) 16. W.C. closing report
( ) 17. Subrogation
( ) 18. ______

BODILY INJURY (Include, MEDPAY, WC, PIP)

(✓) 1. Medical Authorization
(✓) 2. Employee Authorization
(✓) 3. Medical bills
( ) 4. Physician's report
( ) 5. Hospital report
( ) 6. Employer Lost Wage Verification Report
(✓) 7. Projection Sheet
(✓) 8. Reserve Still adequate
( ) 9. BI worksheet
( ) 10. Activity Check
( ) 11. Other specials
(✓) 12. Treating Physician Identified
( ) 13. Photos of injury
( ) 14. ______

Draft(s) in payment have been issued with this report as follows:

MP Draft $ 285. No. 100401 Issued to Insured Date 9-16-8

COLL. Draft $ 3986. No. 100402 Issued to Insured Date 9-20-8

COVERAGE QUESTION: None

FACT SUMMARY: Insured controlled by stop sign collided with Vehicle 2 who was speeding. Illegally parked car a factor. Witness says Morgan speeding but Insured didn't come to full stop. Also, says Jones' van hindered visibility.

LIABILITY: Questionable

INJURY: Scott--facial scars healing well, deviated septum
Morgan -- bruises to head and nose.

ADDITIONAL INVESTIGATION/CLOSING REPORT: Insured's med pay and collision paid. (See attached for additional investigation and comments.)

EXAMINER COMMENTS: Andy, Agree on your assessment of case. Morgan's claim is one for compromise. Keep control of Scott and follow up on results of surgery. If no complications, let's get it settled when you summarize medical and hospital expenses and prognosis of scarring and nasal injury.

Claim Examiner Susan Supervisor **Date**

		BR.	POLICY	SEQ.
Teddy Smith	8-8-8	01	1 000 000	
Name of Insured	Date of Loss	Claim No.		

Witness Williams identified and located through a canvass of accident scene. Williams (R/S attached) was standing outside Star service station while car being worked on and eyewitnessed accident. He states that Morgan was driving at about 45 mph in a 35 mph zone but also says that insured failed to come to a complete stop at stop sign. Williams also confirms that both drivers mentioned that Jones' van affected visibility but thatthe insured considered this more important then did Morgan. The illegal parking factor combined with the curve in the road (see diagram and police report) might make visibility a factor here in spite of Insd's alleged failure to come to a full stop. Insd. indicates in his statement that he did come to a full stop.

Liability appears questionable with all three parties sharing some responsibility. Have agreement with Morgan's insurer to contribute to Scott's BI claim. I will attempt to compromise Morgan's BI claim in view of his contributory negligence which I feel is fairly substantial and will attempt to get contribution from Jones personally or from Buckeye Lake Gazette. (Morgan's insurer paid his collision claim and will subrogate against us.) I have confirmed repair cost for $7,600 and since we may only owe for a portion of this, please lower PD reserve to about $4,500 to be safe.

On Scott's claim, I saw her last week and her scars are healing well. Only superficial scarring now and only visible on forehead. She is going into hospital for corrective surgery of minor displacement of nasal bone on 9-1-8_. Projected she will be in hospital for 2 or 3 days at the most. She initially was in the hospital for 3 days and lost three weeks from work and will lose another week because of surgery. She is a bank teller and felt she would have trouble meeting the public with her scars but she admits this is less of a problem than originally anticipated.

I have put Buckeye Lake Gazette on notice of their involvement by virtue of vicarious liability since Jones was within scope of employment when accident occurred. Received a call from Gazette's insurance manager who says they are self-insured. He seems fairly agreeable to some contribution on Scott's BI claim and may be willing to talk about a contribution on Morgan's claim.

Control being maintained with Scott and Morgan and I expect that if there are no complications from surgery, I will be able to settle Scott's claim in 30 to 60 days. Will look for substantial contribution from Morgan's insurer and from the Gazette. I will not get into possible seat belt defense in settlement negotiations with Scott unless she becomes unreasonable in her demands.

illustration purposes only. More often than not, the reports are hand written by adjusters.)

Full Formal Report A full formal report is required by some companies when the claim is particularly complex or serious and has been active for an extended period of time. It is a very detailed report with all the conventional captions such as liability, injury information, recommendations, and so on, as well as other captions unique to the particular claim. The objective of a full formal report is to help the adjuster as well as claim management organize the file in a manner in which they can see precisely what has been accomplished on the claim and what yet remains to be accomplished. This is done in order to make the file as complete as possible and to offer specific recommendations for future handling which will enable the company to make the best possible decision regarding disposition of the the claim.

Dictated Reports Some companies prefer adjusters to dictate reports, especially with regard to claims of any consequence. Many adjusters find dictating for the first time rather uncomfortable. With practice and experience, speaking into a microphone becomes rather routine, but initially there may be some minor problems adapting to what is for many a new style of communicating. It is helpful to develop some kind of plan or outline for the report and it may even be advisable for new adjusters to write out an outline of the report.

Time saving is perhaps the greatest advantage of dictation. It is easier and faster to dictate a report than it is to write it out, especially if the report will be longer than one page. A disadvantage of dictation is that there may be a significant time delay in receiving the typed report from the clerical unit if the latter is particularly busy.

As mentioned earlier, companies have different requirements regarding the nature and format of their claim reporting. Some companies feel that in the large majority of claims which are essentially routine, hand written reports are sufficient and even preferable. Such reports do not tie up a clerical staff nor do they create the occasional time lag associated with waiting for dictated reports. If adjusters write legibly and if the claim is not particularly complicated, hand written reports usually are sufficient and can actually facilitate the claim handling process and increase adjuster productivity.

Lawsuit Reports When a claim goes into suit, that is, when a lawsuit is instituted by an injured party, many companies require that a lawsuit summary report be made which summarizes the file for the supervisor's or examiner's benefit as well as for that of the defense attorney. An example of such a report is included in Exhibit 6-8.

Exhibit 6-8
Lawsuit Summary

INSURED:	CLAIM NO.:
ADDRESS:	DATE OF LOSS:
COVERAGE & LIMITS:	DEMAND:
SUIT FILED:	RESERVE:
TYPE OF SUIT:	COURT:
SUIT AS FILED:	
PLAINTIFF ATTORNEY:	
DEFENSE ATTORNEY:	
LIABILITY:	
WITNESSES:	
ACCIDENT:	

Potential Problems with Discovery

Traditionally, investigative material (including claim reports) has been considered to be the adjuster's work product. Therefore, it was not subject to discovery by the plaintiff's attorney. Rules concerning whether a plaintiff may have access to material from a company claim file have, however, undergone considerable liberalization by the courts in recent years. Companies face more of a risk today than ever before of having their claim files scrutinized by the plaintiff, judge, or jury. Based on this development, claim people must exercise the utmost discretion in reporting their activities and evaluations in the claim file.

The situation varies somewhat by jurisdiction and claim people should check with their supervisors and/or local defense counsel to be sure that they are not unwittingly exposing themselves and their companies to potential bad faith claims.

As mentioned previously, adjusters must also avoid the use of derogatory or unprofessional remarks concerning the insured, the claimant or, for that matter, anyone associated with the claim (attorneys, doctors, and so on) in their reporting.

In summary, claim people must develop an awareness of the need to exercise discretion in their claim reporting. If there is any uncertainty regarding what is expected and required of adjusters with respect to reporting, they should seek direction from claim management.

Claim Reports to Underwriting

Claim people often are in an excellent position to provide a valuable assist to their underwriting departments with respect to furnishing information about the condition of a particular risk. Since claim people often meet personally with the insured and observe the condition of the premises or the vehicle, they may discover important information about the insured which should be conveyed to the underwriter. Yet the same problems concerning reporting to the claim file apply with respect to reporting to the underwriting department. This information may also be subject to discovery by an insured's attorney when an insured has instituted suit against the company on a claim.

Although much of the information about insureds that is gathered by adjusters is information which is gained from personal observation, other information is obtained through a more *subjective* process. An adjuster who personally observes the insured or the condition of his or her home or property is seeing the situation first hand. If done so discreetly, the adjuster may communicate this information in writing to the underwriter. Information about the physical condition of the premises, i.e., overloaded electrical outlets, appliances in poor or hazardous condition, broken windows, or a cracked stoop which the adjuster observes first hand should be communicated to the underwriter, preferably in a written memorandum.

The situation changes, however, when an adjuster attempts to "judge" the character or integrity of the insured. At this point, the adjuster is in the subjective realm and impressions are based on feelings rather than on facts. There are occasions too where the adjuster will be furnished adverse information about an individual by another person. This is *secondhand* or *hearsay* information. Such information should be communicated to the underwriter but it should be offered with qualifications. It should be emphasized to the underwriter that it is only an opinion, or information which was learned secondhand.

This type of information should probably be communicated orally and the underwriter should be discreet about his or her use of the information. Hearsay information about an insured being a kleptomaniac, for example, which is included in both the claim and underwriting files could subject a company to accusations of bad faith should either one or both of these files be subject to discovery by the insured's attorney. This kind of information should not be reduced to writing and placed in company files.

Once again, it is essential that claim people be familiar with their company's position regarding reporting on the claim as well as reporting to the underwriting department.

STATEMENT TAKING[6]

In a very real sense, the *statement* is the essence of a liability claim investigation. A *statement,* as that term is used in claim handling, is a written or recorded account or declaration of the pertinent facts and circumstances of an accident as related by someone directly involved or by a witness.

Statements are taken for several reasons. The basic purpose of a statement is to gather information so that the claim person can make a proper decision with respect to disposition of the claim. A statement also enables the person giving the statement, hereafter referred to as the *interviewee,* to later remember and review what was said at an earlier time if that becomes necessary. Finally, a statement may be used to confront (or impeach the testimony of) an individual who previously gave a statement and later changes his or her version of the accident.

Claim people should also be conscious of the potential value of statements as a means of reducing claim and litigation expenses. A comprehensive statement which intelligently covers the details of an accident may eliminate the need for defense counsel to take the interviewee's deposition. Claim people should question their counsel's need for a deposition when a good, detailed statement of the individual to be deposed is already available in the claim file.

Furthermore, a detailed statement enables both the claim person and counsel to see all possibilities regarding the claim and to know all pertinent facts so that there will be no surprises later on or at trial. A good, detailed statement also helps the adjuster and counsel see whose testimony may hurt the insured's case so that the individuals will not be deposed or called to testify.

In short, good statements not only help to clarify matters of liability but may be a factor in minimizing claim and legal expenses as well.

The two kinds of statements taken by claim adjusters are *written* statements and *recorded* statements. A written statement is simply that—a statement written in longhand by the adjuster and, after it is read and accepted, signed by the interviewee. Recorded statements are those which are recorded on a belt, disc, or cassette recorder. Recorded statements may be taken in person or by telephone.

At one time, written statements were the norm in claim handling but in the interests of increased efficiency and production, many companies have turned almost exclusively to the recorded statement. Because recorded statements can be obtained in a matter of minutes, compared to the hour or so typically required to take a comprehensive written statement, the former approach can actually accelerate the claim handling process. The adjuster who learns to take a good, comprehensive recorded statement (in considerably less time than it would take to obtain a comparable written statement) has more time to spend on other facets of the claim, or on other assignments. In addition, more claims can be handled by fewer people. Thus, telephone recorded statements fit in logically with the increased use of inside telephone claim units.

This text will not necessarily attempt to teach adjusters how to take written or recorded statements. It is debatable whether adjusters actually can be "taught" how to take a statement. Rather, adjusters need to "learn" how to take statements through regular practice. In essence, there are limits to what can be learned about statement taking in a textbook. The emphasis must necessarily be on the actual practice of statement taking, and much less on the theory. An adjuster's statements should be reviewed and critiqued periodically by his or her supervisor so that the adjuster's statement taking skill can be enhanced.

This text will, however, endeavor to examine the mechanics of statement taking, to furnish sound guidelines for statement taking, and to share with readers the experience of the authors regarding the aspects of good statement taking. If some "learning" takes place in the process, then so much the better.

Both written and recorded statements will be examined in the text. Though recorded statements may be the norm today, some companies believe that it is helpful for new adjusters to start their careers by taking written statements. It is felt that such an exercise helps the adjuster to understand the mechanics and format of statement taking. It also enables the claim person to review the statement in an effort to see what he or she might have neglected to cover. The missed information can then be added at the end of the statement.

Ordinarily, this opportunity is not available during the recorded statement process. Thus, the adjuster's experience with written statements allows him to recognize the problem and condition himself to deal with it later when taking recorded statements.

In addition, some adjusters prefer to take written statements on the more serious cases which are likely to go to trial. Generally, the problem of admissibility of the statement for the purpose of impeaching the testimony of a claimant or witness is minimized with written statements. Furthermore, adjusters wish to minimize situations in which the plaintiff alleges that leading or entrapment types of questions were asked by the statement taker. Such allegations are sometimes presented with respect to recorded statements.

Written Statements

The manner in which claim people actually approach the statement taking process varies by adjuster. Both the personality of the adjuster and that of the interviewee will influence how the subject of taking a statement is introduced. Thus, there is no set or stereotyped approach which can be recommended.

There are, however, several common sense guidelines that can be suggested for adjusters. When meeting a claimant or witness for the first time, adjusters should be friendly and courteous and properly identify themselves. Whether the meeting is prearranged or unannounced will naturally have a bearing on the adjuster's approach.

The adjuster should be businesslike but not to the extent that he or she is remote or highly impersonal. Efforts should be made to put the interviewee at ease and gain his or her confidence. With practice and experience, the adjuster will learn what works best for him. While it is often beneficial to start with light conversation, even to the extent of being somewhat casual, eventually the subject matter will turn to the accident. At that time, the adjuster should be sitting down with the claimant and have his or her statement pad ready.

It is recommended that adjusters refrain from using the term "statement" in describing the information they are seeking from the interviewee. It is wise to avoid any official or legal sounding terms. Rather, the adjuster should use words such as "report," "account," or "version." For example: "Okay, Mr. Claimant, now I need to get your report of the accident."

As noted earlier, a claimant or witness is under no legal obligation to furnish a statement. The adjuster, however, ordinarily needs the claimant's version of the accident, whether it be oral or in the form of a written or recorded statement, before a decision can be made regarding the disposition of the claim. If the adjuster meets with resistance, he or she should explain this to the claimant in a courteous and professional manner. More often than not, such a courteous but firm explanation encourages the claimant's cooperation.

Frequently, it is helpful to set the atmosphere for the statement taking process by requesting the interviewee's assistance in drawing a diagram of the accident on the statement pad. The diagram is usually a necessary preliminary step to taking the statement and there is little or nothing about a rough sketch of a diagram which should alarm the claimant.

Once an atmosphere of relative cooperation is established and the interviewee shows a willingness to talk about the accident, the adjuster is ready to take the statement.

Format of a Written Statement In general terms, a statement comprises three parts: the *introduction,* the *body,* and the *closing.* The introduction will include such items as the date, time, and location of the statement, identification of the interviewee, and so on. The body will include accident data such as the date, time and location of the accident, vehicle identification (if an auto accident), physical description of the scene, accident description and injury information. The closing or conclusion will include a closing statement by the interviewee in which he or she states: "I have read the above ( ) pages and ( ) lines and they are true." Where required, there should be a brief acknowledgment by the interviewee that he or she has received a copy. The closing should also include the interviewee's signature and the signature should be witnessed.

With specific reference to a written statement, the following parts or captions should be included:

1. *Identification of date, time and location of the statement.* This information is indicated in the upper right-hand corner of the statement. (See Statement Guide in Exhibit 6-9, and sample statement of Teddy Smith in the following pages.)
2. *Identification of the interviewee.* The interviewee should be immediately identified. The identification should include age, address, telephone number, marital status, occupation, etc. (See statement guide).
3. *Date, time, and location of the accident.*
4. *Vehicle identification.* Cover bailment situation here, if applicable.
5. *Background or origin and destination of trip.* Include identity of any passengers, activity of driver and passengers before accident, and whether any drinking or drugs were involved.
6. *Physical description of scene.* Include weather and road conditions in detail.
7. *Accident and injury description.* Gauging precise distances is extremely important.

Exhibit 6-9
Written Statement Guide

Insured or Claimant Driver — Auto
(Prepare a Diagram as a Preliminary Step)

Date, time and place of statement — upper right corner of each page. Have person initial all corrections and sign at bottom of each full page and at end of statement. (The sub-headings are for outline purposes only — do not include them in the actual statement.)

A. IDENTIFICATION

1. Name, age, address and phone number (lived there how long?), marital status, spouse's name, children's names and their ages.
2. Social Security Number
3. Employer, address, duties or title, how long employed, telephone number
4. (BI claimant or UM claimant). Present income — hourly, weekly, monthly or annual. If retired, how long — source of income — amount.
5. Driver's license, number, date of issue, type, restrictions, years driving experience. (If minor and applicable, who signed for driver's license?)
6. If claimant: Accident experience and violations

B. DATE, TIME AND PLACE OF ACCIDENT

1. Date, time, exact place of accident, streets, highways, city-town-village or nearest town
2. County and state

C. IDENTITY OF VEHICLE

1. Year, make, model, color, mileage, license number and state
2. Title holder, when and from whom purchased?
3. Previous damage
4. Condition of car — lights, brakes — when last tested
5. Seat belts available — fastened?
6. Wear glasses? Wearing them?

BAILMENT POINTS

a. (If auto owned by someone else) did driver have owner's permission?
b. Did owner restrict its use
c. (Employer owned car) nature of errand. Within scope of employer's business?
d. Purpose of trip

D. BACKGROUND TO ACCIDENT

1. Origin of trip
2. Intended destination
3. Passengers: Names, where seated, ages, marital status and spouse's names, address, phone, occupation — place of employment
4. Reason and purpose of passenger being in car
5. Any complaints about way car was driven
6. Intermittent stops, drinking, other activities enroute. Using drugs?

E. WEATHER

1. Raining, snowing, sleeting, sun shining, sun reflected on windshield or road. Night or day.

F. ROAD CONDITIONS — DESCRIPTION OF ACCIDENT SCENE

1. Road surface, lanes, lane dividers, direction of road, curved, straight, hill-gradual, steep, etc., width, condition, shoulders, traffic conditions, obstructions, traffic controls, speed limit.

G. THE ACCIDENT

1. Name and address of other driver or drivers. Phone numbers.
2. Names and addresses of passengers in other car
3. Make and year model of other car or cars, license numbers and colors
4. Direction of travel: all cars involved
5. Speed of each car prior to and at time of collision
6. Windshield wipers, headlights high or low beam, dirt on windshield, etc.
7. Location of each car when first seen (exact location — feet, yards, car lengths, etc.)
8. When realized accident was imminent?
9. Who entered intersection first — stop signs or traffic lights violated? Who had right-of-way? Which car collided into whose car?
10. Signals given, horn, use of brakes, attempts to avoid accident
11. Position of cars at point of impact. Position on road, in what lanes, points of impact on cars.
12. Did either car move after impact, how far, facing in which direction when they came to rest; upright, upset, etc.?
13. Anyone thrown out of cars? Who they were and from what part of car, where they came to rest, conscious, unconscious.
14. Describe fully all injuries both cars, persons and degree of injuries. Hospitals — doctors
15. Skid marks — length and exact position, debris (dirt, glass, etc.) and position

H. EVENTS SUBSEQUENT TO ACCIDENT

1. Statements made after accident and to whom (drivers, passengers, other driver, occupants of other car)
2. Names and addresses of eye witnesses and their location.
3. Names and addresses of observers who came after the accident.
4. Police or highway patrol at scene and who called them. When did they arrive. Any arrests. Names of officers, measurements made, photos taken. What did police say to other driver, witnesses, passengers?
5. Doctor or ambulance called to scene by whom. Name of doctor or ambulance. First aid to anyone at scene. Where were injured taken?
6. Parts damaged on car. On other car.
7. Car driveable or towed. Who towed, to where, and by whose authority?
8. Other car or cars driveable or towed? By whom to where?
9. Other damage (personals in car; trees; telephone pole, lawn, etc.
10. Any pre-existing damage on the other car?

I. CLOSING

"I have read the above ( ) pages and ( ) lines and they are true, and I have received a copy"

100 Lane Drive
Buckeye Lake, Ohio 43244
August 11, 198-
1:05 p.m.

I am Teddy Smith, (no middle initial) age 32, married to Frances B. Smith, and we live at 100 Lane Drive, Buckeye Lake, Ohio. We have lived here for the last five and one-half years. My home phone number is 222-0000 and my business phone number is

Andy Adjuster Teddy Smith

345-0000. For the last five years I have been employed as a plant supervisor for Good Food, Inc., located at 1508 Balsam Road in Columbus, Ohio. My manager's name is Edward Vernacular. I am paid a salary of $2,000.00 per month. My Social Security Number is 125-00-0000. My Ohio drivers license number is NS 000 100 which was issued on March 16, (year) and which is valid for ( ) years. There are no restrictions to my driving such as corrective lenses, etc., and I have been driving for 16 years. On August 8, 198-, at about 2:00 p.m., I was driving a 1983 brown Chevrolet Citation which is titled in my name, on Connell Avenue in Buckeye Lake, Ohio. Mileage on my car at that time was about 22,000 miles and my Ohio license plate number is ABC-162. I use the car to drive to work and as a family car. The car is in good shape with no previous damage and I have had the car serviced regularly. I had my seat belt fastened at this time. There were no passengers in my car. I was driving northbound on Connell Avenue to go back to work after having a late lunch at Angie's Restaurant located at Connell Avenue and Revenue Road in Buckeye Lake. I did not drink any alcoholic beverages at lunch nor was I taking drugs of any kind. The weather was fair and clear and the roads were dry as I approached the intersection of Connell Avenue and Main Street. The speed limit on Connell Ave. is 35 miles per hour and I believe it is the same for Main Street which runs east and west. Connell Avenue is about thirty (30) feet wide with parking lanes on each side of the street and just enough room for two driving lanes, one for northbound traffic and the other for southbound traffic. Main Street is a little wider with parking lanes on each side and quite enough space in between for two driving lanes, one for eastbound traffic and the other for westbound traffic. Both streets have asphalt surfaces with no lane markings on either street. The part of Main Street which is west of Connell Avenue curves somewhat and is not a straightaway as is the eastern side of the street. I would say that the curvature on Main Street begins about 75 feet west of Connell Avenue. Connell Avenue traffic is controlled by a stop sign while there are no controls for Main Street traffic. As I appraoched the intersection of Connell Avenue and Main Street I was driving at a speed of approximately 30 miles per hour. I came to a full stop at the stop sign, looked to my left and right and then pulled slowly into the intersection to cross Main Street. I believe I was in a stopped position for about one full second. To my left, a black van was improperly parked facing eastbound on Main Street. The van, combined with a line of parked cars and the curve in Main

Andy Adjuster Teddy Smith

Street, hindered my view somewhat so I had to pull slowly into the intersection. As I pulled into the intersection, I looked again to my left and then to my right and the way looked clear, so I proceeded through the intersection. All of a sudden I heard the screech of brakes to my left and as I turned to my left, a 1984 Oldsmobile Cutlass Ciera which I later found out was driven by Ralph Morgan in an eastbound direction on Main Street struck my car in the left rear quarter panel and spun the car around. I ended up in the lot of the Star Service Station which is located at the northeast corner of the intersection. I cannot estimate Morgan's speed but judging from the suddenness of the impact after I had checked to make sure the intersection was clear, I believe that he was speeding and that his view of the intersection was also hindered by the improperly parked black van. At the time of the impact, the front of my car was a few feet beyond the middle or center point of Main Street. At this point I couldn't have been travelling at more than five (5) or ten (10) miles per hour since I had started from a stopped position at the stop sign. After the impact, my car came to a stop across the intersection at Star's Service Station. Ralph Morgan's car came to a stop over the curb of the south side of Main Street facing in an easterly direction. The car ended up about two car lengths from Connell Avenue. After my car came to a stop, I sat there momentarily as I was too emotionally shaken to move. Several bystanders came over to see if I was all right and they finally helped me out of the car. An unknown bystander called the police and about five minutes later, two police cars from the Buckeye Police Department arrived at the scene along with an ambulance. Upon impact, I bumped against the door and I must have hit my head on the steering wheel as I had a large bruise on my forehead. Ralph Morgan was bleeding from the nose and holding his head when I first saw him and he was very concerned for his passenger whom I later found out was Sandy Scott. Her face was bleeding and she was holding her nose. The Buckeye Lake Rescue Squad took Ralph Morgan and myself to the Buckeye Lake Clinic but I believe another ambulance which came to the scene took Scott to General Hospital because she was complaining of difficulty with her breathing. There were about 20 or 30 feet of skid marks which were left from Morgan's car on Main Street. There were no accusations that I am aware of which were made after the accident by either myself or Ralph Morgan. I did point out to the police officer that the black van was improperly parked and I believe that the owner of the van was cited for being illegally parked. I did not talk to Ralph

Andy Adjuster   Teddy Smith

Morgan after the accident but while we were together in the ambulance on the way to the clinic he asked me where my car came from and whether I stopped at the stop sign. I believe there were witnesses to the accident because immediately after it occurred several people came to the scene trying to help but I did not get the names of any eyewitnesses. Neither Morgan nor myself was cited for traffic violations as a result of the accident. The police questioned me briefly and I told them I stopped at the stop sign, pulled slowly into the intersection and the van had hindered my view. I do not know what Morgan told the police about the accident. At the clinic, I was X-rayed and released in about 45 minutes. Morgan was treated for a bloody nose and X-rayed and I believe he was released shortly after me. I do not know what treatment Sandy Scott received at General Hospital. The rear bumper of my car was hanging from the car and the left rear quarter of the car was demolished. Ralph Morgan's car had extensive damage to the front end and the windshield was cracked. There was debris from the accident lying in the intersection and fluids, probably oil or antifreeze, were leaking from Morgan's car. Neither car was drivable after the accident. My car was towed to Tamborine Auto Body and Morgan's car was towed to Morgan Auto Body. I suspect that this is his business or a relative's business. I could not tell if there was any pre-existing damage to Morgan's car. I have read the above three pages and the lines and they are true.

Andy Adjuster Teddy Smith

8. *Events after the accident.* Accusations, conversations, witnesses, police, identity of ambulance, hospital, doctors, etc., condition of vehicles, etc.
9. *Conclusion.* As mentioned previously, it is important to have the interviewee read the statement and actually write, at the close of the statement, "I have read the above ( ) pages and ( ) lines and they are true." Then the adjuster should have the interviewee sign the statement.

The authors recall a trial in which this closing sentence written in the plaintiff's own handwriting was decisive in bringing about a defendant's verdict.

Originally, the claimant, in a premises fall-down case, had signed a written statement to the effect that she did not know what caused her to fall on a stairway. The adjuster took a comprehensive statement and ruled out any debris or foreign objects which might have contributed to the fall. He also confirmed that the surface of the stairway was not slippery and that there was in existence a sturdy railing on the stairway. In addition, the claimant stated that the lighting was fine and that there were no witnesses to the accident. In effect, the adjuster had obtained a signed statement which ruled out any liability on the insured landlord's part. Consequently, the claim was denied. Soon after the denial, a summons and complaint were served upon the insured by the plaintiff. The insurer defended the case.

When the plaintiff testified at trial, she stated that the reason she fell was poor lighting and some unidentified, slippery substance on the stairway. On cross-examination, the defense attorney read her earlier signed statement into evidence. When asked if this was the plaintiff's statement, she replied that she did not recall. The defense attorney, showing the plaintiff her signature, asked if, in fact, that was the claimant's signature. Her reply was something to the effect that, yes, that was her signature but she did not remember ever giving such a statement or signing it.

The defense attorney then showed her the closing sentence which read: "I have read the above two and a half pages and they are true." The attorney asked if she had written that sentence and she answered in the affirmative. Thus, the witness was unsuccessful in implying that she was pressured into signing the statement without reading or accepting it.

In short, her testimony was impeached by a good complete statement and this resulted in a defendant's verdict.

10. *Signature.* The statement should be signed immediately below the closing sentence and on the right side of the page. The left side of that line is reserved for someone to witness the interviewee's signature, preferably a family member or neighbor. Each page of the statement should be signed and witnessed.

    If, in reading the statement, the interviewee wishes to make a change or delete something, the adjuster should strike through the word(s) and write in the change or correction above it. Then the interviewee should initial the change or deletion.

Rules for Taking Signed Statements In summary, the following guidelines for taking signed statements are helpful in assuring that the format and mechanics of the statement will be correct.

1. At the top right of the first page, note the date, time, and place the statement is being taken.
2. Number and date each consecutive page.

3. No margins should be used.
4. No paragraphs or indentions should be used.
5. No gaps should be left any place on any page.
6. No erasures should be made; all errors should be struck through, the correction inserted above it and the interviewee should initial the correction.
7. No abbreviations (or shortcuts in writing) should be used.
8. Statements must be taken in ink or indelible pencil. (Ballpoint pens or typewriters are satisfactory.)
9. Use the language of the person being interviewed—if he or she uses slang, use slang in the statement.
10. Make the statement clear, concise, chronological, legible and complete in every respect. A written statement should flow naturally and lead up to the happening of the accident on a step by step basis. In other words, the accident should not be presumed to have already occurred in the statement, but rather it should be worked up to in a natural step by step sequence. (Use a Statement Outline or Guide.)
11. The interviewee should read the statement and certify, in his or her handwriting, that he or she has read and understands the statement. Example: "I have read the above two pages and eleven lines and state that they are true."
12. The interviewee should sign at the end of the statement and at the bottom of each page of the statement, and his or her signature should be witnessed.

Teddy Smith's written statement should be reviewed carefully in conjunction with the Statement Outline in Exhibit 6-9.

Recorded Statements

The Approach Much of what has just been said regarding the technique of taking written statements applies equally to taking recorded statements. The difference, of course, is that the adjuster who records a statement is either bringing an electronic device into the interviewee's home or using such a device in conjunction with the telephone. The adjuster should be considerate of any fears a person may have regarding a recorded interview. The recorder should be introduced in a natural manner without undue attention or emphasis. With experience, adjusters learn what works well for them and develop their own techniques.

The adjuster may introduce the recorder in anyone of the following ways:

"We ordinarily record these interviews so we can obtain the facts quickly. You probably have one of these cassettes yourself."

Or:

"We use cassettes (recorders) so we can get your version in your own words." Optional: "And you don't have to sign anything."

Or:

"We know your time is valuable and the cassette (recorder) is much faster than writing a report."

Or:

"We can take a written report in about an hour or we can take a recording in about ten minutes. I prefer and suggest the recording, but it's up to you."

Once again, adjusters should not use the word "statement." Also, if the interviewee requests a copy of the recorded statement, if and when it is transcribed, a copy should be sent accordingly.

Guidelines for Taking Recorded Statements The key in statement taking, as in the investigation of a claim, is to answer the questions who, what, when, where, and why as they relate to the happening of the accident.

Statement guides or outlines have been mentioned previously and can be quite helpful. In some cases, they may be adequate for gathering the necessary facts about the accident while in other cases they may even be too complete. In many cases, however, structural statement guides are insufficient as a means of gathering all the important information about an accident. A guide helps remind adjusters to cover certain points so that an additional statement will not be necessary. But it is only a guide and as such has a limited purpose. Adjusters need to keep this in mind when they are taking statements. This is especially important with respect to recorded statements where the adjuster cannot go back, review the statement, and make additions before concluding it as he or she can with written statements.

The one element which must accompany the statement guide is the adjuster's *ability to listen and think.* Since the circumstances surrounding an accident vary, adjusters will need to obtain different kinds of information for each accident. The statement guide can help but it usually cannot do the entire job. Adjusters must supplement the guide with questions which are relative to the particular case. This means that generally the adjuster must analyze the accident situation and determine if any questions need to be answered which are not included in the statement guide.

The following guidelines should be helpful in reinforcing the basic principles involved in taking recorded statements:

1. All parties to the interview must be identified. Date and time of the interview and location of all parties at the time of the interview must be established. Identity of the interviewee must go beyond his or her name, age, and address.
2. It must be clear in the recording that the interviewee was aware that a recording was being made and that it was with his or her permission.
3. All proper names, unusual sounding locations, and any other words that may not be clear should be spelled out.
4. All interruptions must be explained. The machine should not be stopped after the recording begins unless there is a valid reason and this reason must be explained in the recording itself.
5. Continuity of the recording is necessary. If recording with a belt or disc and a second belt is necessary, or if the cassette must be turned over, the interruption of the recording must be explained both before changing the belt or turning the cassette and after this has been accomplished.
6. The interview must deal with all aspects of applicable and pertinent facts surrounding the loss or accident.
7. At the end of the interview, the interviewee must be given an opportunity to make additions or corrections and an offer extending this opportunity must be part of the recording.
8. The interviewee must be asked if the questions were understood and the answers given true to the best of his or her knowledge.
9. The interviewee must again be made aware of the fact that the interview was recorded.
10. When the interview has been completed, the adjuster should play back the last few words to make sure the interview has been recorded.

Pre-recording Accident Discussion Adjusters should keep their review of the physical facts of the accident with the interviewee relatively brief so that an adverse atmosphere is not created. The date and time of the accident, the location of the accident, and the names of all persons involved should be reviewed with the interviewee. The interviewee may have this information written down and kept in a safe place. It is important that the adjuster and the interviewee have the correct factual information before the interview is begun.

As mentioned earlier, it also is important that prior to recording the interview, the adjuster enlist the interviewee's assistance in preparing a brief sketch of the accident scene. This should be done for telephone as well as in-person interviews so that the adjuster will have an accurate understanding of directions, streets, width and lanes, distances, intersections, traffic controls, obstructions, sidewalks, stairs or steps, handrails, lighting, etc.

Once again, gauging precise distances is extremely important. The statement should indicate how many feet, yards, or car lengths apart the vehicles were when the drivers first noticed each other as well as distances from intersections, curbs, traffic controls, obstructions, and so on. In addition, distances and dimensions associated with the location of a fall-down should also be clearly covered using terms with which the interviewee is fimiliar and understands.

Instructions to the Interviewee Before the interview is actually started, the adjuster needs to explain the procedures:

1. The adjuster should tell the interviewee that this will be a question and answer type of interview.
2. The adjuster should let the interviewee know that he or she will be asked his or her age, marital status, occupation, employer, salary (if a claimant), and social security number. This is necessary in order to identify the person being interviewed.
3. The adjuster should not be afraid to ask the interviewee to speak up if the telephone reception is unclear or if the interviewee is speaking too low for the microphone to pick up the responses during the personal interview.
4. When an adjuster is about to conduct an in-person interview and a second person is present, the adjuster should ask that person not to interrupt the interview. The adjuster can explain that he or she will be glad to answer any questions after the recorded interview is completed. If the person does interrupt, the adjuster must identify the person and have the person state his or her relationship to the accident.
5. The adjuster should explain to the interviewee that he or she is interested only in the physical facts of the accident during the interview and that other unrelated factors can be discussed after the interview. (Do not negotiate the claim during the recorded interview or discuss the insurance policy. The adjuster is only interested in the facts, just as he or she would be when writing a longhand statement.)
6. The interviewee should be asked if he or she remembers:
   - The date and time of the accident
   - The names of his or her passengers, witnesses, other parties and their addresses.
   - The exact place of the accident—highway, stairs, intersection, city or county, and state.
   - The adjuster should instruct the interviewee to have his or her social security number handy.

7. Even with a telephone recorded interview, the adjuster should ask the interviewee to draw a sketch of the accident scene, as this will help the interviewee keep his or her thoughts in order.
8. Prior to recording a telephone interview, the adjuster should ask the interviewee not to hang up when the interview is completed so that the adjuster may make arrangements to visit the interviewee and inspect damages.
9. The adjuster should advise the interviewee that the recorder will be turned on and that he or she will make a short introduction of the interview.

Other Suggestions Developed from Experience The importance of planning ahead, of studying the accident report, cannot be overemphasized. Ideally, adjusters should analyze the accident situation before recording an interview with a party to the accident. However, situations will occur where an adjuster has the opportunity to record an interview of a claimant or witness before he or she has had a chance to review the accident report, or the adjuster may not even have received the accident report. In these situations, it is advisable that the adjuster take advantage of the opportunity and obtain the recorded interview.

Adjusters need to recognize opportunities for facilitating claim handling when they are presented. If a claimant calls to report an accident and is willing to discuss the accident, the adjuster should attempt to obtain the claimant's consent for a recorded interview. Even when coverage has not as yet been confirmed or liability appears questionable, the adjuster should still take the statement. The adjuster should not commit the company to paying the claim but rather indicate that coverage needs to be confirmed and the liability aspect needs to be investigated before a final decision can be made. The adjuster should further inform the party that once these matters are clarified, he or she will be contacted and informed of the company's decision.

At times, an interviewee will be quite talkative and stray from the central points of the accident. The adjuster must be in control of the interview and keep it on the track. The adjuster should get to the important points of the accident quickly and be as precise as possible in his or her questioning. The interview should be kept conversational and informal but it needs to be kept moving as well.

Another problem occasionally encountered in taking recorded statements is that either the adjuster or the interviewee will speak too fast or will not speak clearly. Adjusters must make efforts to speak distinctly and at an even pace and should not hesitate to ask the interviewee to speak up when that becomes necessary.

It is strongly recommended that adjusters incorporate the following two steps into their statement taking technique:

1. Adjusters should write brief notes prior to the interview so that they will know *beforehand* what they are seeking to cover and then check them off as the items are covered.
2. Adjusters should jot down notes regarding important points or questions that come to mind *during* the interview so that these points or questions can be covered before the interview is concluded.

These two steps should supplement the statement guide or outline.

Handling Interruptions When recording a statement in person, adjusters should attempt to select an area where the interview will not be interrupted. If the situation appears hopeless in that bothersome or excessive noise cannot be avoided or interruptions will be frequent, the adjuster should seriously consider writing out the statement, especially when a claimant or witness is involved. In other words, if the choice is between getting a written statement *now* or coming back at a later date to attempt another recorded statement, the wiser decision may be to obtain the written statement at that moment. This is a judgment call since there is no guarantee that a claimant or witness will be receptive to giving a statement at a later date. Adjusters must be careful not to lose an opportunity which may only be available for a fleeting moment.

Although the adjuster may decide that the setting is proper for a recorded interview, interruptions may nevertheless occur. When this happens, adjusters should explain the interruption in a natural manner. The following suggests possible approaches to handling interruptions:

1. SHORT DELAY: "(Name of interviewee) is leaving to (answer the door, check on a disturbance, or whatever). We will leave the machine continually running." When the interviewee returns, say, "(Name of interviewee) has returned and we can continue our interview." Then the adjuster may proceed.
2. LONG DELAY: When it is or becomes obvious that there will be a long delay, the adjuster may handle this in the following manner: "There will be an interruption of this interview while (name of interviewee) leaves to (give the reason for his or her leaving). The time is _____a.m. _____p.m." Then the adjuster may turn off the machine. When the interviewee returns, the machine may be turned on and the adjuster may say, "(Name of interviewee), I see you have returned from (whatever was the interruption) and we may now continue our interview. Have we had any discussion while the machine was turned off?" When

the interviewee answers, say, "The time is now ____a.m. ____ p.m.," and continue.

3. WHEN INTERVIEW MUST BE CONTINUED ON A SECOND BELT OR SIDE TWO OF A CASSETTE: The adjuster should get into the habit of observing the grooves being cut on the belt or the tape on the cassette and when it becomes apparent that the end is approaching, say "(Name of interviewee), we have reached the end of the recording belt (or cassette) and it will be necessary to interrupt the recording and change the belt (or turn the cassette). The time is ____a.m. ____p.m." The adjuster then should remove the belt, insert a new one (or flip the cassette) and turn on the machine. Then say, "This is (adjuster's name) talking to (name of interviewee). We may now resume our interview. Have we had any discussion while the machine was turned off?" The adjuster awaits the reply and then should say, "The time is ____a.m. ____p.m." and proceed with the interview.

Common Mistakes Some common mistakes made by adjusters in recording interviews include the following:

1. Introductions (including claimant data) are drawn out. Identification of the person may fill a transcribed page. Sometimes the introductions are so lengthy that the facts of the loss are almost overlooked. Adjusters should move through the introduction rapidly, using the guide. Adjusters should remember to get pertinent telephone numbers.
2. Adjusters frequently neglect to spell out proper names or unusual sounding words. Occupation and place of employment often cannot be heard.
3. In obtaining a statement from an insured or witness, adjusters should make it a practice either in the beginning or at the end of the statement to get the name of a close relative or friend and the address of that person who will always know where the interviewee can be located. This can be crucial when a case has progressed to the point where depositions become necessary or where it becomes evident that the case will be tried.
4. Adjusters should make every effort to break the habit of asking *leading* questions. Leading questions are those in which the question suggests the answer. In addition, adjusters should attempt to minimize situations in which the response by the interviewee is simply a yes or no, when a more detailed answer is necessary. Adjusters should learn to phrase their questions so that they get detailed responses from the interviewee when required, rather than just a yes or no. Efforts should be made to

get the interviewee to do the talking. The purpose of a recorded statement is not to get the adjuster's statement, but rather the interviewee's version of the accident.

5. It is worth repeating the recommendation that adjusters get into the habit of preparing a diagram or sketch of the accident scene before conducting the actual recorded interview. Adjusters should make this a habit.
6. Adjusters need to prepare the interviewee. The interviewee should be instructed to have his or her driver's license and social security card out so that when these questions are asked, he or she can furnish the information immediately without a delay in the recording. It is also necessary to explain the general format of the interview so that the interviewee will not be surprised or embarrassed by the adjuster's questions.
7. As mentioned earlier, not only must the adjuster plan the investigation but he or she must also plan the interview. Additional questions which may not appear on the statement guide occasionally need to be prepared so that the interview can be complete.
8. Adjusters should keep the subject of insurance out of the interview. That can be covered after the recorded interview. If a coverage question exists which needs to be investigated, a separate statement should be taken from the insured as well as from anyone else involved with the coverage issue. The statement should cover in detail the circumstances causing and surrounding the coverage question. It is best to avoid reference to insurance in the statement dealing with the *facts of the accident* since this statement could be entered into evidence at trial. A number of states still do not permit the introduction of insurance information in the trial of a negligence case.
9. The best advice that can be given to adjusters with respect to taking statements, is that they use their judgment, listen, and think.

As a way of summing up, the following represents a brief list of some "Don'ts" with regard to recording statements:

1. Don't make reference to insurance during the interview. (If coverage is an issue, take a separate statement concerning the coverage question.)
2. Don't ask leading questions. Instead of asking, "You were in the left lane?" or "Were you in the left lane?" ask "What lane were you in?" Or instead of asking, "Did you slip on the ice?" ask, "What caused you to fall?"

3. Don't ask argumentative questions which tend to create an adverse or hostile environment.
4. Don't give your opinions.
5. Don't express excessive sympathy.
6. Don't invite a settlement demand during the interview.
7. Don't use legalistic words or phrases.

The Written Summary of the Recorded Statement Since recorded statements are utilized in large part as a timesaving device and are not routinely transcribed, it is important that the written summary of the statement be highly accurate yet relatively brief. This will serve to refresh the adjuster's memory when he or she subsequently reviews the file and will also enable anyone reading the file to become quickly familiar with the statement content.

The recorded statement summary may be written on an envelope designed for this purpose or in a separate summary sheet. The particular manner of handling this varies by company. A sample recorded interview summary form appears in Exhibit 6-10. Note particularly the caption for "Impression of Interviewee," which is an important factor in many claims.

Special Problems Associated with Statement Taking

A caution must be raised with respect to taking statements from claimants who are hospitalized. Many jurisdictions have rules which preclude or restrict taking the statement of a hospitalized patient. (The patient may be under medication or may be in pain or under stress from the accident.) Adjusters need to be familiar with the situation in their states so that their claim handling will be in compliance with such rules.

Statements may be taken from children provided they are literate and old enough to know the difference between right and wrong. Older children, in the middle or late teens, ordinarily require no special handling. Their statements may be taken in the same manner in which adult statements are taken.[7]

With younger children, a parent should be present during the statement-taking process. The parent, along with the child, may be introduced in a recorded statement and the adjuster should obtain the parent's permission to record the child's statement. If a written statement of the child is taken, the parent should witness the child's signature and the adjuster should obtain a separate statement from the parent noting that the parent was present during the child's statement and that the child's account of the accident was accurately recorded.

Statements may also be taken from illiterates. At times, a recorded statement, if feasible under the circumstances, may be the best method of securing such an individual's account of the accident. In other situations, perhaps where the individual has difficulty speaking, the adjuster may elect to take a written statement. If a written statement is taken, a disinterested person will need to be present to read the statement to the interviewee.

There is a typical manner of handling the interviewee's signature in a written statement. The adjuster may sign the witness's name, leaving a space between the first and last names. Above the space, the adjuster should write "His" or "Her" and below the space, the adjuster should write "Mark." The interviewee should be directed to place an X in the blank space. A separate statement should then be obtained from the disinterested person to the effect that he or she read the statement to the interviewee and that the latter acknowledged it to be true and made his or her mark accordingly.

In the case of someone who can neither *read, write,* nor *speak* English, a written statement will need to be obtained, if that is feasible. In such cases, it is necessary to find an interpreter, usually a relative or neighbor of the interviewee. The adjuster must direct his or her questions to the interviewee through the interpreter. The interpreter should speak and ask questions in the interviewee's native language and then translate his or her answers into English.[8]

Upon completion of the statement, the interpreter should read and explain the statement to the interviewee so that the latter understands it. The interviewee should sign and then the adjuster should write a separate statement, indicating that the interpreter translated the interviewee's statement and the interviewee stated that it was true and signed it in the interpreter's presence. The separate statement of the interpreter should also note that the interpreter understood and translated both the English and the interviewee's native language. The interpreter should then sign the separate statement.

Conclusion

Transcribed recorded statements of witness David Williams (in-person interview) in the *Teddy Smith* case and of claimant Marilyn Jones (telephone interview) in the *Ajax Supermarket* case are included in the following pages. Statement guides for a witness interview concerning an auto accident and a claimant interview concerning a premises fall-down case are also included. These statement guides and transcribed recorded interviews should be examined along with the accident reports in an effort to understand how this material fits together and how recorded statements are taken. The transcribed statements demonstrate how the actual interviews with these parties would be conducted.

Exhibit 6-10
Recorded Interview Summary (Prepare in Duplicate)

Name of Insured ______________________
Claim No. ______________________
Date of Loss ______________________
Date of Interview ______________________

Name of Interviewer ______________________ Tel. Inter. ________ Per. Inter ________

Name of Interviewee ______________________ Age ______ Marital Status ______________________

Spouse ______________________ Address ______________________

Status: Name Insured ☐ Insured Driver ☐ Insured Passenger ☐ Claimant ☐
Claimant Driver ☐ Claimant Passenger ☐ Claimant Pedestrian ☐
Witness ☐ Other (Specify)

Diagram Incl: Yes ☐ No ☐
Liability: Clear or Probable ☐ Questionable ☐ Doubtful ☐
Coverage: Confirmed ☐ Question ☐
Subrogation: Favorable ☐ Unfavorable ☐
Injury: Rules out BI ☐ Alleges BI ☐

Impression of Interviewee: (Comment here on appearance and impression interviewee would make on jury.)

____

Summary: Be concise (Include Nature of Injuries)

____

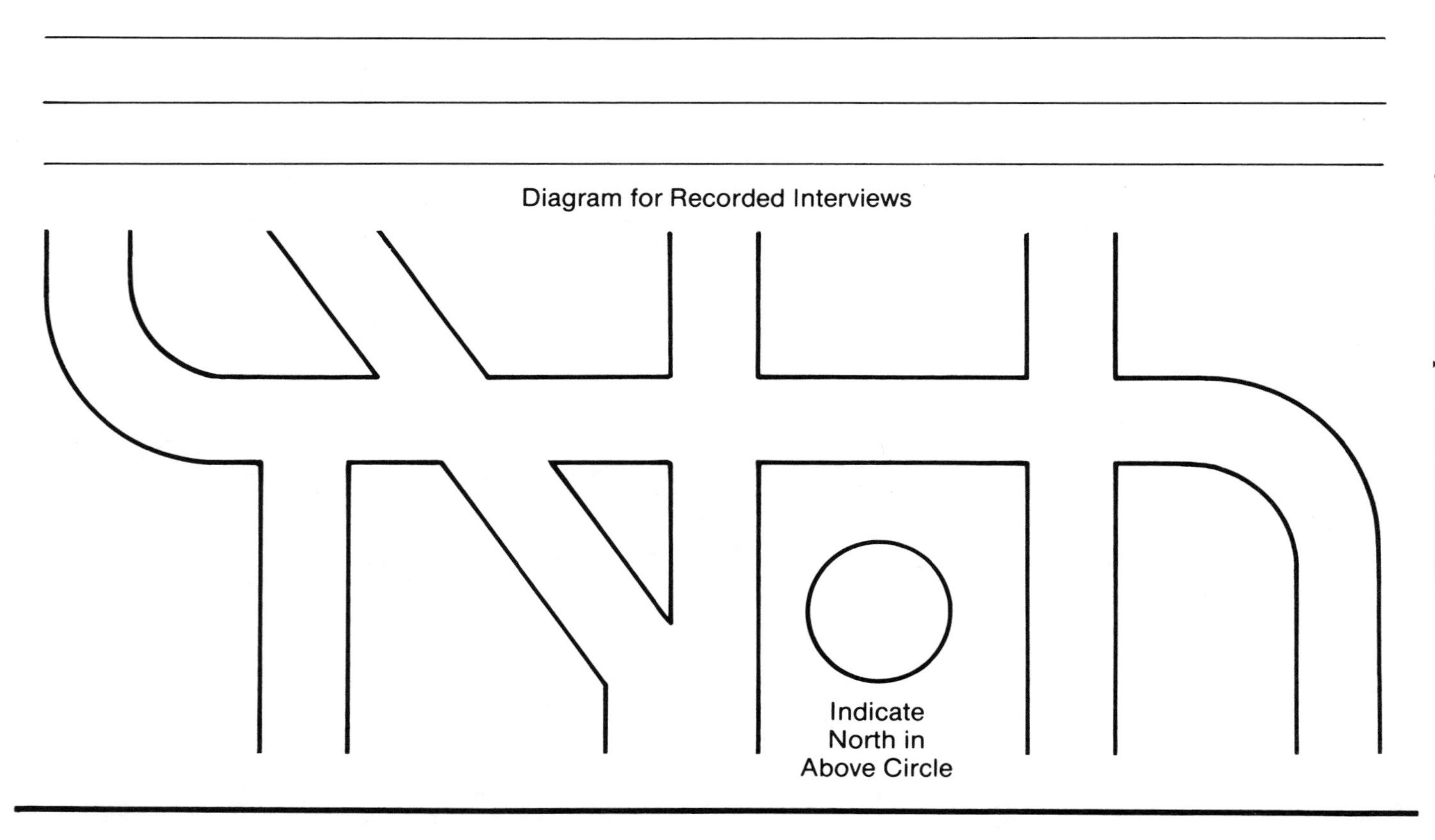
Diagram for Recorded Interviews
Indicate
North in
Above Circle

Chapter Notes

1. Kenneth J. Brownlee, "How to Adjust Almost Anything," *Insurance Adjuster,* January 1984, p. 28.
2. Harry Bacas, "Challenge to Business: America's Changing Face," *Nation's Business,* July 1984, p. 19.
3. Ibid., p. 22.
4. James H. Donaldson, *Casualty Claim Practice* 3rd. ed. (Homewood, IL: Richard D. Irwin, Inc., 1976), p. 622.
5. U.S. Dept. of Commerce, National Climatic Data Center, Federal Building, Asheville, NC 28801—NOAA, April 1984—*Local Climatological Data.*
6. Much of the material on statement taking was culled from the State Auto Claim Manual covering this subject.
7. Donaldson, p. 646.
8. J. C. Penney Insurance Company Claim Manual, Andy Tanler, Claim Director.

Appendix to Chapter 6

AUTOMOBILE RECORDED STATEMENT GUIDE (IN PERSON)

WITNESS

INTRODUCTION: (By Adjuster)
"My name is ____________ and I am speaking with ____________.
Today's date is ____________ and it is ____________.
The address here is ____________. This interview concerns an accident which occurred on ____________________ at ____________________."

PERMISSION:
"You realize that I am recording this interview?"
"And you have given me permission to record the interview?"

WITNESS DATA:

1. Name (check spelling), address, age, marital status—spouse's name, occupation, place of employment, home and business phones, social security number.
2. "Could you give me the name and address of someone who will always know where you can be located?"

ACCIDENT DATA:

1. DATE, TIME AND PLACE OF ACCIDENT. Number of lanes and their direction. Upgrade, downgrade, level, curve—direction of curve. Road surface, lane dividers, weather conditions, and lighting.
2. EXACT LOCATION OF WITNESS AT TIME OF ACCIDENT. Specific location when accident occurred. Distance from accident. Direction from which witness viewed the scene.
3. "WHAT, IF ANYTHING, ATTRACTED YOUR ATTENTION TO THIS ACCIDENT."

ACCIDENT DESCRIPTION:

1. "In your own words, please describe how the accident occurred." (Make notes for follow-up.)
   a. Speed and direction of cars?
   b. Are there any traffic controls?
   c. Which car entered intersection first?
   d. Where in intersection did cars make contact? Points of impact?
   e. Who hit whom?
   f. Parts of cars that were damaged?
   g. Position of cars following the accident?
   h. Were there any attempts to stop by either party?
   i. Were there any skid marks?
   j. Can you identify the drivers or passengers in the vehicles?
   k. Conversations after the accident?
   l. Are you related to any of the parties to the accident?
   m. Do you know any of the parties?
   n. Was anyone's attention distracted that you know of?
2. Police Report:
   a. authority responding and making report?
   b. anyone cited for violation?
3. Any other witnesses? Identify by name and address.
4. To whom, if anyone, did you give your name as a witness to the accident?

INJURY:

1. Any complaints of injuries?
2. Describe injuries.
3. Ambulance at scene?
4. Identify doctors, hospitals, if known.

CLOSING:

(Before concluding, check your notes or diagram to see if any additional questions or issues need to be asked or clarified.)

1. "Is there anything further you would like to add concerning this accident?"
2. "Have you understood all the questions asked?"
3. "Were your answers true to the best of your knowledge?"
4. "Did you understand that our conversation was being recorded? Was this with your permission?"
5. "Thank you, (*name of person*)."

This concludes the recorded interview. The time now is ________.
(a.m. or p.m.)

PREMISES RECORDED STATEMENT GUIDE (TELEPHONE)

CLAIMANT

INTRODUCTION:
My name is ____________and I am calling from telephone number ________________________. Today's date is ____________and it is ____________. I am speaking to ____________at____________. This interview concerns an accident which occurred on ____________at ____________________.

PERMISSION:
"You realize that I am recording this interview?"
"And you have given me your permission to record the interview?"

CLAIMANT DATA:

1. What is your full name?
2. How do you spell your last name?
3. May I have your age, please?
4. What is your mailing address and phone number?
5. What is your social security number?
6. Are you married? (If so) What is your spouse's name?
7. Do you have any children? (If so) What are their names and ages?
8. Where do you work? What is the address? What do you do there? Can you be seen there? Do you know the telephone number there?
9. What is your present income? (hourly, weekly, monthly, or annually)
10. Retirement (how long retired and outside source of income—how much?)

ACCIDENT DATA:

1. Date, (month, day and year)
2. Time of accident

3. Exact location of accident (sidewalk, driveway, entrance to house or building, steps, stairway, in house, store, etc.)
4. Weather conditions (if outside)
    a. raining, snowing, sleeting, etc.,
    b. condition of premises affected by weather?

ACCIDENT DESCRIPTION:
"In your own words, please describe how the accident occurred." (Make notes for follow up)

1. Condition of accident scene
    a. *If outside*
        1. composition and condition of surface. Give its general condition, e.g., uneven, full of holes, broken edges, etc.,
        2. give measurements of locus, e.g., measurements of driveway, sidewalk, steps, etc.
        3. is accident scene actually part of insured premises? (If not, determine owner of property e.g., city, neighbor.)
    b. *If inside*
        1. Give room or location where fall took place. Dimensions.
        2. Condition of floor—carpeted, linoleum, heavily waxed floor, throw rugs on top of waxed floor or linoleum floor, terrazzo, etc.
        3. Lighting conditions
        4. If foreign substance or debris, get description.
2. Were you alone at time of accident? (If not, obtain name, age, address and relationship of other person or persons present.)
3. What was the purpose of your being at the location of accident scene? (House guest, visitor, baby sitting, door to door selling, customer, etc.?)
4. Exact route traveled to point of accident.
5. Actions prior to accident. (Walking, running, looking at ground or floor, looking upward, in process of sitting down, etc.)
6. Describe how fall occurred. (Which foot slipped first?)
7. How did you fall? (Forward, backward, sideways, etc.)
8. Position after fall, (On back, on side, on face and near what object?)
9. Observation of floor or area *after* the fall. (Invite subject to give any peculiarities observed.)
10. Was a specific cause of the fall noted? (Banana peel on floor, toys, marbles, or any other item or substance on the floor that may have caused fall)?
11. Skid marks or any other evidence of fall?

12. What kind of shoes were you wearing? (Rubber or leather soles, height of heels, type of shoe.)
13. Previous falls when same shoes were worn?
14. Bundles or objects carried or pushed? (Describe in what hand or arm, weight, size, etc.)
15. Do you wear glasses? (If so, worn at time of fall? Are glasses with or without bifocals?)
16. Did subject use any artificial aids? (Cane, crutches, artificial limbs, etc.)
17. Witnesses? Identity. (Did they observe hazard involved?)
18. Any remarks made by witnesses? (Obtain verbatim details.)
19. Assistance needed to get up? (Who helped, or what assistance in general?)
20. Was ambulance called? (If so, by whom and what ambulance? Where was claimant taken?)
21. If no ambulance was called, describe how subject left premises.
22. Any drinking or drugs involved?
23. Was there any prior notice of hazard?
24. General condition of accident area OTHER than accident scene, e.g., rest of floor, or floors, clean and free of debris?
25. Were police called? Obtain details.

INJURY:

1. Any complaints of injuries?
2. Describe injuries.
3. Ambulance at scene?
4. Identify doctors, hospitals, dates and type of treatment; in particular, date of first treatment.
5. Doctor's diagnosis and prognosis.
6. If employed, any lost time from work?
    a. extent of time lost
    b. Is employer continuing to pay wages?
7. Any prior accidents, injuries or serious illness?
8. What was the extent of your injuries received in the accident?
9. Was any other part of your body injured in this accident. (If yes, follow up.)

CLOSING:

(Before concluding, check your notes or diagram to see if any additional questions or issues need to be asked or clarified.)

1. "Is there anything further you would like to add concerning this accident?"
2. "Have you understood all the questions asked?"
3. "Were your answers true to the best of your knowledge?"

4. "Did you understand that our conversation was being recorded? Was this with your permission?"
5. "Thank you, (name of person)."

This concludes the recorded interview. The time now is ______________.
(a.m. or p.m.)

My name is Andy Adjuster and I am speaking with David Williams. Today's date is August 24th, 198____ and it is approximately 9:05 a.m. The address here is 1508 Beechmont Avenue, Buckeye Lake, Ohio, which is the home of David Williams. This interview concerns an auto accident which occurred on August 8th, 1984 at the intersection of Connell Avenue and Main Street in Buckeye Lake, Ohio.

Q: Mr. Williams, do you realize I am recording this interview?
A: Yes
Q: And do I have your permission to record the interview?
A: Yes, you do.
Q: Okay. May I have your full name and can you spell your last name, please?
A: David Williams, W I L L I A M S.
Q: And your address?
A: 1508 Beechmont Avenue, Buckeye Lake, Ohio
Q: And your age and marital status?
A: 40 and I'm married.
Q: May I have you wife's name?
A: Pamela.
Q: Okay. And what do you do for a living, Mr. Williams?
A: I'm a high school teacher.
Q: And what's the high school; where do you work?
A: Buckeye Lake High.
Q: How long have you taught at Buckeye Lake High?
A: About six years.
Q: Okay. And may I have your home phone and your business phone number, please?
A: My home phone number is 899-4216, business number is 895-5542.
Q: And your social security number?
A: 123-78-7789.
Q: Okay. Can you give me the name and address of someone who will always know where you can be located?
A: My father, Robert Williams.
Q: And his address, please?
A: 17 Riverview Road, Buckeye Lake, Ohio.
Q: And his phone number please?

A: 899-4241.

Q: Okay. Can you tell me the date, time and place of the accident?

A: It was August the 8th at about two in the afternoon.

Q: And the location of the accident?

A: The accident occurred at the intersection of Main Street and Connell in Buckeye Lake, Ohio.

Q: Can you describe Connell and Main Street at the point where the accident occurred? As far as number of lanes, surface and so forth?

A: Well, Connell goes north and south, it's a two-lane road; and Main Street is basically an east-west street and it also has two lanes. Main is a little wider than Connell.

Q: Is there any room for parking on these streets, parking alongside the street?

A: On Connell there's parking. Also on Main Street.

Q: And the surface of Connell Avenue and Main Street?

A: They're both paved roads.

Q: Any lane dividers? Any way of distinguishing lanes?

A: I don't think there are any lane markings.

Q: Okay. Thank you. Any curvature in the road that you recall, or were the streets pretty straight?

A: Fairly straight, there's a little curve on Main Street to the west, but uh, just a small curve.

Q: What were the weather conditions at the time of the accident?

A: It was very pleasant. Clear and dry, as I recall.

Q: Now, where were you at the time this accident occurred? Where were you located?

A: Well just before the accident I was at Star Service Station, I was getting my car worked on and was just walking outside for a few minutes to get a breath of air waiting on my car to be done.

Q: Could you estimate approximately how far from the accident scene you were where when you noticed the impact? In feet or car lengths.

A: I would guess maybe 70, 80 feet.

Q: Okay. What attracted your attention to the accident?

A: While I was looking over at the intersection, just sort of looking around and I noticed this car, I think going north on Connell and I also saw another car about the same time headin' down Main Street going, uh, east. And, uh, it sort of looked like the car on Connell wasn't going to stop for the stop sign and the car on Main Street also looked like it was going pretty fast. I thought they might've collided and kept watching and sure enough they did.

Q: In your own words, Mr. Williams, can you please describe the accident?

A: Well the car on Connell Street, as I said, was headin' north. It was comin' up to the stop sign; it slowed down but it didn't stop, just sort of rolled out into the intersection, and about that time this other car on Main Street, as I said it was going pretty fast, uh, just went right out into the intersection and the front of that car on Main Street, it was traveling on Main Street, the front of that car hit the, uh, the left rear of the car that was traveling north on Connell.

Q: Do you know the speed limit on Main Street?

A: I believe it's 35.

Q: Okay, And you indicate that the car driving east on Main Street might have been speeding. Could you estimate the speed of that car?

A: Mmm, I'm sure it must have been going at least 40.

Q: Okay. And do you recall the speed limit on Connell Avenue?

A: I think it's the same, 35.

Q: Okay, You say that the car on Connell Avenue slowed, did you say there was a stop sign controlling traffic on Connell Avenue?

A: There's a stop sign on Connell both at, uh, the intersection of Main Street, both for northbound and southbound traffic.

Q: Okay. Is there any traffic control on Main Street?

A: No, it's a thru street.

Q: You say that the car slowed on Connell Avenue. Can you give me an idea approximately how much it slowed down?

A: Mmm, maybe—

Q: Can you estimate the speed?

A: —maybe five, ten miles an hour, something like that. But it never actually came to a full stop.

Q: Do you recall which car entered the intersection first?

A: I'm really not sure. Perhaps, uh, perhaps the car that was on Connell, I'm not sure; it might have been there first because that other car was going pretty fast.

Q: Can you tell me where exactly in the intersection did the cars make contact?

A: Well, the car on Connell was just about halfway into the intersection. It was just starting to go into the westbound lane of Main Street. And the car on Main Street, when he stuck the car on Connell, was just into the northbound lane on Connell where Connell would meet Main Street.

Q: Okay.

A: Pretty close to the middle of the intersection.

Q: Okay. And what part of each car was damaged as a result of the impact?

A: The front end of the car on Main Street the left rear of the car on Connell.

Q: Can you identify the kind of car that was on Main Street and describe the damage to that car?

A: I believe it was an Oldsmobile, a Cutlass I think. There was a lot of damage. I mean the whole front end was pretty well smashed.

Q: And the other car, the one on Connell Avenue?

A: I believe it was a Chevy Citation. It was hit on the left rear side and it got pushed in pretty good. It looked like both cars may have been totaled.

Q: Do you recall the color of the Citation?

A: Well, yes, it was brown.

Q: Can you tell me what happened after the impact? Where did the cars end up?

A: Oh, the car that was on Main Street just continued on to the east a little bit and pulled off just past the intersection on Main. Uh, the car on Connell, it made one complete turnaround and went off across the intersection and, uh, into, the service station parking area.

Q: Okay. Did the car on, uh, Main Street, make any effort to stop? Did you hear, did you notice any effort to stop on the part of the Main Street vehicle?

A: Right before he hit that car on Connell I heard brakes squeal, but just right before the impact.

Q: Did you notice if there were any skid marks left by either vehicle?

A: Yes, there were skid marks for the vehicle that was on Main Street; they started, oh maybe 20 feet to the west of the intersection, and they ended where the cars collided.

Q: Can you identify the drivers of the cars?

A: I think the driver of the Cutlass was a Mr. Morgan. I believe Teddy Smith was driving the Citation. Smith was on Connell Avenue.

Q: Okay. Do you recall any conversation after the accident between the drivers?

A: Yes. The car on Connell, the driver of that car said something about his view being obstructed by a van that was parked along Main Street.

Q: Okay. Did you see that van parked there?

A: Yes I did. I happen to recall seeing it after the accident.

Q: After the accident. Okay. And can you tell me what color that van was.

A: I think it was black.

Q: Do you know whom it was owned by?

A: I believe it was owned by the Gazette, the local paper there. They have an office just across the street on Connell and Main.

Q: Aside from the conversation, aside from that aspect of the van obstructing, uh, visibility, were there any other comments, conversations between the drivers, or any statements made by anybody after the accident?

A: Not that I can recall.

Q: Okay. Are you related, Mr. Williams, to any of the parties to the accident?

A: No.

Q: Do you know any of the parties to the accident?

A: No, I do not.

Q: Did you notice if either driver's attention was distracted in any way which could have led to the accident.

A: No, I don't recall thinking that at the time of the accident.

Q: Did the police come to the scene?

A: Yes.

Q: Do you recall the identity of the police department?

A: That was the Buckeye Lake Police department.

Q: Okay. Did they make a report of the accident?

A: I believe they did.

Q: Do you know if there were any other witnesses to the accident?

A: Well, there were a lot of people in the area. I don't know any of them. I don't know if anybody came forth and talked to the police or not.

Q: Have you given your name to anyone as a witness to the accident, Mr. Williams?

A: No one besides you.

Q: Can you tell me if anyone was injured as a result of the accident?

A: Yes, the driver of the car on Connell; he bumped his head or something and, uh, there was the driver and a passenger in the other car, and I think the driver also bumped his head. I believe the passenger hurt her head and her nose.

Q: You say that the driver of the car on Connell bumped his head.

A: Mm-hmm.

Q: Could you describe the injuries to the driver and passenger in the other car in as much detail as you remember?

A: They both were bleeding. The driver hit his head and had some blood on his head. The passenger had blood all over her face.

Q: Was everybody able to get out of their own cars after the accident?

A: Well, the driver of the car on Connell got out and so did the driver of the other car. But the passenger in the car on Main Street, she was hurt pretty bad, kind of shaken up, and she stayed in the car until the ambulance came and took her away.

Q: Okay. And again can you explain what injuries she had?

A: Well, it looked like her face was pretty cut up and it looked like she might have been bleeding from the nose. She was having trouble breathing there at the time.

Q: Okay. Was an ambulance called to take the drivers from the scene?

A: Yeah, there was another ambulance which came later and took them, uh either to General Hospital or the clinic.

Q: Is there anything further you'd like to add concerning the accident? Anything else you can think about which might be pertinent that we have not talked about?

A: Mmm, nothing I can think of right off hand.

Q: Okay. I do have one further question. Do you know if the police cited anybody for a traffic violation?

A: As I recall, yes, that van I was telling you about that was parked there at the intersection, I think he was cited for illegal parking, the one that the Daily Gazette owned.

Q: Okay. And were the drivers cited in any way that you know?

A: I don't think so.

Q: Okay. Let me ask you once again if there is anything further that you would like to add concerning the accident?

A: I don't believe so?

Q: Okay. Have you understood all the questions I've asked you?

A: Yes.

Q: And were your answers true to the best of your knowledge?

A: They were.

Q: Did you understand that our conversation was being recorded?

A: Yes.

Q: And was that with your permission?

A: Yes it was.

Q: Well I thank you, Mr. Williams, and with your permission I'll turn off the recorder.

A: All right.

Q: Thank you. This concludes our interview. The time now is 9:24 a.m.

My name is Andy Adjuster and I am calling from telephone number 776-1600 in Philadelphia, Pennsylvania. Today's date is November 5th, 198__ and it is approximately 4:30 p.m. I am speaking to Marilyn Jones at telephone number 532-6403. This interview concerns an accident which occurred on November 2nd, 198__ at the Ajax Super Market on Indian Mound Road in Andover, Pennsylvania.

Q: Do you realize that this interview is being recorded, Mrs. Jones?

A: Yes, I do.

Q: Do I have your permission to record the interview?

A: Yes.

Q: Can you please state your full name and spell your last name, please?

A: Marilyn Jones, J O N E S.

Q: Okay. And your age and address?

A: I'm 54 and I live at 604 Panoramic Way, Apartment A here in Andover.

Q: And may I have your phone number please?

A: It's 532-6403.

Q: And your social security number, please?

A: It's 897-55-1349

Q: Are you married, Mrs. Jones?

A: I'm a widow.

Q: Do you have any children?

A: No, I do not.

Q: Are you employed?

A: Yes.

Q: Can you please state the name of your employer and the location where you work?

A: I'm a telephone operator for Pennsylvania Bell in Philadelphia.

Q: Do you have the address? Can you tell me the address of Pennsylvania Bell in Philadelphia where you work?

A: Yes, it's 1200 West Poplar Street, Philadelphia, Pennsylvania.

Q: Can you be reached there by telephone?

A: I hope so.

Q: May I have your telephone number there, please?

A: It is 779-5200.

Q: Can you tell me what your salary is at the telephone company?

A: $275 a week.

Q: Okay. Can you state the date, time and place of this accident?

A: It happened on November the 2nd at about four in the afternoon and I was shopping at the Ajax Market on Indian Mound here in Andover.

Q: And can you give me the exact location of the accident?

A: It was in the produce section of the store, close to where the lettuce is.

Q: Can you describe the accident in your own words?

A: Well, I was in there doing a little shopping along with my niece, Matilda. We were over by the produce section and I stopped the cart and was walking over towards the lettuce and I stepped on somethin' and I fell down, right down on my backside. I tried to get up and my foot and ankle were hurting me, and so was my back, and I noticed there was a piece of lettuce there on the floor I must have stepped on. There was some water in the area too.

Q: Okay. Can you tell me how wide the aisle was in this particular location?

A: I guess maybe eight, ten feet, something like that.

Q: What is the composition of the floor where you fell?

A: I guess it's a tile floor.

Q: How was the lighting in the area?

A: Uh, fine.

Q: Okay. And can you state once again how you fell? What was the reason for your fall?

A: As I said, I stepped on something, I believe it was my right foot, which was very slippery and I just, my feet came out from under me and I fell down. It was that piece of lettuce.

Q: Okay. Can you describe the piece of lettuce?

A: Well, it was green, it was a normal piece of lettuce, oh, about the size of my hand, maybe. It was kind of wet, there was some water around it.

Q: Okay. Can you tell me, the condition of the lettuce? You say it was green. Were there any other aspects about it that you recall?

A: Not really. It looked a little dirty. It was—just looked like a piece of lettuce you'd have in your salad.

Q: Was it a fresh, crisp piece of lettuce?

A: It looked like it might've been wilting just a little bit.

Q: Did you see the lettuce before you fell?

A: No.

Q: Can you describe—you mentioned there was a wet spot on the floor. Can you describe the size of the wet spot?

A: Oh, it was a small pool of water maybe a foot, foot and a half around.

Q: Can you tell me—describe the condition of the water, how it appeared to you, color-wise?

A: It was colorless.

Q: Colorless. Was there any other, any other, uh, was there anything else on the floor besides the lettuce leaf and the water in the vicinity of where you fell?

A: No.

Q: You mentioned that the lettuce was green, but it looked somewhat wilted and dirty?

A: Mm-hmm.

Q: Was the water also dirty?

A: Well, perhaps, a little.

Q: Anything else about the condition of the floor which might've been a factor in your fall that you can think of?

A: Just that it was a rather smooth surface, and once I stepped on the lettuce it was easy to slip on.

Q: Aside from the lettuce and the water, was the floor unusually slippery?

A: No, I really think the floor was okay except for the lettuce leaf and the water.

Q: Was anyone with you in the store?

A: Yes, my niece.

Q: Did your niece see you fall?

A: I think so, maybe not the beginning of it but she was close enough to me to see me on the floor immediately afterwards.

Q: And your niece's name?

A: Matilda Winters.

Q: And where does she live?

A: In Andover.

Q: Do you have her exact address?

A: Yes, she lives in my apartment building, apartment D at the same address as mine.

Q: Okay. And her age?

A: Oh, Matilda must be about 30.

Q: Was anyone else with you at the time of your fall?

A: No.

Q: Okay. Can you tell me why you were in the store, Mrs. Jones?

A: I was just picking up a few groceries along with my niece.

Q: What were you doing prior to the time that you fell?

A: You mean while I was in the store?

Q: Yes.

A: I was just doing some shopping. I had a few things in my shopping basket and I was just walking over to pick up a head of lettuce when I fell.

Q: Okay. What kind of shoes were you wearing?

A: Tennis shoes

Q: And how did you fall, forward, backward?

A: I fell backward. My feet went out from under me and I landed on my posterior.

Q: Did you notice any skid marks from your tennis shoes?

A: No. I stepped on the lettuce. I don't think there would have been any.

Q: Okay. Have you fallen before in the last six months or a year?

A: No. I don't have a habit of falling.

Q: At the time that you fell were you carrying anything?

A: No. I had my purse with me but it was in my shopping basket.

Q: Okay. Were you pushing the shopping basket when you fell?

A: No. I was over beside the aisle. I left it to the side and was walking toward the lettuce.

Q: How close to the side of the aisle, to the counter, in other words, was the lettuce leaf?

A: Oh, maybe a foot and a half or so.

Q: Do you wear eye glasses, Mrs. Jones?

A: Yes, I do.

Q. Were you wearing them at the time of the fall?

A: Yes, I was.

Q: Do your glasses have bifocals?

A: No.

Q: When was the last time you, uh, how old is the prescription for these particular glasses?

A: Oh, couple three years I guess.

Q: Okay. And how do you consider your vision with, uh, with the glasses on?

A: I see real well.

Q: Were you using any artificial aids such as a cane or crutches when you fell?

A: No.

Q: Were there any witnesses to the accident?

A: Well, as I said, my niece was there and I think she saw it. I don't think there was anyone else; there were people shopping, but I don't think they saw me fall. Some of them came over afterwards to help try and get me up, but I don't think they saw the accident.

Q: Was there any conversation made at the time of the accident by anybody—Matilda, or store employees, or any people who came over to assist you?

A: Well, Matilda, I pointed out the lettuce, and Matilda, she saw the lettuce too. She said that must have been what I fell on. And the store manager came over and I told him my foot hurt, my back hurt, and he went and had someone call an ambulance, and I think Matilda showed him that lettuce too. There were a lot of other people around at the time trying to help me up but I just wanted to stay there because my foot hurt too much.

Q: Do you know if the manager took a report of the accident?

A: I think so.

Q: Do you know if anybody came forth and gave their name as a witness to the accident besides Matilda?

A: I don't believe anybody did.

Q: Uh, were you assisted, did you need to be assisted after you fell?

A: Yes, the people from the ambulance squad came out and they put me on a stretcher and I was taken by ambulance to the hospital.

Q: Did anyone in the store help you to get up? You stayed sitting until the ambulance arrived?

A: Oh, a couple of them tried but I told them I wanted to stay put.

Q: And you say there was an ambulance called by the store manager; is that correct?

A: Yes

Q: What ambulance was that?

A: The Andover Rescue Squad.

Q: And where did the ambulance take you?

A: Andover General Hospital

Q: Mrs. Jones, this accident occurred at approximately four o'clock in the afternoon, uh, were you working on this day?

A: Yes, I had gotten off work about 2:30, something like that, because we're experimenting with flex hours. Then I picked my niece up and decided to get some shopping done.

Q: Okay. Did you have lunch that day?

A: Yes, Matilda and I ate over at her place.

Q: Okay. And did you have a drink for lunch?

A: No sir, I don't drink.

Q: Do you stop at Ajax Super Market on Indian Mound Road on a regular basis?

A: Sure, about once every week or so.

Q: Okay. So you're familiar with the store; is that correct?

A: Yes.

Q: Generally, what have you noticed the condition of the floor to be at the supermarket?

A: They keep it up okay. Once in a while you see something in the store. I've seen, in the produce section, vegetables on the floor once in a great while. I don't see how I missed the lettuce; normally I look out for that.

Q: Where were you—at the time just prior to the fall, what were you looking at, do you recall?

A: I was looking at the lettuce, trying to pick one out.

Q: What was the general condition of the store, particularly the produce area at the time of your accident?

A: To my recollection, it was in pretty good shape but I can't recall in any detail.

Q: Were the police called to the scene?

A: Not that I know of.

Q: So there was no police report made of your accident?

A: That's right, as far as I know.

Q: Can you tell me the injuries you sustained as a result of the fall?

A: Well, after I got to the hospital they told me I broke my ankle. My back hurt, and they said it was a sprain or something, and I bruised my knee. They wrapped my ankle and put a cast on it and I went home later that night.

Q: And what hospital were you treated at?

A: Andover General.

Q: How long will you have the cast on?

A: They said at least six weeks.

Q: Okay. Can you tell me, do you recall what kind of fracture it was diagnosed as being?

A: No, they said it was pretty bad.

Q: Okay. So you did not stay overnight in the hospital?

A: No.

Q: And the name of the doctor who is treating you now?

A: Dr. Jackson.

Q: And do you know his first name?

A: Robert.

Q: And where is he located?

A: He's at Andover General. I don't know his exact address.

Q: Okay. Is he the doctor who treated you at the hospital?

A: Yes.

Q: Were you taken there right from the scene?

A: Yes, he is an orthopedic man, I believe, and he had to determine if my ankle was broken.

Q: When is your next visit with Dr. Jackson?

A: I'm supposed to see him at the end of the week.
Q: Do you plan to see any other doctor about your injuries?
A: Not yet. I'll probably go to my family doctor, have him check me out, but I think I'll go to Dr. Jackson first.
Q: May I have the name and address of your family doctor?
A: Yes, he's Dr. Michael Farraway, on Broad St. in Andover. I don't have the number on Broad St.
Q: Do you have any idea how much time you will lose from work?
A: Well, I imagine until I get the cast off I'm not going to be able to go back, because I can't drive and get around very well with the cast on my foot.
Q: You normally drive to work?
A: Yes, sir.
Q: Which ankle did you break?
A: My right.
Q: Are you receiving a salary while you're out of work?
A: Yes, I am.
Q: Do you know what your hospital bill was for your treatment in the hospital?
A: Mm, it was around $300.
Q: Okay. And has this bill been paid?
A: Not yet. I have the name of my hospitalization carrier at the hospital, but I figured you'd be taking care of it.
Q: Okay. We can't make a decision on that as yet. Uh, have you ever injured your back before?
A: Mm, no, you get cricks in the back once in a while when you get my age.
Q: Have you ever been treated for back problems with either a medical doctor or chiropractor?
A: I've been to a chiropractor once or twice.
Q: Can you tell me the nature of the problem, what part of your back it was that was bothering you?
A: Just my low back once in a while; all that sitting being a telephone operator sometimes gets to you.
Q: And what part of your back is bothering you right now as a result of this, or after this fall, what part of your back is involved?
A: About the middle of my back. My back goes into spasms every so often.
Q: Have you ever been treated for problems with the middle of your back before?
A: Not really.
Q: Can you tell me the name of the chiropractor who treated you?
A: Dr. Robertson, I believe.

Q: Okay. Do you remember his first name or his address?

A: No, he's just down the road from the supermarket. It's there on Indian Mound Road.

Q: And when was the last time you treated with him prior to the accident?

A: Mm, maybe six months, eight months ago, something like that.

Q: Did you ever get a diagnosis of what the nature of the problem was with your back?

A: I don't go to him that often, just every once in a while. I call it old age.

Q: Have you ever injured your ankle before, this particular ankle, your right ankle?

A: No, neither ankle.

Q: Once again, can you tell me the extent of the injuries you sustained as a result of this fall?

A: Well, I broke my right ankle, as I said, I sprained my back and kind of bruised my knee.

Q: Was any other part of your body injured as a result of this accident?

A: No, that's it.

Q: Going back just a bit, Mrs. Jones, do you recall if there were any comments or remarks made by the store employees after your fall, or any of the people who came to assist you after the accident?

A: Well, the manager, he apologized, said that he was real sorry I fell. I told him it was the lettuce but he didn't say anything about it. A couple of the other people I talked to asked me how I was feeling, but that was about all.

Q: Okay. Is there anything further that you would like to add about the accident?

A: Just that if the lettuce hadn't been there I wouldn't have fallen in the first place.

Q: Did you understand all the questions that I asked you?

A: Yes.

Q: Have your answers been true and correct to the best of your knowledge?

A: Yes, they have.

Q: And do you understand that this interview has been recorded?

A: Yes.

Q: And the recording was made with your permission?

A: That is correct.

Q: Okay. Thank you, Mrs. Jones, for the interview. This concludes the interview. The time now is 4:45 p.m.

CHAPTER 7

Types of Claims Investigation

AUTO CLAIMS

Introduction

Under the tort system, negligence consists of conduct falling below the standard of care established by law for the protection of others against reasonable risk of harm within the scope of foreseeability. Thus, the motorist has the duty to act as a reasonably prudent person in the course of driving an automobile, exercising ordinary care. Deviation from reasonable activity creates both negligence and liability for any damage resulting from such negligence. Duties created by statute produce degrees of care as a matter of law under certain conditions.

Degrees of Negligence Degrees of negligence as characterized in some jurisdictions are ordinary, gross, and slight. *Ordinary negligence* involves, for example, the failure of a motorist to stop for a red light or a stop sign, thereby causing an accident with ensuing damage or injury. *Gross negligence* would probably obtain if a motorist failed to stop for a red light, caused an accident involving bodily injury and property damage, left the scene of the accident, and was subsequently arrested and charged with driving under the influence of alcohol.

Slight negligence is involved in failing to meet a high degree of care, such as that expected of a taxi driver to a passenger. If a taxi driver failed to reduce speed at an intersection and caused an accident that resulted in injury to a paying passenger, the driver's negligence to the passenger would be slight but would be violating a high degree of care. On the other hand, the driver's duty to the occupants of the other vehicle involved in the accident would require only ordinary care.

Auto Ownership One of the basic phases of the claim representative's investigation in an automobile claim is the identification of the vehicles involved in the accident. This consideration is significant in relation to the car driven by the insured, as coverage and payment of the claim are determined by the identification.

If the auto is owned by the insured, it must be described in the policy by year, make (perhaps model), and vehicle identification number (VIN), which is also known as the serial number. The VIN plate is usually located on the left side of the dash panel where the panel joins the windshield. As the adjuster inspects the auto, the numbers on the VIN plate must coincide with those listed in the policy. If they are the same, the adjuster can proceed with other needed investigation as that part of coverage has been confirmed. Should the numbers on the auto differ from those in the policy, additional attention must then be given to determine if the difference is merely a typographical error or a nonowned automobile.

Since people sell and purchase cars periodically, provisions are present in the policy to cover newly acquired vehicles which are either replacement or additional autos. In such situations, coverage is afforded immediately, but the insured has a policy-specified period of time in which to advise the insurer of the change. If an accident occurs with the newly acquired vehicle and it is not described in the policy, the claim representative must conduct sufficient investigation to verify coverage.

In the event that the insured was driving a nonowned auto, coverage may still be available if other insurance does not apply and providing that the insured had permission to drive the car and that the car was not furnished for the insured's regular use.

Permissive Use. If a person is driving a nonowned vehicle and reasonably believes that he or she has permission to do so, the policy describing that car would afford primary coverage. If the nonowned auto is uninsured, the driver's own automobile policy would provide coverage on a secondary basis. This version of permissive use is based on the "plain language" personal auto policy. In comparison, other older policies required specific or implied permission of the owner of the vehicle before coverage could be afforded. It is evident that establishing permissive use of a nonowned auto is easier in the personal auto policy than in the older policies.

Diagrams The purpose of preparing a diagram for the claim file is to provide visual representation of the accident scene to whomever may review the file. Although it is not a photo, the diagram serves the same purpose as it affords a great deal of factual information. The details of the diagram may range from the basic "driver A rear-ends driver B on a two-lane street" to a complex informative scale drawing of an accident scene involving a fatality. The essential criterion is that the diagram includes all relevant data pertaining to the accident and that it is available in the file when needed.

Photographs As with the diagram, photographs are an essential ingredient of the investigation. They are useful in revealing and preserving the damage to autos, personal property, and real property. In the case of auto damage, it is important to include views of the front, rear, and both sides of the car to establish the presence or absence of damage in all areas. It is equally important to include the license plate in at least one photo to identify the auto. The file should contain a minimum of two photos of the vehicle, taken at diagonally opposite corners. In this manner, each photo will include one side and the rear, and the other side and front. If needed, additional photos should be taken to capture close-up views of specific damage. If the claim relates to real property, at least one photo should include the address to establish the identity of that property.

Photographs are also useful in preserving the characteristics of the accident scene by depicting skid marks, ice or snow conditions, stop signs hidden by foliage, high shrubs that block views, and other conditions can prove beneficial to the defense.

The adjuster must use judgment when taking photos. For example, a vehicle covered with snow should be cleaned first by removing the snow; otherwise, the damage may not be visible. If ice or snow are a critical factor in the accident, the photos should be taken immediately to depict those elements. Likewise, if a stop sign is hidden by foliage and may be the proximate cause of the accident, it is essential that the photos be taken with the foliage present and not after the foliage has fallen, otherwise losing the critical value of that evidence. Such a delay may mean the difference between being able to transfer the liability to the entity responsible for maintaining the stop sign and the necessity of absorbing full liability.

Professional Photographs. As the claim representative proceeds through the investigation it may be necessary to consider the need for professional photographs in circumstances associated with serious injury or damage claims. In these situations, the adjuster is advised to discuss these needs with the supervisor as the expense related to such services must be justified.

As with other professional services, attention must be given to the possibility that discovery rules may prove to be a disadvantage if the photos should be detrimental to the defense. If the plaintiff is aware of their presence, they may be subpoenaed for plaintiff's review and use during the trial of the case.

Uninsured Motorists Claims

Prior to the availability of uninsured motorists coverage, the adjuster's legal concern of the covered person's injury was only the cost of the medical expenses, up to the limits of the medical payments coverage, where such coverage had been provided.

When the uninsured motorists coverage became available, the covered person's injury acquired new dimensions for the adjuster, as the element of liability was added, making a full investigation necessary to determine the liability aspect, as well as the value of the claim. This coverage was designed to "pay for damages for which a covered person is legally entitled to recover from the owner or operator of an uninsured motor vehicle because of bodily injury (1) sustained by a covered person, and (2) caused by an accident."[1]

The theory of this coverage is to provide an insured with protection for injuries sustained as the result of the liability of an auto owner or operator who is uninsured and thus permits the insured to transfer the risk without having to rely "on the other person." Although this coverage is contractual, it puts the insured into the shoes of a third-party claimant, an adversary role.

Because of this liability aspect, it is of utmost importance to determine if the tortfeasor were insured, and if so, by whom. At times, this question may be difficult if not impossible to answer as the tortfeasor often proves to be uncooperative or impossible to find.

This portion of the investigation must include an attempt to secure a statement from the wrongdoer, specifically covering the availability of liability coverage for that person. In addition, the statement must include all other questions that are normally asked of the adverse party in an automobile claim, including the intended destination and the purpose of the trip. This information is valuable in the event that the wrongdoer is uninsured but is acting in the capacity of an agent or servant of someone, such as an employer or other principal. Such vicarious liability circumstances would then activate the principal's liability coverage and thus eliminate the need of applying the Uninsured Motorists coverage.

If the insurance information is not available from the tortfeasor it may possibly be obtained from other sources. For example, some police reports include insurer identification for all cars involved in the crash. If the vehicles were towed from the scene, the towing company may be able to provide information as to who paid the towing bill—perhaps an insurance company. Also, the towing company may be able to direct the adjuster to the garage where the wrongdoer's car was towed for repairs, and that source can be questioned as to whether an insurer is paying the repair bill. After the insurer's identity is known, it can then be contacted to determine if liability coverage exists. Aggressive investigative activity by the adjuster may mean the difference between paying an expensive claim and closing the file without payment.

Once it is established that the other driver is uninsured, the injured insured must be informed so that an uninsured motorist claim may be made if the insured so desires. The claim representative is cautioned to be sure to advise the insured of the availability of the medical payments and uninsured motorists coverage if one or both are afforded by the policy in accordance with requirements of Unfair Claims Practices regulations.

The process of settling the covered person's uninsured motorist claim is similar to that of any third-party injury claim, requiring the customary investigation, evaluation and negotiation. When the claim is settled, the closing document to be signed by the covered person is called a *trust agreement,* rather than a release as in a third-party claim.

A trust agreement is used because the claim results from a contractual coverage and thus requires different terminology from that of a release. Also, since the insurer is paying the insured for the tortfeasor's negligence, the insurer will pursue recovery from the wrongdoer, through the insured. However, subrogation by the insurer itself cannot be pursued; most jurisdictions do not allow bodily injury claims to be assigned. Therefore, the trust agreement requires the insured to bring the action against the tortfeasor at the expense of the insurer.[2] In case of successful recovery, the insured would then reimburse the company for all or part of the payment made under uninsured motorists coverage.

Should settlement not be possible through the negotiation process, the insured must submit to arbitration as required by the policy. Each party selects an arbitrator, and the two arbitrators select a third. Local rules of law and evidence are applied and an award or decision agreed upon by two of the three arbitrators will be binding. An exception is made if the award exceeds the financial responsibility limits in the state where the covered person's car is principally garaged. In that case, either party can demand a trial and the demand must be made within sixty days of the arbitrator's ruling.[3]

Statute of Limitations

Since this coverage is provided in the contract, the statute of limitations for uninsured motorist claims would be that of a contractual statute, which may differ from one jurisdiction to another. Moreover, statutes of limitation for contracts and torts also differ from each other and, since the latter are shorter than the former, if legal action is to be taken against the wrongdoer, it must be done before the tort statute expires.

Underinsured Motorists Claims

Underinsured Motorists coverage has become available in many states, covering the insured for the amount of his or her claim that exceeds the tortfeasor's liability limits, up to the higher limits of the insured's own policy.

The notice of claim is given to the insurer in the usual manner, for the most part, as the collision and medical payments claims must be attended to. While working on the latter, the adjuster is in a position to determine the nature and extent of the covered person's injuries and if they appear to be serious, the adverse carrier should be contacted in order to ascertain the bodily injury limits of that policy. Should those limits be less than the insured's, an underinsured motorist exposure exists and steps should be taken to investigate the claim to the degree needed to permit proper disposition. Statements must be obtained to determine negligence, including the possibility of the presence of more than one tortfeasor. If there are several, their limits combined may exceed those of the insured, eliminating the underinsured motorist claim.

As in the case of third-party liability claims, up-to-date medical reports must be obtained to ascertain the severity of the injury.

When the claim is being negotiated, the adjuster must make sure that the insured or his attorney understands that any amount paid by the adverse carrier would be applied as a set-off against any claim paid by the insured's own carrier.

A serious problem exists in reference to settlement procedures in the claim between the adverse party and the insured. After a settlement or award has been arrived at, the adverse party requires a general release in exchange for the amount paid. Unfortunately, the underinsured motorist coverage contains a subrogation in favor of the company clause which would be nullified by the insured's signing the release. In these circumstances, if the insured intends to pursue an underinsured motorist claim as well, he or she must first obtain the consent of his or her own underinsured motorist carrier whose potential subrogation right might be jeopardized.

The underinsured motorist coverage contains the same arbitration provisions as the uninsured motorist coverage applicable in the event that negotiations do not produce a settlement.

The statute of limitations is based on contract; thus again, that time factor must be kept in mind by the adjuster.

Auto Damage Claims

While processing an auto accident claim, one of the principal duties of the claim representative is to adjust and conclude the claim for the car damage. Following confirmation of coverage, an initial task is to identify the car by comparing the vehicle identification number (VIN) on the VIN plate with the VIN listed on the policy. There may be occasions when an insured may own two similar cars with only one being covered by the policy. The undeclared car, of course, would not be covered.

In the past, the VIN consisted of thirteen digits with the last six numbers acting as the actual serial number of the car. The preceding digits codified the type of car, where it was made, and the model year.

Presently, the VIN is comprised of seventeen digits with the digital increase designed to describe the car in more detail, primarily to assist authorities to curb auto thefts.

The VIN plates are fastened to the auto by rivets that have a plain round head or engraved head, called rosettes. When the adjuster inspects the VIN, care should also be taken to inspect the rivets and the entire plate. If any part of the plate or rivets are scratched or defaced or if the letters and numbers do not look natural, the adjuster must determine if the VIN plate is genuine or if it was tampered with. If tampering is involved, the auto may well be a stolen car with a switched VIN plate. Also, particular attention should be given to identification plates that are manually stamped on a plastic strip. Such a plate will surely prove to be fraudulent.

Illustrated in Exhibits 7-1 and 7-2 are examples of the older thirteen digit VIN plate and the newer seventeen digit plate, respectively.

Determining Extent of Damage There are various ways of determining the extent of damage. Estimates may be prepared by several body repair shops and then compared by the adjuster, whose duty is to eliminate overcharges such as "overlap" and "included operations." By the same token, the claim person should be alert to items that may have been unnoticed or hidden by other damaged parts. This not only assures the insured or claimant of a complete service with no oversights and a fair price, but also eliminates additional inspection trips and complaints.

An "overlap" is present when two or more components are contiguous to each other and all require repair. Since the time has

Exhibit 7-1

Thirteen Digit Vehicle Identification Number Locations: Chevrolet — 1979*

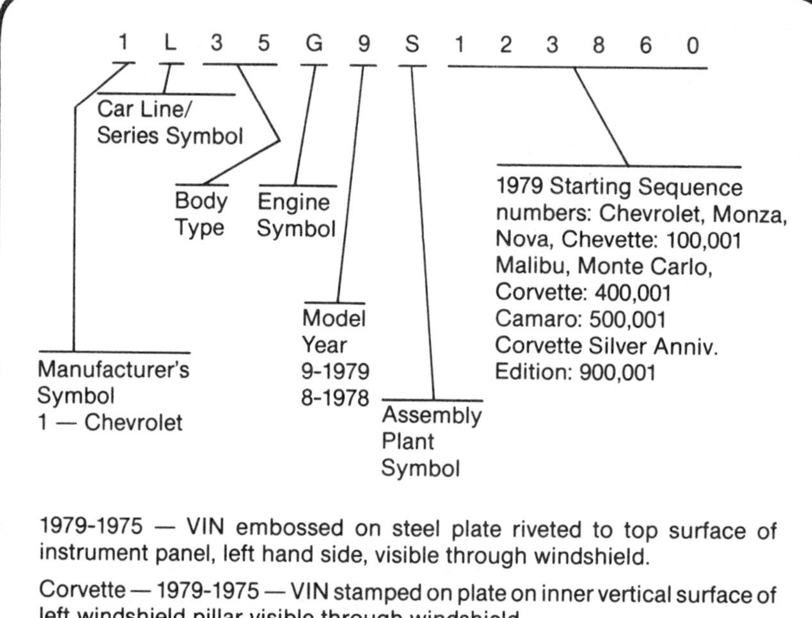

*Reprinted, with permission, from *National Automobile Theft Bureau 1979 Passenger Vehicle Identification Manual* (Jericho, NY: National Automobile Theft Bureau, 1979), pp. 42, 46.

already been spent to gather the necessary tools to repair one item, it is not proper to charge the same time to the contiguous items. Also, less protective care is required while repairing one panel as the panel next to it must also be repaired and refinished. In the painting operation, less time is needed to cover (mask) and tape multiple panel areas as it would take to protect each panel individually.

An "included operation" pertains to damage which is not on the surface of the car. For example, the water pump is located behind the radiator and if the pump has been damaged, it is logical to assume that the parts preceding or in front of or the side of the pump have also been damaged. The proper way to estimate such damage is to allow the full time to remove and replace the pump by first removing the preceding parts which were also damaged. In this manner, a fair time is allowed to replace all of the parts. Unfortunately, many shops charge the time for each unit, thus duplicating removal time with the result of an

Exhibit 7-2
Seventeen Digit Vehicle Identification Number Locations: Chevrolet (USA)*

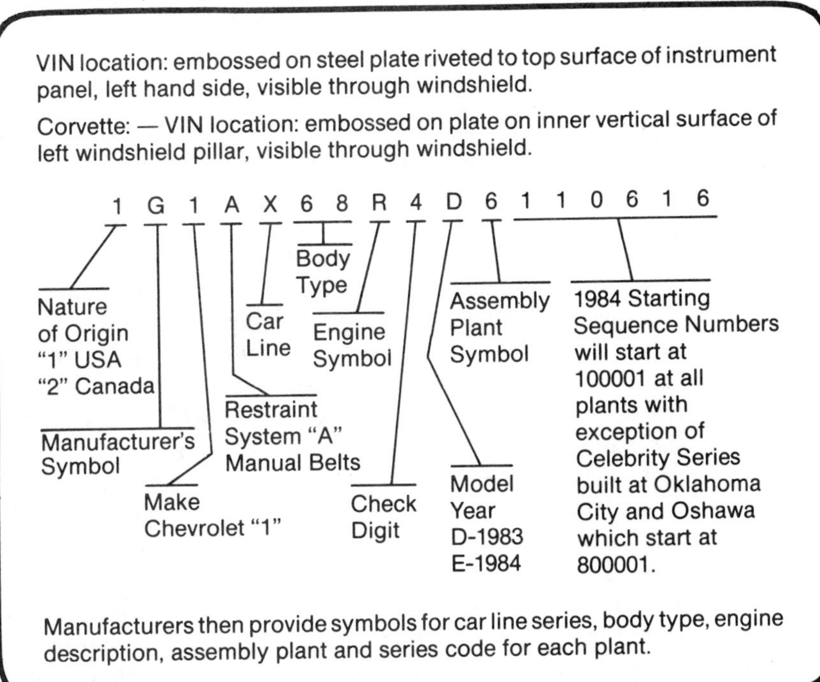

*Reprinted, with permission, from *National Automobile Theft Bureau 1984 Vehicle Identification Manual* (Jericho, NY: National Automobile Theft Bureau, 1984), pp. 53-56.

inflated estimate. Adjustments of this nature require technical knowledge on the part of the adjuster when dealing with the repair person and car owner.

Determining Repair Charges There are several manuals available to assist the claim person in determining repair charges. Basically, they all provide the same information. The manuals first categorize each auto by make, model, and year. Then, in each area, the various components are broken down into individual parts with information dealing with costs and time to remove and replace each item.

The time for straightening sheet metal requires experience to assure a fair allowance. The best method, even though time consuming, is to observe and time various straightening operations at a body shop.

The recommended practice in preparing a repair estimate is to start at a point in the front of the car, then covering one side, followed by the rear, the second side, and completing the cycle at the point where the estimate started. If there is damage to the roof of the passenger compartment, it can be included at the end of the estimate. The foregoing presents an organized method of estimating and reduces the chance of oversight.

Due to the age and inferior condition of many cars, it is necessary to consider the depreciation factor if new parts will be used on an older model. It is important to discuss the matter with the owner not only to the point of understanding, but also agreement. Failure to do so will create problems as to who will pay the difference, with the adjuster most often making the payment.

Many insurers require competitive estimates to assist in arriving at a fair agreed price to repair the damaged car. By comparing the estimates and inspecting the car, the adjuster may be able to arrive at the proper repair figure; however, since all available estimates may be inflated or may miss some damage, it is recommended that the repair manuals be used to obtain the accurate parts cost and time charges, preceded by a detailed inspection of the damage.

If a drive-in estimating facility is available at a claim office, the insurer must staff it with an estimator during business hours to prepare estimates on driveable damaged cars, making it unnecessary for the owners to secure additional estimates. If the drive-in estimator is fair and competent, there should be no difficulty encountered with the repair shop and payment can be made "on the spot." In the event that hidden damage is uncovered during repairs, an inspection should be made immediately upon notice from the repairer.

The nondriveable auto requires an inspection at the location where it is stored. Many insurers employ estimators whose only duty is to estimate nondriveable damaged cars.

Appraisal At times, there may be a disagreement on the amount of the loss between the insured and the insurer. The policy provides a possible solution for this problem, permitting either party to demand an appraisal of the loss. Each party selects an appraiser and the two appraisers select an umpire. If the appraisers fail to agree on the amount of the loss, they submit the differences to the umpire and a decision agreed to by two of the three parties is binding as to amount of loss.

The insured and the insurer each pay its own appraiser and share the expenses of the appraisal and the umpire equally. During this process, the insurer does not waive any of its rights by submitting to appraisal.[4] This procedure is less expensive then litigation and a speedier conclusion can be realized.

Computerized Estimates In this era of computerization, it is now possible to prepare auto damage estimates with portable terminals placed on-line in the central computer with the aid of a telephone. The computer must be programmed to contain all of the components of all autos that are being marketed, including replacement costs and labor charges. By entering the damaged part information into the computer terminal, the computer is capable of selecting the proper data from the memory bank and transfers it to paper via the printer. If a part is to be repaired instead of replaced, the estimator must first arrive at a proper repair time and that information is then entered. The paint charges are handled similarly as are all charges, such as sublet items, towing, and storage. When the computerized estimate is complete, copies are then provided for the repair shop, the auto owner, and for the claim file.

A computerized estimate saves time and is more accurate, but an insurer must have a sufficient volume of auto claims to make this procedure cost-effective as the expenses of such an operation are high.

Unibody Vehicles Until fairly recently, most cars were built with the motor and other basic components attached to the frame, providing a product that was solid, heavy, and large. Auto body mechanics were trained to repair these cars in the typical "bump and grind" method and were able to produce a commendable finished product. In this process the mechanic knew that if the frame was straight, the replacement parts would fit with no difficulty.

In order to meet the demand for lighter, more fuel-efficient vehicles, manufacturers began using a unitized body shell with all basic components being bolted directly to the body. In addition to the elimination of the weight of the frame, the currently used material is lighter in weight and is reported to be stronger, that is, "high-strength steel." Other innovations replaced the "ball-joint" suspension with McPherson struts and "collapse points" in the metal, designed to protect the passengers by dispersing and absorbing the impact within the metal panels. The factory specifications of the unibody allow extremely close tolerances where the joints are welded, thus permitting all panels and other components to be aligned with one another.

Auto repairs discovered that many of the old repair techniques were no longer applicable to the damaged unibody models. If a panel was to be repaired on an older model car, the mechanic applied heat with oxyacetylene heat to shrink or stretch the metal, reshaped it and worked it back to original design. This procedure is difficult with high-strength steel as the application of excess heat destroys the metal's integrity by completely changing its molecular structure.

The problem in applying the oxyacetylene heat to the high-strength steel is the great amount of heat (well over 1,200° Fahrenheit) is dispersed throughout the metal, thereby weakening it. The newer models are assembled at the factory with MIG welders and spot welders which also produce a high degree of heat, but in a localized manner. Although there is still some controversy related to this subject matter, most manufacturers are now recommending the use of MIG and spot welders when replacing panels.[5]

Bench Machines Due to the major significance of the relationship of the unitized body to its component parts it is strongly suggested that straightening operations be performed with the use of a bench machine to realize the original accuracy of the factory specifications. A bench machine is designed to anchor the vehicle, making it possible to hydraulically push or pull the damaged parts back to their original shape. A number of brands are presently being marketed, all with the ability to properly accomplish the straightening process, providing that the mechanic has sufficient skill to use the machine. Also, with some bench machines, a "pull" can be made to factory specifications only to move out of alignment when a second or third "pull" is made, necessitating repeated measuring to be certain that all parts remain true.

Bench machines require training for body shop mechanics and adjusters alike, and failure to acquire this training can result in several areas of high expense. First, the adjuster's inability to correctly estimate the damage may result in declaring the car to be a total loss instead of a repairable car with thousands of dollars at stake. Further, if the vehicle is improperly repaired with excessive heat or by not complying with factory specifications, the adjuster and repair garage may be involved in a serious liability claim after the repaired automobile crashes due to losing its steering ability, injuring the occupants. The importance of the difference in repair technology may not be understood by all repairers, thus the adjuster cannot always rely on the advice of those experts.

Constructive Total Loss In order to determine whether the damaged auto is a total loss, the adjuster must arrive at the actual cash value prior to the loss and the present salvage value of the car in a damaged condition. If the repair figure exceeds the difference between the two, the vehicle should be considered a constructive total loss and the adjustment should proceed on that basis. An example of this process would be as follows:

Actual cash value of auto prior to loss	$8,500.00
Salvage value after crash	−$2,575.00
	$5,925.00

If the repair estimate amounts to $6,100.00, it would not be economically feasible to fix the car as the combination of the salvage value and repair value exceed its actual cash value.

If the repair estimate is less than the difference described above, the strict mathematical application would indicate that repairs should be made. Depending on the severity of the damage, however, caution should be taken as hidden damages may later surface and far exceed the difference. Also, consideration must be given to whether car rental charges will be involved. If so, these charges, when added to the cost of repair, may place the car in a total loss category. Should the adjuster not consider these contingencies, the settlement will result in an overpayment. Further, when damage is severe, the body shop may experience difficulty in repairing the vehicle to the extent that the owner will not accept the car and may insist on a replacement. When this occurs the problems are multiplied and a final conclusion may prove to be costly.

Actual Cash Value and Replacement Cost

The factors to be considered in arriving at the actual cash value (ACV) include depreciation and obsolescence. *Depreciation* represents the reduction in value due to wear and tear (use) and general deterioration of the condition of the item. In using the automobile as an example, ordinary use produces wear to tires, brakes, the exhaust system, and other parts of the car. In addition, exposure to the elements of nature causes the paint to fade and the body to rust. *Obsolescence,* on the other hand, reduces the value of an object through the process of going out of style or becoming outdated.

There are several ways to arrive at the value of an object, with the local jurisdiction often deciding which method will be used. Examples are market value, replacement cost less depreciation, and the broad evidence rule.

Market Value. This method utilizes current market values of similar items to assist in evaluating the damaged property. In the case of an automobile, this information may be obtained from a number of local auto dealers as well as the newspaper advertisements and used car books. By securing information from these sources, the adjuster can arrive at a reasonably accurate market value of the automobile.

Some jurisdictions may require the adjuster to go one step further in considering the market value of a car. In the Arizona Court of Appeals case, Farmers Insurance Co. of Arizona v. R.B.L. Investment Co., 675 P. 2d 1381, the car owner argued that when a new car sustains substantial damage as the result of a crash, it is worth less than another of the same type and newness. The court ruled that the measure of damages for injuries to personal property is the difference in value of the property immediately before and immediately after the injuries, thus finding for the owner on the theory that there is a difference between an automobile that is "new" versus one that was new but was in an accident and is now repaired. In the same case, the court also ruled that the interest-expense for the time that it took to repair the car was also a compensable loss because it was the result of the negligence of the tortfeasor.[6]

Replacement Cost Less Depreciation. Replacement cost is simply the cost of an item when purchased new. If it is damaged after it has been used, a depreciation factor is applied and that amount is subtracted from the new cost to establish the actual cash value. The replacement of a tire serves as an illustration of this method. The tread in the used tire is measured to determine the percentage of wear. If the tire gauge indicates 75 percent tread remaining, the adjuster should pay only 75 percent of the cost of a new tire.

Broad Evidence Rule. This method is targeted toward buildings that have been destroyed and where coverage is provided under a first-party property policy; however, these same principles of evaluation may apply to real property if damaged by the negligence of a tort-feasor.

The court in the case of McAnarney v. Newark Fire Insurance Co. 247 N.Y. 176, 159 N.E. 902 (1928), stated:

> Where buildings have been destroyed, the trier of fact may, and should, call to its aid, in order to effectuate complete indemnity, every fact and circumstance which would logically tend to the formation of a correct estimate of loss. It may consider original cost and cost of reproduction; the opinions upon value given by qualified witnesses; the declarations against interest which may have been made by the insureds; the gainful uses to which the buildings might have been put; as well as any other fact reasonably tending to throw light upon the subject.

As stated, the rule permits the court to consider all information available to assure that proper payment is made to the insured.[7]

Auto Theft Claims

In order to combat the problem of increasing car theft claims, some insurers have instituted special investigation units (SIU) whose full-time duties are to investigate suspected fraudulent claims, especially auto thefts. Initially, the insured is required to complete a detailed questionnaire designed to supply pertinent information regarding general background. When the form is returned the information is reviewed and if a number of items provide specific information, the claim is reassigned to the SIU for further handling. If sufficient evidence develops, the claim is denied. Obviously, the file must be developed in a professional manner and the insurer must work closely with its defense counsel to correlate the investigation.

Since there is a strong possibility that the sale of salvage is directly related to auto thefts, some insurers make sure that salvage that is not repairable is destroyed. In this way the certificate of title is required to be returned to the issuing authority of the jurisdiction, thus preventing its use on an identical stolen car. With the destruction of the salvage, the VIN plate is also destroyed, making it even more difficult to secure the necessary identification to place a stolen car on the road.

Additional support against auto theft is provided by the National Automobile Theft Bureau (NATB). One of its main efforts is to receive statistical information on auto thefts from their subscribers, the insurance companies, which is then entered into a computer for cross-reference purposes. In this manner, multiple-theft insureds are identified and reported back to the insurer. Although the insureds may be innocent of any crime, the insurer is put on notice of the multiplicity of thefts and the information can be used as potential evidence if the person is responsible for the crime. In addition, the NATB also enters data pertaining to total loss autos damaged by collision. These entries are limited to newer models. This bank of information is cross-referenced with those autos reported stolen and will detect the VIN of a car that was previously reported as a total loss. An investigation can then be instituted to determine if the car was truly rebuilt or if the certificate of title and VIN plate were used on a stolen car.

Other methods of disposing of auto salvage, whether totally damaged by theft, collision, or other perils, range from securing salvage bids from independent salvage buyers to the use of salvage pools where buyers may inspect a number of cars and bid on those that they desire. Also, salvage may be purchased by the owner if he or she so desires.

Auto Arson Claims

Fires of normal causation occur in automobiles and these losses are covered in the Comprehensive section of the automobile insurance policy. In most cases, they are confined to the engine compartment or passenger compartment and very seldom does the fire consume the entire car. While investigating the fire loss, the claim representative must be aware of factors that separate the legitimate fire from arson.

According to arson investigators, a stray lighted cigarette by itself will seldom cause total destruction of the car; therefore, if that is the alleged cause of the fire, the adjuster should concentrate on looking for evidence of an accelerant. An accelerant can consist of any flammable material, such as gasoline, kerosene, and other similar liquids. Also, rags or papers may be stored in the car to help a fire along. The use of accelerants can be detected by burn patterns or excessive charring in the area where the highly combustible fluid was spilled. Often, more than one pattern will be detected as the arsonist wants to be certain that the car will be a total loss.

If the fire was accidentally caused by a cigarette or a live ash, the damage area would be more evenly burned with no evidence of patterns described above. The following data explain the results of tests that were made on fires involving various seat cover materials:

> *Seat Cover Materials* As a result of our tests it appears the plastic materials used in automotive seat coverings burn only during the application of a test flame.
>
> Test made with rayon cloth material showed this fabric can be ignited with a match. Burning was slow but steady and never so rapid that it could not have been easily extinguished.
>
> Various experiments were conducted using lighted cigarettes in efforts to ignite foam rubber seat cushion material. The material would char as long as the cigarette remained in contact with it, but would not ignite. If the cigarette was entirely consumed, deep char holes resulted.
>
> Lighted cigarettes were placed upon cotton padded and foam rubber type automobile seats, some with and some without plastic coverings. These tests produced evidence only of scorching and flame did not result from cigarettes during any of these experiments.
>
> As a result of numerous experiments, the conclusion was reached that a smoldering fire may result from lighted cigarettes on upholstery but such fire generally will not flame or rapidly consume the interior.
>
> Flame from a torch was applied to an automobile seat cushion containing foam rubber and covered with a plastic upholstery material. After application of the torch for approximately ten seconds, it was discovered the plastic material had melted and the upholstery had scorched but no flames were produced. The torch was again applied for approximately the same period of time with the same results. A third application of the torch for a slightly longer period caused the material to flame briefly. The flames continued for about seven seconds and died out.
>
> The experiment was repeated using gasoline poured over the seat cushion. Vigorous burning resulted consuming all combustible material in the seat cushion.[8]

An incendiary fire (arson) must be accompanied by a motive to start the fire, such as money, revenge, or domestic problems.

Financial Motive No longer being able to meet the monthly payments, the insured may decide that it is easier to satisfy the loan by having the car destroyed by an intentionally set fire. In such a case, frequently all valuable personal property is removed from the car and, at times, the new tires are replaced with worn ones, and the fire takes place in a desolate area to avoid witnesses. In this situation it is important to contact the mortgagee to determine if the insured was in arrears in the monthly payments on the car. A statement must be secured to ascertain the insured's financial position, work status, and possible previous fire history. During this questioning, the adjuster must be careful not to commit an act of defamation of the insured. This same type of investigation would also prove valuable in the case of an insured whose car had a history of expensive mechanical problems followed by a total loss by fire. In this instance, the repair mechanic may be able to provide valuable information regarding the mechanical condition of the car.

Revenge Motive Reasons for this motive may vary, but the end result may be the torching of the target's car with the use of incendiary material. During the investigation of such a fire, developments should show that the insured has no personal motive. Although arson is the cause of the fire, coverage would be in order as the act is that of a person other than the insured.

Domestic Problem Motive As with other motives, a complete investigation is mandatory, including checking court records for divorce proceedings, although this is not to cast aspersions on persons who are divorced. Other investigation can be developed by interviewing neighbors who may be familiar with the insured's domestic situation. Bank accounts should also be checked as should the various charge accounts.

Automobile Flood Claims

Water damage to a car, caused by flood, is covered in the Comprehensive section of the policy and when such claims are reported, the adjuster must make every effort to minimize the cost. As flood waters rise to the highest level, the water leaves its mark. Immediate attention should be given to all parts that were totally or partially submerged. Failure to do so may cause various types of damage—metal rusts, fabrics become stained and retain an odor, and finally, mildew appears. Electrical connections also rust and must be replaced.

Upon first inspection, if it is noted that the water mark has reached the level of the instrument panel (dashboard), insurers generally agree that the car should be declared a total loss. Experience has shown that attempts to disassemble, clean, repair, and reassemble the components would exceed the car's actual cash value, less its salvage value.

Should the water mark not reach the instrument panel, caution must be exercised before it is decided to proceed with repairs. More often than not, additional damage is found at a later time. Careful attention must be given to all values involved to determine the extent of necessary repairs as to provide the best service to the insured. If repairs do proceed, proper consideration should be given to parts of like kind and quality if the vehicle is of an earlier vintage.

No-Fault Auto Insurance Claims

An overview of no-fault auto insurance was presented in Chapter 5. The no-fault system parallels that of workers' compensation insurance in the manner in which injured persons eligible for coverage are compensated. Like recipients of workers' compensation benefits, individuals injured in auto accidents are entitled to receive benefits promptly and without regard to fault.

The benefits package generally includes coverage for medical expenses, lost income, replacement services (household help, and so on), funeral expenses, and sometimes survivors' loss benefits. Although some states provide unlimited medical and rehabilitation benefits, the majority of no-fault states place monetary limits on the benefits received by injured persons.

Some states provide an *aggregate* limit for all benefits paid under the law, while others provide specific limits for each category of coverage, i.e., medical expenses, lost income, replacement services, and so on. Still other plans contain an aggregate limit for all categories of coverage, which are further subject to internal limits for each specific benefit category. (Most state no-fault plans offer their residents an opportunity to purchase higher benefits for an additional premium.) Adjusters, of course, need to be familiar with the provisions of the applicable no-fault law in their jurisdictions.

The provisions of no-fault auto insurance laws are ordinarily made a part of the auto insurance policy by endorsement. No-fault endorsements for Florida and Michigan appear in Exhibits 7-3 and 7-4, respectively.

As indicated previously, there are three types of no-fault auto insurance plans: *modified, add-on,* and *voluntary* plans. A modified plan is the only type which actually changes the tort liability system by placing restrictions of the right to sue. The mechanism which is used to accomplish this end is called a "threshold." Both *monetary* and *verbal* thresholds are utilized for this purpose. The distinction between these types of thresholds were examined in some detail in Chapter 5 when the threshold provisions of the no-fault plans of Massachusetts and Michigan were contrasted.

Exhibit 7-3
Endorsement Personal Injury Protection Coverage—Florida

The Company agrees with the **named insured**, subject to all of the provisions of this endorsement and to all of the provisions of the policy except as modified herein, as follows:

Section 1

PERSONAL INJURY PROTECTION

The Company will pay, in accordance with the Florida Motor Vehicle No-Fault Law, as amended, to or for the benefit of the injured person:
(a) 80% of **medical expenses**, and
(b) 60% of **work loss**, and
(c) **replacement services expenses**, and
(d) funeral, burial or cremation expenses,
incurred as a result of **bodily injury**, caused by an accident arising out of the ownership, maintenance or use of a **motor vehicle** and sustained by:
(1) the **named insured** or any **relative** while **occupying** a **motor vehicle** or, while a **pedestrian** through being struck by a **motor vehicle**; or
(2) any other person while **occupying** the **insured motor vehicle** or, while a **pedestrian**, through being struck by the **insured motor vehicle**.

Exclusions

This insurance does not apply:

(a) to the **named insured** or any **relative** while **occupying** a **motor vehicle** of which the **named insured** is the **owner** and which is not an **insured motor vehicle** under this insurance;

(b) to any person while operating the **insured motor vehicle** without the express or implied consent of the **named insured;**

(c) to any person, if such person's conduct contributed to his **bodily injury** under any of the following circumstances:
(i) causing **bodily injury** to himself intentionally; or
(ii) while committing a felony;

(d) to the **named insured** or dependent **relative** for **work loss** if an entry in the schedule or declarations indicates such coverage does not apply;

(e) to any **pedestrian**, other than the **named insured**, or any **relative**, not a legal resident of the State of Florida;

(f) to any person, other than the **named insured**, if such person is the **owner** of a **motor vehicle** with respect to which security is required under the Florida Motor Vehicle No-Fault Law.

(g) to any person, other than the **named insured** or any **relative**, who is entitled to personal injury protection benefits from the **owner** of a **motor vehicle** which is not an **insured motor vehicle** under this insurance or from the **owner's** insurer;

(h) to any person who sustains **bodily injury** while **occupying** a **motor vehicle** located for use as a residence or premises.

Limit of Liability; Application of Deductible; Other Insurance

Regardless of the number of persons insured, policies or bonds applicable, vehicles involved or claims made, the total aggregate limit of personal injury protection benefits available under the Florida Motor Vehicle No-Fault Law, as amended, from all sources combined, including this policy, for all loss and expense incurred by or on behalf of any one person who sustains **bodily injury** as the result of any one accident shall be $10,000; provided that payment for funeral, cremation or burial expenses included in the foregoing shall in no event exceed $1,750.

SCHEDULE

Except as otherwise provided in the declarations, the insurance for PERSONAL INJURY PROTECTION is subject to the following deductible:
DEDUCTIBLE of $ ____________ applicable to
☐ the following named insured only: ____________
☐ each named insured and each dependent **relative**
If stated in the declarations, the insurance for Personal Injury Protection is subject to the following option(s):
Option 1 ☐ **Work loss** for **named insured** does not apply
Option 2 ☐ **Work loss** for **named insured** and dependent **relative** does not apply
Option 3 ☐ Coverage reduced by military benefits for **named insured** and dependent relative

This endorsement forms a part of the policy to which it is attached.

The spaces below need not be completed unless this endorsement is issued subsequent to preparation of the policy.

Effective Date (12:01 A.M. STANDARD TIME)	Date of Issue	Issued To	Policy Number

Any amount payable under this insurance shall be reduced by the amount of benefits an injured person has recovered or is entitled to recover for the same elements of loss under the workmen's compensation laws of any state or federal government or the Medicaid program.

If benefits have been received under the Florida Motor Vehicle No-Fault Law, as amended, from any insurer for the same items of loss and expense for which benefits are available under this policy, the Company shall not be liable to make duplicate payments to or for the benefit of the injured person, but the insurer paying such benefits shall be entitled to recover from the Company its equitable pro rata share of the benefits paid and expenses incurred in processing the claim.

The amount of any deductible stated in the schedule or Declarations shall be deducted from the total amount of all sums otherwise payable by the Company with respect to all loss and expense incurred by or on behalf of each person to whom the deductible applies and who sustains **bodily injury** as the result of any one accident, and if the total amount of such loss and expense exceeds such deductible, the total limit of benefits the Company is obligated to pay shall then be the difference between such deductible amount and the applicable limit of the Company's liability. Such deductible shall not apply to funeral, burial or cremation expenses.

If an entry in the schedule or declarations so indicates any amount payable under this insurance to the **named insured** or dependent **relative** shall be reduced by any benefits payable by the Federal Government to active or retired military personnel and their dependent relatives. If such benefits are not available at the time of loss the Company shall have the right to recompute and charge the appropriate premium.

Definitions

When used in reference to this Section:

"bodily injury" means bodily injury, sickness or disease, including death at any time resulting therefrom;

"medical expenses" means reasonable expenses for necessary medical, surgical, x-ray, dental, ambulance, hospital, professional nursing and rehabilitative services, for prosthetic devices and for necessary remedial treatment and services recognized and permitted under the laws of the state for an injured person who relies upon spiritual means through prayer alone for healing in accordance with his religious beliefs;

"named insured" means the person or organization named in the declarations of the policy and if an individual, shall include the spouse if a resident of the same household;

"motor vehicle" means any self-propelled vehicle with 4 or more wheels which is of a type both designed and required to be licensed for use on the highways of Florida and any trailer or semi-trailer designed for use with such vehicle;
a **"motor vehicle"** does not include:

(a) any motor vehicle which is used in mass transit or public school transportation and designed to transport more than 5 passengers exclusive of the operator of the motor vehicle and which is owned by a municipality, a transit or public school transportation authority, or a political subdivision of the state; or

(b) a mobile home;

"occupying" means in or upon or entering into or alighting from;

"insured motor vehicle" means a **motor vehicle**: (a) of which the **named insured** is the **owner**, and (b) with respect to which security is required to be maintained under the Florida Motor Vehicle No-Fault Law, and (c) for which a premium is charged, or which is a trailer, other than a mobile home, designed for use with a **motor vehicle;**

"relative" means a person related to the **named insured** by blood, marriage or adoption (including a ward or foster child) who is usually a resident of the same household as the **named insured;**

"pedestrian" means a person while not an occupant of any self-propelled vehicle;

"owner" means a person or organization who holds the legal title to a **motor vehicle**, and also includes:

(a) a debtor having the right to possession, in the event a **motor vehicle** is the subject of a security agreement, and

(b) a lessee having the right to possession, in the event a **motor vehicle** is the subject of a lease with option to purchase and such lease agreement is for a period of six months or more, and

(c) a lessee having the right to possession, in the event a **motor vehicle** is the subject of a lease without option to purchase, and such lease agreement is for a period of six months or more, and the lease agreement provides that the lessee shall be responsible for securing insurance;

"work loss" means with respect to the period of disability of the injured person, any loss of income and earning capacity from inability to work proximately caused by the injury sustained by the injured person;

"replacement services expenses" means with respect to period of disability of the injured person all expenses reasonably incurred in obtaining from others ordinary and necessary services in lieu of those that, but for such injury, the injured person would have performed without income for the benefit of his household.

Policy Period; Territory

The insurance under this Section applies only to accidents which occur during the policy period

(a) in the State of Florida; and

(b) as respects the **named insured** or a **relative**, while **occupying** the **insured motor vehicle** outside the State of Florida but within the United States of America, its territories or possessions or Canada; and

(c) as respects the **named insured**, while **occupying** a **motor vehicle** of which a **relative** is the **owner** and for which security is maintained under the Florida Motor Vehicle No-Fault Law, as amended, outside the State of Florida but within the United States of America, its territories or possessions or Canada.

Conditions

(1) **Notice.** In the event of an accident, written notice of the loss must be given to the Company or any of its authorized agents as soon as practicable.

If any injured person or his legal representative shall institute legal action to recover damages for **bodily injury** against a third party, a copy of the summons and complaint or other process served in connection with such legal action shall be forwarded as soon as practicable to the Company by such injured person or his legal representative.

(2) **Action Against the Company.** No action shall lie against the Company unless, as a condition precedent thereto, there shall have been full compliance with all terms of this insurance, nor until 30 days after the required notice of accident and reasonable proof of claim has been filed with the Company.

(3) **Proof of Claim; Medical Reports and Examinations; Payment of Claim Withheld.** As soon as practicable the person making claim shall give to the company written proof of claim, under oath if required, which may include full particulars of the nature and extent of the injuries and treatment received and contemplated, and such other information as may assist the company in determining the amount due and payable. Such person shall submit to mental or physical examinations at the company's expense when and as often as the company may reasonably require and a copy of the medical report shall be forwarded to such person if requested. If the person unreasonably refuses to submit to an examination the company will not be liable for subsequent personal injury protection benefits. Whenever a person making claim is charged with committing a felony, the company shall withhold benefits until at the trial level the prosecution makes a formal entry on the record that it will not prosecute the case against the person, the charge is dismissed or the person is acquitted.

(4) **Reimbursement and Subrogation.** In the event of payment to or for the benefit of any injured person under this insurance:

(a) the company is subrogated to the rights of the person to whom or for whose benefit such payments were made to the extent of such payments. Such person shall execute and deliver the instruments and papers and do whatever else is necessary to secure such rights. Such person shall do nothing after loss to prejudice such rights.

(b) the company providing personal injury protection benefits on a private passenger motor vehicle, as defined in the Florida Motor Vehicle No-Fault Law, shall be entitled to reimbursement to the extent of the payment of personal injury protection benefits from the **owner** or insurer of the **owner** of a commercial motor vehicle, as defined in the Florida Motor Vehicle No-Fault Law, if such injured person sustained the injury while **occupying**, or while a **pedestrian** through being struck by, such commercial motor vehicle.

(5) **Special Provision for Rented or Leased Vehicles.** Notwithstanding any provision of this coverage to the contrary, if a person is injured while **occupying**, through being struck by, a **motor vehicle** rented or leased under a rental or lease agreement which does not specify otherwise in bold type on the face of such agreement, the personal injury protection coverage afforded under the lessor's policy shall be primary.

Section II

MODIFICATION OF POLICY COVERAGES

Any automobile medical payment insurance, any uninsured motorists coverage or any excess underinsured motorists coverage afforded by the policy shall be excess over any personal injury protection benefits paid or payable or which would be available but for the application of a deductible.

Regardless of whether the full amount of personal injury protection benefits have been exhausted, any medical payments insurance afforded by this policy shall pay the portion of any claim for personal injury protection medical expenses which are otherwise covered but not payable due to the limitation of 80% medical expenses contained in Section I but shall not be payable for the amount of the deductible selected.

Section III

PROVISIONAL PREMIUM

It is agreed that in the event of any change in the rules, rates, rating plan, premiums or minimum premiums applicable to the insurance afforded, because of an adverse judicial finding as to the constitutionality of any provisions of the Florida Motor Vehicle No-Fault Law, as amended, providing for the exemption of persons from tort liability, the premium stated in the declarations for any Liability, Medical Payments and Uninsured Motorists insurance shall be deemed provisional and subject to recomputation. If this policy is a renewal policy, such recomputation shall also include a determination of the amount of any return premium previously credited or refunded to the **named insured** pursuant to Section 12 (2) (e) of the Florida Motor Vehicle No-Fault Law, as amended, with respect to insurance afforded under a previous policy.

If the final premium thus recomputed exceeds the premium stated in the declarations, the **named insured** shall pay to the Company the excess as well as the amount of any return premium previously credited or refunded.

Exhibit 7-4
Endorsement Personal Injury Protection Coverage—Michigan

The Definitions and General Provisions of the policy apply unless modified by this endorsement.

SCHEDULE

Benefits	Limit of Liability
Medical Expenses	No maximum dollar amount
Funeral Expenses	Up to **$1,000** per person
Work loss benefits consisting of income benefits and replacement services	Up to $2,195* for any 30 day period subject to a $20 per day maximum for replacement services
Survivors loss benefits consisting of income loss benefits and replacement services	Up to $2,195* for any 30 day period subject to a $20 per day maximum for replacement services

*or whatever amount is established under Chapter 31 of the Michigan Insurance Code for accidents occurring on or after the date of the change in the maximum.

The following options apply as indicated in the Declarations or by an X in the box below:

COORDINATION OF BENEFITS

☐ Coordination of medical expenses applies to you or any **family member.**

☐ Coordination of work loss benefits applies to you or any **family member.**

DEDUCTIBLE

☐ A deductible of **$** __________ applies to you or any **family member.**

I. DEFINITIONS

The following words and phrases are defined for Personal Injury Protection coverage. They are boldfaced when used.

"Auto" means a motor vehicle or trailer operated or designed for use on public roads. It does not include a motorcycle or moped, or a vehicle:

1. Operated by muscular power; or
2. With fewer than three wheels.

"Auto accident" means a loss involving the ownership, operation, maintenance, or use of an auto as an auto regardless of whether the accident also involves the ownership, operation, maintenance, or use of a motorcycle as a motorcycle.

"Covered person" means:

1. You or any **family member** injured in an **auto accident**,
2. Anyone else injured in an **auto accident:**
   a. While **occupying your covered auto**; or
   b. If the accident involves any other **auto:**
      (1) which is operated by you or a **family member**; and
      (2) to which Part A of this policy applies.
   c. While not **occupying** any **auto** if the accident involves **your covered auto.**

"Your covered auto" means an **auto:**

1. For which you are required to maintain security under Chapter 31 of the Michigan Insurance Code; and
2. To which the bodily injury liability coverage of this policy applies.

(over)

This endorsement forms a part of the policy to which it is attached.

The spaces below need not be completed unless this endorsement is issued subsequent to preparation of the policy.

Effective Date (12 01 A M Standard Time)	Date of Issue	Issued To	Policy Number

In Witness Whereof, we have caused this endorsement to be signed by our duly authorized Officers.

Charles H. Elliott Secretary

President

II. PERSONAL INJURY PROTECTION COVERAGE

We will pay personal injury protection benefits to or for a **covered person** who sustains bodily injury. The bodily injury must:

1. Be caused by accident; and
2. Result from the ownership, maintenance or use of an **auto** as an **auto.**

These benefits are subject to the provisions of Chapter 31 of the Michigan Insurance Code. Benefits consist of the following:

1. Medical expenses. Reasonable and necessary medical expenses incurred for **a covered person's:**
   a. care;
   b. recovery; or
   c. rehabilitation.

   Only semi-private room charges will be paid unless special or intensive care is required.
2. Funeral expenses. Reasonable funeral and burial expense incurred.
3. Work loss benefits:
   a. Income benefits. Up to 85% of a **covered person's** actual loss of income from work. We will pay a higher percentage if the **covered person** gives us reasonable proof that net income is more than 85% of gross income.
   b. Replacement services. Reasonable expenses for obtaining services to replace those a **covered person** would have done:
      (1) without pay; and
      (2) for the benefit of that **covered person** or that **covered person's** dependents.

   The most we will pay in any 30 day period for the total of these benefits is the amount shown in the schedule unless another amount is established by law. Any income a **covered person** earns during the 30 day period is included in determining the income benefits we will pay. These benefits are payable for loss sustained during the 3 years after the accident. They do not apply after a **covered person** dies. We will prorate these benefits for any period less than 30 days.
4. Survivors loss benefits:
   a. Income loss. The contributions a deceased **covered person's** spouse and dependents would have received as dependents, if the **covered person** had not died. The contributions must be tangible things of economic value, not including services.
   b. Replacement services. Reasonable expenses incurred for obtaining services to replace those a deceased **covered person** would have done for that **covered person's** spouse and dependents.

   The most we will pay in any 30 day period for the total of these benefits is the amount shown in the schedule, unless another amount is established by law. These benefits are payable for loss sustained during the 3 years after the accident. A deceased **covered person's** spouse must have either:
      (1) resided with; or
      (2) been dependent on;

   the **covered person** at the time of death. The benefits for a spouse at remarriage or death.

Any other person who was dependent upon the deceased **covered person** at the time of death qualifies for benefits if, and as long as that dependent is:

(1) under age 18, or
(2) physically or mentally unable to earn a living; or
(3) in a full time formal program of academic or vocational education or training.

EXCLUSIONS

We do not provide Personal Injury Protection Coverage for bodily injury:

1. To any person who intentionally caused the bodily injury.
2. Sustained by a person using an **auto** which that person had taken unlawfully. This exclusion does not apply if the person had a reasonable belief that he or she was entitled to use the **auto.**
3. Sustained by any person while not **occupying** an **auto** if the accident takes place outside Michigan. However, this exclusion does not apply to:
   a. you; or
   b. any **family member.**
4. To you while **occupying,** or struck by while not **occupying**, any **auto:**
   a. owned or registered by you; and
   b. which is not **your covered auto.**
5. Sustained by the owner or registrant of an **auto** involved in the accident and for which the security required by Chapter 31 of the Michigan Insurance Code is not in effect.
6. Sustained by anyone entitled to Michigan no-fault benefits as a family member under another policy except while an operator or passenger of a motorcycle involved in the accident. This exclusion does not apply to:
   a. you; or
   b. any **family member.**
7. Sustained by anyone entitled to Michigan no-fault benefits as a named insured under another policy except while an operator or passenger of a motorcycle involved in the accident. This exclusion does not apply to you.
8. Sustained while **occupying,** or struck by while not occupying, an **auto** (other than **your covered auto)** if:
   a. operated by you or any **family member**; and
   b. the owner or registrant has the security required by Chapter 31 of the Michigan Insurance Code.

This exclusion does not apply to:

a. you; or
b. any **family member.**

9. Sustained while **occupying** an **auto** located for use as a residence or premises.
10. Sustained while **occupying** a public auto for which the security required by Chapter 31 of the Michigan Insurance Code is in effect.
    This exclusion does not apply to bodily injury to you or a **family member** while a passenger in a:
    a. school bus;
    b. certified common carrier;
    c. bus operated under government sponsored transportation program;
    d. bus operated by or servicing a non-profit organization; or
    e. taxicab.
11. Sustained by you or any **family member** while **occupying** an **auto** which is owned or registered by:
    a. your employer; or
    b. any **family member's** employer; and

for which the security required under Chapter 31 of the Michigan Insurance Code is in effect.

12. Sustained while **occupying** an **auto** other than **your covered auto**:
    a. for which the owner or registrant is not required to provide security under Chapter 31 of the Michigan Insurance Code; and
    b. which is being operated by you or a **family member** outside Michigan.

This exclusion does not apply to:
a. you or a **family member**; or
b. medical or funeral expense benefits.

13. Arising out of the ownership, operation, maintenance or use of a parked **auto.** This exclusion does not apply if:
    a. the **auto** was parked in such a way as to cause unreasonable risk of the bodily injury; or
    b. the bodily injury resulted from physical contact with:
        (1) equipment permanently mounted on the **auto** while the equipment was being used; or
        (2) property being lifted onto or lowered from the **auto**; or
    c. the bodily injury was sustained while **occupying** the **auto.**

However, exceptions b. and c. to this exclusion do not apply to any employee that has Michigan worker's disability compensation benefits available and who sustains bodily injury in the course of employment while loading, unloading, or doing mechanical work on an auto, unless the injury arises from the use or operation of another vehicle.

14. For medical expenses for you or any **family member**:
    a. to the extent that similar benefits are paid or payable under any other insurance; service, benefit or reimbursement plan; and
    b. if Coordination of Benefits for medical expense is indicated in the Schedule or Declarations.
15. For work loss benefits for you or **any family member**:
    a. to the extent that similar benefits are paid or payable under any other insurance, service, benefit or reimbursement plan; and

    b. if Coordination of Benefits for work loss benefits is indicated in the Schedule or Declarations.

16. Sustained in an **auto accident** by you or any **family member** while an operator or passenger of a motorcycle, if the owner, registrant or operator of the **auto** has provided security for that **auto** as required under Chapter 31 of the Michigan Insurance Code.

LIMIT OF LIABILITY

The limit of liability shown in the Schedule for this coverage is our maximum limit of liability for each **covered person** injured in any one **auto accident.** This is the most we will pay regardless of the amount of:

1. **Covered persons**;
2. Claims made;
3. Vehicles or premiums shown in the Declarations;
4. Vehicles involved in the accident; or
5. Insurers providing no-fault benefits.

Any amount payable under this insurance shall be reduced by:

1. any amounts paid, payable or required to be provided by state or federal law except any amounts paid, payable or required to be provided by Medicare; and
2. any deductible you elect. However, the deductible applies only to you and any **family member.**

III. DUTIES AFTER AN ACCIDENT

We must be notified promptly of how, when and where the accident happened. Notice should also include the names and addresses of any injured persons and of any witnesses.

A person seeking coverage must:

1. Cooperate with us in the investigation or settlement of any claim.
2. Submit, at our expense and as often as we reasonably require, to physical or mental examinations by physicians we select.
3. Authorize us to obtain:
    a. medical reports;
    b. statements of earnings; and
    c. other pertinent records.
4. Submit a written proof of claim when required by us.
5. Promptly send us copies of the legal papers if a suit is brought.

IV. GENERAL PROVISIONS

OUR RIGHT TO RECOVER PAYMENT

If we make a payment under this policy and the person to or for whom payment is made recovers damages from another, the person shall:

1. Hold in trust for us the proceeds of the recovery; and

2. Reimburse us to the extent of our payment.

Our right is subject to any applicable limitations stated in Chapter 31 of the Michigan Insurance Code.

DUPLICATION OF BENEFITS

No one will be entitled to duplicate payments for the same elements of loss under this coverage regardless of the number of:

1. Motor vehicles covered; or
2. Insurers (including self-insurers) providing security in accordance with Chapter 31 of the Michigan Insurance Code or any other similar law.

A **covered person** who sustains bodily injury resulting from an **auto accident** which shows evidence of the involvement of an **auto** while an operator or passenger of a motorcycle shall claim personal insurance benefits in the following order of priority:

1. The insurer of the owner or registrant of the **auto** involved in the accident.
2. The insurer of the operator of the **auto** involved in the accident.
3. The **auto** insurer of the operator of the motorcycle involved in the accident.
4. The **auto** insurer of the owner or registrant of the motorcycle involved in the accident.

LEGAL ACTION AGAINST US

No legal action may be brought against us until there has been full compliance with the terms of this coverage. In addition, no legal action may be brought against us after one year from the date of the accident causing the injury unless:

1. Written notice of the injury has been given to us within one year from the date of the accident: or
2. We have already paid any personal injury protection benefits for the injury.

If either 1. or 2. apply, you may bring action against us. Action must be brought within 1 year from the date the most recent medical or funeral expense or work or survivor's loss was incurred. No one may recover benefits for any portion of the loss incurred more than one year before the date on which the action was begun.

PREMIUM RECOMPUTATION

Chapter 31 of the Michigan Insurance Code places certain limitations on a person's right to sue for damages. The premium for this policy reflects these limitations. A court from which there is no appeal can declare any of these limitations unenforceable. If this occurs we will have the right to recompute the premium. You can choose to delete any coverage as the result of the court's decision. If you do we will compute any refund of premium on a pro rata basis.

OTHER COVERAGES

Any amount payable under either:

1. Uninsured Motorists Coverage, or
2. Underinsured Motorists Coverage;

will be reduced by any personal injury protection benefits paid or payable to a **covered person** under this or any other **auto** policy.

With the brief review of no-fault insurance completed, the focus must turn to the question of how much investigation is necessary regarding no-fault auto insurance claims. While admittedly no-fault auto insurance is on a first-party basis with payment being made regardless of fault, investigation is still necessary in many claims for several important reasons.

Perhaps most obvious is the fact that the only type of no-fault law which actually limits tort claims is a *modified* plan. The investigative requirements in states with *add-on* or *voluntary* plans should not be affected since tort liability is not changed in such states. (It is believed, however, that the availability of first-party no-fault benefits in these states eliminates the need for many people to pursue third-party claims.)

With respect to modified plans, third-party liability claims can be made when the claimant's medical expenses exceed the tort threshold or when the claimant's injuries are considered "serious" as described in the verbal threshold provision of the particular plan. In view of this, adjusters frequently need to be concerned with determining both liability and the nature and extent of the injuries sustained by the individuals involved in the accident.

Another reason investigation is still necessary in no-fault states is that *property damage* is not subject to no-fault auto insurance laws. (The only exception is Michigan.) Property damage claims are handled on a tort liability basis and, therefore, fault continues to be the basis upon which payment is made.

Third, many no-fault laws provide for subrogation of no-fault benefits and since liability is often questionable, investigation may be necessary in an effort to clarify the liability situation.

Furthermore, a no-fault insured who has an accident in a state which has not enacted a no-fault law limiting tort liability can be sued by an injured party without restriction. A careful investigation of such out-of-state accidents needs to be conducted.

Finally, the uninsured and underinsured motorists exposures continue to exist, even where compulsory auto insurance and no-fault laws are in effect. If the seriously injured insured finds that the negligent third party is uninsured and uncollectible, he or she will turn to his or her own insurer for general and special damages.

It is evident that bodily injury and property damage liability exposures continue to exist in no-fault auto insurance states. Although the need for investigation may be reduced, it certainly is not eliminated by no-fault auto insurance plans. It is understandable, however, why claim people might be less concerned about conducting substantial investigations in claims of minimal injuries. Where the tort threshold is relatively high, chances are good that in routine claims with minor injuries, third-party liability claims will not be made. The injured person's expenses are paid promptly by his or her own insurer without the need to pursue recovery elsewhere. In minor injury cases where liability is doubtful (from the standpoint of the no-fault insurer), there is even less reason to be concerned with investigation.

For the above reasons, recorded statements may not be obtained, especially when a police report establishing fault is available. In these routine situations, there may be a tendency to qualify questions about injury or liability by telephoning the parties to the accident rather than by specifically obtaining recorded statements. The objective of most insurance companies in these cases is to strike a balance between the need for investigation and the need for a cost efficient claim operation.

In many respects it is true, as some claim people contend, that handling routine no-fault auto claims more closely resembles clerical work, with emphasis on issuing drafts, and so on, rather than investigative work. Specific investigation may be necessary, however, regarding causal relationships and possible malingering on the injured person's part.

Generally, no-fault laws provide for the right of no-fault insurers to have the injured person submit to an independent medical exam. In addition, insurers ordinarily obtain medical and wage authorizations to verify injuries, medical expenses and lost earnings incurred by no-fault claimants. (See the Application for Benefits form for Michigan, shown in Exhibit 7-5, which includes both a medical and wage authorization.)

The potential problem with minimizing investigative requirements on small, seemingly routine no-fault claims is that the seriousness of the injury may go undetected or be underestimated. In addition, a turn for the worse in the injury may go undetected until the insured is served with a lawsuit.

Ordinarily, the claim person has access initially to the accident report which describes the accident and indicates the extent of the injuries. From this report, he or she must decide what course of action to take with regard to handling the claim. While frequently the accident report is all the information necessary to make this decision, in many cases, the accident report may contain insufficient information and further inquiry will need to be made concerning liability and injuries.

The decision the adjuster often needs to make is whether to contact the parties in the adverse vehicle. These individuals are ordinarily entitled to no-fault benefits either from the vehicle owner or from their own no-fault insurance policies. If injuries appear minor, many claim people do not contact these potential third party claimants. If there is a question about the nature and extent of the injuries, the claim person has an important decision to make with regard to contacting these third

Exhibit 7-5
Application for Benefits

Date	Our Policyholder	Accident Date	File Number

The no-fault law provides benefits for medical expenses, wage loss and replacement services, as well as survivors' loss. To enable us to determine if you are entitled to any of these benefits, please complete this application form and return it promptly

IMPORTANT — TO BE ELIGIBLE FOR BENEFITS, YOU MUST:

(1) Complete, sign & return this application no later than one (1) year from the date of the accident.
(2) Submit bills for expenses promptly, but no later than one (1) year from the date the expense was incurred.
(3) Sign the attached authorization(s).

general

Applicant's Name	Home Phone	Business Phone

Address (No., Street, City or Town, State, Zip)	Birthdate	Soc. Sec. No.

Date & Time of Accident am pm	Place of Accident (Street, City or Town, State)

Brief Description of Accident:

Describe motor vehicles owned by you, your spouse, or relatives of either you or your spouse residing in the same household on the day of the accident:

Vehicle	Lic. Plate No.	Owner	Insurer	Policy No.

☐ Check here if there are no vehicles in the household.

medical

Describe the injury which resulted from this accident:

Were you treated by a doctor? Name, Address & Phone of doctor(s) providing treatment?

☐ Yes ☐ No

If treated in a hospital, were you ☐ In-patient ☐ Out-patient ?	Hospital Name and Address

Do you expect to have more medical treatment?
☐ Yes ☐ No ☐ Undetermined

Have you received any benefits under a medical plan or health insurance?
☐ Yes ☐ No

Name of your medical plan, ins. company, govt. program or HMO:

Policy or plan number:

Name

Address

Identification No.

City State Zip

( )
Telephone No.

Have you received any medical treatment for the same or similar symptoms prior to this accident?

☐ Yes ☐ No

If yes, list name, address & phone of physician(s) providing treatment:

Were you on the job working when the accident occurred? ☐ Yes ☐ No

Date Disability from Work Began | Date Returned or Anticipate Returning to Work | Avg. Weekly Wage/Salary

wage loss

Have you received any benefits under workers' compensation, social security, or any wage or salary continuation plan?

☐ Yes ☐ No

If yes, indicate source of payment: ______

Amount of payment per month: ______ Per Week: ______

Are you currently receiving unemployment benefits? ☐ Yes ☐ No

List names, addresses & phones of present employer(s):

Name, address & phone | Occupation | Date Hired

Name, address & pbone | Occupation | Date Hired

exp.

As a result of your injury, have you incurred any other expenses, such as transportation costs or expenses for services you would have performed for yourself or your dependents?

☐ Yes ☐ No If yes, explain on a separate sheet and attach.

These statements are true and complete to the best of my knowledge:

______ Date: ______
Signature of applicant or parent or guardian

Do Not Detach

AUTHORIZATION FOR MEDICAL INFORMATION

This authorization or photocopy hereof, will authorize a physician, hospital, clinic, or other medical institution to furnish all information you may have regarding my condition while under your observation or treatment, including the history obtained, x-ray and physical findings diagnosis and prognosis. You are required to provide this information in accordance with the Michigan motor vehicle no-fault insurance law, P.A. 294 of the Public Acts of 1972.

______ Date: ______
Signature of applicant or parent or guardian

Do Not Detach

AUTHORIZATION FOR WAGE AND SALARY INFORMATION

This authorization or photocopy hereof, will authorize you to furnish all information you may have regarding my wages or salary while employed by you. You are required to provide this information in accordance with the Michigan motor vehicle no-fault insurance law, P.A. 294 of the Public Acts of 1972.

________________________ Date: ________________________
Signature

____
Social Security Number

parties and possibly stirring up a claim which otherwise would not have been pressed.

Ordinarily, the adjuster representing the negligent driver cannot contact the injured claimant's insurer and expect that insurer to furnish injury information about the claimant. To furnish such information (without the permission of its insured) would subject that insurer to possible claims of invasion of privacy. In many jurisdictions, such action would violate the insurer's duty of good faith and confidentiality to its insured.

When confronted with questions of whether to contact third party claimants when it is unclear whether their medical expenses or injuries will exceed the tort threshold, adjusters must analyze the claim in the same manner as they analyze tort liability claims. They must examine the accident report and try to determine the seriousness of the injuries, if any. It is frequently helpful to question the insured about the extent of the injuries sustained by the claimant(s). In addition, the police report may be helpful in providing information as to the severity of the impact and the extent of any visible injuries observed by the reporting officer.

After considering all factors, the adjuster may decide that the wisest course of action is to conduct the investigation from the insured's side only. Statements are secured from the insured and any witnesses, the police report is obtained and photographs are taken, but the adjuster refrains from contacting the claimant. If a claim eventually is made, at least the major portion of the investigation will have been completed.

Whether potential third-party claimants should be contacted in cases where the extent of the injuries is unknown is really a matter of judgment. Adjusters should be guided by their own feelings about a case and, where necessary, seek the advice and counsel of their supervisory or management personnel.

In concluding, it should be noted that in many no-fault states, evidence of no-fault benefits received by the claimant is not admissible in a civil suit for damages. Since the situation varies somewhat from state to state, adjusters should be familiar with the actual situation in their state regarding this question.

PUBLIC LIABILITY CLAIMS

Slip, trip, and fall claims enter into an adjuster's workload as a result of personal liability or commercial liability policies and may involve injuries of various degrees of severity.

Status of Claimant

While investigating the claim, one of the most important duties is to determine the legal status of the claimant, as only then can the degree of care be ascertained. The legal principles pertaining to the duty owed by the possessor of land to others coming onto the premises was discussed in Chapter 5.

Causes of Falls

Slip, trip, and fall claims can be the result of various causes. Some examples are:

- parts of vegetables or other slippery objects on a grocery store floor (leaf particles, grapes, broken glass, and so on)
- torn carpeting
- waxed floors
- stray objects (brooms, mop, pail, boxes, and so on)
- defective stairs
- defective handrails
- lack of adequate lighting
- defective walkways
- ice and snow accumulations

It is recommended that these investigations start with contacting the claimant, not only to maintain control but also to establish the allegations and facts as known by the claimant. At the same time, arrangements can be made to secure signed medical authorization forms.

When the insured is contacted, a statement should be obtained from the person or persons who are the most familiar with the facts. In addition, a copy of the lease must be obtained to determine the insured's duties with respect to the condition of the premises.

Defective Stairs Falls resulting from defective stairs occur frequently, causing injuries that often are serious. In the process of investigation the stairs should be inspected before a statement is taken, to determine the general condition of the area, including maintenance, housekeeping, lighting, and the presence or absence of handrails.

At the same time, photographs should be taken, including the step where the fall originated, and the entire staircase looking down and another looking up. They should also include the presence or absence of windows, artificial lighting, and handrails.

When the statement is taken from the insured, the preceding topics should be covered, including the number of steps in the staircase, type of covering if any is present, description of any defects, when the insured had first knowledge of the defects, and when the last repairs or maintenance were done and by whom. Equally important is to ask who cleans the stairs and the material that is used. Is the staircase used only by the tenant or is it a common stairway, used by others? If it is a stairway intended only for the tenant and the tenant is the injured party, the chances of the owner's liability may be nil as most jurisdictions hold that the tenant accepts the premises as they are. If, however, the owner had actual or constructive notice of a defect, many jurisdictions will find him liable.

The following data should be obtained from the claimant while taking a statement:

- Date, time and exact place of accident
- Exact location of fall on stairs. Exact step if known. Going up or coming down?
- Carrying packages or objects? Number and size? Which arm?
- Wearing glasses? Bifocals or trifocals? Not wearing glasses and should have?
- Claimant's pre-accident familiarity with the scene.
- Description of stairs, covered with material or treads? How fastened? Condition? Metal edges?
- Stair traffic? Crowded? Pushed or knocked off balance?
- Alone? Accompanied by others? (get names and addresses)
- Lighting? Windows present? Ceiling lights? Other lights?
- Type of shoes? Height of heels? Leather, rubber, composition soles and heels?
- Hand rail(s)? Was it being used? Not used? Why?
- Type of fall? Backward, forward, to knees. Struck head? Where? One or both feet slipped? Attempt to catch self?

- Nature of injuries? Go to hospital? How taken? When? To doctor's office? When recovered? Medical bills? Lost time from work?
- Talk to anyone after the fall? Who? (get name and address)
- Witnesses? (get names and addresses)

Sidewalks Falls occurring on sidewalks may be caused by a variety of conditions, with ice and snow being responsible for many. Coverage is available in homeowner policies, Section II, for personal liability of the homeowner, or in commercial liability policies for the merchant or other business person.

As a general rule, natural accumulation of ice and snow does not constitute liability in itself, as these are natural phenomena and pedestrians have a duty to act prudently in efforts to avoid accidents and injury. In some areas, courts have held that failure to remove snow as required by local ordinance does not create liability; however, it would seem that such a defense would be weak at best.

Another variation may be involved as when the ice or snow covers a deep hole or a defective walk. In such a circumstance the question of notice to those in control takes on great importance. Other questions that must be answered are, Where is the sidewalk located? Where did the fall occur? Was it on personal property or city-owned property? Local ordinances must be checked to ascertain the city's liability in these cases.

As with any other claim involving a tenant, a copy of the lease must be secured to determine the responsibilities of exterior maintenance. If the tenant-insured is free of responsibility, a "take-over" letter should be sent to the owner immediately.

When considering defective sidewalks, the defects should be photographed in detail as well as including the insured dwelling or building to show relationship to the insured premises and general location. If a depression or hole is present, the photograph should include a ruler measuring the depth and the picture should be a close-up view. In such a case, the question of actual or constructive notice must be investigated.

Of course, in determining liability, the prevailing law of contributory or comparative negligence must also be considered.

The following questions are recommended while taking a statement from the claimant in ice and snow claims.

- Why was the person on the premises?
- Direction of travel? Witnesses? (names and addresses)
- Carrying packages? Which arm? How many packages?
- Claimant's apparel? (overshoes, boots, coat, etc.)

- Description of accident scene (diagram)
- Describe accident in detail. How injured? Treated? By whom? Lost work?
- Unusual conditions? Signs, barricades? Defective eaves or downspouts? Leaking water? Where?
- Snow and ice accumulated? If removed prior, was job well done? By whom? If not removed, was accumulation natural?
- Wearing glasses?
- Police investigation?
- When was the last snowfall before the accident? Amount of snow?[9]

Lighting Along with ice and snow fall down claims, those caused by alleged defective lighting may provide an element of assumption of risk to the defense of the claim, as these conditions may be within the knowledge of the claimant, thereby placing a burden on that person to act prudently.

Suggested questions while taking a statement include:

- Purpose and status of claimant on the premises?
- Was claimant a frequent visitor on the premises?
- Was the person carrying objects? Which arm? How many?
- Was claimant running or walking?
- Type of shoes worn—describe bottom surface.
- Wearing glasses? Or should have worn glasses?
- What source of light was present, if any?
- Describe presence and location of windows and artificial lighting.
- Were artificial lights working properly? Were they on or off?
- Any foreign substance on walking surface?
- Other defects contributing to the fall?
- Actual cause of fall?
- Describe injuries, treatment—in hospital or doctor's office? Medical bills—length of disability—lost work? How long?
- Witnesses—names and addresses

Debris Any foreign substance on a walking surface may create a potential cause for someone to slip or trip and fall with resultant injury. Many of these falls occur in the produce department of supermarkets. Since many customers handle the produce, it is not unusual for particles of lettuce, carrot tops, or other vegetables to drop on the floor. For this reason, management has to arrange for frequent clean-up procedures in an effort to avoid such occurrences.

Other claims caused by debris may originate from contents spilled from broken containers, merchandise dropped from shelves and cluttered aisle-ways.

Questions for statements follow the usual line as found in preceding types of fall-down claims and, as always, photographs should be taken to depict the fall area. The statement from the insured must include the procedure of how floors are cleaned, by whom, and how often.

PRODUCTS LIABILITY CLAIMS

In comparison to auto liability claims, the products liability field provides a widely diversified range of causes of injury or damage. Consequently, the adjuster must employ creative concepts while investigating the facts. There are untold numbers of products that are capable of causing injury or damage and many more are being marketed annually. The fact that many of these claims have resulted in large awards and settlements dictates the need for thorough and exacting investigations.

The coverage for these claims is afforded in commercial liability policies, requiring an additional premium for products liability coverage and is intended to cover injury or damage which results from the insured's product. This includes injury or damage from any form of packaging used to contain the product.

The policy period is one of the determining factors deciding coverage as the injury or damage must occur within this time frame. The resultant damages are considered as occurrences within the contract, which also defines an occurrence as an accident. The date on which the product was manufactured has no bearing on the policy period; rather, the time of the injury or damage is the factor to be considered.

At the present time many questions prevail relating to products that are ingested or the exposure to which might cause illness at a later time. Does the policy in force at the time of ingestion or exposure apply, or is the one at the time of the manifestation of the ill effects? Asbestos-caused illnesses are a prime example of this question, as the particles of the product may have been breathed in many years prior to the resultant illness.

Exclusions

Quality of Product Certain areas of exposure are not intended for coverage. If the product fails to accomplish its purpose, the policy does not guaranty the item for the insured. Nor does the policy intend to guaranty the quality of work done by or for the insured.

Alcoholic Beverage Exclusion Coverage is excluded for the insured who distributes or sells alcoholic beverages to a minor, to an already intoxicated person, or in any other manner which is in violation of the law. Should the alcohol contribute to injury or damage to a third party, in some jurisdictions the insured could be held liable, but coverage would be excluded.

Workers' Compensation Exclusion Since employees are covered by workers' compensation coverages, a duplication of coverage is not intended by general liability policies, and thus, this exposure is excluded.

Recall Exclusion It is no longer uncommon for a production run of a product to be recalled for repair or replacement due to a potential for injury being present. Such a procedure is costly, not only from the aspect of the defective part, but also from the standpoint of the expense of notification to the consumer and the time spent in the entire process. Coverage for this type of loss is not intended by the insurers and, therefore, is specifically excluded.[10]

The foregoing represent only a few of the exclusions that appear in the products liability section of the policy. In the course of the investigation, the adjuster must be certain that all exclusions have been reviewed to determine if any could apply to the claim at hand.

Privity

Historically, common law provided that a claim could be successfully pursued only if the claimant was a party to the contract, or was "in privity" with the defendant. An early case that developed the theory of privity, Winterbottom v. Wright (10 Meeson & Welsby, 109) (1842), involved a mail coach driver injured as the result of alleged negligence of the coach's repairman. The court held that since the driver was not in privity with the repair contractor, the latter owed no duty to the driver.

In 1852, however, in the case of Thomas v. Winchester the New York Court of Appeals ruled that when a manufacturer negligently made a product that was imminently dangerous to others, he was liable whether or not a contract is involved. In this case the plaintiff's husband purchased medication which turned out to be mislabeled poison. The fact that imminent danger was present proved to be significant in this case.

In 1916, a New York case, MacPherson v. Buick Motor Co., 111 NE 1050, provided the impetus to further erode the application of privity. The court held:

> The manufacturer of a product is liable for harm caused by lawful use of the product in a manner and for a purpose for which it was manufactured, if he has failed to exercise reasonable care in manufacturing the product which he should have recognized, if it was not carefully made, involved unreasonable risk of harm to those lawfully using it for the purpose for which it was manufactured and to those whom the supplier should expect to be in the vicinity of its probable use.

In this case, MacPherson purchased a car and was injured in a crash caused by a defective wheel. The manufacturer claimed that there was no privity and there was no imminent danger, but the court's ruling set aside the requirement of imminent danger and cleared the path for plaintiffs to sue manufacturers in the absence of privity.[11]

Legal Basis of Products Liability Claims

The principles on which products liability claims are based are the theories of warranty, negligence, and strict liability. Warranties may be express or implied and are within the concept of contractual obligations of the manufacturer to the consumer, who buys or uses the product. Express warranties are promises made verbally or in writing by the manufacturer.

Implied warranties are imposed by law and are divided into two types, the implied warranty of fitness and the implied warranty of merchantability. The "fitness" warranty is applicable when the consumer can prove that the seller knew the purpose of use of the product and that the buyer depended on the seller's recommendation of which product to purchase. (UCC-Sec. 2-315)

A warranty of merchantability requires that the product be made in accordance with the standards of the industry. (UCC-Sec. 2-314)[12]

Negligence as a concept in products liability is identical as in other liability claims, since it requires the exercise of ordinary care of a reasonable person. It applies equally to manufacturers and designers of products.[13]

Res Ipsa Loquitur

Translated, this term means "The thing speaks for itself"; thus, in the field of products liability, a defect in a product speaks for itself and the manufacturer may have to prove that it was not liable for the injury caused by its product.

Initially, the plaintiff has the duty to establish certain criteria to place the claim into the realm of *res ipsa loquitur* by showing that:

- the accident was of a kind which ordinarily does not occur in the absence of negligence,
- the accident was caused by an agency or instrumentality within the exclusive control of the defendant,
- the accident was not due to any voluntary action or contribution on the part of the plaintiff (contributory negligence), and
- there is not direct evidence as to the cause of the injury.[14]

The injured party having shown that these criteria have been met, there arises a rebuttable presumption of negligence on the part of the manufacturer and/or seller. To rebut this presumption, the defendant must prove:

> the accident could have occurred without anyone's negligence, someone other than the defendant was negligent, the plaintiff was negligent, there was a lack of control of the agency or instrumentality by the defendant or due care was exercised by the defendant.[15]

The basis for strict liability in tort may be found in the Restatement of Torts, (2d) Sec. 402A. It, in effect, eliminates the need for proving negligence by the "user" or "consumer" on the part of the seller, including the manufacturer:

> (1) One who sells any product in a defective condition unreasonably dangerous to the user or consumer or to his property is subject to liability for physical harm thereby caused to the ultimate user or consumer, or to his property, if (a) the seller is engaged in the business or selling such a product, and (b) it is expected to and does reach the user or consumer without substantial change in the condition in which it is sold. (2) The rule stated in subsection (1) applies although (a) the seller has exercised all possible care in the preparation and sale of his product, and (b) the user or consumer has not bought the product from or entered into any contractual relation with the seller.[16]

Duty to Warn

Experience demonstrates that a large number of products claims are the result of the failure of the manufacturer to properly warn the users of a product as to a potentially dangerous situation present in the goods. It has been generally held that if a dangerous condition is apparent to the user, the duty to warn is not necessary, but it must be remembered that the current leniency of the courts may eventually erode that premise. If a danger exists that is not apparent, a warning must be provided, sufficient enough to make its presence known in the prudent person's mind. The court will determine if the warning is adequate, thus the manufacturer can control its own destiny relating to such matters.

The manufacturer's duty to warn relates to instructions on labels and for the proper assembly of products.

Proximate Cause and Intervening Acts

During the investigation of a products claim, care is recommended to ascertain if the product that caused the injury is in the same condition as when it was first sold, or if modifications were made to change its design and function. Such changes may well be an intervening cause directly attributing to the injury.[17]

Investigation Procedures

Unlike the auto claim, where the insured is usually contacted first, the products liability claim investigation should start with the claimant, as it is important to obtain as much information as quickly as possible and gain possession of the product which caused the injury or damage. Frequently, the product is immediately disposed of for fear of sustaining additional injury. Thus, immediate contact is essential; otherwise the item may be irretrievably lost, causing critical defense data to be gone forever.

A statement must be taken from the claimant covering all of the facts in detail. The injury description should be reported in full, depicting the relationship of the injury to the product. Included in the statement should be the data pertaining to the product, such as when it was purchased, from whom, and its general condition, as well as the manner in which it was packaged and all warnings and instructions that came with the product. In addition other routine information should be included, such as how the product was used, witnesses, and where the injury took place.

On occasion, the claimant may not be willing to release the defective product and if this occurs, photographs should be taken to illustrate the defect or portion which caused the injury. It may be prudent to employ a professional photographer to obtain enlarged photos of the item to graphically reveal the defect.

If the product produces a significant injury or damage, defense counsel should have the opportunity to select the appropriate expert if indeed an inspection and opinion are needed at that stage of the claim. Should the necessity exist, it is suggested that the product be retrieved by the expert who will identify it, can testify that no other person handled the item and that no changes occurred to the product after it left the possession of the claimant. The expert should be qualified to closely inspect and analyze the product and testify as to his or her findings and opinion. Short of the foregoing, the adjuster should take possession and immediately deliver it to the expert, if it is an easily movable object.

In an injury claim, the usual medical authorization forms must be secured and control maintained as long as possible.

Contact with the insured includes a statement from the person who is most qualified to provide pertinent data, including the insured's activities relating to the product. For example, did the insured manufacture and assemble the entire product or did they manufacture a component and ship it to an assembler? It may be possible that although the product failed, the insured's component part had performed as intended, thereby potentially relieving the insured of any responsibility and liability.

The procedure in such an instance is to put the whole-product manufacturer on notice by letter, of its apparent liability and demand that it take over the entire handling of the claim. The letter should [illegible] sent "Certified Mail—Return Receipt Requested" and should also demand the costs of any judgments and expenses, should they fail to take over. In the meantime, if the insured is named as a defendant in ensuing litigation, the insured must be protected with a legal defense.

While investigating the claim with the insured, it is wise to secure as much information about the product as possible. Items that should be obtained are package instructions, warnings and copies of labels pertaining to the product. In addition, a tour of the premises will provide an accurate insight relating to the manufacturing process or the general operations. Quality control of the product is important, particularly if the product is connected with food or items which are to be ingested or applied to the skin. A more efficient defense can be provided if the adjuster and defense counsel have maximum knowledge of the product and its manufacturing process.

At times, a manufacturer creates a product at the request of the purchaser. A transaction of this nature may include specifications supplied by the purchaser and a written contract agreed to by both parties. Should this be the case, copies of the specifications and contract should be obtained and preserved as they will play a large part in deciding the presence or lack of liability on the insured.

Consideration must also be given to the material used in the manufacturing process. It is possible that the insured performed in a proper manner while working on a piece of stock but the stock was defective, thus causing a failure. In this event, the previously decribed "take-over" letter must be sent to the supplier of the stock, requesting that it take over in the entire handling of the claim.

As the investigation proceeds and more knowledge is gained by the adjuster, the required information for a good defense becomes clearer. It must be determined if the plaintiff was negligent in the use of the product. The defenses to be considered are improper use, unintended use, use with knowledge of defect or danger, disregard of warnings, use contrary to instructions, abuse, or "as is" sale.[18] Examples of these defenses are as follows:

- *Improper Use.* Consumer takes a bath and while in the tub of water, attempts to change the radio station, resulting in electrocution, creating improper use of the radio.
- *Unintended Use.* Consumer purchases an aerosol product and used it to sniff to produce a "high," causing serious brain damage.
- *Use with Knowledge of Defect or Danger.* Purchaser of a new automobile is aware that a tire is defective with a "ballooning" sidewall, but takes an extended trip and the tire "blows," causing a crash and injuries.
- *Disregard of Warnings.* Purchaser uses a battery jumping cable and fails to follow instructions by attaching each cable to the corresponding terminal on the battery, instead of "grounding" the negative cable as instructed. Such disregard causes the battery to explode in the user's face, causing serious injury.
- *Use Contrary to Instructions.* The "Disregard of Warnings" example may apply to this defense also.
- *Abuse.* Consumer purchases a punch press which is completely equipped with appropriate hand guards. In order to increase production, the operator who is on piece-rate removes the hand guards, resulting in the loss of a finger in the subsequent operation of the machine.
- *"As Is" Sale.* Frequently, a product is sold in a used condition on an as is basis. For instance, after a used tire is purchased from a friend, it "blows" and causes a crash, resulting in injury. Proving that the purchaser knew the tire was used is pertinent to such a defense.

Depending on the severity of the injury in these claims, it is advisable to discuss the defense strategy with the examiner and also with local defense counsel to be certain that necessary information will be available in the claim file.

While the adjuster engages in the products claim investigation, it may be well to maintain a complete perspective of the defense. It may be divided into five segments, each requiring serious consideration by defense counsel:

1. Did the product fail as compared to injury or damage being caused by the product that performed as it was designed to perform?
2. Extent of injury and/or plaintiff background. Is the injury visible (objective) or not visible (subjective)? Is the plaintiff pathetic — one who will derive sympathy?
3. What is the competency and experience of plaintiff's counsel?
4. Amount and validity of special damages and the plaintiff's resources to try the case?
5. What is the nature and character of the defendant? (High exposure company?)

Although these segments of the case are general in nature, they can assist to guide the adjuster in the direction that should be followed during the investigation.

Duty of Safe Design

As the requirements of express and implied warranties indicate, the manufacturer of a product must produce merchandise that performs or can be used as advertised. This includes its safety of design. Closely related is the "state of the art" theory which provides that the manufacturer must use or improve the latest design of any similar product where such application applies to safety. If an automobile manufacturer fails to provide "collapse points" in the sheet metal and it can be shown that a consumer was injured because the metal did not collapse in an accident (as it would with collapse points), it probably would be determined that the maker was liable.

Statute of Limitations

The adjuster must be aware of local law pertaining to the statute of limitations. In the past, the question arose as to whether the claim was triggered when the injury took place or when the product was made. Most courts have ruled that coverage is not involved until the injury occurred, making the insurer of record at the time of the injury responsible for the coverage and defense.

PROFESSIONAL LIABILITY CLAIMS

Professional liability policies are designed to cover the professional person for negligence committed in the course of practice and to provide the insured with a legal defense. This coverage, also known as malpractice coverage, can be obtained by physicians, nurses, hospitals, lawyers, architects, accountants and other professionals.

In the recent past, the premium rates have increased sharply due to the number of claims that have been presented and associated with large court awards. In some states, the high premium rate has caused professional groups to band together to form their own insurance companies to reduce individual premiums. To a great extent this action has proved successful.

Generally, a physician is legally responsible to provide reasonable care to the patient, according to the regularly accepted practice of the community involved. If physicians are specialists in a field of medicine and hold themselves out as such, they would owe a greater degree of care than a general practitioner.

Within the same reference frame, other professionals are held responsible for the same degree of care if injury or damage befalls the patient or client due to the professional's actions.

Professional liability policies contain an agreement that the usual liability policy does not include: the necessity of prior approval of the insured, before an offer to settle the claim can be made to the claimant. Since the professional has acquired a great deal of knowledge and skill through an extensive educational and training program, her reputation may be at stake if the insurer capitulates and settles a claim. In recognition of this factor, insurers agree that they must first receive the insured's approval before such an offer is made. If the insured refuses such approval, the claim must be defended until it is decided by the courts.

The statute of limitations in professional liability claims is a matter with which the adjuster must be especially cognizant. Initially, statutory time periods began to run when the negligent act occurred. For example, if a surgeon committed a negligent act during surgery, the statute of limitations began at that time, even though the patient was not aware that the surgeon was negligent and thus responsible for the ensuing medical problems. Some states now do not permit the statute of limitations time to start until the patient discovers that malpractice has been committed.[19]

WORKERS' COMPENSATION CLAIMS

Prior to the enactment of Workers' Compensation laws, an employee who was injured in the course of and arising out of his employment, was required to prove negligence against the employer before he could recover damages for the injury. The employer, on the other hand, was permitted to argue the defenses of contributory negligence, assumption of risk, or the Fellow Servant doctrine. Experience showed that all too often, the employee was defeated in his legal action and was left penniless, perhaps unable to work and unable to pay the medical bills or support his family. If the employee was killed on the job, an unsuccessful claim by the survivors left them without financial means.

The defenses of contributory negligence and assumption of risk are self-explanatory in that they are the same as might apply in automobile cases. The Fellow Servant doctrine was applicable to cases where the injury was caused by a fellow worker and did not otherwise involve the negligence of the employer.

In the early 1900s, the first Workers' Compensation Acts were legislated in several states and by 1948, all states enacted some form of compensation law.[20]

Although the Acts differ from state to state, the specific intent was to guaranty payment for injury or death of an emplyee on a scheduled basis, without the need to show negligence on the part of the employer. With this guaranty, the Act also protects the employer by providing immunity against liability claims of the employee.

Benefits

The benefits are available only if the injury is accidental and one which "arises out of" and "in the course of" employment. Injuries are categorized into three groups: medical benefits, compensation benefits, and benefits to dependents in the case of fatality.

Medical Benefits Those represent payment of medical, hospital and rehabilitation costs based on fees allowed by the individual act.

Compensation Benefits These are payments to the employee based on a percentage of weekly earnings for the period of time that the employee is not able to work. These benefits are classified as temporary total, permanent total, or permanent partial disability; and payment amounts are determined by schedules included in the individual act.

In addition, depending on state law, settlements are made with the injured person who has sustained permanent disability after the percentage of disability has been established. Lump sum payments can be made at a discounted figure to permanently close the claim, if the provisions of the act so permit.

Benefits to Dependents in a Case of Fatality As in the other benefits, the amounts paid in this classification are determined by each individual act, payable to the dependents of the deceased employee.[21]

Sources of Coverage

Depending on the state law applicable, the sources of the coverage may originate from private insurers, from the state itself, or the employer may be self-insured. It is also possible that some jurisdictions will permit combinations of these sources to operate within its boundaries.

Since the coverage does not usually involve the question of liability, that aspect does not enter into the investigation. The adjuster's main concerns are whether the injured person was an employee, whether the injury was accidental and whether it arose out of and in the course of employment, and, of course the nature and severity of the injury. As these questions are being answered, the claim representative then pursues other details such as what type of work was being done, rate of pay, permanency of the injury and the number of dependents the employee has. It should also be determined if the injured employee has children from another marriage as they too may qualify as dependents.[22]

Specific questions to be asked for statement purposes from the claimant are as follows:

1. Complete identification—name, address, age, social security number, marital status, name and age of spouse
2. Identification of all dependents
3. Employment—name and address of employer
4. From whom are wages received? Hourly rate? Piece rate? Salary? Be specific on amounts. Are bonuses paid?
5. Are deductions made from the pay? Income taxes, social security, other benefits?
6. Full-time work or part-time? What are established work hours? How may work hours per day, per week?
7. Date employment started.
8. Name of union if a member.
9. Date of accident.
10. Complete details of how accident occurred.
11. Details of injury.
12. Names of witnesses if any.
13. Establish claimant's background regarding medical condition, previous injuries and/or disabilities.[23]

Subrogation of Workers' Compensation Claims

If it is determined that the injury is the result of the failure of a product, such as equipment used by the employee, or was caused by the negligence of another, the adjuster must be alert to the possibilities of subrogation and conduct the investigation to sufficiently strengthen a recovery after the payments have been made. In such a case the claim representative must place the responsible party on notice of his company's subrogation claim.

Occupational Illness or Disease

Occupational diseases may be covered under the Workers' Compensation or the Employers' Liability portion of the policy and often involve serious medical conditions, with cancer being the most notable. In such investigations, it is necessary to establish the employee's relationship and exposure to the source of the disease, the length of the exposure and the date that the disease was first discovered. This information is required in addition to the previously mentioned list of questions and as the investigation is obtained, all pertinent information should be confirmed by the employer.[24]

Chapter Notes

1. Personal Auto Policy, PP 00 02 (6-80) BF, Insurance Services Office, 1980, Part C, p. 5.
2. Pat Magarick, *Successful Handling of Casualty Claims* (New York: Central Book Co., Inc., 1974), p. 442.
3. Personal Auto Policy, Part C, p. 7.
4. Personal Auto Policy, Part D, p. 9.
5. *Auto Damage Reports* (Chambersburg, PA: Vale Labs Publications, February 1982), No. 229, p. 2.
6. Ken Brownlee, ed., *Crawford Educational Newsletter,* vol. IV, no. 9, September 1984.
7. "Actual Cash Value Revisited," *UAC Update,* no. 1, Winter 1983, p. 3.
8. *Manual for the Investigation of Automobile Fires* (Palos Hills, IL: National Automobile Theft Bureau), pp. 48, 49, and 50.
9. *Field Claim Procedure Manual* (Columbus, OH: Southern Home Insurance Co.), Section 10—Part 1, p. 62.
10. Pat Magarick, pp. 548, 549.
11. B. David Hinkle, "An Adjuster Looks at Products Liability," (Atlanta, GA: Crawford and Co., 1974), pp. 5, 6, 7, 8.
12. B. David Hinkle, pp. 11, 12.
13. Franklin D. Beohm and Fritz M. Stoller, "Introduction to Rules of Evidence and Theories of Liability in Products Liability Actions," *Products Liability—Trial Notebook* (Milwaukee: WI: Defense Research Institute).
14. Corydon T. Johns, *An Introduction to Liability Claims Adjusting,* 3rd ed. (Cincinnati, OH: The National Underwriter Co., 1982), p. 39.
15. Corydon T. Johns, pp. 39, 40.
16. B. David Hinkle, p. 13.
17. Pat Magarick, pp. 553, 554.
18. Edward C. German, "Substantive Products Defenses," *Defense of a Products Case* (Milwaukee, WI: Defense Research Institute, 1982).
19. James H. Donaldson, *Casualty Claim Practice,* 3rd ed. (Homewood, IL: Richard D. Irwin, Inc., 1976), pp. 315, 319, 331, 336.
20. Pat Magarick, pp. 613, 614.
21. Pat Magarick, pp. 616, 617, 618.
22. Pat Magarick, p. 653.
23. Pat Magarick, pp. 653, 654, 655, 656.
24. Pat Magarick, p. 658.

CHAPTER 8

The Evaluation and Settlement of Injury Claims

INTRODUCTION

The investigation of a bodily injury claim must be completed before it can be fairly evaluated for settlement purposes. The only exception might be a claim that is settled on a *first call* basis where reasonable liability exists. Ordinarily, then, the claim person must verify *coverage,* determine *liability,* and obtain detailed information about *damages* before a claim can be evaluated and settled.

Specifically, the adjuster must establish claimant control (in cases where the claimant is not represented by an attorney) secure the necessary medical authorizations and verify special damages, and, if necessary, interview the treating doctor. On occasion, it will be necessary to have the claimant submit to an independent medical examination as well.

Once the investigation of coverage, liability, and damages has been completed, the claim person is ready to evaluate the claim. It is at this time that efforts are made to settle and close the claim, usually through the exchange of a claim payment for a release.

Unlike the situation under which case reserves are established, where limited injury information may be all that is available so that reserves are based largely on estimates or projections of future damages, claim people ordinarily require documentation of actual expenses incurred before attempting to evaluate injury claims. These expenses include medical expenses, lost wages, and other special damages. An exception to this settlement rule is a serious injury case, perhaps with permanency, where lost earning capacity must be projected over the course of the work life of the injured person. But even in such cases, the claim person will require documentation of those medical expenses and lost wages actually incurred up to the point of settlement.

FACTORS AFFECTING CLAIM EVALUATION

In order to evaluate a bodily injury claim, certain factors must be considered. The primary factors that affect claim evaluation are:

- *Damages*
    - *Special*—represented by actual, identifiable expenses such as medical, surgical, and hospital charges, past and future lost income, and so on.
    - *General*—no specific showing of a monetary loss, e.g., pain and suffering, inconvenience, disfigurement, scarring, mental anguish, and so on.
- *Nature and extent of injuries*
    - *Diagnosis*—determination of the identity of the disease or injury from symptoms or signs.
    - *Prognosis*—a forecast of the probable course or result of an injury.
    - *Disability*—inability to function normally due to injury. Disability may be total or partial.
    - *Permanency*—an injury where the effect lasts indefinitely.
- *Legal liability*—in determining the liability situation, it is necessary that the claim person be familiar with the laws in effect in his or her jurisdiction. This includes knowing whether the law of contributory or comparative negligence applies. It is also necessary that the adjuster be familiar with any laws or court decisions that may affect claim handling, such as intra-family or governmental immunity, guest statutes, no-fault laws, and so on.

Other factors which generally need to be considered in evaluating injury claims, depending upon the seriousness of the case, are:

- Insured's, claimant's and other potential witnesses' appearance and impression on a jury
- Claimant's age and occupation, i.e., whether young, or of legal age, productive, retired, strenuous work, and so on
- Claimant's marital status, dependents
- Skill, appearance and impression of plaintiff's and defense attorneys (Does plaintiff's attorney prefer to *settle* or *try* cases? Does *defense* attorney prefer to settle or try cases?)

- Local verdict value. Generally, verdict value needs to be considered in evaluation since claims that cannot be settled may ultimately be decided by jury verdicts. The importance of verdict value as a factor in claim evaluation varies from claim to claim. Verdict value is a significant factor, for example, in a case where the insured's dog, known to be vicious, attacks a young teenage girl, leaving her with severe facial scars which cannot be completely corrected by plastic surgery. It will be a less significant factor in a claim involving soft tissue injuries with no disability or permanency.
- Emotional or horror factor. This is related to verdict value and refers to the emotional atmosphere that may sometimes be generated by a trial. The dog bite situation, described above, may create an emotional atmosphere at trial which might result in a high verdict. Any situation involving serious injuries where the defendant was excessively careless or grossly irresponsible in causing the accident tends to have an inflating or punitive effect on the ultimate award.
- Physician's appearance and impression on jury. A doctor's testimony can be crucial in deciding the outcome of a trial. Claim people should be cognizant of the appearance and impression of the plaintiff doctor as well as the defense doctor who conducted a physical exam of the plaintiff and will appear on behalf of the defendant.

(Note that while some of these factors may not be directly related to the merits of the claim, reality dictates that they be considered in claim evaluation since they may weigh heavily on the ultimate outcome of the trial. It should be noted that these factors are influential in setting case reserves as well.)

Importance of Medical Report and the Doctor Interview

A doctor's report which furnishes detailed information about the claimant's injury is essential in properly evaluating a claim. Whether the information is furnished in a typical insurance medical report form as illustrated in Exhibit 8-1, or in letter form usually is unimportant. The main thing is that the doctor address the essential questions of *diagnosis, prognosis* and, when applicable, *disability* and *permanency.* Once this information is received, along with information about special damages, the claim person is prepared to begin the evaluation process.

In order to properly and fairly evaluate a claim, the adjuster must know the extent of the claimant's treatment as well as all special

Exhibit 8-1
Attending Physician's Report

DATE OF REPORT ____________________

NAME OF PATIENT ____________________ AGE ______ MARITAL STATUS ____________

ADDRESS ____________________ OCCUPATION ____________

CITY AND STATE ____________________ TELEPHONE ____________

DATE OF FIRST EXAMINATION ____________________ WHO WAS PRESENT ____________

PLACE OF FIRST EXAMINATION ____________________

EVIDENCE OF OLD INJURIES ____________________

OF DISEASE ____________________

OF INTOXICATION ____________________

PATIENT RECEIVED FIRST AID OR OTHER PRIOR TREATMENT FOR THIS INJURY FROM ____________

PREVIOUS MEDICAL HISTORY ____________________

____

PATIENT'S ACCOUNT OF INJURY

DATE AND HOUR OF INJURY ____________________

PLACE AND MANNER OF OCCURRENCE ____________________

____

DESCRIPTION OF INJURY

____

____

TREATMENT

DATE OF TREATMENTS ______ WHERE GIVEN? ______

NATURE OF TREATMENT ______

WERE X-RAYS TAKEN ______ BY WHOM ______ DATE ______

FINDINGS ______

NUMBER OF STITCHES TAKEN ______ LOCATION OF STITCHES ______

DISPOSITION OF CASE

TAKEN HOME OR TO HOSPITAL ______ NAME OF HOSPITAL ______

DATE OF DISCHARGE ______

DIAGNOSIS ______

______

PROGNOSIS AND PERMANENCY OF INJURY

______

______

______

PERIOD OF DISABILITY:

TOTAL DISABILITY FROM ______ ,19____ TO ______ ,19____ PARTIAL DISABILITY FROM ______

____ ,19 ____ TO ______ ,19 ______

NATURE AND EXTENT OF ANY PERMANENT DISABILITY ______

AMOUNT OF BILL TO DATE $ ______ PHYSICIAN'S SIGNATURE ______

EST. AMOUNT OF FINAL BILL $ ______ CITY ______ STATE ______

damages incurred, including not only doctor and hospital expenses but charges for X-rays, medication, prosthetic devices, if any, lost income and any other reasonable expenses incurred by the claimant.

Not infrequently, the adjuster obtains the medical bills and doctor's report but finds that the information is inadequate to accurately evaluate the claim. Perhaps the doctor has not furnished sufficient information about the prognosis or has failed to assess the length of disability in any detail. When available injury or medical information is insufficient to evaluate the claim, the adjuster ordinarily must take the additional step of contacting the doctor for more information.

In most cases, the doctor already has possession of the medical authorization signed by the claimant and a follow-up telephone call by the adjuster usually presents no problem on the doctor's part with regard to furnishing additional information. It needs to be emphasized at this point that the adjuster should never attempt to obtain information about a claimant's injury from a treating doctor without providing the doctor with a signed medical authorization from the claimant.

If the doctor, or the medical receptionist or secretary, is approached courteously, the information usually is obtained without complication and within a reasonable time. Experience suggests that the doctor's secretary or receptionist often will make the arrangements for a meeting between the doctor and the adjuster or relate the requested information to the adjuster. In requesting additional information, the adjuster simply desires sufficient information about the claimant's injury so that a fair evaluation of the claim can be made. Once the adjuster is able to demonstrate the purpose of his or her call to the doctor, the information should come rather freely.

Quite often, the information is obtained over the telephone. Actually, many doctors prefer telephone contact over a face-to-face meeting because of their busy appointment schedule. In those complex bodily injury claims where the adjuster believes a face-to-face discussion is in order, he or she should attempt to persuade the doctor of the necessity of such a meeting and arrange the meeting at a mutually convenient time. The key is to be courteous and honest with the doctor. Once the doctor realizes the purpose of the adjuster's call—to obtain sufficient information to fairly evaluate the claim—he or she ordinarily provides the requested information. It may even be advisable to offer to pay the doctor's usual office call fee.

In cases where the claimant is represented by an attorney and additional medical information is needed, the adjuster can often persuade the attorney to see that the necessary information is provided by the treating doctor. As an alternative, the adjuster may arrange for a physical examination of the claimant to which the insurance company is ordinarily entitled. The fact that some attorneys prefer to go at their own pace and may seem unwilling to provide what the adjuster feels is necessary medical information should not discourage the adjuster from continuing the pursuit of such information. Eventually, the attorney will be in a position where he or she wants to move the case, and the adjuster usually is able to get the necessary information at that time.

Medical Terminology

Any claim person who handles bodily injury claims needs to develop a familiarity with medical terminology as well as a knowledge of the human skeletal system. It is desirable that claim people memorize the more frequently encountered terms and the major bones of the body. When engaged in the handling of bodily injury claims, claim people should have a medical dictionary within easy reach.

Exhibits 8-2 through 8-4 should be helpful in familiarizing claim people with some of the essential medical information necessary to effectively handle injury claims. Exhibit 8-2 defines various medical specialists; Exhibit 8-3 contains a sketch of the human skeleton with the major bones identified; and Exhibit 8-4 includes illustrations of major types of bone fractures. See the appendix to this chapter for a list of frequently encountered medical terms.

Other Considerations or Issues

Loss of Consortium Loss of consortium refers to the services and companionship that one spouse normally receives from the other, but which are suspended because of injury to the other spouse. In a case in which one spouse is injured, the other spouse has a cause of action against the wrongdoer and may be compensated for the loss of services of the injured spouse. The adjuster must consider this aspect of the claim when evaluating it for settlement. This is a factor in securing the release as well which will be discussed subsequently.

Courts in some states have held that a "loss of consortium" claimant has a *separate* cause of action from that of the injured spouse. What this means with reference to an auto liability insurance policy, for example, is that *each* spouse may be entitled to the policy's "per person" limit of liability in a split insurance policy. Claim people need to be aware of the situation in their states regarding this issue.

Treatment by Chiropractors Traditionally, insurers have resisted or have been reluctant to accept expenses for chiropractic treatment of a claimant. The resistance was based essentially on the

Exhibit 8-2
Medical Specialists

The following are the generally accepted designations of the more common medical specialists:

Anesthesiologist — Expert in the administration of anesthetics.

Cardiologist — Expert in the disorders of the heart.

Dermatologist — Expert in the disease and conditions of the skin.

Diagnostician — Expert in the art of recognizing the presence of disease and deciding as to its character.

Gynecologist — Expert in treatment of the diseases of women.

Internist — Physician who specializes in the diseases of the stomach and abdomen.

Laryngologist — Expert in the disorders of the larynx and throat.

Neurologist — Treats diseases of the nerves.

Neurosurgeon — Handles diseases or injuries to the nervous system by operative methods.

Obstetrician — Expert in the management of childbirth.

Ophthalmologist — Expert in the diseases of the eye.

Optometrist — Scientifically examines the eyes to prescribe glasses to correct defects of vision.

Orthopedist — Corrects deformities and diseases or injuries to bones.

Otologist — Expert in the diseases and disorders of the eye.

Pathologist — One who studies tissues (usually microscopically) to discover diseases.

Pediatrician — Expert in the treatment of children.

Physician — Treats disease or disorders by medicine — as distinguished from a surgeon.

Plastic Surgeon — Repairs defects by transferring tissue such as skin from one area to another.

Proctologist — Expert in the diseases of the colon and rectum.

Rhinologist — Expert in the diseases of the nose.

Roentgenologist — Interprets X-rays.

Surgeon — Treats disease by operative procedures. He must cut into the body to repair or remove some organ.

Vascular Specialist — Expert in disorders of the blood vessels, especially in the legs.

Exhibit 8-3
The Human Skeleton

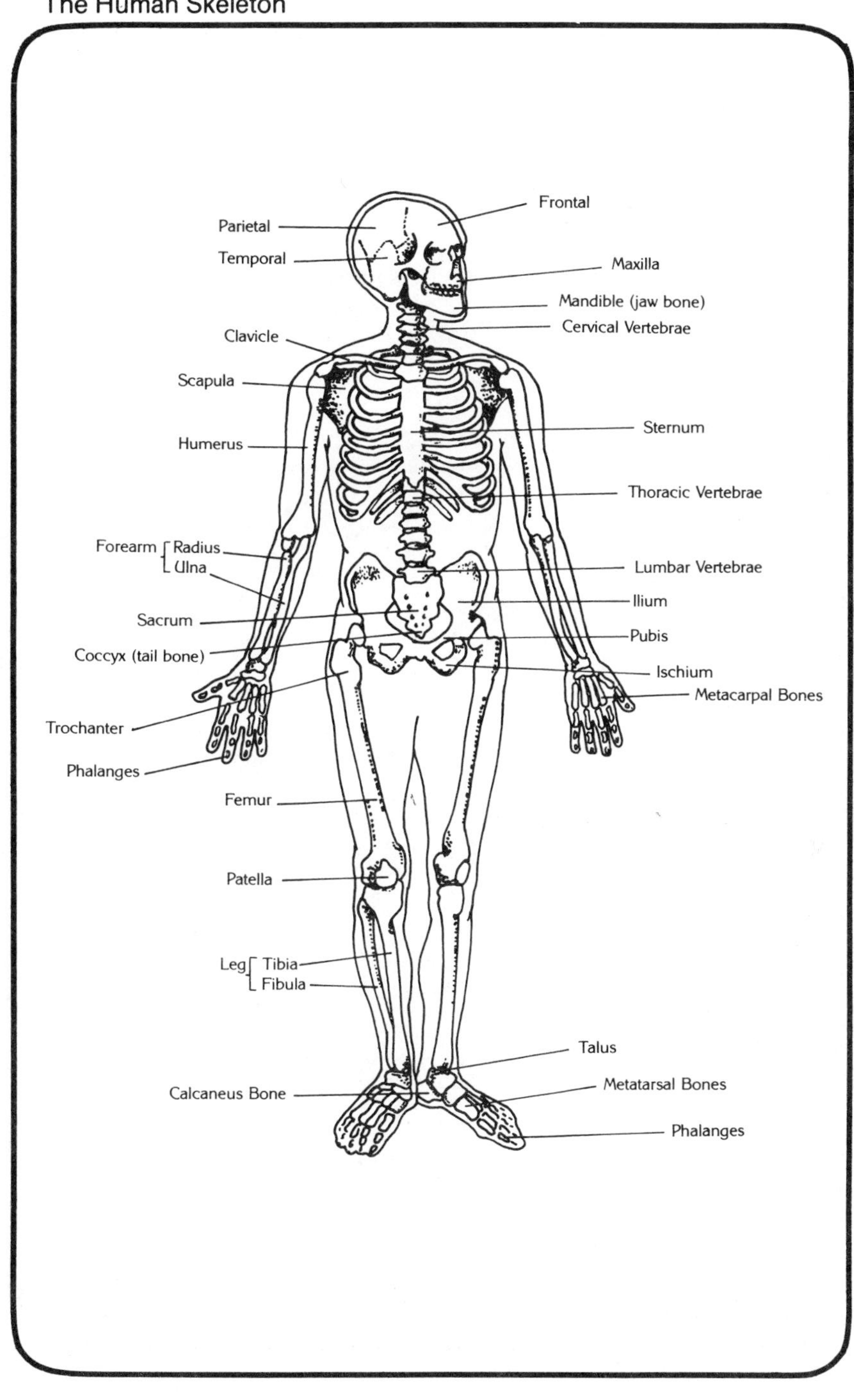

Exhibit 8-4
Bone Fractures

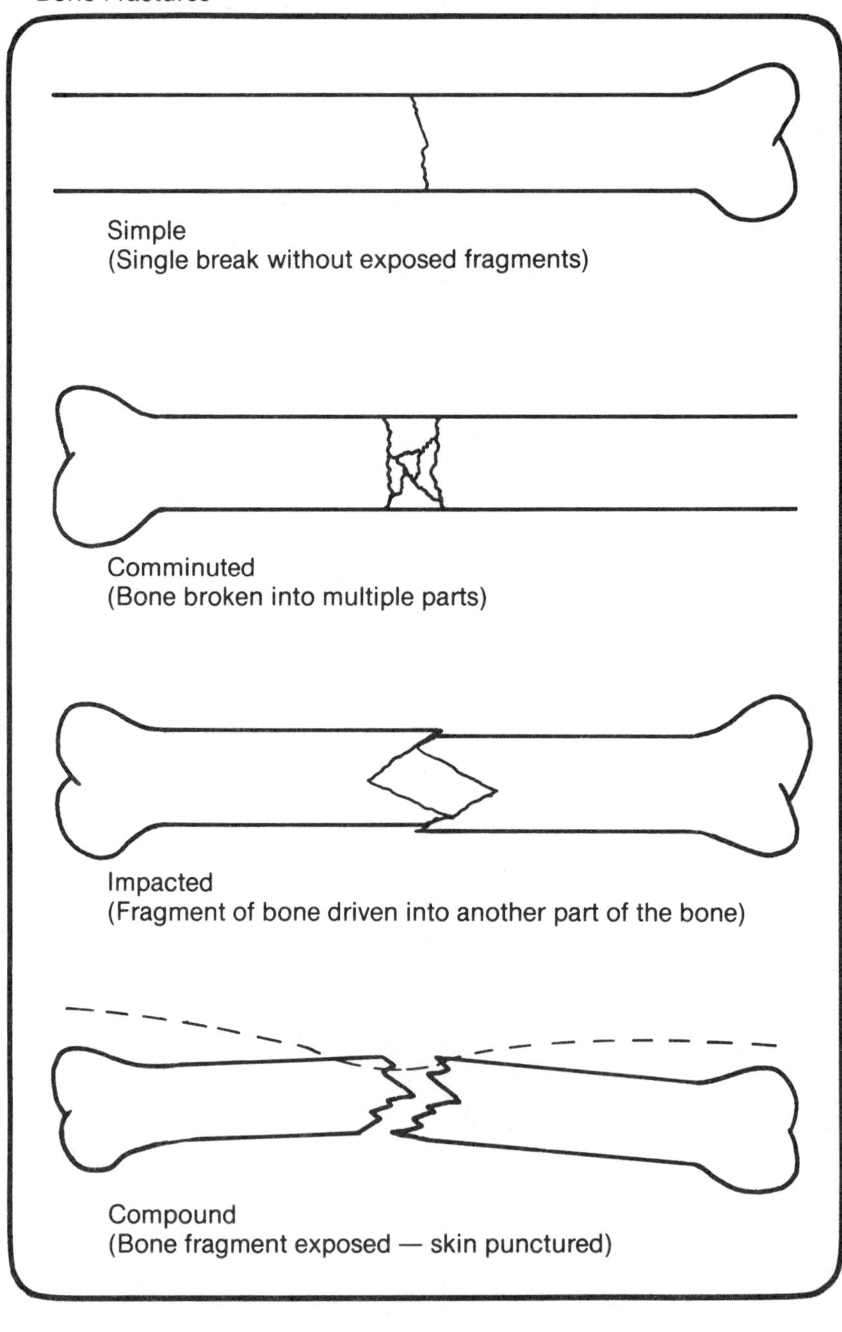

fact that a chiropractor is not a licensed physician and, according to many physicians, treats patients in an unscientific manner. More recently, however, chiropractic treatment or therapy has become more accepted, with a segment of the medical profession believing that it is useful in treating certain musculoskeletal conditions.[1]

There may, however, be legitimate reasons for questioning the treatment of some chiropractors in disputed claims. And such questioning can be particularly effective if the case gets to the courtroom. If chiropractic treatment is a significant issue in a claim, it is recommended that defense counsel carefully question prospective jurors about their attitudes toward chiropractors.[2] Despite the opinion held by many medical doctors, some people are devout believers in the effectiveness of chiropractors.

Areas in which the chiropractor's qualifications may be questioned include the following:[3]

1. Education
   In some states, chiropractors may not be required to have undergraduate college degrees and many practice without a college education. In some circumstances, the educational background of the chiropractor should be pursued and questioned by the defense counsel.
2. Board Certification
   Chiropractor board certification is available in orthopedics and roentgenology and requires completion of certain post-graduate courses and a period of residency training before the chiropractor is eligible.
3. While in most states medical doctors may practice medicine without limitations, chiropractors are subject to significant statutory practice limitations. By closely examining the treatment reports and records of a chiropractor, it may be determined that a practice violation has occurred.

In response to the growing use of chiropractic treatment by claimants, insurance companies have begun to strike back, so to speak, by utilizing defense-oriented chiropractors to assist them in claims involving chiropractic treatment. These chiropractors conduct physical examinations of the claimant and review chiropractic bills and treatment. Such examining chiropractors can comment upon the necessity of treatment, the justification for use of certain procedures, and the propriety of the charges.

Since many chiropractors are taking a "holistic" approach to treatment of their patients, that is, treating the whole person rather than just the specific ailment, they may be prescribing somewhat unconventional approaches to treatment such as consumption of multiple vitamins, natural or health-oriented foods, etc. The consumption of these items may have no real connection with the treatment of the specific injury sustained in the accident. The examining chiropractor should be able to determine when such charges are not causally related to the specific injury sustained.

Chiropractic therapy, while beneficial in certain cases, has its limitations. In a disputed claim, effective cross-examination which demonstrates these limitations to a jury can be instrumental in mitigating damages. In the same sense, a claim person should be aware of these limitations to chiropractic treatment when negotiating a claim in which extensive chiropractic treatment was an issue and justification for the treatment is questioned.

Thermography Thermography is described as the science of heat photography. One medical dictionary[4] defines it more precisely as: "A technique wherein an infrared camera photographically portrays the body's surface temperature, based on self-emanating infrared radiations; sometimes used as a means of diagnosing underlying pathologic conditions such as breast tumors." Thermography is a fairly new diagnostic technique which purports to show evidence of pain and its diagnostic value is subject to varying opinions among doctors and lawyers. It is not necessarily a "picture of pain" as some allege, and outside influences such as previous injuries, surgery, disease, mechanical problems involving blood vessels or nerves, mental conditions and environmental conditions affect a thermographic reading.[5]

In addition, the technique apparently has faced some problems with respect to admissibility into evidence, although it has been introduced into evidence in the courts of some states.

It is too soon to tell whether thermography will become a well established and accepted means of objectively demonstrating otherwise subjective pain as well as revealing a malingerer. In the meantime, where it is alleged by plaintiff counsel that thermography proves objectively that a plaintiff has suffered injury and pain, the claim person should seek the advice of both local defense counsel and medical practitioners regarding the value and admissibility of this technique.

Claimant's Duty to Establish and Mitigate Damages The burden of proving liability and damages ordinarily is placed on the claimant. The claimant must establish precisely what damages he or she sustained as a result of the accident. (It should be recalled that the element of *damages* is one of the four elements of tort liability which must be established by a claimant before recovery can be made.)

Along with the duty to establish damages, a claimant has a duty to *mitigate* damages as well. This usually means that an injured claimant cannot neglect himself and expect the tortfeasor or defendant to be responsible for any additional medical expenses brought about by that neglect. The claimant must exercise reasonable care in the treatment of his or her injuries. The duty to mitigate damages includes seeking reasonable treatment and avoiding excessive treatment just because another individual may be responsible for the accident and ultimately will be paying the medical bills.

Preexisting Injuries Where an injury to a claimant aggravates a preexisting condition, the wrongdoer is responsible for the aggravation. The adjuster's objective in such cases is to determine the extent of the aggravation of the preexisting injury or disease. This is necessary because the insured's responsibility is limited to the period of the aggravation or flare-up of the preexisting condition. Once the aggravation subsides and the claimant's condition returns to the same status as prior to the accident, the insured's responsibility ceases.

It is important, therefore, that the adjuster secure medical information from the treating physician which will establish the period or extent of the aggravation. It may be necessary in such cases for the adjuster to interview the doctor either by telephone or in person.

In cases where the medical attention required to treat the injury is greater because of the claimant's preexisting condition, the wrongdoer ordinarily is responsible for the additional expenses incurred. The claimant, however, must prove through medical evidence that the treatment was necessitated by the injuries sustained in the accident in combination with the preexisting condition.

Collateral Source Rule The collateral source rule holds that even though the claimant has other resources available to pay for medical expenses, the wrongdoer cannot take credit for these benefits. The same is true in cases in which the employer continues to pay the claimant's salary or wages during his or her period of disability. In short, the wrongdoer is still responsible for the damages sustained by the claimant, regardless of any benefits which may be received by the claimant from collateral sources. Frequently, these benefits are available from other insurance plans for which the claimant has paid a premium, such as accident and health plans like Blue Cross or Blue Shield, medical payments insurance, or wage continuation plans.

As a practical matter, the collateral source rule permits the claimant to "double dip," or to be paid more than once for the same expenses. For this reason, many insurance people have criticized the rule and have called for its elimination as a necessary means of containing insurance costs, or of reducing insurance costs, by prohibiting duplication of benefits.

The rationale behind the collateral source rule, however, is that if the wrongdoer is allowed to take credit for collateral benefits received by the claimant, he or she would escape the full burden of compensating the injured claimant.[6]

The rule does not apply (which means a claimant *cannot* duplicate payments) to workers' compensation payments nor, in many instances, to medical payments benefits received by the claimant from the wrongdoer's insurance policy.

Thus, the set-off provision in the medical payments section of the personal auto policy, which reduces expenses payable under medical payments coverage to the extent that the same expenses are payable under the liability coverage of the policy, is applicable. The set-off provision would apply to a case in which a passenger in the insured's car is injured through the insured's negligence. The injured party is entitled to medical payments coverage and can seek a liability recovery from the insured as well. The practical effect of this provision is that the claimant cannot recover his or her medical expenses more than once under the insured's auto policy.

In addition, the provisions of many no-fault auto insurance laws prevent the injured person from receiving no-fault (PIP) benefits from the no-fault insurer and then recovering the equivalent expenses again in any recovery from the liability insurer of the responsible party.

Claim people need to know the status of the collateral source rule in their states and to what extent it has been eliminated with regard to any applicable no-fault law.

Although it is true under the rule that the tortfeasor's insurer is not entitled to take any credit for collateral benefits received by the claimant, it is usually helpful in settlement negotiations for the adjuster to know the actual out-of-pocket expenses, if any, incurred by the claimant. Such knowledge may help the adjuster and the claimant gain some flexibility and reach agreement on other matters such as general damages which may lead to the eventual settlement of the claim.

Fraudulent Claims It is difficult, if not impossible, to find precise statistics concerning the extent of insurance fraud in the industry. Probably all that can be said with relative certainty is that fraud exists and tends to increase during times of economic hardship.

Though fraud is a recognizable factor in some claims, an equally troublesome concern is that of padding or inflating claims. Some claim practitioners and attorneys feel that no distinction should be made between fraud and padding. Others, likely the majority, concede that padding may not be fraud but agree that often there is a very thin line separating the two elements. At some point, in other words, padding may become fraud.

Insurance fraud may be committed by a variety of people. While sometimes it is the work of an organized ring of individuals who defraud insurers as a means of livelihood, it may be committed by the "average, good citizen," as well. Padding claims, in particular, appears to be a more common practice than might be expected.

It is not particularly difficult to understand why insurance companies might be the target of people intent upon committing fraud or making a few dollars off an inflated claim. Insurance companies, like many large enterprises, are generally seen as having no *personal* identity. Gaining an advantage over a big insurance company or making a few dollars on a claim is not seen as hurting anyone *personally.*

By contrast, a case in which the insured deliberately burns his or her car or home to collect the insurance proceeds, either because the car is a "lemon" or the home is a financial burden and cannot be sold, is downright fraud. Experience suggests that in times of economic difficulty, some people may see the insurance policy as a way out of a crisis.

Occasionally, the insurance industry is the object of criticism, perhaps from legislators, law enforcement officials, or even from within the industry itself, for not putting up more resistance to questionable or suspicious claims. This type of criticism has waned considerably in recent years as most companies realize that claims where evidence of fraud is relatively clear must be vigorously resisted. To do otherwise, invites more of the same. It is fairly well established that the "defrauders," especially those who engage in such activity on a regular basis, know which companies have a policy of resisting such claims, and which companies do not.

Claim people must learn to recognize potential fraudulent or padded claims. There are a number of "red flags" which may indicate the presence of fraud. Once recognized, claim people should seek the assistance of claim management or counsel to decide what course of action to take with regard to handling the fraudulent claim.

Various organizations are available to assist companies in handling and defending fraudulent claims.[7] A particularly prominent organization is the Insurance Crime Prevention Institute (ICPI). The organization has special agents throughout the country and investigates suspicious claims reported by its member companies.

The National Automobile Theft Bureau (NATB), with several regional offices and special agents throughout the country, monitors the auto theft claims of member companies for possible indications of fraud. In addition, automobile total loss claims are entered into the NATB computer to guard against individuals "insuring" a piece of salvage as a conventional automobile with the intent to fabricate phony theft claims.

The Central Index Bureau, discussed in Chapter 6, provides a means for insurers to learn about the claim history of bodily injury claimants. In addition, the local police can often be of help in investigating fraudulent claims, and some state insurance departments have formed insurance fraud bureaus for this specific purpose.

According to ICPI, the following indicators of casualty fraud should alert claim people to the possibility that they may be dealing with a fraudulent claimant or insured.[8]

Automobile Accident Schemes

Manner of Claimant or Insured

- Claimant or insured is overly aggressive in demanding an immediate settlement.
- Insured is overly anxious to take the blame for an accident.
- Claimant or insured is unusually knowledgeable with regard to insurance, medical, or vehicle repair terminology.
- Insured is adamant in insisting that the claimants caused the accident. (The insured may have been targeted by a "caused" accident ring.)

Common Elements of Fraudulent Claims

- A rental vehicle is involved in the accident
- Three or four unrelated occupants in the claimant or "struck" vehicle.
- Over-the-counter police report for a major collision (suspicious in jurisdictions where the police typically respond to most auto accident scenes).
- No police report.
- Accident occurred shortly after one or more of the vehicles was registered and insured, or within a short period before the termination of the policy.
- Accident occurred shortly after coverage was increased to include comprehensive and collision (especially for single vehicle accidents).
- One or more claimants list a P.O. box or hotel as an address.
- Index Bureau return indicates an active claim history.

Elements of Property Damage Fraud or Inflation

- All vehicles taken to the same body shop for repair.
- Major accident with *no* special damages, or with only minor, subjectively diagnosed injuries.

- Minor collision results in excessive repair costs.
- No towing charge although repair estimates suggest that the vehicle could not have been driven from the scene of the accident.
- Appraiser reports difficulties getting into the body shop to look at the car.

Elements of Medical Fraud

- All injuries are of the subjectively diagnosed variety, e.g., headaches, strain, sprain, spasm, whiplash, etc.
- Some or all of the medical bills submitted are photocopies. Third or fourth generation photocopies are especially suspicious.
- Minor collision with large special damages based on subjectively diagnosed injuries.
- Summary medical bill submitted without itemization of office visits and treatments.

Elements of Lost Earnings Fraud

- Employment information provided is for a small or unknown business and/or business address is a P.O. box.
- Business telephone number is answered by a tape recorder/answering device, an answering service, or secretarial service.
- Claimant started employment shortly before accident.
- Lost earnings statement is handwritten or typed on a blank sheet of paper instead of a business letterhead.
- One or more elements of lost earnings claim is questionable, e.g., length of absence, rate of pay, income incompatible with claimant's residence.
- Letter of intent for a prospective job for a currently unemployed claimant.

Claim Inflation Indicators

- Minor accident produces major medical costs, lost wages, and unusually expensive demands for pain and suffering.
- Past experience demonstrates that the physician's bill and report, regardless of the varying accident circumstances, is always the same.
- Treatment prescribed for the various injuries resulting from differing accidents is always the same in terms of duration and type of therapy.

- Medical bill indicates routine treatment being provided on Sundays, holidays, or usual doctor's day off.
- Efforts to verify lost wage statement with employer raise doubts about employer's legitimacy or about the actual employment of the claimant.
- The same doctor and attorney repeatedly handle major medical and lost earnings claims following minor accident.
- Hand delivered documents to avoid the use of the mails.

It must be emphasized that experience strongly suggests that the great majority of claims are legitimate. Most people, if dealt with openly and honestly, will respond in like manner. Adjusters must guard against becoming the perennial cynics who view most claimants and insureds with distrust and suspicion. Insureds and claimants should be dealt with in a positive manner.

A final note about handling suspected fraudulent claims is in order. A number of unfair claim practice acts contain provisions which require that insurers notify claimants of any delay in the investigation or settlement of a claim. In addition, a reasonable explanation of a denial of a claim must be provided as well. Some of the acts relieve the insurer from these requirements when there is reasonable evidence that the loss was caused by arson or fraud. It is essential that adjusters be familiar with the unfair claim practice law in their state and understand what effect, if any, such law has on the handling of fraudulent claims.

To Compromise or Defend—Economic Considerations A recurrent conflict for claim people is whether to defend a case which (with relative certainty) can be won or to compromise that case because of the economic factors involved. A questionable to doubtful liability claim with moderate injuries, for example, technically may be a case to defend, but the legal expenses incurred to defend the claim may far exceed its compromised settlement value. Faced with the option of defending or compromising the claim, many insurers choose, for economic reasons, the latter alternative.

Claim people find themselves in the position of having to make this choice in a fairly large number of claims. The claim person often must choose between standing on principle and incurring substantial investigative and legal expenses for defense, or taking the practical solution of compromise with the risk of encouraging similar claims in the future.

Companies vary in their response to these kinds of claim situations and to so-called "nuisance" claims where the claimant is aware of the mild dilemma he or she has created for the insurer. (A nuisance claim can be described as a small claim where liability is doubtful but which probably is more economical to pay and close than to maintain on an open claim file status.) Some insurers vigorously resist such claims while others believe the best course of action is the most economical one. Then again, each case is somewhat different and the company's decision will be influenced by the individual circumstances of each claim.

A similar problem confronts insurers with respect to handling possible fraudulent claims. At times, such claims need to be compromised because the available evidence is simply insufficient for the insurer to prevail in a lawsuit by the claimant. Where evidence is sufficient to defend its position, many companies are standing on principle and enthusiastically resisting such claims. To do otherwise, many companies reason, will make the industry an easy target for defrauders and encourage fraudulent or inflated claims from otherwise legitimate claimants as well.

As noted, companies vary in their response to claims which create a choice between defending or compromising. The decision made often depends upon the individual circumstances of the claim and, to a large extent, the attitudes of the local community as well as those of the company's top management.

METHODS OF EVALUATING CLAIMS

Though there are a number of methods available for evaluating bodily injury claims, each injury claim has its own unique set of circumstances and this tends to discourage the application of any precise formula which might apply to all injury claims. In the final analysis, each claim is different and the adjuster will need to use his or her experience and judgment to evaluate it.

Nevertheless, these various methods provide claim people with some assistance in the form of general guidelines for evaluating claims. In addition, attorneys will sometimes base their settlement demands on one or more of these methods or formulas. For these reasons, it is beneficial to examine the various approaches to establishing settlement values.

Since *special damages* ordinarily are known, the real challenge in settling claims is to arrive at a fair evaluation of *general damages,* such as pain and suffering, discomfort, or inconvenience. The objective of the following evaluation methods, therefore, is to consider the value of general damages.

X Times Special Damages

This is a formula approach whereby an arbitrary figure is

multiplied by the medical specials to arrive at the total value of the claim. In effect, the multiplication produces an amount which includes *both* special damages and the pain and suffering or general damages aspect of the claim. Implicit in this formula method is the assumption that there is a direct relationship between medical special damages and general damages.

Although claim people generally do not subscribe to such formula approaches, there is some indication that formulas are occasionally considered, at least as guidelines, in evaluating claims. The numbers three and five, for example, have been associated with this particular formula method. It has been suggested that when dealing directly with a claimant, "three times the medical specials" may provide a general guideline for evaluation. When the claimant is represented by an attorney, "five times the medical specials" apparently is more appropriate to account for the attorney's fee. (The fact that this formula approach exists is not an endorsement of the method. It is doubtful that any company would actually promote, without certain qualifications, this evaluation approach.)

The following is an example of how the formula might work:

Medical Specials	\$375
Pain and Suffering, Discomfort (General Damages)	3 × \$375 = \$1,125.00
Lost Earnings, One Week	\$275.00
Total Settlement Value	\$1,400.00

There are several variations of this method which may affect the total value of the claim substantially. Precisely which special damages are included in the multiplication process will significantly influence the ultimate settlement value of the claim.

In the previous example, it was assumed that the \$375 figure involved medical expenses incurred purely for actual *treatment* of the injuries, and not for diagnostic type expenses, such as X-rays, blood tests, or medication. Assume now, however, that the claimant has incurred such diagnostic expenses in addition to the \$375 and the formula to be used in "three times *all* medical specials." The claim would be evaluated as follows:

Medical Specials

Treatment	\$375.
X-Rays	75.
Blood test	25.
Medication	15.
Total Medical Specials	\$490.

General Damages (inclusive of medical specials)

Pain and suffering, discomfort (3 × $490)	=$1,470
Lost Earnings	275
Total Value	$1,745

Note that the settlement value increases from $1,400 to $1,745 when the focus is on *all* medical specials instead of just those medical expenses related to actual treatment.

Still another variation of the "X times the specials method" is to multiply X by total specials, *including* lost earnings. In that case, the total value of the claim would be $2,295 (3 × total specials of $765—$490 + $275).

It is easy to see the many fallacies inherent in this approach to evaluating claims. Once again, the method presumes that there is a direct relationship between special damages and general damages such as pain and suffering and discomfort. Yet, there is no scientific basis for this presumption.

The method also provides an incentive to "run up" treatment as well as diagnostic expenses such as X-rays and various testing procedures. The claimant who can afford to accumulate a large amount of medical bills from repeated office visits or extensive X-rays and the like, and who can take considerable time off from work, has a distinct advantage over the less fortunate claimant. The large medical expenses will increase the total value of the claim. Is it fair to relate the amount of medical expenses incurred to the amount of suffering and discomfort sustained? Or is it fair to take the view that the claimant who has incurred greater special damages should be entitled to a larger recovery?

With this method, the claimant who is treated by an expensive doctor or who is hospitalized at an expensive hospital, will generate higher general damages whereas another claimant who is treated by a doctor who charges less or who uses a less expensive hospital will be given less consideration for his or her suffering, discomfort, or inconvenience. Clearly, the "X times the specials" method is subject to serious criticism as a rational means of establishing the settlement value of a claim.

Total/Partial Disability Approach

The concept of disability is an important factor in estimating general damages. This method is designed to measure pain or discomfort based on the claimant's length of disability. An *arbitrary* amount is usually assigned on a weekly basis for total disability, and a lesser amount for partial disability. For example, a figure of $250 may be used to measure each week of total disability while $150 might be used to measure each week of partial disability.

If a claimant is totally disabled and cannot work, and the disability is confirmed by both the doctor and the employer, this ordinarily is sufficient evidence that the claimant suffered pain and discomfort. The fact that he or she eventually returned to work on a part-time or reduced work basis suggests that some pain or discomfort persisted during the partial disability period. This, of course, can be confirmed by the doctor and employer as well.

On occasion, a third arbitrary figure is used to measure a lesser degree of discomfort such as when a claimant has returned to full-time work but is still being treated occasionally and has not yet been discharged from the doctor's care. The fact that the claimant is still inconvenienced by having to see the doctor and may have occasional discomfort, is worth something in the form of general damages.

To illustrate, the general damages of a claimant who sustained two weeks of total disability, one week of partial disability, and one week of inconvenience might be calculated as follows:

Total Disability (two weeks at $250 per week)	$500
Partial Disability (one week at $150 per week)	150
Inconvenience (one week at $75 per week)	75
Total General Damages	$725

The problem with this method is that the amounts used to measure pain and discomfort are the same regardless of the nature of the claimant's injury, occupation, or his or her style of living or working. Thus, there is little or no consideration of the personal impact or effect of the injury on the particular claimant. If attempts are made to observe the nature of the injury and assess its effect on the particular claimant on a week to week basis, thereby verifying the weekly changes in disability, this method might have more validity.

Unit of Time

This method is similar to the total/partial disability approach in that both methods attempt to arbitrarily measure pain and discomfort according to the length of disability or inconvenience. An amount representing pain and discomfort is assigned for each unit of time (minutes, hours, days, weeks and so on) for which the claimant was disabled or inconvenienced as a result of the accident. Since the average person sleeps about eight hours a day, the calculations are based on sixteen hours a day of actual pain or discomfort. Assuming an arbitrary value of $35 a day has been assigned for pain, disability that lasts thirty days will produce general damages of $1,050.

The weakness of this approach is that it is virtually impossible to rationally set a dollar value for pain on an hourly or daily basis. Furthermore, in all likelihood, the level of pain fluctuates over periods of time to the extent that attempting to fix a set dollar amount for pain is unreasonable. This method is rarely, if ever, considered by claim people but occasionally may be advocated by plaintiff's counsel.

An interesting approach has been suggested as a means of countering the unit of time method.[9] The plaintiff's attorney might suggest a seemingly conservative amount for measuring pain, say $30 a day, but take the position that the plaintiff, age thirty-two, will experience pain for the rest of his or her life. An award of only $30 a day can result in a jury verdict in excess of $400,000 if the jury merely multiplies the $30 figure by the number of days remaining in an average lifetime.

To counter this argument, the claim person might consider using expert testimony by a member of a firm specializing in *structured* or periodic payment settlements. (The subject of structured settlements is discussed later in this chapter.) Testimony could be given to the effect that the same benefits ($30 a day over the plaintiff's lifetime) could be produced by the purchase of an annuity at the cost today of $90,000. This type of testimony might assist the jury in arriving at a fair verdict by placing the "unit of time" argument in proper perspective.

Judgment/Experience Method

This method, while essentially subjective, encompasses consideration of many factors and probably is the most common method used by claim people to evaluate bodily injury claims. The evaluation process is based to a large extent on the claim person's experience and knowledge of general settlement values in his or her particular locale. It entails looking at a number of factors which could affect settlement value, such as the liability situation; applicable law, e.g., contributory or comparative negligence; intra-family immunity; appearance and impression of the insured, plaintiff, key witnesses, and doctors; attorney skills and reputation; presence or absence of horror factor; and local verdict value.

Depending upon the seriousness of the injury, the liability situation, and the degree of likelihood the case will actually approach trial or be tried, the aforementioned factors may be of little or great concern to the claim person. In a case where injuries are minor and liability is clear, for example, the adjuster may look only at special damages, the nature of the injury and its effect on the claimant and, from this information, subjectively determine the total value of the claim.

On the other hand, if injuries are serious, liability is questionable, and the plaintiff's lawyer has a reputation for being a skilled trial attorney, all of these factors should be of concern to the adjuster.

It is difficult, if not impossible, to prescribe any definitive approach to evaluating injury claims. As mentioned previously, each claim or each injury and its effect on the claimant, are different. Ordinarily, any attempt to generalize or standardize such a personal misfortune as an accident which causes bodily injury will be wrought with error.

While some of the previous methods discussed occasionally may be of some assistance as a general guide to evaluation, the more rational approach seemingly is to examine each case individually, using one's judgment and experience. With this in mind, one suggested approach to evaluation looks at the injury, special damages, and liability and then attempts to determine what a jury comprising individuals who possess a strong sense of justice and fair play would award the claimant.

Admittedly, there is a subjective element here, both in attempting to portray such a jury and in calculating what it might award a particular claimant. But claim evaluation is *not* an exact science and since there are so many variables in each claim and a degree of chance in each trial, subjectivity is an inescapable part of the evaluation process. Furthermore, adjusters who use this approach are compelled to focus on the individual claimant and his or her particular injuries and damages, and this individual attention is what is necessary to get claims settled.

In using this method, the adjuster looks at the injury, medical specials, lost wages, and disability in an effort to gauge what this hypothetical "fair and just" jury would award the claimant. The adjuster needs to determine what kind of general damages have been generated by the injury. How has the injury affected the claimant in terms of disability, pain and suffering, discomfort or inconvenience? How has it affected the claimant's ability to live and work; in other words, the claimant's life-style?

Once sufficient thought has been given to these questions, the adjuster must decide what all this is worth in monetary terms. He or she decides this question by trying to ascertain what the jury would award the claimant after considering all of the medical and injury information just considered by the adjuster.

Usually, the adjuster sets a range for settlement value, acknowledging the subjective aspect of evaluation and the fact that ordinarily some negotiations are necessary before a settlement figure is agreed upon with the claimant or attorney. The adjuster may attempt to settle the claim for a figure in the middle of the range or may be willing, if necessary, to go to the upper limit in order to settle the case.

With this approach, it is immaterial whether or not the claimant is represented by an attorney. If the claimant is represented, consideration is made for the attorney's fee in the evaluation. Furthermore, if liability is questionable or comparative negligence applies, that is taken into consideration and the settlement figure is adjusted accordingly.

Unlike the formula methods discussed earlier, this method utilizes a more individual approach to the case and considers the unique aspects of the claim. It is not unusual for claim people to combine this method with the total/partial disability method explained earlier. In other words, in addition to attempting to determine what a fair-minded jury would award the claimant, the adjuster may also use the disability approach to obtain a reasonable idea of what the disability is worth in monetary terms. This should help the adjuster to evaluate general damages.

As adjusters gain experience and become more familiar with claim values, they build confidence and knowledge about the claim evaluation process.

Round Table

The objective of "round tabling" a claim is to use more than one opinion regarding its value. Two, three, or even more individuals may be involved in the evaluation discussion.

Round tabling actually is more an exercise in brainstorming than it is a specific method of evaluating claims. Claim people involved in the process ordinarily utilize their own individual method for evaluating the claim. Once values are determined, they are discussed and debated so that a general settlement range can be established.

The advantage of this approach is that the person responsible for settling the claim gets the benefit of the thinking of his or her associates. A possible disadvantage may be that sometimes no consensus is reached, leaving the responsible claim person with more uncertainty about the claim. Generally, however, round tabling is a fairly common practice and one generally regarded as producing positive results.

EXAMPLES OF CLAIM EVALUATION

In the following two case examples, sufficient information is provided for evaluation purposes. The first case involves a situation in which the adjuster has established claimant control. The claimant has sustained soft tissue injuries and liability is considered clear or probable.

The second case involves a more serious injury, a fracture of the radius, with the claimant being represented by an attorney. Liability is considered questionable but a comparative negligence law (50 percent rule) is in effect. The locale of both accidents is a moderate to large, fairly conservative, midwestern city.

Three experienced claim people were asked to evaluate these claims by establishing a range within which they felt the cases should be settled. At the outset, it must be repeated that claim evaluation is not an exact science and that judgment and experience play a vital role in such evaluations. The three evaluators reviewed the fact situations and developed settlement ranges which actually are quite similar. Readers probably will wish to establish their own settlement ranges for these cases. They should use their own judgment and experience and try to gauge what a fair-minded jury in this type of location would award the claimants.

Before the evaluation process begins, readers should keep in mind that there are many variables associated with claim evaluation. In addition to the injury, disability, and extent of special damages, the particular locality of the accident (i.e., community values and attitudes), the relationship developed between adjuster and claimant or claimant attorney, the personalities of the individuals, the expectations of the claimant, and the attorneys' skill and reputation all affect, to varying degrees, the value of the claim.

The facts in these cases are as follows:

1. *Case One*

    Claimant: John Davis, age twenty-eight, married

    Occupation: Carpenter, earning $8 an hour; works a forty-hour week.

    Accident Description: Claimant entered the insured's hardware store and slipped on the floor, falling against the counter. The floor had been waxed about an hour earlier by a store employee and excessive wax had been used. Prior to the claimant's fall, two customers had slipped on the floor, yet no steps were taken by the storekeeper to warn customers or correct the condition.

    Injuries: Hematoma left knee, eccyhmosis side of forehead, headache, abrasions to face. Claimant treated and released at the hospital emergency room.

Special Damages:	
Skull X-rays	$ 80.00
Emergency Room treatment	$100.00
Total Emergency Room bill	$180.00
2 doctor visits @ $25 each	$ 50.00
Total medical specials	$230.00

Lost two days from work	
$55 a day	$110.00
Total Specials	$340.00

Assume that based on information from the claimant and his employer, the adjuster determines the claimant was totally disabled for two days and continued to be in some pain and discomfort for an additional six days. Furthermore, the prognosis was for full recovery and there were no complications.

With these facts in mind, establish a settlement range for this claim, keeping in mind that the claimant is not represented by an attorney.

2. *Case Two*

Claimant: Barbara Day, age thirty-two, married, two children

Occupation: Bank Loan Supervisor, annual salary $20,000

Accident Description: Claimant and insured involved in an auto accident at an uncontrolled intersection (driver versus driver). Assume that the investigation reveals a questionable case of liability (50 percent versus 50 percent) with perhaps a slight edge in claimant's favor, due to points of impact and location of the vehicles in the intersection.

Applicable Law: Comparative negligence (50 percent rule)

Injuries: A simple fracture, shaft of right radius, and bruised shoulder. (Claimant is right-handed.) The fracture was treated by closed reduction (plaster cast). Estimated disability is six weeks according to the doctor's report (see Exhibit 8-5). Claimant, however, returned to work after three weeks on a reduced-work basis (with cast on). The cast was removed after six weeks with the fracture well healed, with no complications.

Adjuster confirms that the claimant sustained three weeks of total disability, three weeks of partial disability, and estimates two weeks of further discomfort and inconvenience after the cast is removed.

Special Damages:	
Hospital emergency room	$525.00

(The claimant spent about two hours in the emergency room where X-rays were taken, a plaster cast was set, and medication was administered.)

Doctor Visits	
5 visits at $22 each	$110.00
X-rays	40.00
Medication	50.00
Total Medical Specials	$725.00

Exhibit 8-5
Attending Physician's Report

DATE OF REPORT 11-6-8

NAME OF PATIENT Barbara Day
AGE 32 MARITAL STATUS married

ADDRESS 100 Dutro Lane
OCCUPATION Bank Loan Supervisor

CITY AND STATE Central City, Ohio
TELEPHONE

DATE OF FIRST EXAMINATION 9-26-8-
WHO WAS PRESENT

PLACE OF FIRST EXAMINATION Office

EVIDENCE OF OLD INJURIES No

OF DISEASE No

OF INTOXICATION No

PATIENT RECEIVED FIRST AID OR OTHER PRIOR TREATMENT FOR THIS INJURY FROM Mercy Hospital Emergency

PREVIOUS MEDICAL HISTORY N/A

PATIENT'S ACCOUNT OF INJURY

DATE AND HOUR OF INJURY 9-14-8-

PLACE AND MANNER OF OCCURRENCE Auto Accident

DESCRIPTION OF INJURY

Simple fracture, shaft of right radius.

TREATMENT

DATE OF TREATMENTS 9-15, 9-22, 9-29 10-15, 11-1 WHERE GIVEN? Office

NATURE OF TREATMENT observation, X-rays

WERE X-RAYS TAKEN Yes BY WHOM office DATE 11-1-84

FINDINGS well healed

NUMBER OF STITCHES TAKEN ____ LOCATION OF STITCHES ____

DISPOSITION OF CASE

TAKEN HOME OR TO HOSPITAL ____ NAME OF HOSPITAL ____

DATE OF DISCHARGE ____

DIAGNOSIS ____

PROGNOSIS AND PERMANENCY OF INJURY

Fracture well healed after closed reduction

PERIOD OF DISABILITY:
TOTAL DISABILITY FROM Sept. 14 ,19 8- TO Oct. 7 ,19 8- PARTIAL DISABILITY FROM Oct 8 ,19 8- TO Nov. 1 ,19 8-

NATURE AND EXTENT OF ANY PERMANENT DISABILITY None

AMOUNT OF BILL TO DATE $ $110.00 PHYSICIAN'S SIGNATURE Richard Sawyer MD

EST. AMOUNT OF FINAL BILL $ - CITY Central City STATE Ohio

Lost Income (Three weeks)	
Weekly salary ($327 × 3)	$981.00
Total Specials	$1,706.00

The claimant's attorney's demand is $15,000. He concedes little, if any, contributory negligence on his client's part.

Establish a settlement range for this claim.

Case One Evaluation—Clear or Probable Liability

This is a case of clear or probable liability, soft tissue injury claim with $230.00 in medical specials, and $110 in lost wages (two days). The claimant suffered some pain and discomfort for about a week after the accident. He is not represented by an attorney. The evaluations by the three evaluators could be as follows:

Evaluator 1	*Evaluator 2*	*Evaluator 3*
$590---$840	$500---$800	$600---$900

These are the settlement ranges established by the three evaluators on the basis of their judgment and experience. The ranges represent to them what a fair and just jury in this locality would probably award the claimant who has sustained this injury and incurred these special damages.

In essence, the case may be worth anywhere from $250 to $500 over the special damages, although one evaluator's range began below $250 while another's slightly exceeded the $500 figure.

Case Two Evaluation—Questionable Liability

This case involved a questionable liability case with a fact situation which slightly favored the claimant. A comparative negligence law (50 percent rule) applied, meaning that the claimant could recover as long as her contributory negligence did not exceed 50 percent. However, the recovery would be reduced by her percentage of comparative negligence.

The claimant sustained a simple fracture of the right radius which was treated by closed reduction. Medical specials were $725 and she underwent treatment for six weeks but returned to work on a reduced work basis after three weeks. Her lost income for three weeks was $981. The adjuster estimates that the claimant was totally disabled for three weeks, partially disabled for an additional three weeks, and in discomfort for another two weeks.

The evaluations (on roughly a 50-50 comparative fault basis) may be as follows:

Evaluator 1	*Evaluator 2*	*Evaluator 3*
$3,000--$3,600	$3,000--$3,500	$3,200--$3,900

(The evaluators might feel that with attorney representation this case has a total value—*with clear liability on the insured's part*—of around $6,500.)

In arriving at these settlement ranges, the evaluators would be looking at a claimant who sustained a fracture of her right radius and incurred total specials of $1,706. Of that figure, $725 represented medical specials and $981 was lost income for three weeks. With regard to disability, the claimant sustained three weeks of total disability, three weeks of partial disability, and an additional two weeks of some pain and discomfort.

With a fracture of the right radius, $1,706 in special damages, and eight weeks with either some disability or discomfort, the settlement ranges established represent what a fair and just jury would award the claimant in this questionable liability situation in this particular locality. The settlement ranges also reflect consideration of the attorney's fee, which ordinarily is one-third of the recovery unless the case is actually tried, in which case it may be as high as 50 percent of the recovery.

It must be kept in mind that if the fracture had been more severe or if the prognosis had been less favorable, the case would be worth more money. In addition, if the liability situation were slightly different—perhaps an eyewitness was found who slightly favored one of the drivers—the evaluation could be substantially altered.

Since, in all likelihood, this case could involve some extended negotiations because of the liability question, the claim person might want to establish an even greater range. This would depend on the adjuster's knowledge of the claimant attorney's negotiations style and skill.

In effect, this case was roundtabled by three claim people who established a general settlement range of $3,000 to $3,900. The precise figure at which the settlement negotiations process should begin depends to a considerable extent on the adjuster's perception of how much negotiating will be necessary and on how reasonable the attorney will be. The adjuster's initial offer may be for an amount less than $3,000, if the claimant attorney is known to be a tough negotiator who strenuously resists moving off his original demand, or comes down to reality at a painstakingly slow pace.

It needs to be emphasized that lost wages or income is calculated on a *net* basis in evaluating these claims. This is because claim settlements are *not* subject to income tax and, therefore, a deduction of about 15 percent can be taken from gross salary figures when negotiating a settlement. Although gross income loss can be reduced in the *negotiations* process, the courts have generally held that the fact that lost income damages are not subject to income tax is not admissible at trial. It appears, however, that this issue is undergoing some transition at the current time and claim people are advised to check with their local defense counsel on the status of this matter.

SETTLEMENT NEGOTIATIONS

Generally, the negotiation of a claim is the prelude to its final disposition. To negotiate is to meet or confer with another to reach agreement on a matter. With regard to insurance claims, the parties are attempting to reach agreement on the settlement value of the claim.

Much of what is said about settlement negotiations in this text is grounded in basic common sense and courtesy. These two basic ingredients are essential in achieving agreement between two or more individuals. In order for negotiations to result in agreement, the dignity and self-respect of each party must be considered and maintained throughout the negotiations process.

It is advisable for adjusters to participate in both the evaluation and negotiation processes early in their careers. Under the guidance of their supervisors, adjusters should analyze and make decisions concerning the value of the claims they handle. In addition, once their evaluations are approved or modified by supervisory counseling, they should attempt to negotiate their claims to a close. The evaluation and negotiation aspects of claim handling can only be learned through practice, and the sooner adjusters initiate the learning process, the quicker they will develop competency in these areas.

Determining Case Readiness for Negotiations

Though the general goal of claim handling is to close claims, adjusters must be careful not to unduly hurry the settlement process and risk jeopardizing a good relationship with the claimant. At a certain point in the claim process, the claim will be ready for settlement negotiations. The claim person can do much to hasten the arrival of this time by completing the investigation and evaluation in a timely manner, by communicating clearly with the claimant regarding what he or she must do to process the claim, and by making oneself accessible to the claimant's needs and questions.

It is worth repeating that experience strongly suggests that claims do not get any less expensive with time. In fact, just the contrary appears to be true. One notable weakness of many adjusters seems to be an all too common *passive* claim attitude which often results in bodily injury claims remaining open indefinitely and not getting the attention necessary to finalize them. When investigation reveals that a claim is one for settlement, aggressive action should be taken by the claim person to secure the information necessary to conclude the claim.

Before the negotiations process can begin, however, certain actions must be taken in preparation for settlement negotiations:

1. Coverage must be verified.
2. Liability must be determined.
3. Medical treatment by the claimant ordinarily must be completed (an exception is an "open end" settlement which will be discussed subsequently).
4. Special damages must be verified and the file must be documented with medical reports and bills. (The extent of documentation will depend upon the seriousness of the claim.)
5. The claim must be evaluated and the claim person must have authority to settle at the evaluated figure.
6. The claimant must be ready to settle, both from a medical as well as a psychological standpoint.

Planning the Approach to Negotiations

If negotiations are to lead to agreement, it is essential that the adjuster know every detail of the claim file. This includes being familiar with the facts of the accident, being aware of the existence and version of any witnesses, and knowing the details of the claimant's injuries and special damages. The adjuster also must have established a settlement figure or range and must be equipped with the necessary tools to dispose of the claim, such as drafts, releases, and so on.

The adjuster must demonstrate in convincing fashion that he or she is well prepared and well informed about the details of the accident as well as the damages being claimed. Such preparation on the adjuster's part adds dignity to the negotiations process by demonstrating to the claimant that the adjuster thinks enough of the claimant to have done the homework and prepared well for their meeting.

It is also necessary that the adjuster be aware of the strong and weak points of the case so that he or she will be able to respond intelligently to objections or arguments raised by the claimant. The adjuster must have thought about how he or she would present the arguments which are favorable to the insured without losing control or alienating the claimant with technical or legal jargon.

In a fall-down case, for example, the adjuster may meet with substantial resistance when he or she offers only out-of-pocket expenses in a serious injury case because the cabbage leaf on which the claimant slipped was fairly "crisp and clean." Indicating that the "clean" condition of the cabbage leaf suggests that it was on the floor for only a short time, making liability questionable or doubtful, might result in the adjuster's early departure from the claimant's home. Yet, there is a principle of law involved in such cases which ordinarily needs to be explained to the claimant. The challenge is to explain it in a way that is understandable and, at the same time, demonstrates concern for the claimant.

In the above case, the adjuster might try the following approach:

> "Now this may sound a little unusual at first, Mrs. Claimant, but let me explain how I arrived at my position before you reject it entirely. The Ajax Supermarket has a responsibility to its customers to use reasonable care in the maintenance of the store. And I emphasize *reasonable.* The produce department makes regular sweeping runs anywhere from five to seven times a day, depending upon traffic, and you yourself, Mrs. Claimant, have said that you are a regular shopper there and generally find the store to be clean. Once in a while, there's going to be debris on the floor. It's unavoidable, and I think it would be 'unreasonable' to expect the floor to be spotless at all times. My investigation at the supermarket indicates that the floor was swept about an hour before you fell. As strange as it may sound at first, one of the first things I try to find out is the condition of the debris, especially if it's produce of any kind. With a cabbage leaf, I ask about color, crispness, and dirt. If I'm told that the leaf looked fairly clean and crisp, that tells me that in all probability it wasn't on the floor very long and bears out what the produce manager told me about his maintenance procedures on the day of your fall."

Depending on the degree of customer traffic, the specific condition of the leaf, the presence of any witnesses, and the type of comparative negligence law in effect, such a claim will likely be compromised or denied.

With an auto accident, adjusters must undergo a similar process, analyzing the various aspects of the claim—points of impact, speed, witnesses, and visibility—that tend to favor the insured and that they will emphasize in presenting their case.

If the claim is serious or complicated enough to warrant it, it might help adjusters to actually conduct a "dry run" of their negotiations approach either on their own or with a work associate. At the very least, the adjuster should go over the basic approach in his or her mind to develop a general familiarity with it.

Above all, in planning the approach to the negotiations, the adjuster must know something about the claimant; that is, the claimant's personality and style and his or her expectations about the claim. The adjuster needs to ask, "How will this particular claimant respond to my negotiations approach?" "How can I convince this particular claimant that my reasoning is fair and sound?"

If the relationship established between the adjuster and claimant has been one of trust and confidence from the start of the investigation the adjuster must be careful not to lose this trust by maneuvering for advantage or by making an insincere offer. If the adjuster established good claimant control through sincerity and honesty, these qualities must be maintained throughout the negotiations process.

Negotiating a settlement often involves give and take, making a concession here, getting a concession there. With this in mind, the adjuster must come to the claimant with some flexibility and be prepared to bargain to some extent. The negotiations approach and the extent of the bargaining that will be necessary is determined, in large part, by the personalities of the parties and the relationship they have established.

Some claimants place considerable trust in the adjuster to deal with them fairly. Others are ready to "horse trade" from the start and will do everything possible to get the upper hand in settlement negotiations. Still other claimants have developed what can best be described as an "arm's length" relationship with the adjuster, reflecting neither trust nor distrust, but exhibiting a sort of "wait and see" attitude before they start looking for an attorney. Understandably, the adjuster's approach to each of these claimants will vary considerably.

In summary then, when planning the negotiation strategy, the claim person should:

1. know the claim file, e.g. the liability situation and damages;
2. know the strong and weak points of the case and how to use them to his or her advantage; and
3. know the claimant—his or her personality, style and expectations. The adjuster's approach to the negotiations process will be strongly influenced by the style and personality of the claimant.

Characteristics of a Good Negotiator

Certain characteristics or behavior traits usually are evident in adjusters who negotiate effectively. Certainly, a friendly attitude on the adjuster's part is helpful in breaking the ice and getting the negotiations started. Adjusters must be careful, however, to maintain sincerity in their efforts to be friendly. An insincere attempt to be friendly often will be recognized by the claimant.

The claimant must be informed of what he or she must do to process the claim. Communication and information are interwoven in a claims situation and both are necessary if a settlement is to be reached. A lack of communication generally leads to a lack of information, and vice versa.

The adjuster must empathize with and be conscious of the claimant's position and feelings as a result of the accident. In addition, the adjuster must focus on the needs of the claimant because "need" is the motivating factor in negotiations. The claimant has material as well as emotional needs which must be considered and understood. By observing the claimant and by listening to him, the adjuster usually learns much about the claimant's personality and his or her needs and desires. With a better understanding of the claimant's needs, the adjuster can modify his or her negotiations style to meet those needs. For example, the claimant may have an immediately recognizable *material* need such as the need for a new household appliance or a second car. Such material needs present opportunities for adjusters to move the settlement negotiations in the direction of meeting those specific needs.

Adjusters need to be patient with claimants. Delay in the settlement negotiations process is sometimes an indicator of a lack of information or communication. If the adjuster has explained the claims process fully to the claimant, delay should be minimal. If the delay stems from some basic uncertainty or fear on the claimant's part, the adjuster must try to understand the motivation for this fear and work with the claimant in disposing of or minimizing it.

The adjuster must be professional at all times and maintain an even temper. He or she must treat the claimant with respect, no matter how difficult this may become at times. A good adjuster maintains control of his or her emotions no matter how adverse the conditions may become. In addition, adjusters should attempt to speak the claimant's language and avoid what might appear to the claimant to be a condescending attitude. Using repeated legal or claim terminology should be avoided by the adjuster.

Self-confidence on the adjuster's part is essential if he or she is to persuade the claimant to accept his or her positions and ideas on liability or settlement value. If the claimant detects anxiety or uncertainty on the adjuster's part, this could impede the negotiations process. Being well prepared and well informed about the claim and the claimant should enhance the adjuster's self-confidence.

Confidence also includes knowing when the timing is right to attempt to close the negotiations process and secure a release. Some claimants require a calm, attentive, serious approach to negotiations while others only understand, and actually prefer, the utmost candor on the adjuster's part. Such people may even become a little suspicious if the adjuster does not react with some sincere emotion from time to time. As the adjuster gains experience and self-confidence, he or she will be able to judge what approach will work best with each claimant.

Finally, adjusters should be honest throughout the negotiations process. They should not make promises they cannot keep and should be certain that they are negotiating within their limits of settlement authority.

Initiating the Negotiations Process

One common approach to initiating the negotiations process is for the adjuster to review the claim with the claimant. A brief summary of the accident facts along with an itemization of special damages are presented for background purposes by the adjuster. This approach usually creates a positive atmosphere because the adjuster and claimant are simply agreeing on the basic facts of the claim. Once the positive atmosphere is established, the adjuster can begin the process of making an offer or soliciting a demand from the claimant.

Another approach is for the adjuster to set out a basic objective which he or she intends to achieve by meeting with the claimant. For example, the adjuster may emphasize to the claimant that they have established a cooperative and honest relationship from the start and that based on this cooperation, they should be able to reach a fair settlement agreement which is satisfactory to both parties. With the foundation laid, the adjuster explains why he or she is making the following offer, or asks the claimant what he or she has in mind as a fair settlement figure.

It is important that settlement discussions between the adjuster and claimant begin on a positive note. The adjuster, therefore, should seek as subjects of the initial discussion areas on which they can reach general agreement.

The adjuster needs to be careful not to embarrass the claimant or create a situation which allows the claimant to lose face or self-respect. Ego and self-image are crucial aspects of the settlement negotiations process. As the adjuster gains experience and develops judgment, he or she will be able to determine when it is appropriate to initiate settlement discussions and make an offer. In time, the adjuster will learn which claimants like to bargain and "horse trade" and which prefer to avoid the theatrics and deal matter of factly with the adjuster.

With respect to the negotiations process, both the adjuster and the claimant have the same general goal—to settle the claim. The potential conflict stems from the distinct perceptions of value which each party may hold. The adjuster, for example, seeks a generally conservative figure in which to settle the claim because he or she is dealing with the company's money. The adjuster has been trained to be fair and reasonable, but somewhat frugal, with those funds. The claimant, on the other hand, has often been "warned" that the adjuster's goal is to save money and that the claimant should ask for more than he or she really wants in order to balance the opposing goals of each party so that a fair settlement may be achieved.

It is possible in this day and age to dispense with much, if not all, of these potentially negative elements in the negotiations process. Certainly, in cases where liability is clear and injuries are not severe and an atmosphere of confidence and trust has been built by the parties, all things are possible. Where the case is clearly one for settlement, it should be settled in a timely manner, and the adjuster can usually justify paying a substantial but reasonable figure in such cases. It is the questionable liability cases, perhaps where the claimant has sustained some disfigurement or permanency, which seemingly pose the more difficult and challenging problems for the claim negotiator.

Handling the Attorney Threat

Frequently, in cases where the adjuster is negotiating directly with the claimant and an obstacle or dispute arises, the claimant may indicate that he or she will seek the services of an attorney. This may be an idle threat designed to instill fear in the adjuster or there may be genuine substance to the claimant's threat. Regardless of the claimant's motivation, however, the adjuster should not express alarm over the possibility that the claimant may retain an attorney. Unquestionably, the claimant has the right to do so, and claim people may not advise a claimant to refrain from seeking legal advice.

As a matter of fact, experience suggests that perhaps the best way to handle the claimant's threat to seek counsel is to immediately affirm the claimant's right to do so. It should be explained that in that case, the adjuster is required to work directly with the attorney and may not maintain contact with the claimant.

By not demonstrating alarm or panic in the face of such a threat the adjuster quickly dispels any notion the claimant may have that his or her bargaining position has been elevated by this threat. And this is ordinarily accomplished without insulting the claimant. All the adjuster has done is to agree with the claimant that he or she has the right to the services of an attorney and that the adjuster may not stand in the claimant's way. The claimant is free to do as he or she chooses but should be made aware that the presence of an attorney does not necessarily increase the value of the claim. With this said, the adjuster should then reiterate the fact that the relationship between the adjuster and the claimant has been one of cooperation up to now and that it is important to the adjuster that negotiations continue, if that is the claimant's wish.

This reemphasizes the adjuster's desire to negotiate directly with the claimant and affords the claimant a chance to regain any self-esteem which might have been lost when the attorney threat was deflated by the adjuster. It should not be mentioned, however, that if the claimant retains an attorney, the claim may continue for a long period of time, since the claimant may already be aware of this.

THE OFFER

The offer to settle the case may be made by either the adjuster or the claimant (or the claimant's attorney). Although the term "demand" is most commonly associated with an offer made by the claimant or his or her attorney, a *demand* is just as much an offer of settlement as is an offer by the adjuster. The different terms are used merely to distinguish between an offer made by the claim person and one made by the claimant or attorney.

It is strongly suggested that the term "demand" not be used in the negotiations process. The adjuster should never ask the claimant or attorney for a demand. A "demand," as that term is used in settlement negotiations, represents more of an upper figure for the record than a genuine evaluation of the claim by the claimant or the claimant's attorney. For this reason, claim people should talk to claimants and attorneys in terms of what they would settle the case for rather than what their demand is on a particular claim.

Some general guidelines with regard to making an offer which might be helpful to claim people, include the following:[10]

1. Do not make an offer unless there is a possibility of settling the claim for a figure approximating the amount offered. If the claimant's demand is grossly excessive, it may be best for the adjuster to suspend negotiations until such time as the claimant presents a more realistic settlement demand. The adjuster should present reasons why he or she feels the claimant's figure is unrealistic by focusing on the nature of the injuries and the special damages and ask the claimant to provide reasons why he or she feels the figure is reasonable.

Through a persuasive discussion of values based on the injuries and special damages, it may be possible to demonstrate to the claimant the unreasonableness of his or her demand.

2. Do not increase the offer unless there is a corresponding decrease in the demand. An enhanced bargaining position may be gained by the claimant if the adjuster begins to increase the offer without getting corresponding concessions from the claimant. If, for example, the adjuster increases a $1,500 offer to $1,750 and then to $1,900 without the claimant moving down from his or her demand of $5,000, the claimant may get the impression that the adjuster has some money to spend and was not serious about the initial offer. Before offering $1,900 the adjuster should persuade the claimant to reduce his or her demand of $5,000.

   In addition, the adjuster should increase his or her offer conservatively so as to avoid creating the impression that the adjuster has a considerable amount of money with which to negotiate.
3. Avoid ultimatums to the claimant. Adjusters should always leave the door to settlement open, regardless of whether the adjuster is negotiating directly with the claimant or with an attorney. As noted earlier, if negotiation is to lead to agreement, the dignity and self-respect of the parties to the claim must be maintained and the chance to save face must always be available.

The First Offer

The question of whether the adjuster or the claimant should make the first offer is one which is frequently debated. The simple answer is that it depends upon the circumstances.

Some claim people feel that from the standpoint of professionalism, the adjuster, who ostensibly is the expert on claim value, should present an offer of settlement to the claimant. This is especially true if the adjuster has established a good rapport with the claimant and has secured the claimant's trust through the handling of the claim.

If the adjuster has effectively taken charge of the claim handling process to the extent that the claimant relies on his or her knowledge and direction, it may confuse the claimant if the adjuster suddenly passes the ultimate decision of settlement value to the claimant. The claimant has relied on the adjuster to give him or her a fair assessment of the value of the claim.

The claimant may not feel confident enough to make this judgment on his or her own. The adjuster's attempt to turn over the responsibility of determining settlement value to the claimant may convince the claimant that neither the adjuster nor the claimant is capable of determining the claim's value. In that event, the claimant may seek the services of an attorney or, at the very least, lose confidence and trust in the adjuster.

Experienced adjusters can usually recognize situations where the claimant's reliance is such that it is appropriate for the adjuster to initiate the offer.

On the other hand, if the claimant has demonstrated that he or she likes to bargain or horse trade, it may be appropriate for the adjuster to outline the special damages and ask the claimant for his or her idea of a fair settlement value based on these specials. (Of course, the adjuster should avoid the use of claim jargon such as "specials," and use instead terms the claimant can understand such as "expenses.")

There are potential advantages and disadvantages to both approaches. By making the first offer, the adjuster sets the tone by establishing a general price range around which the discussion may begin. This serves to mitigate any exaggerated view of the claim's value which the claimant might hold.

A possible disadvantage of having the adjuster make the first offer is that the claimant may have been quite willing to accept less money than the figure offered by the adjuster. This is no great problem if the adjuster feels confident that the offer was fair because there are instances, though seemingly rare, where claimants underestimate the value of their claims.

Another possible disadvantage is that the adjuster's offer may be such that it infuriates the claimant and convinces him or her to seek the services of an attorney. If the adjuster has priced the case fairly and cannot bring the claimant down to reality, this is the kind of claim which might be more effectively resolved through negotiations with the claimant's attorney. The attorney should be able to reason with the claimant and inject a sense of reality into the settlement process.

An advantage of having the claimant make a demand first is that the adjuster can determine the claimant's perception of settlement value without committing to a figure himself. The adjuster can then decide whether the claim can be settled or whether the negotiations should be suspended until the adjuster can persuade the claimant to be more realistic.

On the other hand, by asking the claimant to indicate a figure first, the adjuster may help affirm the claimant's exaggerated perception of value and make it more difficult to get the claimant to move down to a more realistic figure.

The approach used in opening settlement negotiations will vary among adjusters. With proper supervision and experience, adjusters develop the style which works best for them. Regardless of the approach used, the adjuster eventually reaches the point where it is appropriate to make an offer.

Whether the first offer should be for out-of-pocket expenses, for total special damages, or for special damages plus a sum that represents pain and suffering and discomfort depends on the particular claim. The extent of special damages, the nature and scope of the injuries, the liability situation, the expectations of the claimant, all must be considered in determining the amount of the first offer.

In some relatively small claims, pain or discomfort may not be a factor as far as a particular claimant is concerned. It may be that the claimant has already collected his or her medical expenses from a collateral source and the fact that he or she is being offered duplicate benefits representing these expenses may be quite sufficient to close the claim. Other claimants feel that regardless of whether they have been reimbursed for actual out-of-pocket expenses, they are entitled to compensation for the intangible aspects of the claim such as pain, discomfort, or inconvenience.

Perhaps the most that can be said here is that the adjuster must look at the special damages, the injury, the claimant, and the liability and then establish a settlement range and make an initial offer which ordinarily should reflect a conservative figure. Company claim philosophy will determine to a considerable extent whether initial settlement offers are made for specials only or for specials plus an amount reflecting general damages. Seemingly, though, the most important considerations in determining the amount of the first offer are the adjuster's perception of the claim situation and his or her judgment regarding what the first offer should be.

Negotiating with Attorneys

Most of what has been said about negotiating directly with claimants applies equally to negotiations with attorneys. It needs to be emphasized, especially with newer adjusters, that attorneys, like adjusters, are human beings. Some attorneys are well versed in negligence law and are good negotiators. Others engage in negligence work only as a sideline and may not be that familiar with legal or claim issues. At times, adjusters will sense that they are in control of the negotiations process or that they are more informed about the liability situation and relevant aspects of a particular claim than the attorney. The point is that the background and knowledge of attorneys vary considerably.

Generally speaking, reasonably experienced adjusters who have undergone training in coverage analysis, tort law, and claim investigation principles should be well prepared to deal with even the most knowledgeable attorneys. As noted earlier in the text, once a claimant has retained an attorney, the claim person can no longer contact the claimant or negotiate directly with him. All correspondence and communications must be conducted with the attorney who acts as agent for the claimant.

Summarizing the ideas expressed earlier with regard to negotiations, the adjuster must know the claim file, i.e., special damages, injuries, disability, liability situation, insured's version (and appearance and impression), and identity of any witnesses. The adjuster should also know his or her adversary. Is the attorney generally cooperative? Does he or she furnish medical information, submit special damages, discuss liability, and agree to a medical examination? Does the attorney try cases, or does he or she have a reputation for settling virtually all his or her cases?

If the attorney is not a trial attorney, the adjuster should be aware of this fact. When a claimant attorney must refer cases to other attorneys for trial purposes, the original attorney must share his or her fee with the trial attorney. Understandably, this is an incentive for the original attorney to settle cases with the adjuster so that there will be no need to make such referrals to trial counsel. Such knowledge on the part of the adjuster can be to his or her advantage from a negotiations standpoint, and may facilitate the settlement process. Adjuster can sometimes learn much about plaintiff counsel from their fellow claim employees and from claim people associated with other insurance companies with whom they come in contact.

Another factor in settlement negotiations of which adjusters should be aware is the concept of *contingent fees.* Ordinarily, attorneys handle bodily injury liability claims on a contingent fee basis. This means that whether the attorney receives a fee for his or her services depends upon whether the claimant makes a recovery. The usual attorney fee is one-fourth to one-third of the recovery, but it may be as high as 50 percent, especially if the case goes to trial.

The fact that claimants need not pay legal fees unless there is a recovery creates an incentive for them to use the services of attorneys. This, in turn, increases general claim activity. If claimants had to pay their attorneys on a conventional basis, i.e., an hourly rate or flat fee, fewer claimants would be able to employ the services of attorneys. The contingent fee concept has been criticized by those who favor reform of the tort liability system because it encourages questionable and groundless claims and increases litigation as well. On the other side of the coin, defenders of the system contend that it enables numerous people, who otherwise would be unable to do so, to pursue recovery of their legitimate claims.

From the claimant attorney's standpoint, he or she receives no revenue until and unless the claimant makes a recovery, either by settlement or through a court award. When it is considered that no income is generated by the attorney until there is a recovery, and that the outcome of a trial almost always carries some risk, it becomes clear that it is frequently in the attorney's best interest as well as the client's to settle claims.

Adjusters should be cognizant of those factors which tend to provide an incentive for attorneys to settle cases. In claims which the adjuster feels should be settled or compromised, it often is to the mutual benefit of the parties that the cases be resolved by settlement, without assuming the expense and the risk associated with the trial process.

Who Makes the First Offer When Attorney Represents Claimant? The general guidelines regarding when to make an offer with respect to negotiating with claimants apply equally to claims in which the claimant is represented by an attorney. There is, however, one notable exception. When negotiating with attorneys, the customary approach is for claim people to seek the attorney's demand before making an offer. The attorney is presumed to know something about settlement value. Claim people ordinarily can expect the attorney to begin the negotiations process without the need for them to reveal their own thinking regarding claim value. With few exceptions, that initial demand is likely to be an inflated figure and adjusters should try to persuade the attorney that the sooner he or she makes a realistic demand, the sooner serious and meaningful negotiations can begin.

Though obtaining the attorney's demand before making an offer may still be the customary approach, today many claim people, in an effort to aggressively dispose of the more probable liability cases, are initiating the settlement process by making the first offer themselves. As a limited agent of the claimant, the attorney has no authority to settle the claim unless he or she is authorized to do so by the claimant. The attorney, therefore, ordinarily must communicate the adjuster's offer to his or her client, and usually makes a recommendation whether or not to accept it. While the adjuster's offer may not settle the case, it starts the process and may get both the attorney and the claimant seriously interested in moving the case toward disposition.

Claims which are considered to be cases for settlement should be given constant attention and evaluated as early as reasonably possible. Once a settlement range is established, the claim person should contact the attorney with the goal of settling the claim. If the claim is evaluated fairly and realistically, and if the attorney is equally realistic, the prospect for early disposition of the claim would seem promising.

With regard to questionable liability cases, there may still be an incentive for settlement, on a compromised basis. The fact that comparative negligence laws apply in the majority of states today compels claim people to seek settlement opportunities even when the claimant's comparative negligence approaches 50 percent. Of course, in states with pure comparative negligence laws, the claimant will be entitled to some recovery even when his or her negligence exceeds 50 percent. Thus, insurers have some exposure which encourages their efforts to settle such claims.

From the attorneys' viewpoint, they face substantial expenses if the case is tried and, with considerable liability on the claimant's part, they could conceivably lose the case as well. Clearly, there are incentives for both sides to investigate settlement opportunities.

Finally, adjusters need to be sure that they document the claim file with respect to any offers or demands which have been made. It is advisable to follow up the negotiations session with a letter to the attorney, either reiterating the offer or responding affirmatively or negatively to the demand, so that there is no chance of misinterpreting the intent of the parties regarding settlement.

CLOSING THE CLAIM—THE RELEASE

A *release* is a legally binding contract and, as such, must embody all of the elements of a contract in order to be valid. (The elements of such a contract were examined in Chapter 2.)

A release provides that in consideration for the specific sum paid to the claimant, the claimant releases the insured from all claims arising out of the particular accident. Thus, there are two aspects of consideration here: (1) the claimant's promise to refrain from bringing suit in return for (2) the payment by the insured (or on behalf of the insured) of a specified sum of money in settlement of the claim.

In actual practice, the claimant often signs the release before receiving a settlement draft or check with the understanding that it will be issued shortly. If the claimant expresses concern over the fact that the draft will not be exchanged immediately, the adjuster might explain that the contract between them is not binding until the consideration, in the form of a draft or check, is actually received by the claimant.

The effect of a release is that the claimant relinquishes the right to bring legal action against the insured to enforce his or her claim. Although most people understand the binding effect of a release, it is advisable that prior to obtaining a signed release, adjusters make sure that claimants fully understand that the release terminates their claim.

Probably one of the more commonly used settlement agreements is the *general release,* shown in Exhibits 8-6 and 8-7. A general release is customarily used in cases in which there is only one tortfeasor. The common law rule that a release of one tortfeasor releases all tortfeasors, while substantially eroded, still applies in some states. For this reason, a general release, which would serve as a complete release of the injured party's claim against *all* tortfeasors, has limited application in a claim involving multiple tortfeasors. This is because an adjuster representing one insured in a multiple tortfeasor case frequently can settle the portion of the claim for which that insured is believed liable, but the claimant will not release the remaining tortfeasors because he or she wishes to reserve the claim against them. In such cases, a general release is inappropriate and other approaches, such as a *joint tortfeasor release* or a *covenant not to sue* (explained later) are more suitable.

The general release ordinarily is used, as stated earlier, when the insured is the only tortfeasor or where the amount being paid to the claimant represents the full amount of the claim and the claimant has no objection, under the circumstances, to releasing all tortfeasors.

In a claim involving injuries to a married person, the release should be signed by both spouses. This is because many states grant a wife as well as a husband a cause of action for loss of consortium. A release which contains only the signature of the injured spouse leaves the other spouse free to make a claim for the loss of services of the injured person. Regardless of the type of releases being taken, therefore, the release should be signed by both spouses when the claim involves injury to a married person. Ideally, releases should be notarized as well but this is impractical in most less serious claims.

In addition, it is important that the names of all individuals (or firms) covered under the insurance policy be specifically named as persons released. For example, if the driver of the car is someone other than the insured owner, the names of both individuals should be included in the release.

Many different types of releases are available to meet the special circumstances encountered by claim people, such as where multiple tortfeasors or children are involved. Releases for these special circumstances are discussed shortly.

Before describing some of the various types of releases used in the claim business, a word of caution about the design and format of releases is in order. Since adjusters are not permitted to engage in the practice of law, they may not design or create a release in order to individually tailor it to a specific claim situation. Such release must be

Exhibit 8-6
Release

Know all men by these Presents, That we, the Undersigned, for the sole consideration of ....

.... dollars,
the receipt of which is acknowledged, have released and discharged, and by these presents do hereby forever release and discharge ....

.... heirs,
executors, administrators, employers, employees, principals, agents, insurers, successors and assigns, for and from any and all liability, claims, demands, controversies, damages, actions and causes of action on account of personal injuries, death, loss of services or consortium, property damage and any and all other loss and damage of every kind and nature sustained by or hereafter resulting to the undersigned or any person or persons for whom the undersigned is acting as executor, administrator

or guardian, from an accident which occurred on or about the.............................. day of ...., 19.......,

at ....

....
and of and from all liability, claims, demands, controversies, damages, actions, and causes of action whatsoever, either in law or equity, which the undersigned, individually or in any other capacity, their heirs, executors, administrators, successors and assigns, can, shall or may have by reason of or in any wise incident or resulting from the accident hereinbefore mentioned.

As inducement to the payment of the sum aforesaid the undersigned declare that we fully understand the terms of this settlement, and that we voluntarily accept said sum for the purpose of making full and final compromise, adjustment and settlement of all loss, damages and injuries hereinbefore mentioned or referred to, and that the payment of said sum for this release is not an admission of liability by the payor, but that the payor expressly denies liability.

It is understood and agreed by the parties hereto that the undersigned, by the execution of this instrument, do..................

not release or discharge ....

...., who was also involved in the above accident, from any claim or claims for damages arising out of such accident, which the undersigned may have against said ....

....

...., but on the contrary all such claims, demands, and causes of action against said .... are hereby specifically reserved.

It is agreed that distribution of the above sum shall be made as follows ....

....

....

....

....

In Witness Whereof, We hereunto set our hands and seals this .... day of ...., 19......

In presence of

Name	.... (Seal)
Address	.... (Seal)
Name	.... (Seal)
Address	.... (Seal)
Name	.... (Seal)
Address	.... (Seal)
Witnesses sign here	**Claimants sign here**

Exhibit 8-7
Release in Full of All Claims and Rights (General Release)

For and in consideration of the sum of ______________________ ____ ($________________), receipt of which is acknowledged, I release and forever discharge ____ their principals, agents, representatives and insurance carriers from any and all rights, claims, demands and damages of any kind, known or unknown, existing or arising in the future, resulting from or related to personal injuries death or property damage, arising from an accident that occurred on or about the ________ day of ________, 19____, at or near ______________________________

This release shall not destroy or otherwise affect the rights of persons on whose behalf this payment is made, or persons who may claim to be damaged by reason of the accident other than the undersigned to pursue any legal remedies they may have against the undersigned or any other persons.

I understand that this is a compromise settlement of all my claims of every nature and kind whatsoever arising out of the accident referred to above, but is not an admission of liability. I understand that this is all the money or consideration I will receive from the above described parties as a result of this accident. I have read this release and understand it.

Signed this __________ day of __________ 19_____, at __________

______________________	______________________
WITNESS	SIGNATURE
______________________	______________________
WITNESS	SIGNATURE

drawn by lawyers. Filling in the blanks of a preprinted release form, however, is acceptable because it does not constitute the practice of law. Claim people need to keep this distinction in mind as they go about the daily business of handling claims.

Types of Releases and Settlement Agreements

Joint Tortfeasor Release This type of release is designed for claims involving multiple tortfeasors. As mentioned earlier, the common-law principle that a release of one tortfeasor releases all tortfeasors has been substantially eroded. Many states have modified the common law through the enactment of the Uniform Contribution

Among Tortfeasors Act. This statute creates a right of contribution among joint tortfeasors in favor of the joint tortfeasor who settles with the claimant, a right the common law does not recognize. The law in these states requires the use of special types of releases which are commonly referred to as *joint tortfeasor* releases. (See Exhibit 8-8.)

An example of a release which might be used in a comparative negligence state is shown in Exhibit 8-9. In the last paragraph, the release indicates that no representation is made as to the percentage of liability of any party, but the claimant releases the insured from whatever percentage of negligence may hereafter be determined to be the percentage of causal negligence attributable to the insured.

Joint tortfeasor releases vary somewhat by state and the actual release language may be influenced by local law such as a comparative negligence law. For this reason, also, they must be drawn by counsel.

Generally, a joint tortfeasor release provides a means of releasing all the insured's liability to the injured person while leaving the latter free to make claim against the other joint tortfeasors. It is used where an adjuster is able to settle his or her insured's portion of the claim but a general release is inappropriate because the claimant wishes to retain his or her claim against the remaining tortfeasors. Ordinarily, it also protects the insured from a possible claim for contribution if the claimant is successful in an action against the remaining tortfeasors.

Covenant Not to Sue A *covenant not to sue* serves essentially the same purpose as a joint tortfeasor release. Both documents are used in claims involving multiple joint tortfeasors. Like the joint tortfeasor release, a covenant may be used when an adjuster, representing one of several joint tortfeasors, can settle his or her insured's portion of the claim with the understanding that the claimant is free to make claim against the remaining tortfeasors. Both the covenant and the joint tortfeasor release include language which indicates that the claimant reserves such rights against the other tortfeasors.

Ideally, adjusters representing several joint tortfeasors agree on an acceptable apportionment of the injured party's claim and usually one adjuster obtains a general release for the full settlement, naming all tortfeasors in the release. In actual practice, however, such agreements among claim people are sometimes difficult to achieve. In that event, if one adjuster has developed a rapport with the claimant and is able to settle his or her insured's portion of the claim, a covenant or joint tortfeasor release (depending upon the jurisdiction) may be used.

Not all states permit the use of covenants. In states which have enacted the *Uniform Contribution Among Tortfeasors Act,* or a variation of it, special or nonstandard releases, such as a joint

Exhibit 8-8
Release (Joint Tortfeasor Act)

We, the Undersigned, in consideration of ($900.00)- -- Nine Hundred and 00/100 dollars, the receipt of which is acknowledged, do hereby forever release and discharge (Names of Insureds responsible for the loss) ______ herein after called the Payor, their heirs, executors, administrators, employers, employees, principals, agents, insurers, successors and assigns, from any and all liability, damages, actions and causes of action on account of personal injuries, death, loss of services or consortium, property damage and any and all other loss and damage of every kind and nature sustained by or hereafter resulting to the undersigned, his heirs, successors and assigns or any person or persons for whom the undersigned is acting as executor, administrator or guardian from an occurrence on or about the loss date day of month of loss, 19 year, at (location of loss -- address -- street -- highway -- city -- county -- state.).

It is further understood and agreed that all claims or damages recoverable by the undersigned against all other persons, firms, partnerships or corporations, jointly or severally liable to the undersigned in tort for injury to person or property as a result of said accident are hereby reduced by (amount of settlement -- $900).

The undersigned hereby warrant that I/we have not heretofore released any person, firm, partnership or corporation from any claim or liability for damages arising from said occurrence.

As inducement to the payment of the sum aforesaid the undersigned declare that we fully understand the terms of this settlement, and that we voluntarily accept said sum for the purpose of making full and final compromise, adjustment and settlement of all claims against the Payor, and that the payment of said sum for this release is not an admission of liability by the Payor, but that the Payor expressly denies liability.

This release is not intended to nor shall it be construed as releasing or discharging any other tortfeasor who may be liable for the injury and damage sustained in the above occurrence.

It is agreed that distribution of the above sum shall be made as follows Entire amount to be paid to the undersigned.

In Witness Whereof, We hereunto set our hands and seals this today's date day of this month, 19 year.

In presence of

Name (Signature of witness)	To be signed by claimant (Seal)
Address ______	To be signed by claimant's spouse (Seal)
Name ______	______ (Seal)
Address ______	______ (Seal)
Witnesses sign here	**Claimants sign here**

Exhibit 8-9
Release (Comparative Negligence)

I/we, the Undersigned, in consideration of ______________________________
____________ dollars, the receipt of which is acknowledged, do hereby forever release and discharge ______________________________
herein after called the Payor, their heirs, executors, administrators, employers, employees, principals, agents, insurers, successors and assigns, from any and all liability, damages, actions and causes of action on account of personal injuries, death, loss of services or consortium, property damage and any and all other loss and damage of every kind and nature sustained by or hereafter resulting to the undersigned, his heirs, successors and assigns or any person or persons for whom the undersigned is acting as executor, administrator or guardian from an occurrence on or about the ____________ day of ____________ 19____, at ______________________________
____

This release is not intended to nor shall it be construed as releasing or discharging any other tortfeasor who may be liable for the injury and damage sustained in the above occurrence and I/we specifically reserve the right to make claim and prosecute actions against any other tortfeasors not a party to this agreement for damages arising from the said occurrence.

The undersigned hereby warrants that I/we have not heretofore released any person, firm, partnership or corporation from any claim or liability for damages arising from said occurrence.

As inducement to the payment of the sum aforesaid the undersigned declare that I/we fully understand the terms of this settlement, and that we voluntarily accept said sum for the purpose of making full and final compromise, adjustment and settlement of all claims against the Payor, and that the payment of said sum for this release is not an admission of liability by the Payor, but that the Payor expressly denies liability. Further, no representation is herein made or intended as to the percentage of liability of any party, but the undersigned releases the Payor from whatever percentage of negligence may hereafter be determined to be the percentage of causal negligence attributable to the Payor.

It is agreed that distribution of the above sum shall be made as follows: ____________
____
____

In Witness Whereof, We hereunto set our hands and seals this ________ day of ____________, 19____.

In presence of

Name ____________________ ____________________ (Seal)
Address ____________________ ____________________ (Seal)
Name ____________________ ____________________ (Seal)
Address ____________________ ____________________ (Seal)
Witnesses sign here Claimants sign here

tortfeasor release, may be used. In some of these states, a covenant not to sue may be used as well. Claim people should be guided by company claim policy regarding which document is used in such multiple tortfeasor situations.

It needs to be emphasized that a covenant not to sue is *not* a release. The claimant simply agrees not to sue the individual named in the covenant. The claimant is still free to sue the other tortfeasors. In the event that the claimant also sues the settling tortfeasor, that tortfeasor may countersue for breach of contract. The tortfeasor should ordinarily recover the amount of the claim settlement as well as the legal costs incurred in bringing the counterclaim. (A sample covenant not to sue appears in Exhibit 8-10.)

High/Low Agreements A *high/low agreement* can be described as a settlement arrangement in which the parties to a lawsuit agree to guarantee minimum and maximum settlement figures. The jury's verdict decides the actual payment to be made. The parties do not agree upon a settlement figure but rather a settlement *range,* from which the settlement figure is determined when the jury renders its verdict.

A high/low agreement might work as follows. The settling defendant guarantees a specific minimum payment for the plaintiff, regardless of the jury's verdict. The plaintiff, in turn, agrees to limit the settling defendant's liability by accepting a *maximum* or upper limit on the defendant's potential liability. These agreements are usually made with the understanding that regardless of the verdict, there will be no appeal. Thus, a defendant's verdict or a verdict below the guaranteed minimum, would result in the minimum amount being paid as a settlement figure. A judgment in excess of the maximum would be reduced to the maximum figure. In the event that the jury's verdict is rendered for an amount between the guaranteed minimum and maximum, the verdict itself becomes the settlement figure.

This type of agreement has particular application to cases in which the defendant's liability is doubtful or questionable but due to the seriousness of the injuries, the potential exposure is significant. The plaintiff benefits in that he or she is guaranteed some recovery even if the case is lost whereas the defendant has a ceiling on his or her liability should a verdict be rendered for the plaintiff.

High/low agreements have several advantages. Setting a maximum figure allows the defendent to limit his or her exposure to a huge verdict and removes the threat of a bad faith claim stemming from an excess verdict against the defendant. In addition, the expense and time delay of an appeal is avoided by the parties. Finally, since the case still goes to trial, both plaintiff and defendant gain the satisfaction, after a long period of case preparation, of knowing the jury's decision. In short, both parties benefit from the process.

One possible disadvantage of high/low agreements is that the concept might tend to encourage litigation because plaintiffs believe that they can recover something even when liability against the defendant is doubtful. In addition, the idea that the jury ordinarily is not informed of such agreements and may have been misled as to its role in the case, might tend to create some resentment.

In the final analysis, however, it would seem that high/low agreements do much to expedite cases, reduce legal expenses associ-

Exhibit 8-10
Covenant Not to Sue

FOR AND IN CONSIDERATION of the payment to me/us at this time of the sum of ________________ Dollars ($________),the receipt of which is hereby acknowledged, I/we, being of lawful age, do hereby covenant and agree jointly and severally, that I/we will never at any time make any demand or claim, or commence, prosecute, cause or permit to be prosecuted, any action at law or in equity, or any proceeding of any description against ________________

____

because of any or all damages, costs, loss of services, expenses and/or compensation, on accout of, or in any way growing out of, any and all known and unknown personal injuries and property damage resulting, or to result, from an accident that occurred on or about the ________ day of ________ 19______, at or near ________________

____

I/we further promise and bind myself/ourselves jointly and severally, my/our heirs, administrators and executors to indemnify and hold forever harmless the said ________________

____

heirs, successors and assigns and agree to repay any sum of money and expense, that he/she/they may hereafter be compelled to pay because of the said known and unknown personal injuries and property damage.

I/we hereby declare and represent that the injuries sustained are permanent and progressive and that recovery therefrom is uncertain and indefinite, and in making this covenant and agreement it is understood and agreed that I/we rely wholly upon my/our own judgment, belief and knowledge of the nature, extent and duration of said injuries, and that I/we have not been influenced to any extent whatever in making this covenant by any representations or statements regarding said injuries, or regarding any other matters, made by the persons, firms or corporations herein mentioned, or by any person or persons representing him or them, or by any physician or surgeon by him or them employed.

I/we specifically reserve the right to make claim and prosecute actions against any and every other person, firm or corporation not a party to this agreement for damages arising from the said accident.

It is further understood and agreed that this settlement is the compromise of a doubtful and disputed claim, and that the payment is not to be construed as an admission of liability on the part of ________________ ________________ by whom liability is expressly denied.

This Covenant Not To Sue contains the ENTIRE AGREEMENT between the parties hereto, and the terms of this agreement are contractual and not a mere recital.

I/we further state that I/we have carefully read the foregoing instrument and know the contents thereof, and I/we sign the same as my/our own free act.

WITNESS ____________ hand ________ and seal ________ this ________ day of ________________ 19 ________

CAUTION! READ BEFORE SIGNING

________________ ________________(SEAL)

________________ ________________(SEAL)

State of ________________
County of ________________ ss.

On this __________ day of ______________ 19 ________, before me personally appeared ______________ to me known to be the person.. described herein, and who executed the foregoing instrument and ________ acknowledged that __________ voluntarily executed the same.

____
Notary Public

My term expires, ________ 19 ____

(If this agreement is acknowledged before a Notary Public, no witnesses' signatures are necessary)

ated with the appeal process, and allow both sides some degree of victory. Claim people should be open to the use of such settlement agreements in appropriate cases, provided, of course, that they have the approval of claim management.

Mary Carter Agreements A *Mary Carter agreement* secretly guarantees the plaintiff a specified recovery which will be reduced or extinguished by any recovery from the other defendant(s). For example, suppose one defendant, the so-called *settling* defendant, guarantees the plaintiff $10,000—to be reduced or eliminated depending upon the amount the plaintiff recovers from the other defendants. If the plaintiff recovers $20,000, the settling defendant is released from paying anything. If the recovery against the other defendants is $5,000, however, the settling defendant must pay $5,000 so that the plaintiff will receive the $10,000 guaranteed amount.

In addition to the guarantee agreement, the settling defendant remains in the lawsuit and can benefit from a verdict which is favorable to the plaintiff, to the extent that it will reduce or eliminate the guarantee obligation. (A Mary Carter agreement may also include a loan receipt provision.)

Mary Carter agreements can benefit both the plaintiff and the settling defendant. The plaintiff benefits from such agreements because he or she gains the security of a guaranteed recovery regardless of the outcome of the trial. In addition, the plaintiff can make a double recovery, as in the case above where the verdict was $5,000 but the plaintiff gained an additional $5,000 from the settling defendant. The advantage to the settling defendant is that his or her potential exposure is limited or, better yet, eliminated, if the verdict is high enough.[11]

Mary Carter agreements have been criticized for encouraging collusion between a settling defendant and the plaintiff. The possibility that the settling defendant's potential liability may be reduced or eliminated (depending upon the outcome of the trial) provides an incentive for the settling defendant to help the plaintiff obtain as large a verdict as possible against the nonsettling defendant(s).[12] In addition, these agreements are viewed by many as being unfair because of the secrecy aspect of the agreement.

The courts are not necessarily uniform in their position on the validity of Mary Carter agreements. Some courts have ruled that such agreements are void as against public policy while other courts have held the agreements to be valid.

Probably the most significant issue associated with these agreements concerns disclosure.[13] Disclosing the agreement to the trial judge and perhaps to the nonsettling parties would avoid the chief concern of collusion and the possible prejudice to the nonsettling defendant which could result. In addition, dismissing the settling defendant from the suit is another possible solution being suggested to minimize the problems associated with these agreements.

Mary Carter Agreements have limited application and must be discussed with counsel regarding their possible use in certain settlement situations.

Release for Injury to Minor A minor is a person who has not attained legal age. In some states, the legal age is eighteen; in others it is twenty-one. A minor is under a legal disability and cannot give an effective release for his or her injuries.

Some states regard a release given by a minor as voidable at the minor's option, while others regard it as totally void. In either case, such a release provides the insured with little or no protection. In a claim involving injuries to a minor, there are actually two causes of action which arise:

1. The claim of the minor for his or her injuries, including pain and suffering, discomfort, and permanency, if any. The release is executed by a guardian (usually the parents) or custodian upon approval by the court.
2. The claim for medical expenses and loss of the minor's services (consortium) by the parents.

While the parents can release their claim for expenses and loss of services, they cannot legally release the claim of their child. In order to effectively release a minor's injury claim, therefore, the release must be obtained in accordance with the statutory provisions of the state in which settlement is made. In cases involving serious injuries, the claim should be closed only by means of a court approved settlement through a guardian or by the procedure known as a "friendly suit."

When the claimant is represented by an attorney, the adjuster should have the attorney prepare the necessary documents to process the agreed upon settlement through the court. In the event the claimant is not represented, the adjuster may have local defense counsel prepare the papers and finalize the settlement through the court.

In serious injury claims, court approval is for the benefit and protection of the injured child. Ordinarily, the court will not approve the settlement unless it has reviewed a current medical report from the treating physician and is satisfied that the settlement fairly compensates the injured child. Since the procedure may vary by jurisdiction, claim people need to be familiar with the accepted procedure in their jurisdiction.

Parents' Release and Indemnity Agreement When a minor's injuries are slight and a full recovery is anticipated, many companies forgo the time and expense of the court approval process and use a *Parents' Release and Indemnity Agreement.* (See Exhibit 8-11.)

Although specific criteria may vary by company, this release should only be used under the following circumstances:

1. The injury is slight and medical expenses are nominal or the medical report indicates that the minor was examined by a physician and released.
2. No fractures are involved.
3. No scarring is involved.
4. There is no likelihood of future disability or impairment.

In any other circumstances, it is usually required that the settlement be submitted for court approval.

The release also contains an indemnity agreement that states, in effect, if the minor later makes a recovery against the insured, the parents will indemnify (or reimburse) the insured for any payment he or she must make to the claimant. The legal effect of the indemnity agreement is open to question.[14] Some courts have held the agreement void as against public policy. Before attempting to enforce such a provision, claim people should check with local counsel on the propriety of such an action.

In addition to the release, some companies require adjusters to obtain a statement from the parents which indicates that the child has fully recovered and is performing his or her usual activities. The settlement should be further supported by a current medical report showing complete recovery.

The release should be signed either by both parents, surviving parent, or the parent having legal custody, if the parents are divorced. The draft or check should be made payable to both parents individually and as parents and natural guardians of the minor child; e.g., "John Jones and Mary Jones, individually and as parents and natural guardians of Thomas Jones, a minor."

The release purports to release both the parents' and the child's claim. While it effectively releases the parents' claim for medical expenses and loss of services, as noted earlier, it does not legally release the claim of the minor child. As a practical matter, when the minor attains legal age, he or she may make claim for injuries sustained in the accident. The claimant would then be subject to the applicable statute of limitations with regard to the time in which suit must be instituted. Thus, while the release has some psychological value, it has no legal weight as far as the minor's claim is concerned.

If used with discretion—that is, in claims with slight injury and full

Exhibit 8-11
Parents' Release and Indemnity Agreement

IN CONSIDERATION of payment to me/us of Seven Hundred fifty and 00/100 Dollars ($ 750 00/100), receipt being acknowledged at this time, I/we, parent(s) and/or guardian(s) of John Claimant a minor, age 16 release and discharge Insureds heirs, executors, administrators, successors and assigns of and from any and all actions, causes of action, claims, demands, damages, costs, loss of services, expenses and compensation on account of or in any way arising out of any personal injuries or property damage which we may now or in the future have as parent(s) and/or guardian(s) of said minor, and also all claims or rights of action for damages which the said minor has or may have in the future, either before or after—he/she has reached his/her majority, resulting from an accident which occurred on or about March 16, 1980 at or near intersection of Berwick Avenue and Titus Road, Buckeye Village, Ohio

I/we further agree jointly and severally, my/our heirs, administrators and executors to repay to the said Insureds heirs, successors and assigns any sum of money, except the above mentioned sum, that he/she/they may be compelled to pay in the future because of the said accident.

It is further understood and agreed that this settlement is not to be construed as an admission of liability on the part of Insureds ________ by whom liability is expressly denied.

I/we have read the foregoing release and understand the contents of this agreement.

WITNESS TO SIGNATURES DATE May 15, 1980

Mrs. Ralph Neighbor

John Claimant Sr.
Parent or Guardian

Address ________

Mrs. Jean Aunt

Myrtle Claimant
Parent or Guardian

Address ________

recovery—it can be beneficial to both the claimant and the insurance company. In these small claims of little or no consequence, both the claimant's interests and the company's are served by avoiding the court approval process.

If the release is used properly (in small claims with no complications), it is likely that nothing more will ever be heard from the claimant. Proper use of the release depends to a large extent on good judgment. Claim people should be well aware of their company's position with regard to the limited use of such releases.

Uninsured Motorists Release and Assignment Agreement This release is used when an insured is injured in an accident with an uninsured motorist. (Some states require that insurance be provided for property damage as well as for bodily injury which is caused by an uninsured motorist.) The form also assigns to the company the right of subrogation to make claim against the wrongdoer for the amount of the uninsured motorists claim paid to the insured.

For uninsured motorists coverage to apply, there must be negligence on the part of the uninsured motorist and the insured must be legally entitled to recover damages from such motorist.

An important provision in the agreement concerns the insured's statement that he or she has not previously settled or signed a release with the uninsured motorist. If the insured has signed such a release, he or she ordinarily has extinguished the insurer's potential subrogation claim against the wrongdoer. The personal auto policy, under the heading, "Our Right To Recover Payment," prohibits the insured from taking any action after loss which would prejudice the insurer's rights. Thus, if the insured signed a release in favor of the wrongdoer, the uninsured motorists insurer could point to this provision in the policy as an indication of a breach of contract on the insured's part and refuse payment accordingly. (The policy also contains an exclusion which precludes coverage if the insured settles the bodily injury claim with the company's consent.) A sample Release and Assignment appears in Exhibit 8-12.

Nominal or Dollar Releases Frequently, adjusters encounter claimants who, while involved in an accident, have not sustained any physical injury or actually made a bodily injury claim. Some adjusters may take a "no consideration" release from such claimants, essentially for psychological reasons. In the past, a so-called "dollar release" was often secured from the claimant so that the claim file could be closed. Despite their possible psychological value, these releases have limited legal effect since no money (consideration) is exchanged.

Another alternative in such situations is for the adjuster to attempt a first-call settlement for a nominal amount, provided that some liability is present on the insured's part. Many claim people, however, feel that the better approach in such situations is to take a "no injury" statement from the claimant in combination with a release, or to forget entirely

Exhibit 8-12
Family Protection and Uninsured Motorist Coverage

RELEASE and ASSIGNMENT

Know all men by these Presents, that we, the undersigned, for and in consideration of

____________________ Dollars,

to us in hand paid by ____(Company Name)____, receipt of which is acknowledged, have released and discharged and do by these presents hereby forever release and discharge said ____(Company Name)____, its successors and assigns, for and from any and all liability, claims, demands, actions, and causes of action under Family Protection and/or Uninsured Motorist Coverage afforded under policy number ________ issued to ____________, resulting from an accident which occurred on or about the ________ day of ________, 19 ________, causing bodily injury, death or other loss to ____________. Furthermore, in consideration of such payment, the undersigned hereby assigns and transfers to the ____(Company Name)____ ____________, each and all claims and demands against any person, persons, firm or corporation, and particularly against ____(Operator uninsured vehicle)____ and ____(Owner uninsured Vehicle)____ arising from or connected with such loss or injuries to the extent of the amount named above. The undersigned further states that no monies have been paid to them by or on behalf of the party alleged to be at fault and that they have executed no release of their claims against such party and that they will assist the Company in the prosecution of all claims against the party alleged to be at fault and will execute any and all papers necessary to the prosecution of said claims and further agree that said claims may be prosecuted in their names by and on behalf of the ____________ ____(Company Name)____.

In Witness Whereof, we hereunto set our hands this ________ day of ________, 19 ________.

____________________ ____________________
Witness

____________________ ____________________
Witness

____

about taking a release which might, at best, have only some psychological value.

Release Draft Many companies utilize *release drafts* with specific release language on the reverse side of the draft. Such releases are most commonly associated with small to moderate property damage claims. The claimant's endorsement of the draft or check serves as a release of the claim.

Adjusters need to keep in mind that many unfair claim practice laws place restrictions on the use of release drafts. As a result, adjusters should be familiar with any such restrictions in their states.

On occasion, release drafts will be used in such a manner that adjusters will need to cross out the release language of the draft. Such situations might include an instance where the draft constitutes a partial payment or where it represents an advance payment to the claimant.

Telephone Recorded Releases Telephone recorded releases are occasionally taken by adjusters in smaller claims in which the claimant is not represented by an attorney. The acceptability and use of telephone releases vary by company and, to some extent, by jurisdiction. Telephone releases appear to fit in relatively well with telephone adjusting and, at times, may be obtained in place of a telephone recorded statement on small claims.

To obtain a telephone recorded release, the adjuster should introduce himself in the same manner as if a recorded statement is being taken. Then the recording might continue as follows:

> Adjuster: This recording will confirm that we have made an agreement to settle your claim arising out of the previously described accident. Do you agree to the settlement?
> Claimant: Yes, I do.
> Adjuster: Please state your full name, address, and date of birth and please spell your last name.
> Claimant: Does so accordingly.
> Adjuster: Do you understand that I represent __________?
> Claimant: Yes, I do.
> Adjuster: Have we reached a settlement agreement in your claim against __________ in the amount of __________?
> Claimant: Yes, we have.
> Adjuster: Do you understand and agree that the payment I am forwarding to you for the amount of settlement is a full and final settlement for any claims you may have as a result of an accident which occurred on __________.
> Claimant: Yes, I do.

Adjuster: The adjuster concludes the recorded release in the same manner as he or she would conclude a recorded statement.

Release When Claimant Is a Corporation or Partnership When a release is taken from a corporation, it must be signed by an officer of the corporation who has the authority to release claims. The signature should include the name of the corporation along with the particular officer's signature as follows:

"AJAX, Inc., by James Smith, Secretary."

Many insurers require that the corporate seal of the company be affixed to the release as well.

When the claimant is a partnership, a partner should sign the release and include the name of the partnership as follows:

"Joe and Tom Sign Company, by Thomas Jones, partner."

Setting Aside of Releases

With the discussion of the various types of releases and settlement agreements completed, it is now appropriate to examine the general question of setting aside or "avoiding" releases.

Generally, there has been a reluctance on the part of the courts, in the absence of clearly justifiable circumstances, to allow a claimant who has signed a release to subsequently avoid it. This reluctance was based on the courts' view that upholding releases is necessary in order to promote the orderly settlement of disputes and to reduce litigation. If releases were so easily broken, the resulting chaos in the settlement dispute process would tend to make releases meaningless.

Despite the traditional emphasis on the binding nature of releases, however, there are circumstances in which a release may be set aside. A release may be avoided by *mutual mistake* of the parties to the release or by *fraud* or misrepresentation in the execution of the release.

Mutual Mistake The concept of mutual mistake usually applies to cases in which a claim is settled without the full extent of the injuries being known to the claimant and adjuster. Based on the concept of mutual mistake, many courts hold that a release may be avoided if subsequent to signing the release, an injury is discovered which was not known to exist at the time the release was signed. The unknown injury is treated as a matter which was not within the contemplation of the parties at the time of settlement.[15]

A mutual mistake, therefore, which does not take into consideration an unknown injury at the time the release was signed may void the release. An example of such a situation might be a case where an accident causes a back injury upon which the settlement is based, and then, several weeks after signing the release, the claimant begins to experience epileptic seizures which are traced back to the accident.

In order to avoid the release, the mistake must relate to a past or present fact, material to the release, and not to an opinion concerning future consequences of a known injury.[16] Unforeseen or unanticipated complications arising out of *known* injuries are ordinarily not sufficient to avoid a release, in the absence of fraud or misrepresentation. Furthermore, a mistake on the claimant's part concerning his or her opinion or estimate of when recovery for the injury would be complete was held by one court to be insufficient to avoid the release.[17] In this case, the court stated that if there was a mistake, it was *unilateral,* or a mistake self-induced by the claimant and this would *not* be grounds to set aside the release.

Other courts which have addressed the distinction between a unilateral and mutual mistake have ruled similarly. For example, a release could not be avoided when a claimant, who was aware that she was suffering back pain but did not inform the adjuster, chose to sign a release because she believed the injury was minor.[18] The court concluded that had the claimant exercised reasonable care for her own safety, she could have ascertained the extent of her injuries, since there was no pressure on her to sign the release.

In addition, a claimant who signed a release before undergoing medical examination because he believed the injury was minor was considered by the court to have made a unilateral mistake which did not provide grounds for rescinding the release.[19]

Essentially then, if an injury is known at the time of settlement, the release is binding, even if unknown or unexpected consequences result from that injury. If the injury is unknown, and if the intent of the parties is to settle for all injuries sustained, then the release will not be binding as to the injury which was unknown at the time the release was signed. Generally, a release cannot be avoided merely because the injuries have proved more serious than the claimant believed them to be.

It needs to be noted, however, that there appears to be a growing view that avoidance of a release on the grounds of mistake should not depend on whether the mistake concerns unknown injuries, or unknown consequences of known injuries. Rather, it should depend on whether upholding the release produces an unconscionable (or grossly unjust) result.[20]

Another factor which may influence whether a release may be avoided is the specific language in some releases which relinquishes claims even for *unknown* injuries.[21] The courts are divided on whether such language will bar the claimant from avoiding the release. Some courts look to what was actually contemplated by the adjuster and the claimant when the release was signed in determining whether a mistake sufficient to justify avoidance existed. Other courts take the view that express language which relinquishes claims for both known and unknown injuries is conclusive.

Adjusters should also note that claims involving certain types of injuries may be more susceptible than others to attempts by claimants to break releases.[22] Neck and back injuries, in particular, appear to be the subject of considerable litigation, apparently because substantial injuries to these areas often defy detection or definitive diagnosis for long periods of time. Head injuries and injuries to internal organs also seem to produce a considerable amount of litigation which is aimed at avoiding releases.

It would seem that, in many cases, the chances of avoiding a release on the grounds of mutual mistake will diminish somewhat when the claimant is represented by an attorney. Attorneys are presumed to have adequate legal sense to properly advise claimants regarding an intelligent course of action on a claim.

Fraud A release may be avoided if there is evidence that the adjuster fraudulently secured the release from the claimant. Where an adjuster takes advantage of an illiterate or a person with extremely poor eyesight, for example, by telling that person that the document he or she is signing is merely an advance payment receipt or acknowledgement, this is fraud in the execution and the release will not be valid.

Even where the claimant is aware that the document being signed is a release, if the adjuster tells the claimant that the document will be regarded as only a partial release, this is fraud in the inducement. The release is voidable at the claimant's option, which means that he or she may accept or disaffirm it.[23]

Some states have enacted statutes which impose a specific waiting period before a release can be executed so as to minimize the chances that a recovering claimant might be exploited. It is advisable in serious injury claims that claim people refrain from taking a release until the claimant has obtained an accurate prognosis from the treating doctor.[24]

Most situations in which a claimant attempts to avoid a release will possess their own unique set of circumstances. In addition, existing case law in a particular jurisdiction will have a significant bearing on the claim person's response to the case. Claim people should be aware that there are circumstances in which a release may be avoided, but that resolving such questions ordinarily requires the assistance and advice of claim management and defense counsel.

Alternative Approaches to Settlement

Where circumstances warrant, adjusters may depart from the conventional method of settling claims in which a full and final release is secured from the claimant before a settlement check is issued. Claim people actually have a variety of options available with regard to the manner in which they finalize the settlement process. The following methods are frequently used by adjusters in appropriate circumstances and have proven to be helpful in maintaining claimant control and facilitating the settlement process.

Advance Payments The settlement technique known as *advance payments* can be effective in building good will for the adjuster and his or her company and in solidifying claimant control as well. With this technique, the claim person issues periodic drafts or checks to the claimant so that he or she may meet the various expenses incurred as a result of the accident. The payments are made without the requirement that a release be signed by the claimant.

Frequently, the claimant is in a position where he or she needs funds to pay mounting medical or related expenses necessitated by the accident. The money may be needed to pay doctor or hospital expenses, household help, repair or replacement of damaged property, replacement of lost income, or even for prosthetic devices such as a walker or wheelchair which have become necessary as a result of the accident.

The advance payments approach is generally used in cases of clear or probable liability where injuries are fairly serious and the claimant has demonstrated both a financial need and a cooperative attitude. With comparative negligence laws in effect in the majority of states, adjusters may use this approach even in cases where the claimant's contributory negligence is fairly substantial. By offering to alleviate any financial burden placed on the claimant as a result of the accident, the adjuster has created a positive claim handling environment by relieving the claimant's concerns about meeting medical and related expenses. The company is seen as an ally rather than an adversary and the attitude which ordinarily emerges is one of cooperation and trust. The claimant has a valid reason to believe that his or her claim will be handled fairly and this helps the adjuster establish and maintain claimant control.

Many companies which use this settlement technique require that an advance payment *receipt* be obtained from the claimant each time that a payment is issued. (A sample receipt is shown in Exhibit 8-13.) The receipt states that it is not a release and indicates that the advance payments will be credited to the total amount of the final settlement or judgment. A *distribution* section allows the adjuster to distribute the

Exhibit 8-13
Receipt for Advance Payment

(This is not a release)

This is to acknowledge receipt of $ __________ paid on behalf of ____________________________ to be credited to the total amount of any final settlement or judgment in my/our favor for alleged damages resulting from an accident on ________________, 19__________ at ____

I/We authorize that the above sum be distributed as follows: ___
____
____

Date ______________________ ______________________ (L.S.)

______________________ ______________________ (L.S.)
Witness
______________________ (L.S.)

______________________ ______________________ (L.S.)
Witness

drafts or checks in any number of ways. The payment may be made directly to the claimant or to a treating physician or hospital, or to both the claimant and the physician.

If the claimant is married, the receipt should be signed by both spouses. When possible, the claimant's signature should be witnessed by a third party such as a neighbor or friend of the claimant.

Many companies require that the words "advance payment" be included on the face of the draft or check. Other companies are less formal and simply issue a partial draft to the claimant. If the company issues drafts with preprinted release language on the reverse side, adjusters must be sure to cross out that language before issuing the advance payment draft.

When treatment has been completed and the claimant has returned essentially to his or her normal, pre-accident condition, the adjuster should initiate final settlement negotiations. When the claimant's recovery is not complete and some permanency is involved, the case will need to be evaluated on that basis as discussed previously. Once the settlement figure is agreed upon, a full and final release should be secured from the claimant. The total amount of the release should equal the total sum of the advance payment(s) and the remaining portion of the settlement figure, which represents general damages.

For example, if three advance payments were made for (1) $750, (2) $850 and (3) $1,200 respectively, for a total of $2,800, and the *total* settlement figure is $7,500, the release should be completed in the following manner: The total amount of the settlement is shown as $7,500 with the distribution section showing the three individual advance payments including the dates issued, totaling $2,800, and a final payment of $4,700 being made on this date. (The sum of these figures equals $7,500, the total amount of the settlement).

Advance payments may be used when the claimant is represented by an attorney as well but with less effect. Adjusters, of course, must follow their individual company's claim policy regarding the use of this settlement technique with attorneys. Generally, the courts look favorably upon the use of advance payments and allow the payments to be credited against the final settlement or judgment.

As a caution, claim people need to be conscious of both the insured's policy limits and the applicable statute of limitations when using advance payments. If the sum of the advance payments will approach or equal the policy limits, the company cannot use this settlement technique without the agreement of its insured. This is because once the policy limits are paid or exhausted by advance payments, the company's duty to defend ordinarily ceases. Since legal expenses incurred in defending the insured are payable *in addition to* the policy limits, the payment of such expenses represents a very important benefit to which the insured is entitled. The insured, therefore, probably will be reluctant to agree to use of the advance payments technique if it appears that through its use, the company may be relieved of its obligation to later defend a lawsuit because the policy limits have been exhausted.

With regard to the statute of limitations, if an adjuster is in the process of settling a claim and the statute is about to expire, the adjuster's failure to notify the claimant of this fact may waive the statute. (A statute of limitations refers to the period within which suit must be instituted on a claim.) If the statute has been waived, the claimant is not barred from instituting a lawsuit even though the statutory period within which the suit must be started has passed.

When adjusters are confronted with a situation in which an applicable statute of limitations will soon expire, it is advisable that they notify the claimant in writing of such limitation. The claimant should be informed that his or her rights will be affected by the statute of limitations and then efforts should be made to settle the case. If the case cannot be settled, the claimant will usually seek the services of an attorney so that his or her rights may be protected if the statute is not waived.

Ordinarily, the adjuster will have developed good claimant control and will have explained the situation in advance of forwarding the claimant a letter indicating that the statute is about to expire. In such cases, the letter is merely a formality, but a waiver must be in writing.

Adjusters must keep in mind that many Unfair Claim Practice acts require that when a claim is in the settlement negotiations stage and a statute is about to expire, claimants be notified in writing anywhere from thirty to sixty days in advance of the expiration date of the statute. The requirement is necessary to protect individuals who are in the process of negotiating the settlement of a claim with an insurance adjuster and who are unaware of the effect of the statute's expiration on their claim. When a claimant is represented by an attorney, the notification requirement ordinarily does not apply.

Although it would be naive to suggest that every claim handled on an advance payment basis results in a smooth disposition, it is probably safe to say that if used in cases which meet the previously mentioned criteria, chances are good that the ultimate outcome will be beneficial to all parties concerned. Experienced claim people often can differentiate between those claimants who will respond favorably to offers of advance payments and those who will simply use the payments to finance a lawsuit. Even where control is lost or a lawsuit eventually ensues, the advance payments issued can be credited against the final settlement or judgment figure. The benefits to be gained from this settlement technique seem to far outweigh its possible shortcomings.

In summary, the advance payment settlement technique is used widely and serves as a positive public relations tool for insurance companies. Equally important, it often helps establish and maintain claimant control and creates a favorable environment which facilitates the overall settlement process. If used in appropriate situations with cooperative and honest claimants, it can be beneficial to both claimants and insurers.

Open End Release Settlements While closing liability claims with a full and final release is the primary goal of claim people, there are occasions when securing a conditional release with limited open items is appropriate and necessary in order to dispose of the claim. A claimant may be unwilling to sign a full and final release because he or she anticipates that additional medical expenses may be incurred. In such situations, the adjuster may relieve the claimant's fears and obtain a signed release by agreeing to pay for additional medical expenses incurred within a specified time and up to a specified monetary limit.

An *open end release* is usually appropriate in situations where the claimant has completed treatment but where it is possible that he or she may need to see the doctor for a follow-up visit or incur slight additional medical expenses. By making allowances for these possibilities, the claimant's fears are relieved and the adjuster is able to obtain a release and close the claim file.

The maximum period of time and maximum amount to be allowed for future medical expenses vary somewhat by company and by the nature of the claim. If a claim is settled on an open-end basis and additional medical expenses are presented, it is not necessary to take an additional release. The original release is all that is necessary.

It is suggested that when a claim is settled and the claimant signs an open-end release, he or she should be given a blank attending physician's report, a medical authorization form, and a stamped, self-addressed envelope with the claim number written on the envelope. The adjuster should have the claimant sign the authorization and afterwards the adjuster should place it in the claim file. The claimant should be instructed that in the event a claim for future medical expenses is made, the doctor should complete the medical report and forward it to the adjuster. Upon receipt, the adjuster will review it to confirm that the expenses are accident-related and were incurred within the allocated time. If there is any question, the adjuster may use the claimant's signed medical authorization to question the doctor.

Open-end releases should not be used when a claimant is represented by an attorney or when the advance payment procedure would be more appropriate. For example, an open-end release should not be taken early in the case where treatment is continuing and it is expected that considerable medical expenses will be incurred by the claimant. In such cases, the advance payment technique if appropriate, should be used. This is not to say, however, that a claim which has been handled on an advance payment basis up to the final settlement discussion cannot be disposed of with an open-end release. The open-end release should be viewed as a closing document, whereas advanced payments are more appropriately seen as an *initiating* technique. (A sample open-end release is shown in Exhibit 8-14.)

Drop Drafts Frequently, settlement negotiations reach a point where neither side appears willing to move from its last offer or demand. When such a standstill exists, a claim person may wish to take a chance and send the claimant or attorney a *drop draft.* A drop draft is simply a draft in the amount of the last offer, or perhaps a slightly higher amount, which is either delivered or mailed to the claimant or attorney with the aim of finalizing the claim. The draft is ordinarily enclosed with a letter expressing the offer to the claimant or his or her attorney. It is believed that with check in hand, the claimant or attorney may be more willing to accept the offer.

A prime case for a drop draft is one in which the adjuster and claimant (or attorney) are fairly close to agreement but cannot actually

Exhibit 8-14
Open End Release

RELEASE OF ALL CLAIMS EXCEPT FUTURE MEDICAL EXPENSE

Know all men by these Presents, That we, the Undersigned, for the sole consideration of ______________________ dollars, the receipt of which is acknowledged, and in further consideration of the promise to pay such additional reasonable medical expenses as may be incurred within the next ________ months up to a maximum of ____________ dollars ($ ________) as a result of the accident described below do hereby release and discharge, and by these presents do hereby forever release and discharge ______________________ heirs, executors, administrators, employers, employees, principals, agents, insurers, successors and assigns, for and from any and all liability, claims, demands, controversies, damages, actions and causes of action on account of personal injuries, death, loss of services or consortium, property damage and any and all other loss and damage of every kind and nature sustained by or hereafter resulting to the undersigned or any person or persons for whom the undersigned is acting as executor, administrator or guardian, from an accident which occurred on or about the ________ day of ____________, 19 ________, at ____________

____

and of and from all liability, claims, demands, controversies, damages, actions, and causes of action whatsoever, either in law or equity, which the undersigned, individually or in any other capacity, their heirs, executors, administrators, successors and assigns, can, shall or may have by reason of or in any wise incident or resulting from the accident hereinbefore mentioned.

As inducement to the payment of the sum aforesaid the undersigned declare that we fully understand the terms of this settlement and that we voluntarily accept said sum for the purpose of making full and final compromise, adjustment and settlement of all loss, damages and injuries hereinbefore mentioned or referred to, and that the payment of said sum for this release is not an admission of liability by the payor, but that the payor expressly denies liability.

It is understood and agreed by the parties hereto that the undersigned, by the execution of this instrument, do ____________ not release or discharge

______________________,

who was also involved in the above accident, from any claim or claims for damages arising out of such accident, which the undersigned may have against said ____

______________________,

but on the contrary all such claims, demands, and causes of action against said

____

are hereby specifically reserved.

It is agreed that distribution of the above sum shall be made as follows ______

____

____

____

____

In Witness Whereof, We hereunto set our hands and seals this ________ day of ____________, 19 ________

In presence of

Name ____________	____________ (Seal)
Address ____________	____________ (Seal)
Name ____________	____________ (Seal)
Address ____________	____________ (Seal)
Name ____________	____________ (Seal)
Address ____________	____________ (Seal)
Witnesses sign here	Claimants sign here

settle the matter. The technique may, however, be used in cases where there is a greater disparity between offer and demand, especially in cases where the adjuster believes the claimant's demand is unreasonable and that the drop draft may bring the claimant down to reality.

A release may or may not accompany the drop draft. In smaller claims, the company may wish to waive a release while requiring one on larger claims. Some companies require a release to be executed when a claimant is represented by an attorney while other companies waive releases even when an attorney is involved.

No Release Settlements Some companies permit their adjuster to settle claims, usually claims under a specified dollar amount, without securing a release from the claimant.

This approach can create a positive public image for the company in that the claim is paid without placing any restrictions on the claimant in the event that additional medical expenses are incurred. The claimant is paid with the understanding that any future medical bills incurred will also be considered. This technique is sometimes referred to as a *walk-away* settlement as well.

A frequent result of such settlements is that the claimant appreciates the direct and open manner in which the claim is handled and no further claim is ever presented. Companies vary on their attitude toward settling cases without securing a release and adjusters must be guided by their individual company policy on this matter.

Structured or Periodic Payment Settlements Although the lump-sum cash settlement is the traditional method of settling bodily injury liability claims, a relatively new settlement device, which serves as a viable alternative to the traditional method, has emerged in recent years—the *structured or periodic payment settlement.*

A structured settlement involves periodic or installment payments which are made to the claimant. Usually these payments are made on a monthly basis either for a fixed period or for the claimant's life. In addition, scheduled lump-sum payments, often at five- or ten-year intervals, may be included. These lump-sum payments may be used by the claimant to pay for anticipated medical or rehabilitation expenses or for the future educational needs of the claimant or his or her children.

Along with the structured settlement, the settlement agreement often includes an initial cash payment that may be used by the claimant to pay for such items as unpaid medical or hospital expenses, other financial needs, or attorney fees. A separate structured settlement agreement may be arranged to pay the attorney's fees as well if the attorney is interested in such an agreement.

Actually, considerable flexibility and creativity may be exercised, depending upon the individual needs of the claimant and the imagination of the structured settlement broker or consultant. Structured or periodic payment consultants are available to assist claim people both in identifying cases appropriate for such settlements and in negotiating such cases.

The primary method of funding structured settlements is through an *annuity* which is usually purchased through a life insurance company. (An annuity is a type of life insurance policy or contract which makes periodic payments to the recipient for a fixed period or for life in exchange for a specified premium). Other options, however, including trusts or the purchase of stock/bond portfolios are also available to fund such settlements.

Advantages of Structured Settlements. While the desire to reduce claim costs in the wake of rising jury awards (which may include assessments for punitive damages) is largely responsible for the increased use by insurers of structured settlements, significant benefits are received by the injured party and his or her attorney as well.

With regard to the benefits received by insurers, a structured settlement costs an insurer less than a lump-sum settlement. This is so because the cost of an annuity, which is based on the present value of future benefits paid out over the claimant's lifetime is substantially less than the lump sum settlement amount. For example, a case worth anywhere from $100,000 to $125,000 on a lump-sum basis might be structured at a cost to the company of, say, $75,000 or less (the cost of the annuity), but the structured settlement will generate considerably more than $125,000 in benefits over the claimant's lifetime.

Probably the prime benefit to the claimant of a structured settlement is the *tax-free* nature of such a settlement tool. The proceeds of the settlement (which may be paid out regularly over the claimant's lifetime) are not taxable to the claimant recipient as income. The Internal Revenue Code excludes from gross income claim payments received by a claimant for injury or sickness regardless of whether they are received as a lump sum or as periodic payments. (Sec. 104(a)(2).)

While it is true that a lump-sum settlement which is received by the claimant is also tax-free, any income generated by investing that sum *is* taxable. On the contrary, the benefits received by the claimant over his or her lifetime from a structured settlement are *not* taxable as long as the custody and control of the annuity is not with the claimant. (The casualty insurer, in other words, most exercise control over the periodic payment process). Thus, in order to maintain the tax-free status of a structured settlement, the claimant cannot alter the original settlement agreement in any way.

Another related benefit is that a structured settlement provides sound money management for the claimant because a steady flow of funds is guaranteed over the claimant's life and, in many instances, for a longer period to his or her beneficiaries. This builds financial security for the claimant and may tend to enhance his or her credit rating as well.

The money management/security feature is particularly important in cases involving minors, uneducated claimants, or individuals who have a great difficulty in holding on to or managing money. Indications are that many recipients of windfalls from lotteries or court awards spent the money within a few years. A structured settlement protects such individuals from their own shortcomings.

Unlike the situation with the claimant, money received by the claimant's attorney is treated as income and is, therefore, taxable. However, the attorney may mitigate the tax impact by spreading payments over several years. In this way, the attorney is able to defer taxes that would otherwise be payable all at once had he or she settled on a lump-sum basis and received his full contingent fee at one time.

Finally, society benefits from structured settlements to the extent that these settlement devices relieve court congestion and minimize situations in which lump-sum settlements are squandered by claimants causing them to be without proper care or to be placed on welfare.

Which Cases Are Appropriate for Structured Settlements. Probably before a case should be considered for a structured settlement, it should be evident that the settlement technique will benefit both the company and the claimant. The structured settlement should enable the company to reduce the cost of the claim as well as provide the claimant with long-term financial benefits beyond those afforded by a lump-sum settlement. Once again, the particular needs of the claimant will substantially influence whether a structured or periodic payment settlement is utilized to dispose of the claim.

Although originally, structured settlements were seen as being applicable only to large claims involving serious injuries and disability, particularly to claims involving children, this is no longer the case. While at one time $100,000 might have been viewed as a starting point for a structured settlement, many companies are now proposing such settlements for claims valued at much lesser amounts. In fact, one claim executive has indicated that of forty-six structured settlements in which his company has been involved, more than half were for less than $25,000, and several were for under $15,000.[25] These settlement figures included not only the cost of the structured settlement but attorney fees and initial payment as well.

The kinds of claims for which structured settlements may be appropriate include those, as mentioned earlier, where individuals have difficulty managing money. Children, whose settlements frequently require court approval, are good subjects for structured settlements. In addition, structured settlements seem most appropriate in cases where claimants are seriously injured or disabled. Brain damage, paralysis, spinal cord injuries, loss of a limb, or burn cases are examples of the kinds of injury claims which seem suitable for structured settlements. Death claims where dependents are involved represent ideal cases for structured settlements as well. Another possibility for structured settlements is a comparative negligence case where the amount generated by the structured settlement can overcome the plaintiff's objections to a reduction in value due to liability.

Admittedly, this is an incomplete list because the creative nature of the parties to the settlement process in addition to the needs of the particular claimant often make additional situations suitable for such settlement devices.

Structured Settlement Example.

Facts:

The insured's automobile made a left turn into the path of the claimant, age twenty-nine, who was driving his motorcycle. The claimant's motorcycle was being operated without a functioning front brake, which probably reduced his ability to stop.

Liability:

Questionable to probable. Claimant can be charged with some negligence in this comparative negligence state in view of nonoperating front brake.

Injuries:

Compression fracture of L-2 with impingement of the spinal cord. The claimant suffered initial paralysis but in time improved to the point where he is now ambulating fairly well with some loss of sensation. Claimant's annual income is $12,500.

Approximately $8,500 in medical bills plus lost wages of about $10,000. Total Specials of about $18,500.

Evaluation:

Case evaluated on a lump-sum basis at about $85,000, to be raised or lowered depending upon the actual extent of recovery. As this amount reflects what the claim person feels the case would be worth on a clear liability basis, it can be reduced somewhat due to the fact that the claimant can be charged with some contributory negligence.

Final Settlement:

The case was closed on a structured settlement basis. Two annuities were purchased for a total of $26,549. One annuity cost $20,549 and funded the payout for the claimant; the other annuity cost

$6,000 and represented the loss of consortium claim of the claimant's spouse, and funded periodic payments for her.

The periodic payments were to be received as follows:

(a) Claimant
   (1) $200 per month for life or for 30 years (360 months) guaranteed, whichever is longer.
   (2) Deferred periodic payments to be received on:

Date	*Amount*
September 1, 1992	$3,750
September 1, 2002	7,500

(b) Claimant's spouse
   (1) $50 per month for life or for 30 years (360 months) guaranteed, whichever is longer.
   (2) Deferred periodic payments to be received on:

Date	*Amount*
September 1, 1992	$1,250
September 1, 2002	2,500

(c) Initial payment in the amount of $30,000 representing the claimant's attorney's fee. $8,500 had been previously paid to the claimant as an advance payment.
Total cost of settlement to the company: $65,049.

The general attitude among insurance people and defense attorneys, as well as many plaintiff attorneys, is that structured settlements have considerable merit and are beneficial to all parties participating in the settlement process.

There are some plaintiff attorneys, however, who insist on lump-sum payments for their clients because they question the extent to which benefits really accrue to the claimant in typical structured settlement agreements. In the opinion of one notable plaintiff attorney, the wise investment of a lump-sum settlement is preferable to a nontaxable annuity, the present value of which has no relationship to the real value of the case.[26] This attorney believes that court approval should be required in all structured settlements as it is in the case of infant claims and wrongful death actions. In addition, he believes that actuarial proof of present value should be disclosed to the claimant and attorney.

Another issue which occasionally creates some concern about structured settlements is the so-called *contingent liability* of the settling casualty insurance company. Despite the fact that typically an annuity is purchased from a life insurance company, the *settling casualty company* owns the annuity and remains responsible for the continued funding of the payments to the claimant. If the life insurance company becomes insolvent, the settling insurer is obligated to continue making the periodic payments. For this as well as for tax reasons, casualty insurers which make structured settlements should maintain their claim files until all stipulated payments are made. The claim file may be closed but should not be destroyed in the normal destruction process. (Some companies believe that a reserve should be carried even after a structured settlement is executed because of this contingent liability aspect.)

Obviously, it is important that casualty insurers be selective in the choice of life companies from which they purchase the annuity. Many insurers insist that the life company issuing the annuity be rated A + (excellent) by Best's Insurance Reports. (The A. M. Best Company evaluates insurance companies annually on the basis of their management, underwriting competence and reserve adequacy, to name a few of the criteria. Such ratings are widely accepted by industry executives and consumers as an accurate measure of a company's overall competencey and financial stability.)

On the other hand, if a *settling casualty insurer* becomes insolvent, the claimant faces a dilemma because he or she has no rights to the life insurance company annuity, but can only look to the casualty insurer for continued payments. In effect, the claimant becomes a general creditor of the casualty insurer and, as such, must share this status with all other general creditors of the company. The chances of the claimant collecting on future payments may be reduced under such circumstances.

Remedies are available to settling insurers, however, whereby they may transfer or assign the responsibility for making future periodic payments to a third party. In such cases, the settling insurer obtains a full release from the claimant and is relieved of its contingent liability for making future payments. Among the more common methods available for transferring the contingent liability of the settling insurer are reinsurance and bonding.

It is clear that structured or periodic payment settlements are currently being used with considerable frequency and in a large variety of cases. In addition, the settlement device appears to have the general approval of all parties involved in the settlement process, with perhaps some limited exceptions. It should be kept in mind, however, that the device involves some complex tax and security questions which must be closely examined by the parties to the settlement process. As long as structured settlements are perceived as providing benefits to all parties concerned, they should continue to be used and promoted as a means of settling many liability claims.

Reducing Claim Costs

Subrogation Subrogation is the right of the insurer (which has paid a loss to its insured) to be put in the position of the insured in order to pursue recovery from a third party legally responsible for the loss.[27] It is the substitution of one party (the insurer) for another (the insured) with reference to a lawful claim or right.

The right of subrogation is founded on the basic concept of equity or fairness which holds essentially that the party responsible for the loss should ultimately bear the loss. Thus, when because of a contractual obligation under an auto insurance policy, the insurer pays the insured's collision loss which was caused by a negligent third party, the insurer acquires the insured's rights and may sue the wrongdoer in order to recover the amount it has paid. Without the right of subrogation, the collision insurer could not recover from the negligent third party in which case the latter would be unjustly enriched. (It should be kept in mind that the subrogating insurer is subject to the same defenses which could be asserted against the insured by the wrongdoer.)

Occasionally, an insured will be asked to sign a "loan receipt" which enables the insurer to bring the subrogation action in the insured's name rather than the insurer's. The insured agrees in the loan receipt to repay the amount received from any recovery which is made in the subrogation action against the wrongdoer.

It needs to be emphasized that an insurer which pays its insured's claim on a *voluntary* basis—that is, when there is no contractual obligation to do so—does not acquire a right of subrogation against the wrongdoer. Should an insurer pay a technically not-covered claim (for agency reasons, perhaps it cannot later make a subrogation claim against the negligent third party. The third party could successfully argue that the insurer's payment was made on a voluntary basis in the absence of a legal or contractual obligation. This is known as the *volunteer* doctrine.

While the right of subrogation is based on the principle of equity, an insurer is usually entitled to subrogation by contract as well. Most insurance policies contain a subrogation clause. The subrogation provision in the personal auto policy reads:

OUR RIGHT TO RECOVER PAYMENT

A. If we make a payment under this policy and the person to or for whom payment was made has a right to recover damages from another we shall be subrogated to that right. That person shall do:

1. Whatever is necessary to enable us to exercise our rights; and
2. Nothing after loss to prejudice them.

However, our rights in this paragraph do not apply under Part D, against any person using your **covered auto** with a reasonable belief that that person is entitled to do so.

B. If we make a payment under this policy and the person to or for whom payment is made recovers damages from another, that person shall:
   1. Hold in trust for us the proceeds of the recovery; and
   2. Reimburse us to the extent of our payment.

Clearly, subrogation represents an important means of recovering a substantial portion of the claim dollars paid out to insureds. For this reason, claim people should be especially alert to claim situations in which subrogation may be a factor. Subrogation may be available in the following types of claims: collision, fire or other property, automobile damage, no-fault or medical payments, uninsured and underinsured motorists, workers' compensation, or claims involving bailment situations.

Many jurisdictions place limitations on set-offs involving medical payments as well as subrogation of medical payments as the coverage relates to uninsured motorists insurance. Some insurance policies simply do not provide for subrogation of medical payments. Adjusters should be familiar with the situation in their jurisdictions.

Notification of Third Party. Generally, the negligent third party or his or her insurer will be liable to the subrogating insurer if it settled the damaged party's claim with knowledge that the latter had already recovered from its own insurer. With this in mind, adjusters should be sure to notify the wrongdoer or his or her insurer in writing when they pay first-party claims which will be subrogated.

If after receiving payment from his or her own insurer, the insured settles with the third-party insurer and releases the wrongdoer, the release ordinarily voids the insurer's right of subrogation. If, however, the first-party insurer had notified the wrongdoer's insurer of its subrogation claim through a letter or lien, it ordinarily will be able to recover from the third-party insurer. Such notification is clearly an important means for a subrogating insurer to protect itself.

In the event that the insured collects from both the first party subrogating insurer and the wrongdoer's insurer before the latter has been put on notice of the subrogation claim, the subrogating insurer may make claim directly against its insured for breach of contract.

Note that the subrogation provision in the personal auto policy requires that the insured do nothing after loss to prejudice the insurer's rights. It also requires that the insured hold the proceeds of any recovery in trust and reimburse the subrogating insurer to the extent of its payment.

Means of Pursuing Subrogation. Subrogation may be pursued by simply making a claim, by filing a lawsuit or, in many instances, by fiing for arbitration. The preferred method of settling such disputes among insurers is through the routine claim process without the necessity of instituting suit. In this way, the costs of bringing the subrogation claim are kept to a minimum. Where there is a dispute between insurers which cannot be resolved through discussion and negotiation, many insurers use one of the various forms of arbitration which may be available. Arbitration allows the dispute to be heard by a disinterested third party and the cost of the process is minimal when compared to the cost of litigation.

One frequently used type of arbitration program, the *Nationwide Inter-Company Arbitration Agreement,* serves as a means of settling automobile collision subrogation claims between *signatory* companies. Only companies which have signed the arbitration agreement may use this program. Inter-Company Arbitration is inexpensive and ordinarily achieves fairly prompt results. The general subject of arbitration is examined in more detail in Chapter 9.

When to Subrogate. Claim people must use their common sense in determining when to subrogate. Subrogation probably should not be instituted when the amount of the damage is minor and liability is questionable. Particularly with respect to claims involving comparative negligence, initiating subrogation in certain situations can be unwise. There have been cases where collision claims were subrogated only to stir up a much larger counterclaim by the other party. A company which pays a $1,000 collision claim in a comparative negligence state when liability is questionable, had better make sure the damage to the adverse vehicle is not extensive before it pursues subrogation. If damage to the adverse vehicle was, say, $5,000, a counterclaim by the adverse driver's insurer, whose chances of recovery are as good as the insured initiating subrogation, could prove embarrassing and costly for the latter insurer should the adverse insurer win the case.

The amount of the claim as well as the expenses anticipated in bringing the subrogtion claim must be considered in deciding whether to pursue the action. In addition, the collectibility of the adverse party is obviously a prime consideration here as well.

It should be noted that an insurer may waive its right of subrogation by specific agreement. Many property and multiple-line policies provide a limited waiver of subrogation provision which reads:[28] "This insurance shall not be invalidated should the Named Insured waive in writing prior to a loss any or all right of recovery against any party for loss occurring to the property covered herein."

Indemnity, Contribution and Other Insurance In addition to subrogation, claim people should be alert to other possibilities of legitimately reducing claim costs. When investigating liability claims, adjusters should determine whether parties other than the insured are responsible for the accident. When investigation reveals the presence of other parties which may be negligent, the adjuster should seek, on behalf of the insured, either indemnity or contribution from these parties. (Indemnity and contribution were discussed in Chapter 4.)

Adjusters need to be particularly conscious in handling products or public liability claims of hold harmless or indemnity agreements which run in favor of their insured, since such argreements may indemnify the insured in the event that he or she is compelled to pay a claim.

Before determining liability in an auto accident or in claims involving machinery or equipment, adjusters should consider whether a mechanical defect in the automobile or equipment might have caused the accident. With regard to automobile claims, adjusters should check to see if the particular vehicle has been subject to any manufacturer or government recalls.

In fire losses, adjusters should investigate (or where necessary and warranted, call in a special investigator or expert to investigate) the *cause* and *origin* of fires resulting in substantial property damage. Aside from the arson issue, there may be subrogation possibilities in that a third party may be responsible for the fire loss. This is particularly important where the fire originated in a furnace, water heater, or in a TV set or other appliance.

Claim people should develop as standard practice the conscious pursuit of the often elusive negligent third party in claims which they handle. Adjusters should ask: How did this accident happen? Why did it happen? Who was responsible? What were the contributing causes? Where warranted, potentially negligent parties should be identified and placed on written notice of their involvement in the claim.

Finally, adjusters should be conscious of the possiblity that other insurance may be available to their insured which will act to reduce their company's claim payment. Frequently today, the broad policy definition of insured, along with the use of endorsements which further broaden that definition, results in coverage being available from multiple policies. Adjusters should continually look for instances where an insured may be entitled to the protection of other policies as well as the one in which he or she is specifically named as the insured.

Clearly, there is much adjusters can do to reduce their company's claim costs by being alert to situations which present opportunities for subrogation, indemnity, contribution, or other insurance. It is important that adjusters work toward fulfilling this responsibility by staying mentally alert and by conducting intelligent and concentrated claim investigations in all such instances.

Chapter Notes

1. Thomas D. Jensen, "Chiropractic Cross-Examination," *For The Defense,* Chicago, Ill: The Defense Research Institute (June 1984), p. 15.
2. Jensen, p. 16.
3. Jensen, pp. 16, 17.
4. *Dorland's Pocket Medical Dictionary,* 22nd edition (Philadelphia, PA: W. B. Saunders Company, 1977).
5. Peggy Mika, "Chiropractic Claims Can Be Challenged—Lawyer," *The National Underwriter* Property & Casualty Insurance Edition, 11 November 1983, p. 40.
6. Pat Magarick, *Successful Handling of Casualty Claims* (Brooklyn, NY: Central Book Company, Inc. 1974), p. 53.
7. The Insurance Training Group of Ohio (ITGO), a consortium of four Ohio based insurance companies, has produced a series of fraud training programs for use by the industry. Robert Cecil, trustee, Insurance Training Group of Ohio, 650 South Front Street, Columbus, Ohio 43216.
8. Insurance Crime Prevention Institute (ICPI), Westport, Connecticut, Wendall C. Harness, Director. The "Indicators of Casualty Fraud" are reprinted with the permission of ICPI.
9. This approach was proposed in a letter by Kevin P. Richter, Settlement Planning Incorporated, Minneapolis, to the editor of *For The Defense,* August 1982.
10. James H. Donaldson, *Casualty Claim Practice,* 3rd ed. (Homewood, IL: Richard D. Irvin, Inc., 1976), pp. 819–822.
11. Richard J. Nygaard and Janice K. Cook, "Settlement Agreements" (Minneapolis, MN: Rider, Bennett, Egan and Arundel).
12. Ronald W. Eubanks and Alfonse J. Cocchiarella, "In Defense of Mary Carter," *For The Defense,* February 1984, pp. 20-25.
13. Eubanks and Cocchiarella, pp. 22–25.
14. Donaldson, p. 837.
15. Thomas R. Trenkner, Managing Editor, *American Law Reports* 13 ALR 4th (Rochester, NY: The Lawyers Co-operative Publishing Co. 1982), p. 699.
16. Magarick, p. 288, citing case of *Melvin vs. Stevens, 458 P2d 977 (1969) Arizona.*
17. *Davis vs. Flatiron Materials Co., 511 P2d 28 (1971) Colorado,* as cited in 13 ALR 4th, pp. 703 and 704.
18. *Nogan vs. Berry 193 A2d 79 (1963) Delaware,* as cited in 13 ALR 4th, p. 704.
19. *Boccarossa vs. Watkins 313 A2d 135 (1973) Rhode Island,* as cited in 13 ALR 4th, p. 704.
20. 13 ALR 4th, p. 691.
21. 13 ALR 4th, pp. 691, 692.
22. 13 ALR 4th, p. 692.

23. Donaldson, p. 175.
24. Magarick, *Successful Handling of Casualty Claims,* p. 287, 288.
25. Alfred G. Haggerty, "Structured Settlements Advocated" *The National Underwriter,* (Property and Casualty Insurance Edition, 21 May 1982, p. 41. The article was based on a speech by Ralph W. Arnold, Vice President Claims, American Family Mutual Ins. Co., Madison, WI.
26. Aaron J. Broder, "Structured Settlements: Insurance Gimmick," *The National Underwriter* Property & Casualty Insurance Edition, 29 August 1980, pp. 25, 26.
27. Ronald A. Anderson, *Couch on Insurance,* 2d (Rev. ed) 61:1 Volume 16 (Rochester, NY: The Lawyers Co-operative Publishing Co., 1983), pp. 74, 75.
28. James J. Lorimer, Harry F. Perlet, Jr., Frederick G. Kempin, Jr. and Fredrick R. Hodosh, *The Legal Environment of Insurance,* Volume I (Malvern, PA: American Institute for Property and Liability Underwriters, 1978), p. 355.

Appendix To Chapter 8—Medical Terms

Abrasion—A rubbing or scraping off of the skin or mucous membrane.

Acetabulum—The cavity at the hip that receives the head of the femur.

Aneurysm—A sac formed by the dilation of part of an artery and filled with blood.

Angina Pectoris—Pain and oppression about the heart.

Ankylosis—Abnormal immobility and consolidation of a joint.

Anomaly—Deviation from normal, not standard.

Anorexia—Loss of appetite.

Anterior—Situated before or in front of—the front.

Arteriosclerosis—Hardening of the arteries.

Ataxia—An incoordination of muscular action.

Atrophy—A wasting or diminution of size.

Bursa—A small sac interposed between moveable parts of joints.

Bursitis—Inflammation of bursa.

Callus—A new bony deposit about a fracture by which union between ends of a fractured bone is effected.

Carcinoma—Cancer, a malignant tumor.

Cardiac—Pertaining to the heart.

Cauterize—To apply an agent that burns the flesh, e.g., hot iron or acid.

Cerebral Hemorrhage—A hemorrhage into the brain.

Cervical—Pertaining to the neck.

Clavicle—Collar bone.

Closed Reduction—External means, such as a plaster cast, used to set a fractured bone.

Coccyx—The lower end of the spine or tail bone.

Concussion—Severe jarring, commonly refers to concussion of the brain causing temporary unconsciousness. Usually the result of a blow.

Congenital—A developmental condition existing at or from birth.

Contusion—A bruise.

Cranial—Pertaining to the skull.

Cutaneous—Pertaining to the skin.

Diastolic—Pertaining to the phase of the heartbeat when the heart is expanded—the opposite of systolic.

Diathermy—The generation of heat in the body tissues due to the resistance offered by the tissues to high frequency electric currents passing through them.

Diplopia—Double vision.

Distal—Away from the central; the outer end.

Dorsal—Pertaining to the back—that part of the spine between the cervical and lumbar regions.

Duodenum—The first part of the small intestine nearest the stomach.

Dura—The outer fibrous membrane of the brain and spinal cord.

Ecchymosis—Discoloration from hemorrhage of blood under the skin (black and blue mark).

Edema—Accumulation of fluid in the tissue.

Effusion—The escape of fluid into a part or tissue.

Embolism—An obstruction of a blood vessel by a blood clot or other body.

Encephalitis—Inflammation of the brain.

Encephalography—X-ray examination of the brain.

Femur—Bone of leg between hip and knee.

Fibula—Outer bone of leg between knee and ankle.

Flexion—Act of bending.

Fracture—The breaking of a bone.

Frontal—Pertaining to the anterior part—forehead.

Fusion—The fixation of a joint by surgery—the abnormal coherence of adjacent parts or bodies.

Gastroenteritis—Inflammation of the stomach and intestines.

Hematoma—A blood tumor, blood blister.

Humerus—Bone between shoulder and elbow.

Hypertension—High blood pressure.

Hypertrophy—An abnormal enlargement of a part of an organ.

Hypotension—Low blood pressure.

Ileum—Distal end of small intestine.

Ilium—The upper part of the innominate bone or pelvis.

Impacted—Driven firmly in—closely lodged.

Inguinal—Pertaining to the groin.

Intravenous—Within a vein.

Ischium—The lower hind part of the hip bone.

Keloid—A fibrous tumor of the skin—an overgrowth of scar tissue.

Laceration—A wound produced by tearing.

Lamina—An arch of bone between the transverse and spinus processes of the vertebra.

Laminectomy—A cutting out of the lamina of a vertebra.

Lateral—Pertaining to a side.

Ligament—A tough fibrous band connecting bones or supporting viscera.

Lordosis—Curvature of the spine with a forward convexity.

Lumbar—Pertaining to the lower part of the back.

Malingerer—One feigning injury or illness. A faker.

Malleolus—Inner-lower end of tibia; outer-lower end of fibula. The "knobs" of the ankle.

Mandible—The lower jaw bone.

Maxilla—A jaw bone. Usually refers to upper jaw bone or superior maxilla. Inferior maxilla refers to lower which is also known as mandible.

Medial—At or toward the midline of the body.

Metacarpus—Part of hand, one of short bones between wrist and phalanges.

Metastasis—Transfer of disease from one organ to another.

Metatarsus—Part of foot, one of short bones between tarsus and toes.

Myelogram—Examination of the spinal canal by means of fluoroscopy (X-ray) after the injection of a contrast medium.

Myopia—Nearsightedness.

Necrosis—The death of tissue or bone.

Neuralgia—A painful infection of the nerve caused either by functional disturbance or by inflammation in the course of the nerve.

Neuritis—Inflammation of a nerve.

Neurologist—One specializing in the treatment of nervous disease.

Neurosis—A nervous disease.

Non-Union—Failure of the ends of a fractured bone to unite.

Objective—Perceptible to the senses of another person as opposed to subjective. (Where a physician can see, feel, etc. the ailment.)

Occipital—Referring to back part of head.

Olecranon—The large process forming head of ulna, elbow.

Open reduction—Use of surgery to repair a fractured bone.

Orthopedic—Pertaining to the correction of deformities of the bones.

OS Calcis—Heel bone.

Osteoarthritis—Inflammation of bones and joints.

Osteomyelitis—Inflammation of marrow and bone.

Parietal—Pertaining to the walls of a cavity, usually refers to the two bones forming the roof of the skull.

Patella—Kneecap.

Pectoral—Pertaining to the chest or breast.

Phalanx—Any bone of a finger or toe. The various phalanges are called proximal (nearest to hand or foot), middle, and distal (farthest).

Phlebitis—Inflammation of a vein.

Post Concussion Syndrome—A complex of symptoms usually alleged to be the result of a violent, jarring blow to the head.

Posterior—Situated behind or toward the rear.

Quadriplegia—Paralysis of all four limbs.

Radius—Bone of forearm between wrist and elbow located on thumb side of arm.

Renal—Pertaining to kidneys.

Roentgenogram—X-ray film or plate after exposure and development.

Scapula—Shoulder blade.

Sciatica—Neuritis of the sciatic nerve which runs down the back of the thigh from the ischium bone of the hip region.

Scoliosis—Abnormal curvature of the spine, usually laterally.

Septum—A dividing wall or partition. Deflected septum frequently means fractured nose.

Spina Bifida—A congenital defect of the spine in which the spinous process and/or the laminae are missing from one or more vertebrae.

Spinal tap—Removing spinal fluid by use of a needle—spinal puncture.

Spleen—A blood-processing, gland-like organ in the upper left part of the abdominal cavity.

Spondylitis—Inflammation of the vertebrae.

Sternum—Breastbone.

Subdural—Under or near the dura.

Subjective—Not perceptible to the senses of another person. (Where the claimant says he or she hurts but there is no objective evidence.)

Subluxation—Incomplete or partial dislocation.

Suture—A surgical stitch or seam.

Systolic—Pertaining to the phase of the heartbeat when the heart muscle is contracted—the opposite of diastolic.

Tarsus—Ankle region of the foot or the small bones supporting it.

Temporal—Pertaining to the temple.

Tendon—A fibrous cord of tissue connecting bone and muscle.

Thoracic—Pertaining to chest.

Thrombosis—The formation of thrombus. The effect of a thrombus.

Thrombus—A plug from a blood clot in a vessel at point of formation.

Tibia—Large bone between knee and ankle.

Trauma—A wound or injury.

Traumatic Neurosis—A nervous functional disease caused by trauma. (It was once described by a doctor on cross-examination as: "A functional nervous disease born of fear, stimulated by avarice and kept alive by the attorney for the plaintiff.")

Trochanter—Either one of the two processes below the neck of the femur.

Ulna—The larger bone of the forearm between wrist and elbow. It is on the little finger side of forearm.

Urethra—The passage through which urine is discharged from the bladder.

Varicose Vein—A greatly enlarged and contorted vein.

Vascular—Pertaining to or full of vessels.

Vertebra—Any one of the thirty-three bones of the spinal column.

Vertigo—Dizziness.

CHAPTER 9

When the Negotiation Process Breaks Down

FIRST-PARTY DISPUTES

The claim representative will probably experience a breakdown in the negotiation process early in his or her career, since the entire nature of claims adjusting relates to adversary problems and situations. When this occurs the adjuster should make every attempt to prevent the adjustment of the claim from becoming unmanageable or ending up in litigation before final disposition can be made. It should be noted that such breakdowns do not necessarily reflect the incompetency of the adjuster. Many factors may contribute to this type of aggravated status, such as unreasonable insureds, repairmen, or attorneys. Should the claims person in any way be responsible for the breakdown, the best method of changing the direction of the claim is to acknowledge the shortcomings and proceed with the intent of disposing of the claim in a fair and equitable manner.

An unreasonable insured must be dealt with as diplomatically as possible and perhaps the best way to proceed is to be certain that the insured understands what the adjuster is trying to accomplish and why. Good communication is imperative.

Coverage Disputes

There are any number of ways that a coverage dispute may present itself in relation to facts not fitting the available coverage, including:

1. accident not occurring in the policy period,
2. exclusion applying to facts of the claim,
3. late notice, and
4. comprehensive coverage versus collision coverage.

Other coverage controversies will certainly occur during an adjuster's career, but those listed are probably the most prevalent.

Accident Not Occurring in the Policy Period The obvious illustration of this type of dispute involves an accident that occurs on a date preceding or following the dates shown in the policy. This example was more prevalent when all or most policies were written on an annual basis and renewal of coverage necessitated the issuance of a new policy. Presently, the majority of insurers issue policies for three- or six-month periods, with renewal consisting of the payment of the premium before the due date, through direct billing by the insurer. The same policy is used for the new coverage period and the new policy dates are shown on a new declarations page, usually sent with the premium billing. Also, any changes, such as a replacement auto or addition or removal of coverages, are noted on separate endorsements.

With this latter method of renewing coverage, there are times when the insured fails to pay the premium in time, or the insurer fails to receive the payment before the due date. If an accident occurs after the due date, a serious question of coverage is presented and it is the adjuster's duty to investigate the coverage question before the insurer can take a position related to coverage. Before the investigation proceeds, the first step is to obtain a signed nonwaiver agreement from the named insurer or to send a reservation of rights letter to the named insured.

Following, a statement must be secured from the named insured to determine what activity took place regarding the premium payment. At times, the insured will state that the payment was mailed in time, thus hoping to put the burden on the postal service. The adjuster should ask for some evidence of that payment, such as a copy of a certified check, receipt of a money order, or an entry in the insured's check register. Copies of this evidence should be obtained.

It may also be necessary to secure a statement from the agent if that party was involved in the transaction. In addition to the statement, copies of the agent's notes or records should also be secured if applicable to the issue.

All facts should then be presented to the examiner with the claim representative's recommendation regarding the coverage question.

There is another consideration to be aware of, related to direct-billing policies. Often, the insurer allows a "grace period" or a "continuous cover offer" following the due date. Both references relate to an extension of time if the premium is received by the insurer before the end of the period. If an accident occurs prior to the end of the grace period and the premium has been paid, the insurer will grant the coverage. If not paid within the grace period, the policy lapses retroactively on its original expiration date.

Overall, coverage questions are usually sensitive in nature and care must be taken to obtain all facts before the insured is advised of the insurer's position. Conversely, the investigation must be secured as early as possible, so that it cannot be said that the insurer took an unreasonably long time to resolve the coverage question.

As the preceding discussion suggests, the adjuster must be familiar with the employer's corporate policy regarding the coverage problem, and take action promptly.

Exclusion Applies to Facts The investigation of the claim will establish the facts and they must then be compared to the coverage and exclusions to determine if coverage applies. An example in the general liability policy under the completed operations section is illustrated by the contractor who installs a new roof on a dwelling and rain water leaks through to damage the interior. The coverage of this section would apply to the interior damage, but not to the roof, as it was work done by or for the insured (contractor) and excluded in the policy.

Late Notice On many occasions, the loss report is not received by the insurer for many days or months after the date of loss. If the agent was aware of the loss immediately thereafter, but did not report it to the insurer, it is usually agreed that notice to the agent constitutes notice to the company and the late notice becomes a moot point. If the loss is unknown to the agent or company until an unreasonable lapse of time, a non-waiver agreement must be secured or a reservation of rights letter must be mailed to the insured so that the insurer does not waive any of its rights in the process of investigation. If it is determined that the late notice did not prejudice the insurer's position, coverage should be granted, as that is what most courts would undoubtedly rule in such a situation. If there is any element of doubt connected with the coverage decision, it should be resolved in the insured's favor as courts have ruled that any ambiguity in the policy provisions must be interpreted in favor of the insured. Caution must be applied by discussing the matter with the examiner, as most times the adjuster does not have authority to make such a decision.

Comprehensive Coverage versus Collision Coverage This type of question usually is presented in claims where there is a deductible applicable to the collision coverage, but none to the comprehensive coverage. To illustrate, the insured reports striking an object which is stationary on the road, damaging the undercarriage. At times, insureds feel that these circumstances indicate a comprehensive loss, but such is not the case. Since the object was stationary, striking it constitutes a collision. Had the object been in motion, as being airborne, it would be a flying missile and coverage would be granted under the comprehensive section. The same situation could prevail if the insured carried comprehensive and no collision coverage.

Declaratory Judgments When a coverage dispute cannot be disposed of in any other way, the last alternative is to litigate in the form of filing an action for a declaratory judgment. This is the process employed when parties to a contract cannot agree to its meaning. However, in the case of the insurance policy, any ambiguity will be found in the insured's favor as the insurer had the opportunity to construct the contract, whereas the insured had to accept it as written. For this reason, the insurer must be realistic in arriving in its position in such a case.

This litigation can be filed by the insured or the insurer and is the basis for many legal decisions made in the past. The process is a lawsuit and is subject to appeals in higher courts, including state supreme courts. As in any lawsuit, the appeals are expensive, from the standpoint of defense costs as well as pre-judgment and post-judgment costs and expenses if the insured prevails.

Damage Disputes

Depreciation, Betterment, and Preexisting Damage Although many claims are settled with little or no difficulty, more than a few involve disputes relating to the cost of damage, particularly in the automobile damage field. They include the areas of depreciation, betterment, and preexisting or old damage. It was mentioned in an earlier chapter that the difference between depreciation and betterment is that the former takes a reduction of value into consideration. Thus, if the car is a total loss, the settlement is predicated on the actual cash value of the car, at the time of the loss. To further illustrate, a settlement will be based on the current value of a 1980 Buick, a four-year-old auto, and not on the basis of a 1984 Buick, as the car has been driven for four years and has accumulated the customary wear and tear for that length of time.

On the other hand, betterment is an improvement, thereby requiring the car owner to proportionately contribute to the cost of a new part when it is included in the repairs. For example, the insured is required to contribute that portion of the wear of a damaged tire that is registered on the gauge.

When discussing old damage, it is at times difficult to separate the cost from new damage, since the damaged part may consist of old and new damage. The deduction for the old depends on the extent of damage present. The old damage is easily detected when comparing it with new which is relatively fresh, disclosing clean metal under the surface where the damage appears. The old damage often contains areas of rust and/or dirt.

In dealing with any of these factors, the adjuster should take a positive, yet diplomatic approach by properly explaining the applicable factor and emphasizing the fairness of the position being taken. Various examples can be cited by the adjuster to explain the fairness of the insurer's position.

Appraisal This method of disposing of a dispute is described in detail in Chapter 6 and as stated, is a preferred method as compared to time consuming and costly litigation. The claim representative should make it a point to be familiar with the Appraisal section in the auto policy.

Other Insurance Clause The personal auto policy contains an "Other Insurance" clause which states, "If other insurance also covers the loss we will pay only our share of the loss. Our share is the proportion that our limit of liability bears to the total of all applicable limits."[1] This means that the policy will not duplicate payment of an amount that has already been provided by another policy. Rather, this clause states that this policy will cover only a proportionate share of the loss as it bears to the total of limits. If there are two applicable policies providing coverage and each policy has limits of 50,000/100,000 for bodily injury, each policy with this clause would pay 50 percent of the amount of the loss as both policies contain the same limits. If the limits differed, such as 25,000/50,000 in one policy and 50,000/100,000 for the other, the former policy would pay 33 1/3 percent of the loss and the latter pays 66 2/3 percent. Mathematically, the total coverage available is 75,000/150,000 and since 25,000/50,000 constitutes one-third of the total limits, that is the proportionate share of that policy. The second policy constitutes two-thirds of the total limits and thus a two-thirds portion of the loss is owed. This clause is generally present in both contracts and must be adhered to by both parties. If this provision were not present, the insured would be in a position to profit from a fortuitous circumstance and that is not the intent of the policy.

THIRD-PARTY DISPUTES

This section discusses the effect of a coverage dispute with the insured on a third-party claim. Not only does the claim representative have to contend with the insured who is upset with the possibility of there being no coverage for an accident, but he or she must also deal with the claimant who has property damage, or an injury, or both. An immediate coverage investigation is required and the insurer must determine its position as to coverage as soon as possible. Failure to do so may result in unfavorable complications including not only a waiver of the insurer's rights if the investigation is unreasonably delayed, but also the possibility of a claim of bad faith against the insurer.

While the coverage investigation is in process, if it does not violate the state Unfair Claims Practices Act, it may be suggested to the claimant that he or she pursue his or her own collision coverage so that repairs can be started on the car. If the claimant is not so insured, a great deal of pressure may be exerted by that party as well as by the insured. Since it may take some time before the claimant is ready to discuss settlement of injury claim, pressure on that account may not be as severe.

Another interested party in such a situation may be the state Insurance Department if the claimant or the insured complains of improper or slow service. Should this occur, the insurer must immediately acknowledge the Department's correspondence and explain the circumstance of the delay.

Frequently, a coverage problem of this nature results in losing control of the claimant at an early date and all ensuing communication must be directed to the claimant's attorney.

Damage Disputes with the Claimant

The same disputes as with the insured relating to actual cash value, betterment, and old damage can also be experienced with the third-party claimant. There are a few claimants who seize the opportunity to attempt to improve the condition of their automobile by claiming old damage, rust, or simply insisting on new parts for an older car, without paying betterment. Such demands should be resisted as they are not owed and the additional costs eventually increase premium rates for the entire class of insureds. Unfortunately, the claimant who is also injured may use the injury as leverage to obtain the unreasonable demands as described. The trainee adjuster should discuss these cases with the examiner, to be certain that the insurer's interests are best protected.

In contrast, persons do have honest differences of opinion while trying to settle their own claims. In such a case diligent communication may avoid misunderstandings and result in a proper conclusion. Occasionally, a compromise might be the only way to satisfactorily conclude a debatable issue.

Liability Disputes

It is not unusual to encounter a dispute concerning liability as the adjuster develops an investigation of a claim as the parties involved relate the facts that they remember or imagine. For various reasons, they may even fabricate facts that are self-serving, thereby hoping to avoid liability. It is also possible to receive factual information from witnesses where the facts are diametrically opposed to each other due to their positions at the scene. In such circumstances, the importance of a complete investigation cannot be stressed too much.

When all the facts are gathered the claim representative must determine the position to be taken and proceed with the settlement, denial, or compromise.

In the past, additional complications appeared in cases where two or more tortfeasors were involved in the same accident. If the tortfeasors disagreed on the distribution of liability, it was impossible for one to pay the claimant for the total claim and then attempt to recover contribution from the others. The reason is that such a payment was considered a voluntary act and such an act was legally precluded from recovery. As a result, the claimant was placed in the position of being forced to sue all the tortfeasors in order to obtain payment of damages.

In order to circumvent such complications, many states have passed legislation known as Joint Tortfeasor Contribution Acts, which rule out the voluntary act concept and enable one tortfeasor to pay the claimant for the total damages and then pursue the claim for contribution against the other tortfeasors. As in other legal questions, it is mandatory that the adjuster be familiar with the law of his or her jurisdiction.

A similar difficulty has presented itself when a question of coverage was at issue between two or more insurance companies. If they could not decide as to whose coverage would apply, the settlement would be delayed as neither insurer would pay the claim due to the voluntary act concept. This problem area was resolved in many states, by a directive from the Insurance Commissioner providing that contribution or indemnification could be pursued by the insurer who volunteered the payment. In this manner, relief for the claimant is not delayed and the volunteering insurer is protected regarding recovery.

If contribution is expected, caution must be taken to name all tortfeasors in the release document, thus granting them immunity from any further claims from the third party. If this precaution is not heeded, recovery might be impossible.

Contributory Negligence and Comparative Negligence

The subjects of contributory and comparative negligence have been discussed in detail earlier and are mentioned here to stress the importance of a thorough investigation. The adjuster must recognize the relevant prevailing law in the jurisdiction and develop all facts that are available in effort to establish a defense.

In the field of contributory negligence, the importance lies in discovering whether there was some degree of negligence on the part of the third party so as to preclude liability to him or her. Since the facts are usually reduced to a jury question, the preponderance of the evidence must be in favor of the defendant if the defense is to be successful.

When considering comparative negligence, the claim representative must be familiar with the type of the comparative negligence law in question. The investigation must be thorough enough to enable the adjuster to determine the percentage of negligence to be charged to each party.

Need for a Thorough Investigation

As has been urged throughout this text, a thorough investigation is of extreme importance either to recognize that liability is present or to establish a defense to a claim. It does not matter if the law is based on contributory or comparative negligence or whether the claim is large or small, as the only method of determining the position to be taken is through an investigation.

The presentation of facts is the backbone of a claim file and serves to establish the evidence after it has been gathered, in the form of statements, diagrams, photos, reports, and the assistance of an expert, if necessary.

On occasion, an adjuster may wonder why statements are needed when the claim is to be defended, since the defense attorney usually deposes those who will provide testimony. Such a question may seem logical except for the fact that depositions are usually not taken until some time after the crash has occurred. By that time, memories have faded and facts have a way of changing. With a statement in the claim file, the defense attorney is in a position to review the facts that were given shortly after the accident with the insured or witness and in this manner, the accuracy of the information is more likely.

At times, a witness who gives a negative statement, to the effect that the witness did not actually see the crash or the color of the traffic light, may change his or her mind at a later date and vividly describe what occurred in detail, including the color of the light. When such a circumstance presents itself, defense counsel can impeach the witness through the use of the statement taken by the adjuster.

Investigations relate to more than just gathering facts. When an insured or claimant is involved in an accident, an early contact assures both parties of the insurer's interest. Such a contact not only strengthens the chances of securing all available information, but also improves the chance of maintaining control of some claims.

To further illustrate the importance of investigation, Unfair Claims Practices Acts specifically require a complete investigation within thirty days after notification of the claim. (See NAIC Mode Regulation—Section 7). Failure to comply may result in various penalties for an insurer.

During and immediately after the investigation, the claim representative is required to submit reports which describe all developments of the claim. This process should consist of factual information pertaining to the claim. All effort must be exerted to avoid any type of editorializing or assumptions of any kind. The latter may cause someone to believe an assumption to be a genuine fact and reliance on such information can prove to be disastrous. For example, an adjuster may state in a report that "the insured is a crook because he tried to include a new paint job on his car, but I wouldn't budge from my stand of painting only the needed portion." This obvious example illustrates how an adjuster would become embarrassed and humiliated if these lines were read back to him or her while on the witness stand, during a bad faith trial.

The test for the adjuster is to ask himself or herself if he or she would like to be responsible for such a statement in court. Of course, the answer is no. As a result, all information must be carefully worded to avoid such predicaments.[2]

Inter-Company Arbitration

Frequently, disputes arise relating to the subrogation aspect of a claim in that neither insurer feels that its insured was negligent, or the insurers cannot agree on the percentage of liability to be charged to each party when considering comparative negligence. Since a great deal of money may be at stake, the matter must be litigated or arbitrated.

Litigation is costly, usually requiring a large percentage of the recovery (often 33 1/3 percent) to be paid to legal counsel. In addition, court costs must be paid by the insurer pursuing the recovery, and the time involved in litigation is quite lengthy.

Another factor that may arise is when the defendant files not only the answer to the complaint, but also a counterclaim alleging both property damage and bodily injury. When this occurs, the plaintiff is placed in the position of paying defense costs which can amount to more than the initial subrogation demand.

An alternative to litigation is available in the form of inter-company arbitration, through the organization called Insurance Arbitration Forums, Inc. In this arbitration process, subscribing insurers agree to arbitrate disputes among themselves and to be bound by the decision as to liability reached by the arbitration panel.

An insurer can participate in one or all of the programs that are made available by this organization, which include:

1. Fire and Allied Lines Subrogation
2. Special Arbitration
3. Automobile Accident Reparations Arbitration
4. Nationwide Arbitration
5. Accident Arbitration
6. Executives Arbitration
7. Medical Malpractice Inter-Insurer Agreement
8. Workers' Compensation Arbitration (California)
9. Workers' Compensation Arbitration (Michigan)
10. Uninsured Motorist Arbitration
11. International Reciprocal Arbitration Agreement
12. Reinsurance Arbitration

Each program contains a separate agreement which outlines the rules to be followed in determining liability and each agreement must be signed by the insurer who wishes to participate in any given program.

The procedure starts with an applicant insurer completing a contentions form (see Exhibit 9-1) which provides pertinent information relating to the companies, representatives, insureds, and the file numbers. The applicant's allegations on the left side of the form are also completed and signed, and the form along with pertinent portions of the applicant's investigation is submitted to the local forum representative. A copy of the contentions form is then sent to the respondent insurer who completes the Respondent's Allegations section, signs the form, and also submits it with pertinent portions of their investigation.

The cost of arbitrating an auto claim is nominal and, in a comparatively short time, the local panel reviews the merits and makes an award based upon all of the information presented.

Although the arbitration process described is intended for signatories to the agreement, it is also available to non-signatory companies on a voluntary basis.

Should one of the insurers fail to conduct a thorough investigation, the chances of recovery are reduced considerably; therefore, all statements, photos, diagrams, and applicable law should be included for review by the panel.

Exhibit 9-1
Contentions Form

Docket no. N ____ - ______ - ____ **Committee** ____________
Type Committee name above

Received ______ M M D D Y Y

(N)

(Lower right hand section to be filled in by respondent.)

APPLICANT Original and 3 copies to Arbitration Secretary. 3 copies direct to Respondent.

1 copy to Arbitration Secretary. 1 copy direct to Applicant. **RESPONDENT**

______ COMPANY ______

______ REPRESENTATIVE* ______

______ ADDRESS* ______

______ INSURED ______

______ INSURED'S ADDRESS ______

______ REP. FILE NO. ______

______ CO. FILE NO.* ______

DATE OF ACCIDENT ______ PLACE OF ACCIDENT ______

APPLICANT'S ALLEGATIONS

Is this a counterclaim? ☐ Yes ☐ No
If this is a counterclaim the original case MUST be identified here!
Docket No. ______
Applicant Co. ______ Insured ______
Respondent Co. ______ Insured ______
Date of filing ______

Damages claimed By Company $ ______
(Company Interest Only)

Applicant's Insured's Deductible, If Any, $ ______

Are Companion Claims or Suits Pending? ______
(Rule 7 – General – Arbitration Rules & Regulations)

If yes – Do you waive deferment? ______

RESPONDENT'S ALLEGATIONS

Do You Admit Coverage? ☐ Yes ☐ No
(A failure to answer the question, or an affirmative answer, prior to an award shall be deemed a waiver of ANY coverage defense)
A negative answer must be explained under contentions.

Do You Admit Liability? ______

Amount of Damages Contested, If Any $ ______

Respondent's Insured's Deductible, If Any, $ ______
(This applies to policies with a liability deductible.)

Are Companion Claims or Suits Pending? ______
(Rule 7 – General – Arbitration Rules & Regulations)

If yes – Do you waive deferment? ______

*Has Settlement Been Attempted? ____________

*(If affirmative, respondent representative's name, address and respondent's file number must be included in upper right section where marked by asterisk. If this information is not available attach explanatory memorandum to application on compliance with condition precedent).

Do you waive Notice of Hearing? ____________

NOTE: Case will be heard by one arbitrator, unless checked here ☐

SEND ONLY ONE COPY OF YOUR FILE - NOT THE ORIGINAL.

IF WE MAY DESTROY YOUR FILE AFTER HEARING, CHECK HERE ☐

CONTENTIONS: (Use reverse side if additional space is required for Contentions)

Applicant Representative (Signature) ____________ Date ______

Area Code Tel. No.

** Has Contact With Applicant Been Attempted? ______

(**If negative, attach explanatory memorandum to your answer.)

Do you waive Notice of Hearing? ____________

NOTE: Case will be heard by one arbitrator, unless checked here ☐

SEND ONLY ONE COPY OF YOUR FILE - NOT THE ORIGINAL.

IF WE MAY DESTROY YOUR FILE AFTER HEARING, CHECK HERE ☐

CONTENTIONS: (Use reverse side if additional space is required for Contentions)

Respondent Representative (Signature) ____________ Date ______

Area Code Tel. No.

DECISION

Panel members ____________

____

____

Date closed M M D D Y Y

Check if closed without hearing ☐

Basis of findings ____________

Mark appearance in space below:
F – File only.
N – No appearance by file or representative.
P – Personal representative.

☐ Check if respondent did not file answer.

			Dollar amounts*	Leave Blank	
______	Applicant	Amount claimed	DDDDDD•CC		ps
______	1st respondent	Award vs 1st resp.	DDDDDD•CC		d
______	2nd respondent	Award vs 2nd resp.	DDDDDD•CC	N	d
______	3rd respondent	Award vs 3rd resp.	DDDDDD•CC	N	d

*Excluding insured's deductible.

1/83

Special Arbitration

This program can be valuable to insurers as it was created to resolve two areas of dispute:

1. Disagreements between two or more casualty insurers with insureds allegedly negligent for the same loss in the same claim.
2. Disagreements for liability for loss between casualty insurers who have overlapping coverages.

Insurers must submit to arbitration if they have signed the compulsory provision with Insurance Arbitration Forums, Inc. and if the following six conditions have been met:

1. a special arbitration committee is operating in the state where the claim or lawsuit is pending;
2. the controversy involves the insureds of signatory company;
3. the dispute involves casualty coverages;
4. the dispute involves either: (a) overlapping casualty coverage, or (b) two casualty insurers whose insureds are named as liable for the same loss;
5. one of the insurers involved has settled with the claimant for an amount not exceeding $50,000; and
6. there was contact between the insurers prior to settlement.

In proper situations, arbitration serves a worthy purpose and fulfills a need in the disposition of auto damage or other casualty disputes.[3]

FORCES INFLUENCING THE DECISION TO SETTLE THE CLAIM

A number of factors may be instrumental in persuading an insurer to settle a claim after considering the facts that have been developed. They may relate to local statutes and ordinances, regulatory requirements, or various consumer protection agencies, all of whom take an interest in claims with problems.

Local Statutes and Ordinances

The jurisdiction that an adjuster is working in will determine the method of evaluating claims and whether the claim will be settled or denied. For example, if contributory negligence is the law to be followed in an area, a claim involving that factor may result in a denial or compromise, depending on the strength of the evidence. If comparative negligence is to be followed, the percentage of liability must be determined and the claim concluded in that manner. Perhaps a jurisdiction follows the bailment rule, where the negligence of the bailee is not imputed to the bailor, thus necessitating settlement when a bailment is present.

Regulatory Requirements

Unfair Claims Practice Acts and other directives published by state insurance departments may have some bearing on the settlement of a claim. In Ohio, for instance, when there is a dispute of coverage between two insurers, payment may not be delayed while it is decided whose policy is liable. An Insurance Department regulation requires that one of the companies pay the loss promptly without it being considered a voluntary payment, and the insurers can resolve their differences thereafter.[4]

Consumer Protection Agencies

A number of agencies exist on state as well as local levels for the purpose of consumer protection in relation to defective products and alleged lack of service in many areas, including insurance claim complaints. On the state level, the Insurance Department and the Attorney General's office may provide a "hot-line" to receive complaints from the public. Locally, television stations and/or newspapers may become interested in complaints which are received through public service departments.

Just as the above mentioned statutes, ordinances, and agencies assist in settling a claim, the same sources can be utilized in not settling if the claim investigation supports a defense of the claim. For example, if a claimant is proven to be 80 percent negligent in a jurisdiction that is ruled by a "not more than 50 percent" comparative negligence law, that statute will serve to strengthen the insurer's defense of the claim and enable the adjuster to stick to his denial. The same theory can be applied if the Insurance Department or consumer protection agency are brought into the dispute.

Another argument might be that an unwarranted payment serves to increase premiums, thus creating a condition contrary to public interest.

THE LEGAL PROCESS

The objective of the claim representative is to settle meritorious claims after they have been investigated, evaluated and negotiated. Failure to do so represents a breakdown in the adjusting process and necessitates time-consuming litigation, additional expenses and longer lasting claim files. In addition, a degree of control is lost as the lawsuit is subject to the rules of the court, and further, the defense must be prepared to withstand all allegations presented by the plaintiff. This requires the filing of answers, interrogatories, various briefs and taking depositions.

When settlement negotiations fail, plaintiff's attorney prepares and files a lawsuit in the court of proper jurisdiction. It must be recognized that anyone can initiate a lawsuit for any reason and it is the duty of the insured's company to provide a legal defense as promised in the liability insurance policy, as long as the allegations are covered by the policy.

The lawsuit consists of a complaint which contains the designation of the court, docket number, plaintiff's name(s), defendant's name(s), causes of actions, allegations, prayer (*ad damnum*), and the plaintiff attorney's name and address. The plaintiff is the party who has been damaged and is filing the suit against the defendant, who allegedly is responsible for the damage or injury. There may be several plaintiffs and defendants, known as co-defendants, all of whom are the litigants in the legal action.

After the lawsuit is filed, in some jurisdictions the clerk of court prepares a summons addressed to the defendant and the summons and complaint are then served on the defendant by a process server or the sheriff, or through the mail.

The date of service represents the date that the summons and complaint are received by the defendant and in accordance with the instructions in the summons, the defendant is permitted a designated length of time in which to file an answer to the complaint, depending on local rule.

One of the insured's duties described in the policy is to "promptly send us copies of any notices or legal papers received in connection with the accident or loss."[5] The insured should notify the insurer immediately of the receipt of the suit papers and arrange to transfer them to the insurer personally if possible or by registered mail. It is also necessary for the adjuster to determine the date that the legal papers were served on the insured so that the answer due date can be ascertained.

When the complaint is received by the claim representative its allegations should be reviewed to learn if there are any obstacles to the insurer's defense of the claim. For example, the wording may be framed with the use of the words "intentionally, or willfully and wantonly," which conceivably could preclude a defense due to the "intentional act" exclusion in liability policies. Caution must prevail, however, as some courts are broadening their interpretation of policies to the extent that if there is any question of providing a defense to an insured, they will rule in favor of the insured. (See Willoughby Hills v. Cincinnati Ins. Co. (1984), 9 Ohio St. 3d 177.)

In addition, many lawsuits include a prayer for punitive damages against the defendant. Jurisdictional position in this matter must be ascertained as some states do not permit coverage of punitive damages as being against public policy. Also, the prayer of the complaint for compensatory damages may exceed the limits of the policy. Should punitive damages not be permitted to be paid by the insurer in a jurisdiction, or should the prayer exceed the policy limits, the claim representative must immediately advise the insured, in writing, of the exact problem presented and what the insurer's position is in that regard.

In relation to the excess amount, the letter invites the insured to retain separate counsel if he so desires and requests identification of that counsel in order that the two defense attorneys can work together.

In reference to punitive damages, the broadening of coverage is again evident as some courts have ruled that the literal construction of the policy also includes this type of award since the policy reads, "We will pay damages for bodily injury or property damage for which any covered person becomes legally responsible because of an auto accident."[6] In the absence of an exclusion, some courts have ruled that punitive damages are included in this agreement. (See Price v. Hartford Accident and Indemnity Co., 108 Ariz. 485, 502 P.2d 522 (1972) and Lazenby v. Universal Underwriters Ins. Co. 214 Tenn. 639, 383 S.W. 2d 1 (1864).

By definition, compensatory damages represent payment to a person for injury or damage caused by the negligent action of a tort-feasor, and punitive or exemplary damages are awarded in cases where the court feels that the tort-feasor should be penalized for extreme negligence or willful misconduct.

In the past, the court's logic was that an award for punishment would have no effect if the insurer were to pay the award; however, such reasoning is being changed in some states.

After the summons and complaint have been reviewed and coverage is in order, it is recommended that the insurer's representative call the defense counsel to assign the case over the telephone, advising the docket number, the designation of the court, the litigants, and the answer date. Such verbal assignment precludes mail. At an early date, the legal papers, a copy of the file, and a cover letter containing instructions, opinions, and values must be delivered or mailed to the defense counsel who can then decide the best action to be taken in reference to the answer date.

Upon receipt of the new lawsuit, the defense counsel is expected to review the file and report back to the insurer, covering opinions on liability, injuries, values and the necessity for additional investigation, should it be required.

Throughout the life of the case, it is also expected that the defense attorney will provide the insurer with timely reports, especially if developments may change the outlook on liability or value. Such developments may include the discovery of a new witness, an opinion of how the insured or witnesses will appear to a jury, or the results of any ongoing negotiations.[7]

If there is a possibility that the claim can be settled in a short time, the defense attorney may request the plaintiff's attorney for an extension of time before the answer must be filed. Should settlement not be possible, the attorney must file the answer within the designated time of the answer date.

Protecting the Insured

The insurance liability policy is designed to provide three primary functions: the fiduciary obligation to investigate the claim properly, to pay for bodily injury and damage for which the insured becomes legally liable, and to provide a legal defense for the insured. The former have already been discussed in the form of settling and paying claims. The latter is equally important as it protects the insured against the cost of the legal process.

Once a lawsuit is initiated, it cannot be ignored even though the insured feels no responsibility for the damages claimed. Should the insured fail to respond to the legal proceedings for any reason, the suit would go into default and the court would rule in favor of the plaintiff, up to the amount of the prayer.

Following the initial activities, future developments should be reported to the insured by the defense counsel or by the claim representative. Such status reports not only render a service to the insured, but also present an opportunity to maintain contact with the insured, whose presence may be needed during various phases of the litigation.

As the case nears trial, the location of favorable witnesses must also be confirmed as their availability at trial will be equally important if the defense is to sustain any possibility of success.

Discovery Procedures

These procedures include interrogatories, depositions, expert testimony, and securing medical and lost-wages information.

Interrogatories Interrogatories are questions designed to secure pertinent information relative to the plaintiff or defendant and to the facts of the accident. They are allowed by the court and may be filed at any time during the course of the lawsuit, as long as they are reasonable.

Deposition In the process of developing a case, the attorneys are permitted to question opposing parties and witnesses to determine as many facts as possible. Present at the deposition are the attorneys of both sides, the person to be deposed, and the court reporter. The deponent provides testimony under oath that is in most cases admissible in court.

At times, depositions are recorded on videotape in lieu of a shorthand record and the tape is also admissible. It is shown on a video monitor, thus saving time and expense of the witness' actual presence in the courtroom at the time of trial. The videotape method is particularly advantageous in the case of deposing expert witnesses.

Expert Testimony As the need presents itself, experts are called in to analyze medical conditions, products or other technical subjects and may be requested to testify in behalf of one of the litigants. This testimony includes the expert's technical or medical background, the details of the expert's findings and his or her opinion as to the medical prognosis or technical opinion relating to the subject of the analysis.

Medical and Lost-Wages Information It is the defendant's right to be supplied with sufficient data relating to these special damages. Frequently, this information is made available at an early date, but when it is not, defense counsel may petition the court to order the plaintiff to provide the material.

Pretrial Conferences

A pretrial conference is a meeting of the parties in the lawsuit and is conducted in the judge's chamber or in the courtroom. Attendance is mandatory for the plaintiff's attorney, defense counsel and often, the plaintiff and the insurance company representative. In some jurisdictions, the latter's attendance is absolutely mandatory and the representative must have sufficient authority to settle claims eliminating the need of calling his or her supervisors in order to obtain additional authority.

The merits of the case are discussed at the pretrial conference with the intent of settling the claim. At times, if plaintiff's attorney delays submitting medical reports, bills, or other needed information, the pretrial is an excellent time to impress the plaintiff and the judge that these items are necessary before an evaluation can be made. The results of such a request are often successful.

If the claim is settled, arrangements are made for the signature of the release, the filing of a dismissal and the payment of the claim. Should settlement not be realized, a date is set for trial.

As the trial date approaches, the defense attorney must be certain that all preliminary work is completed. Consideration must be given to the need of a medical or technical expert if not already arranged. Witnesses must be located and facts discussed so that their testimony will follow as expected. The insured is counseled as to current developments, and arrangements are made for the insured's presence and testimony. In the meantime, unless all chances of settlement have vanished, negotiations may still continue.

Statistically, very few cases reach the trial stage. Both sides realize that expenses will be high and if at all possible, serious attempts will be made to dispose of the claim.

The Trial

The trial procedures start before the scheduled date in the form of subpoenas, which must be served on witnesses to notify them of the date and time of their court appearance.

Before the trial starts, the attorneys meet again in the judge's chamber to discuss last minute negotiations toward settlement. Should these talks fail, the trial is started and the length of the hearing is contingent on the issues of liability and/or injury and may last for days or weeks. During this time, the developments are constantly analyzed by both sides with the hope of detecting strengths or weaknesses, which may initiate further negotiations for settlement.

After all testimony has been given and the judge gives the jury instructions regarding the applicable law, the jury retires to deliberate. As instructed in the charge, they must find for the party who presents the preponderance of the evidence, which means the strongest evidence, but not necessarily the most in terms of quantity. In a criminal trial, on the other hand, the defendant's guilt must be beyond a reasonable doubt.

If the case has not been settled while the jury is deliberating, the court is reconvened and the verdict is read.

In trying a case, the plaintiff and defendant may be subjected to substantial expenses that may not be justified by the eventual result. For the defendant, expenses may consist of expert's fees and legal fees that are charged by the hour before trial and usually by the day during trial. Similarly, the plaintiff may have to incur considerable outlay for expert fees. This suggests that in many instances it would benefit both parties to settle the claim, especially since the unexpected may always occur, leaving the question of success hanging in the balance.

The Appeal

The verdict reached by the jury may be reasonable in the opinion of all parties and if so, the matter will end with the execution of releases, payment of the claim and the recording of the satisfaction of the judgment. If the verdict is excessive in the opinion of the defense attorney or insurer, it will be discussed before a decision is made regarding appeal. Several factors must be considered before the decision is made. These consist of the probable length of time the appeal will consume, the probable additional legal costs and the potential amount of post-judgment interest charges that would accrue. In addition, it must be determined if there is any chance of success regarding the appeal of judicial error, or other reasons, e.g., excessiveness of the verdict.

From the plaintiff's viewpoint, an appeal includes the expense factor and whether the plaintiff is willing to wait for payment, assuming that an award was granted in the verdict.

If judicial error is found in the appeal, the case may be returned to the lower court for retrial, thus exposing everyone to another jury, another verdict, and additional costs.

The Negotiation Process After Suit Has Been Filed

After a claim has been investigated, the adjuster must evaluate and attempt to settle it in a reasonable manner. If the negotiations are unsuccessful and litigation follows, additional evaluations are made to be certain that the position that has been taken is correct.

Procedures may vary between insurers, but the most common methods include individual, roundtable and defense counsel evaluations.

Individual Evaluations The claim examiner prepares an evaluation based on all known factors of the injury or damage, which is then applied to the liability of the insured. If the law of comparative negligence is applicable, the total value of the claim is multiplied by the insured's percentage of liability to arrive at a value. For example, if the total claim value is $6,000, that amount is multiplied by the insured's percentage of liability, in this case 70 percent.

$6,000	Total claim value
× .70	Percent of liability
$4,200	Net value of claim

Should the law of contributory negligence apply and it is found that the plaintiff is partially liable, then theoretically, the insurer owes nothing on the claim. Realistically, a value must be applied as to how much the insurer wants to pay; otherwise, the case will go to trial and the insurer will take the chance of losing and will have to pay the verdict in addition to the expensive legal fees.

With some insurers, the individual evaluation is the only method used to arrive at a claim's value, although the file may be reviewed by others of higher authority who may either agree or disagree with the value. If there is disagreement, the value likely will be changed.

Roundtable or Committee Evaluation This method of evaluating a claim involves a minimum of two people, with no set number as a maximum. Ideally, four or five claim persons may participate, resulting in a fairly accurate value. Although any claim can be "roundtabled," it is recommended that a minimum value be established, such as $10,000 or $25,000.

One format used in conducting such a discussion is for the person who requests the evaluation to complete an analysis form (see Exhibit 9-2) that provides significant facts relating to the claim. Should the injury be serious, it may be desirable to include medical reports and a list of special damages to assist in comprehending the degree of injury. The same person leads the discussion by briefly reviewing the material. It is recommended that he or she be thoroughly knowledgeable with the details of the file as various questions may be presented relating to any aspect of the case. Some pertinent questions may be:

1. Has a defense medical report been obtained?
2. Is there a possibility of contribution from a joint tortfeasor?
3. What is the demand?
4. Have any offers been made?
5. Does the claimant's attorney try his own cases or refer them to a trial attorney?
6. Have there been any pretrial conferences?
7. Has a trial date been scheduled?

During the discussion, it may be discovered that additional

Exhibit 9-2
File Analysis for Roundtable Discussion

Insured	D/Acc.	File #

Answer Date	Plaintiff Age at Acc.	Co-defendant

Plaintiff Atty.	Our Defense Atty. Co-defendant Atty.

Case Summary

Injuries

Special Damages

Policy Limits	Excess Letter	Non-Waiver	R/Rights Letter

Full Liability Value	Chance of Successful Defense %
Max. Settlement Value	Our Liability %
Demands Date of Demand	Offers Date of Offer
	Co-Defendant Agrees to Pay

Investigation Needed

Submitted By Date	Attended By

Notes

Reserve_____ Is Reserve Adequate?

investigation is required such as obtaining additional medical reports or making contact with the joint tortfeasor's insurance company.

When all questions have been satisfactorily answered, each participant voices an opinion as to value and should there be disagreement regarding the value range, further discussion should follow until the range is agreed upon.

Consideration should then be given to the current reserve amount. It should be noted that an accurate reserve must be established as early in the claim as possible so that the insurer's financial position properly reflects all outstanding claim reserves.

The roundtable or committee method of evaluation holds several advantages, one of the most prominent of which is relieving the responsibility of a single individual to make a decision involving perhaps hundreds of thousands of dollars. Using this method the person responsible for the file is required to express a value, yet is protected by the safety valve provided by the other participants' opinions and evaluations. In addition, this process exposes participants to claims other than their own and serves as an educational tool for all. Finally, this method enables the claim department to conduct this portion of handling claims in an organized manner and assists in eliminating potential errors.

Plaintiff Counsel and/or Defense Counsel Evaluations As the claim representatives conduct their evaluations, defense and plaintiff counsel may follow the same procedures depending on the severity of the claim. In addition to their own evaluations, roundtable discussions may also be conducted with their colleagues in addition to discussing the legal strategy to be employed in the case.

Authority to Settle

As previously discussed, authority to settle claims varies among insurers and these procedural rules must be observed for reasons of control needed by management. The adjuster must report to the supervisor when the evaluation exceeds his or her authority and, progressively, the supervisor and manager must obtain authority to settle a claim from higher management. For example, the adjuster may be authorized to settle claims up to $5,000 before approval is necessary from the supervisor. The supervisor might have $25,000 authority and any claims valued beyond that figure would require the approval of the claim manager, who might have a maximum of $50,000 authority. Claims valued over $50,000 would require approval from a designated person in the insurer's regional or home office.

Some insurers provide the claim manager with policy limits

authority enabling him to operate autonomously, and require only skeleton files for home office use. The procedures are always outlined to the adjuster by each insurer and they must be adhered to as directed.

Insurers may also differ in their procedure relating to negotiations on a claim after a lawsuit has been filed. Some companies feel that the defense attorney should conduct all negotiations when litigation commences, on the basis that the claim has become a legal matter. Other insurers take the opposite approach and direct their adjusters and/or supervisors to negotiate all or most of the claims that are in suit. When this method is prescribed, it is important to advise defense counsel of such procedures and all negotiations, including demands and offers, must be communicated to the attorney promptly. Theoretically, closer attention can be devoted to the claim by the adjuster as compared to the attorney who must attend pretrials, file briefs and prepare for trials. The expense factor is also involved as the attorney's fees are considerably higher than the costs involved when an adjuster does the work.

During the process of handling the claim, including negotiations, an adjuster must exercise caution not to engage in the practice of law unless licensed to do so. In accordance with the Statement of Principles referred to in Chapter 1, an adjuster is permitted to negotiate settlements, but unless the adjuster is a lawyer, the practice of law is illegal. In this respect, the adjuster is permitted to use forms that have been drawn by an attorney, but may not prepare special releases or other agreements. Also, the claim representative who is not a lawyer is not permitted to dispense legal advice in any way, and should situations be presented in this area, he or she should contact the supervisor immediately for advice.

Balancing the Interests

On occasion, a claim may pose circumstances that require balancing the interests of liability, exposure, and expense. The facts of the case can indicate little or no liability; yet the circumstances may project an exposure far beyond the limits of the insured's policy. The questions presented to the claim representative are whether to attempt to settle the claim within the policy limits or to take a firm stand and try the case. Settlement may represent the payment of a large amount and may prompt criticism from the agent and persons within the company who may not understand the technicalities at hand. Conversely, if the case is tried, other factors arise which represent an even greater dilemma. Legal costs increase substantially as a result of the additional time and work expended, including the actual time devoted to the trial. Other uncontrollable contingencies must be considered, such as the make-up of the jury, the capabilities of the plaintiff and defense lawyers and the impressions that witnesses will leave on the jury. The strength of the defense must be compared with that of the plaintiff. Consideration must be given to the possibility that a verdict for the plaintiff may be in excess of the policy limits, thereby requiring the insured to apply personal funds to the payment. Such exposure of the insured may precipitate a bad-faith lawsuit against the insurer, requiring additional legal costs and the possibility of payment of punitive damages in addition to the verdict.

In the process of deciding the direction to be followed, the claim representative must take into account any legal precedent that may apply to the case in comparison to the facts that have been developed and after discussing all aspects with the defense attorney, making an intelligent appraisal on whether to settle or try the case.

SUMMARY

The responsibilities of the claim representative are great in that the finances of the insurer are directly affected by his or her decisions, and these responsibilities become even more complicated by the erosion of defenses in the past several years. Whether the erosion is due to consumerism, more lenient courts or any other reason is not material. What is important is that the claim person recognizes the constant change that is prevalent in most jurisdictions and that those factors are given due consideration. The adoption of comparative negligence by many states, permitting payment to a plaintiff who would have received nothing under the contributory negligence rule; expanded wrongful death statutes that not only allow for pecuniary injury as before, but now allow for loss of support, services, society, companionship, consortium, inheritance and mental anguish; the elimination of guest-passenger laws in more states and the disintegration of various family and governmental immunities and the concept of strict liability in product liability cases are but some of the most important examples.

Chapter Notes

1. Personal Auto Policy, PP 00 02 (6-80) BF, Copyright, Insurance Services Office, 1980, p. 8.
2. Pat Magarick, *Successful Handling of Casualty Claims* (Brooklyn, NY: Central Book Co. Inc., 1974), pp. 125, 126, 127, 128.
3. *Arbitration Facts, 1983-1984 Edition,* Insurance Arbitration Forums, Inc., 200 White Plains Rd., Tarrytown, NY, pp. 9–15.
4. State of Ohio, Department of Insurance, *Newsletter #71,* September-October, 1966, p. 12.
5. Personal Auto Policy, p. 9.
6. Personal Auto Policy, p. 2.
7. Magarick, pp. 694–695.

CHAPTER 10

Reserving

INTRODUCTION

A reserve, stated simply, is a sum of money which is set aside from surplus into the liability column to meet some future obligation. Since reserves represent future obligations of an insurance company, they are classified as liabilities on the company's balance sheet.

The two principal types of reserves established by insurance companies are *claim* reserves and *unearned premium* reserves. Unearned premium reserves represent that portion of the premium which has not been earned or used up at any particular time. For example, the *earned* premium on a one-year policy generating $100 in premium which is canceled after three months is $25. (One-fourth of $100 has been earned.) The *unearned* portion of the premium at this point is $75. Since the company has not yet earned the $75, it must be set aside as a reserve.

Although it is true that unearned premium reserves are an important factor in determining a company's financial position and future production capacity, they are of little concern to claim people. For this reason, the discussion of reserving deals primarily with claim reserves.

In order to understand the significance of claim reserves, it is necessary that three basic questions be answered. They are:

1. *What* is a claim reserve?
2. *Why* are claim reserves necessary?
3. *How* are claim reserves established?

What Is a Claim Reserve?

Essentially, a claim reserve is an estimate of what a claim will cost. The reserve represents money which is set aside for the eventual payment of a claim. From the company's standpoint, a claim is incurred when it happens, regardless of when in the future it is paid.

Some companies include *estimated claim expenses* in the reserve amount while other companies establish a separate reserve for the claim and a separate reserve for anticipated expenses which will be incurred in conjunction with the claim. Such claim expenses include independent adjuster fees, legal fees, charges for police reports, hospital records, appraisals, and so on.

Why Are Claim Reserves Necessary?

As mentioned previously, insurance is often characterized as an "intangible" product. This characterization is based on the view that an insured does not receive anything material or tangible for his or her premium dollar until a claim is paid. The payment of a claim then is what consummates the insurance contract. It is especially important, therefore, that when claims become due, money is available to meet these obligations.

With respect to liability claims, and particularly *bodily injury* liability claims, years may pass before a claim is paid. This might be due to the fact that time is needed for the injury to heal or because the claim is in litigation. Because of the extended time involved before such claims are finally settled and closed, bodily injury liability claims are sometimes referred to as "long tail" claims.

Since an insurer has an obligation to pay covered claims, it is understandably important that funds be available for this purpose when claims are ultimately settled. Claim reserves are necessary to properly recognize, at any given time, a company's future obligations.

The importance of proper reserving is further demonstrated by the fact that claim reserves are required by insurance regulatory law. In addition, the reserving practices of companies are periodically audited by state insurance departments in an effort to recognize potential problems and to take corrective action so as to avoid company insolvencies.

Improper reserving, both under-reserving and over-reserving, adversely affect a company's financial position. Inadequate reserving understates a company's liabilities and overstates its surplus. The following example, although admittedly an oversimplification, should help demonstrate the effect of under-reserving.

Keep in mind, first of all, the basic accounting principle that *assets minus liabilities equal surplus.* In this hypothetical example, assume that assets are $100 and liabilities are $75. For purposes of illustration, assume further that liabilities are comprised totally of claim reserves.

Assets − Liabilities = Surplus

$100 − $75 = $25

Suppose, however, that this particular company has a serious under-reserving problem and as claims are ultimately settled, they actually cost $95 instead of the $75 originally estimated.

Under these circumstances, the balance sheet would appear as follows:

Assets − Liabilities = Surplus

$100 − $75 = $25 estimated

$100 − $95 = $5 actual

It is evident here that as claims are settled, the company must draw from its surplus in order to meet its settlement obligations. If such a situation continues unchecked and surplus is depleted, the company faces insolvency.

In addition to the fact that inadequate reserving understates the company's liabilities and overstates its surplus, it also may have a devastating effect on rate making. Since reserves are an integral part of rate making, inadequate reserves can result in rates which are lower than they should be and this may hasten the company's decline.

Over-reserving can create problems for insurance companies as well. Over-reserving understates a company's financial strength and may create the false impression that rate increases are necessary or justified. In addition, since earnings are understated, the company pays less taxes. A company suspected of over-reserving invites audits by the tax authorities which could result in penalties being assessed against the company for its over-reserving practices.

In summary, claim reserves are necessary to properly recognize a company's future obligations. Proper reserving is important in order to accurately reflect a company's financial position. The importance of proper reserving is further demonstrated by the attention given to companies' loss reserving practices by the various state insurance departments.

How Are Claim Reserves Established?

Claim reserves are established essentially in two ways: (1) *statistically* or actuarially by monitoring past loss experience and by projecting future loss experience, and (2) *subjectively* by the claim person's judgment.

Types of Reserves

Average or Formula Reserves Average or formula reserves are set statistically by the actuarial or accounting department and are based on past loss experience and adjusted periodically.

This reserving method usually is applied to high-volume type claims such as auto collision, comprehensive, property damage, medical payments, and accident and health where payments generally are minimal and claims are settled fairly quickly. The extent to which average reserves are used varies by company and by lines of insurance.

Since such reserves are set, for the most part, by the accounting or statistical department, they are not of primary concern to claim people.

Incurred But Not Reported (IBNR) Frequently, accidents which have already happened are not reported for weeks, months, or even years after the incident. Despite the fact that these claims have not been reported, they are *incurred* from the company's standpoint when they happen. Hence, the phrase "incurred but not reported" is used to describe this type of reserve.

Accident reports may be delayed for a variety of reasons. Aside from the normal time lag in reporting claims, the insured may be initially unaware that insurance coverage is available for the claim or the claimant may not immediately recognize that the policyholder may have been responsible for the accident. Products liability, medical malpractice and latent disease claims (i.e., asbestos-related claims) where injuries may not be evident for years after the accident or exposure, have magnified the reserving problems associated with properly estimating IBNR reserves.

Whatever the reason for the delayed report, it is reasonably safe to assume that a company always has outstanding claims which have not yet been reported.

Estimates for IBNR reserves ordinarily are based on past experience. They may be further modified by what statisticians believe are relatively certain projections regarding claim frequency and severity. In any event, such reserves are established by actuaries or statisticians and, like average reserves, do not require the attention of claim people.

Case Reserves Individual case reserves are reserves set subjectively by the claim person on an individual claim basis. After considering the many factors associated with the claim, the claim person uses his or her judgment to set the individual case reserve. Case reserves are typically applied to claims that remain open for an extended period of time and are most commonly associated with bodily injury liability claims. Many companies modify case reserves statistically, thus adding in what is perceived as a safety cushion based on past and projected loss experience.

There is no magic or proven formula for setting individual case reserves. Case reserves are established essentially by the judgment and experience of the claim practitioner.

Factors which need to be considered in setting case reserves include the following:

1. Nature and Extent of the Injury
    a. Diagnosis
    b. Prognosis
    c. Pain and Suffering
    d. Disability
    e. Permanency
    f. Disfigurement
2. Medical Specials
3. Lost Earnings
4. Insured's Impression on Jury
5. Claimant Profile
    a. Age
    b. Occupation
    c. Economic Status
    d. Impression on Jury
6. Attorney Skills—Plaintiff and Defense
7. Economic and Social Inflation (Social inflation refers to noneconomic conditions which influence jury verdicts such as society's attitude concerning an individual's right to recover from an insurance company, and so on.)
8. Local Verdict Climate
9. Legal Liability Factor
10. Application of Comparative Negligence or Contributory Negligence—Type of Comparative Negligence Law (49%, 50%, pure).

Establishing Individual Case Reserves

Proper and realistic case reserving is one of the primary responsibilities of the claim department. Who sets the reserve, whether it be the adjuster, the supervisor/examiner or the manager, is determined by individual company claim policy. Regardless of who sets the reserve, however, the claim adjuster is in an ideal position to furnish the kind of information necessary to set accurate and realistic reserves. While in many companies, the adjuster does not actually establish the reserve, he or she is expected to obtain the information during the course of the claim investigation which is required to set accurate case reserves. This necessary information includes the adjuster's opinion of legal liability, specific information about the injuries, specials, claimant profile, and so on. The adjuster's investigative report should convey this information to the claim person responsible for setting the reserve.

Precisely when in the life of a claim a case reserve is established varies by company and by line of insurance. Some companies require that case reserves be established within thirty days from notice of claim while other companies defer setting case reserves for as long as three or even six months.

The more specific the information which the adjuster obtains about a claimant's injury, the more accurate the reserve will be. If the adjuster knows the diagnosis and prognosis as well as the amounts of the medical specials and actual lost earnings and confirms the claimant's disability, the chance of reserving accurately is considerably enhanced. With this information, the person responsible for setting the reserve can make a fairly accurate assessment of the company's exposure and decide upon a monetary figure which represents the ultimate cost of the claim.

Ordinarily, the ultimate cost of a claim is the amount that will finally be necessary to conclude it. This could be its *ultimate* settlement value (as opposed to *current* settlement value) or its verdict value, although there is a reluctance, as explained later, to equate reserve value with settlement value. Then again, in those cases in which no payment is contemplated, such as where liability is doubtful and the case will be defended, the ultimate cost is viewed in still another manner. Even though the company might believe that it will prevail in the lawsuit, there is always the chance that an unexpected and adverse verdict could be rendered. In such cases, most companies establish a case reserve based on the degree of probability that they could lose the case. At the very least, an expense reserve will be established to reflect the fact that considerable investigative and legal expenses will be incurred to defend the claim.

Claim case reserving philosphy varies by company. Some companies may rely totally on the claim person's judgment in establishing case reserves, while others modify case reserves by some statistical formula based on past and projected loss experience. Even the specific approach to individual case reserving is not uniform and varies somewhat by company.

Generally, companies attempt to set reserves on the basis of what the ultimate probable cost of the claim will be. There are serious risks involved, in the opinion of the authors, in reserving bodily injury liability claims on the basis of what it would cost to settle the claim today. In the interests of accuracy and realism, the reserve should be based not necessarily on what the claim person believes the case can be settled for, but on *ultimate probable cost*. The latter concept recognizes that the claim may not be settled in the immediate future and acknowledges the fact that important information about the claim or injury may not be known at the time the reserve is established. It also takes into consideration such things as the eventual impact of inflation and the general uncertainty about what might develop as the claim ages with time. Facts which are unknown at the time the reserve is set often are uncovered later in the life of a claim and frequently this information can be adverse to the insured's position. A turn for the worse in the claimant's injury, for example, may render the initial reserve inadequate.

In addition, it is generally difficult to gauge the future impact of economic and social inflation. Reserves, therefore, should be set with the distinction between what it would cost to settle the claim today and *ultimate probable cost* in mind. The distinction between these two concepts is that ultimate probable cost recognizes such real life factors as inflation, possible adverse developments, and general uncertainty whereas "settlement value" may not because it tends to focus on the present. A company may find itself with an under-reserving problem if its claim people set reserves on the basis of settlement value—without attempting to project the longterm developments referred to above which ordinarily are associated with bodily injury claims. If all the aforementioned factors are considered in setting the reserve, the risk of setting inadequate case reserves should be minimized.

It must be kept in mind, however, that there is a danger in setting the reserve too high as well. While it may be a common and sound practice among companies to reserve cautiously—that is, to add in a safety cushion in recognition of the uncertainties which may develop with the claim—the variation between settlement value and the reserve should not be too great. The company may be vulnerable to a claim of bad faith if the claim file is reserved for policy limits and then a "low ball" offer is made. In other words, a company should not take the position that a claim is worth a minimal amount and simultaneously carry a reserve which substantially exceeds that amount.

Claim people should develop the practice of checking the reserve every time a case reserved claim file is reviewed. While most companies prefer that the initial case reserve reasonably and accurately reflect the ultimate probable cost of the claim, reality suggests rather strongly that reserves need to be adjusted periodically. As new developments occur in a claim, whether favorable or adverse, reserves should be revised to reflect those developments.

The following hypothetical example or analogy might help newer adjusters understand the case reserving process more clearly.

Assume that a family is planning a one-week vacation. The family estimates that the entire vacation will cost $1,000. Will the family simply carry $1,000 (or the equivalent in travelers' checks) on the vacation? Probably not. It is evident that there is an element of uncertainty in making a trip of this nature and unforeseen events could arise which increase the cost of the vacation. For this reason, it usually is necessary to carry additional funds in order to meet these potential contingencies. In all likelihood, the family will add in a cushion for safety and may actually carry $1,200, $1,300, or more on the trip, for emergencies.

While the family will make efforts to keep within its $1,000 budget, chances are relatively good that the cost of the vacation will exceed the $1,000 estimate. Likening this to a claim reserving situation, some companies use the $1,000 as a reserve while others take a more cautious view and add in an allowance for uncertainty and would reserve the claim at $1,200 or $1,300.

Projecting Claimant's Total Special and General Damages—The Projection Sheet

When injury information and special damages are known, it is a relatively simple task to set the case reserve. Experience suggests, however, that in reality the claim person has only sketchy information about the injuries and special damages at the time the claim reserve needs to be established. Therefore, the claim person must make an educated guess as to the amount of the reserve. Some companies encourage their adjusters to engage in the practice of "projecting," from limited medical information, what special and general damages ultimately will be incurred. Of course, the more detailed injury information the adjuster can obtain, the easier it will be to project damages. This is why it is so important to effectively question the claimant's attorney so that sufficient injury and damage information may be initially obtained.

One company, acknowledging the need to properly project special and general damages, has developed a form for this purpose.[1] Adjusters are required to complete what the company refers to as a "projection sheet" early in the life of the claim. The end result of the projection sheet is the adjuster's suggested reserve, which is reviewed by the claim examiner or manager and either approved or revised. The claim examiner may call for a new projection sheet at any time during the life of the claim. In fact, it is required that projection sheets be completed periodically to account for increases in medical and hospital expenses as well as changes in labor and wage rates, and so on. The projection form enables the adjuster to participate in the reserving process even if he or she does not ultimately establish the case reserve.

The projection sheet provides a logical method for projecting the claimant's total special and general damages, both incurred and anticipated. The device can be especially helpful when the attorney has furnished only limited information about the injury and special damages.

Detailed information about special damages, although preferred, is not essential to project the reserve. It is true that some injury information, such as diagnosis, prognosis, general treatment, estimated disability, and so on, is necessary as a basis upon which to estimate damages. However, the purpose of the projection sheet is to help adjusters or examiners analyze the injury situation and make reasonable estimates with regard to the special and general damages which will be incurred. Obviously, adjusters must use their intelligence and imagination to complete the projection sheet from the often limited medical information which is available in many circumstances. (Claim people need to keep in mind that "projecting" implies going forward, not backwards, and this entails some analysis and imagination on the adjuster's behalf.)

Three variations of projection sheets are found in Exhibits 10-1, 10-2, and 10-3. The adjuster's common sense and imagination are necessary ingredients for completing a projection sheet.

Perhaps the best way to develop an understanding of how to complete such a form is to actually go through the process on a step-by-step basis.

The following hypothetical case needs to be case reserved:

- Date of Loss—(assume that the accident happened four weeks ago and that the case reserve is now due to be established.)
- Coverage—$300,000 single limit bodily injury and property damage liability.
- Liability—probable.

Exhibit 10-1
Projection Sheet

Project the claimant's total special and general damages, both incurred and anticipated, so as to arrive at a realistic reserve figure.

Case#__________ Ins.__________ D/L__________

Claimant__________ Age______ Occupation__________ Sex______

Injuries__________

Ambulance $__________ $______

Hos. - Emer. Room______ $______

Hos. ______day @$______ $______

X-Rays__________ $______

Lab__________ $______

Other __________ $______ Total Hos. & Related Expenses $__________

Doctor:

Dr. V. _____@$__________ $______ Total Doctor & Related Expenses $__________

Consultation $_____ Future Treatment

Therapy_______@$________$_____ Projected Dental

Rx____________________$_____ Total Medicals $__________

Optional:

Disability____________$_____

Total__________Weeks

Partial________Weeks

Total Wages $_______________

Total Other $_______________

Total Non-Med.$__________

Wages_____@$_________$_____

Total Specials$__________

Optional:

Disfigurement or
Permanency factor$________

Reserve:

Verdict Range - Low $_____________High $___________

Average $___________x Liability Factor___% =

Reserve $____________

Exhibit 10-2
Reserve Projection

Line No. ____________ Claim No. ____________

Damages Remarks (Describe claimant, age, occupation, injury, etc.)

Hosp. ____________

Doctor ____________

Wage Loss ____________

Misc. ____________

Total: ____________

Verdict Range ____________ to ____________

Average Verdict ____________ X Liab. Factor ____________ % = ____________

PROJECTION DATE ____________ EVALUATION BY ____________

Line No. ____________ Claim No. ____________

Damages Remarks (Describe claimant, age, occupation, injury, etc.)

Hosp. ____________

Doctor ____________

Wage Loss ____________

Misc. ______________________

Total: ______________________

Verdict Range ________________ to ______________

Average Verdict ______________ X Liab. Factor ______________ % = ______________________

PROJECTION DATE ______________ EVALUATION BY ______________

Line No. ______________________ Claim No. ______________________

Damages

Remarks (Describe claimant, age, occupation, injury, etc.)

Hosp. ______________________

Doctor ______________________

Wage Loss ______________________

Misc. ______________________

Total: ______________________

Verdict Range ________________ to ______________

Average Verdict ______________ X Liab. Factor ______________ % = ______________________

PROJECTION DATE ______________ EVALUATION BY ______________

Exhibit 10-3
Projection Sheet

Project the claimant's total special and general damages, both incurred and anticipated, so as to arrive at a realistic reserve figure. *NOTE:* This is *not* your view of settlement value, but rather your projection of our realistic claim exposure.

Claim #________ Ins.________ D/L________

Claimant________ Age________ Occupation________ Sex________

Injuries________

Claimant's Impression on Jury good ☐ fair ☐ poor ☐

Insured's Impression On Jury good ☐ fair ☐ poor ☐

Claimant Attorney Skills outstanding ☐ able ☐ fair ☐

Hospital Related Expenses

Ambulance $________ $________
Hos. - Emer. Room $________ $________
Hospital ________ day @ $________ $________
Surgery ________ $________
X-rays ________ $________
Lab ________ $________
Other ________ $________

Total Hospital & Related Expenses $________

Doctor Related Expenses

Doctor:
Dr. Visits ________ @ $________ $________

Consultation $______

Therapy ______ @ $______ $______

Rx. ______ $______

Total Doctor & Related Expenses $______

Total Medical $______

Disability

Total ______ Weeks

Partial ______ Weeks

Wages______ @ $______ $______

Total Disability/ Wages $______

Other Expenses

______ $______

______ $______

Total Other Expenses $______

Total Non-Med $______

Total Specials $______

Disfigurement or Permanency Value

Disfigurement or Permanency Value $______

Description of Disfigurement or Permanency:

______

______

Reserve: Estimated Verdict Range - Low $______ High $______

Average $______ x Liability Factor ______ % =

Suggested Reserve $______

Date______ ______

Claim Representative

- Description of Accident—Insured turned left in front of claimant. It is alleged that claimant was speeding but physical circumstances of the accident indicate that insured was primarily responsible. In the adjuster's opinion, the insured is 80 percent at fault while the claimant bears the remainder of fault.
- Applicable Law—Comparative negligence law (50 percent rule).
- Injuries—Claimant, a 40-year-old male, is alleged to have sustained a broken nose, low back strain, and bruises to the thigh and knee. It is also alleged that he lost a tooth. Claimant removed from the scene in an ambulance.
  —Claimant attorney informs the adjuster that the claimant spent three days in the hospital and has incurred a $500 doctor bill to date.
  —The claimant is still out of work but expected to return to work shortly. Claimant is a shoe salesman. Case reserve this claim.

Step-by-Step Completion of Projection Sheet Looking at the completed projection sheet in Exhibit 10-4, the adjuster will note there are various captions (ambulance, hospital emergency room, X-rays, and so on) in which projected or actual figures, if they are available, must be inserted. In the hypothetical case, little or no medical and wage loss information is available but there is enough information, with the help of the adjuster's imagination, to project special and general damages.

Since it is indicated that the claimant was removed from the scene in an ambulance, a figure is inserted adjacent to that caption. (Adjusters should have some idea of the ambulance fees in their local territory so that they can insert an appropriate amount under this category.) It is also probably safe to assume that there was some immediate emergency treatment in view of the claimant's injuries; and the adjuster should include an amount for emergency treatment, considering the nature and extent of the injuries sustained. It is also known that the claimant spent three days in the hospital. The adjuster is expected to have some idea of the semi-private room rate in his or her area and an amount should be inserted accordingly. (Keep in mind that if the injury is such that intensive care is required, the daily rate is sometimes two and a half to three times the semi-private rate.)

The adjuster will continue to make these projections with regard to doctor visits, treatment, therapy, and prescriptions. It is already known that the doctor bill to date is $500. The adjuster has also inserted $500 for future treatment (assuming that plastic surgery will not be necessary in this case) and has projected the dental bill to be $1,500. In addition, $50 is inserted under the prescription category. These figures would be insufficient if the claimant's broken nose involved complica-

Exhibit 10-4
Projection Sheet

Date TODAY

Project the claimant's total special and general damages, both incurred and anticipated, so as to arrive at a realistic reserve figure.

Case # 01000000 Ins. ____ D/L ____

Claimant ____ Age 40 Occupation SHOE SALESMAN Sex M

Injuries FX NOSE, TOOTH KNOCKED OUT, LOW BACK STRAIN, BRUISES TO THIGH AND KNEE.

Ambulance $ ____ $ 50

Hos.-Emer. Room ____ $ 500

Hos. 3 day @ $250 $ 750

X-Rays ____ $ 100

Lab ____ $ 30

Other ____ $ 50 Total Hos. & Related Expenses $ 1,480

Doctor:

Dr. V. ____ @ $ ____ $ 500 Total Doctor & Related Expenses $ 2,550

Consultation $ 500 Projected treatment

Therapy ____ @ $ ____ $1,500 Projected dental

Rx ____ $ 50 Total Medicals $ 4,030

Optional:

Disability ____ $ ____
Total 6 Weeks
Partial ____ Weeks

Total Wages $ 1,500
Total Other $ ____

Wages 6 wks @ $250 $ 1,500

Total Non-Med. $ 1,500

Total Specials $ 5,530

Disfigurement or Permanency factor $ ____

Reserve: Verdict Range - Low $ 15,000 High $ 25,000

Average $ 20,000 x Liability Factor 80 % =

Reserve $ 16,000

tions or would require plastic surgery for correction. Since the claimant is expected to return to work shortly and the attorney has indicated that no future surgery is anticipated, the adjuster views these figures as being sufficient.

At this point, total hospital and related expenses are estimated at $1,480 and total doctor-related expenses are estimated at $2,550. Total medicals are, therefore, estimated to be $4,030.

Note that two sections of this report are indicated as "Optional." Since the projection process views the reserve in terms of average verdict range, there is some validity to the position that the captions for Disability and Disfigurement or Permanency are redundant and therefore unnecessary. On the other hand, including these captions on an optional basis encourages the adjuster to think in terms of disability and permanency and to recognize their impact, if any, on the claim.

The adjuster estimates the lost time at six weeks in view of his recent interview with the claimant's attorney. The claimant's weekly salary as a shoe salesman is unknown but the adjuster estimates this at $250 per week. The estimated lost wages are $1,500. When total medical and total nonmedicals are added, total specials are $5,530.

The final step is for the adjuster to consider verdict range in his or her local area. In determining verdict range, both the adjuster's experience and the opinion of local defense counsel will be important factors. It must be emphasized that determining verdict range is a very subjective process. The adjuster needs to consider the jury sympathy which might be generated by the claim, the claimant's impression on the jury, the nature and severity of the injury, social and economic inflation, the general uncertainty about what might develop with the claim, the plaintiff and defense attorneys' skills, etc.

After the adjuster has considered verdict range, he or she must estimate a low-verdict range (which should be a conservative figure) and a high-verdict range. From these two figures, the average reserve is determined. (The projection process hypothetically assumes that the case is being handled by competent trial counsel and that it will be tried to a conclusion.)[2]

It is also important to keep in mind that some companies include expenses in the reserve figure. In such cases, expenses (including legal expenses) should be accounted for in the ultimate reserve which is established.

Once the average verdict range is calculated, that figure is tempered by the liability factor which in this case the adjuster believes is 80 percent. The end result of this process is the suggested reserve. Since the adjuster is in the best position to develop the information necessary to set a realistic reserve and because the projection exercise enables the adjuster to develop his or her own skills in setting reserves, there is much benefit to be gained from the projection process.

Once again, this figure may or may not be representative of the settlement value of the claim. In order to calculate the reserve, the claim person has "projected" future damages from limited information in an effort to reasonably estimate the ultimate probable cost of the claim. When a case is ready for settlement, presumably the adjuster is dealing, for the most part, with *known* facts regarding injuries and specials and evaluates the claim based generally on today's value, not projected value.

Ideally, when the claim is ultimately settled months or even years later, the amount of the settlement should approach the case reserve figure; provided, of course (and this is significant), that the adjuster's projections were reasonably accurate. (It is also important that claim people remember to adjust case reserves, if warranted, when new information is learned about the claim.)

Perhaps the best way to explain this sometimes confusing distinction is to say that the *reserve* is a reasonable estimate or projection of the ultimate probable cost of a claim while the *settlement value* of a claim is its worth at any given time with essentially all relevant factors being known. (Ordinarily, claims are not settled until detailed injury information is available and verified.) As more information is learned or becomes available regarding injuries and special damages, the less disparity there should be between a claim's reserve and its settlement value.

When a claim is in its early stages then, and injury information is sketchy, a more realistic reserve is established when claim people think in terms of ultimate probable cost rather than in terms of what the claim can be settled for. In order to set a realistic and accurate reserve, the claim person must "project" future damages from the limited information available, an exercise which is often unnecessary when actually evaluating a claim which is ready to be settled. This is so because when a claim is ready for settlement, the claim person ordinarily has obtained all of the claimant's special damages and relevant medical reports and has sufficient information to evaluate the claim for settlement purposes. This is frequently not the case when a bodily injury case reserve is being established for the first time on a claim.

Chapter Notes

1. Much of the credit for originally implementing reserve projection theory must be given to LeRoy E. Kennedy, President, Northwestern National Insurance Group, Milwaukee. Forms for this specific purpose, known as "projection sheets," were later developed by Thomas A. Savignac, Assistant Vice President, Northwestern National Insurance Group. The company makes the regular completion of reserve projection sheets by claim personnel an essential part of its claim handling procedures.
2. Ibid., Thomas A. Savignac.

CHAPTER 11

The Role of the Claim Department in the Company

INTRODUCTION

Although the claim department's main function is to investigate and settle claims, the claim person also contributes to the proper functioning of other departments and to the general well-being of the company. Several departments that derive such benefit are underwriting, agency (sales), accounting, data processing, and marketing.

Underwriting Department

The adjuster may sometimes uncover a discrepancy in the vehicle identification number (VIN) of an insured automobile and must investigate to determine if the difference is a typographical error on the policy or if it is an undisclosed vehicle owned by the insured. In either case, the underwriting department should be notified for the correction and to collect additional premium if due. Perhaps the vehicle is not garaged at the address indicated, producing a further reason to notify the underwriter.

The underwriter would also be concerned if an independent contractor ventures into a field of business other than that shown on the application for insurance. This information may lead to an additional premium charge or possible cancellation, if the new exposure is not acceptable to the insurer.

Other factors may appear that are significant in post-underwriting consideration by the underwriter, such as:

1. Revocation of driver's license of the insured, any driver who lives with the insured, or any driver who customarily uses the covered auto.[1] This condition usually applies when an insured or other driver is arrested and convicted of driving while intoxicat-

ed and results in the revocation of that person's driver's license. In such a circumstance, the underwriter may wish to cancel the policy.

2. Moral hazard, a condition involving the insured's character which could lead to a false claim or to the exaggeration of an otherwise legitimate loss.[2] For example, the likelihood of an arson loss would be much greater if an insured had previously been convicted of arson and the underwriter should be advised of the insured's previous loss experience.
3. Morale hazard involves the insured's indifference toward loss and loss-causing activities in the expectation that the insurance company will pay for the damage.
4. Improper quality control in manufacturing a product may result in additional injury claims. In such a case, the underwriter may want to suggest proper controls, or consider refusing to renew the policy.

In today's legal climate, caution must be used in the manner in which a report is made to the underwriting department. If the report is written, the adjuster's comments should be limited to conditions that are factual, avoiding insinuations or charges that cannot be proven. These precautionary measures are necessary since the adjuster's report is placed in the policy folder and may serve as a basis for ensuing actions taken by the underwriter. Should the insured file a lawsuit alleging bad faith against the insurer, company records may be subpoenaed and the adjuster may subsequently be required to explain her comments on the witness stand. Embarrassment and even punitive damages may result if the comments were merely the defamatory feelings or opinion of the adjuster.

Agency (Sales)

Since many insurers depend on agents to sell their policies, it is important for the adjuster to maintain a proper business relationship with the agent. For example, if the claim representative determines that no coverage exists for a claim, the agent should be advised before the denial is made. Thus, an agent will be prepared to answer any questions which the insured may later ask; or, due to a close relationship with the insured, the agent may want to inform the insured of the basis for the disclaimer personally.

Accounting Department

The accounting department frequently becomes involved with

claims in several areas, with the reserving process being the most predominant. Although reserving is actually a claim activity, the accounting department records the reserve figures to the company's financial record. Consequently, if the reserves are inaccurate or are reported late, it is the accountant who must make the corrections, additions or assumptions.

The Accounting Department also records all expenses, including the adjuster's expense account, if there is one. Thus a proper and timely report is always essential.

Data Processing Department

Most insurers have already adopted electronic data processing (EDP) into their business systems and other companies are expected to follow. If the adjuster is not directly involved with computer terminals, others use information supplied by the adjuster to enter data into the system. These entries must be accurate and timely, imposing additional constraints on the information submitted by the adjuster.

Some claim representatives are equipped with portable computers for use in preparing damage estimates. Due to the high cost involved, this equipment must be suitably maintained and properly protected.

Marketing Department

Insurance policies and services are the only commodities that insurance companies offer to the public. The adjuster performs the service when claims are processed quickly from the beginning to the final payment and such service may leave a long-lasting impression on both the insured and the claimant. The quality of the performance often determines whether the insured continues the coverage with that insurer or if dissatisfaction causes the insured to place the coverage with another carrier.

The quality of the performance also affects the claimant, who is often pleased to the extent of placing his or her coverage with the adjuster's company.

CORPORATE STRUCTURES

Insurance companies may be structured in a number of ways. The common denominators are the goals of smooth and efficient transaction of business and the ability to provide service to the consumer. In most cases, a claim department chain of command has a wide base of examiners and supervisors who are responsible for the technicians who, in turn, deal directly with the public and agents on a daily basis. The structure narrows toward the top of the organization until ultimately the level of the chief executive is reached. Often this is the president who reports to the Board of Directors, whose task is to make the policy decisions for the company.

Here are several diagrams illustrating some of the organizational structures used by insurance companies.

Exhibit 11-1 depicts a functional organization consisting of vice presidents who report to the president in reference to their own specialized fields. As this illustration indicates, the Vice President of Branch Administration is responsible for the physical operation of all branches or the individual profit centers. These responsibilities include all segments of each branch's operation, such as proper work flow, number of personnel needed and budgetary controls.

Each branch manager is directly accountable for all operations within the branch to the Vice President of Branch Administration. Often a branch is a full-service operation that includes claims, sales, and underwriting departments.

All department managers report to the branch manager and, in turn, are responsible for all personnel and duties pertaining to their departments.

In this form of structure, the departmental vice presidents and their support personnel in the home office serve on a staff level and act in an advisory capacity to the branches. For example, the Home Office Claim Department usually consists of well trained claim specialists, examiners, attorneys, and a training unit, all of which are available to the branches on an advisory basis. Also, the branches may be required to report specified claims that involve high reserves or lawsuits, so that the home office examiner may periodically review these files and lend his or her expertise in an effort to conclude the claim in a proper manner.

In this illustration, Exhibit 11-2 would represent a moderate-sized insurer that operates in a specific geographic area. For a larger insurance company operating on a national scale, a regional level of command may exist between the branch manager and vice president.

The disadvantages of the regional structure centers in the duplication of departments in each branch, the region, and the Home Office. However, a moderate-sized company may overcome some of these difficulties through controlling the size of the regional staff.

This type of structure permits the company to provide a full-service operation in a local area, eliminating the need for the agent to deal with telephone voices located hundreds or thousands of miles away. In addition, with each branch operating as a profit center, the spirit of competition between the branches prevails and it is possible for

Exhibit 11-1
Organizational Chart—Type A

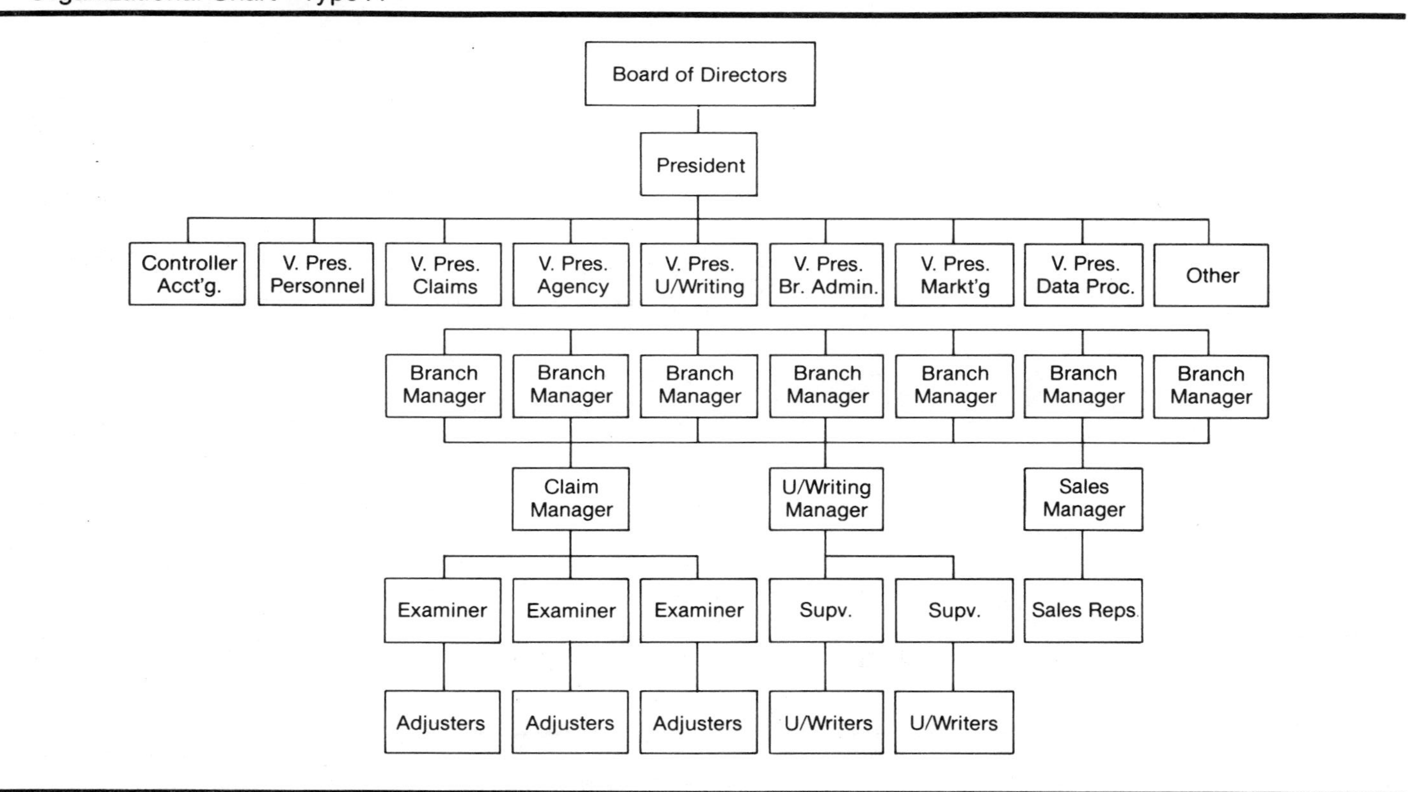

Exhibit 11-2
Organizational Chart—Type B

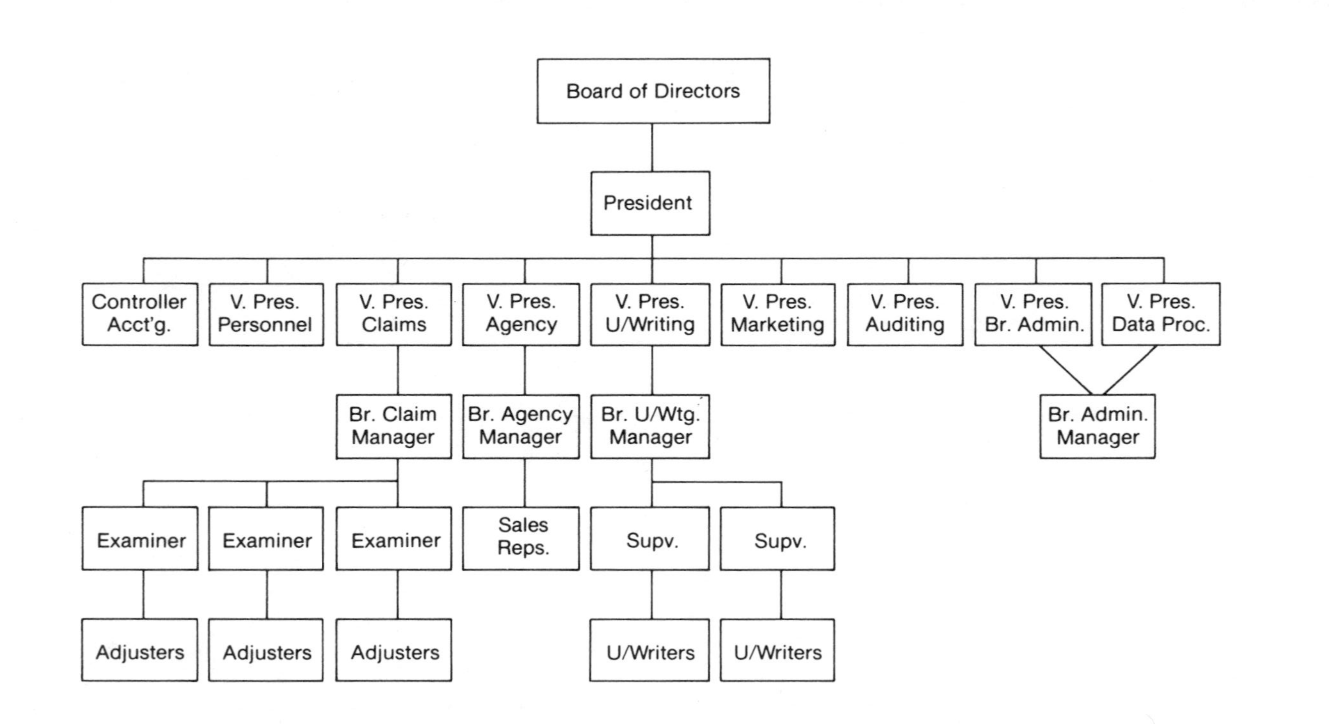

management to isolate problem areas and make recommendations that are successful in other branches. Finally, much of the authority is decentralized, permitting within limits, the local personnel to make their own decisions.

Exhibit 11-2 presents a more direct chain of command by eliminating the need for a branch manager, thus permitting the vice presidents to deal directly with their department managers in the branch in a technical manner, as well as in supervision.

In this illustration, the Branch Administrative Manager is responsible for the general administration of the office, with duties such as ordering supplies, keeping attendance records, responsibility of the maintenance of all equipment including computer hardware and conducting preliminary employment interviews for the other department managers. In some offices, this manager may also supervise the clerical employees.

As in Exhibit 11-1 a larger company may require the level of a regional manager in the various departments, located in the chain of command between the vice president and branch department manager.

The advantages to this structure include full branch operations with each branch being a profit center and being in close proximity to the agents. A large part of the company authority is decentralized and the need for a branch manager is eliminated, providing direct supervision from the home office. The disadvantage of this structure is the duplication of full-service facilities in each branch location.

Other variations of corporate structure may be found throughout the industry with an example of the transfer of underwriting services from a branch level to a regional or home office. In such instances, agents are required to deal with the underwriters on a long-distance basis via telephone and/or by direct computerized facilities.

Other companies process their claims from a regional or home office location using long-distance telephones and the mails. Local appraisers are utilized when the need of appraisals or inspections arises. Overall, most insurers still maintain local staff or independent adjusting services in all areas in which the company writes insurance and where it is cost effective.

A direct benefit of utilizing centralized operations is that there is no duplication in services occurring in the local offices, thus resulting in decreased operational expense.

Types of Insurance Companies

The two most prominent types of insurers are stock and mutual companies, both of which provide similar policies. The difference lies in the structure of the ownership of the company.

Stock Insurance Companies These insurers sell their stock to raise capital and the stockholders who buy the shares of stock become part-owners of the corporation. They elect the Board of Directors and the Board then formulates the company policy and elects the company officers.

The insurance policies may be sold by independent agents or directly by the company. In the latter case, premiums may be lower as the agents' commission is eliminated provided that these savings are passed on to the consumer.[3]

Mutual Insurance Companies Mutual companies are owned directly by the policyholders who elect the Board of Directors. Most mutual companies now sell nonassessable policies; in the past, the policyholders participated in the profits or losses incurred by the insurer.[4]

Mutual companies historically had more restrictive coverages in their policies, but for all intents and purposes, the present-day coverages in both types of companies are similar.

Some of the mutuals as well as some stock companies market their product through direct-writer agents who sell exclusively for the one insurer and generally receive a smaller commission as they also receive other benefits from the company. The book of business developed by the direct or captive agents is owned by the insurer, as contractually agreed upon.

Other mutual companies market their policies through independent agents who are in business by themselves and own their own book of business. As independent entities, they must pay their own expenses and as a result, receive a larger commission.

Reciprocal Insurance Exchanges In this type of organization each subscriber (insured) purchases insurance coverage for a needed amount and, in turn, agrees to underwrite other subscribers at a premium rate that is determined actuarially, based on the law of large numbers, plus expenses. The liability of each subscriber is predetermined and agreed upon, and consists of the premium charged.

A reciprocal insurance exchange is operated by an attorney-in-fact, who may be a natural person, partnership or, most often, a separate corporation, and is responsible for the operation of all functions within the organization and usually is paid a percentage of the premiums collected. This percentage may include all operating expenses, except losses.

Many of the fire insurance reciprocals return savings to the subscribers and, when necessary, may charge assessments to assist in meeting unanticipated losses. Auto reciprocals usually do not return savings and charge a fixed premium with no assessment charges. These conditions place the auto reciprocals in somewhat the same category as a mutual insurance company.[5]

Self-Insurers Self-insurance is an approach utilized by entities to assume their own losses, based on the law of large numbers and the probabilities of loss which may occur as a result of their industrial or commercial operations. The difference between this form of risk treatment and the purchase of an insurance policy from an insurer is twofold: (1) the risk is not transferred to an insurer but is retained by the self-insurer; and (2) the self-insurer eliminates the acquisition costs that are incurred by an insurer. Those costs include the agent's commission, underwriting costs and any other expenses incurred in the promotion of the purchase of policies.

As a self-insurer, a company must be prepared to pay both for the cost of investigating the claims and for the losses themselves.

Some business entities structure their protection by self-insuring their first layer of exposure up to a certain limit, depending on the size of the entity and the degree of exposure. For example, a smaller company's self-insurance retention may be $100,000, whereas the larger entity's retention may be established at $1,000,000.

In essence, the theory of self-insurance is not merely a case of paying a loss if one should occur; rather, it is a planned and organized manner of a company's method of self-protection in the event of loss. It should set aside sufficient funds to provide for the payment of losses and expenses. Otherwise, these obligations would have to be paid out of surplus or capital.

Risk Management/Investment of the Insurer

In the insurance company's process of conducting business, consideration must be given to the type and volume of coverages written as well as making proper investments to capitalize on the use of their available funds.

The type of coverages that are to be written is determined by the insurer who may wish to write multi-line or specialty coverages. For example, many stock and mutual companies are diversified and are in a position to write the multi-line coverages. Others restrict their writings to a certain specialty, such as floral or hardware risks. Also, some carriers only write fire and allied coverages, while others confine their business to casualty risks. The amount of coverage written is determined by the financial capacity of the insurer, based on surplus, which is the amount of funds left over, after all financial liabilities on the company's balance sheet have been satisfied.

Insurance regulators, who periodically audit the insurer's financial records prefer to see a ratio of 2 of 1, meaning the premiums written should not be more than twice the amount of surplus. Higher ratios of 3 to 1 or 4 to 1 may be permitted; however, the chance of insolvency is greater with higher ratios, as the chance of adverse loss experience is that much greater.[6]

The surplus funds of the carrier are invested so as to permit long-term as well as short-term gains while maintaining liquidity to provide necessary cash flow. Most investments consist of stocks and bonds.

Economics of the Insurance Company

As with any other commercial entity, an insurance company is in business to make a reasonable profit and thus must conduct its operations as efficiently and professionally as possible. Unfortunately, in today's business climate, few insurers realize an "underwriting" profit, as to do so, their combined losses and expenses must be less than the amount of premium earned. This measure of experience is determined in percentage points; thus if the company's expenses amount to 30 percent (30 cents of each premium dollar), the permissible loss ratio would have to be less than 70 percent if the company is to realize an "underwriting" profit.

The experience of most insurers in today's market indicates that their combined loss and expense ratios exceed the 100 percent mark and, in fact, some ratios reach the magnitude of 120 percent and 130 percent. As a result, they must rely on investment income or the company's surplus to make up for the underwriting loss. Neither of these alternatives is healthy as they not only retard growth, but also increase the possibility of insolvency of the company should losses and expenses become extreme.

In order for an insurer to grow, it must have adequate funds available to pay acquisition costs of new business as most of these costs are incurred at the beginning of the life of the new policies. The premium received from the sale of new policies cannot be used for these costs or losses as it does not become fully earned until the policies expire and it must remain in the unearned premium reserve account until such time.

An insurer can proceed in several ways to properly reduce its combined loss and expense ratio. Expenses must be reduced in such a manner as not to lose efficiency. Some companies proceed by systematically eliminating expense items that are not absolutely essential to the operation. Occasionally, some companies find it necessary to lay off employees, with the remaining personnel absorbing the work of those who were laid off. Such activity may be disruptive not only to the remaining employees, but also to the agents who sell that insurer's policies.

Other alternatives to reduce the loss and expense ratio may be an increase in new business without hiring additional employees, careful underwriting to reduce future losses and reduction of employees by attrition.

Chapter Notes

1. Personal Auto Policy, PP 00 02 (6-80)-BF, Copyright, Insurance Services Office, 1980, p.10.
2. Robert I. Mehr and Emerson Cammack, *Principles of Insurance,* Seventh Edition (Homewood, IL: Richard D. Irwin, Inc., 1980), p. 20.
3. Pat Magarick, *Successful Handling of Casualty Claims* (Brooklyn, NY: Central Book Co., Inc., 1974), p. 14.
4. Magarick, p. 14.
5. Mehr and Cammack, pp. 535–536.
6. Mehr and Cammack, p. 705.

Bibliography

"Actual Cash Value Revisited." *UAC Update,* No. 1, Winter 1983, p. 3.

Anderson, Ronald A. *Couch on Insurance.* Rochester, NY: The Lawyers Co-operative Publishing Company, 1959.

______________*The Insurer's Tort Law.* 2d ed. Ephrata, PA: Science Press, 1971.

______________and Kumpf, Walter A. *Business Law.* 9th ed. Cincinnati, OH: South-Western Publishing Co., 1972.

Arbitration Facts, 1983–1984 Edition. Tarrytown, NY: Insurance Arbitration Forums, Inc., p. 9.

Atiyah, P. S. "No-Fault Compensation: A Question That Will Not Go Away." *The Insurance Law Journal,* November 1980.

Auto Damage Reports. Chambersburg, PA: Vale Labs Publications, February 1982.

Bacas, Harry. "Challenge to Business: America's Changing Face." *Nation's Business,* July 1984, p. 19.

Beohm, Franklin D. and Stoller, Fritz M. "Introduction to Rules of Evidence and Theories of Liability in Products Liability Actions." *Products Liability—Trial Notebook.* Milwaukee, WI: Defense Research Institute.

Broder, Aaron J. "Structured Settlements: Insurance Gimmick." *The National Underwriter,* Property & Casualty Insurance Edition, 29 August 1980, p. 25.

Brownlee, Kenneth J., Ed. *Crawford Educational Newsletter.* Vol. IV, No. 9, 9 September 1984.

______________. "How To Adjust Almost Anything." *Insurance Adjuster,* January 1984, p. 28.

Dey, Dorothy H. "Recent Insurance Cases." *For the Defense,* November 1982, p. 10.

Donaldson, James H. *Casualty Claim Practice.* 3d ed. Homewood, IL: Richard D. Irwin, 1976.

Dorland's Pocket Medical Dictionary, 22d ed. Philadelphia, PA: W. B. Saunders Co., 1977.

Eubanks, Ronald W. and Cocchiarella, Alfonse J. "In Defense of Mary Carter." *For the Defense,* February 1984, p. 20.

FC&S Bulletins. Cincinnati, OH: The National Underwriter.

Field Claim Procedure Manual. Columbus, OH: Southern Home Insurance Co., Section 10—Part 1.

German, Edward C. "Substantive Products Defenses." *Defense of a Products Case.* Milwaukee, WI: Defense Research Institute, 1982.

Haggerty, Alfred G. "Structured Settlements Advocated." *The National Underwriter,* Property & Casualty Insurance Edition, 21 May 1982, p. 41.

Harney, Gerald P. "A Little Known—But Crucial—Decision." *The National Underwriter,* Property & Casualty Insurance Edition, 26 March 1982, p. 19.

Hinkle, B. David. "An Adjuster Looks at Products Liability." Atlanta, GA: Crawford and Co., 1974, p. 5.

"Important Supreme Court Election." *The Ohio Underwriter,* June 1982, p. 60.

"The Indicators of Casualty Fraud." Westport, CT: Insurance Crime Prevention Institute, Wendall C. Harness, Director.

Jensen, Thomas D. "Chiropractic Cross-Examination." *For the Defense.* Chicago, IL: The Defense Research Institute, June 1984, p. 15.

Johns, Corydon T. *An Introduction to Liability Claims Adjusting.* 3d ed. Cincinnati, OH: The National Underwriter Co., 1982.

Lorimer, James J. *et al. The Legal Environment of Insurance,* Vol. I. Malvern, PA: American Institute for Property and Liability Underwriters, 1978.

Magarick, Pat. *Successful Handling of Casualty Claims.* Brooklyn, NY: Central Book Co., 1974.

Manual for the Investigation of Automobile Fires. Palos Hills, IL: National Automobile Theft Bureau.

Mauney, John H. "Waiver and Estoppel: Creation and Prevention." *Update.* New York: Underwriters Adjusting Company, Summer 1983.

Mehr, Robert I. and Cammack, Emerson. *Principles of Insurance.* 7th ed. Homewood, IL: Richard D. Irwin, 1980.

Melvin, John. *The Claims-Gram.* Vol XXIV, No. 4, December 1982 and Vol. XXV, No. 1, April 1983.

Mika, Peggy. "Chiropractic Claims Can Be Challenged—Lawyer." *The National Underwriter,* Property & Casualty Insurance Edition, 11 November 1983, p. 40.

Nygaard, Richard J. and Cook, Janice K. "Settlement Agreements." Minneapolis, MN: Rider, Bennett, Egan and Arundel.

Rokes, Willis P. *Human Relations in Handling Insurance Claims.* 2d ed. Homewood, IL: Richard D. Irwin, 1981.

Smith, David M. "Watching Out for Bad Faith." *CQ, Claims Section Quarterly,* Vol. 2, No. 3, Spring 1984, p. 3.

Trenkner, Thomas R., Managing Editor. *American Law Reports,* 13 ALR 4th. Rochester, NY: The Lawyers Co-operative Publishing Co., 1982, p. 699.

Webster's Encyclopedia of Dictionaries. Ed. John Gage Allee. Cedar Knolls, NJ: Wehman Brothers, 1975.

Webster's New Collegiate Dictionary. Springfield, MA: G. & C. Merriam Co., 1981.

Witt, Robert C. and Urrutia, Jorge. "An Overview and Assessment of No-Fault Plans." *CPCU Journal,* March 1984, p. 10.

Index

A

Abuse, *333*
Acceptance, *35*
Accident, definition of, *49*
  unavoidable, *176*
Accident not occurring in the policy period, *432*
Accident reconstruction experts, *229*
Accountants, *230*
Accounting, adjuster's knowledge of, *18*
Accounting department, claim department and, *478*
ACORD forms, *200*
Act of God, *177*
Activity check, *213*
Actual cash value (ACV), *16, 303*
Ad damnum, 90, 445
Add-on no-fault plan, *153*
Adhesion, contracts of, *40*
Adjusters, assigning claims to, *2*
  field and office, compared, *9*
  fields of knowledge of, *17*
  functions of, *1*
  hiring, *6*
  independent, *10*
  personnel functions of, *6*
  role of, *12*
  staff, *8*
  successful, attributes of, *20*
  training, *7*
  types of, *8*
Adjusting, telephone, *198*
Advance payments, *406*
Ady decision, *80*
Agency, *120*
Agency versus bailment, *142*
Agency (sales) department, claim department and, *478*
Agent's daily, *206*
Agents, *11*
Agreement (as used in contracts), *35*
  high/low, *394*
  Mary Carter, *396*
  parents' release and indemnity, *398*
  trust, *295*
Aircraft, definition of, *43*
Alcoholic beverage exclusion, *328*
Aleatory, *39*
Ambiguity, *41, 43*
Annuity, *413*
Apparent authority, *36*
Appeal, *450*
Appeal bonds, *58*
Applicant (for arbitration), *440*
Appraisal, *435*
  auto, *300*
Arbitration, inter-company, *439*
  special, *443*
As is sale, *333*
Assault, *98*
Assumption of risk, *175*
Attorney, claimant's, *25*

obtaining information from, *213*
defense, *27*
handling the threat of, *378*
negotiating with, *382*
role of, in insurance claims, *25*
Attractive nuisance, *107*
Attributes of a successful adjuster, *20*
Authority to settle, *453*
Auto arson, domestic problem motive for, *307*
financial motive for, *306*
revenge motive for, *307*
Auto arson claims, *305*
Auto business exclusion, *65*
Auto claims, *291*
Auto construction and repairs, *17*
Auto damage, determining extent of, *297*
Auto damage claims, *297*
Auto liability claims, *29*
Auto ownership, *292*
Auto repair charges, determining, *299*
Auto theft claims, *304*
Automobile accident schemes, *356*
Automobile flood claims, *207*
Automobile guest statutes, *135*
Automotive engineers, *230*
Autopsy, *234*
Autopsy report and death certificate, *234*
Average or formula reserves, *460*
Avoidable consequences, *176*

B

Bad faith, sources of, *165*
Bad faith and excess liability, *163*
Bail bonds, *58*
Bailee, *140*
Bailments, *140*
agency versus, *142*
Bailor, *140*
Battery, *98*
Bench machine, *302*
Benefits to dependents in a case of fatality, *336*
Betterment, *17*, *434*
Bodily injury, definition of, *48*
Bodily injury liability claims, *458*
Bonds, appeal, *58*
bail, *58*
release of attachment, *59*
Breach of duty, *99*
Broad evidence rule, *304*
Building construction, adjuster's knowledge of, *19*
Burden of proof, *112*
Business invitee, *105*
Business pursuits, *43*
"But for" rule, *100*

C

Car rental situation, *63*
Care, degrees of, *109*
"Care, custody or control," *44*
Career, claim field as, *32*
Carrying persons or property for a fee, *65*
Case reserves, *461*
individual, *462*
Categories of liability, *197*
Causal relationship, *210*
Causal relationship—proximate cause, *100*
Cause, intervening, *104*
Central index bureau, *232*
Chemical engineer, *229*
Children, contributory negligence and, *174*
Chiropractic treatment, *347*
Civil law, *96*
Claim costs, reducing, *418*
Claim department, functions of, *1*
role of, in the company, *477*
Claim evaluations, *5*
examples of, *365*
Claim field as a career, *32*
Claim file reporting, *167*

Claim function, self-insured firm's need for, *11*
Claim inflation indicators, *357*
Claim investigation, types of, *291*
Claim reports to underwriting, *246*
Claim representative, field, *9*
  office, *9*
Claim reserves, *457*
  establishment of, *460*
Claimant, damage disputes with, *436*
  status of, *323*
    in a premises liability claim, *105*
Claimant control, *209*
Claimant or insured, contacting, *217*
Claimant's attorney, obtaining information from, *213*
Claimant's cooperation, obtaining, *218*
Claimant's duty to establish and mitigate damages, *352*
Claims, assigning, to adjusters, *2*
  auto, *291*
  auto arson, *305*
  auto damage, *297*
  auto flood, *307*
  auto liability, *29*
  auto theft, *304*
  closing, *385*
  forces influencing the decision to settle, *443*
  injury, evaluation and settlement of, *241*
  investigation of the injury aspect of, *231*
  liability versus property, *30*
  methods of evaluating, *359*
  no-fault auto insurance, *308*
  nuisance, *358*
  personal and general liability, *29*
  products liability, *29, 327*
  professional liability, *334*
  providing procedures for reporting, *2*
  public liability, *323*
  role of the attorney in, *25*
  types of, *28*
  underinsured motorists, *296*
  uninsured motorists, *294*
  workers' compensation, *335*
Clause, other insurance, *435*
Climatological experts, *230*
Collateral source rule, *189, 353*
Collision coverage versus comprehensive coverage, *433*
Common law, *95*
Common and statutory law, *95*
Comparative negligence, *112, 126, 437*
  operation of, *131*
  relationship of, to other actions, *134*
Comparative negligence laws, kinds of, *127*
Compensation benefits, workers' compensation, *336*
Compensatory damages, prayer for, *446*
Competent evidence, *221*
Competent parties, *37*
Completed operations liability claims, *30*
Comprehensive coverage versus collision coverage, *433*
Compromising, *358*
Compulsory auto insurance laws, *149*
Computer, *206*
Computerized estimates, *300*
Concurrent liability, *117*
Conflicts of interest, *27*
Consideration, *37*
Consortium, loss of, *182*
Construction engineer, *229*
Constructive total loss, *302*
Consumer protection agencies, claim settlement and, *444*
Contacting the claimant or insured, *217*
Contacting witnesses, *220*
Contingent fees, *383*
Contingent liability of a settling insurance company, *416*
Continuous cover offer, *432*
Contract, elements of, *35*

insurance, distinctive features of, *39*
legal liability based on, *115*
Contracts of adhesion, *40*
Contractual liability limitation, *70*
Contribution, *118*
Contributory negligence, *112, 126, 171*
and comparative negligence, *437*
Control, *209*
Controlling, *15*
Conversion, *98*
Coordination of benefits, *157*
Corporate structures, *479*
Costs, controlling, *15*
Court hearings, traffic or criminal, *235*
Covenant not to sue, *386, 390*
Coverage, determining, *2*
importance of knowledge of, *77*
importance and meaning of, *35*
out of state, *74*
Coverage disputes, *431*
Coverage information, sources of, *205*
Coverage versus liability, *73*
Coverage problems, *82*
Coverage questions, procedures for, *207*
recognizing, *205*
Covered auto, *51*
Covered person, *50*
Criminal law, *96*
Current settlement value, *462*

D

Daily, agent's, *206*
Damage, auto, determining extent of, *297*
preexisting, *434*
Damage disputes, *434*
with the claimant, *436*
Damage to property owned or transported, *62*
Damage questions, recognizing, *209*
Damages, *104*
claimant's duty to establish and mitigate, *352*
definition of, *48*
first-party, *180*
general, *181*
intangible, *15*
negotiation of, *195*
role of, *180*
special, *181*
verification of, *184*
Damages in the form of interest, *190*
Dangerous activity, *124*
Data processing department, claim department and, *479*
Date of service (of summons), *445*
Death certificate, *234*
Debris (as used in public liability cases), *326*
Declaratory judgment action, *89*
Declaratory judgments, *434*
Defamation, *98*
Defective stairs, *324*
Defense, inadequate, *166*
Defense attorney, *27*
Defenses, *171*
Degrees of care, *108*
Degrees of negligence, *291*
Demand, *379*
Depositions, *448*
Depreciation, *16, 434*
Depreciation (of automobiles), *303*
Diagnosis, *343*
Diagrams, *225*
claim file, *292*
Diary system, *22*
Dictated reports, *244*
Direct bill receipts, *207*
Disability, *183, 343*
Discovery, potential problems with, *245*
Discovery procedures, *448*
Discovery process, claim personnel and, *168*
Discovery rules, legal consideration of, *186*
Disfigurement, *182*

Disputes, coverage, *431*
first-party, *431*
third-party, *435*
Disregard of warnings, *333*
Distribution section of an advance payment receipt, *406*
Divorce proceedings, *236*
Doctor interview, *343*
"Double dip," *353*
Doubtful liability, *197*
Drop drafts, *410*
Duties, nondelegable, *124*
Duty, breach of, *99*
legal, *99*
Duty to defend, PAP, *56*
Duty to warn, *330*

E

Economic considerations of compromising or defending a claim, *358*
Economic loss, *154*
Economics of the insurance company, *486*
Elements of a contract, *35*
Emancipated child, *137*
Emergency defense, *178*
Emotional distress claims, *189*
Emotional or horror factor, *343*
Employer-employee relationship, *120*
Engineers, automotive, *230*
Estimated claim expenses, *458*
Estimates, computerized, *300*
Estoppel, *82*
Evaluation, *14*
Evidence, *209*, *220*
Excess letter, *90*
Excess liability, *89*
bad faith and, *163*
Exclusion applies to facts, *433*
Exclusions, personal auto policy, *61*
products liability, *327*
Exclusions applying to persons, *61*
Expert testimony, *448*
Experts, accident reconstruction, *229*
use of, *228*
Express warranty, *329*
Extended nonowned coverage, *68*
Extra-contractual liability, *164*

F

"Fair amount," *14*
Falls, causes of, *323*
Family member, PAP definition of, *62*
Family purpose doctrine, *116*
Fault, *147*
Fees, contingent, *383*
Field claim representative, *9*
Field and office adjusters compared, *9*
Files, reviewing, *3*
Financial responsibility laws, *148*
First call settlement, *219*, *341*
First-party damages, *180*
First-party disputes, *431*
Foreseeability, *110*
Form, report, *236*
Form required by law, *38*
Forms, report, preprinted, *237*
Fraud (as it relates to release), *405*
Fraudulent claims, *187*, *354*
common elements of, *356*
Friendly suit, *397*
Friendly witness, *222*
Full formal report, *244*
"Furnished for regular use," *45*

G

General business exclusion, *66*
General damages, *181*
General provisions (as used in the personal auto policy), *46*
General release, *386*
Genuine assent, *37*
Governmental functions, *139*

Governmental immunity, *138*
Grace period, *432*
Gross negligence, *110*, *291*
Guest, *136*
Guilty plea, *115*

H

Healing factors of injuries, *186*
Hearsay information, *246*
High/low agreement, *394*
Hionis decision, *78*
Hiring adjusters, *6*
Holistic approach, *351*
"Horse trading" attitude, *375*
Hospital records, *233*
Hostile witness, *222*
Human relations abilities, adjusters', *23*

I

Imminent danger, *329*
Immunity, *136*
  governmental, *138*
  interspousal, *137*
  intrafamily, *137*
  parent-child, *137*
Implied warranty, *329*
Improper use, *333*
Inadequate defense, *166*
Included operation, *298*
Income tax returns, *235*
Incurred but not reported (IBNR) reserves, *460*
Indemnity, *118*
Independent adjusters, *10*
Independent contractor, *123*
  negligent selection of, *124*
Independent medical examination report, *188*
Independent medical examinations, *186*
  reasons for requesting, *186*
Individual case reserves, establishing, *462*
Individual evaluations, *450*
Information, coverage, sources of, *205*
  hearsay, *246*
  for investigation, sources of, *225*
Initial reports, *237*
Injuries, preexisting, *353*
  unknown, *404*
Injury claims, evaluation and settlement of, *341*
  factors affecting evaluation of, *342*
  investigation of, *231*
Inquiring mind, adjuster's, *20*
Insurance, joint and several liability and, *143*
Insurance Arbitration Forums, Inc., *440*
Insurance claims, role of the attorney in, *25*
Insurance company, economics of, *486*
  types of, *483*
Insurance contracts, distinctive features of, *39*
Insurance Crime Prevention Institute (ICPI), *355*
"Insured," *44*
Insuring agreement, personal auto policy, *48*
  undefined terms in, *48*
Intangible, *39*
Intangible damages, value of, *15*
"Intangible" product, *458*
Integrity and honesty, adjusters', *23*
Intentional act, *45*
Intentional injury or damage, *61*
Intentional tort, *97*
Interest, conflicts of, *27*
Interests, balancing, *454*
Inter-company arbitration, *439*
Interim or status report, *238*
Interpleader action, *58*
Interrogatories, *448*

Interruptions to an interview, handling, *262*
Interspousal immunity, *137*
Interstate driving, *156*
Intervening cause, *104*
Interview with treating physician, *233*
Interviewee, instructions to, *260*
Interviews, common mistakes made during, *263*
planning, *215*
Intrafamily immunity, *137*
Investigation, *12*, *195*
bad faith claims and, *165*
claims, types of, *291*
information for, sources of, *225*
need for, in comparative negligence claims, *133*
in third-party disputes, *438*
planning, *200*
planning the work schedule for, *214*
of the injury aspect of the claim, *231*
Investigation procedures, products liability claims, *332*
Investigative process, *195*

J

Joint and several liability and insurance, *143*
Joint tortfeasor, *117*
Joint tortfeasor release, *386*, *389*
Joint ventures, *122*
Judgment/experience method, *363*

K

Knowledge and information, sources of, *31*

L

Laboratory or test results, *236*
Last clear chance, *178*
Late notice, *433*
Law, adjuster's knowledge of, *19*
civil, *96*
common and statutory, *95*
criminal, *96*
evolutionary process of, *170*
principles of, affecting liability claim handling, *116*
Laws, comparative negligence, *127*
financial responsibility, *148*
Lawsuit reports, *244*
Lawsuits, defending, *4*
Legal duty, *99*
Legal liability, meaning of, *95*
Legal liability based on contract and statute, *115*
Legal liability questions, counseling adjusters in the resolution of, *4*
Legal process, *445*
Legal purpose, *38*
Legally responsible, definition of, *49*
Liability, categories of, *197*
concurrent, *117*
contingent, *416*
coverage versus, *73*
doubtful, *197*
excess, *89*
joint tortfeasor, *117*
legal, *95*
parental-family, *125*
probable, *197*
questionable, *197*
vicarious, *119*, *174*
Liability analysis, personal auto policy, *46*
Liability claim handling, principles of law affecting, *116*
Liability claims, completed operations, *30*
personal and general, *29*
Liability coverage exclusion, *71*
Liability disputes, *436*
Liability without fault, *98*

Liability questions, recognizing, *209*
Liability versus property claims, *30*
License requirements, *124*
Licensee, *106*
Lighting, *326*
Limit of liability, *75*
Loan receipt, *418*
Local statutes and ordinances, claim settlement and, *443*
Local verdict value, *343*
"Long Tail" claims, *458*
Loss of consortium, *182, 347*
Loss and expense ratio, *485*
Lost earnings fraud, elements of, *357*
Loyalty, adjuster's, *24*

M

MacPherson v. Buick Motor Co., *328*
Malicious prosecution, *98*
Market value, *303*
Marketing department, claim department and, *479*
Mary Carter agreement, *396*
Material evidence, *221*
Material need, *376*
Medical benefits, workers' compensation, *336*
Medical charges, verification of, *185*
Medical examinations, independent, *186*
Medical examiner or expert, selection of, *187*
Medical examiner's qualifications, *187*
Medical fraud, elements of, *357*
Medical knowledge, adjusters', *18*
Medical and lost-wages information, *448*
Medical report, *343*
Medical specialists, *229*
Medical terminology, *347, 425*
Military records, *236*
Minor, release for injury to, *397*
Mistake, mutual, *403*
 unilateral, *404*
Modified no-fault plan, *153*
Motor vehicle reports, *235*
Mutual insurance companies, *484*
Mutual mistake, *403*

N

National Automobile Theft Bureau (NATB), *305, 355*
Need, material, *376*
Negative statement, *223*
Negligence, *98*
 comparative, *112, 127*
 contributory, *112, 126, 171*
 degrees of, *291*
 determining, in premises liability claims, *105*
 elements of, *99*
 gross, *110, 291*
 legal liability based on, *98*
 ordinary, *110, 291*
 slight, *110, 291*
Negligence per se, *96, 114*
Negligent selection of an independent contractor, *124*
Negotiation, *14*
Negotiation process, after suit has been filed, *450*
 breakdown of, *431*
Negotiations, determining case readiness for, *372*
 initiating, *377*
 planning the approach to, *373*
 settlement, *372*
Negotiator, effective, characteristics of, *375*
Neighborhood check, *213*
No contact considerations, *218*
No-fault auto insurance, *151*
 strengths and deficiencies of, *158*
No-fault auto insurance claims, *308*
No-fault laws, types of, *153*
No-fault provisions, *156*

No release settlements (walk-away settlements), *412*
Nominal or dollar releases, *400*
Nondelegable duties, *124*
Noneconomic loss, *154*
Nonwaiver agreement, *57, 85*
Nuclear energy exclusion, *67*
Nuisance claims, *358*

O

Obsolescence (of automobiles), *303*
Occupational illness or disease, *338*
OCR (office claim representative), *9*
Offer, *35, 379*
  first, *380*
Office claim representative (OCR), *9*
Official reports, *234*
Omnibus clause, *54*
Open end release settlements, *409*
"Operated or used by the insured," *44*
Operation, included, *298*
Oral evidence, *209*
Ordinary negligence, *110, 291*
Ordinary witness, *220*
Orris vs. Claudio, 81
Other insurance clause, *435*
Out of state coverage, *74*
Overlap, *297*
Over-reserving, *459*
Owned by or furnished for any "family member's" regular use, *68*
Ownership, auto, *292*

P

Pain and suffering, *182*
Parent-child immunity, *137*
Parental-family liability, *125*
Parents' release and indemnity agreement, *398*
Partnerships, *122*
Passengers, contributory negligence and, *175*
Passive claim attitude, *373*
Periodic payment settlements, *412*
Permanency, *232, 343*
Permissive use, *292*
Personal auto policy (PAP), *46*
  additional limitations under, *70*
  duty to defend under, *56*
  exclusions of, *61*
    applying to vehicles, *68*
  insuring agreement, *48*
    undefined terms in, *48*
  liability analysis, *46*
  limit of liability in, *74*
  other insurance provision in, *75*
  out of state coverage in, *74*
  supplementary payments under, *58*
Personal contract of the utmost good faith, *41*
Personal injury protection (PIP), *153*
Personnel functions, *6*
Photographs, *226*
  claim file, *293*
Physical evidence, *209*
Physician, treating, interview with, *233*
PIP (personal injury protection), *153*
Plaintiff, *25*
Planning for future needs, *7*
Planning the interview, *215*
Planning the work schedule for an investigation, *214*
Police report, *225*
Policy, readable, *46*
Policy language, ambiguous, *43*
Prayer (*ad damnum*) as used in legal terminology, *445*
Preexisting damage, *434*
Preexisting injuries, *353*
Pre-judgment interest, *191*
Premises, maintenance and control of, *108*
Premises liability claims, determining negligence in, *105*

Prenatal injury claims, *190*
Preponderance of the evidence, *112*
Preprinted forms, *237*
Pre-recording accident discussion, *259*
Pretrial conferences, *448*
Primary/excess situations, *75*
Privity, *328*
Probable liability, *197*
Product, quality of, *327*
Product manufacturing, adjuster's knowledge of, *19*
Products liability claims, *29, 327*
investigation procedures for, *331*
legal basis of, *329*
Professional liability claims, *334*
Prognosis, *232, 343*
Projection sheet, *464*
step-by-step completion of, *472*
Proof, burden of, *112*
Property damage, definition of, *49*
Property damage fraud or inflation, elements of, *356*
Proprietary functions, *139*
Proximate cause, *100*
illustrations of, *101*
Proximate cause and intervening acts, *331*
Public adjusters, *11*
Public liability claims, *323*
Punitive damages, *93*
prayer for, *446*
Pure comparative negligence, *130*
Pure no-fault plan, *153*

Q

Questionable liability, *197*

R

Readable policy, *46*
Reasonable expectations, *41*
Recall exclusion, *328*
Reciprocal insurance exchanges, *484*
Recorded statements, *247, 257*
guidelines for taking, *258*
written summary of, *265*
Recorded statement guide, automobile example of, *271*
premises, example of, *273*
Records, hospital, *233*
military, *236*
school, *235*
"Red flags" (indicators of casualty fraud), *355*
Reducing claim costs, *418*
Regulatory requirements, claim settlement and, *444*
Release, *385*
general, *386*
joint tortfeasor, *386, 389*
nominal or dollar, *400*
setting aside of, *403*
telephone recorded, *402*
types of, *389*
Release of attachment bond, *59*
Release when claimant is a corporation or partnership, *403*
Release draft, *402*
Release for injury to minor, *397*
Relevant evidence, *221*
Remedies, *148*
Rented to, used by, or in the care of, *62*
Repair charges, auto, determining, *299*
Repairs, auto, *17*
Replacement cost less depreciation, *304*
Replacement value, *16*
Report form, *236*
Reporting, *236*
Reporting claims, providing procedures for, *2*
Reports, dictated, *244*
full formal, *244*
initial, *237*
interim or status, *238*
kinds of, *237*
lawsuits, *244*
motor vehicle, *235*
police, *225*

toxicology, *234*
weather, *228*
Reservation of rights, *57*
Reservation of rights letter, *83*
Reserves, average or formula, *460*
case, *461*
claim, *457*
establishing proper, *5*
IBNR, *460*
types of, *460*
unearned premium, *457*
Reserving, *457*
Res ipsa loquitur, 112, 329
Respondant (for arbitration), *440*
Respondeat superior, 120
Reviewing files to ensure proper disposition, *3*
Risk, assumption of, *175*
Risk management/investment of the insurer, *485*
Role of the adjuster, *12*
Role of damages, *180*
Roundtable, *365*
Roundtable or committee evaluation, *451*
Royal Globe vs. Superior Court, 167
Rule of purpose, *42*
Rules of strict construction and ambiguity, *41*

S

Safe design, duty of, *334*
School records, *235*
Seat belt defense, *179*
Self-discipline and work organization, *21*
Self-insured, *11*
Self-insured firm's need for the claim function, *11*
Self-insurers, *485*
Set-off provision, *354*
Settlement, *14*
alternative approaches to, *406*
authority to proceed with, *453*
claim, forces influencing, *443*
first call, *341*
Settlement agreements, types of, *389*
Settlement negotiations, *372*
bad faith claims and, *165*
Settlement value, *462, 475*
Settlements, first call, *219*
Settling casualty company, *416*
Sidewalks, *325*
Slight negligence, *110, 291*
Source of primary coverage (no-fault), *157*
Sovereign immunity, *138*
Special arbitration, *443*
Special damages, *181, 359*
Special and general damages, projecting, *464*
Special investigation units (SIU), *304*
Specialists, medical, *229*
Staff adjuster, *8*
Stairs, defective, *324*
Standard Venetian Blind decision, *79*
Stare decisis, 81
Statement, *247*
negative, *223*
recorded, *257*
signed, rules for taking, *256*
written, *249*
Statement of principles, *25*
Statement taking, *247*
special problems associated with, *265*
Status of claimant, change in significance of, *108*
in a premises liability claim, *105*
in public liability claims, *323*
Statute, legal liability based on, *115*
Statute of Fraud, *38*
Statute of limitations, *295*
Statutory law, *95*
Stock insurance companies, *484*
Strict construction, rules of, *41*
Strict liability, *98*
Structured or periodic payment settlements, *412*

Structures, corporate, *479*
Subpoena, *449*
Subrogation (no-fault), *158*
  reducing claim costs and, *428*
Subrogation claims, pursuing, *5*
Subrogation of workers' compensation claims, *337*
Substantial factor test, *101*
Successive negligence, *117*
Suit, friendly, *397*
Summons, *445*
Supporting witness, *222*
Surplus, *458*

T

"Take-over" letter, *325, 332*
Technical functions, adjuster's, *1*
  claim department, *1*
Telephone adjusting, *198*
Telephone recorded releases, *402*
Testimony, expert, *448*
Thermography, *352*
Third-party damages, *181*
Third-party disputes, *435*
  need for investigation of, *438*
Tort liability system, imperfections of, *147*
Tort threshold, *154*
Torts, *97*
  intentional, *97*
  types of, *97*
Total/partial disability approach, *361*
Toxicology reports, *234*
Traffic or criminal court hearings, *235*
Training adjusters, *7*
Treating physician, interview with, *233*
Trespasser, *106*
Trial procedures, *449*
Trust agreement, *295*
Types of adjusters, *8*

U

Ultimate probable cost, *463*
Ultimate settlement value, *462*
Unauthorized use of vehicle, *66*
Unavoidable accident, *176*
Underinsured motorists claims, *296*
Underinsured motorists insurance, *150*
Underwriting, claim reports to, *246*
Underwriting department, claim department and, *477*
Underwriting file, *206*
Underwriting profit, *486*
Unearned premium reserves, *457*
Unemancipated child, *137*
Unfair claim practices acts, *167*
Unfriendly witness, *222*
Unibody vehicles, *301*
Uniform Contribution Among Tortfeasors Act, *118, 390*
Unilateral mistake, *404*
Uninsured motorists claims, *294*
Uninsured motorists insurance, *149*
Uninsured motorists release and assignment agreement, *400*
Unintended use, *333*
Unit of time method, *363*
Unknown injuries, *404*
Unreasonable risk of harm, *329*
Use contrary to instructions, *333*
Use with knowledge of defect or danger, *333*
Utmost good faith, personal contract of, *41*

V

Vehicles covered (no-fault), *157*
Vehicles having less than four wheels, *68*
Vehicles owned by or furnished for the "named insured's" regular use, *68*
Vicarious liability, *119, 174*

Voluntary no-fault plan, *153*
Volunteer doctrine, *418*

W

Waiver and estoppel, *82*
Warranty, implied, *329*
Warranty of merchantability, *329*
Weather reports, *228*
Winterbottom v. Wright, 328
Witness, *220*
  classification of, *222*
  ordinary, *220*
Witnesses, sources of, *223*
Workers' compensation, *64*
Workers' compensation claims, *335*
  sources of coverage, *337*
  subrogation of, *337*
Workers' compensation exclusion, *328*
Written statements, *247*, *249*
  format of, *250*

X

"X times the specials" method, *359*